LIVINg ON ROCKS

A Memoir of Sangria and Cyclones

copyright 2003-2018, James B Rieley
cover photo: Nigel's Beach Bar at Smuggler's Cove, Tortola
cover photo credit: the author

Abandoning country, friends and family to live on a rock in the Mediterranean. Rieley's tales from the village will entrance and delight readers as local characters and customs come leaping from the page. Faced with adversity through a series of illness culminated in surviving Hurricane Irma in the BVI where sailboat home was destroyed.

Author Dr James B Rieley has had a varied working life, from owning a plastics manufacturing business, an Arabian horse stud farm and subsequently becoming an international guru on business solutions, he changed nationality, moved from the US to Europe and cannot spend a day without working on a project.

Alison Lawrence

"You can never discover new lands if you are afraid to lose sight of the shore."

- The cover of a brochure from Class Afloat, West Island College

CONTENTS

Introduction — 1
01 - Deciding What to Do — 4
02 - Settling in to a New Life — 38
03 - Almost Really Believing I am Living Here — 67
04 - Joys of Village Life — 109
05 - The Indefatiguable Mysteries of Being Here — 170
06 - Amêlie — 207
07 - La Clinica, Otra Vez — 332
08 - A New Rock — 352
09 - Irma Comes to Visit — 385
10 - Wretched Excess of Waffles — 403
11 - Getting on With It — 420
About the Author — 449

James B Rieley

Living on Rocks

As friends or clients of mine will tell you, I have been known to often say, "Life is full of choices." One of life's biggest choices we all have is where to live. I am not sure when I first became aware that people don't necessarily need to spend their entire lives within close proximity to where they were born, but one day, it hit me like a meteor from space. And since that day, parts of my head and heart have always been devoted to seeing what is out there, waiting for me to discover it. This doesn't mean that I was desperate to find the lost cities of Tanis or Shambhala; not at all. For me, it is all about living on islands and/or boats. This vision most definitely would not have the black-hole-like attraction to me if the islands or the boats were in shite latitudes. No, clearly, I am happiest when I am in an environment that is bathed in warm, sunny weather. And I have to tell you; living on a (relatively) small island isn't for everyone. There is this whole "island fever" thing that some island livers claim to suffer from. They are good for a while, but then feel the need to return for a while to a piece of land that is not surrounded by water. For some reason, I don't suffer from this self-perceived malady, thankfully. I am quite content to be living on some rock in the middle of the sea.

Like all choices in life, this kind of life does come with unintended consequences, but to me, they are outweighed by being able to live a life I have chosen. To paraphrase something I saw years ago, "Some people want things to happen. Some people wait for things to happen. Some people make things happen." Having a vision, and making choices to realise that vision is what making things happen is all about.

Living on Rocks is pretty much a story that has evolved over time. I began writing the parts of this story that is inside these covers as a way to share what was going on in my life with family and friends. But as time when on, the number of people whom I knew increased, and with them came more requests to vicariously experience my life on boats and on islands through my words.

For most of my life, I was a product of a life in a fast-moving, high-tech, pretty highly sophisticated environment. It wasn't until I had retired that it became clear to me that the life I had been living had never been the life I wanted to live. We are all impacted, to one level or another, by the expectations of others. In my case, the prevalent expectations were those of my parents. After I retired, I had one of those, "Oh-my-God-I-feel-so-comfortable-being-able-to-actually-be-James-for-a-change." It wasn't that I wasn't competent to leave that previous life, it was just that it was never the life that was my choice. In hindsight, it was clear that we often find ourselves in an environment in which we do what is expected and deal with it, because that is what is expected of us.

For me, everything changed when I bought my first boat after I had retired. I *found that being on water was so very special for me, and by the time I had sold that boat for one a bit longer, I was convinced that this was part of my DNA. I sold my house and moved onto the boat, and this convinced me even more. The final shift in my life happened with my next boat. I had sailed from Barcelona to the island of Mallorca with the "plan" being to stay there for a couple of weeks. I stayed for over 15 years, and have lived on rocks (islands) ever since. The need (or desire) to live on rocks must be part of my genes.*

Living on rocks is different than living in places like London, or Barcelona, or even a small town. For comparison purposes, the city of London is a tad larger than 600 square miles. The entire island of Mallorca is only about double that. Antigua is only 108 square miles. Tortola is about 55 square miles; and Virgin Gorda is 8 square miles. Size means that just about everything in life itself is different. And I suppose that is one of the reasons why it seems to suit me. It is the whole, "living in a third-world environment" thing that works for me. Life is not about having "stuff" and in my previous "first-world" life; I was, admittedly, pretty focused on getting "stuff." It wasn't until I realised that having "stuff" wasn't what was important. Living on a boat helped me realise this. My second boat (the first one I actually lived on-board) would have fit in the sitting room of just about any of the houses I had owned. And because of this size parameter, it caused me to realise that I really didn't need all the "stuff" I had accumulated. Life became simpler, and because of that, it became better.

Writing about this life has been a way to share with family and friends (for whom I wrote all these stories) what I was experiencing. And have no doubt, many of the things I have experienced in the past years has been pretty different than what my life had been like. Because I had been writing these stories for friends and family; i.e. people who already had some context of my life; you might be some references that don't make sense. Sorry about that. With the patience-laden assistance of my editor, I have tried to clean some of these references up a bit.

And in the sense of full-disclosure, as part of my statement about feeling comfortable in a third-world environment, I do like having access to technology; but I don't need to have choices of 15 types of greens or 25 types of toaster-waffles. I am just happy when my local market wherever I am actually has lettuce or bread. Life living on rocks does not work for everyone…but I am not everyone. Living on rocks works very well for me.

Two more things: First a disclaimer of sorts, followed by some sailing wisdom. The disclaimer: throughout this book, you will see some names of some of the people who have been part of my life. I was considering changing the names in case these people wanted to hide their identity, but as I only use first names, it shouldn't be too big an issue. Besides, none of the people who I have talked about were real twats, so all this should be okay. Next, the sailing wisdom.

When I learnt to sail, I noticed that, standing on the deck of my first boat, the horizon was about 10 miles away. I found I could sail all day in the same direction, and yet, at the end of the day, the horizon would still be about 10 miles away. If you are someone who would feel that this meant you hadn't accomplished anything, I suppose it might also mean you would not like sailing. But for me, the fact that the horizon is always out there, and that I will never reach it is all good news. Sailing, for me, wasn't about being someplace; sailing was all about...well, sailing. The longer I could be out on the water, the better it all was. If I was sailing beyond where I could see land, it was even better. Being surrounded by water was about as good as things could ever be. Living on rocks was right up there with sailing for me.

The story begins several years after I moved to Mallorca.

01
Deciding What to Do

2005

The weather was quite the opposite of what I felt. It had been personally a very long, hard winter – a winter that felt like it had lasted several years – but here I was in Mallorca, and suddenly the sun and warmth were brightening my outlook. I had come to Mallorca on my boat on a visit, but after a few weeks, I just knew that this is where I wanted to be. I sold the boat and rented a flat in Palma to use as a base whilst looking for a home.

Mallorca is a pretty spectacular place, but as there are so many tourists here, it is almost easy to lose track of where you really are. Walking down the streets of Palma, it is audibly visible that this is a favourite holiday destination for Germans and English alike. I had rented a flat in Santa Catalina, part of the old quarter of the city, and was desperate to use my Spanish. Okay, this was a bit of a problem for me, as the Spanish I knew had worked well in the Americas, and even in central Spain, but this was Mallorca, and here, Spanish was in reality Mallorquin. The only way I can describe Mallorquin is that it is sort of a cross between Spanish, French, Catalan, Paella, and red wine. So I found myself connecting mainly with ex-pats from all over the world. My best friends here are from Australia, and although listening to them is quite enjoyable, what they speak is not Mallorquin, nor is it even Spanish. I was living on a Spanish island, only 100km from the mainland, and I was determined to find an environment in which I would improve Spanish, or probably just wilt away from lack of sustenance.

I began to look for properties that were outside of Palma. Well, the reality was that I began to look for properties in little villages that are not filled with visitors from other parts of the English-speaking world. Last autumn, my friends and I were driving around looking for a fab restaurant on our semi-frequent Sunday journeys out of the city, and we drove through Puigpunyent. Puigpunyent (poooeeej-poon-yent) is indeed a small village. According to one of my friends here, it is actually just a "T-junction" that filled up with houses over the years. No big central square where the locals gather; no proliferation of shops; no hustle and bustle; just a little sleepy village about 14km from Palma. As we drove through looking for the right road to Valdemossa, Puigpunyent registered itself in the back of my mind as a place to consider settling in.

I looked at all the trendy, four-colour glossy adverts put out by estate agents on the island, only to find out that the German influx in the 1990"s had driven prices into the stratosphere. So that meant I had to readjust what I considered appropriate housing choices. Out went the idea of large finca surrounded by hectares of orange, lemon, and olive trees; out went the idea of having a swimming pool the size of a football pitch; and out went the idea of having spectacular views of the sea surrounding the island. All of which upon reflection was probably a good thing. It became apparent that a nice village house would (hopefully) be available in my budget range, and living in a village would be better for immersing myself in the real culture of the island. So I kept looking at the cleverly worded adverts – *"reformation possibility"* meant that the house was in a state of ruin that approximated Coventry after the war; *"spectacular vistas"* meant that if you stood on your toes with your face smashed up against an upstairs window, you might actually see something other than the house across the street; and *"incredible possibilities"* meant you would have just as much of a chance of making it liveable as winning the lotto the same day that Cindy Crawford rings you for a date.

(2004)

Whilst on a business trip to London, I was talking to a friend and our conversation slowly drifted toward signs. Not street signs, not traffic signs, but signs from above. You know, those signs we see or don't see, believe or don't believe, that can foretell our future. Signs of very special things. Signs about our lives. Signs. Gabriel was telling me about someone he knew in Singapore that was able to reveal incredible information about his life, just from the exact time and date of his birth. It made me think back to one of those times several years ago where everything was lined up so as to be a once in a lifetime sign.

It was February 2002, and we were living in Barcelona. It suddenly struck me that my birthday was going to be a *very* special day. I was born on February 20th, and I realised that this year (2002) was truly a once in all-of-time occasion. "All-of-time" was clearly more impressive than simply "once in a lifetime," so I began to check and double-check everything.

On my birthday that year, I realised that (using the European numbering schemes, which is where we were living), the resultant numbers would be 20-02-2002. Not bad...2002-2002. A duplication in numbers. *Very, very special.*

But then I took it once step further. Yes, the term anal retentive might have applied to me that day, but I was on a roll. At exactly 8:02 that night, the number sequence would triple. The hour, 8:02, would be represented in a 24-hour clock as 20:02. And when you added that to the date (20th of February, the second month of the year); and to the year, you would have 2002-2002-2002. How cool was that. My God, a triple numerical sequence, and it clearly could occur only once-in-all-of-time. It was surely the signal that something *very, very, very* special was to occur in my life.

So I pondered what I should be doing at that exact moment of my life, the moment when all the stars were lined up, when all the planets must surely be synchronised in their orbits, the time when every Tarot card deck was ready to tell of glorious things, the time when the small bones thrown by voodoo doctors would signal nothing but good. I was always told that birthdays are when we become older and wiser; and this time, I was to be incredibly lucky as well.

I rushed about trying to see if there was some lottery someplace that would be drawn that date. I checked websites on numerology to see what I should be doing at that precise time. I began to notify friends so that we could all be together at this very, very, very special time for me. And for the planet itself. I was convinced that this was *the* time, and I had to get ready for it.

I wondered if this could have happened for my father. He was born on the 20th of May, so it wasn't a workable start to the numbers ever lining up right. And the fact that he died in 1974 mucked up any chance for him. My brother was born in November but his sequence would have been 2411 to begin with, so that wouldn't have worked out either. And then I realised, this occurrence, the one time in all of time when the time, date, and year all were identical was truly special. And it was to happen on my birthday. Unbelievable.

So we assembled a group of friends, ostensibly to go out to dinner that night. But deep down inside, I knew that this was *the* night of all nights.

At about 7:45, we set out to walk to the restaurant with friends. It was one of my favourite restaurants in Barcelona, and I thought it would be an appropriate place to celebrate such a special, special, special, once in a lifetime, once in the entire history of the world event. I kept checking my watch – subtlety, of course – all the way toward the restaurant, all the time immersed in conversation about the supernatural and astrology and other stuff that I really knew nothing about. Just setting the stage for the big occurrence.

And as we all crossed the street a block from the restaurant, I looked down at my watch again…and saw that it was now 8:04h. I had missed the magical moment. And it would never happen again. Well, to be more precise, whatever was supposed to have happened wouldn't happen again. But dinner was great. I had the four-cheese ravioli.

After talking to Gabriel about signs the other day, I thought I would have another go at the timing of my next birthday. After investigating every possible combination of numbers, dates, times, and astrological symbols, I have figured it out. In the year 2005, my birthday will result in me being another year older…on a Sunday. Not sure about the "wiser" part.

(Back to 2005 again)

Earlier this year, I found a house in an advert that looked super. I clicked on the estate agent's website and saw more photos of it and instantly fell in love. It was two old (old means very old) connected houses that had been reformed by a previous owner into one two-bedroom, two bath home with a small terrace off one of the bedrooms and a patio that was filled with an overgrown palm tree. And it was in Puigpunyent. After a phone call to the agent, off I went to see it. It was, in a word, spectacularly wonderful (okay, that may look like two words, but I am trying to keep the word count down for the editors, and that is what it was). In my budget, sort of. Nice location. Serious vistas of the mountains. Fab kitchen in the centre of the house. In Puigpunyent. But for the next three months, I waffled about it. I would spend hours trying to "see myself" in the house, trying to imagine what it would be like to live there, but I didn't make an offer.

In early April, I was with a friend looking at a flat for her and when she was done talking to her estate agent, he turned to me and asked if I needed any help finding a property. "*Well*," I replied in my increasingly acceptable local language, "*I have seen a house I like in Puigpunyent. Do you have any homes for sale there?*" He did. And I ended up buying it.

Buying a home in Spain is an experience. I come from a culture where home buying is all about scurrying about, rushing to wait, dealing with appraisers and legal minds, and hard bargaining. But my experience here was a tad different. Yes, step one was to find the house you want to buy – did that. Step two was to make an offer. But according to my estate agent, an ex-pat Brit who had been here since Franco was a just gleam in his father's eye, the way the offer thing worked here was to only make a money offer. No real conditions required at this point. No parameters of the deal. Just figure out how much over the asking price you wanted to pay and he would tell the seller. "How much *over* the asking price?" No, the way I was brought up is that purchasing a house is about as adversarial as any financial transaction could be. The seller wants X, I will offer X minus a bunch, with more conditions that a hypochondriac has on a bad day. Then the seller says no and counters with a mild compromise. Then I am supposed to halve the difference, and eventually, all this compromising and "halving" differences ends up with a deal.

So I made my offer, but I added about fifteen contingencies to it, clearly demonstrating my home buying competence and my desire to stay in my home-buying safety zone. The estate agent tells me that there is no way the seller will accept it. So I, feeling that someone is just trying to attach a Hoover to my bank account, tell the estate agent to actually find out by ringing the seller (I thought that was his job anyway). He does, and comes back with the message he predicted. Buggers. Now I needed to figure out how badly I want this house.

The house that I was keen on is a village house. Originally a house and a barn that were connected; a previous owner broke through the common walls on both floors and made it into one. Three bedrooms, two bathrooms, one ensuite for the master bedroom, a living room the size of a small aircraft carrier, a kitchen of almost equal size, fireplace in the living room and one in the kitchen, a roof terrace, and a tiled courtyard with orange trees and a completely out of control bougainvillea plant/tree/bush that appears to have been on steroids for some time. The house is over two hundred years old, and the external walls are almost a metre thick. Nice tiled roof, great shutters on the windows, and a wall providing privacy from the street. (I use the term street a bit loosely here, as the street is actually a relatively narrow mews-like alley, but passable by car... if you are careful) Then there was the thing about the sign.

When I first saw the house, the estate agent took me up the street to a long cream-coloured rendered stonewall. In the middle of the wall was a massive wooden door, and on one side of it, an etched brass plaque with the name of the house. I loved the sign, and I loved the fact that the house had a name. Apparently the artist who etched the plaque also put his initials in the plaque, because in the lower right-hand corner was a "JR." As these are my initials, it was clear to me that this was a sign from heaven's property Gods, and that my having this house was pre-ordained. Those are some of the good bits. The bad bits are that there is no garage, and living in a village away from Palma means I would need to buy a car. The village doesn't really have a centre to it, just some streets that come together every once in a while. One "super market" as far as I can tell, but even the supermarket is about the size of a newsagent's shop. But the bottom line was that I really did like the house, so I decided to increase my offer up to the asking price.

Before doing this, I had more homework to do. Due to the fact that so many houses on the island are older, many owners have "reformed" them so they are more suitable for today's buyers needs and wants. All this is fine, but I had been told that in many cases, the rehabilitation process for houses was not recognised by local authorities, so this suddenly became a potential issue. Was the house legal? If I bought it would I be able to obtain legal title to the property as it now stands? Were the two older houses really considered to be one property now? After consulting with the local government in Puigpunyent, I received assurances that all was well. Then there was the minor issue that as I was not a resident of the island – residency is an important issue, as you cannot purchase property in Spain without holding a NIE number. I had never got one when I arrived in Mallorca as I was initially living on a boat, and had no idea how long I would stay. So I began to talk to solicitors here about how to obtain the all-permitting number. Whilst there does seem to be a fixed process for doing this for UK citizens, every solicitor I spoke with gave me varying information. Then I mentioned it to my bank here and was told that they would take care of it all for me. So I thought I was good to submit my offer.

It wasn't just my emotions that were driving the increase in my offer. I had got my hands on a valuation of the house from two years ago, and it was more than my latest offer, so I felt pretty good that I would be safe in buying it. Besides, Mallorca is an island, so land availability is pretty much non-existent unless you look in the middle of the island. Even in recent housing price falls in the UK and continental Europe, the housing market has been not slipping on the island. So I raised my offer, added even more conditions with it and sent it to my estate agent. Within hours after its submission, I had the answer…my offer was accepted.

Moving from my flat in Palma, whilst an exciting prospect, was fraught with worries. I had been enjoying living where I was. Overlooking the harbour in Palma, I currently had two terraces, each with spectacular views, and windows on all four sides. Each flat occupied a separate floor of the lift-equipped building, so I had lots of privacy and because I didn't own a car, I had become quite comfortable with walking everywhere.

The neighbourhood I had been living in is called Santa Catalina, and it's very special. It was only a five-minute walk to the fresh fish/meat/poultry/flower market that was open from 0800 to 1400 each day. I was only five minutes as well from a pretty-well stocked super market. I was only five minutes from a plethora of restaurants of which many became favourites. And I was only a bit more than five minutes from downtown Palma. Actually, I could find almost anything I wanted within a five-minute walk from the flat – I felt like I was in the centre of the Palma world. But it was time for me to move on, and I was very excited about the prospects of the new house.

Being not as young as I used to be, and with those annual chronological increases comes corresponding slippage in the ability to keep everything straight in my head, I began to make lists. Lots of lists. One list was of all the things I would need to do to finalise the paperwork on the purchase; one list identified all the things I had to do to make my flat rentable again; one list detailed all the things I wanted to do to the new house to make it truly mine; one list included all the miscellany that comes with transferring utility services to a new owner; and one list identified all the stuff relating to the actual move. It was this last list that became the most complex.

For over four years, I had been paying a storage facility outside of London to keep the furniture I had in my London flat, all packed sardine-like in a 16 cubic metre space. Yes, I know, four years of monthly storage bills was pretty excessive, and even whilst making the list, I tried to avoid doing the sums of how much I had paid these people over the years just to keep my things in case I needed them again. I rang the London facility to give them the good news that I was finally going to get my belongings out of their locker-filled building, but for some reason, they didn't seem as excited as I was; probably because they were losing one of their sure-thing annuities, but they did understand. We talked through how much I owed them for the final month, what part of the security deposit I had given them years ago I would get back, and how the removal company would get access. As I didn't plan on being there to help put everything in a removal lorry, I asked if there was some way they could get past the very expensive, super strong padlock that I had put on the door of the locker when I rented it. *"Oh, not a problem; we cut them all the time."* So much for security.

I found several companies that said they specialised in weekly removals between Spain and the UK, so after bartering back and forth, committed to use one of them. This was a bit tricky (or just new to me). The deal was, I was told, that they would collect everything from my storage locker thing and take it to a depot where it would be containerised for the trip south. But whilst they were keen to get their lorry over to the storage place and fill it up, they wouldn't ship it until they were paid in full. Fair enough I supposed, but a serious pain in my bum as I struggled to make sure that getting them the funds did not slow down the shipping process. I offered to have the local agent come to my flat to collect the check, but he was too busy with removal work to do this quickly; and when I offered to come to his office, I was reminded of the fact that he just didn't sit around waiting for someone to come strolling in with sterling. It was the beginning of several catch-22 scenarios; they won't ship until they get paid, and they are too busy to take the money, the word *delay* started to spin around in my head. Eventually I was able to sort it all out, but it was a nuisance that I didn't need.

Then there was the little thing about getting my Palma furniture to Puigpunyent. Whilst I didn't have too many things here, the catch was that the removal company was quoting me two prices; one for two men in a van, one trip; and the other was two men in a van, two trips. "*Why would you suggest two trips?*" I asked. "*Well, we may not be able to use a van big enough for one trip that will make it down the village streets.*" Oh fine. I hadn't expected an over the road, double trailer lorry to do this; all I had to move was some tables, terrace chairs, large palm plants, pictures, and clothes. No appliances, no beds, no sofas...just normal stuff, and not much of it. This discussion went on for a week until the agent managed to come over to the flat and have a look. One trip, one van, two men...four hours, give or take a bit. Done.

All I had to do now was wait for the bank to finish their paperwork – a mortgage note, various notary signatures, reviewing the new valuation on the property, and the filing of new ownership documentation with the local authorities. The new valuation had come in about 25% higher than the purchase price.

The whole thing of having to wait once I was ready is frustrating. For some reason, in my mind, I couldn't understand why, if I was ready, the current owner of the house wasn't. Okay, so that might be a cheeky attitude, but here I am, having waited for months to even find a house I wanted to buy, having made my decision, made the offer, all fired up, and now I am sitting waiting.

From a rational perspective (something that gets thrown out of the pram with the toys when emotions kick in), I should have been able to get my head around the delay. After all, the current owner wasn't about to take steps to move out until he knew for sure that the deal was on – fair enough. And I don't think that he was even that keen to sell the house anyway. Something about the fact that selling the house was the only way to sort out finances due to an upcoming…okay, I think you may have a clear picture of what was going on so enough about his problems.

I spent part of one day trying to figure out how to have the local removal people safely move the palm plants from my flat – palm plants that had been expanding about as fast as the start of the Big Bang theory. What were nice little palms in cute little pots when I bought them last year had gone jungle on me. Don't get me wrong; I loved the fact that they became highly motivated to grow once I re-potted them. But they had gone from being about 1.5 metres tall and ¾ metre wide to over 2 metres tall and by a sprawling 2 metres width. I was beginning to feel like I was on one of those celebrity-get-me-out-of-here programmes when walking through the flat. I suppose I could have just purchased a pith helmet, but buying the house seemed like a better idea.

Plan one to move the plants was to just leave them as they were and keep my fingers crossed. I wasn't too keen on this idea, as the local removal staff might break off the palm branches. Plan two was to wrap some light twine around the branches, holding them up in a semi-mummy-shaped configuration. I tried this idea on one of them, but was using so much twine to keep all the leaves in place that I was worried that the movers would assume I was the head of the Palma S&M club. Probably not a good idea either. On to plan three. This one sprang into my head whilst lying out in the sun on the terrace (all part of my daily health regimen). I got up from the sun lounger and went to my closet. For some time, I had been washing and ironing my own shirts instead of taking them to one of the neighbourhood laundries, but in the back of the closet, I still had some shirts that they had done… and they were covered with those clear poly-what's-their-name bags. After whipping one of the bags off a shirt (and trying to figure out why I hadn't binned that shirt years ago), I cut the top off of the bag and gathered it up into a poly-donut thing shape. I then put the ring of clear plastic on the floor and manhandled one of the palm pots into the centre of it. After a bit of pulling and stretching, I was able to slide it up around the palm leaves. A great way to ship the plants – all protected into a poly-wrapped tube. Nice. Yes, of course I had to slide it off, as I it didn't appear that I would actually make the move for another two weeks, and didn't think that Mr. Palm would enjoy being wrapped up in a cling-film like container that long.

Now just in case you are reading this thinking to yourself, *"I think he has too much spare time on his hands,"* don't worry. I have plenty to do; I just want to get into my house and it admittedly is becoming on an equal standing as finding the Holy Grail for me. Next, I pulled out my handy-dandy measuring stick and began to measure all the paintings for the local removal people. You know, so they could ensure to bring the correct containers for them. *"Let's see; one that is 102 x 72cm, one that is 150 c 100cm, three that are 92 c 60cm,"* and on and on until I had the exact dimensions of all 15 paintings. After compiling a rather exhaustive list, I rang up the removal company to give them the news. His reaction? *"Thanks mate, we will bring a couple of big boxes."* Fine. So much for trying to help him.

All this "hurry-up and wait" may have been getting to me, I admit. I began to stare at the photos I had taken of the interior and exterior of the house. I scrutinised the floor plans. I compared the floor plans to the photos. I went out and bought copies of trendy home magazines to look for clever ideas of how I could enhance the ambiance of the house. I studied the photos of interiors of other houses that I saw on websites. And suddenly I realised the most important thing I could do, the thing that all people who are eager to move into a new house but have to wait should do; I opened a bottle of red wine…and fell asleep.

The actual move to the village of Puigpunyent went well. Or as well as any human being could expect in a country where everyone speaks a language that I don't know as well as I should by now. No last minute hitches, so major problems…well, sort of. At the last minute, I had received a phone call from my friendly banker – anyone who was nice enough to give me the money to buy the house deserves to be called friendly. The message was pretty clear – I had to get over to the bank to supply them with one additional document before I could sign the mortgage note. The request was fair enough, but what was confusing was what they wanted. They wanted to see a copy of my last will and testament. *"My will? Why?"* I enquired. *"Because of your age and the length of the mortgage, we want to make sure that you have children."* I am sure that my sons will be very excited to know that a bank in the middle of Mallorca thinks that they will pay off my mortgage after I die. I took it in; they photocopied it; and went back home, happily with the knowledge that everything was set for the hand-over.

I went to my Mallorquin bank and met with the bankers, the sellers, the notarios, and my estate agent; signed way too many papers; received a series of keys and instructions on how to operate all the appliances, and a list of contact details for anyone important connected to my new home. You know, the names and phone numbers of the fireplace wood supplier, the local newsagents, and the various utilities. I had asked for a list of all the little idiosyncrasies of the house, but I was told that there were none. Right. I have never owned a property that doesn't have little quirks, so this should be either, A) a wonderful experience, or B) quite an interesting experience of discovery. I really didn't care at that point – I just wanted to get back to my soon-to-be vacated flat in the centre of Palma to help the movers get everything packed and on its way to Puigpunyent.

I had been packing for several days, and as these things go, had ended up with far more boxes than I had planned on. I had taken care to make a small floor plan of La Antigua and labelled each box with a huge blue letter that identified which room at the house the lads from the removal company should put them. So much for planning.

James B Rieley

The boxes were all stacked as close to the door as possible; the plants were all wrapped in their clear polyethylene sleeves, and I had previously dragged what furniture I had all into the centre of the living room. I was ready. I was excited. I was chomping at the bit. And I was waiting for them to arrive.

The actual moving expedition went like clockwork. And as if I suddenly became lucky, I received a phone call from the movers who were bringing my furniture from the UK that it was already in Palma and would be out for delivery the next day. So within a twenty-four hour period, everything was in the house. Okay, so it was a bit hectic – the international movers arrived and were carrying everything from their lorries to the house along the narrow road; my food delivery people arrived and carried enough supplies to feed an army for a month to the house; and a package delivery service arrived with a house-warming present from a good friend in the UK. A very busy two days…but I am in La Antigua, and am very happy.

The cast of characters for this week's missive includes; Luis – the previous owner of La Antigua; Paulo – sort of Luis" handyman; Vesca – the woman that Luis has been using to clean the house once a week; myself – the new proud owner of La Antigua; Tony – the owner of my local café; four German tourists; and Pedro – the cabinet maker. Bet you just can't wait…So here is how things went.

When I arrived at La Antigua, my plan was to unload my hire car before the movers arrived, but for some reason unknown to modern man, the moving van managed to catch up to me on the road from Palma to Puigpunyent. So by the time I pulled up in front of Calle Es Forn (the name of the street I now live on), they were stuck on my tail so close I think that my little Ford Fiesta had a Velcro bumper. Okay, so that part of the plan didn't work out that well, but I knew that they wouldn't be able to get their van up the street because it is a tad narrow. Narrow means that the street is only 2.3 metres wide, which in other, non-metric worlds, means it is 89 inches wide. (Apparently, when the houses along my street were built almost 200 years ago, not too many people were driving cars). So my cunning plan to get there first sort of shifted a bit, and I decided to back up the street and unload the car in front of the house. Ever try to back a car down a street that is 89 inches wide? Not only was I able to (softly) touch both side of the street repeatedly, I almost burned out the clutch. The problem (okay, MY problem) is that I live in a village, and on either side of the street are houses. Houses whose exterior walls are literally the edge of the street. No walk path, no extra space, just street and house on both sides. Looks great, feels great…except not to the fenders of the car. And to top it all off, the street is about a 15-degree incline. So whilst trying to avoid my neighbour's houses, I was riding the clutch quite a bit. But eventually, I did make it up to the outside gate, just in time because the interior of the car was beginning to smell a lot like burning clutch. My next challenge was to open the door far enough to get out and unload the stuff that I brought…just about the time that the movers had most of their van unloaded and placed on the ground in front of my car that was, as you might imagine, blocking the gate. Think I was having fun yet? It was only beginning.

When I managed to move the car backwards a bit further so that the movers could carry all my things in, I met Paulo and Vesca. And why do you suppose they were there? Of course, they were finishing moving Luis" stuff out. Well, that was what Paulo was doing at least. Vesca was there to clean the house completely for the new proud owner of La Antigua. A nice gesture on the part of Luis, but apparently Vesca may have skipped out on a few classes in the Cleaning Academy of Bulgaria. Don't get me wrong; Vesca was a very nice lady...it is just that she and I have different views of what the word "cleaning" means. The big wooden gate was spotless – she wiped that down more than once whilst I was telling the movers which room to put which stuff. But she did miss a few other areas...like the floors, ceilings, walls, closets, refrigerator, stove, oven, and counter-tops. But the outside gate looked fab.

Yes, everything did get unpacked AND put away. No sense waiting for days trying to figure out exactly where things should be – just get the clutter cleaned out and make the house liveable was my motto. Within two days largely spent trying to figure out where things were, and why I put them there; I decided I needed a break, so off to my local café. Can Domingo is a very special place. Not too big, not too modern, just your typical local Mallorquin café. I walked up the hill (Puigpunyent is not exactly a flat village) to the café and sat down. I really like Can Domingo, probably because one of the reasons I wanted to live in the village was to work on my Spanish, and it seems that everyone that goes there is a local resident. Tony came over and said hello and explained what was on the "Menu del Dia" that day and brought me some water and a glass of red wine. I was in heaven. I was surrounded by the sounds I wanted to hear. Okay, so I didn't understand everything I was hearing, but one of the best ways for me to learn a language is to surround myself with it, and that is what I was doing. And then I heard a melange of German and English. It seems that two older couples (if I am 60, and am saying that they were "older," you can just imagine how old they were) had sat down at a table near me and were trying to order. "You have menu?" was the first thing I focused on. Well, Tony doesn't have menus. In a restaurant that has a Menu del Dia, you get what they make, and that day, it consisted of a seafood salad, pork in an incredible sauce, desert, coffee, and wine. So the two couples finally figured out that the menu was set, but when Tony's wife brought the salads, one of the women began to try to explain that they didn't eat any meat, fish, or anything that closely resembled them. It took a few tries, but eventually, her salad was replaced with some lettuce and onion slices. As I devoured my lunch, I began to feel sorry for the tourists – I know how difficult it can be when you don't speak or understand a foreign language, so I borrowed a pen from Tony and wrote something on my place mat for the lady. *"Soy vegetario y no es posible comer carne o pescado. Gracias."* (I am a vegetarian and do not eat meat or fish, thank you). Not sure, but I think I earned my merit badge for being a good person that day. Too bad I didn't wait around for them to finish; I suppose I could have earned another one by helping them across the street, but the streets are so narrow and traffic is not exactly a major problem in Puigpunyent, I figured that they could handle it on their own.

Today, after another day of looking for things in closets and drawers that I know I put someplace, but can't find; I decided to go talk to Pedro. Pedro is a neighbourhood cabinetmaker and I had found out from Luis that he is the one who built the kitchen of La Antigua. Why would I go see him? After several days in the house, I realised that I wanted an island built for the open space in the kitchen and a cabinet for under the stairs on the south wall of the kitchen. So down the hill I walked (See? I don't always have to go uphill except on my way home from Pedro's I guess) and gave Pedro a semi-accurate artist's representation of what I wanted him to build for me. That's all, no traumas, no problems, just the news that it would take him 15 days to make the stuff. And then Pedro helped me understand the Spanish culture a bit more. He said that 15 days in Spain meant a month...and then he smiled. I will let you know how the things look in two weeks...hopefully.

I have some friends who, for some unknown reason, refer to Puigpunyent as "Hermit Valley." Well, I suppose I do understand why. When I began to talk about moving here, I used words like,

countryside, little village, and truly Mallorquin. And I suppose if I was hearing these words from someone who leans toward being an introvert, I might come to the same conclusion. Whilst my descriptors are accurate, they might also be a bit mis-leading.

Clearly, Puigpunyent is not a metropolis, but equally, I really wasn't looking to live in something the size of London again. The population here is (allegedly) 1,500 people; it does have a supermarket (okay, so it only has three aisles); it does have a post office; and it does have more than one restaurant. Yes, the streets tend to be quite narrow; yes, many of the homes were built around the time Ben Franklin and Thomas Jefferson were hanging out together; and yes, the village has more character than Sybil has personalities. Puigpunyent *feels* like a village. And that is what I was after.

I have made it a point to meet some of the other residents here. Here's how this goes...I see someone walking down the streets in my neighbourhood (Yes, Puigpunyent has multiple neighbourhoods, but more about that in a bit). I walk up to the person and immediately tell them (in Spanish) that I just purchased a home here, AND apologetically, I admit my Spanish is crap. Well the fact is that I probably don't need to tell them that last bit after listening to me for three seconds. But everyone is so polite, and they all respond with "no, your Spanish is very good." Right. So then we kibitz back and forth for a few minutes about the weather, or where I can buy something, and I go on my way…having made a new friend in the village. Now all this sounds great, but my first problem is that I can never remember who they are. Last night, one of my neighbours knocked on the big wooden gate of the courtyard. I went rushing outside to find out that he was interested in knowing if it was my car blocking the road. "No, my car is parked down the road a bit" I responded. But it was an opportunity to meet a neighbour and dazzle him with my Spanish (which he said was very good. Right) Just as he left, I once again asked his name, and then rushed back inside to write it down. I figured that not remembering the names of every person I assaulted with poor Spanish in the village was okay, but it would be good if I could remember my neighbour's names. Tomeu. Nice name. TOE-MAY-OOH. I suppose I should have checked to see if that was his Christian name or his surname. Tomaeu. The whole name thing is different in Spain. Most people have three names, as I do – James Brown Rieley. But in Spain, it is the first two that are what people are known as. I, on the other hand, am not Spanish, and everyone knows it. Almost every person I have met in Spain refer to me as one of the following: *"Dr. James;" "Mr. Realley;"* or just *"Señor."* (I keep waiting to hear, "hey, YOU.") Whatever works is my motto, so I respond to pretty much anything when I think that someone is talking to me. In the case of Tomeu, he called me "el dueño nuevo" (the new owner). I imagine, in a village where people have lived here for generations, I will be the "new" owner of La Antigua for the next 200 years.

Puigpunyent isn't too out-dated in everything. The village has a very serious re-cycling programme. Of course, due to resources, the programme does appear (to me) to be a bit "interesting." Every house has its own numbered trash container. That is the good news. The bad news is that the container is about big enough for a litre of water. And to make things even more interesting, the village people who collect the refuse only pick up certain types of trash on certain days. As far as I can understand it so far; Mondays, Wednesdays and Fridays are "food garbage days;" Tuesdays are for bottles; Thursdays are for paper and cardboard; and the weekends are dedicated to drinking wine. So as a recently arrived person, who needed to dispose of multiple kilos of crap that I shouldn't have even moved, I was trying to figure out how to put all this stuff into this little plastic box. And then I found out that Puigpunyent has its own recycling centre. Separate places for bottles (four huge green bins), cardboard and paper (four more huge containers), electrical appliances (yes, how many discarded appliances can there be in a village of 1,500 people does seem like a fair question); metals of various types; grass and plant clippings; motor oil; rubber; and non-recyclable items. Pretty nice. So what do I do? Easy peasy. I begin to fill up monster bags of junk and haul it to the centre in the boot of my hire car. One day, I was so pumped up about the whole concept, that I loaded one of my black polyethylene bags full of cardboard and chucked it onto the little carry-rack on the back of my

James B Rieley

bicycle. How ecologically minded am I, anyway? Well, the recycling centre is at the bottom of a large hill, and as I was coasting down towards it, I was beginning to think I could do this everyday. Then I had to get back home. I took the car ever since. As of today, I have been in the village for 8 days, and have made 9 trips to the recycling centre. I don't" think I will ever get to the point of using the adorable Barbie-sized home container, but at least I am recycling.

I have been in La Antigua for a week and a half, and the fun is just beginning. Tomorrow is Tuesday, and I have been told that Tuesday's are the day for the open market in the centre of Puigpunyent. So tomorrow morning, I will wake early and walk / ride my bicycle / drive into the town centre and have a look around. (You can pick my method of transportation yourself, but my money is on the car).

After my shopping excursion, I will probably come home and resume the routine I have seemed to have established for myself: sometime between 0630 and 0900, I wake up and do my exercises. Not exactly the highlight of my day, but part of my post-GBS life is lots of stretching exercises to keep all those muscles and joints operational. I do my exercises to the melodic sounds of Mietta, an Italian singer whose CD I bought whilst living on a previous boat in America. Still have no clue what she is singing about, but with her singing, my exercises are not quite as frenetic as they were when I was listening to Aretha Franklin egging me on with "Who's Zooming Who?"

After a shower, it is breakfast time, and as I live in a little village in Mallorca, AND, I am working really hard to assimilate into the culture of the island, I have a typical Mallorquin breakfast. When pigs fly. After my toast, yoghurt and tea, it is email time. I love email time...(yes, you are now thinking that this guy has no real life. But I do; it is just that email keeps me connected to the non-Puigpunyent world...which is pretty sizeable.

Usually, what shows up in the morning is adverts for low-interest loans; adverts for a couple hundred variations of Viagra; offers to help out some poor bloke whose father squirreled away millions in Zimbabwe and has picked me to help him get his money from some mythical account in a mythical bank; as well as the rather bizarre myriad of methods to increase the length and breadth of some of my body parts. Next, it is time for the semi-religious experience that I do daily of looking at various websites to see what is going on in the rest of the world. This usually means surfing through the Telegraph, the Times, bCentral (a Microsoft website that has been publishing some of my writings), and my brother's website. By then, it is time to get cracking, and getting cracking means going out to sit in the courtyard and just pondering.

Wednesday was a good example of the trouble that pondering can get one in. I was thinking of how wonderful all the trees and plants looked, and then I noticed that some leaves had fallen from the trees. As I was always taught that a clean courtyard is good, I decided to sweep the fallen leaves up. And as I was doing this (almost daily) chore, a couple more fell. So, being proactive, I took my magical red-handled broom and whacked the trees a few times, expecting that more loose leaves might fall, saving me from repeating the sweeping exercise tomorrow. Well, fall they did, and within a couple of minutes, the stones on the courtyard floor were completely covered in leaves. So after filling up *another* big black garbage bag for the recycling centre, I rewarded myself by having one of the oranges that had been growing in my trees that had fallen with the downpour of green.

By 1000h, I was about ready to get back to serious work, and decided to fill in a form to send to my friends at the internal revenue service in America, explaining to them that, as a British citizen, living in Mallorca, I would no longer need their always exciting, annual form-filling-out exercise. I read the directions, filled in all the blanks, double-checked it all, then, following the instructions, placed the four-page form into an envelope addressed to Philadelphia. I was feeling pretty good about doing this, so with a feeling of exhilaration, walked to the main post office in Puigpunyent. Okay, so there is only one post office here, but that would make it the main one, wouldn't it? After a brisk 10-minute walk, I found the building, and as I went to open the door, was practising to say, "I need to send this by certified mail to America." And then I noticed the sign on the door. Hours: 0800 – 1000. The (main) post office in my town is only open for two hours per day! And I had walked all the way there. Buggers. On the walk back home, with my letter firmly in hand, I realised that being open only two hours per day makes sense; after all, that gives THE employee the rest of the day to deliver the post. And go to lunch. And have a siesta. Ahhh, village living.

When I purchased La Antigua, I was given the names of several people by the former owner. One of these names was Pau. Pau was the "gardener and wood-suppler" of La Antigua I was told, although for the life of me, I couldn't figure out why a gardener was even needed. The house doesn't really have a garden, only a courtyard that is filled with trees and bushes and plants. But I was beginning to think that, as my grape vines were beginning to produce what appeared to be a bumper crop of grapes, I should ring Pau. After all, I was told that one of his jobs was to spray the vines to avoid a flock of wasps from appearing along with the grapes.

Today Pau came. He looked strangely like someone from the next George Lucas Star Wars sequel, with this huge spray tank on his back with hoses sticking out all over. I was trying to figure out how to ask him if he was one of the cast members of Revenge of the Grape-Sucking Wasps, but I was sure that there was no possible way to say it, luckily for me. For all I knew, it would have come out sounding like your mother sucks grapes. Yes, still working on the language thing. So after the mandatory "hello" and "how are you today Pau," he began his work. He pumped up the pressure on the tank and went about his work. After a couple of minutes, I looked out the window, and noticed that the overspray was falling down on top of him. So being a good little homeowner – and a concerned employer – I went outside and, in my best Spanish, asked Pau if all that spray falling on him was safe. There was a bit of background in my question. I used to be the owner of a company in America, as well as a business consultant in the United Kingdom; and was painfully aware of all the health and safety regulations that are designed to protect workers. Technically, as I had contracted with Pau for him to spray my grape vines, he was my employee, and I certainly didn't want him to become sick from his efforts. I have seen photos of people spraying pesticides in the past, and they are all covered up with protective clothing and breathing masks, and here was Pau, dressed in a t-shirt and jeans, with nothing over his face, spraying away. When I asked if this was safe for him, his response was that, in small amounts like he was using, it was completely safe...and then he let out a series of coughs that made me think his lungs were coming out. Life here certainly is different than where I came from. P.S. can't wait for the grapes to appear.

I knew that moving from Palma to Puigpunyent would require several serious changes in my life. I had existed quite well in the city without a car. Everything I needed was within walking distance, with my only automobile requirements being getting back and forth to the airport when I did my monthly trips to London. And whilst taxi's solved that for me, I realised that living in the village would mean that I would need a car. So a week or two before my actual move, I began to look for a suitable car.

Sort of torn between practicality (a VW Golf or Polo) and fun (a Mazda MX5), I, in my decidedly pragmatic thinking mode, sought out all the adverts I could that were auto-specific. It didn't take long to find that my eyes kept coming back to an advert for a silver MX5 for sale at a used car dealership in Palma. One day I walked over to see it and was smitten. Yes, it was a bit small (only two seats, with barely room enough behind them for copy of Vanity Fair, and a boot that might be able to carry my travel bag. But it had a removable hardtop and a folding convertible top. I checked under the bonnet; I examined all the wheels and brake discs; I prowled around through the boot (whatever prowling means in a space that was exceedingly small); and most importantly, I sat in it and started it up. I was hooked. I kept thinking about what would happen when friends and family would come and visit me. What would I do if there were more than one person? How would I transport the guests and their luggage? Screw-em. They could take a taxi...I was primed for the Mazda. So I went into bargaining mode with the dealer, and after about 30 minutes of hard, but somewhat understandable offer, counter-offer, counter-counter-offer, we were on the same page with the price. Now came the minor little details of actually writing the deal up.

The dealer, a very helpful name named Antonio, asked me for the spelling of my name, followed by a request to see my NIE number and insurance information. In Spain, an NIE number is required whenever you buy anything serious, like a car or a house. I explained that I didn't actually have one yet, but had applied for it because of the house purchase. Not a problem replied Antonio, but I would need to provide a photocopy of my application. I was feeling pretty good. But then he asked again for my insurance information. *"Don't have any yet, but I will get it straight away,"* I replied. Antonio gave me the name of an insurance agency in Mallorca that was staffed largely by Brits, so as soon as I returned home (with visions of driving around with the wind blowing through my hair in the soon-to-be-my-Mazda), I rang them up. Yes, I wanted to obtain an automobile policy for a Mazda MX5. Yes, I have been driving for over 40 years. Yes, I have a driving license. No, it is not from the United Kingdom, it is from America. Oh. America may have all the money in the world, but they don't seem to have the ability to convince Spain that a US driver's license is the same as a European one. Interestingly enough, it is possible to rent a car with a US permit, but not to buy a car. (Note: If anyone who reads this can explain the logic behind this, please do feel free to write me.) So I decided to simply get a Spanish drivers permit; after all, I was living here, had bought a house here, and was feeling very Spanish.

Obtaining a driver's license in Spain could be the Webster's unabridged definition of bureaucracy. First, you have to go through a driver's school. Yes, I know I have been driving for over 40 years, but this is how it works. The driver's school arranges for the medical examination you have to take (yes, you need a medical exam to get a driver's license, and whilst it only consists of an eye test, a hearing test, a blood pressure check, and a two-hand coordination test; you still need it). So I did that, but must admit that the coordination test did seem like an updated version of one of the first computer games, with the instructions being to not let the little horizontal bars slip outside of the curvy, moving white line. Next, you have to take a written test.

Making sure I was getting all this straight seemed like a bigger challenge than the test itself, for the people who worked at the drivers school didn't speak a bit of English. I do love (attempting) to speak the local language, but when it comes to technical things or specific legal instructions, it sure is nice to double check what I am hearing with my native language, but that wasn't to be. So I kept asking them to repeat everything a couple of times, and far slower than they are used to talking. For the written test, I was told that I needed to study the "book." Okay, fair enough. *"Tienes este libro en ingles?"* I asked (do you have the book in English?). No, sorry, we don't have one in English. Shit. But instead of just taking what was going to be offered, I then asked, *"Es possible para obtener un libro en ingles?"* (Can you get a copy in English for me?) Yes, that they could do, but I would have to come back the next day. Not a problem. So the next day I was back in the office to pick up my trendy little study book, only to find that it had 560 questions that needed to be studied. FIVE HUNDRED SIXTY QUESTIONS!!!! Scheisse. Luckily, there are only 40 questions on the actual test, but it sure would have been nice to know which ones to worry about.

I apparently should have just taken the test in Spanish, as the English version was totally depressing and confusing. It seems that whomever translated the test questions sort of, as we say, mucked it up. Of the forty questions on the test, a passing score was to be 36 correct. I managed a 35, so now on to plan B (which I haven't even figured out yet).

The weekend, as most of us know very well, is a time for rest and relaxation; a couple of days to recharge from the turmoil and stress of the workweek. And it is the same here at La Antigua, with a few minor exceptions. Exception 1: my typical workweek is either full on, or semi-non-existent (according to some of my friends here on the island); Exception 2: I like to do stuff, and just sitting seems so non-productive; Exception 3: There are lots of things I could do each day here to convert La Antigua from a great village house to MY great village house. So quite often, my weekends blend in with my weekdays.

Last night (Friday), I had been invited over to see some of my new neighbours and had a lovely time, but after a couple of G&T"s during the evening, I think I overslept this morning. My day began normally, except for the fact that it began later than normal; whatever normal is for me. A few days ago I had purchased 15 flowering Oleander's from my favourite garden store in Palma (this is a serious garden store, and I think it actually could be on a par with all of Puigpunyent size-wise), and quite unexpectedly, they were delivered this morning. Early. About the time I had just gotten into the shower.

After helping the delivery man haul the 15 potted plants, the 15 larger pots so I could replant them into something larger than the cheesy little pots they came in; and the 300 cubic litres of potting soil up to the house, I decided that they probably weren't going to re-pot themselves, so I began the ever fun job of seeing how much potting soil a person can jam up under his finger nails. I had purchased these beauties for the roof terrace, but as I was flying to London for a few days next week, I decided that I should leave them in the courtyard where there is some shade until I returned. I had been told that the Oleander's would be good in direct sun, and that is what the roof terrace is full of. But being gone meant that there would be no one to water them for three or four days, and I reasoned that being newly re-potted, they might need some adjustment time. And besides, now in their new, more spacious injection-moulded imitation clay pots, they were heavy…and I was tired. So I hosed them down for a while in the courtyard and then set about my next task for the day.

My original plan for Saturday was to do some research for the books I had been contracted to write. Doing research (in my lexicon) usually means lying in the sun and thinking. And I reasoned that after the adventure in re-potting, this exercise was well deserved. So I hustled my ex-American, semi-

British, Mallorquin wannabe butt up to the terrace and began the process of getting things ready for the day. "Getting things ready" included positioning one of the sun lounges so that it would be perpendicular to the sun (for increased intensity, of course); looking for a some sunscreen that had a number on it that was higher than 1; turning on the music on the terrace (that days choice was Luther Vandross; and ensuring that I had something cold to drink. And because I have children who think that I spend too much time in the sun to begin with, I even committed to myself to actually turn over prior to needing a total skin-grafting operation. Four hours later – yes, I did turn over a couple of times…I think – I was back in the courtyard examining the Oleanders and wondering what I could do next to feel productive.

Doing creative things is pretty high on my list of things I like to do, so I dug up some heavy (heavy in terms of paper means "stiff," not "weighs a lot), a couple of photos that I like, my container of Cola Blanca (which is just white glue for wood or paper), my straight edge, and a matt-cutting knife. Hours later, I had accomplished what I set out to accomplish; sort of a modified "three-panel picture." When viewed from one side, it is one picture, from the other side, it is a different picture, and head on, still another picture. So I hung it on the wall…as I do with almost everything I make for La Antigua. And by the time I had made dinner, my mind was already rolling about what I would do the next day.

And I think Pau was right when he told me the other day that I would have a bumper crop of grapes this year. Or did he say that the grapes would be green? Or that the bumper on his car was green?

It was, in the words of Charles Dickens, the best of times and the worst of times…or something like that. Whilst my time living in La Antigua has been an incredible experience so far, I awoke the other morning to my worst fears. It was something that I had known might occur but after feeling so comfortable living here for the past month, I think perhaps that my fears had dissipated over time. After all, the past month had been glorious; great weather, meeting new people, getting my house sorted, being pretty productive with my writing and painting. But here I was, hit with something that I had all but forgotten could happen. Yes…it was cloudy.

The clouds did bugger off after an hour or so and the sun resumed its rightful place in the sky over La Antigua; and I decided that a cloudy day once in a while might not exactly qualify for razor blades on the wrists. By 1000, I was at the pool following the JBR-modified-health-regimen prescribed by my doctor as a way to keep up with my GBS episode of last year. I try to follow my doctor's orders explicitly – that is to say that when he says to exercise as much as I think is appropriate on any given day, and then to get lots of sun (for vitamin A or E or some other letter I think); I do actually do what he says. Although I must admit, sometimes the "exercise time" and the "sun time" do sort of blur together into something I recognise as "laying in the sun thinking about exercising."

James B Rieley

The public swimming pool is very, very nice. If you arrive shortly after they open at 1000, the pool is virtually deserted, with only two or three "regulars" (well, three or four now counting myself). It isn't until around lunchtime that all the mothers arrive with their darling children. So when I arrive, I have my morning conversation with Pablo, the all purpose lifeguard, card-checker, maintenance person, and Baywatch wannabe. We talk about just about anything…well, anything that I can say in Spanish that is. I made a deal with Pablo – each day, he needs to help me learn another word or two in Spanish, and for this service, I promise not to splash. Well I think that is what I promised. (God, I hope that is what I promised) Today I did a series of laps in the pool, did my compulsory lying in the sun, cleverly using some of that time to thank the sun for breaking through the clouds earlier. Then when the children arrived, I headed into Palma to do a bit of serious shopping.

I have been very fortunate in Puigpunyent in the fact that I am able to buy almost everything I need here. If my market doesn't have what I am after, I ask Guillem (one of the two brothers who own the shop) if he can get it for me. Which he always seems to be able to do. The only things that I need to go into Palma for are canvases, furniture, and visiting friends. I had asked Guillem to bring in some red wine that I quite enjoy that I couldn't find on his shelves, along with other necessities (white wine for friends, beer for friends, still water for friends, fizzy water for friends, coke light for myself, tonic water for mixing with Gin, and cranberry juice…for myself. The whole thing about finding cranberry juice has been interesting. First of all, the word for juice is "zumo," so when you order orange (naranja) juice, you say, "*Zumo de naranja por favor.*" But as I have yet to find the word for cranberry in this apparent non-cranberry part of the European Union, when I order orange and cranberry juices mixed together, as I tend to do, I end up saying "*Zumo de naranja y zumo de cranberry por favor.*" And the waiter looks at me like I am from a different world – and seeing as how I was born in Milwaukee, he might be right. When I asked Guillem to bring in a case of cranberry juice, I brought an empty brick with me (most juices and milks come in "brick-like" cardboard containers that are fabulous for storage). So I said, "*Guillem, este bric es zumo de cranberry.*" (Brick is bric in almost any language apparently.) And he blurted out some word that apparently is the translation for cranberry, but I missed it. So there we were, me saying "zumo de cranberry" and Guillem saying "*Zumo de something-or-other.*" I really do need to A) listen more closely; B) get Guillem to speak slower; C) find a better dictionary; or D) start drinking things I can pronounce.

I must admit, I have never really been the big "festival guy," but as one of the reasons I was keen to move to a small village was to become part of the culture. And today the culture came to me. The Festa de Sant Joan is an annual festival that Puigpunyent celebrates, and as luck would have it, the celebration takes place just around the corner from La Antigua.

According to the brochure that the local government had delivered to each home, all the village people are invited to participate. Come to think of it, I wasn't even sure exactly who Sant Joan was before the festa began, although, about mid-way through the evening's festivities, I was beginning to think that Sant Joan was a reference to Joan Wilder in the movie "Romancing the Stone" – lots of people enjoying the evening in the little plaza with couples dancing the evening away. The reality is that the Festa de Sant Joan is all about the life of John the Baptist, and traditionally, it is at this time of the year to celebrate the arrival of summer. Of course, relatively speaking, summer weather has been here for months.

After a dinner (there was the choice between Italian and Mallorquin food), a band began to play, and the music was wonderful. It was a truly Spanish evening; even when the band broke into Achy-Breaky Heart in Spanish. Well, okay, so maybe that was a stretch, but it did sound far better in Spanish than I thought it ever did in English. It could have been the environment, it could have been the evening, and it could have just been Puigpunyent. At a quarter after midnight, the band stopped playing and fireworks began to rocket off into the evening sky. And whilst the concept of fireworks in Puigpunyent may not be the same as it is in Barcelona, or London, or even Milwaukee; they were everything fireworks are supposed to be; loud as thunder, bright as a million flashbulbs popping in front of your eyes, and fabulous as they whizzed up into the night over the village. Actually, as the plaza where the festival occurred is only about 100 metres from La Antigua, the fireworks and the music completely filled my house. And after the fireworks were over, the music continued, but now with a different band. But for the rest of the night, the sounds that managed to filter through the walls of La Antigua were a melange of Rescue Me, Sex Bomb, I Will Survive and Lady Marmalade. It was then that I decided to go to sleep. Well, at least I decided to try to sleep. A very special evening in a very special place. And the weekend wasn't even over yet.

I had decided that I needed to have a little get together to celebrate my purchase, and several weeks ago, I picked Sunday to have it. Living in the village was a big driver in my planning – I wanted to serve typical Mallorquin dishes, and consequently, began to try to find ideas for recipes that I thought I would be able to make myself. I went online; I looked in cookbooks; I spoke to friends who I thought would know what would be good to have. After enough of trying to sort out what would be best, I went to my market to talk it all through with Guillem. I, in my faltering Spanish, went through my planned menu and asked how many of these things I could get there. And then, in one of my best moments, told Guillem it would be a lot easier if he prepared it all and brought it to the house a few hours before the party was to begin. Which he did. The food was great; the friends were fabulous; and the day, whilst being a tad warm, was wonderful. I just finished loading the dishwasher and am pondering how many trips to the recycling centre

James B Rieley

I would need to make tomorrow to bin all the wine bottles that somehow were now empty. A(nother) good day in Puigpunyent. Not all my days in Mallorca had been this good.

(2003)

I am not even sure exactly when I first noticed the rash, but there it was, sort of monopolising a major part of my upper back. I couldn't really see it, but I could feel that it was lurking back there…and I didn't like it. And then about a week later, it had somehow snuck on over to my chest as well. But, it was just a bit of a rash, so I didn't think too much of it. I was pretty focused on the impending spring, as I had been able to spend the previous several weeks on-board Angelina in Palma and whilst the weather had not been the best, at least it was better than in England, where I was headed.

London was great – with the exception of the cold, damp, grey skies that seem to be present whenever I visit – and I was able to accomplish most of the client work, ghost-writing an article for a CEO I had worked with. And then it was off to Paris for a few days; and that is when things began to change.

First, I found that my legs were getting stiffer than a teenager who just devoured a bottle of Viagra. Really painful to stand and walk, so I did what most people like me do – I took as many Advil and Panadol as I could get my hands on. Problem solved…or so I thought.

After my three days, I flew back to Palma and immediately rang a physiotherapist I knew on the island. A taxi took me directly to her office from the airport and after a quick overview of what was happening to my body, she began to bend me into pretzel-like shapes, all the time whispering things like, "*oh yes, this is good*," and my favourite, "*Hmmm.*" I have no idea what all that means, but from my perspective, it was not quite as much fun as I would expect getting polio might be. She filled in her contortionist merit badge check sheet and told me that I should probably really see a doctor. Well, thank you very much. How nice that I only had to pay you €40 for that advice. At least she gave me the name of a doctor who was close to her office, as right about then, I was only marginally able to even think about walking.

My visit to the doctor only ended up costing me €60, and for this fee, I was told, "*Whew, I have no idea what this could be. Have you thought about seeing a specialist? I know one.*" Oh yes, then he gave me the bill for the 60 euros. Needless to say, I didn't call his guy. But instead, I actually did something quite clever – I rang my insurance agent and asked him who was good, and of equal importance, who would be covered by my policy.

Okay, so I did get connected with a very good doctor. He is Spanish and whilst he does speak several Spanish dialects, as well as French, his English probably doesn't appear on his CV in the category of "high skills and competencies." But that's okay, as my Spanish is not exactly world class either. So we muddle through trying to sort out what this thing is that I have.

The first plan he came up with was for me to take some medication in the form of pills, two different types to be exact. These were to counteract the virus that he thought I had. And the virus idea sounded pretty good to me – a virus lodged in my spine would be able to muck up my walking, give me lots of lower back pain (something I had in copious amounts), and probably surface the rash that was the first symptom. This actually did make sense. So we went off to treat the virus with these meds. And because we were by now really buddies, he said I could keep taking the Naprosyn I found on the boat as an anti-inflammatory painkiller thing. Nice Naprosyn. So, go home and do this for a few days and we will see how it goes I was told. Or at least that is what it sounded like. So off I went, but by the time I had returned to Angelina, I had a secret ace-up-my-sleeve.

Yes, I did plan on taking the meds, but my real plan was to visualise the virus into submission. You know, "*see the virus*" and then "*see it going away.*" Shoot, this method is really good and it did work for me years ago when I had a stomach ulcer (or maybe just the change in my diet and the reduction of stress helped out a bit). Anyway, that was my plan.

Visualising something like a virus is not easy work. First, I have no idea what it really would look like if it walked up to me in the street and hit me (as it apparently did). But I have seen enough pictures of "virusy" looking things in Electron Microscope Monthly and other scientific journals that I read all the time (note the sarcasm), so I at least had that going for me. My plan was get a good solid picture of the virus in my mind, then hit it aggressively with medical thoughts such as, "*be gone with you,*" and "*do not pass go, do not collect anymore body functions,*" and the ever popular, "*just fuck off.*" Quite the plan, eh?

And just in case this plan wasn't good enough, I actually considered something that I learned about from some friends in high school in America. Dave, John, and Bob were all Christian Scientists, and as you may know, this is the religion founded by Mary Baker Eddy, a woman who believed that.... well, I never really did get the gist of it. But what I do remember is being told one night out that this religion really did work, and my friends had the evidence of it.

When he was about 9 or 10, I was told, Bob had broken his arm in some sporting event (who puts their kids into arm-breakable sporting events at that age I still wonder) and as they were Christian Scientists, this meant that Bob was not allowed to be treated by a doctor. Really, this is what it is all about – instead of going to a doctor or hospital, Bob's mother sat home and read to him from Mary Baker Eddy's literary version of DIY. I repeated what I had been told – "*Your Mom just read to you and your arm healed?*" "*Yes,*" was the reply from not only Bob, but Dave and John too – both witnesses to the near miracle they said.

Well I would have considered my reaction to this to be gobsmacked but I didn't learn that expression until I moved to London in 1999, so my reaction was probably more like "wow, cool." But then Bob did let it slip that his Mom had read to him for 8 weeks. *"Eight weeks? You mean you just laid in your room without moving your arm for eight fucking weeks while your Mom read to you?"* Well no shit it healed. And I'll bet he would have healed faster if she had not read to him day after day.

Okay, back to my little problem. I knew that I wouldn't be able to even find Bob's Mom or have any desire to have someone sit and read to me for weeks, so it was now up to the doctor's new solution of daily shots of some mystical medication or spend a few days in hospital. Don't like shots, and probably like hospitals even less.

Last time I was in hospital, I ended up with two semi-smiley 10cm long scars that weren't even symmetrically placed, and they gave me shots too. Bastards. And to top it all off, I have never been that great about following doctor's instructions apparently. After the dual operation event, the doctor told me that I would need to rest for 45 days before resuming normal activity. So the day after the operation, whilst I was still pretty well packed with God-knows-what hard-core medication, I checked myself out of the hospital and three days later flew up to London. The day after that, I flew to Amsterdam. And the day after that, I was back in hospital. Okay, so not the best at following medical instructions. This time, I thought that maybe, just maybe, I should listen to the doctor, so I checked into a very nice new hospital in Palma where my doctor is a senior medical-type person. And here I sit…well; actually here I lie in a hospital room.

The doc's (lucky me, I get more than one doctor, probably because I am either very special or just have a great insurance card) that are seeing me think that they have it sorted out, or at least what it is that has taken up residence in me. They say it is a virus called the Guillain-Barré Syndrome, which in my experience, translates to *"the really bad bastard nasty mean old virus that doesn't like James"* or something like that. It is hard to do a perfect translation from the Latin medical terms to Spanish to English. But I think that is about the best translation.

Feel like shit. Getting shots every couple of hours. Tired beyond belief. Managed to already drop a thermometer onto the floor as the nurse came back to the room to retrieve it – it broke into lots of little thermometers. And did I mention being bored? But I am here, resting, and I am listening to the doctor, for a change. Trying to do the patience thing. Thank God friends smuggled my computer into my hospital room…resting is one thing, but doing nothing resting is well beyond my scope.

18 March - So for those of you who know me (and I mean *really know me*) you probably have learned over time that patience is not exactly my middle name. But the past couple of weeks have taught me that patience is not only a virtue, it is the only way to go sometimes. Did the hospital for two

weeks, learned how to careen down the hall to the lift in a wheel-chair (only did run into one poor soul whilst trying to back the bloody chair up, sorry Señor), took all the injections and pills and capsules and blood tests and MRI"s and other assorted less than fun tests…and now I am out of hospital and recovering slowly. And here is where the word patience kicks in. Am recovering *slowly*.

This Guillain-Barré Syndrome should not be on anyone's wish list. And whilst many people who are unfortunate to get it have it far worse than I have had it, it still has not been fun. But I am doing pretty well.

Patience. According to some online dictionary site I found, patience is defined as "a good natured tolerance of delay." Okay, I can work with that definition I suppose. Well, with the minor exception of the "good natured" bit. I am crap at demonstrating patience. I get all cranky when things don't go really well, and being sick is one of those times. And of course, *we all* know that a "boy cold" is *far worse* than just about anything on this planet. So this has been a real bitch. I really thought (someplace deep in the back of my mind where people are not supposed to go) that I could just whack this GBS out of me in a couple of days. Oooooh baby, was I ever wrong. So now I am an active, dues paying member of the congregation of those who have learned that patience can be a good thing – especially considering the fact that I suppose I could actually still be in hospital.

So the past two days (have been out for two whole days now – whoopee) I have been doing what the doctor ordered. I take lots of adorable little pills. Adorable means I take some round white ones that are chocker with anti-GBS medication; I take some really cute pink oval ones that are laden with vitamins of all sorts of B–numbers; I take some that are blue and white (they must have something of redeeming value inside of them but for the life of me, can't figure out what it is) and of course, the normally prescribed pills that are supposed to counteract the negative effects of the other pills. Wouldn't you think by now that medical science would have some of this sorted out – why take a pill and then have to take a different pill to offset the effects of the first pill? This is way to confusing to me, but then again, I am on meds, so I don't have to understand everything. Or at least that is my excuse today.

Patience. So part of the therapy – needing to get the body working again as the GBS does some mean things to muscles and joints – is to do a lot of resting, some light stretching and slow walking. Slow is defined as S-L-O-W. Very slow. So today I walked almost a whole block to a café to sit outside in the sun and have a tea with friends. It felt like it took forever, and guess what? Friends lead to new friends, who lead to more friends, and then once in a while, you get to meet someone who has all the answers about any disease known to mankind. And today, I met such a person.

There we all were – me sitting there with my tea, trying to get my back and legs comfortable, and this Brazilian woman comes over and sits down to say hello to the other friends I was with. And then she looks at me as says *"Hola."* I replied with *"Hola."* Really, all I responded with was Hola and she says to me, *"Oh, you are Canadian?"* Well, I am not, but the citizenship thing is another whole story. I still don't get how when all I say is *"Hola."* (How can I mispronounce "Hola"?) And then someone else says, *"Oh, you sound like a Canadian."* Mind-boggling.

Anyway, then Urs (a friend of a friend of a friend) who was there, says, *"James just got out of hospital with Guillain-Barré Syndrome."* He had a big smile on his face so I took the comment as some sort of a badge of honour apparently just to get out of hospital at all, and the woman says, *"What you need is Reiki."* So just for clarification; here is what she knows – I must be a foreigner because of the apparently dysfunctional way I say *"Hola;"* she has just heard that I was in hospital with the GBS; and because of those two meagre facts, she has made a diagnosis. Welcome to the land of mysticism I guess.

What the fuck is Reiki, I begin to think. But being cordial and not wanting to seem overly stupid, I just responded with the internationally recognised, *"Hmmm."* (Of course, that probably came out in English too). So after receiving the lecture on why Reiki is *the* cure for most anything other than mouldy bread, I hobble home and go online and check it out.

According to what I read online, Reiki is a holistic remedy process that involves the laying on of hands (now that sounded pretty good to me, but with all the meds in my system, I wasn't sure why) and lots of energy transfer. And the website of the Reiki international association of believers of the gospel according to Mr. Reiki or whomever came up with this, even tells where the hands go. So I keep scrolling down through the site looking for the real cure, but all I keep seeing is two hand silhouettes on someone's head probably pushing like crazy. Didn't look that great to me, so just for the hell of it, I actually decided to read what the website said.

Part of the energy transfer part consists of saying words in an almost prayer-like way to purge the bad shit from your system. You know, words like, *"Help me use my hands to remove this illness from this poor souls body"* or something like that. So I am not sure if I can really get around that kind of thing, but my view of the energy transfer process being improved would be to place the hands on the part of the body where the problem is, and then saying something like, *"Hey, fuck off you mean bastard syndrome. Get the hell out of this guys body. Piss off."* But apparently, this is not the way the Reiki programme works. And besides I had the bizarre notion that part of the way that the Brazilian woman was thinking of a cure also involved some small dolls with pins stuck in them. So being of (semi) sound mind, and relatively well educated (and one big chicken-shit), I think I will pass on Reiki for now.

Then again, there are other alternative treatments that are available that are, as we say in the "West," non-traditional. Non-traditional in my vernacular means that the "Doctor" has not necessarily spent eons of time in a proper medical school, but instead just knows how to help people get and stay healthy. Now have no doubt, I have had great experiences with doctors, especially in the past several years, but I also have had great experiences with things like acupuncture, which by most medical standards, is seriously non-traditional.

When I used to live in Barcelona, I had a serious back issue going on from dragging my carry-on bag through at least five airports every week. So after talking about it for too long, I heard from another boater that there was someone in the marina who could sort out back pain. I found out who it was, made an appointment and went to "get better." Kirstie and her husband had been sailing for quite a few years and whilst he was rebuilding their boat, she would make extra money doing massage, acupressure, and acupuncture.

She looked at me and told me to stand up straight. Then she asked me if that was what I considered standing straight was. This was followed by saying my posture was pure crap and said we should go right for the needles. Ah, the needles.

Now I never thought I was too squeamish, but the thought of someone from Sweden sticking little needles into me wasn't that great. But, I figured that it couldn't be too much worse than the back pain, so I said (is a truly manly voice), "*Needles, yes, of course.*" I soon had needles in my chest, needles in my hands, needles in my head, and needless in my legs. Think about this picture – I go to her because of back pain and now I have needless in my chest, hands, head and legs. I was a bit caught off guard and said to Kirstie, "*Excuse me; the problem is in my back. Hello? My Back?*" That was when she replied in a lovely Swedish accent, "*Oh, I'm sorry. I didn't realise you were the one who was trained in acupuncture.*" Ouch. Patience.

And then she said, "*I think I should put some needles under your thumbnail. You won't mind that will you? I know that when I do that to my husband he always screams. What do you think?*" Oh, this is terrific. I have just heard that her husband screams from needles under the thumbnail and she is asking me if I want them? "*Not a problem*" I responded with a sense of panic running through my system at the speed of light – which, as you know, is pretty flippin' fast. And guess what.... I fell asleep. And when I woke up, I felt better. My posture was still crap, but Kirstie yelled at me enough times about that I worked on that too. Patience.

Today I went back online – okay, so as I have a broadband connection here in the flat, I *never really am off line* - to look for more stuff to learn about GBS. And then my neurologist rang me. I like it when the doctor actually calls the patient to check up. What a refreshing thing that is. His news was good. I have several prescriptions that I am taking, one (the little white pills) of which is "*Take four of these little pills each morning.*" Well the four pills are pretty nasty tasting – even when you just try to avoid them touching any part of your mouth, they seem to latch onto my tongue with little gripping fingers just waiting to see if you can swallow enough water to slosh them down. So taking the pills is not exactly the same taste quality that one would associate with, say, M&M"s Peanuts. Which as medical science has clearly shown is God's gift to those with chocolate adoration syndrome, which I clearly have as well. The good news from "el doctór" was that on Saturday, he thinks I should go from taking four of those little yucky pills to only three in the morning. And then on Wednesday, maybe get it down to two each morning. My assumption is that either, a) he is happy with my progress and is working on weaning me from the harder medication, b) there is a world-wide shortage of these pills and he wants to save some for a rainy day, or c) Martha Stewart has sold her stock in that company too. I am betting on assumption A. And then he told me to have patience. So I am working on it.

Thursday of the following week I had an appointment to go back to the doctor for some more blood tests, and some follow-up tests on my progress. Sounded pretty good to me. And shoot, Thursday was only a week away. If I have made it this far, this patience thing may be really working.

24 March - Part of all the stuff I have been going through involves getting my body to work again. The GBS does nasty things to muscles and joints due to the way the immune system gets smacked around by the virus, so this has been a major challenge.

Yesterday, I began physical therapy. Now, some might say that James doing damn near anything physical is sort of an oxymoron. But, as I am (desperately trying to be) a good patient and listening to my doctors, they say physical therapy and I say when. And it has been a while since I did any exercise anyway.

Before this the GBS landed in my body and got me, I was doing exercise – actually quite a bit of it. Almost each morning, I would do between 150 and 200 sit-ups (clearly going for that abs of steel appearance that would enable me to hold a line-dancing contest on my stomach.) Well, I suppose I should clarify the term "sit-ups." Sit-ups to me are stomach crunchy things. You know, the kind of stuff that they teach you in Pilate's class. Was I doing Pilates? Of course not, but I had seen enough adverts on television where for one minute, they show some guy who as absolutely zero body fat doing little crunchy things and that didn't look that difficult, so I followed suit. An easy regimen – put on some Ronettes or Martha and the Vandellas, crank up the volume, and a few minutes later was on my way to abs of steel. Unless of course, it was a really sunny day and my exercise programme then consisted of lying on deck in the sun. Still would have the Ronettes on, but the physical effort would be a tad diminished.

Years ago, I had decided to take up running as a form of getting in shape. I was living in Milwaukee at the time, and as a card-carrying lazy person, my first step after determining that running would be "my thing" was to go out and obtain the necessary equipment. It was clear to me at the time that running was very serious stuff, and I knew that there was no way I would be able to achieve my "running goals" without having appropriate running kit. Appropriate running kit included some really great Nike Air Step shoes (this was a while ago when they first came out with those cute little air pockets glued into the sole), some great red shorts (I thought a really committed runner should always have red shorts), a couple of trendy t-shirts to run in (with highly appropriate running logo crap on them), and the thing that is the most important for any runner – a new portable music player so I could run with Aretha Franklin whilst she was doing "Freeway of Love" or "Who's Zoomin' Who." These songs, by the way are almost mandatory for a new runner, if you are amongst those who still think that running is a fun thing to do. And no, I do not have stock in Atlantic Records and do not receive commissions on records sold for Ms. Franklin.

So there I was...my first day of running...very excited. I put all the new running kit on, got my Aretha tape all set to play "Who's Zoomin' Who" first, and tried to touch my toes once or twice – I never was able to do that before I took up running so it was just put into the column of "physical impossibilities for me" or "birth-defect" – and headed out down the block. This was easier than I thought. In no time, I was at the end of the block and between Aretha's verses, was speculating on whether I should do five miles or a bit further. My mind was calculating exactly where five miles would be, where seven miles would be, and even where ten miles would be. After all, it was my first day and I didn't want to overdo.

By the end of block two, I was hitting a good stride, feeling pretty damn great. Aretha flowing through my ears, the sun shinning on me as I was rhythmically bouncing down the street, and a gentle breeze blowing over the visor of my semi-official Nike running hat (also matching red, of course). By the end of block three...well, I never actually made it to the end of block three. Something about being totally out of breathe. Clearly a problem. At first I couldn't figure it out. I had all the right kit to run in, I had great Aretha running music. The only thing I neglected to so (I finally figured out) was to try to get into shape so I would be able to run. And that seemed like way too much work, so I sort of just chucked the idea of running. Besides, the shoes, whilst they were great, were a pretty tacky red colour that never really did match the shorts or hat.

So now I have found myself in a "mandated by the doctors" physical therapy programme. And this I will do. When I went to the hospital yesterday afternoon to begin the programme, I found my way down to the physical therapy area and did something that I learned to do the first time I visited my doctor here. It is a custom in Mallorca that when you come into the doctor's waiting room to say to whomever is already sitting there, *"Hola, Buenos Tar-*

des." Which means, "*Hello, Good afternoon.*" It is just such a nice thing to do. Shows some respect for others, adds a bit of familiarity to it all. Just a nice thing. So yesterday, I go into the therapy area and look around and see about six other people sitting there. They all look up as I am being wheeled in, and I say, "*Hola, Buenos tardes.*" In a courteous, respectful way, of course. And all six people replied with, "*Hola, Buenos tardes.*" Hey, sitting in my wheel chair I am thinking that my entrance went pretty well. But within a minute or two, most of them are talking amongst themselves and I am convinced they are all saying, "*Shit, what a crap accent from that Brit who actually sounds like an American in the wheel chair.*" Bastards. HOLA. Like I wrote in my last little essay...how many ways can you say something that is pronounced OH-LA. Well, there is OH-LA, or OH-LA or OH-LA. That's the entire combination of pronunciations. And they are all the same. And that is what I said. HO-fuck-ing-LA. HOLA. Buggers.

Okay, so now I am just sitting in the corner in the wheel-chair – God, I hate just sitting in the wheel-chair anyway – and waiting for my name to be called. Looking around for a mirror to see if I have "HAS BAD ACCENT" tattooed on my forehead or something. I was thinking that if I were really prickly, I would wait until they pronounced my name correctly (or at very minimum, the way that my father taught me to pronounce it), but then I figured I would be sitting there for about 26 years, so I just waited until I heard anything that sounded close to Rieley. And wait I did, not even sure what this therapy would consist of.

A few months earlier was my only real experience with physiotherapy. I had done something less than kind to my back. I had for some bizarre reason decided to clean out one of the lockers on the aft deck of Angelina – why in God's name I decided to take everything out just to put it back is still beyond me, but it was the chore for the day.

So I had been pulling all sorts of bits out of the locker when all that remained was the transformer that I used to convert 220v to 110v to run some or my computer stuff. Now I am not sure if you can get your head around a transformer that does this, but the best way to describe it is that it is a yellow-moulded plastic container about 38cm x 38cm x 38cm that weighs approximately 127,586 pounds, or so. Okay, that might be a tad of an exaggeration, but the thing is bloody heavy and because it was semi-buried in this locker, and it was a bugger to pull out. But I managed to manipulate it out through a space that was about ½ as big as it should have been; looked at it for about five minutes wondering why I did that, and then rammed it back in its hole. And then began to notice a slight twinge of pain in my back. Setting a new world-speed record, within 30 minutes, I was in such pain that the annual output of the company that makes Advil would not have sufficed. So I hobbled down the road to the next marina where there was a physiotherapist whom, I was told, had magic hands.

Now not having been to a physiotherapist before, my expectations were mixed, but all I wanted was to feel better. So in a few minutes, I was called into a small poorly lit room and told by the runner-up in the Slovenian refrigerator-throwing contest to get on the bed. After about 30 minutes of having my back manipulated, bent, twisted, rubbed, pulled, and otherwise brutalized, Olga (or whatever her name was) said that she would now use the Tens machine on me. Well, shit, by this time I was thoroughly confused, having assumed that she only had 10 fingers to begin with. But what she meant was the "tens" machine. Oh good. The Ten's is a cute little electrical device that she connects up with pads to various parts of my back and then proceeds to crank up the power until I can feel my muscles twitching in time with almost any Shania Twain record. And then after a bit, she came back into the room and spun the dials up to turbo level. My body was damn near bouncing off the table, but I was feeling an exceptional amount of rhythm. And after about 15 minutes of that, Olga said I could get dressed and go home. Oh, almost forgot. She told me to take lots of ibuprofen and not try to lift the transformer again. Well thank you very much.

So my expectations of the hospital physical therapy were, as you might imagine, a bit mixed. Suddenly I sort of snapped out of my dream world of physio-flashbacks when I heard a nurse saying, "*Señor Reeeeeely?*" I was actually thinking of helping her learn how to pronounce my name but then thought fuck-it – just let's get on with this. "*Oh yeah, that's me, Señor Reeeeely.*" I wheel myself into a small office where my new doctor – it does seem that about every other day I get another doctor. What a special person I must be – or, what great insurance I must have.

This doctor, who didn't speak any English (which is clearly good for my Spanish utilisation and improvement) asks me to get out of the wheel chair and get onto the examination bed. Oh shit. I am fully expecting that another version of Olga will suddenly reappear, but no, a bit of luck. All the doctor wanted to do was to test how much strength I had in my arms and legs. Okay, well I can get into this.

Just a simple set of tests. She has me lift my right arm vertically, then puts her hand against mind and tells me to push. Well, although this doctor looked like she went about 50 kilos soaking wet, I couldn't move her arm if a strong wind blew in the room. Okay, how about the left arm? Hmmm, what a powerhouse she is probably thinking through her yawn. My legs were a bit better, but it was pretty obvious that the GBS had caused me to lose so much of the incredible muscle tone that I once had. (Yeah, I know, more exaggeration, but writing this in this way makes me feel better so bugger off). More questions about the illness, questions about what exercise I normally do (let's see, does eating M&M"s count as exercise? They should.... it's not easy to get all those little chocolate peanuts out of those bags, is it?) Then she proceeds to tell me how lucky I am because I am not paralyzed, was not paralyzed, and didn't die (thank you very much for the reminders, but I do realise how lucky I am). And then discussed the physical therapy programme that she wants me on.

Initially, it will be for twenty straight days. Oh, I get weekends off. What a treat that will be. Oh fuck, everyday, physical therapy. Okay, I obviously need it, but I was taken a bit back by the plan. But as you all know, my middle name is now patience, so I am good with it. And then I asked her to describe the actual therapy regimen. It became apparent that it would be easier for her to show me, so a nurse comes and wheels me out into this very large room. A room that has all sorts of bits and bobs attached to walls and tables. A room that has large mirrors on the wall so you can see how you are progressing. A room that is full of chrome stuff that doesn't look like that much fun. A room that looked at first glance like something that Dr. Mengele had in Germany during the war. And the highlight was over in one corner where there was a wire-cage room with a bed smack in the middle of it and hanging from all the wire cage walls are assorted pulleys, leather straps, and other nasty looking stuff. I am assuming that this is the Hannibal Lechter memorial transformation specialty centre. Can't wait to get into there. And then they send me home, as I can't really begin the therapy sessions until Friday anyway. So that's okay. At least things are moving forward. But at 1100 each weekday, ooh baby, ooh baby. Look out.

Oh, almost forgot. This morning I had an appointment with my neurologist – just a check-in to monitor blood-flow and see how I was doing. So I get to his office, check in with the nurses to let them know I am there and then am told to go sit in the waiting room. I walk in, look around, and see about five other people sitting there reading magazines and otherwise killing time. And I say, *"Hola, Buenos Dias."* And they all looked up and said, *"Hola, Buenos Dias"* and then go back to their magazines, like I am actually fitting in. How cool is that? Things *are* looking up.

17 April - So I have been doing physical therapy each morning. And it is pretty brutal. Not always brutal physically, but clearly brutal mentally. The first real day of therapy, Andreas (my therapist at hospital) went over my programme – he said we would work on the total body, but very slowly. So I said, *"Sure, not a problem,"* after all, before I was hit with this nasty bastard disease, I was in semi-good shape…for a 59 year old male who was living onboard a boat. Andreas walks me over – okay, so I hobble over – to the first "station" of what loomed to be potentially easy exercises. And then he tells me that all I have to do is grab a hold of this rubber thing that looks like a bicycle inner-tube tied to a wall, and then pull it five times. *"Cinco?"* I ask, just trying to be a good patient and not wanting to do anything wrong. *"Si,"* he replies, and then goes on in Spanish to tell me that I should do this very easy. Okay. My right arm grabs the trendy orange stretchy-thing and I begin to pull. No, I don't think bicycle inner-tubes are orange in Spain – this most certainly is some very expensive physical therapy device…but a nice inner-tube would have worked fine I was thinking. Shit. I barely was able to pull it all the way five times. This is not good, and I am beginning to take all this therapy stuff

a bit more seriously. Then Andreas tells me to now turn around and pull it the other way with the same arm. Bastard – this is even harder, and I am marginally able to begin the fifth pull. Thank you Andreas. Ooops, a bit too early...he then tells me to now use the other arm. And that goes about the same. One weak person I am thinking, but after all, I am in physical therapy for a reason, so I do the same exercise with my left-arm and then almost fall into a chair, totally knackered. "*Que bueno James*," Andreas mutters with a huge smile on his face. But before I can bask in the delight of "doing good," it is time for lifting weights. And then time to try (and try is the operative word here) some semi-deep knee bends. Almost was able to get to two on that one. How good am I? Then he takes me over to a bed-like thing and tells me to lie down. This bit of fun is something that I never really did catch onto the name of, but the essence of it is that I lay down on my back, then pull my legs up at my thighs, then bend at my knees so my calves are parallel with the table (and the rest of me). Then Andreas tells me to push with my hands on my knees and breath in and out – deep breaths he says, or so I think he says. Buggers, I can't even lift my legs up without using my arms to lift them. Shit. Can't do that exercise. This is not doing much good for my ego, or my emotions. So what does he have for the big finish of the day? Oh, another simple weight-lifting one he tells me. Still lying on my back, he produces from seemingly nowhere, a long wooden stick to which he attached a lead weight on each end. And Andreas tells me to push this weighted thing into the air five times – by now I am beginning to think that there must be something magical about the number five...like it is either Andréa's favourite number, or this is the slow start for the semi-crippled, like me. I try my best, but can barely manage the push the weight to arm's length the five times. I am totally exhausted. Totally. So whilst laying there trying to catch my breath, I casually ask how heavy the weight was. Andrés tells me, "*Un kilo*." Now although my Spanish is not that great, it didn't take a simultaneous translator at the U.N. to understand what he said. I was struggling to lift that stick that only weighs 2.2 pounds. Shit, I am buggered and I know it. And this knowledge is devastating beyond belief. I finally realise that this will be truly a long recovery process – yes, I know, that is what the doctors all told me, but you know, someplace deep in my mind I am sure I just assumed really long meant a few weeks. My body was wracked with GBS, and it will take a major effort on my part to get rid of it. The meds are great, but I will have to really work to get anywhere close to where I was physically. And remember, me? Mr.-I-need-to-work-on-having-patience? Shit. So I drag my body back to the reception desk of the hospital and order a taxi to go home... and within minutes of arriving home, I do fall asleep.

By day four, things are looking up. The "rule" of five is pretty much out the window (even though the physical therapy room is in the basement of the hospital and has no windows. As a matter of fact, to get to it, I have to walk down about 40 steps. What is that all about? To get to physical therapy, they make you walk down 40 steps? Shit, there must be a lift someplace around the building that gets you there, but for the life of me, I can't find it; and when I ask someone where I might find it, they all smile at me and point to the stairs. At least going down is easier than going up). By the end of day four, I am doing 10, yes, count'em, TEN of each of the painful, but helpful exercises. Whoooweee baby. I am seeing improvement, and I like it. Of course, by the end of the session, I am ready for about five days of sleep, but I am getting better and seeing the improvement.

Day 10 in physical therapy, and things are even better now. Okay, "better" is sort of a relative term when talking about physical therapy for GBS. I do have some days in which I can see real differences in my abilities, but there are other days where I am just not too thrilled with the time it is taking. Yes, I can do far more "repetitions" of all the exercises, and I am doing about the same amount at home during the rest of the day, but it is the "not knowing" how long I will have to do all this before I am back in shape that just drives me mad. Then I think back to where I was less than two months ago – barely able to stand or walk, in hospital with the knowledge that I could become paralysed, barely able to lift a one-kilo weight. And then I think of what all my doctors have told me – patience. Whew, this patience thing is far more brutal than the physical therapy itself. It was just about this time that I began to realise how much I loved living on rocks.

02
Settling in to a New Life

I bought a car. I know, in an earlier letter I talked about the complexities of the entire "automobile purchase" bureaucracy in Spain, but I managed to come up with a "Plan B." In order to buy some time to retake the Spanish driver's licensing test, I gave in an figured out how to obtain an International Driver's License. And as soon as it arrived in my hands, I began to get back into my car search mode.

I was kind of torn between something expressly fun and exciting; or something that would be practical and comfortable. And after doing an exhaustive (well exhaustive in my terms) I found a nice sedan. Yes, I know…I ended up going down the practicality route. It is nice…a used SEAT Cordoba, made here in Spain several years ago. Three doors; five speeds; lots of trendy dials, some of which I will figure out in a year or two; a boot big enough to hold most of the Spanish Royal Family; an ironing board; and it is white. Yes, white. I do live on an island where the prevalent characteristic of weather is an intense sun that bestows light and heat (heat being the key word here) on everything. So a white car made sense to me. Besides, the last hire car I had was dark blue and it shows up dust and dirt and damn near everything that lands on it. So white it is. The ironing board. Right. Well in automotive parlance, it would be called a spoiler, but come on…why would a used SEAT Cordoba need a spoiler? Sure looks like an ironing board to me.

This morning I returned my hire car and took a taxi to the auto dealer where I purchased Amelia (yes, I am a firm believer that cars should have names to match their personalities, and this car is most appropriately named Amelia). I gave the dealer money, I signed lots of papers, Debbie (the daughter of Antonio the auto dealer) gave me the keys, and off Amelia and I went. Well, it didn't exactly go that smoothly as it turned out. I did sign everything; I did have my auto insurance documentation with me; and I did give Debbie a cheque, but because the cheque was not a bank cheque, the two of us walked a couple of blocks to one of the branch office of my bank to get them to say the cheque was indeed good. Then I was given the keys to Amelia and drove off.

Our first trip ("Our," as in James and Amelia) was to El Corte Ingles, a Spanish department store that has two sites in Palma and has just about anything that one person could imagine. I like shopping at El Corte Ingles, but I usually do walk out of their stores with many more things that I went in for. And quite often, I am so busy shopping impulsively, I completely forget about what I went there for. But today, I was a man on a mission. I wanted to buy a picnic basket. On my last trip to London, I went shopping for them, and for some reason, had difficulty in finding exactly what I was looking for.

Yes, I did find some pretty great ones, but I really didn't want one that had the Burberry plaid pattern all over it, nor did I need one that had Harrods printed on everything inside of it. Besides, the ones I found in London were a tad on the expensive side (a "tad" means two to three hundred pounds Sterling for a wicker-looking basket with a couple of cheesy plates in it). I did find one in El Corte Ingles (actually, they only had one style, but it was perfect) and after exercising my Visa card again, walked out with my new purchase. That was the good news. The bad news was that I now had to locate Amelia, parked somewhere underground near Plaza de España.

Palma, to help cope with the tens of thousands of cars that can't seem to find a place to park, have built underground parking garages in many parts of the city. The problem is that the garages are huge and if you don't pay serious attention to where your car is, you may spend days looking for it. As Amelia and I were new to each other, we hadn't worked out any special ways for her to let me know through mental thought projection (yes, I just made that up) where she was. After a few well-intentioned excursions down aisles that were chocker-block with cars that all looked like Amelia, I finally found her and we drove home.

The distance between Palma and Puigpunyent is not that far, with only 14 kilometres separating the two cities (okay, one city, Palma - and one village, Puigpunyent). The road, one lane travelling each direction, is a bit narrow at times, and has more curves than the entrants in the Miss World contest, but it cuts through some of the most spectacular countryside of the island. As Amelia was whisking me along through the woods, suddenly I came up on something I had never seen before. There was a police car on the side of the road with its driver motioning for everyone who came along to slow down. And just around the next curve, here was a car that apparently had gotten a bit too close to one of the many trees that line the road. It did appear that no one was hurt, and I was quite impressed to see several police cars and a tow truck there; but the thing that stuck in my mind was to make sure that I had every emergency number plugged into my mobiles. You just never know when, out on the road, you might need assistance. But for now, as soon as I made it past the road disruption, I geared down and went whizzing along through the woods and along the grapevine-laden fields in my new car.

It was about early evening and I was on the phone with one of the organisations I write business articles for in the UK when I heard the noise. It was almost like a car crash, except of course I realised that it couldn't be that, as my street is so narrow that only one car can fit on it at any given time. And then I heard it again. It was a sound that I had heard before, but I just couldn't place it for a few moments; and then I remembered…it was thunder. I rang off of the phone call and went bouncing outside to feel gloriously cooling rain falling from the soon-to-be-dark skies.

Rain. Oh My God. Rain. Haven't seen rain since I had moved to Puigpunyent. My mind started flashing through all sorts of thoughts; good for the plants; a welcome washing down of the courtyard; a free car wash for Amelia; an opportunity to help re-fill the cistern...THE CISTERN!!!

La Antigua is a typical old village house, and most of them have cisterns that act as back-up water supplies. I have even been told that putting a cistern in is a requirement for many homes on the island as a way to deal with potential water shortages that do seem to occur every so often on this rather arid island. And as with most older homes, the cistern has a kind-of-sort-of semi-automatic refilling system.

A good idea I thought; to have a cistern that would collect rainwater and store it for later use. The system itself isn't that complicated. Coming down from the roof edges of the house, there are three drain downspouts. One funnels off the water that collect on the roof terrace; another one funnels off the rain water and deposits it in the courtyard via an angled spout, or, through an adjustable valve of sorts, funnels the rain water into the cistern. How innovative is that? So as I was standing in the doorway watching the rain change the appearance of the courtyard stones from dry and grey to grey with water on it (I know what you are saying, but it did look different), I realised that if I wanted to funnel the water into the cistern, I would have to venture out and move the connector pipe from direct courtyard soaking mode to cistern refilling mode. I thought I should wait a few minutes however, in order to have some of the rain water wash out all the dust and dirt from the roof channels, so I just stood there for a few minutes, not knowing how long I should wait until the water that would soon replenish my cistern was clean. I am not even sure how clean the water needs to be in a cistern, after all, I only use the cistern water supply for nourishing the garden some days; although I had been told when I purchased La Antigua, that there is a submersible pump and valve so I can send cistern water throughout the house in an emergency situation. After ten minutes, I felt I had waited long enough and out into the rain I went.

By now, it was getting dark; the combination of the rain clouds and the time of night were making it difficult to see exactly what I needed to do, so I came back in to get a torch. Hey, at least I had a torch for just such occasions. Back out into the rain to manipulate the angled input pipe from one exhaust pipe (the courtyard) to the other one (the cistern). This wasn't a difficult task, only a bit wet. But I didn't care; my cistern would be refilled, my car would be clean, my garden would be happily moist again. And then, just as I managed to disconnect one pipe and connect the other one, the rain stopped. I imagine that my cistern, if I could measure it, would now be almost a tenth of a millimetre more full. Okay, maybe a hundredth of a millimetre. I came in to dry off.

Sunday, a day of rest...or so they say it should be. Sunday is also the day for the big market in Consell (CON-SAY) so off I went. The road to Consell is interesting, to say the least. Winding back and forth over the mountains behind Puigpunyent, the road is almost wide enough for two cars and the fact that

James B Rieley

it does wind back and forth more times than an epileptic snake makes it an interesting drive. Once over the top of the mountains, the road settles down to a smooth ribbon of tarmac all the way to Santa Maria. Then it is only another seven kilometres to Consell.

The market takes place amongst some industrial buildings on the south end of the town and by 1000 in the morning, the car park is chocker-block with cars. Walking through the throngs of a combination of tourists who come looking for something to do other than sit on the beach in front of their hotels recovering from the previous nights mass consumption of stimulants, and locals for whom the market is just another place to socialise.

I was there on a mission. Having seen one too many home magazines from Spain, Italy and France, I was beginning to look for bits to put in my courtyard. Specifically, I wanted to find some decorated pottery and classically designed floor tiles. With an anticipated number of local vendors approaching fifty, I was sure that I would be able to find what I was looking for. And after seeing a melange of discarded computer kit that was out of date several years ago, newly antiqued furniture pieces, and other forms of bric-brac that one might encounter when strolling through a recycling centre (some of which I have no idea what they were for), I finally did locate the vendors that were selling what I was looking for. I immediately went into bargaining mode.

Trying to barter with locals who have seen every type of consumer, and already apparently graduated from the school of *"pick a price, double it, then be willing to haggle back and forth until the price is where you wanted it in the first place,"* engaging in the back and forth was a challenge, but great fun. Although I never did locate the exact things I was looking for, I did make purchases from three different vendors; and the final score was vendors 1, me 2 (or so they made me think). All in all, it was great, and although I never did get the pottery or the floor tiles I had gone for, I did go home with five fabulous bulbous green glass bottles that are now happily resting in the courtyard.

The previous week, I had gone to the post office to send a letter to my insurance company in Palma. As I did remember that they were only open from 0800 to 1000, I walked into the village centre shortly after 0900 with my letter firmly in hand. Luckily, I was the only customer that day, and after watching the clerk distribute incoming post into those cute little shelf compartments that most post offices had, the clerk came over to see what I wanted. Having been there before, the clerk recognised me and asked how I was. I replied that I was fine, very happy living in Puigpunyent, and had a letter to post to an address in Palma. She weighed the envelope (following a tried and true process, but as the envelope only contained a single sheet of paper, I didn't think that it would even register on the scale), she said that it would require 40 cents worth of postage. *"Bueno,"* I replied, and passed over a five-euro note. *"Hmmm,"* it appeared she said as she looked first at the five-euro note, and then the almost completely empty cash drawer. It was apparent that the options were minimal. I could walk back home and return with 40 cents; I could walk to a store and get some change; the clerk could do either of my choices; or, I realised, there was another option.

Puigpunyent is not exactly Palma, and the entire life-style is a bit more relaxed. In the short time I have lived here, I have realised that this is a real community, and we all live together in the community. I offered a suggestion (in my best, but still marginal Spanish). Why didn't she post my letter, and then in a day or so, just put my change – when she had it – in an envelope and deliver it when there was something else addressed to La Antigua. Not a problem she said, and I walked back home happy in the belief that I was making more connections in my choice of a village to live in. The next day, nothing came to my house. Fair enough. The day after that, nothing. The following day, still nothing. And today, I received a nice bill from Vodafone (nice being a courteous way of referencing big business" way of getting lots of money for me using a phone), and a beige envelope with 4.60 euros in it. I smiled.

Life has proved not to be dull in Puigpunyent. As a matter of fact, this summer, Puigpunyent seems to have become the centre of the island universe for entertainment. I received another flyer from the local government that listed all the upcoming events in the village, and was pleasantly surprised by what I found.

I know that many of my friends were concerned that I would just spend all of my time in the village hidden away in La Antigua typing – sort of the hermit lifestyle that we introverts quite often lean towards. But I have actually been doing stuff.

Two weeks ago was the "Teatre a La Placa de Son Bru," which translated to a play that was put on in the plaza within eyesight (and ear-shot) of La Antigua. Okay, so the play was done in Mallorquin and I had no flippin' clue what it was about, other than the kept playing music from movies that I recognised, but seeing as how it was two weeks ago, I have completely forgotten what they were. But I do remember from the applause that the crowd in the plaza seemed to enjoy the play.

Last night was a jazz concert. And luckily, it didn't take place next to my house. It is nice that some community events take place so close to La Antigua, but the sound systems they use apparently were designed for Woodstock, and it is possible to hear the sounds so well as they come wafting through the air, that even when inside my home, with the windows closed, and my head buried under a pillow, it can be a bit deafening. But the jazz took place in the plaza in front of the local government offices in the centre of Puigpunyent. It said in the flyer that the performance was to be by the Molly Duncan Quartet. Okay, I assumed it would be at least one woman in the group (the reference to "Molly" was my tip off), but Molly turned out to be the nickname of Malcolm Duncan, and he and three other musicians warmed the already warm (and humid) crowd that had assembled. A nice evening.

The next event scheduled is set for the 23 of July and this time it will be at the "Polisportiu," which is the community sports centre. The sports centre is piece of land consisting of the pool, a football pitch, tennis courts, a café and bar, and a set of table-tennis tables and swing-sets for children. It is nice – well, the pool is the only part I have experienced so far and that is very nice – but I have no clue where the event will actually be. In the flyer, it says that the event will be a showing of "The Incredibles," and as the write-up said "Los Increibles," (IN-CRAY-EEE-BLAYS) I am sure it will be in shown in Mallorquin. I don't care, I am going anyway, if for no other reason that to see where they will put the big movie screen (assuming they have a big movie screen). I think I need to find out what the Mallorquin word is for "popcorn." Oh yes, I almost forgot. The last community sponsored event this month will be a magician performing at the sports centre. I wonder if he will gesture hypnotically and rain with cooler weather will materialise?

I spent yesterday working on a new creative project. When I moved to La Antigua, in a corner of the courtyard was this little upholstered stool. The wood was old and weathered and the upholstered seat had clearly seen better days, but it did look like it was something to save. After a few days, I had placed a large potted plant on the seat, but after a few weeks, I realised that the upholstery was a lost cause, so I took it off. Not a big job – just take off the four screwed that held the seat onto the legs, but as the screws had apparently been rusting for the past 100 years or so, it was a knuckle-cruncher. But I did manage to get it off, and underneath the seat was a wood platform. So I put the plant on the little platform until I could figure out what I wanted to do with the stool. And Saturday morning, I had figured it out.

I like mosaic work, and after spending several years in Barcelona – the home of Gaudi, one of the masters at using decorative mosaic work – I had made my decision. No, my plan wasn't to some bizarre Gaudi-like design. I decided to make a surface of small smooth stones. That was the good news. The bad news is that I didn't have any. So I got into the car and drove to a local DYI store and found a vast assortment of ceramic tiles, and eventually, small stones that could be used as tiles. I knew how many square centimetres the surface area of the stool was, so I did some rough calculations of how many stones I would need and, after buying them, raced back home full of anticipation of a soon-to-be-completed stone mosaic stool.

I had done quite a bit of tiling and mortar work when reforming a house I owned in America, and other than the mess it all generated, didn't remember what fun it was to mix the mortar. Well, just mixing the mortar isn't bad; getting the right combination of water and powder is the pain. And as it had been such a long time since I had done this, I think I miscalculated a bit. Okay, a lot. I put a couple of litres of water into a bucket, and then gently began to pour some of the mortar powder in. And then some more, alternating stirring the slurry until it was the right consistency and gently pouring in more powder. It didn't take too long before I had dumped the entire 5 kilo bag of beige mortar powder into the bucket. And seeing as how my little stirring stick promptly broke when it ran into the mass of powder that seemed to be solidifying rapidly under water, I jammed my hand in to make sure that the solution was just right. Hmmm, interesting. I swirled the solution; I kneaded the muck; and swirled and swirled and swirled. I had placed the stones on the surface where I thought they would look the best before the mixing festival, and so I was ready to pour the liquid in between them, filling up the voids created by the stones. This process lasted about two seconds before I just ended up pouring the solution all over the top of the stones. I took my already beige and mortar encrusted hand to smooth the mortar out and then looked back into the bucket. It was almost still full of mortar. Ooops. I think I made too much.

The stool, or should I say, my new stone-covered mosaic table, looks great. And I am sure that in another couple of weeks I will be able to chip the rest of the dried mortar out of my bucket. As for now, I think I will just go back and type for a while.

Life in Puigpunyent was quickly becoming "normal." Well admittedly, normal for one person may not seem normal to all people, but for me, life in the village became *my version* of normal. And whilst some might think that I don't do anything, this couldn't be further from the truth.

Yesterday was pretty typical…I have been working for quite a while on writing two books for a UK publisher on, yes, you guessed it, business. I had completed the first several weeks ago, and yesterday managed to complete the second. (I had been writing them concurrently, which is an interesting experience). So after finishing the writing and checking, and checking, and checking, I rang the publisher to let them know of my progress and found out I needed to reformat them both into double-spacing in order for their editors to do their "red pencil" job on them. Okay, not a problem, but changing two 300 page books currently set at 1-1/2 line spacing to double line spacing does muck up all the formatting I had done. But on the other hand, the 300 pages skyrocketed to over 400 pages for each book. (of course, now I have to carry all of this to London tomorrow). I put them both on a CD-ROM, and drove into Palma to find a printer who could whack them out for me. I suppose I could have just run them through my trendy combination printer-scanner-copier, but I was pretty conscious that it would take longer to print them at home than it did to write them, so a trip to Palma seemed advisable.

During the day, I had several visitors. First, Jordi and his son Tomeu came over. Jordi is an electrician who lives in Puigpunyent, and because I thought La Antigua could use some electrical changes, I had asked him to be the one to make them – it is always nice to deal with the people from your own community. Jordi and I explained to Tomeu what I wanted done exactly (always a challenge, as Jordi and his son were both born in Puigpunyent and their English is non-existent, and I, not born in anyplace even remotely near Spain...well, you know). Jordi had to leave to do whatever other jobs he had, and Tomeu and I went at it. Okay, so the reality is that Tomeu did anything that remotely had anything to do with electricity, and I used the time and opportunity to practise my Spanish.

Two lights that didn't work were simply a matter of connecting some bad wiring, but the major accomplishment was the connecting up of a light switch that was never connected to anything. Yes, drilling through walls, pulling wires through buried tubing, making lots of dust, and for me, learning new ways to say things that I am sure Tomeu didn't learn at church. But now I have a functioning light in a previously dark corner of the kitchen.

After Tomeu finished, Dani came over. Dani is the proprietor of an Internet café in Palma who I know, and he came over to sort out some of the wireless problems I have been enduring at La Antigua. Not a major problem – the wireless function for my computers does work fine, but the almost metre thick stonewalls play serious havoc with the signal roaming through the entire house. So after installing another signal transmitter thingy, I can now be connected online in every room of the house. I know, some readers are probably wondering, *"why does he need to be connected all over the house?"* The answer is because I am who I am, and sometimes it is nicer to be doing my computer stuff in the kitchen whilst waiting for dinner to be ready, or sitting out in the courtyard enjoying the warmth of the sun. I don't think I will be doing this too much during the day however, as the sun is so bright I can't see anything on the computer screen. Perhaps after the sun goes down a bit. And besides, many of my friends are as anal retentive about connectability as I am, so now when they visit, they can get their emails from one of the guest rooms.

After sweeping the courtyard, which is a daily activity (the bougainvillea is spectacular, but every day, flowers fall from it onto the courtyard floor - visualise the adverts for American Beauty, but without the blond cheerleader), I resumed working on a painting for some friends in Palma. John and Ms. Ely already have one of my paintings hanging on their walls, but had asked if I would do another one for them. I replied that I would be more than happy to do so, if they would buy me the canvas to paint on. They did, so I have been laying down paint almost every night for a while. And last night, I finished it.

And then I just sat and relished the peace and extraordinarily mystical beauty of an evening in Puigpunyent.

I remember sending an email to my sons (who still live in America) on 12 September, 2001. It was the day after the World Trade Centre attack, and having witnessed the destruction of the buildings on a video link in Amsterdam where I was, I felt I needed to share something with them. In part of my email I said, "I hope you can remember what life was like on the 10th, because life as we know it would never be the same again." It isn't, and today, I was on the edge of the new world we all live in.

I had flown to London to attend a business meeting last week, and after arriving at Heathrow airport, I went downstairs to catch the Heathrow Express into the city. After managing to get on-board just as the train's doors were about to close, I sat there for five minutes, trying to figure out why the train hadn't zoomed out of the terminal toward Paddington Station on its almost always prompt timetable. And then there was a policeman walking through the coaches telling everyone to evacuate the train immediately. On the platform, police had a young man wearing a large rucksack sprawled out, and clearly, there were concerns about what was in the rucksack. Eventually, we all were permitted back on the train and it departed into the city. After the arrival at Paddington, I managed to find a taxi to take me to my hotel, and on that part of the journey, found out about the extremely heightened state of security in London.

Living in Puigpunyent, we are very conscious of what goes on in the outside world. But seeing news alerts and broadcasts about terrorism threats is different than being caught in the middle of them. Life has indeed changed, for all of us. And I fear it will never be the way it was ever again. And I learned, once again, we just don't know about tomorrow so…well I think you know.

So, I am back in La Antigua. My flight back from London was interesting, as always. But the plane was chocker with tourists coming to Mallorca and the ever-present sun and warmth. And if all the tourists plugging up the airport queues weren't enough, I was bringing home a large pastel I purchased whilst in London. Not a pretty sight; a briefcase, a little trolley that I pack my clothes in, and now I was manhandling this framed picture too. Not even sure where to put it yet in the house, but I think it will end up on one of the guest rooms walls.

This morning, I experienced more of the Spanish way of doing things. Shortly after purchasing La Antigua, a friend had mentioned to me that wills drafted in countries other than Spain were either not valid here, or at very minimum, fraught with problems. Several weeks ago, I had met with a solicitor here to find out what I needed to do, and before going to London, had taken him a copy of my current will. Alejandro looked at it and smiled, mentioning the fact that in Spain, all the pages weren't necessary. Here what is needed is a simple document that states that all my possessions simply are transferred to my sons. That's it. So this morning I went to see Alejandro again to sign my new will. In the past, when I had drawn up a will, it was typed up and signed by myself and by witnesses. But in Spain, the process is that a solicitor draws it up – in my case, both double-spaced pages – and then I sign it in front of a "Nortario" (a notary). And because of the legal system – solicitors work privately, and notarios are publicly employed – we had to walk several blocks to the notaries office for the big signing...which lasted about three minutes. All done and dusted, and on its way to be filed in Madrid with everyone else's wills in Spain. I did some small shopping at a great store in Palma and raced home.

As luck would have it, when I walked through the courtyard gate into La Antigua, there was the post lying on the courtyard floor. I had missed the delivery, which was too bad, because I received notification of a delivery from China. And I missed it, meaning that I would have to wait until tomorrow to see what it was. Not sure, but I think (and hope) that it is a copy of one of the books I have written that is being re-published in Taiwan for the Chinese market. A month ago I received several copies of the "formal Chinese version" of the book, but I had been told in London that copies of the "simplified Chinese version" of the book was on its way to me. And whilst it will be good to have it, I am sure that I won't have any more clue as to what it says than the formal Chinese version.

Okay, so maybe Puigpunyent may not exactly qualify as a "city," it does certainly qualify as summer here. And to steal a quote from the Lovin' Spoonful, *"Hot town, summer in the city; Back of my neck getting dirty and gritty."* When I had purchased La Antigua, one of the things that I thought was highly attractive was the part of the courtyard where the shade provided by the Yellow Jasmine, Orange tree, Grape vines, and Bougainvillea created an outside room that I fell in love with. I put some nice wicker chairs out there and a table or two and made the space into one of my favourite "rooms." But over the past weeks whilst sitting out in the shade, I kept noticing that the "ceiling" of my new "room" was a disaster. According to Pau, my magical mystery gardener, the previous owners had given him explicit instructions to not touch the vines, branches, and other green things that had merged together and become more entwined than teenagers in the back seat of a Chevy at the drive-in.

I have talked to Pau about this spaghetti-like mess several times when he has come over to spray my grapevines, and we agreed that in autumn, he would come and clean it all out. Pauls idea was to cut away at least ½ of it all, with the intent being that next spring, it would all grow back, but much more organised and healthy. The idea made sense to me, but this morning, there I was; sitting outside, looking up at the mass of dead stuff above my head and decided to not wait until autumn. Did I call Pau? Not on your life. I went into the laundry room and grabbed my leather gardening gloves and a branch shears and had at it. (Yes, I do own gardening gloves; hell, I even own a trowel). So up on a chair I went (no, I don't own a ladder...yet) and began hacking away. Two hours and about 35 litres of perspiration later, I had filled up several 200-litre garbage bags and began to sweep up the courtyard. It was hot, it is summer, and the back of my neck was dirty and gritty; but the "ceiling" of the outside space is beginning to take shape. I wonder if Pau will even notice?

After an extremely long and cooling shower, I was on a roll. Last week I had completed two serious projects that I had been working on: I finished writing the two books I had been contracted to produce, and I had put the finishing touches on a large acrylic that I had done for friends here on the island. I suppose it should have been a great feeling to know that I had completed them, but part of me was wondering, "what project will I work on next?" Over the weekend, I had figured out what it was, and after the jungle-like episode outside, I began. I do like to paint, and for some time, I had been thinking about painting on pottery. Nothing too terribly cheesy; but I had done some water-colours whilst recovering from my encounter with the evil GBS last year that I thought might look nice on plates or pitchers. So I had purchased four large ceramic plates from an art supply store in Palma that would be suitable to test out my new project idea. It seemed like such an easy plan – buy the pottery; sketch out what I wanted to paint on the pottery; paint it; and then take it back to the shop to be fired (I do have a fab oven, but to fire pottery, apparently it needs to be at a temperature of about 1250 degrees, my oven doesn't quite make it that high I think). Step one; buy the pottery – done. Step two; sketch out the design on the pottery – done. Step three; apply the paint in the aforementioned design – done (more or less). Step four; get the pottery fired in the shops apparently steroid-laden oven – tomorrow. I can't wait to see how they come out, and as the process involves actually painting the picture on the plates, then covering it with a clear glaze that actually goes on quite pink in colour, I can't even see what I painted now. But hopefully, the pink will turn clear in the firing process (well they told me it would), and I will end up with some samples so I can figure out if this is a good idea or not. Stay posted for an update.

By now it was almost 1600h, and I thought I heard a faint cat-like noise coming from the roof terrace. Well, as I know that there is a cat that seems to enjoy vaulting over my south wall and spending time on the terrace, I assumed that it actually was a cat. And I don't like cats. To be fair, it isn't that I just don't like them; I am allergic to them. So I flew into the house, scampered up the stairs and flung open the door to the terrace, only to find it empty, except for the throng of Oleanders that I had put on it in big pots a few weeks ago. No cat. Shit. But then again, I really didn't have a plan, other than trying to convince him (or her) to stay away from La Antigua. I have asked friends and neighbours about how to keep them away, but the suggestions have sort of covered the gambit of dealing with pesky animals. Suggestion 1 was to make it a pet – not a good suggestion for someone who is allergic to cats. Suggestion 2 was to put out some poison. That did seem a bit harsh – I don't hate cats, I just don't want them around. Suggestion 3 was to sprinkle pepper where he was walking. The logic of this (I actually did ask why) was that the cat would get the pepper on his cute little paws and not like it. With any luck at all, the cat will associate the bad pepper experience with my roof terrace and stay away. But as an avid fan of The Far Side years ago, I thought I recalled that the only thing dumber than a cat was a rock, so it seemed like a daft idea. None-the-less, I have sprinkled pepper several times along the wall that the sneaky little furry thing comes over, with the total result so far is that the pepper blows around in the breeze as I am sprinkling it and I end up sneezing a lot. Then there was suggestion 4 – when I see the cat, I should spray it with water. I have heard that cats don't like getting sprayed with water, so on the surface that seemed like a good idea. But as the cat has not been neighbourly enough to provide me with a schedule of his visits, I think that this idea isn't the best either. So that left suggestion 5 - get a dog. At first, this did sound like a nice idea to think about, but then I realised that few dog breeds are competent to edit all the writing I do, and when I do bugger off to London, he (or she) would be alone and probably wrack up big bills to Lassie Fan Club chat rooms on the internet. And if I did have a dog, I would end up sweeping up more than just bougainvillea leaves in the courtyard. I think I will stop at the market tomorrow and buy some more pepper first.

Spain is clearly not England, and even more clearly, it is not the same as the United States. Growing up in the latter country, I was raised with a certain sense of "how things are done." I spent a half-century in a climate where business, or more appropriately, making enough money to live at least as good as the bloke next door, was everything. And when I moved to the United Kingdom, I felt like I was in the same environment, only on then the environment was on steroids. Work, work, work. And when you come from one of these environments, working at the speed of light becomes the norm. And now I live in Spain. And it is different.

I first encountered the difference in Barcelona a few years ago whilst living on Angelina. Living on a boat suited me; after all, everyday required working on the teak or some other boaty project. And as with most projects, this required going off most days to purchase supplies with which I could do the work. The first day I had to do this, I just assumed that my teak-cleaner supplier was closed for some really great reason, but I had no idea that it was because it was the part of the day set aside for siesta. Siesta – a noun that seems to mean that you get to close your shop from about 1:30 to 4:30 pm because there are more important things to do than make money…or something like that. I can imagine that siesta was a great idea back in the preair-conditioner days, when summer in Spain was blistering hot mid-day. But we do have air-conditioning today and the stores still close each afternoon. Okay, whilst I am still mystified about the whole siesta thing, I am used to it. But then there is the whole August thing.

Whilst living on Angelina, I had a mechanic do some engine work for me – I don't do that whole greasy engine thing well, so I hired a mechanic which enabled me to stand around and look the part of a boat owner instead. The work entailed taking apart the fuel injection system on the engine, or so I thought. Not a big problem, it only took him an afternoon to crawl into a space the size of a shoebox, but then he said that he needed to take the injectors to an injector-rebuild shop. That was the good news. The bad news was that it was the last day of July. An anticipated two-day job took a month. Why? Because most of Spain closes for the month of August!!!! WTF?!?!?!

So here I am in Puigpunyent, and whilst I *know* about these little cultural things – siestas and the August holiday time – I still am plagued by them. Remember when I talked about my ceramic painting adventure? Well yesterday I drove into Palma to have my newly painted plates fired in some intense oven that cranks out enough heat to melt most of Antarctica, and found out that they are closed for the entire month. And then in the afternoon, I suddenly got the urge to walk to my local market (the only market in Puigpunyent) at two o'clock, and of course, it was closed for siesta. I must be acclimating to living here however, because after the attempted visit to my market, I just went home and fell asleep. It is a cultural thing…and I like it.

Living in a different country than one is born in can result in different views of what is "right." I can remember when I moved to London years ago. An American friend of mine wrote to me and asked what it was like to drive on the wrong side of the road. My response was that in England, they don't drive on the *wrong* side of the road; they drive on the *other* side of the road. There is no right or wrong when living in a different culture than you are used to; there is however, the opportunity to experience new ways of looking at things.

Today Jordi and Tomeu came over to install a ceiling fan outside in the courtyard. Whilst my "room" outside is wonderful, on days when there is little air movement, I realised that simply by hanging a ceiling fan from the structure that supports all the grape vines, I could make the "room" even nicer. And although it wasn't quite the easy job it appeared to be – I had been able to assemble the fan and hang it from a structure that helps hold up the vines; it did take Tomeu to weave electrical cable around and connect the fan to electricity. Of course, it does look a bit like an old DC-3 is landing through the grape vines. Now the "room" is complete…until I come up with another idea of how to make La Antigua even more comfortable.

They're back; it's that time again; the veritable good news v. bad news. It is…hold your breath…festival time in Puigpunyent once again. I had been tipped off about the mid-August weeklong festival, but had almost forgotten completely about it, until I heard the sounds wafting over my courtyard wall this afternoon. I had been sitting in the courtyard, working on my computer (well?), when I heard the sounds of drums, fife, and bagpipes. I kept typing for a few minutes until it set in; drum, fife, and bagpipe? I put my computer down and opened the gate only to see absolutely nothing… but I could still hear the sounds. Down my street I went, and sure enough, around the corner was a marching band. Okay, it was two men, one playing a bagpipe, and the other playing a drum and a fife. No, I am not kidding about this. They were being followed down the street by a group of children, each passing out flyers about the upcoming festival. Perhaps the two guys are the Pied Pipers of Puigpunyent? I was given one of the flyers, and now I know what the festival will entail. So, cutting straight to the chase because I know you are all on the edge of your seats, here is the line up for the big August festival.

8 August: the semi-finals of Petanca, at the sports centre. Petanca is a group dance activity where the participants dance to constantly changing music. The trick (I think) is to have the entire group you are dancing with keep with the rhythm of the music. I just may pass on this event, having seen it quite a few times whilst living in Barcelona. But then again…it might be worth seeing here.

9 August: the semi-finals of a series of football matches; followed by Cinema a la Fresca, also at the sports centre. No word on what the movie will be, but from the name, the village must have managed to acquire sponsorship from a soft-drink company. Or maybe it will, like last time, just be held outside. Probably the latter…but now I am thirsty. Hang on, I need to get something to drink.

10 August: at 1100, the finals of a children's Ping Pong tournament. At 1930, more football, and at 2030, a presentation by Tomas Vibot, the author of "I Jornades d'Estudis Locals." Sorry, no clue, and whilst my online translator programme does do Spanish to English, it doesn't do Mallorquin at all. Your guess is as good as mine. At 2230 is the Gran Ballada Popular at La Placa de Son Bru. This appears to be a large dance…and it is at the plaza that is very near my house. It will undoubtedly be a late, noisy night for me.

11 August: amongst other activities, there will be the seniors final Ping Pong tournament at 1900 at the sports centre, and at 2230, (oh my God), the IV Gran Nit de Play Back…next door. And guess what? We can vote on our favourite songs via SMS text messaging. Whooooweeeee. And at 2300 (that would be quite late you realise) is the Gran Nit de Rock. No, I don't think it will be the Corrs. A rock concert; almost next door; loud, pounding, heavy metal; yikes!!! I think I will need to buy a couple of kilos of cotton to stick in my ears before this one.

12 August: Not exactly sure – the flyer is printed in Mallorquin and my Mallorquin is about as good as my ability to run the mile in under 12 seconds – but it appears that it will be a series of exhibitions of paintings and sculptures, followed by more music and skits. Probably next door…(note to myself, buy more cotton for ear plugs).

13 August: the finals of the children's Ping Pong (Ping Pong does seem to be a big thing here in Puigpunyent apparently), followed by the finals of the football, a Café Concert (this must be a music dinner) and a magician's performance. The magician is good, and I will do this one for sure, and hopefully, he will be able to gesture hypnotically and restore the hearing that I will probably lose the night before.

14 August: at 1100 are the Festa Aquatica (yes, this will be held at the pool); the Festa Amb Inflables (at the football pitch); and the finals of Petanca. Hmmmm, more Petanca. And at 2300, it is the Gran Orquesta Mallorca. I am assuming that this will be more than a drum, fife, and bagpipe, but will let you know later.

15 August: at 1900 you can either attend a football match, or the finals of senior women's tennis. At 2230, it is a play called "Noces D'Argent", and yes, it will be next door to my house. And even more exciting (???) is the fact that at midnight, there is a programme for residents, but they must be over 14 years old to attend. What? I always thought that 14 year-olds should be in bed by ten o'clock at night to begin with. Oh, that's right...that is what I was told by my parents...who weren't from Puigpunyent. Never mind. Note to myself: buy stock in companies that make cotton balls.

16 August: at 1800 it is the senior men's finals of tennis, followed at 2130 by the Sopar A La Fresca. To be honest, I have no clue what this is, but it will be outside, and should be good – you need to buy tickets in advance (3 euros for residents and 6 euros for non-residents. Place your orders now)

Okay, so let's do a little recap; nine days that are chocker with activities for the community – good. Activities for young and old – good. Various forms of things to do - good. Rock concerts near my house – oh, for joy.

Will I attend a lot of these activities that are put on by the village? Damn right I will. Part of living in the village, is "living" in the village. And maybe whilst I am there, someone can help me understand the drum, fife, and bagpipe thing.

Living in Mallorca, or probably more appropriately, ON the rock that is Mallorca, enables me to find the real culture of the island. No, not the culture of places like Magaluf – which is more like Birmingham that Birmingham is, or Arenal, which I thought was just a suburb of Munich when I first went there. But the real Mallorca; and to do that, one needs to go hang out with Mallorquins. This is quite a challenge for me because whilst my Spanish is good enough to be able to communicate with just about everyone I need to talk to, my ability to communicate in Mallorquin is...well, it is about as good as ability to do a triple-reverse somersault wazoo flip-thingy for the Circ du Soleil whilst wrapped in Day-Glo spandex. But learning to communicate better is important to me, so I work at it.

Remember the ceramic plate-painting extravaganza? Well, the other day, in my frustration of not being able to get them fired in a ceramic oven, I drove to Palma and asked just about everyone I knew in Santa Catalina if they knew anyone that has an oven that was made for firing ceramics. I came up empty, but whilst there, I decided to ring my ex-landlord (and artist) Biel. Biel and his partner Catalina have lived on the island all of their lives, and we got along rather well when I was living in the building they owned in Palma. And although neither of them speaks any English,

James B Rieley

we have always been able to understand each other. So I rang their mobile and as things would have it, Catalina answered. Catalina is adorable, but she does speak rather quickly – when I was renting the flat from them, Catalina would be the one who would stop over on occasion to sort out any requests I had, and invariably, I would end up saying to her, *"Mas despacio por favor Catalina"* (could you please speak a bit slower). She would smile, and start again, pronouncing each word as if I was a four-year old, and in terms of language, that is probably what I was at the time. But within a half-sentence, Catalina would be deluging me with the Mallorquin language at a speed that a U.N. translator would have trouble keeping up with. Regardless, I accepted the challenge and asked Catalina if she or Biel knew of anyone who could fire ceramics. She said that she would have Biel ring me back; which I took as either Biel may know someone, or she had no clue as to what I was asking for.

The next day, Biel did ring back and I asked him if he knew anyone with an oven and he said he thought he did and would ring me back in a few minutes. Which he did. So today, I drove to the airport to meet my new combination Mallorquin friend and ceramic oven provider. Barbara works for Iberia airlines and was getting off her Sunday shift at 1400 and had told me when we spoke to bring my plates to the airport with me. We met; we exchanged pleasantries, we talked about Puigpunyent, we discussed the type of glaze I had used on the plates, and she said that she would take them with her and fire them in the next day or two. I should expect a call from her when they are ready. All this without using any English; and damn, that was fab. I felt good about resolving the plate situation, but even better that my Spanish flowed from my mouth as if I was actually thinking in Spanish.

I think my biggest problem in Spanish is the conjugation of verbs. It hasn't seemed that difficult to learn the root verbs, learning the conjugations for them is about as difficult as me believing that the inquisition was the first example of good customer service. It would be bad enough to learn all the conjugations for all the verbs (assuming I *even knew* all the verbs) if there was one rule that applied to all of them, but the reality is that the number of conjugation rules is only exceeded by the number of exceptions to those rules. And as I don't seem to have the right level of attention span to learn from Michel Thomas or some other language teacher that attempts to help people learn via CD-ROMS, the best way for me to get with the programme is to listen and talk to Spaniards. This afternoon, this method kicked in big time when two Catalan friends from Barcelona who are in Mallorca for a few days came to visit me and see La Antigua. Neither Afrika or her cousin speak any English, but we managed to talk for a couple of hours about her late husband, Josep Maria, about Barcelona, about Mallorca, and just about everything else that we could think of. Josep Maria owned a ferreteria / ironmongerer / hardware store (pick on that makes sense in the language you are most comfortable with) and I had happened to be in his store the day he collapsed and was taken to hospital. We had visited with him whilst he was there, and were saddened when he passed away. Josep Maria was a very special friend, and everyone who knew him misses him, even several years later. Afrika, her daughter Carmen, and the other friends from the store and I have kept in touch, and it was very special for her and her cousin to come and visit whilst on the island. And if their visit weren't special enough, Afrika brought me a ceramic pitcher from Barcelona. The visit was great, the present completely unexpected and wonderful, but just being able to communicate for a couple of hours was the ultimate treat. I must admit, I did ask several times for them to speak a bit slower, but I know that most Spaniards believe that Brits speak English way too fast as well. Language does seem to be a relative thing: when I lived in Houston, I was amazed the first time I heard, *"howyalldoin?"* and *"y'allgoindowntothemall?"* come out sounding like one long word. I think the trick for me, or at least the way I have been able to learn to understand my Spanish friends is to not become fixated on one or two words in a sentence. Screw that. Sure I may not understand every single word that is said to me in a one-breath sentence of two hundred words, but by just listening to what is being said and focusing on the whole sentence, I am able to get the drift of what is being said; and at the same time, be able to learn how to use another word or two when I speak.

It was different when I was in "translation mode." I would listen to a Mallorquin speaking and try to get every single word sorted out in my mind. This, of course, did slow down my ability to comprehend what was being said, mainly because I would get stuck on every fourth or fifth word whilst trying to remember what the words were in English. Not only did it slow down my ability to understand what was being said, by the time I would finally figure out what the speaker was saying, he would be about six sentences further along, leaving me in his dust. And then there was the time when I clearly mis-understood what someone was saying – no doubt because I was lost in the translation process – that I began to think he was telling me that Generalissimo Franco was alive and well and making a living as a waiter in my favourite neighbourhood restaurant.

Actually, I don't even get too worked up about language anymore. I just do what I can, with what I know, and keep trying to learn more. Of course, I have used a secret weapon – trust me, this has worked rather well for me. I simply begin speaking to someone new with the incredibly well pronounced, *"Lo siento, mi Español es muy malo"* (I am sorry, my Spanish is not that good). Then I kick in with my butchered conjugations and disjointed sentences. Perhaps it is a pity reaction on the part of those I am speaking with, but at least they do know I am trying to speak the language of the country I have chosen to live in.

Item 1: Robin MacNeil, of the old MacNeil-Leher Report on America's PBS, when asked what it felt like to become an American citizen, said, *"you never more feel like a guest."* And these are the same sentiments I have about being

James B Rieley

British and living in Europe. When I made my choice to become a British citizen, I knew that it would take a while before I really felt that I was part of a different country. But it wasn't until I settled in Puigpunyent that I really have felt that I am part of Europe. Okay, so it might seem a bit confusing to some of my friends – born in the US, who became a British citizen, and living in Mallorca Spain. But it does work for me, and in reality, I am very comfortable here. One of the things I like the most is that Puigpunyent is a sleepy village...most of the time. But this week is the annual Puigpunyent Festival and the "sleepy" part seems to have disappeared temporarily.

This evening's entertainment was titled, "Gran Nit de Rock", or as most people over the age...well my age, would translate it, *"louder than standing next to a 747 engine."* It was spectacular. There were several live bands that demonstrated their ability to exceed the limits of the human eardrum, and all on stage only fifty metres from my house. Even though the programme didn't even begin until eleven thirty at night, I hustled myself to the plaza to take part in my community celebrations. The plaza was filled with young children (running around with the clear intent of driving their parents a bit crazy); teen-agers (trying to avoid being seen with their parents); hard-core rock and rollers (trying to absorb the sounds that not even a lead-lined brain could avoid); parents (looking a bit perplexed at it all); and grandparents (probably remembering the days when the music was a bit softer and sung in Mallorquin). And then there was me; standing listening to a local band singing Paperback Writer in English; and just absorbing it all. I must admit that after an hour or so, I did head home, safe in the knowledge that I would still be able to hear the music – oh my God, could I hear the music.

Item 2: Living here certainly is different than living in the big city...any big city. Yes, it is true I don't have access to all the things that go on in big cities; yes, it is true I am not even able to see all the big city lights, but everything is a trade off. Whilst I don't have big city lights, I do have a clear view on the spectacular evening sky. Tonight, the view became even more spectacular. I was just about to go over to the plaza for the festival when my phone rang. It was Afrika, who called from Barcelona to let me know that she just saw on telly that tonight it would be the best time to see the "llubia de las estrellas." (YOU-BE-AH DAY LAS ES-TRAY-YAHS) Afrika, as you know by now, doesn't speak any English, and her Catalan comes across at near the speed of sound; but when she said "llubia de las estrellas," it caught my attention. Llubia de las estrellas translates literally to "rain of the stars," so I asked her if she was telling me that some stars would be flying across the sky, and she said yes. A hot night for shooting stars, and because I live in the village and not the big city with the big city lights, I just might be able to see some of them.

Before going up to the roof terrace with my camera, I did a quick web-search to see what exactly I should be looking for and where in the sky it would be. Actually, talking to Afrika made more sense that the website I found...

this weekend would be the best time to see the Kappa Cygnids, and whilst there were projected to be only a few per hour, they would be *"strikingly augmented with the annual August Perseids."* Isn't that special? I wasn't sure if this was a shooting star report, or part of an old Gene Roddenberry script, but armed with all this new knowledge (like I am actually going to remember it), up to the roof I went.

Being on the roof terrace at night is very special, even when the peace of it all is accompanied by the power of 83 billion watts of a rock sound system. I am not even sure how long I sat out there, covered with a blanket of millions of stars overhead (but none apparently zooming across the sky when I was looking).

Tonight I learned several things: the stars at night, are big and bright...oh, sorry, strike that; an apparent lapse into Texas culture again. The stars are spectacular; the night skies over the village let you see so much more than what we see from cities; and the local festivals are equally spectacular, and reinforce my sense of being part of the village. When reflecting on the evening in the weeks to come, I am sure I will remember that, as we used to say years ago, it was good for me.

The inside of La Antigua is just about the way I would like it, but for several weeks I have been pondering what to do about the courtyard gardens. It is lovely the way it is, in a "garden run amuck" sort of way. So I decided to change it. As La Antigua is in Mallorca, and Mallorca is in the Mediterranean, I thought that it would be good to put a bit of structure to the gardens, but in a Mallorquin sort of way.

Ever since I arrived at La Antigua, I had been whittling away off and on at the hanging yellow Jasmine and the grape vines that seemed to wind through everything else. At one time, I was going to go through the effort to actually map out where the vines were, but when my picture began to look like the London underground, I gave up. What I needed was a plan. You know. An overall plan of what I wanted to accomplish. So I began to sort out what I needed to do.

As with most jobs, my first thought was that I could whip through this in a day or so. Right. But it hasn't exactly worked out that way.

Step 1: figure out what I wanted the gardens to look like after I had replanted them.

Step 2: clean out all the plants that I didn't want to have lingering around.

Step 3: dig out some of the soil beds to make room for new, nutrient filled soil.

Step 4: go buy the plants I wanted to have in place of the crazy jumble of green that was there.

Step 5: plant the new bushes, flowers, and herbs.

Step 6: water the shit out of the new glorious gardens.

James B Rieley

Step 7: have a Pym's whilst sitting back and admiring my handy-work.

But as fate would have it, some of my common sense, logical garden construction steps didn't work out as planned. I did actually make some sketches of what I wanted it to look like. Then I went out and bought and borrowed some garden books to see if what I wanted made any sense – growing plants in constant sun and heat can be a bit challenging, especially when the village authorities send out cleverly worded flyers that talk about the need to conserve water. In a Puigpunyent summer, the word conservation seems to evaporate from the vocabulary as fast as the sweat appears whilst pruning bushes that seem to be in turbo regeneration mode all the time. So after a few more sketches and consultations with gardeners and friends, I thought I had a good idea of what the courtyard would look like.

I began step 2 one day when there was a cloud off in the distant sky that I had hoped would somehow scoot over my house and then stay for the rest of the day, providing a bit of shade. Right. I attacked the offending vines and bougainvilleas that had been growing at an exponential rate. I was well equipped for this task, having nice leather gloves (thorns are not nice to have stick in your hands); one of those handy-dandy garden pruning clipper things that looked as if it would cut through my fingers without even feeling guilty; a very large recycling green polyethylene bag for the cut-off stuff; and the most important thing of all for you perspective gardeners – a vocabulary that would make a Spanish sailor blush. And as with all life experiences, there were lessons learnt from all this. Lesson 1: no matter how big a garbage bag you have to put cut up branches and stuff in, it will not be big enough. Lesson 2: If you have two big bags, you will really probably need four. Lesson 3: leather gloves are no match for nasty thorns, but if you don't have access to something that Sir Lancelot wore, make sure you have plasters nearby. Lesson 4: thorny plants about to be hacked away seem to take offence at being called *"puta-madre,"* and tell their thorny plant friends to be mean to the person with the clippers. Lesson 5: God invented machetes for a reason.

After entire day – I probably lost about 3 stone from perspiration, but I wouldn't recommend this as a weight loss programme – I had managed to get the bougainvillea back to where I wanted it to be, and had done some serious adjustments to the Jasmine. When I stood back and looked at the mound-like pile of branches and crap that I cut out, and then looked at my two garbage bags, I knew there would be a problem. So I next cut up all the branches into nice little pieces no longer than 10cm – no, I didn't measure them, I just kept cutting them into smaller and smaller pieces, trying to avoid my fingers getting in the way of my trendy action clipper that was moving at a speed that would have impressed even Edward Scissorhands. I even dragged out all the odds-and-ends plastic pots that had been loitering on the garden beds. Plastic pots are okay, if you believe everything from the soundtrack of The Graduate; but I knew that I would end up binning them and eventually replacing them with seriously Mallorquin clay pots.

Step 3, digging out the garden beds to make room for new, nutrient rich dirt began to look at bit intimidating for me. So maybe intimidating isn't the most appropriate word. Instead, how about, it seemed way too much like nasty work, so I modified the big plan. Modify is a Mallorquin word that means I hired a professional gardener to finish up the hard part of the work. I did pick out the new plants; I did decide where they would go; but I realised that playing in the dirt is not exactly my area of expertise. Or maybe it just seemed like too much hard work in the sun, so I slagged off the job to Miguel, who slagged off all the nasty bits to Michel, his worker. I must admit, sitting in the shade watching them dig up the garden beds made me feel like ol'Ben Gunn, but after watching the work, I am sure that paying for someone to do it was alot smarter than doing it myself.

Steps 4 and 5 were handled by Miguel – part of the newly revised cunning plan, of course. And steps 6 and 7? Well I figured out I could hold the hose in one hand and the Pym's in the other, so once again, life is good in Puigpunyent.

The entire ceramic adventure has been going along well. I did, however, run into a slight glitch when I went to collect all the pieces I had previously delivered for firing. It seems that the oven that the shop uses to heat the painted ceramics only does hold so much, and whilst they were able to fit almost everything into it, the water pitcher didn't quite make it so I had to make another trip into Palma to collect that. Everything else did turn out pretty much as I had hoped for – plates, saucers, cups, serving platters, a large fruit bowl, and the azulejos (AH-ZOO-LAY-HOES) I painted to put around the kitchen window near the sink.

Not only did the ceramic extravaganza go well, the garden changeover well brilliantly as well. Miguel (the man who either has a better back than I do, or seems to love sweating more than I do) and his worker did a wonderful job in converting my chaotic jungle of green stuff into a well-planned Mallorquin garden patio.

I had picked out quite a few photos from magazines and gardening books and had asked Miguel to go buy what he thought was appropriate from my list of favourites (my list did occupy two pages of A4 paper I might add). I was going to go with him but I had to wait for the repairmen for my dishwasher (pump motor went to dishwasher heaven) and refrigerator (ice maker was acting stupid…as ice makers can do I am told).

After several hours, Miguel and Michel returned with some of the things from my photo list (apparently, if he had purchased everything I had chosen, it would have been able to fill Kew Gardens). So now, after much thought, much planning, solid effort by the lads, and a draining of the garden budget for La Antigua, I am the proud owner of courtyard gardens that contain; Dracina Marinates; Asplenium Nious; Chlorophytum

Comosum Variegatum's; Cordyline Australis'; Hibiscus; Cyca Revoluta, as well as Thelma and Louise. Thelma is the lucky one who is now living in a huge maceta (MAH-SAY-TA, ceramic pot) that I received as a gift from the friends from London who also have a home in Soller. I have no idea how Tim managed to lift this mother-of-all-macetas into his car, but he brought it over when he visited La Antigua last week. A wonderful surprise pressie.

And if all that wasn't good enough, today, on my way back from the ceramic store (the bloody water pitcher still wasn't out of the oven yet), I stopped at Magatzem Verde (a huge garden store in Palma) and bought a rather oversize Aloe Vera plant (good if my body decides to become sun burnt some day) and a huge variegated spikey plant thingy. I am not sure, but I think its Latin name is "largium greenium and yellowium spikeium plantium." Or maybe it was Raquel, which may not be Latin, but does seem like a great name for a fab plant.

It has been a busy time for me lately. Life in the village has been good, but I have been pretty occupied with my work (writing for the Telegraph and Microsoft) and my relaxation (cranking out decorated ceramic bits at a level that one might have if I was really doing this for money). In recent days, things have changed quite a bit in Puigpunyent.

It is early October, and autumn has been covering Mallorca for almost a month. The days are usually sunny and warm, but the evenings are beginning to be cool. The most obvious change in the weather has been the autumn rains that usually arrive in September, and this year has been no different. I am not even sure how many days it has rained here in the past month, but the gardens are extremely happy. Lots of green, with the new plants flourishing and perhaps the best news of all is that I haven't had to spend almost an hour each night watering everything. Outside of the courtyard quite often being wet, the change of seasons has been good. It has enabled me to actually rummage through my closets to find jumpers and long pants to swap for my shorts by late afternoon each day.

With any luck at all, this week Miguel will come over and clean my chimneys – it is almost evening fireplace time. I had spoken to a friend about who I should ring to have them cleaned, and was given a choice. I could either A) clean them myself using the tried and true method that used to be the way to go on the island; or, B) call Miguel. So I enquired as to what option A was. It seems that years ago, the way you cleaned a chimney was to catch a chicken, tie its legs together, and then slowly lower it down the chimney. It would flap its wings trying to get out of the small vertical tunnel, and in the process, clean all the soot off the chimney walls. As I don't have a chicken to catch, and don't think that doing this would match my concerns about cruelty to animals, I opted out to ring Miguel.

Last week, Amelia fell ill. I had gone into the city, and upon returning to my car, I discovered that the clever little electronic component that some cars have to frustrate potential car thieves had died. Amelia's engine spun like a roulette wheel every time I turned the key, but it just wouldn't fire up. I ended up ringing my auto insurance company and they sent a grua (which is a flatbed truck) to take Amelia to a garage for repairs. But as luck would have it, the garage was closed for the weekend, so it was a return to La Antigua by taxi. And because the little component is something that is not usually in stock, I had to wait until I returned from a business trip to London to get my car back. The bad news: I have once again become accustomed to having a car and being able to drive into Palma when I feel the need. The good news: the mechanic who came with the lorry didn't speak a speck of English, so I was able to learn some new words (which I am sure I can use if Amelia ever again decides to not start).

I had woken up today, and after the usual proper tea and toast, had gone up to the roof terrace to do what I do many days…ponder the world's problems whilst enjoying the brilliant warmth of the sun. This was to be a very special day in the village. I had been waiting for today for several weeks, and I think that I noticed it the local animals began making more noise than usual. On a typical day, it is possible to hear the odd rooster calling out in rooster-eze to his friends, or telling neighbours that it was well past sunrise and they had better get cracking. And because of the orientation of where La Antigua is in the village, it is also possible to hear dogs barking, even if they are halfway across town. But today, suddenly, it was if all the animals were talking to each other. Well, actually, it sounded like they were howling and screeching as if the world was coming to an end. And then I realised, it was getting darker. At first, I thought that some cloud who hadn't read the instructions to not cast shadows on my terrace whilst I am up there had gotten it all wrong, but even when I lifted my sunglasses, it was noticeably darker…at 1100h. Animals howling? Roosters screeching? The sun going dark? Could it be that Keith Richards was coming to the village?

Sorry, it was an annular eclipse. An annular eclipse is when the moon slides in front of the sun, blocking the blinding rays for a time, and in the process, creating a visual ring of fire in the sky. I had read about this several weeks ago, and had even sent out information to my friends in Spain so that they could see it as well. And because looking directly at the sun, even when it is partially covered by the moon, is frowned upon by the eyes (unless you have decided to learn braille), I had even picked up a pair of the almost unbelievably dark "eclipse watching glasses" from my local newsagent. I scrambled back inside to get my special glasses and my camera and went leaping (okay, so I can't actually leap, but I did go quickly) back up to the roof terrace to see the solar/lunar event.

The newspapers had said that the path of the eclipse would track right over Ibiza, but because we are so close, Mallorca would have an 88% visible eclipse. But just after seeing the moon begin to pass in front of the sun, some rogue clouds appeared, and within minutes, the sun was totally blocked by them. No eclipse visible, so off to the market I went.

Autumn is firmly in control over Mallorca. It seems that almost everyday is has been raining, but the reality is that the rains have been visiting only sporadically. But for someone who does love the sun and warm, more than a few days does tend to be a bit tiresome. Everyday I go online to check out the weather forecasts, but apparently all the Ph.D.-laden meteorologists using the latest of technology can only do as good as flipping a coin. And to complicate things, even the online forecasts tend to differ with each other. One ten-day forecast touts day after day of rain, whilst another one pledges sun on a daily basis. So I have given up on the forecasts and instead look at the satellite pictures of Europe; and lately, it has been difficult to spot my island, as the autumn clouds keep drifting in. So to be prepared, a couple of weeks ago, I made a serious psychologically devastating purchase. Wellies. But now, I am ready for more wet weather.

On the days when the sun does come blasting through the clouds, it has been brilliant here. Yes, I have managed to do what any serious sun-baker does and sit on the roof terrace doing reading, painting, thinking, and the most important of all – just ask any sun person – resting in the warmth that envelopes all below. Today was a mixture of both days – it rained in the morning and then the sun came out to dry everything off. When this happens, I don my new Wellies and head out into the courtyard to sweep up the leaves that have fallen (yes, one might call this a bit of anal retentiveness, but it is my courtyard, so I get to keep it the way I like it). Sweeping up rain-soaked leaves has to be one of life's challenges, but I do manage.

And after the courtyard was cleaner, I sat down to just enjoy my home. It was then when I noticed a visitor had arrived. No, I didn't hear the round steel doorknocker make its distinctive clunking sound; I just looked up and there he was. Or maybe there she was. As a child, my father had introduced me to butterfly collecting, and in the process, had given me a nicely illustrated book of just some of the most common butterflies that I might be able to capture (and as I look back on it all, sadly kill and stick pins and display in an old museum box with a glass top). I can still remember reading the pages of the book that described some rather exotic bugs that I probably would never see in my life. But here one was. On the chair opposite where I was sitting in the courtyard, there was a Praying Mantis. Not exactly one of God's most beautiful pieces of work, it is, to say the least, fascinating to watch as it waited for a fly to land close enough to have for a snack. These green miniature monsters must have more patience than I have, because for almost an hour, he didn't move, just waiting. I finally decided that he could wait elsewhere, and carried him outside the courtyard walls to forage for whatever looks tasty to a Praying Mantis.

A friend just rang to see what I have been up to lately (besides waiting for the occasional rains to bugger off). So in the spirit of not having to say this over and over again, this is what has been occurring lately at La Antigua. I received the proof copy of one of the two books I wrote this summer, and that has been an interesting time-eater-upper. I do find it difficult to proof read my own writing. I can remember asking someone to proof read an article I wrote a couple of years ago, and after some silence, was asked what I meant by something I had typed. I said, *"Let me see where you are seeing this;"* but only to find that when I had read my own writing, I was seeing what had been in my mind when I wrote it, not exactly what I had put on paper. So to proof read the entire book was a challenge. Actually, it looked okay, but I did take the opportunity to add a few things I wished I had said whilst writing it – I am sure the publisher will be thrilled to see my additions.

Besides the proof reading (which will resume next week when the other book arrives for my review), I have been working on this year's Christmas card. Yesterday I made several test prints to check colours, and will do more this afternoon probably. Oh yes, then there is the aluminium bas-relief I have been working on. This has been an on-going project for the past month, and I finally was able to finish it a few days ago. Now I just need to find a way to get all the carcinogen-laden sugar substitutes out of my system.

Years ago (actually many, many years ago), I was in the Boy Scouts. And through the years that I ran about being enthralled at the time by Lord Baden-Powell's words on how to become a better person (whilst racking up those Merit Badges for God-knows-what). And even today, I can remember one bit from the Scout's oath (but am a bit foggy on if it was even called the Scout's oath). The bit I remember? Be prepared. So yesterday, in the vein of "being prepared," I drove to Establishments (a town about 6 km from Puigpunyent) to track down a supply of leña (LAIN-YAH) for the winter. Leña is for all you non-Spanish-speakers, firewood.

Yes, La Antigua does have central heat and air conditioning, but over the summer, I never had to use the air conditioning. Not because it wasn't warm; on the contrary, it was bloody hot here for much of the summer, but the walls of the house are almost a metre thick and that much stone and mortar must be the best insulation on the planet. And assuming once the house is warm, I would expect the insulation to keep it warm as well. But because I have two fireplaces, instead of just enlarging the checkbook of the electric utility here on the island, I thought I would have fires at night.

On Monday, Miguel (have you noticed how many people I know named Miguel yet?) the gardener came over to clean my chimneys. Yes, there is a correlation between gardening and chimney sweeping apparently, but I haven't figured it out yet. I had been waiting for many weeks to have the chimney's swept, so when he arrived, I was rather pleased. And after watching Miguel and his helper drag a crumpled up piece of wire mesh up and down the chimneys, all was well. So yesterday I went to Establishments to find wood to burn in my almost-clean-enough-to-eat-off-of fireplaces.

Miguel had told me that there were only three types of wood I would want to burn – Olivo (Olive tree), Almendras (Almond tree) and Encina (Oak tree), so after finding the wood suppliers yard (I did drive past it twice and only found it after looking up and seeing mountains of cut wood), I parked Amelia and ventured in. Jaime, the proprietor, is older than most of the trees he has cut down I thought but was very helpful, in a non-English speaking way. I began by telling him my Spanish is not very good – my standard line when meeting someone new on the island who doesn't speak English – and then said I needed to buy some firewood, and I wanted either Olivo or Almendras, or Encina (to impress him with my knowledge of fireplace propriety). He asked me how much I wanted, whilst glancing over to Amelia and then looking at me with a frown. I said I needed a lot of wood, about a pile 2 metres by 2 metres by one log deep. He kept his frown.

Okay, I enquired, how much would that much wood cost? Well, he said, he sells wood either in bags (kindling-type wood-bits) or by the bucket, but…if I didn't want to come visit him every other day, he suggested I buy his standard amount. Which was "mil kilos." In English, that is 1,000 kilos, or about a ton of flippin' wood. I couldn't imagine how much wood it takes to weigh a ton, but before I could respond, Jaime said it was forty buckets-worth. Well, that didn't seem like too much so I said fine, but he had to deliver it to La Antigua. I gave him directions to my house, and, to be courteous, did tell him that my street is only 2.3 metres wide. I didn't want him to come with some lorry that was recycled from a monster truck event and not be able to get to my door – see, more Boy Scout training being applied here. And more good news; I didn't have to pay him until the wood was delivered, so Amelia and I drove home.

The next morning my mobile rang and it was Jaime's driver letting me know he would be over in about 45 minutes. By now I was getting a bit concerned about where the forty bucket-loads of wood were going to go, so I cleaned out my wood storage area and re-stacked the wood I still had on hand. And shortly after taking some Naprosyn for the back pain that I was already beginning to experience, there was a knock on the compound door. It was the driver, but he did look a tad concerned about getting his lorry up the narrow street. This man must be related to Mandrake the Magician, because after gesturing hypnotically (and driving very carefully), the truck was now at my door. The driver and his helper (everyone here seems to have helpers…I need to find a helper I think, not sure for what, but at least I would fit in more on the island) and I slogged the wood into the courtyard.

In under 30 minutes, all the wood was in, stacked neatly, and they were on their way again. But this is where the real fun began…it was tricky getting their lorry UP the street…but unbelievably tricky to back it DOWN the street. But they did it, and off they went, leaving me to go admire my freshly-delivered-ton-of-nicely-stacked-wood. I think I will light the fireplaces up tonight…after all, I am now prepared for the onset of winter, marginal that it will be here.

Living on Rocks

This was copied from the Mallorca Daily Bulletin, the island English-language newspaper: *"Majorca's first sprinkling of snow this winter is forecast for this week and many will be hoping that the Balearics will have another huge dump of snow over Christmas and New Year like last year when it even snowed on the beaches. The forecast for the week ahead points to a deterioration in the weather tomorrow with snow forecast at 1000 metres, the peaks of the Sierra de Tramuntana with light showers and the odd storm nearer sea level. The temperatures will start to drop slightly from this evening with the worst of this new cold front expected to grip the region this weekend."* And of course, I can see the mountains from my house, so I think I might just hibernate in front of the fireplaces for a bit. The whole spectre of winter seems so remote, as last Sunday morning the sun was shining brilliantly in the eastern sky, and I thought it would be a good morning for a walk. Sunday morning means the Sunday Times from London is at our local village combination bakery, gift shop, newsagent, and tobacco shop, and because last Sunday was fabulous, I thought I would take a stroll to collect the paper.

I live .9km from where the combination-just-about-everything shop is, so with using the normal conversion tables, calculating kilometres into miles, and then factoring in the various hills of the village, I figure I walked about 223.5 miles when I go to get the paper, and then converting that into calories burnt, at least 28,753,694.3. Now perhaps the readers of this chapter who were maths majors in school will differ with my calculations, but, as we ex-pats say, p**s-off. *(note: I would like to report that my body fat is now down to negative numbers from all this exercise, but apparently the Mars and Snickers bars that somehow find their way into my system somehow can counteract all the benefits of all the exercise)*

The village holds a special charm for me. I am not even sure exactly why, but I do both love living here and feel so comfortable in this environment. The people in the village who I come upon whilst walking all greet me, as I do them. And because I am working diligently to "fit in," I am always amazed at the various greetings I am presented with. Some people say, *"muy Buenos;"* some say, *"buenos dias;"* some say *"bon dia;"* and some just nod their head and smile. And however they say "good morning" really doesn't make a difference to me; they are all very welcoming, especially in light of the fact that I have only lived here for six months and clearly am not a village native.

In late November, whilst at the Correo picking up stamps for Christmas cards to send out, I was talking to the woman who works there about the village. She has lived her for twenty years (and she told me that she was "new in the village") and said that one of the reasons that she lives here is that she loves the quiet life of the country. Of course, then she mentioned the weather, and that did send a bit of a shudder through my body. Last year, we had snow in the village for four days. Not that much of it, but it was here for the four days straight. I said that it must have been very pretty - I have always hated winter, and the winter snows that turn a dark, depressing black-grey colour as soon as cars begin to travel over the roads. The fact that snow is a function of incredibly cold (for me) weather is another whole issue. Yes, it was pretty she said, but it was also very slippery as it turned to ice. *"Ice?"* I said, wondering how to walk up and down the hills of the village. She provided me with a very simple solution to a potential problem. She said that she just didn't go outside. I do have firewood that should last me through any storm that drops out of the mountains; I do always have food here; I do have my computer and my paints – let winter come! Now just in case the Gods of Weather are reading this last sentence, what I really mean is that I would be happy to sit in front of the fireplace, watching the snow fall, but would much rather it sunny and warm.

It has been a tad over seven months since I moved into La Antigua, and in a word, it has been fabulous. Yes, there have been challenges; after all, the house is almost 200 years old, and I suppose that I would have a few idiosyncrasies if I were that age too. 1) The walls are almost a metre thick, which was great in summer to help keep the heat out, but in winter, it does take a lot to warm them up. 2) Houses this old, especially in Mallorca, tend to have "interesting" electrical systems. La Antigua was originally two homes and consequently, still has two different systems. Not a major challenge, but when a circuit breaker decides to click off, it is like the world's most bizarre puzzle to figure out why "that breaker" controls "those mains." 3) All the foliage in the courtyard gardens provide much needed shade in summer, but has resulted in the daily activity of sweeping up fallen leaves…and occasionally, fallen oranges from the tree. 4) The stone floor of the courtyard has far more character than a smooth paved floor, but after it rains, some of the individual stones act as little tidal pools that need to be swept empty. 5) The electricity level in the village is marginal, and usually only delivers 210 volts instead of the 220 or 230 that is the norm in most big cities. But would I change anything? Not on your life… okay, it might be nice to have 230 volts all day, everyday, but everything does seem to work. Whilst I have owned some pretty great houses in my day, this one is by far the most special one.

And now it is almost Christmas at La Antigua, and I have been busy. Each year, I like to make my own Christmas cards, and this year was no different. After I had made them, signed them, put them in envelopes, addressed them all and took them to the Puigpunyent Post Office, I realised that the Christmas spirit had invaded my body and I began to do more. I had made some azulejos and ceramic serving platters for my family and decided to wrap them in hand-made wrapping paper. This really isn't that difficult to do (just in case you want to get ambitious). Get a roll of white paper; buy some potatoes, buy some acrylic paint, and get busy. Without a single sliced finger, I was able to make a six-colour paper for wrapping the pressies. A nice feeling of accomplishment, but I didn't stop there. For the past several years, I have avoided having a Christmas tree for a variety of reasons. Whilst living on Angelina, it seemed a bit over the top to put a Christmas tree on-board, plus I have no idea where I would have even had room for one. And last year living in Palma, I just wasn't in the mood. But this year, I thought I would decorate a tree, but instead of going out and buying some traditional Christmas tree, I opted out to decorate one of the large palms I have in La Antigua. And by now, you have probably figured out what I did next. Yes, I made the ornaments for the tree. Nothing major, just something that children could do with a bit of supervision; and seeing as how Christmas is a great time for all of us to enjoy the wonder of the season, I found some coloured paper and made paper garlands. And because *this is what you do,* I made something for the top of my "tree" as well. Something sort of traditional. Well, "sort of" is the applicable term here. I made an Angel for the top of my "tree"....out of aluminium foil. So "sort of" traditional. She looked great.

03

Almost Really Believing I am Living Here

2006

Today, as I was out sweeping the courtyard I noticed that the bulbs that Maryann and Barry gave me a while ago are beginning to come up. Hopefully, daffodils will grace the courtyard in the near future.

At times, it is so hard for me to believe that I have been in La Antigua for almost eight months, but every day when I awake and see the sun creeping over the mountains, it is pretty clear to me that I am home. Okay, it is true… some winter mornings what I see is clouds hovering over the mountains, and even some days the mountains are a bit obscured by the rains, but even on what I tend to think of as "bad weather days," the sun does peek out at some point.

The holiday week has been pretty great. Kel and Lorraine, friends I met whilst living on-board Angelina in Barcelona who now live in Melbourne Australia, came to Mallorca to spend the hols with friends. After spending a couple of days in Palma with other friends, they came out to the village and stayed in the warmth of La Antigua. There was a Christmas party, a New Year's party, and special get-togethers in between with friends. And if all that wasn't enough, there was even an attempt to cook in the kitchen fireplace. Lorraine had said she had a foolproof pizza base recipe, so after a quick trip to my local market, we decided to give the recipe a go. Attempt number 1 sort of failed due to one recipe component being missing. Attempt number 2 sort of failed due to a frozen pizza base not defrosting evenly. Attempt number 3 almost made it into the record books for excellence in home-made-oven-cooked-pizzas had it not been for the apparent excessive heat on the incredibly think pizza pan I had. The end result, whilst marginally edible, resulted in the base resembling something a crematorium might produce. And by then, Kel was near starvation, so the great idea ended up being sandwiches. Overall, having them at La Antigua was very special, and we did manage to catch-up on all the happenings between Melbourne and Puigpunyent quite well. Good friends.

Whilst my friends from Australia were at La Antigua, I thought it would be nice to show them some of the areas that surround Puigpunyent, so after watching the sun come up over the mountains from the roof terrace one morning, we went for a ride through the countryside toward Esporles.

I have never really gotten my head around what is a town, a city, a village, or whatever. Yes, I am sure that someplace, there is definitive data on population being a factor, or perhaps it is governing structure. Not really sure, and not sussed enough to dig up the information, but clearly, there is a difference. Puigpunyent is a village – nice feeling, a few shops, but surrounded by the countryside. And it "feels" like a village. Semi-quiet streets, people who greet you whilst walking about, and just an overall sense that we are all living together. Not exactly like some other places I have lived. Barcelona was grand, but it is so big. It is as much of a city as London or Houston, but with a whole different feeling to it. Yes, it has high rise buildings, horrendous traffic problems, a cathedral that looks like it could hold the entire population of Puigpunyent, and clearly different neighbourhoods, each having its own sense of identity. And one of the things that I loved about Barcelona was the name.

City/town/village names hold special interest to me. When I was looking for a house to purchase, I can remember my estate agent driving me around to various towns and villages that had properties for sale. I think this was one of the days the estate agent realised how difficult his task might be. My estate agent had wanted to show me a property in Esporles and as we approached the town, he was going on about the house I was about to see, but I waved him off saying that I was struggling imagining living in a place with the name Esporles, and on we went to the next property...which happened to be in Puigpunyent.

Last evening, a new restaurant opened in the village. I went with Barry and Marianne to the opening party and was very glad I did, as I met many new people. It is quite amazing to me – for some time after moving to the village, I was beginning to believe that the three of us were the only English-speakers in the village. This was fine with me, as this is one of the principle reasons I moved here. My reasoning was clear – I live in Spain, and therefore, I should speak Spanish and found this difficult to do in Palma as there are so many people who do speak English, or at least want to speak English. But everyone I had met in Puigpunyent (save Barry and Marianne) spoke only Spanish...until last evening. Apparently, Puigpunyent is one of those secret enclaves for Brits, and I was introduced to quite a few other people who envisioned themselves as being bi-lingual.

Whilst it is very early in February, and according to the calendar, winter is still upon us, the weather here has taken a turn for the better. The past several months have seen grey clouds and rain several days each week, but the past two days had been simply brilliant. The temperatures – whilst never being very cold here – are on the rise but even so, every night I have a fire in at least one of the fireplaces. Not so much for heat, but I think it is like living in Puigpunyent...it just feels good.

Whilst it is still on the waning edge of winter, fabulous weather is fast approaching. The daffodils are coming up faster than the lift in a high-rise; the yellow jasmine flowers are beginning to bloom; and the almond blossoms are popping out all over the island. By mid-month, I had been basking in the sun on the roof terrace for several hours each day, enjoying the warmth, reading, and exhausting my leftover selection of single-digit solar protection bottles of lotion.

My son David came to visit La Antigua for my birthday, and whilst I am pretty content to be at La Antigua most of the time, I thought it would be a good time to venture out and do something I hadn't done since I had moved to Mallorca. Our plans included visiting Soller, but to get there, instead of driving up in Amelia, we would take the train.

It may seem a bit odd, but, yes, even Mallorca has a train line. The train, a classically designed train with wooden framed cars, travels between Palma and Soller several times each day. After getting our tickets, we quickly found seats in a relatively empty car for the one-hour trip through the countryside and mountain tunnels. But before the train departed, the car filled with tourists – we were sitting just in front of three generations of a German family that apparently all had hearing defects, as they apparently felt compelled to yell back and forth to each other. But we didn't let that bother us…we were on the train heading north.

The train had a very "Orient-Express" feel to it, except for the lack of food, comfortable seating, an overall First-Class appearance, and an elderly detective named Ms. Marple. We scooted north through fields of flowering almond trees; wound around mountains with only deep valley views on one side, and steep hills on the other; and several times, everything went dark as the train plunged into narrow tunnels that had been cut into the Tramuntana mountain range that covers most of the north-west coast of the island. And just about on schedule, the train pulled into the station in Soller. Whilst I had never taken the train before, I knew that there was another, smaller train that went from Soller to the Port of Soller on the coast. So we boarded that one immediately and continued our journey of exploration. The port train was, well, it was best characterised by the sound of fingernails being dragged across a chalkboard for twenty minutes. The ride, a bit bumpy and not as scenic as the first part, was fine, although it might be nice if they would raise the ticket price from 3 euros to say, 4 euros, if only to be able to afford oil for the carriage wheels, which we figured might cut down on the terrible squeeking sound.

Port de Soller was, well, it was pretty deserted. It is still February, and the tourists haven't inundated the island yet, and tourists are what keep the port alive. So we putzed about, looking for a place to get something to eat before the double return trip to Palma. The trip(s) back were a bit nicer for us. When we boarded the Soller to Palma train, we boarded what turned out to be the carriage that also contains the electrical powerplant that drives (pulls?) the train, and the seats in that carriage were quite plush, with more space and leather-covered cushions. It was very comfortable and the gentle swaying of the train as it crossed back toward Palma lulled David and I asleep within minutes.

The next day, being ever vigilant for things to do for artistically motivated family members, we visited…the cemetery. Yes, we went to the cemetery. It is unbelievably beautiful, in a grey-stone-tombs-filled-with-expired-Mallorquins sort of way. One of my neighbours had told me that there were catacombs under the cemetery that were open some days, but on the day we were there, either they weren't open, or we just couldn't find them - it had been difficult enough to just find a place to park Amelia and walk in.

And then after a few more days, David had to leave, and the island sensed his departure I think because the weather turned foul and very wet. All yesterday it rained as if there was a large wooden boat awaiting the boarding of two of every species. And if the rain wasn't enough, the temperature began to fall and by mid-afternoon, and I could see snow falling into the compound courtyard. Luckily, the temperature nearer the ground wasn't that cold and as fast as the snow would fall, it would disappear into masses of puddles. But this morning when I awoke and looked outside – a sunny dry day once again – I could see that some of the high mountains visible from La Antigua were covered with snow. So, as far as I am concerned, we have had this year's snow and now summer can return. And by now I mean right now.

Living in the village is a real learning experience, and an experience I am enjoying quite a bit. Of course, there are some things that do catch me off guard. The other day I had gone into Palma to pick up some picture frames for a series of photos that I have, and when I returned home, the spot I usually leave Amelia in was occupied by another car. When this occurs, as it has previously, I simply drive around several blocks and come back up Carrer des Sol and quite often, a spot has opened up. If not, I drive around the corner and park in a street that normally has few cars parked there. But that day, I instead parked Amelia in front of the entrance to Plaza Son Bru (where the festival celebrations are during the summer). My intent was to simply unload the frames and carry them to La Antigua and then move the car because I was parked over a yellow line, which means no parking. But I reasoned the chances of a policeman driving along in the next ten minutes was about as good as me moving back to a country I am not fond of, so it wouldn't be a problem. I carried the frames to the house and then the phone rang; and then several important emails came in; then another phone call; and by then I had forgotten about where I was parked. But four hours later, there was a knock on the compound door.

I went out and opened the door only to find a neighbour who wanted me to move my car so she could get into her garage across the street. I muttered Spanish apologies as we walked down the street and I quickly (and neighbourly) moved Amelia to my usual parking spot which was by then open. And that was when I noticed a little yellow piece of paper stuck between the windscreen and one of the windscreen wipers. A note; what fun, I thought. But it turned out to be a parking ticket. Okay, fair enough...I did deserve it, so the next morning I walked down to the adjuntament (the village hall, so to speak) to pay the 30-euro fine. The clerk, whose Castellano was about as good as mine because he is seriously Mallorquin, explained to me that there was a discount if you pay the ticket in a certain amount of time. Great news I thought...the discount was 20%, and whilst I have never been a maths whiz, I was able to determine that the 30-euro fine would now be only 24 euros. I laid my 24-euro penance on the counter, only to have the clerk give me back 3 euros. Now at this point, I could have just said thank you and taken the money, but as a resident of Puigpunyent, I didn't want to have the clerk later discover his mistake and try to collect the 3 euros again. So I said that I think there is a mistake. I borrowed his calculator and showed him that 20% of 30 euros was indeed 6 euros, and 30 euros minus 6 euros was actually 24 euros. I smiled, knowing that I was doing the right thing. And that was when he told me that regardless of what the ticket said about a discount of 20% for paying quickly, he was giving me a 30% discount and the fine was only 21 euros. I certainly didn't want to offend him, so I took the 3 euros (and a receipt that the ticket had been paid), and walked merrily home a bit confused about maths in the village, but 3 euros richer.

Later that same day I heard a knock on the compound door of La Antigua. I was upstairs on the roof terrace, enjoying the sun that seemed to have been coming back to our village, so I went to the terrace wall and said that I would be down in a moment to open the door. As soon as I flung the door open – it is always exciting to see who is coming to La Antigua – I found a woman standing there who began to rabbit on about being sorry but her car was connected to my car in the street. Now whilst my Spanish has improved tremendously in the past eight or nine months in the village, I must admit I was struggling to understand what "connected" to my car meant. So I walked down c/Es Forn with the woman and around the corner to where Amelia was currently parked. Sure enough, she had been trying to park her car in what appeared to be a spot large enough for a car that was one-half the size of her car. And because Amelia has a tow-bar attached to the back of her, the woman had managed to have her grill ingest the tow-bar. Her idea was for me to simply drive my car forward and the two cars would dislodge from themselves, and whilst this did seem like a semi-logical solution (as she couldn't go any further backwards), she had already taken her scissors-jack and lifted her car up a bit figuring that now it would be easier for me to remove Amelia's tow-bar from her grille. Even I thought this was a good idea, except for the minor fact that if the tow-bar wasn't completely disengaged from her grille, when I would ease Amelia forward, it would pull her grille out AND drag her car off the scissors-jack. So we talked about it for a bit (in Spanish of course, with neither of us making any sense what-so-ever probably), and then I had a go at it. Ever so slowly, I let Amelia ease forward until I heard a loud snap, which meant that either the two cars were disconnected, or that her nice Peugeot now didn't have a grille at all. As luck would have it, all was well, although her car now did have a minor re-shaped air scoop on the top of her grille. She thanked me graciously, and I walked home, eagerly awaiting a new merit badge in auto-grille-removal-from-a-tow-bar to be delivered in the post in a few days. It could be a long wait.

If living in the village has taught me anything, it is that, in many cases, going slow is fast enough. This week I had to fly to London for a series of business meetings, and when landing at the Heathrow mega-doo-wah airport, I was fortunate to see something that brought this point home to me. Several years ago, I had the high privilege of flying across the Atlantic on Concorde, and as my plane faffed about looking for a gate that was open, we taxied past one of the Concorde's that British Airways has conveniently left out on the tarmac for everyone to see. I don't think it is there because all the hangars are full – it is probably there as a reminder to everyone that we used to be on the cutting edge of transportation. Concorde flew at about 21,000 metres (double the altitude that today's planes fly at), and at 1.2 times the speed of sound (which, at over double the speed commercial jets fly at, is pretty flippin' quick), and the flight that I took from London to New York only took a hair over three hours. No time for an in-flight movie, only time to eat (an incredible meal) and try to contort your neck to see the curvature of the earth outside the tiny little windows. I loved it. An unbelievable experience that few people have ever been able to have. And at that point in my life, getting places quickly was pretty important. And now I live in a village where some of my neighbours look suspiciously at me if they think I am in a hurry as I barely stroll to the market.

When I am home in the village, my life does slow down. Yes, I do spend quite a bit of time on-line, cranking out book after book and article after article, but I am most content when I am able to just enjoy living where I live. There is much to be said for taking the time to enjoy what surrounds you.

Puigpunyent is a pretty sleepy village, and that was one of the attractions it held for me when I moved here. Of course, in fairness, my perception of it being just that is relative. The other day I was over at a neighbour's house, whingeing with them about the dire cold we have been enduring this March (cold for me has now become anything under 20c), and I mentioned that the "sleepiness" factor of the village was high on my list of favourite things about living here. Barry responded with, "*Sleepy little village? I don't think so.*" But of course, he and his wife have lived here for 17 years and have seen it change so much. Even I can see that there is the "old" part of the village and the "new" part. La Antigua is in the old part. Village homes that were constructed well over one hundred years ago, on narrow little streets that used to be only used by people on foot or in horse-drawn carts. Houses that have walls made of real stone and that are a metre thick and are full of character. And then there is the new part of the village.

Yes, there has been a somewhat serious attempt to make the new houses "look" as if they have been here for years, but the reality is that the construction is that of today in Spain – building blocks glued together with a mortar-like substance that workmen then render with a thin stone veneer to make them look old. And regardless of what the local planning commission tries to do, the new houses all look alike; sort of a series of highly incestuous townhouses all lined up waiting for holiday-makers to come and plop money down on so they have lay claim to their own part of the sun. (Sense any bias here?)

Yesterday, upon my return from London, I could almost feel my internal speed controller begin to slow down as I drove home from the airport. By the time I had parked Amelia and dragged my carry-bag through the compound door, my *"Need to rush about"* factor that had been in force whilst in London had dropped by half, and by the time I was in the courtyard watering the gardens, I was feeling quite good again. Yes, I had a lot to do – unpack the carry bag; unpack the briefcase that was full of business stuff that I had been carrying with me; begin to sort through all the things I had brought home with me – but I was content to just stand in the courtyard and water the plants that had begun to dry out in the now-almost-summer-weather. I was now on Puigpunyent time, and I was loving it.

There are some times where even I admit that living at this speed can be a bit challenging. I am still waiting for a price estimate from Pedro, the woodworker whom I asked over a month ago what it might cost to replace a couple of the pursiannas that are on the kitchen doors; have been waiting for about six weeks for Guillem to make me a simple metal brace for some of the grape vines over the courtyard; and am still waiting for Balthazar to just give me the bill for some things I purchased at his market several weeks ago. But the reality is that they will all get around to doing what I asked them to do when they get to it. And there really is no hurry…I will be here, enjoying living in my village. And the best news of all is that they know it.

And now some breaking news…I had tried to meet a neighbour last month, but he wasn't home, so today I tried again. His house is immediately to the west of La Antigua, and I have exchanged pleasantries with his wife and one of his daughters, but I thought that as I was a neighbour, I really needed to make a formal introduction. So I planned out what I would say, even to the point of looking up a couple of words in my word conversion dictionary, and then strolled over to his house a bit ago. I flicked the bell that is attached to his gate and within seconds, a man came from behind some gardens and said *"Hola"* to me. Okay, here I go, I thought. I knew exactly what I wanted to say, and luckily, it almost flowed out of my adopted Mallorquin mouth. I apologised for having crap Spanish, then told him who I was and that I had been living next to his house for over eight months; then tossed in that I felt bad that I hadn't introduced myself sooner. He smiled, and then said (these are his exact words…) *"Glad to meet you James."* Scheisse. Whilst he is Mallorquin, his English is about as good as 99% of the people I grew up with. Amazing. John (not even Juan…he said his name was John. Amazing) is a doctor – something that I have been known to need off and on, who was born in England, but of Mallorquin parents, and he moved back to the island when he was quite young. Amazing…simply amazing. So now I could tick off the box of having met all of my immediate neighbours, finally. Enough typing for now. Time for me to go back onto the roof terrace…the sun thing, remember?

There have been a couple of interesting things that have occurred in the village since I wrote last, and I thought they were worth sharing. The first of which was the annual village boot sale. No, we don't have an over-supply of Wellies here; it was sort of a trunk sale or as in America, a garage sale. Villagers came together at the plaza in front of the Ajuntament (our centre of government in the village) and browsed through the myriad of tables that had been set up by residents to sell all the things that they had discovered in the past year that they really didn't want anymore. When I had first heard about the sale, I was keen to go, if for no other reason than to meet more villagers and see what was on offer. But as soon as I had arrived – I rode my folding bicycle to the plaza with hopes of selling it as well – it became quite clear that a boot sale is a very English thing, and there more Brits who had brought things to dispose of than there were Mallorquins. And interestingly, most of the people milling about were Mallorquins (probably there just to see what we Brits consider saleable items). With the weather brilliant, there were seriously large crowds walking from table to table, with some actually buying things…that they would probably bring back to sell next year once they discover that they really didn't need them. No, I didn't sell the bicycle, but am fully prepared to take offers online.

Last week, I was over at Marianne and Barry's filling a rather large bag with oranges and grapefruit. They had told me that, as they have over fifty fruit trees in their orchard, it was just plain ludicrous for me to keep buying them at market. And whilst I was there, they showed me something I had never seen before – a tree that produced both oranges and lemons. After a few minutes of me looking a bit gobsmacked, I asked how that was possible. The answer was "Rafael."

Rafael is their Mallorquin gardener, and I use the word Mallorquin with a capital "M." Rafael is a tad old, and he has lived here since birth and he has, apparently, a veritable "green thumb." It didn't take me long to ask to borrow him one day to do some of his magic on my solitary orange tree in the courtyard. A few days later, Barry came over with Rafael to check out my tree. Barry had tipped me off in advance that Rafael only does grafting under certain conditions. These conditions included; the condition of the tree, the time of year, the weather, and the moon. Yes, the moon. Not sure if Barry was telling me this with his tongue firmly planted next to one cheek, but after meeting the tree magician, I was ready to believe anything. Rafael looked at my tree lovingly, then unloaded on me about the way I had cut some branches off previously (which I hadn't done myself, but thought it was pretty useless to try to explain that), felt the branches (assuming to check the age and condition of the bark), then looked to the sky and said he would be back in several days. And here he was.

I wasn't sure what equipment he would bring with him, but half expected him to just have a magic wand and a sorcerer's hat, but what he came with was a pruning saw, some wrinkled old cord, a knife, and a branch off someone else's lemon tree. I had, as I tend to do, done a search on the web for methods to graft branches on trees, and what I found was not what Rafael did.

He looked at my orange tree for a few minutes, seeking to find branches that he could add the lemon grafting's to, and then slowly examined the branch he had brought with him. Now whilst this was interesting, not much was occurring, so I just stood there and tried to look knowledgeable, but not even knowing what that look would be, he probably just thought I was nosey. No, I didn't have any ideas about stealing Rafael's secrets, but I was keen to know how he would do this, especially as we had previously talked about doing several branches, and he had only brought one with him. Suddenly, his knife came out and he started carefully cutting a rectangular shape through the thin bark of the lemon branch. And then even more carefully, he gently picked the rectangle off the branch and put in on the branch of the orange tree that he was going to graft to. He then used the lemon-bark rectangle as a template, and made an exact shaped cut in the orange tree bark, and after lifting that bit off, gently place the lemon piece into the newly cut space on the branch. Notice the notations of "carefully" and "gently?" You might have thought that Rafael was doing open-heart surgery, his hands moving deftly, cutting only through the top layer of bark. I tried to offer my acknowledging comments about what he was doing – "*Ahhh, entiendo*" (I understand), but Rafael didn't even look up to acknowledge my rapidly acquired wisdom; so intent he was on doing what he does. At one point, he did say something to me in Mallorquin, but I didn't know what it was and assumed he said, "*Well duh.*"

After ensuring that the lemon-bark rectangle was in the exact space, he took some of the nasty looking cord and began to wrap it around the branch, firmly affixing the new bit to the old branch. After several dozen wraps of the cord, he put a knot in it and then repeated the entire operation on the next branch. When he was done, (I think) he explained what he had done, with the only part that I really understood was the fact that the lemon rectangles had to contain healthy looking "eyes" that would be where the new branches would sprout from. Two more grafts later, and he was done, or so I thought. He then picked up his saw and began to whack away at my tree, getting rid of orange-tree branches that he didn't seem to like. I did understand why he did this – my first gardening experience was years ago when my father-in-law helped me plant a white birch tree in our front yard, only to then cut almost all the branches off in order to make sure that the nourishment would do what the tree needed. But in this case, the tree was already doing well and a lot of what he cut off looked pretty good I thought. But then again, if I knew what Rafael knows, I guess I wouldn't had to have him come over.

So, according to Rafael, my new friend and gardener, next year, I should have both oranges and lemons ready to pick from the same tree. I can't wait.

I decided a while ago that, whilst I do think that La Antigua has just about everything I need, it would be nice to have a proper shower in the master bathroom. So, as I do, I made a plan on my computer using one of the trendier programmes that the Microsoft lads impale us with when we buy a computer. Next, I began to mock the shower space up using "carton-pluma," which to most artists is known as foam-core. Having pretty well decided that the plan would work, I then set about to get some help from someone has actually has a clue about how to do this. I have done remodelling like this in the past, but never on a house that is three-plus-times older than I am, and never in a country where my language skills are still less-than-competent in my mind. The best advise I received was to find the floor tiles before I started really doing anything.

The tiles on the bathroom floor are great, and I assumed that buying spares would be one of those easy things to do. So I drove to a major DIY store to pick up several square metres of replacement tiles, after all, it seemed a lot easier to just be able to whack away at the old tiles to make room for the shower drain and to accommodate the anticipated move of the loo and the removal of the existing bidet. But, as luck would have it, the store didn't have anything close; so I wheeled Amelia to another store, this one purporting to be a tile shop. After driving past it twice (I must have been looking for a sign that said "Tiles-R-Us" or something), I found their car park and ventured in, full of excitement about buying the replacement tiles so I could get this project going. This shop did have a far more comprehensive selection of tiles, and even had the colour and texture I was looking for. But I needed to find tiles that are 24cm square, and all they had were 25cm and 30cm square. And if that wasn't enough of a problem, the 25cm tiles would take a month to get into stock. After a bit of thought, I realised that cutting off 1cm would be more difficult than cutting off 6cm, so I asked if I could have one of the big boys to take home to compare to the existing floor. Not a problem, I was told; but I did have to drive now to their warehouse depot to collect the sample. Fine. Whilst the last thing I wanted to do was drive around more, I was feeling so good about the almost imminent building of the new shower, so off I went. With sample tile in hand, I drove home, all the way dreaming of my new addition to La Antigua. And after carrying the tile upstairs and laying it on the existing tile floor, my excitement began to diminish a bit. Okay, so the colour was close, but not exactly the same as the tiles that were firmly embedded in the concrete floor under the sink, loo, bidet, and tub. The fact that the sample tile was quite a bit thicker didn't bother me, and I was trying to talk myself into believing that the colour was close enough...until Martin stopped over to see what I had found. Martin lives in Galilea and is in the process of building a new home, and best of all, he is an excellent reference point for me to know what will work and not work in the construction field. What I needed to do, Martin told me, was to carefully remove an existing tile and take it with me when I went to the next tile shop. A good plan, but getting a tile out intact proved to be a bit of a challenge.

Ceramic floor tiles are not only bedded in concrete, but then they are grouted with concrete, and as we all know, concrete is a bit harder than most everything. So I carefully began to chip away at the grouting that was surrounding a tile that sounded like it was loose. The key word here is "sounded." Obviously, this tile had been installed by some clever workman many years ago so when it was tapped, it would emit a hollow sound, whilst still being attached to the floor as if it had been installed with Super Glue for Concrete (assuming that there even is something like that). *"Chip slowly and carefully"* Martin had told me, and that is what I was doing. When all the grout was removed, I gently began to try to slip the chisel-thing under the tile to free it from the nasty hold the concrete had on it. A caution here; don't try this unless you have safety goggles, leather gloves, and an anal retentive compulsion to do things yourself instead of just hiring someone who knows what the hell they are doing. *"Chip slowly and carefully"* kept returning to my ears, only to be obscured by the sound of the tile cracking into several pieces. So I then went after the adjoining tile – the one that hadn't emitted that evilly deceiving hollow sound. This one, when tapped, sounded as if it was connected to bedrock all the way to China, but what the hell, at least it had one side open already from the first attempt. Believe it or not, it almost jumped into my hands after getting most of the grouting chipped away. Okay, now I was all set to resume my search for the Holy Grail of tiles.

I had heard that there was a tile factory (of sorts) just off the road from Palma to Puigpunyent, so I headed off the next morning. After negotiating the turn onto the small road, I began to wind my way up toward SobreMunt, or so the sign said. After managing to not get completely flatted by a car going in the other direction on the road that appeared to be no wider than my car, and after negotiating turn after turn as the road wound its way up the mountain, I finally came upon what I assumed was the tile factory. We really don't have "factories" here on the island, as the word for factory is taller (TA-YER), but as I drove in past the massive stone gates, I had the distinct feeling that I had found myself either amongst a group of artisans or the setting for the movie Deliverance. It was, as we politely say, quite rustic.

Once inside, I found myself surrounded by the biggest grouping of tiles and decorative ceramics that I had ever seen. But it was a bit surreal, as the finished products were all neatly stacked on shelves, but the rest of the space (the inside space was about the size of a football pitch) looked as if they hadn't bothered to clean since the Moors were running the island. There were two young men working at a machine that resembled a meat grinder; one taking gobs of semi-wet mixed sand and whatever else goes into pottery and after kneading them as if he was making a pizza base, plopping them into rough mould boxes, while the other one was pounding the freshly extruded glop to it was compacted tightly into the moulds.

I followed the routine I have mastered quite well since arriving here – in my best Spanish, I introduced myself, followed immediately by my disclaimer that I recognised that my language skills were meagre at best, and then proceeded to enquire if they made a tile of the size and colour I was looking for. The whole anticipatory apology must have worked (again) as one of the lads proceeded to tell me my Spanish was fine, but then swiftly went into Mallorquin and after a sentence of at least 300 words (of which I think I understood 4) left me with a look on my face of complete confusion. Luckily, he recognised my lack of understanding and then told me no. No, they didn't make tiles that size; no, they didn't have the colour I was seeking; and no, they didn't make tiles of the same thickness. How nice. So I did what anyone else who is intrigued by making stuff would do…I stood there for a while and watched them take sand and clay and whatever else goes into ceramics, and make some magic. On the way home, a bit mystified that I still haven't found the tiles I am looking for, I started to ponder on how nice my bathroom looks without a new shower.

As the longest day of the year approaches, it seemed like a good time to reflect a bit on some of the projects I have been working on, and some of the near disasters I have avoided…or not.

The new shower: I did manage to find the magically mysterious tiles I had been looking for, and after several starts and stops, finally did get the project underway. Luckily, I had been introduced to Toni, the brother of the village blacksmith Guillem. Yes, whilst Guillem does have a pretty state-of-the-art plasma cutter and all sorts of welding kit, he also has a typical blacksmith's forge that has probably been in use since the Moors left the island hundreds of years ago. One day, whilst trying to convince Guillem that he really should work on the two little projects I had given him three months ago – patience is truly a virtue in Mallorca – I asked him if he knew of a plumber and he gave me Toni's phone number.

Toni appeared one day and removed the bidet, which I saw no use for in the house, and then moved the loo to where the bidet had been. This day had been precipitated by me whacking away at the floor area where the shower was to go, removing the floor tiles (baldosas) and then breaking up the cement under-floor deep enough to accommodate the slope needed for the shower to drain properly. I had determined the actual sloped required by clever calculations, using basic geometry to determine what angle of finished floor I would need, as well as figuring out that when my arms grew tired from pounding on the floor with my massively brutal five kilo hammer, the slope would be good enough. Luckily, my arms were wasted just about the time I made it down ten centimetres. After Toni disconnected the loo, he then asked me for my floor destruction tools so he could re-route the

James B Rieley

loo drain to where it would be once the job was completed. Even though Toni speaks no English, I knew what he meant when I saw his smile after I produced the hammer and chisel. He said he would only be a few minutes, and disappeared out of the house, only to return with a electric chisel thing, which, must to my amazement, dug out the new path for the loo drain in a couple of minutes. He smiled, I smiled (but muttered several mild obscenities under my breath about why I hadn't thought of that before whacking away at the shower floor). After a couple of hours, the drain piping was all in place and the water supply tubing for the shower was marked out, and he said the next day he would return to actually seat the loo into place. And kindly, just before he left, giving me instructions to cut away enough of the wall so he could bury the water pipes, he told me he would let me use the electric chisel if I wanted. He smiled, I smiled, and just about the time he was sitting in the local bar, probably telling his village friends about this crazy villager who had busted up the floor with a hammer and chisel, I had chiselled out two wall trenches for the hot and cold water pipes.

The next morning Toni returned and soldered the nice shiny copper tubing together and put it in the trenches, telling me to next concrete them in place and call him when the shower was ready for him to install the actual shower fixture – something that I hadn't even bought yet.

I mixed up what appeared to be enough cement to redo the Great Pyramid of Giza and began slapping it on the vertical wall, desperately trying to keep it from sliding down to the floor. After a while, I actually began to think I knew what I was doing. Then, I began to build up the floor again, sloping it toward where the shower drain would be. My previous comment about beginning to think I knew what I was doing disappeared faster than a Snickers bar in kitchen when I ran out of cement. I mixed more. I ran out again. I mixed still more. And, as you might have guessed, I ran out again. But this time, the slope was taking shape and I decided that my back was in dire need of some Ibuprofen, so I gave up for the day.

The next morning, I put another layer of cement on the now gently sloping floor, but this time, it was water-proof cement. I had been told by friends that this was crucially important, as it would not be a good thing to have a small crevice between the floor tiles that would allow many litres of water to suddenly appear in my living room below. I even took the water-proof layer and ran it up the wall a bit, just to make sure that the chances for water seepage would be about as good as me winning the lottery – which would have been a good thing because then I could have just hired a team of experts to do all this work.

The next step – the following day – was to begin to cement the tiles I had acquired down on the floor and up the back wall of the shower. But before I could cement them down, I had to cut them to fit. This had been on my mind, as the slope was compound – it ran both from the high side to the drain, and also formed a slight trench down the middle so the water would not puddle anywhere. Luckily, Toni had also lent me a whiz-bang electric cutting tool so I laid out all the floor tiles; marked them where they needed to be cut, and then without cutting off a single finger, cut all the pieces so the cementing could begin. By now, I was almost having fun. Not sure if this euphoric feeling was from the serious amounts of Ibuprofen I was taking to counter-act the sore back from the previous days, but it really didn't matter. I was finally beginning to see my vision of a new shower take form. Until I ran out of tiles about 1/3 of the way up the back wall. So off to the tile shop in Palma – a nice break for the back – and then back to the La Antigua cementing festival. Late that night, and I do mean late, all the tiles were firmly in place.

The next day was grouting day, followed by a call to the glass man to come and re-measure for the glass walls. Pepe had come and measured before all the real work started, but had told me that when everything was ready he would come back and measure again. I think he said that sometimes dimensions change a tad when things like this were built, and he was right. So, measurements made, he said that he would bring the extremely thick cut glass panels back soon. Well his actual words were that he would bring them in 15 days, more or less. When I mentioned that all he had to do was cut three big panels of glass to size, he said that ten-millimetre glass is not normally on the island and it would have to come from Barcelona. After a week, I rang Pepe and asked if the glass was ready yet, and he repeated the *"15 days, more or less"* story, to which I replied, *"Yes, and a week is less than 15 days."* Ahhh, such a sense of humour. He did bring the glass walls and stainless channel to put them in after another week. By now, Toni had already returned and installed my new wonderously luscious simulated rainfall showerhead, and the next morning, I was finally able to use the new shower.

After a several days of enjoying my creation, I decided that there were two things I needed. I went out and bought a rather long window squeegee – don't like those pesky water-spots on the glass after a shower. I also purchased a wire-formed chrome combination soap dish and shampoo bottle holder. So I marked out where to drill the holes for the soap tray and began to drill…right into the cold water pipe that I had so carefully embedded into the wall with gobs of cement and nice, new tiles. Shit shit shit. Toni should be here in another hour or so to figure out how to fix the leak.

My brother came to visit. I had been trying to get my brother to come visit since I moved to Mallorca, and after some starts and stops, he finally was able to make the trip. Jack and several friends of his flew in from Berlin for several days, and it was great to see him.

A couple of weeks ago, I was doing my almost daily delivery to Parc Verd (the village recycling centre) and whilst I am becoming used to the fact that Parc Verd is full of surprises at times, this visit was especially revealing. Recycling in Puigpunyent is pretty important. We have set the standard apparently for all of Spain, as, according to the village website, we have the

James B Rieley

best record of recycling for the entire country. The centre is divided into sections, so that residents can help the recycling efforts of the village by separating bottles (vidres), plastics, electrical items (electro domesticos), paper (carton y papel), ropa (clothing), and about another seventeen categories of recycleables. And then there is a section for big items (residu volumosos). This day, after depositing my various contributions to the system, I looked over at the residu volumosos section, and there was a 7 metre-long boat. Yes, a fibreglass run-about, semi-buried under piles of discarded tables and chairs...only in Puigpunyent.

It has been warm lately here on the island. Okay, so "warm" may not be the best description of the weather. We haven't seen rain for several months and the temperatures have been in the high 30"s, which if you convert centigrade to Fahrenheit, is bloody hot. And although La Antigua has exceptionally thick stone walls, which does keep the interior cool, I have actually thought about turning on the central air. Note the reference to, "thinking." Haven't done it yet, as when the temperature soars outside, I simply retreat inside the house. Actually, I haven't used the central air system since I bought La Antigua. When I looked at the property, I had been told that the house did have central air and central heat, but that the actual heat exchanger compressor thingy was out for servicing, but would be back by the time I moved in. Well, it wasn't. After a couple of weeks, the unit was back and fully charged. I had no idea how to work it, so I asked the installation man and after several starts and stops due to mis-communications, the system was pumping cold air into the house. And then I turned it off. I really don't like forced air conditioning and would rather just enjoy a cool house, so for the past year-plus, I haven't needed to turn it on. But as summer wraps the village in heat, my thoughts began to think about how warm it actually could be. Last year, it touched forty degrees centigrade more than once, and with all the talk of changing weather patterns, it could be warmer here than before. So I rang an air conditioning service company in Palma to come out to check out my system...just in case.

As I have said many times, living in the village can be sort of a test. For many years, I became accustomed to what most service companies call customer service. You ring them, they set an appointment to come out, and in most cases, they show up. For some foolish reason, I fell into the ex-pat trap of thinking that would apply here. I say "the trap" because I have come to learn that on the island (actually, in most of Spain), setting an appointment is only a relative term. Sr. Pontes told me he would come to La Antigua, but missed the date. So I rang him again, and again, set an appointment date. Again, he missed it; so I rang him again. Guess what? Right. He didn't come. So today I rang him again – I think we are becoming very close phone friends by now. With any luck, he will actually come out this week. And if he doesn't, I will just ring him again.

The whole cultural aspect of living here can be a bit disconcerting sometimes. Not in a bad way; things are just different. A couple of years ago, I was walking down a street in Palma with a friend, and we had to walk around an excavated area of the walkway. There was one of those orange rubber safety cones near the hole – by hole I mean something that a small car could fit in – but otherwise, it was unmarked. As we walked past, I said that this was so different than where I am from. In both the US and the UK, safety cones, flashing lights, would surround the excavated hole and substantial barriers designed to prevent anything on two legs from falling in. Biel asked why. "Well," I said, *"due to the massive amounts of money that could be won in a law-suit if someone were to fall in, the companies that dig the holes have had to protect themselves to avoid problems."* Biel just laughed and told me that if I were to fall into the excavation we just walked past, and decided to go to court to sue someone, the judge would look at me in amazement and ask me why I walked into the hole. After all, it is a hole in the walkway, and if I fell in, I could be hurt. If I would reply that I didn't see the hole, the judge would probably tell me I should have been paying more attention to where I was walking. And then the judge would dismiss the case. Biel said that he thought it was *"what you Brits call common sense."* And of course, he would be right, and it does seem like a breath of fresh air, especially for someone who was raised in a country where you can successfully sue a provider of coffee because it was hot.

Jack and his friends, John, Christina, and Ethan, their son, flew into Palma from Berlin and were here for a long weekend. Whilst La Antigua is not exactly a tiny house, I knew that it would be a tad crowded for everyone to stay here, so I had made arrangements for John, Cristina, and Ethan to stay at the rather fabulous Son Net hotel here in the village. I say *"rather fabulous"* to describe the Son Net as it is a five star hotel and a short drive from my house. Unfortunately, the Son Net was heavily booked, so I could only obtain two nights there for the guests, and had to resort to putting them in the Son Pont for the first night.

The Son Pont is an "agroturisme" hotel, which is to say that it is in reality, the Spanish equivalent of an English stately home (hundreds of years old, 140 hectares of property, nestled amongst orchards, vineyards, and some of the most spectacular vistas available to anyone with eyes). The fact that the Son Pont is an agroturisme property means that at some point, the owners of the property made a deal with the government to convert part of the property into a bed and breakfast for some tax breaks. Business is business.

We all piled into my car and went from the airport to La Antigua, sat around and talked for a while, then I took John, Christina, and Ethan over to the Son Pont. They fell in love with the property, and Hector, the caretaker, was more than courteous; trying to ensure that their stay at the Son Pont would be a good one. Hector had even arranged for a wooden crib in their room for Ethan, who is, after all, only 11 months old. Then I went back to La Antigua and Jack and I sat around, both on-line (as we do), and caught up on things.

James B Rieley

The next morning, when I moved John, Christina, and Ethan to the Son Net, was when things began to go awry. The Son Net is spectacular, but at over three times the room cost per night, it seemed that they had a lot to learn from the agroturisme of the previous evening. We (the five of us) thought it would be nice to eat out on one of the hotel's terraces, but were told that whilst we could have drinks outside, we could not eat outside because they weren't serving outside for another three days. Now we could understand if it was on the edge of winter, with nasty weather looming, or even if there was a swarm of bees hovering about, but the reason was that there is this Son Net rulebook that says that dinner cannot be served outside until the 15th of June, and it was the 12th. Okay, rules might be rules. After some words with Luis, the hotel barman whom I had met previously, we finally were served, but a less than spectacular dinner. Later that night, John had rung down to the hotel's service desk to request the use of two little bowls. Ethan was hungry and John and Christina thought it smart to whip him up some 11 month-old food thing and the bowls would enable that to happen. Yes, they did receive the bowls, only to later find that they were charged seven euros for the use of them. Yes, rules are rules; but apparently, the person at the Son Net who made the rules was too busy rule-making to take a course in customer satisfaction.

The following day it was more catching up – a bit of a challenge because Jack and I were catching up as brothers do; John was playing catch-up on the catching up game as we had never met before and another Rieley to find out about was intriguing to him; Ethan was catching up on his sleep (what a good boy he is); Christina was catching up on her work in Berlin where she was working on a movie script before their trip here; and Jack was desperately trying to catch up on his sleep because he was up most of the night with allergies, phone calls, and emails from friends around the world. And then, almost as fast as they arrived, it was time to take them back to the airport so they could return to their version of normal life (life in Berlin is a bit different than life in Puigpunyent).

Yes, my closest village friends and I do rabbit on in English when we are together, but I do get to speak Spanish to all the other villagers. Well, I suppose that the reality is that I do not "get" to speak Spanish; I am (willingly) forced to speak Spanish if I want to be understood at all. The good news is that this was one of the prime reasons to move here from Palma – I live in Spain and I think that it is important to demonstrate my desire to become part of the culture. To paraphrase some sage, "*When in Puigpunyent, do as the villagers do;*" which means speak their language and participate in local village events.

Two weeks ago was the beginning of the annual summer series of festivals throughout the island. Apparently, one of the measures of a successful village festival is how many events can be packed into the nine or ten days the festival covers. And in the case of Puigpunyent, the answer this year is twenty-nine. Twenty-nine separate events in just over a week....geeeez.

So you might be thinking, *"How many events did I participate in?"* Well, not all that many admittedly. Some of them just didn't hold a lot of interest to me. Typical highlights included; Day one: the semi-finals of local football - not a big item for me. Day two: finals of children's Ping-Pong – hmmm, not a strong draw, nor was the Mozart concert in the main plaza. Day three: the finals of children's tennis – hell, if I don't even like to watch Wimbledon, I am probably not too excited about the future Federer's and Nasal's whapping a tennis ball back and forth. I probably should have gone to this though, as the number two-tennis player in the world, Rafael Nadal, is actually from Mallorca, and his visibility has increased interest in the game here on the island. Also on day three was the (I will tell you what the fiesta brochure called it) V Gran Nit de Playback. Yes, this was a full-fledged, costume-adorned, seriously presented, village version of karaoke. I did go to this, and it was pretty spectacular.

Held in the Placa Son Bru (the plaza about 50 metres from La Antigua which means that I could see it from my roof terrace if I was too lazy to actually leave the house), the Nit de Playback was unbelievable. The plaza had been kitted out with a stage that was something that the Rolling Stones could have been comfortable on; there were crepe-paper streamers that had been strung over the several hundred plastic chairs; there were the typically mandatory stand selling drinks and cotton candy for the children; towers of speakers that would enable everyone to hear clearly (everyone between the plaza and London probably) and – get this – there was even a huge projection screen for those close-ups of the people who were doing their best to emulate Milli-Vanilli. It was in every sense, a rock concert here in my plaza. Well, a rock concert where the performers lip-synced to the music.

Because the various acts that were doing their karaoke thing were all keen to be the best, crowd recognition is very important. Last year as I recall, the people in attendance voted with their applause. A tried and true way of signalling your enjoyment. But this year, hi-tech had come to Puigpunyent. The various people who had decided to stand in front of the throngs and try to replicate an actual performance had been divided into groups – don't ask me how the groups were determined, I haven't a clue. At the beginning of each segment of the programme, two local village girls, both dressed as if they were going to a Hollywood premier, stood on stage and announced which acts would be next. The acts were, at the same time, listed on the large projection screen along with – get this – a phone number and name you could send a text message to. Yes, this year, you would be able to vote which act was the best via text messaging. Sort of a quantum leap of culture in a village in which not that many years ago was the sleepiest place on the planet. Progress I guess.

It was a fun night – I say night, as it didn't even begin until 2230h. I have no idea what time it ended, as the songs were pouring through my bedroom

James B Rieley

windows long after I fell asleep after returning home at midnight.

Day four brought, among other things, a boot-sale in the village centre, with local residents having set up tables and trying to sell most of the same stuff they bought at the boot-sale of last year's festival probably. I didn't buy anything, but did see and talk to some of the local villagers who I have come to know. Whilst my conversations with local life-long villagers are not exactly laden with in-depth discussions about massively important issues, I do think it is important for me to say hello and talk about whatever I am capable of saying. They are all very nice and courteous to me, but I am pretty sure that after I walk on, they are having a real giggle about my verb conjugations.

At just after 1900 on day four, "Cuspidors Restaurant," a children's play was staged at Plaza Son Bru. It was adorable with three actors in clown-like costumes running about trying to entice the mass of youngsters that had come with their parents to interact with them. Then in the evening – this event didn't begin until 2300h– was the "Gran Nit de Rock." Oh my God...four rock bands playing in the town square. I probably didn't even need to go, as I half expected to hear the music all the way back at La Antigua. The plaza had massive speaker towers that looked to be capable of blasting sound throughout most of the known universe. It was a bit deafening, and after a while, I went home. And even though three bands had yet to play, because the breeze was blowing the right direction, La Antigua was pleasantly quiet. The next morning, when I walked to the market, it was clear that the evening must have finished up well as the plaza was filled with soapsuds about two feet deep.

The highlight, as far as I am concerned, of day five was held in my neighbourhood plaza. Every year as part of the summer fiesta, a play is put on, and this year it was "L'Estranya Parella." I was going to look up the translation for the Mallorquin words, but decided to read the description of the play in the brochure first. Miguel Fuliana is playing Oscar, and Joan Carles Bestard is playing Felix, "un perfecte hipocondriac." Yes, it is Neil Simon's Odd Couple... in Mallorquin. Well, whilst I am sure I wouldn't be able to understand the actual dialogue, the play action does not exactly require a UN translator to know what is occurring, so a good way to learn a bit of Mallorquin. It was quite hilarious...in sort of a language-challenged sort of way.

Day six was a children's activity where they get to play around on inflatable-shaped objects. Hmmm, this sounded about as much fun for me as getting ebola, so I passed. Later on day six were the finals of Petanca, a Mallorquin dancing thing, usually populated by people over 50-years old who still believe that dancing involves actual steps and being connected to your partner. A great cultural experience, but as I had seen it several times before, I let this activity slide as well. The last event on day six was comprised of several "cocktail latino orquestra's." This actually did sound good to me, but as it began at 2300h, and I apparently still haven't assimilated completely into a culture where going out for an early dinner begins at 2100h, and entertainment begins at least a couple of hours later, I missed it.

The last several days of the fiesta were filled with a football match in memory of someone who I have no idea who he is; the senior women's tennis tournament; the senior men's tennis tournament; and on the last night, an outdoor village dinner in one of the plazas. This was a must attend event, not just because the dinner last year was fab; it was a great opportunity to just be part of the village I live in.

Just thought you might want to know Amelia is in the hospital. Okay, so Amelia is my car, and the hospital is really the home garage of Onofrey, a mechanic who lives in the village. Nothing too serious, just in for a tune up and according to Onofrey, the catalytic converter had decided to go to converter heaven. I had noticed that Amelia was running a bit sluggish as I was doing my best "boy-racer" impression on some of the better winding roads between Puigpunyent and wherever I decide to go. As I believe that doing as much as I can with shop-owners and local businessmen, I had decided to find a local mechanic to do the work, and after consulting with several friends, heard about Onofrey.

I had been given his phone number and after several attempts, finally managed to talk to him. You guessed it, no English. That was okay with me, but very quickly I discovered that whilst I am able to conduct my normal business on the island, finding the words for "engine tune up" and "my car doesn't seem to have the power it used to" were a bit beyond my skill level. One option would have been to go into Palma to the Seat garage, with the assumption that they would have someone there who understood English, but instead I decided to muddle through. After all, I would probably learn some more words that would prove to be worthwhile in the future.

I did manage to explain that my car's engine (el motor) had a problem and I needed a mechanic to fix it. Onofrey, who lives on the other side of the village, said he would come over in five minutes to see what the problem was. So far, so good. But when he arrived, the real fun began.

"*Hola*," I began authoritatively. "*Mi coche tiene una problema con el motor*" came sliding out of my mouth as if I had lived here for several decades. But it was clear that Onofrey had a cunning plan in mind to suss out my knowledge of Spanish as he replied, "*Si?*" Then he deftly countered my language expertise with what sounded like a two hundred word sentence that appeared to be a question. Hmmm. I wanted to save my standard apology for poor Spanish until later, so believing that he was asking what exactly was the problem, I replied, "*el motor no funciona muy bien.*" The look on his face compensated for the fact that he didn't say "*well no shit. That is why you called me.*" A kind man. After about fifteen minutes with Onofrey pursuing a line of questioning about the actual engine symptoms, and my using words I knew and words I made up that sounded Spanish, we were

86

James B Rieley

both on the same page. The idle speed (velocidad – VAY-LOW-SEE-DAD) of the engine (el motor – MOW-TORE) was slipping due to Amelia's need of new spark plug cables (cables – KA-BLAYS), new spark plugs (enchufes – EN-CHOO-FAYS) and distributor points (puntos – POON-TOES), and this was all aggravated because the catalytic converter (el catalytico) was falling apart causing resistance in the exhaust (la systema de escape – ES-CA-PAY). Okay, so even I thought that this was where we started, but the conversation had been good and I (apparently) was able to communicate the problem to the point that he knew what I was talking about. My next question – something that could perhaps be the most important question when buying a service on the island – was if he wanted to be paid in cash or by cheque. I might as well have been asking if he wanted to breathe air or sulphuric acid.

Onofrey told me that the best way to resolve the engine issues was for me to drive over to his garage Friday afternoon around 1800h, and he would have Amelia all fixed by 1100h Saturday. Okay, so this sounded like a good thing to me. The fact that his garage meant his house didn't bother me. The poor bloke has a day job and auto repair is just a sideline for him. I wouldn't need the car Friday evening, nor would I need it Saturday morning, but then I realised that time on the island is sort of relative. My past experiences with time have included the village carpenter who told me that the kitchen island I had designed would be ready in two weeks, and was finally completed in four; the village metal worker who had told me that he would make some brackets for me "right away" back in March. I still haven't seen them. And then there is a heating and air conditioning specialist, who in July said he would be out to have a look at my central air unit within fifteen days. Still haven't seen him either. Getting things done here requires the right blend of patience and having a back up plan. The brackets I wanted made weren't really needed, just something I thought up one day. La Antigua has immensely thick walls and they manage to keep the house cool regardless of how high the temperature gets, so the air conditioner system hasn't really been needed. But my car? Well, I do need my car. I can (and do) walk to the shops in the village almost daily, but when I need to go into Palma for serious shopping, the 28 kilometres round-trip might be a bit much to walk. So I could be sure of Onofrey's plan to have the car back quickly, I repeated what he said. *"Mi coche sera listo por la mañana el Sabado? Verdad?"* (*My car will be ready Saturday morning? Are you sure?*). He gave me a look that told me my question was way too accusatory about his promise, so I shook his hand and went home to wait for Friday to arrive.

It was shortly after 1100h that I went to collect Amelia. And if past experiences are any opportunities to learn, I should have expected that she wasn't ready yet. It seems my mechanic was in Palma trying to obtain some part that he was changing on the car, so not being too distressed, I came back home. I walked back over about five hours later, but this time, there was no one there. Amelia was in the yard, but as the gate was locked, and I had no

Living on Rocks

idea if the work had been completed yet, I walked home. Around 1900h, my phone rang and off I went...again. Well, Amelia was ready, sort of. New spark plugs, new distributor points, new cables, a freshly cleaned engine, but still waiting for the new catalytic converter. I think I will just do what I have learnt to do best here in the village...and wait.

Ahhh, Sunday. What to do is always the question on a Sunday. This Sunday, after my somewhat normal breakfast of tea, toast and fruit, it was off to collect the newspaper from the village centre, then back home to discover what was going on in London and the rest of the world. Yes, on the way to get the paper, I did stop at Parc Verd to make my deposit of recyclables, thank you very much. I buzzed through the Times rather quickly because whilst at Parc Verd, I heard a sound that was music in my ears. No, Julie Andrews wasn't here in the village – it was Grand Prix day here in Puigpunyent.

I had planned on putting another several coats of varnish on the dining table I am building for the courtyard, but, well, I have had a fondness for sports car racing ever since I had my MGB many years ago. The village racetrack is located behind the recycling centre, and for the past several days, there had been noises drifting into the village from the track. The drivers had been doing their track tests and today was going to be the big race. I grabbed my camera and headed back to the track to watch the Puigpunyent Grand Prix. Now in all fairness, I must tell you that the village version of a grand prix is not exactly the same as it is in Formula 1 racing, nor is the village track exactly the same as it is in Monte Carlo. But auto racing is auto racing, and in the village, it is pretty spectacular.

The cars – a marginal description of what was racing – have all seen better days. They have been pretty well stripped down, with hatchbacks and windows having been removed, roll-bars installed, and names painted on doors and bonnets with spray cans. I am not sure if the paint that had been sprayed on was solely for the purpose of identifying who was who or meant to cover some of the rust and dents that gave the cars the appearance of being entries in the Leprosy Derby.

The cars were all lined up in the village equivalent of pit-lane when I arrived, giving me an opportunity to have a close look at the modifications that had been made to them. It also gave me the opportunity to speculate on the relative value of the individual cars, with my best guess being somewhere in the five to ten-euro range. The other spectators were already there, having arrived early to get the best vantage points of the track. The term "best vantage point" in the case of an auto race in Puigpunyent in August seemed to mean someplace to sit that was in the shade, and not directly downwind from where the dirt track would spiral dust in the air once the race had begun. I had a cunning plan to achieve a good vantage point, and within minutes, I was standing just past the start-finish line, where I would be able to see the sort-of long straight-away before the first turn, as well as turns three and five.

Never having come to this race before, I found someone and asked him (in my best Spanish, of course) when the race would begin. Without missing a beat, he rambled on with me picking up about every fifth word. There had been a series of practise laps earlier, next would be two semi-final races, followed by the big final race. Or at least that is what it sounded like he said. I graciously thanked him, not so much for his answer, but because he didn't give me a look as if to say, "foreigner."

Within about 10 minutes after I found my viewing spot, the track maintenance vehicle slowly went around the track, making sure the surface was conducive for the big race. The reason that it went slow was that walking behind it was a young man directing the hose that was dumping water on the dirt track in order to keep the dust down. Sadly, by the time the water-truck had made it back to the start-finish line, most of the sprayed on water had evaporated in the heat, but it was a nice thought.

The race was about to begin. The cars that had survived the semi-finals (several of them did not after one of them had its bonnet fly open causing the driver to spin around and send two other cars off the track) were all lined up at the starting line. The race steward (apparently the man who had nicked one of his wife's bed sheets and painted black checks on it) met with all the drivers to make sure they were ready and that they knew the rules. Rules? I came to think the only rules were to wear a helmet and try to keep your car upright. Then, with the grace of a ballet dancer, he waved the sheet (sorry, the chequered flag) and rushed out of the way of the surging wrecks as they blasted down the track. The Puigpunyent Grand Prix was underway.

The big race – hey, this is a village of 1,500 people so the word "big" is relative – was strangely reminiscent of a demolition derby. The cars careened off each other as they tried to negotiate the hair-pin turns whilst sliding about in the dirt. As the track is not that wide, and rather short, passing is not the easiest thing to do, but it did happen a few times. Of course passing another car on this track also meant smacking up next to it as you approached a turn, hoping that the driver would simply slide into one of the big piles of dirt that seemed to be all over the place. The tension mounted as there was a real dual between the first place and second place cars, but after a deftly negotiated pass on the long straight lapping the last place car, the driver of car one managed to widen the gap. The second place driver found himself stuffed, as the car that he was stuck behind was having serious engine problems – or else he was just trying to find the exit to Parc Verd so he could drop his car off for recycling. The chequered flag fell after ten laps, and the man who apparently had the greatest death-wish had won.

I plodded home, very hot, completely covered in brown track dust, and happy as a pig in shit. What a village!

I can remember when I lived in big cities prior to coming to Puigpunyent. Milwaukee, Houston, London, and even Barcelona all had something in common. Walking down the street often required a posture of keeping one's head down a bit, just on the oft chance that someone might actually say something to you. But here in the village, it is completely different.

Being in the village on foot means that you will see other people walking about doing whatever it is they are doing. And it also means saying hello to everyone. This, I find, is a very nice habit to have. And whilst it is nice, it can also be challenging. I can remember years ago (quite a few years ago actually) in my high-school Spanish class, we were taught to greet someone with *"Buenos Dias."* This is hard-core, formal Spanish for "Good day." Of course, Puigpunyent, whilst a part of Spain, is more a part of Mallorca and on top of that, it is a small village so the rules of engaging people you encounter are a bit different.

Today I went into the village to buy some vegetables (see, I do eat things other than cereal and yoghurt), and on my walk, I encountered six people, all who greeted me with different greeting. This really isn't a problem, as I do know what they are saying, but my challenge is to respond in a more-or-less correct manner. The greetings included, *"Bon dia," "Muy buenas," "Dia"* (accompanied by a nod of the head), *"Hola,"* and *"Buenas."* The people don't expect some long drawn out conversation about the state of the world, or even about today's temperature. But what is expected is a response. So after over a year living here, I have finally sussed out what to say.

When I came upon the first person, an elderly lady who was undoubtedly coming from the market, judging by the two carry bags filled with groceries and moving at an extremely slow speed up the hill; I beat her to the greeting, coming up with a friendly sounding, *"Hola, bon dia."* She smiled and responded with, *"Muy buenas."* When I was about to pass the next person, an older gentleman who might have been the first woman's local stalker, I chimed up with *"Muy buenas."* His reply was *"Dias,"* as he kept walking, planting his cane firmly on the street with each step not wanting the hot chica in front of him to increase the gap between them. By the time I had reached Balthazar's market, I had said hello to the workman coming out of one of the village's bank with a firm, *"Dias"* whilst nodding my head appropriately with the greeting. He actually stopped counting the fist-full of euros long enough to say, *"Bon dia."*

By greeting a passer-by with the last greeting I had heard, I figured I was sure to have the appearance of actually being part of the village. What a cunning plan. Of course, I have no idea yet what to say when someone I meet hits me with a string of Mallorquin words that I don't understand.

The real trick in saying hello isn't down to making sure that each word is pronounced correctly. The trick is to be able to slur the greeting's words all together. It isn't, *"Hola. Bon Dia."* It is *"Holabondia."* Not *"Buenos dias,"* but instead, *"Buenosdias."* Or *"Muybuenas"* instead of *"Muy buenas."* This can be a bit of a challenge to anyone who has been taught in a formal classroom setting. Luckily for me, most of my Spanish-language skills have been picked up by surrounding myself with the sounds of languages being spoken, or in some cases, slurred together. Besides, I lived in Houston – *"Heyhowyalldoin"* – and London – *"Hiyayouallright?"* - for a few years and am used to hearing greetings that stream together faster than lemmings rushing to the sea. I think that this slurring of words together may be a clue to the origin of the *"Dias"* greeting. Instead of putting the *"Hola"* and the *"Buenos"* in front of the last word, wasting all that voice energy, it is just easier to say *"Dias."* It is, after all, not a situation where someone might mistake the morning greeting with wondering why everyone in the village walks around saying *"Days."*

The other day, again whilst walking to Balthazar's – by now you are thinking that I either eat voraciously, resulting in the seemingly constant need to go shopping, or that I only buy a few things per day as an excuse to do my walking exercise – I was stopped by a car load of tourists. You can always tell who the tourists are in the village, especially the ones in a car. They are evident by a combination of a glazed look on their faces, an open map that they will most likely never be able to re-fold, and they begin asking their questions with either *"Right, habla ingles?"* or *"Sprechen sie Deutsches?"* So there I was, confronted by five people, all crammed into their hired Ford Fiesta like sardines. The driver – the only one who didn't have a camera strapped around his neck – asked me in his version of Spanish where the road was to Palma. Well, as they were on the road that heads away from Palma, my answer was easy. I smiled, but not too much so they would feel that they were total idiots for going in the opposite direction they wanted, and then explained that they needed to follow the street they were on to the end, turn left, then left again and look for the "Palma" signs. I recognised that Spanish wasn't the driver's native tongue, but I figured that if he was trying, then I should reply in the same language. *"Vaya recto, entonces a la izquierda, entonces a la izquierda otra vez. Mire para las muestras a Palma"* flowed out of my mouth as if I knew what I was saying. The driver was duly impressed, but clearly hadn't read his German to Spanish translation dictionary well enough, so I repeated my instructions, a bit slower and with lots of directional arm-waving on my part. I was beginning to feel like I belonged on the runway at Palma airport with my arms pointing straight ahead, then both flashing over to the left. I felt pretty good about helping the poor lost bugger out. Too bad they don't give out Merit Badges for "Good-directions-done-in-a-foreign-language." I assume I would be a sure winner. And as fate would have it, I believed this all the way to the café where I saw the tourists sitting pouring over their maps whilst having several beers. Probably still lost.

It is that time of year once again. Yes, it is just about the autumnul equinox. The equinox, regardless of where you live, is traditionally thought of as signalling the change of seasons. In Mallorca, this means residents of the island getting ready for winter, the onset of cooler weather, and approaching rain. Well, that is what it used to mean at least. But for some reason (climate change does spring to mind), this year the weather cycles have sort of come a bit early. It has been getting cooler…well at least in the evenings. I am still able to keep my windows open all night, but it is cooler. The woodcutters have been busy stockpiling mounds of wood that most of us will buy during the colder months. And the approaching rains? Well, they started a while ago, and whilst we have only had a few days of rain falling, it does seem different. So with the weather changing a bit earlier than in previous years, it does cause one to wonder what the actual equinox will bring.

For me, the equinox was precipitated by disaster. Okay, so maybe disaster is a bit strong, but the past week has been a bit trying. Besides the advising I do with some senior business-types in London, I like to do creative things when at home. And in my case, the term creative means painting, writing, and for the past year, making ceramics. Well I don't actually make ceramics; I buy them and do things to them. It all began when I made a dinner service for myself last autumn. Then it was a large pitcher and bowl. Some serving plates. More pitchers and bowls. I even made some tiles (azulejos) to install around my kitchen window. Doing all this accomplished several things for me. Ceramics gave me a break from all the writing I do; it provided me with an outlet for the creativity thing that seems to run through my DNA; and enabled me to save a shed load of money that I would have had to spend if I bought all this stuff.

This week's project – I tend to think in terms of projects I guess – was to build an outside dining table for the courtyard of La Antigua. Nothing dramatically huge, just a table that would seat four comfortably, and six in a squeeze. Step one was to figure out if I needed to actually construct the table or buy one, and I sort of did a compromise. I found a fab table top, or at least something that would make a fab table top. It was 80 x 145cm and made of actual wood. I mention the "actual wood" part because I really didn't want to have a table that was made of laminate, steel, glass, or the ultimate sin…plywood. No, this was proper wood that had been put together much like a cutting board. Bought it, took it home, and began to gently apply a coat of appropriately coloured stain. I was looking for a colour that would complement the courtyard, and after it was all stained and dry, I realised that the colour, whilst nice, was a bit dark and boring. It might have complemented someone's dungeon, but not my courtyard, so after rummaging around the cans of stain I have acquired since arriving here, I found some teak-coloured stain. A little shaking, a little stirring, and I was ready to fix the colour problem. Of course, I also had to find a new brush to apply it with because the first brush had become stiffer than Elsa Lancaster's hair in Bride of Frankenstein. I could go on and on about the staining exercise, but suffice it to say that it took four different colours (which meant four different applications of the stuff) before I had a colour I was happy with. Job done.

Step two was to attach legs to the tabletop. My original plan was to have the legs fold up out of the way so I could store the table in winter out of the weather. It does rain here in winter, and I didn't want all my work to warp and twist into something that would make me seasick. The folding leg idea was discarded when I found some very nice turned wooden legs that had screw-mounted bases on them. This seemed like a good idea because when I wanted to store the table away, I could simply unscrew the legs. The good news of finding them was doubled when I also learned that the word for legs, as in table, is different than the word for legs, as in body. Bingo, I bought the four patas (don't forget that word if you ever want to embark on a similar adventure) and went home to install them. Job well done.

So now I was almost ready for step three, the real essence of the table. In my mind, I could "see" the completed table having azulejos forming a border just inside the edge of the table. In my vision of what it would look like, I figured out that painting a design that more-or-less looked like grape vines would be nice. After all, the table's future location would be under the grape vines in the courtyard, and I figured that the table and the vines would create the environment I was trying to achieve. So step three was to go to my supplier of all things artsy in Palma and buy the raw azulejos for painting. I had calculated that I would need 16 tiles, so I bought 25, and actually discovered I needed 20 when I laid them out on the newly stained, semi-gloss, brownish-reddish-teakish-oakish coloured table top that was now residing on its own set of legs. After positioning them exactly where I thought they should go to form a border about 4cm in from the outside edge of the tabletop, I began the somewhat labourious job of sketching out the grape vine pattern that was looming largely in my mind. I then painted all the leaves a light green; put some detail into the leaves; painted the shadow-side of the vines; painted the non-shadow-side of the vines; and then painted on the top glaze that would, after firing, make the tiles more long-lasting than Keith Richards. I gently wrapped the azulejos in bubble wrap and took them to my ceramic supplier for firing in their ceramic oven-thingy. Job well done.

So now I had my table with legs; I had my tiles all prepared; all I had to do was route a trench in the tabletop that would accept the azulejos. This part of the project should have been pretty simple, with one minor exception: I don't own a router. I do have a complement of tools, but they are tools that I nicked from Angelina when I sold her and I reasoned that routing a trench in a wood tabletop with a screwdriver and pliers wouldn't be the easiest thing to do. But with ingenuity and creativity flowing through my veins like the Nile in flood season, I resorted to borrowing a router. Ever use a handheld router? Hmmm, nice. It is like holding a small motor in your hands that has a carbide bit on one end that is spinning at the speed of light. The trick was to avoid the cutting end of the router to only touch the wood and not either the power cord or my fingers, and after several hours, the trench was in. All nice and clean, and to make things even better, the trench was the right size. Job well done.

Two days later, I went to collect my custom-designed, hand-painted azulejos from my version of ceramic heaven. I walked into the store all fired up...I was only hours away from having my table completed. Bali, one of the two women who I have come to know at the store, greeted me in Mallorquin with something that resembled *"Why are you here so early James?"* I replied (cleverly) with, *"Hola Bali. Tiene algo para mi?"* (Hi Bali, do you have something for me?) Well of course she did, and we both knew it. But because I had arrived earlier than she expected, she hadn't even opened up the oven yet, so following her, I walked into the back room of the store where the ovens were. Yes, they have a big oven and a small oven and my azulejos had been cooked in the small oven, for two reasons. Reason one: the big oven was full of stuff. Reason two: the little oven wasn't when I brought the azulejos in. The tension was mounting as Bali leaned over to check the temperature on the trendy red digital readout. *"Señor James, todavia el horno hace calor"* (the oven is still pretty warm). I was polite beyond belief and avoided blurting out something like, *"Just open the flippin' oven. I want my tiles."* I instead just smiled, wishing I knew how to say something like, *"I think the current temperature gradient will not affect the overall gloss of the tile surface."* Her hand moved toward the oven door, as if the entire scene was taking place in slow-motion. She unhooked the latch and pulled the door away, exposing...the disaster.

Painting ceramics is a combination of art, science, and a bit of voodoo I think. You have to have the right tiles, the right colour glazes, and you cannot let anything touch the surface of a painted tile (or plate, or pitcher or anything) when it is in the oven. When the temperature inside the oven reaches the 1,400c it needs to reach, the glaze turns liquid and anything that is touching it becomes bonded to it during the cooling down part of firing. All my azulejos had been put on little shelves, keeping a small space between each one in the oven...until most of the shelves decided to fall apart due to the intense heat. The actual technical term for what had occurred was that my tiles, and consequently me, were buggered. Bali felt bad. I felt bad. The tiles had been in a mini-crematorium so they didn't feel much of anything, other than stuck to each other. Job well buggered.

It was an interesting project: I learnt some new words to increase my burgeoning Spanish linguistic capability; I actually did manage to get the colour right on the table; I now know where to borrow a router if I ever decide to play with wood again; and it took me three hours less to paint the replacement azulejos.

I think I may forsake big projects for a while. Between building the new shower and the table, I think I had done something nasty to my right shoulder. Realising that being healthy is important, after suffering from some not-so-nice pain in my upper arm, I decided to go to have it checked out. Okay, so it took me a month to do this, but after consuming most of the annual output of the world's ibuprofen, I finally decided that the pain wasn't going to go away by itself. I drove in to Palma to my favourite hospital and

James B Rieley

explained to the receptionist at the Urgenicas desk that I had a pain in my upper arm. She asked me if I had whacked it on something – okay, she didn't say "whacked" but that is what she meant. I didn't think it was worth an attempt to explain that I had been pounding on tiles whilst building the shower and then probably aggravated it by building the table, so I said, "no." But I did explain that it felt like there was a knife in it when I moved it around. After sitting in the waiting room for a few minutes, my name was called and I nurse took me to an examination room. After another few minutes and a nice conversation with a doctor who was on call, I was ushered off for several x-rays. Nothing. The doctor told me to come back the next day for an MRI.

I have had MRI's before, and whilst it is a good way to catch a 20 minute nap, the constant buzzing and clicking sounds as the electrons (or whatever) are zapping around can be a bit distracting. Two days later, I received a text message on my Spanish mobile from the hospital stating that the results were in and I should return to get the good news. I stopped at hospital on my next trip back from the ceramic supplier and met with the doctor who had seen me earlier. Talking to doctors can always be a challenge as my Spanish has improved quite a bit and I can carry on long conversations, but when it comes to technical or medical terminology, I get a bit lost. The doctor asked how my shoulder was and after telling him that I still had the pain, I asked if he could speak slowly and *"Con palabras para ninos"* (with words you would use when talking to a child). Ha, I figured that this would enable me to catch most of what he would say about the shoulder. He smiled and said he would, and then said, *"Tiene un tendon se rompe."* Perfect. I have a broken tendon. This was one of those times when you realise that some words don't translate well, like the term *"Tendon se rompe."* I figured that he was trying to explain that I had torn the tendon and not that it was actually broken. My arm was still attached to my shoulder so this was a safe assumption on my part.

Okay, I have a torn tendon, which would account for the pain, but what I really wanted to know was what is going to be done about it. I assumed that there would be options, like amputating the arm or, dropping something heavy on my foot so I would forget about the shoulder, or, consuming mass amounts of red wine, which would also cause me to forget the shoulder (and probably my name). He offered none of these and instead prescribed ten treatments with a laser. Hmmm, a laser. Not being someone trained in medicine, all I could visualise was me, laying on the table made famous by Sean Connery in Goldfinger. But after my previous little health problem a few years ago in Mallorca, I have learnt to trust my doctors so I said okay.

The laser treatments take place in the physical therapy department of the hospital, and as of now, I have had two of them. All I have to do is take off my shirt and sit in a chair in front of something that looks like a Dalek junior for a couple of minutes. No noise, no flashing lights, just invisible laser-thingy's zapping into my shoulder. I assume that the laser-doo-wah machine is actually helping the torn tendon heal, but apparently I won't notice anything until the treatments are over. Until then, I will keep taking the fab anti-inflammatory meds that the doctor gave me...and stay away from wielding DIY weapons of mass destruction.

One of my favourite things about living in Spain is the food. Okay, so I am admittedly not a gastronomical snob; actually, some of my friends believe that I eat to live instead of live to eat. But none-the-less, there are several very Spanish foods that I love. One of them is paella (PA-EH-YA).

If you are in Spain, either on the mainland or one of the Balearic Islands, you will see many restaurants advertising paella on picture boards tempting you to come inside. You can find paella mixta (a melange of chicken and seafood mixed in with the rice), paella marisco (a seafood and rice paella), and even paella for vegetarians (probably rice with the rice). Just as there is a range of paellas to have, there is a definite range of the quality of the end product.

I have been trying to improve my cooking skills, and as part of this effort (and it is an effort at times), I have added paella to my list of the gastronomic delights that come out of the La Antigua kitchen. And because one of the purposes of these letters is to share my experiences with you, I thought I would share a paella experience with you.

According to most recipes (allegedly handed down over the centuries from one person to another, but in this case, blatantly ripped off from some website), the ingredients of a good paella marisco are: 1 small onion, finely chopped; 1 green pepper, finely chopped ½ red pepper, boiled until soft and then cut into long thin strips; 2 medium-sized tomatoes, skinned and finely chopped; 2 carrots, finely chopped; 100g peas, cooked; 200g prawns (if using cooked prawns substitute fish stock for the water); 200g small clams; 200g squid; 12 mussels; 350g rice (traditionally short grain rice is used but most prefer to use long grain); 2 cloves of garlic, coarsely chopped; a pinch of saffron strands (if you can't find any saffron, use yellow food colouring instead and add it once you have added the liquid); a sprig of parsley, finely chopped; olive oil; about 800ml water. If you want to make a paella mixta, add some cooked chicken bits. Oh, one last component that will make your efforts worthwhile; a bottle of a good red wine.

Once you have all the bits, you should: Wash the mussels, removing those nasty looking beard-things. Throw away any of the muscles that don't shut on contact with water. Take the squid and rub off the outer dark skin. Pull out the insides (including the transparent back bone – having fun yet?) and pinch the eye away from the tentacles (now I know you are having fun). Save the tentacles. Cut the squid into rings. Take the clams and wash them in water and then put them in a bowl with some salt so that the grit comes out. Throw away any that are open.

James B Rieley

Whether you peel the prawns or not is up to you. If you decide to peel them, save the shells and boil in water for about ten minutes. Save the liquid and add later instead of water. If you decide to leave the shells on, then plan on having a healthy supply of napkins or on finding some new friends. Peeling the shells off prawns is about as messy as doing a liver transplant with bare hands. Take the garlic and beat it into submission with a pestle and mortar (or just use the round end of a spoon like us normal people do), put it in a small bowl and add the saffron (if you actually went to a store to find it), the parsley and a pinch of salt. Next, open the bottle of red wine and begin to pour some down your throat. Do liberally and often during the rest of the paella preparation experience.

Heat some olive oil in a large frying pan. Dump in the onion, green pepper and carrot and fry gently (how do you fry something gently in a pan that is probably at two-million degrees?) for about five minutes. Add the chopped tomato and squid (don't forget those testy tentacles) and fry on a low heat for another ten minutes. Add the rice and stir well to make sure that the rice is thoroughly coated with the previously made slurry. Add water (or the water from boiling the prawn shells), clams and the garlic/saffron/parsley mixture and bring to the boil. Season with salt. Just a personal note here: I don't usually add salt to anything. I actually own some Maldon's sea salt, but I think I just have it in the kitchen for appearances sake. But if you feel the compulsion to add the salt, do it now.

Put a lid on the paellera (the shallow pan that you are cooking all this in), turn the heat right down and cook very slowly for about ten minutes. I am a bit anal when cooking, so I keep looking to make sure that the squid has not managed to put itself together again and try to re-enact the fun part of 20,000 Leagues Under the Sea. Add the prawns and peas and give it a stir. Arrange the mussels and strips of red pepper artistically on top, or, do as I do and just dump them in. Any bit of artistic effort will be destroyed when you stir it all the next time. Put the lid back on and leave for another ten minutes - checking that it has enough water. I have found the best way to check this is to open the lid and, leaning over a bit, say *"Do you want more water?"* to the paella. If it manages to say almost anything to me at all, I take that as a sign to add water. If I hear nothing from it, I assume it is just fine. Once the rice is cooked and the mussels have opened, it is ready to eat.

You can do what you want at this point, but I think paella is best served with French bread, which is a bit bizarre, as this is a Spanish food. This potential confusion should not be a problem if you have consumed the better part of the wine. Open another bottle and sit down and eat.

There are options when cooking paella. You could add peas or corn to the mix; browse through the latest issue of HOLA! Magazine between stirring; listen to a Chakira CD; practise your flamenco steps; or even wear a Zorro mask, but as I am a traditionalist when it comes to paella, I usually stick to what I know works. Which brings me to the next bit of wisdom.

Now, having gone through all this effort to share a paella recipe with you, I thought I might also share with you an easier way to prepare it. Go to a store and buy it pre-packaged. Perhaps not the best, but all you need to do is bung it into a hot pan and stir a bit. You will still need the wine, but at least you will have time to enjoy it.

Autumn is here in the village. Our days are still mostly warm and sunny, but lately, there has been an almost welcome shift in the weather. I say welcome shift because the shift has enabled me to slack off on watering all the plants in the courtyard and terrace; which in summer is a daily challenge. But autumn has brought with it occasional rain, and whilst the plants all seem to be happier, the rain does raise havoc with the other daily challenge of sweeping up the leaves that fall every day.

Autumn is a nice time here in the village. The temperatures shift from the high thirties during the day down to the high twenties, and the evenings cool down to the point of being able to dig out some of the jumpers that I had packed away in early May. The skies are different as well. Instead of the almost constant cloudless blue that surrounds the valley, massive clouds often sneak over the mountains, blanketing the village in a duvet of moisture-laden surprises.

The day before yesterday, the weather forecasts stated that we were supposed to have shed-loads of rain. Well, at least that is what some of the forecasts said. My friend John who lives in Palma rang me to see what I had heard about the weather. Both of us are pretty addicted to being online and he often rings to see what I have read about the potential for rain. Checking the weather forecasts online is a pretty foolish exercise as there are about a half dozen weather sites for the island and for some reason, it is a rare occasion when the forecasts al match up. John had said that of the several sites he was looking at were forecasting varying amounts of rain. I quickly did a check of the other sites and found more variation, with one site only prescribing a light chance of drizzle in mid-afternoon. I looked further, clicking on a satellite photo of Spain, only to see some pretty thin clouds approaching from the mainland. Clearly, the highly paid, well-educated meteorologists who generate the forecasts were doing what they do best; guessing.

The whole issue of looking online for weather forecasts can be a bit frustrating. One would assume that all the websites get their information from the same source – the local weather-reporting station at the airport in Palma. But for some reason, on any given day, the forecasts can vary as much as five or ten degrees, with equal variance on how much sun we are supposed to have.

I think that the only reliable way to find out what the weather will be would be to go ask a local farmer, as these people tend to have a better idea of what nature will be bringing. Whilst this may seem like an exaggeration, I really think that farmers can tell what the weather will be just by looking to see if the chickens are standing on one leg facing the equator or some other low-technology method that only generations of farming can teach. But instead of checking further, I told John that from the best information I had available to me, in the next couple of days it might rain, or it might remain sunny, and if it did rain, the rain could be heavy, or perhaps not. As I had covered just about every option, I felt had done my bit and went back to make dinner.

The weather information that I had given John was spot on. Yesterday actually did bring more sunny, warm weather and life was good. But this morning things changed a bit. I was about to walk into the village to collect the Sunday morning papers, having just finished my breakfast. I looked out into the courtyard and noticed that there were some rain spots on the courtyard stone floor, so I grabbed one of the brollies I keep handy. I didn't really expect to have to use it – an odd raindrop or two wasn't enough to worry about. So out of the house I went, but by the time I had made it to the front gate, it was actually raining. And as I rounded the corner at the bottom of my street – bear in mind that the corner is only about 30 metres from my front gate – the skies had opened up as if a giant loo was being flushed. Before I could even manoeuvre my way back home through the now river-like flow of water careening down my street, the rain had turned to hail, with chunks of ice that were a centimetre or two in diameter bouncing off anything in their path. I did make it back into the house, just in time to see the courtyard awash in leaves that had been beaten off plants, trees, and vines.

The hail ceased falling after about ten minutes, but the rain continued for another half-hour before the sun came back out. And by then, the courtyard was a cushion of green leaves and flowers that had been beaten off the bougainvillea plant. At least I won't have to water anything for a day or two.

Dickens had it spot on when he said it was the best of times and the worst of times. The first lines of "A Tale of Two Cities" began with those incredibly insightful lines, or something like them, and whilst the book was written almost 150 years ago, Dickens could have been writing about recent days in Puigpunyent.

My little village has been working diligently (by Mallorquin standards) to improve the services it provides for its citizens. This, quite often, isn't too easy, especially because over time the village has grown dramatically, and at the rate new houses are going up, it appears that the growth will continue. This may not bode well for the village feeling I fell in love with, but that is a different story. Two months ago, I had received a piece of paper in my post box saying that the village decided that some of the streets in my neighbourhood needed to have their tarmac restored and after a week of the semi-chaos that occurs when you can't park on the street near your house, most of the streets looked shiny and black. I say most of them because for some reason, they only patched up spots in c/des Sol, the street at the bottom of c/Es Forn where I live. At the time I was a bit mystified as to why the village had only patched the street instead of putting an entire new layer of tarmac down, but I assumed that there was: A) some master plan, B) a shortage of asphalt, C) the asphalt crew had gone to lunch...in Buenos Aires, or D) the village would get around to it when they got around to it. Regardless of which of these options seemed to be in play, it really didn't make any difference to me. The potholes on the street had been filled and Amelia was once again able to park near La Antigua.

Last week I received another notice from the village, but this one was about the water system in the village. Now in all fairness, I must say that the notices that the village puts out are quite good, apparently. I really can't tell because they are printed in Mallorquin. My Spanish has improved dramatically since coming to Puigpunyent, but I really don't understand Mallorquin at all. I can pick out the odd word in a written document, but I am completely buggered when listening to the locals talk. I did look carefully at the most recent notice and even asked Guillem, my local metal worker, to translate it for me into Spanish. The basic drift of it was that the village was going to tear up two streets and replace the water supply piping. There would be no parking all of Monday. Okay, I can deal with these types of improvements in the village, so Monday morning I rushed out at 0830h to begin my errands for the day. I started early as I knew that I didn't want to have Amelia being the only car left on the street when the workmen would arrive (which was the case when the asphalting adventure took place). Luckily, there were no workmen in sight when I made it to the car, but it was good I was there when I was, as again, Amelia was the only car on the street. I had a list of about ten things I needed to do in and around Palma but by 1100h, I was already on my way home. I parked on an adjacent street and walked home with my groceries, crossing the trench that was being dug in the middle of c/des Sol. Happy workmen with a huge trench-digging-machine that was crawling along at about $1/10^{th}$ of a kilometre an hour, leaving a trench in the street that was similar to the Marianas Trench, except Puigpunyent isn't in the Pacific Ocean and the my trench was about 10,930 metres shallower. I watched the machine crawl along for a few minutes, but this was about as exciting as watching paint dry, so I went home and headed up to the terrace to read a book I had bought in London.

About 1600h, I came off the terrace and went to make a cup of tea but this process was slowed a bit due to the lack of water coming out of the kitchen tap. Hmmm, the water must still be disconnected I realised, so I went out to ask one of the workmen when it would be reconnected. It didn't take long to find someone. The trench-digging machine was nowhere in sight, but there were several men with pick-axe things and hammers making small trenches heading off the main trench toward houses and side streets. I asked one of them what time the water would be working again. He replied without missing a beat, they hoped sometime tomorrow. WHAT? SOMETIME TO-

James B Rieley

MORROW…THEY HOPED? This wasn't good. I didn't even have to worry that I didn't understand what he was saying. My neighbourhood would not have any water all night. Okay, this wasn't exactly a panic situation. I did have a nice stockpile of bottled water that I could use for drinking and preparing dinner. I could even use some of the bottled water for brushing my teeth I supposed. But I was concerned about how I would water the plants in the courtyard. Okay, so right about now, some of you are thinking that I am a bit too anal about the plants, but I hadn't watered them in several days due to a good soaking they received whilst I was away for my work. I had even thought about watering them the night before the water was shut-off, but I think I was too focused on writing something that by the time I remembered, it was dark out. I was also thinking about how to flush the loos in the house. I wasn't about to use bottled water for that, nor for the plants. It was then I remembered that I was the proud owner of a cistern full of fresh water. A cistern that I hadn't used before, but now was the time, and this, finally, is where Dickens opening line comes in.

Operating a cistern is a pretty straightforward proposition. You lower a bucket down into the cistern, wait until it fills with water, and then hoist it back up. My cistern, like most traditional Mallorquin cisterns even has a pulley situated over the top of the cistern opening to provide a bit of leverage in pulling the bucket back up. I hadn't had a reason to use my cistern up till then, but I thought I would give it a go.

I laid out the very stiff rope that was threaded through the pulley and connected on one end to my official cistern bucket (I say official because it makes it sound as if I really knew what I was doing, don't you think?). The rope was about 3 centimetres in diameter, and felt as if it had been used last just about the time Franco was still in power. Not only was it stiff as the generalissimo, it was a tad mouldy from being coiled up on the cistern pulley-and-bucket-bracket thingy. I cleverly put on my handy-dandy leather gardening gloves and began to slowly lower the bucket into the darkness that was my cistern. Looking down into a well or a cistern can be deceiving. I had no idea how deep the cistern went, but it looked to be about 350 kilometres down to the surface of the water. Okay, perhaps that estimate was a bit further than I knew it must be, but it did look deep. The rope was about 10 metres long, and after half of it had disappeared down the hole, the bucket was at the water's surface, and after figuring out that by playing out more rope, the bucket would actually fill up with water, I began pulling the rope back up. Rather easily, the bucket came back to the top of the cistern, with water right up to the top brim of it. Yes, of course, water went careening out of the bucket before I managed to fill up a container. But after several bucket-loads, I was set for the night.

The next day (the good part of *"the best of times and the worst of times"*), I was watering the garden (yes, with bucket-loads from the cistern) and it was clear to me that spring was here. The oranges were beginning to ripen and my newly planted tomato seeds were sprouting. I know, it is October, but the growing season here is a bit different than where most of you live, and being able to see plants come to life the year through does make living here the best of times.

It was Monday evening, and in about twelve hours, I would be flying to Frankfurt. This wasn't one of those incredibly satisfying but tiring business trips that I do off and on; this was the fabled *"trip home."* The entire concept of going back to the city I was born in was chocker with mixed emotions: I was looking forward to seeing my sons and their families. I was very excited about seeing my grandchildren. I was looking forward to seeing some very special friends whom I haven't seen in what seems to be ages. But that was about as much as I could get excited about. Going back was not something I really was keen on doing. But I was going…and to quote something my father said to me many years ago, I *would* have a good time.

I was struggling to rationalise in my mind the whole flight thing. My tickets would take me from Palma to Frankfurt to Chicago. Now if you paid attention in geography class, you might recognise that Frankfurt is nowhere near a line that can be drawn between Palma and Chicago. But this is where we have found ourselves in this rapidly evolving technologically driven world of supply and demand. It was cheaper and made more sense by far for me to take a two-hour flight headed northeast, switch planes after a two-hour wait, and then fly west for nine hours. As I wrote this I began to seriously have a re-think about this logic. Yes, the delay between flights wasn't too bad. Yes, I would not have to go through Heathrow, which since this summer has been one of the most chaotic places on the planet, with security rules changing almost as fast as planes could land and take off. Yes, this flight plan was actually cheaper than just about anything else I could find online that consisted of two flights that at least headed in the same direction. But no, it just seemed daft to go northeast just to catch a plane that was headed in the right direction.

The whole flying experience has changed so much since I took my first flight at the age of ten or so. Okay, fine. So even though it was fifty years ago; I can still remember what it was like. You would get to the airport terminal and park out in front. Once in the terminal, which was one big room in a semi-cavernous building; you went up to a counter, gave someone some money; received a hand-written ticket; and then walked out onto the tarmac and climbed up the stairs of the somewhat elegant DC-3 that was waiting; almost looking like a praying mantis, about to spring into the air. Now it is quite a bit different, and this trip has brought those differences smack into my face. I booked my tickets online, and only received an acknowledgement with a confirmation number. I drove to the airport and parked in a multi-story building about a half-kilometre from the terminal, but connected by a moving walkway to the terminal itself. Once in the terminal, you check in and after being quizzed about what you have in your baggage, you get to go through a serpentine trail of chrome pylons, guiding you back and forth until you finally reach the large machine that looks like it will devour your carry bag. That is assuming you are game enough to even try to bring a carry bag with you. Then you get to walk down seemingly kilometres of hallways until you eventually find your gate. And with any luck, you actually then are able to walk through the rectangular metal umbilical tube that connects your plane to the terminal. So if these differences are not enough, there always is the time difference. As I recall from being a lad, you used to be able to get to the airport about 15 minutes before your flight. Now, if you aren't there about two hours earlier than the prescribed (or more likely, hoped for) take off time, you will probably miss your flight. I could rabbit on and on about all this, but this is about going Home, not whinging about air travel. Sorry about that.

My flights went…well, okay. According to the in-flight map-thingy, my trip back to the states has now progressed to the point that I am 10,500 metres above Europe, travelling at 900 km/hour, sitting in the very front of the Airbus turbo-tube-in-the-sky, and all I can think about is being home again. Okay, so this is where you may need to pay serious attention. The entire "home" thing has always been sort of a point of contention with me. Yes, I did live in Milwaukee for over fifty years, but I really did want to move away for the last forty of them. And to make things perfectly clear, one of the reasons I didn't think about moving until I was twelve was that I probably wasn't aware that people did move. None-the-less, for a variety of reasons (too young to leave home, in school, locked into an apprenticeship, married, married with children, business responsibilities, business owner) I didn't leave.

Eventually, I was able to move away. My family and I agreed that the time was right, and off we went; all the way to Houston in Texas. And then a couple of years later, we moved again, this time all the way to London. And this is where everything changed…again.

I still live in Europe and this is largely because I feel very much at home here. I feel very comfortable living here; comfortable to the point of actually becoming a citizen of the United Kingdom several years ago. I had no plans to return to America and knew that Europe was where I needed to be, and due to my weather priorities, I purchased a home in Spain.

Earlier this year, one of my sons told me that he was getting married. And then he said how important it was to both he and his fiancé that I would be at the wedding. I responded with a clear and resounding "Yes, of course I will be at the wedding. Where here will it be?" By here I meant where in Europe. I wasn't too particular. They could have had their wedding in France, Italy, Spain, or even England, and I would have been there like a good Dad. But they explained to me that there was this little issue of the wedding party and the cost of getting them to Europe as well. Would I be paying for all of them to fly across the ocean? I bought my ticket to America.

So now, literally as I write this, I am winging my way to America. According to the in-flight display, I should be on the ground in Chicago in about 2 hours. Am I excited about seeing my friends and family? Of course I am. Am I excited about being in the city I grew up in? Not really. Do I think I am going *home*? Not even remotely.

I know that a lot of people hold that where they are from is, and always will be, home. I actually found myself catching the brunt of an "I can't believe you are moving away from your home" conversation with a friend years ago. It was clear to me that this person's mental model of *home*, that I knew that trying to get him to understand why I felt the way I felt would be useless. So instead I went for the stealth approach. *"So"* I began, *"you have lived all your life in this city?" "That's right, I have never even wanted to move away from my home"* he replied, putting that little extra special emphasis on the word *"home." "And your parents? Have they always lived here as well?"* I quickly continued with. *"That's right again. My parents were quite happy to live in the town they were raised in,"* came sliding out of his mouth whilst his eyebrows arched menacingly at me. I went for it. *"And their parents? Were they born here as well?"* I already knew the answer, but was hoping to see how the question would be dealt with. *"Well, no. They moved here from the old country when they were in their 20"s."* I went for the coup de grace; *"Oh my. Are you saying that they actually moved away from their home to start a new life for themselves? They moved away?"* I had made my point, or so I thought. But within minutes I overheard him saying to someone else that he just couldn't understand why anyone (meaning me) would even consider moving away from home.

I am looking forward to being in America again. I do have quite a few friends there. My sons still live there with their families, and I have several aunts and uncles that are still alive and living around the U.S. But regardless of these connections, I will be so happy later in the week when the wedding festivities are over and I can return to *my home*.

Home to me has always been an emotional thing. It is the place you *want* to return to after a long trip. It is the place that you feel most comfortable in. It is the place that you believe is better to be in than just about any other place on the planet. To quote the young lady with the ruby slippers, there is no place like home.

A week later, and I was indeed home. This past Sunday was the arrival in Puigpunyent of the Circo Magic. Whoooo-wee baby, the circus was coming to town. Okay, so maybe I haven't been to a circus since I was quite young, but this one looked like it could be fun; or so I thought from looking at the fab hand-bills that had been posted all over the village. No, it wasn't Siegfried and Roy. No, it wasn't Ringling Brothers. No, it wasn't even Circ du Soleil. It turned out that it was about on the same scale as Puigpunyent, but a fun time none-the-less. After all, a circus is a circus.

James B Rieley

The village is settling in for the winter I fear. I suppose I shouldn't say *"fear,"* but I have never been one who likes cold weather. I remember talking to someone a few years ago about living in Mallorca because of the weather and he replied, *"but you lived in Milwaukee for so many years. You surely must become accustomed to cold weather in winter."* Well I did live there for quite a few years, but being accustomed to something and liking something are two completely different things. Yes, I do like the change of seasons, but to me a good change of season's means that in summer we are bathed in sunlight and warmth, with temperatures in the 30"s. My idea of winter is being bathed in sunlight, with temperatures in the 20"s. Yes, of course I look forward to a day of rain every once in a while – after all, I do have plants in the courtyard and on the terrace that simply adore seriously fresh rain-water. But the sun is pretty important to me, and seeing it in the sky on an almost daily basis is a good thing.

There are ways to tell when winter is approaching in the village. Some of the trees lose their leaves – a normal thing. The winds pick up and the temperature drops considerably at night – also a normal thing. And, residents of the village begin to dress appropriately. This means long pants and jumpers on most days, with the spectre of needing to wear a jacket in the evening… assuming I actually leave the house. I have found that staying home in the evening works quite well for me. Of course, staying home in the evening, especially in winter, means having the heat on and to ensure that this winter La Antigua would be warm as toast, I had a new heating and air conditioning system installed last week.

When I was contemplating this work, I had to think long and hard about the benefits v. the expense. Since living here, I really haven't used the central air system at all. Yes, in the middle of summer, the temperature in the village does reach up to, and often hits, 40c. But when it becomes that warm (notice I refer to 40c as "warm" and not "hot"), I would simply go inside. The almost metre-thick stone walls of La Antigua are the best temperature barrier known to man and inside the house is always a nice temperature. But last winter, I was colder than I wanted to be. Every night I would have at least one of the fireplaces cranking away, providing not only a marvellous environment, but also warmth in the living room and kitchen (where the two fireplaces are). Of course, last year I also went through 2 ½ tons of firewood, and I thought that this year, a new, more efficient and effective heating system would be a good thing.

I was a bit concerned about finding a contractor who would do the work, however. There is some business-cultural thing on the island that goes like this: You ring up a contractor and make arrangements for him to come out to scope out the project. He doesn't show up. You ring him back, reminding him of the set appointment. He doesn't show up. You ring him again. He shows up, but rarely when he says he will. After finally setting out the job plan, he doesn't show up to do the work when he says he will. At this point, you have a choice: A) get incredibly frustrated with the lack of business drive and customer service on the island, or B) realise that this is Mallorca and things are done differently here. The key word concept here is *"tranquillo,"* which roughly translates to *"calm down,"* or in an even more appropriate translation for those of us from the UK, Australia, or America who are used to other business cultures, *"get over it."* Then there is the way that most contractors get paid. The proposal I was given said that the payment schedule was 30% deposit upon the acceptance of the proposal, followed by another 30% when the workmen arrived on-site the first day, and the balance upon completion. Due to many of the horror stories I have heard about island contractors, I said that the proposal was fine, but I wouldn't pay the first 30% until the workmen showed up with the new system, and then I would pay the balance upon job completion.

I have experienced the Mallorquin way of doing business in the past, so I was prepared for arguments about my idea of how to pay, and a long wait from before my new contractor would appear, but he came when he said he would; his workmen appeared on-site when I was told they would, and the work they did was high-quality, on budget, and on-time. Actually, the on budget part was even more interesting because no one asked for any money until the job was completed, and I actually had to ring the head of the company to see if he wanted to get paid.

I made it a point to hang around for the three days the men were here doing the removal of the old system and the installation of the new system. None of the three workmen spoke any English (nor did the owner of the company who I had dealt with), so this seemed like a good opportunity to practise my Spanish. And it was. Of course, it also made me realise that I am sorely lacking in the ability to say certain phrases in Spanish, like, *"are you sure you should be standing on the top of the ladder – the one with the sticker that says,* "do not stand here" - *and on one foot?"*

So now I have a new heating/air conditioning system firmly in place (which works like a dream), enough firewood to make it through the next month or so if I use the fireplaces, and am sitting writing with the doors and windows open...apparently summer has not given up quite yet.

When I was a young boy growing up in Milwaukee, I longed for springtime to arrive. I had this red jacket that my mother would let me wear to school, but only if the temperature would reach 50 degrees Fahrenheit. In Milwaukee, it normally didn't reach that lofty temperature until April or May, and red-jacket-wearing-day was a sign that spring was finally coming. Now, bear in mind that 50 degrees Fahrenheit is the same as 10 degrees Centigrade. It is mid-December here in the village, and whilst the temperature still hasn't fallen to that level, I find it terribly cold. As I was sitting in my living room today, kitted out in my long pants, socks, and jumper, I actually contemplated turning the heat on – today's temperature will only reach the mid-teens. Whilst doing so, I started thinking about how, when I was young, I thought the Fahrenheit-equivalent of 10c was great, and now, at age something-or-other, I shudder at the thought of it being anywhere near 10c (or even 15c). And yet, it is winter and with winter comes cold weather, regardless of what you consider cold to be. Because you really can't rely on the temperatures that are reported online as they often miss the mark by more than five degrees, and I know that some of you do use the various weather websites to see what the tempts are here, I will set the record straight. It is cold here. Bloody freaking cold (well by my standards at least).

In another day, it will be the shortest day of the year, and the shortest day means that the darkness of winter will finally stops its increase and once again the skies will begin to stay brighter longer. At least, that is my wish. The shortest day of the year also means that Christmas is less than a week away. I really can't remember when I found out that Santa Claus was just a good story to explain the gifts that appeared under our tree at Christmas, but I know that at the time, the sudden and sad understanding that Santa Claus wasn't the one bringing the pressies was dispelled quickly as soon as I realised that the presents would still be there. It took me quite a while to understand that the "miracle" that was Christmas had nothing to do with the presents at all.

Since being in the village, I think I have increased my understanding of what miracles can bring. To be able to wake up in the morning at all is pretty much of a miracle. But to be able to wake up to the sun and warmth that usually blankets the village is a very special miracle to me. Yes, whilst growing up there was the miracle of snow, gently falling from the sky on Christmas Eve, with each flake bringing the feeling that something magical was happening. Whilst it would be pretty nice to see snow on the nearby mountains that surround the village at this time of year, I have become more of a snow voyeur than one who actually wants to run out with a couple of bits of coal and a carrot and build a snowman.

To be able to live in a community where people actually talk to each other is another miracle. I just love the fact that everyday I am in the village centre – you know, where the two stores are – I run into people whom I may or may not have met, but it doesn't make any difference. We all say hello to each other. Balthazar and Guillem, the two brothers who own the little market, always ask how I am...and they really mean it. Antonia and Kati, the women who work at the other shop in the village, tell me about the various events planned in the village and help me feel welcome at them. This village has been a miracle for me, and I know that had I not moved here, my life wouldn't have been as full as it is.

To be surrounded by friends who actually are concerned about you is seriously pretty special in my life. Yes, of course I miss my family and loved ones that live in America, England, and Australia, and I wish that we could be together more often. Whether I am able to talk with them every week or not, that doesn't mean I don't miss them terribly. But the miracle of family and friends is that no matter where you or they are on this planet, just knowing that they are there and thinking about you and knowing that you are thinking about them is the best miracle of all. Someone once told me *"good friends are the family you get to choose."* I now have the largest family on the planet I think.

Now if I would just spend less time writing and more time thinking, I might be able to come up with some way to keep La Antigua enveloped in sun and warmth all the time. That would be a real miracle.

04

Joys of Village Life

2007

The year is almost over. Yes, 2006 has come and (almost) gone. And because my father always taught me that there were numbers in everything, it seemed to me on the way back from the airport (I had gone to Berlin to see my brother for Christmas) that this might be a good time to reflect on life in the village numerically.

I have been living in Mallorca now for 3-1/2 years, which as I am sure you all know, is something like 1277 days. I bought La Antigua in May 2005, which means I have lived in the village for 570 days. In that time, I have learnt that some things take longer than others; that having patience whilst waiting for contractors to arrive can be a good thing; that whilst my Spanish has improved tremendously, I will probably never master Mallorquin; and that moving here was the right thing for me to do at the time. 570 days...whew, and it only seems like a year and-a-half.

Amelia came into my life about 500 days ago. Another good decision on my part I think, as she has provided me with faultless transportation ever since I bought her (well with the minor exception being the time that I picked someone up at the airport and one of those highly-technological-electronic-engine-doo-wahs had prevented her from starting). But hey, that is just one little thing...over all, Amelia has been a great car to use to get around. Which brings me to the next numbers.

When I bought Amelia, I set the odometer "trip distance" counter to a big fat zero. Today, on my way back from the airport (Amelia has been working fine since I replaced the doo-wah thing), I noticed that the odometer trip distance counter said 11,500 kilometres. Obviously, I have driven that many kilometres since owning the car, which is fine; but it did cause me to wonder, "How did I manage to crank up that many kilometres when it is only 14 kilometres to Palma, and the entire island is only 3.640 square kilometres in area?" It would have been like driving over the entire island, making sure I drove through every bloody square kilometre three times, and I know I haven't done that. I don't know how many kilometres of roads there are on the island, but I do know that I have never even driven to Pollenca (POI-YEN-SA) on the north-east coast (which by the way is 72 kilometres from Puigpunyent according to a map). Obviously, I have made quite a few trips into Palma. The phrase "quite a few" must represent almost 400 round-trips, which in itself seems odd as I only go to Palma once or twice a week. It appears to me that either, A) I do leave La Antigua and go places on the island more than I would have thought I did, or B) Amelia is driving around the island on her own.

Right about now, some of the metrically challenged readers of this chapter might be wondering how to convert kilometres to miles. The formula (that we all would have learnt in school if we had been paying attention) is Miles = Kilometres X .6 (more or less). Okay? Back to the chapter...

According to some pretty anal website I found, in the year 2000, Mallorca had more than 11,000,000 visitors. Although there isn't any more current data on this marvellously fascinating statistic (I am yawing now as I type because this is B-O-R-I-N-G), I am sure that the number has increased considerably in the past six years. Part of my evidence of that new and even more exciting fact stems from the fact that when I flew back to Palma today, I was able to experience the fact that the Palma airport is recognised as one of the busiest in the world, with 53 airlines having flights in and out of the island, and today I think they were all landing at the same time.

The Island divided into 53 administrative districts, with Puigpunyent being rated as the best one of all...okay, this rating is mine, and it might be a bit skewed, but as this is my story, you can accept this as a fact.

Mallorca does have seasons, with the temperatures ranging from an average high in June through August where the average temperature is 27º c (our high, or best season) to January and February of 15º c (our low, or as I call it, the shit season). Now in all fairness, I must admit that these published temperatures don't reflect my experience on the island. In summer it has hit 40 more times that I have body digits to count on, and in winter...well, I try not to go outside in winter so I just assume that the published numbers are pretty close.

We seem to have a plethora of holidays on the island. Whilst some of them are "Spanish-National" holidays, we also have Mallorquin holidays. Many of the Mallorquin holidays seem to follow some unknown mystical plan that says that everything should close down at least a couple of times per month, and if for some strange reason we miss one, then we usually have a holiday that whose name apparently translates to, *"the holiday that exists because we haven't had a holiday in a few weeks,"* or something like that.

Other interesting but apparently random numbers include:
- The number of times I have swept my courtyard since moving to La Antigua – at least 500. The number of leaves that have fallen causing me to do the sweeping – at least a ka-zillion.
- The number of steps that I walk on an average day (yes, I broke down and bought a pedometer) – about 8,000 on a good day. On a bad day – hmmm, maybe about 20.
- The number of inhabitants of Puigpunyent – 1,500. Palma has a population of 300,000, almost ½ that of the entire island.
- The number of fireplaces in my house – 2; the amount of firewood I used last winter – 2.5 tons. Hey, having a fireplace without a fire is like having

gin without tonic, isn't it?
- The rating of the sunscreen I use – anything with a single digit. The rating of sunscreen I should be using – probably 40. Or 60. Or 90.
- The number of calories in a Snickers Bar – hardly any (I keep telling myself).
- The number of beaches on the island – 76, with 35 of them considered having Blue Flag status. I have no idea what Blue Flag status means, but it is probably better than having a Burberry-plaid flag status.
- The year that Can Domingo (my local restaurant/pub) was founded – 1896. The number of changes that have been made since 1896 to keep Can Domingo current with the world – 1. Maybe 2 if you count adding electricity.
- The number of years that man has been on Mallorca – 6,000. This is one of those statistics that came from a website that stated *"the earliest traces of man discovered on the island date from 4,000BC."* I'm not sure, but it might be possible that the earliest visitors to the island came for a hen party...as they still do.
- The price of petrol on the island – 97 cents per litre. Now, for all you people that are whinging about paying over $2.00 a gallon, bear in mind that .97 cents (of a euro) is the same as $1.23 in US dollars, and there are 3.79 litres to a gallon, so the cost of petrol here equates to $4.69 US dollars a gallon.

I probably could go on and on with more painfully useless numbers, but even I have a life. Besides, the only number that really is important is the next one that we all will encounter...have a fab 2007.

I had thought it would be a good idea to have some friends over for dinner to celebrate the onset of 2007 (sorry if you didn't receive your invitation on time...that pesky postal service), and as the New Year is a very special time, I wanted to have a proper sit-down dinner. Problem number 1 with this seemingly brilliant idea was that my dining table only holds eight people comfortably. Problem number 2 was that I wanted to invite more than eight people. Few problems are insurmountable...I resolved this one easily by simply planning two dinners, on consecutive evenings. Okay, I never spent a lot of time pondering the logistics of having two dinners on consecutive evenings but instead worked out the menu. In the last several weeks of 2006, British television was chocker with holiday cookery programmes, and the one that attracted my interest were the three programmes with Nigella Lawson. Nigella has this...well, style, when she prepares food, and I was mesmerised by some of the recipes she did so I decided to emulate her menu selections.

The starter would be a grilled peach half; sitting on some lettuce, covered (artistically, of course) with some extra-thin sliced Serrano ham, sliced Parmesan, and with Goat's cheese crumbled around it. Once assembled, a bit of Balsamic vinegar was sprinkled over the entire starter tower. Easy-peasy, but to be safe, I tried to make one of these a few days before the big dinner extravaganzas. It was fab, so that was on the menu for sure.

The main course was going to be baked chicken, prepared with lemon-wedges and spiced with sea salt, freshly ground pepper, and a liberal dose of fresh Basil from the garden. My vegetable plan included potatoes (wedged and covered with a blend of sea salt, freshly ground pepper, and Rosemary, also from the garden; as well as sprouts. Cooking Brussels sprouts, as told by the lovely and talented Nigella, can be a trick. Her recommendation was to slop them into boiling water for about five minutes, and then put them in a fry pan that already contained cooked bacon bits and garlic. Add a dollop of butter (to Nigella, a dollop appeared to be about 2 kilos, and I did cut back on that a bit), and cook for another five minutes.

Finally, I had decided that I wanted to have homemade ice cream for dessert. Not just some trendy, carcinogen-laden frozen treat, but orange-zest ice cream. No, I don't own an ice cream maker, and as a matter of fact, I don't even own a mixer. But I borrowed a mixer, bought some double cream and some icing sugar, picked a couple of oranges and went for it. Zest the orange, squeeze the juice out of what is left over, add the sugar and then chuck in 500 ml of the cream...and mix...and mix...and mix. Yes, I did do a test run of this as well, and well I did. Without a proper ice cream maker, this can be a bit time consuming. It took well over 30 minutes standing there with a mixer, whipping the mixture into shape, followed by another 6 hours or so in the freezer before it is ready to eat, but it is soooooooo good, especially when hot melted chocolate is dripped over it.

So, Saturday evening and Sunday afternoon, I did my proper cooking thing, and served everything on the plates and serving platters that I had made last summer (and, as you might imagine, on the placemats that I had designed and screen-printed for the dinners). The only real glitch was that one of my friends is a vegetarian, and I think I don't think she had enough to eat, with just a ham-less salad, potatoes and separately prepared sprouts. I had planned to make some tofu-based chicken for her, but by the time I had everything else going, I had completely forgotten to cook it. Ooops...my kitchen time management needs some work apparently.

I wasn't sure exactly what would happen with the dinners. The options seemed to be; A) the second group of people would get the best of the two dinners, as my learning curve should improve after the first attempt; B) the second group of people would get the worst of the two dinners because I would be so knackered from the first dinner and would muck up the second attempt; or C) I would lose 16 friends due to the effects of food poisoning. Luckily (for both my friends and myself), all seemed to go well, with the minor complaints that I hadn't dressed like Nigella. She does, after all, have this propensity to cook in a red satin robe.

James B Rieley

Enough about my recent cooking exploits. It was another beautiful morning yesterday, with the sun streaming down on the village (and I suppose on the entire island, but I live in Puigpunyent, so that is my concern). It was so warm and sunny that it seemed to be a good day to get out of the house, just to see how some of the areas around the village survived the winter. Okay, even I would agree that it might be a bit premature to say that winter is already over, after all, it is early January; but every good day in January means that the potential for those nasty days that I dislike (the ones where clouds fill the skies and rain falls all over), are diminished. So off on my walk I went.

In the past few days, drives to Valdemossa and Establiments were in order, but today was just perfect for a walk. I put on a jumper and set out from La Antigua. After being here for almost two years, I seem to have identified several walking directions. Today's journey was down on of the back roads that wind around the village, past the winery, coming out on the Puigpunyent-Palma road. Once I had driven the way, just to find out how long it was, but now, with my magical pedometer, the only thing that is important is the number of steps. I do keep striving to get to the magical 10,000 steps per day, but I think the person who came up with that number was probably on some serious medication at the time, but none-the-less, I suppose that being conscious about the amount of exercise I get daily is better than just thinking about it sitting on the terrace reading.

The walk was very special…it was as if winter actually was over. The almost negligible breeze helped to make the apparent temperature soar, and early on, I had to remove my jumper as I strolled (sorry,…as I energetically power-walked…yes, that sounds better) along the narrow road. The only noises I could hear were from the odd dog or two that seemed to be a bit concerned that I was walking past their respective fincas; and the sheep and goats that wander around in the fields, their bells tinkling as they grazed on whatever they graze on.

I like living in Puigpunyent, but you probably already know this. Part of the reason include that being here has been very good for my desire to have a creative outlet for whatever it is I do. The past several days have been, as I can best describe them, as days filled with intensive creativity. Now before I get into this, I think we all need to sit back and realise that creativity is a relative thing, and what one may think is creative and what someone else might deem creative may just be different. There, having said that, I will now tell you what has been going on.

First, the weather has been simply brilliant lately, and I have known for years that when the weather is good (by my standards), my creativity surges. This doesn't mean that I have come up with the solution to global warming, solved world hunger, or even established a plan for real world peace. I tend to work on a different level I guess. My creativity levels focus more on things I can actually do to contribute to what I think is important. So this means I have been writing excessively – I do have a commissioned piece that I need to have done at the end of the month, and to make sure that it is good, I have been conducting a series of phone interviews with people in the UK. Whilst these interviews do sort of cut into my other creativity time, they have produced quite a few good content inputs for the written piece.

I have also been working on the logistics involved in producing this year's holiday card. I usually begin working on my holiday cards in September or October, but this is the time that I come up with the idea of what I want to do. In most years, even make a sample or two to see if the idea is even viable. Two years ago, I made all sorts of tests, only to determine that my idea for the card, in a word, sucked. So at least by starting early, I was able to design something else. Last year's card project began in October, and it took a month to get the cards ready. This year, 2007, my planning began a tad earlier. I visualised the design of the card I wanted to make for 2007 in mid-December, just as I was posting the last of my 2006 cards. Yes, this did seem a bit early, even for someone who lives and thrives on projects, but the only explanation I can give is that when I "*see*" the idea clearly, I need to get cracking on making some samples to test the idea out.

Just after New Year, I had made several tests of the cards. Well, actually, "several tests" means I had by then come up with several variations on the 2007 card. My son David, whom I told what I was doing, began to express concerns that at the rate I was working on this, I would, by mid-summer 2007, I would have enough card designs sorted out to last through 2010, but I assured him that this wasn't the case (but to come to think of it, that might be a good idea). So the part of the past several days has been focused on making sure that the final design was feasible to have ready for posting near the holiday season.

This weekend brings yet another celebration in the village. This one is for Sant Antoni, who I am told "*was born in Egypt in the year 251 and spent most of his life praying and fasting in the desert, where he was tempted many times by the Devil, who would appear dressed as a woman. Since the Middle Ages he has been acknowledged as the Patron Saint of domestic animals.*" Tempted by women and the Patron Saint of domestic animals. Hmmm.

Okay, the flyer for the Sant Antoni celebration that was stuffed into my post box at La Antigua said that this Sunday was the highlight of the celebration, the "Les Tradicional Beneides." I can't wait, or so I thought up to the time I was able to figure out what the text on the flyer actually meant. Here is what it said; "*Totes les carrosses que vulguin participar-hi. Optaran als seguents premis.*" Right. What I *think* this means is that I can bring any animals that I own to the village church and they will be blessed. Now even though I don't own any animals, and even though I am Lutheran, and even though I am really not sure what this is all about, this sounded like a great way to spend the afternoon. With my non-existent Mallorquin, how do you suppose I came to the conclusion of what the flyer said? No, I didn't ask anyone in the village, and I assumed that it didn't mean that everyone could come to the village centre and be tempted by women. I simply looked at the words…and then at all the little photos of cats, dogs, pigs, and horses that were pasted on the flyer. See? Earning that Ph.D. really has paid off. I was thinking I could borrow a friend's pet and have that blessed – that has to be a better option than going to the ceremony with a six-pack of Coke-Light and saying that it is a litter of something – but instead decided to just have a wander over and see what the celebration was all about.

The parade that preceded the blessing of the animals was pretty impressive, with decorated floats, everyone in costume (boys all kitted out as little devils and girls as…well, little girls). I haven't seen this many people in the village in ages. The traffic was at a standstill with all the roads being completely backed up with cars trying to get through the village centre (okay, *both* roads were crowded). I am convinced that some of the tourists that think that a drive in the country on a sunny day is a good thing to do, finding themselves in Puigpunyent after missing some turn, were convinced that the Royal family were in town.

And then there were the animals. I have no idea how many were actually there, but I did see a ferret (I suppose they need all the blessings they can get), a couple of goldfish in a Tupperware-type container, numerous parakeet-type caged birds (all looking rather concerned), cats galore (mostly eyeing up the birds I think), and a plethora of dogs. Cute dogs, nasty-looking dogs, little dogs, big dogs, and even the odd monstrous dog that looked strangely like he (or she) just flew in from the Pyrenees after herding a couple of thousand sheep.

The local Priest, who apparently doesn't have animal allergies, blessed each and every pet that their owners carried/dragged/nudged/cajoled/walked (all of these methods were visible on this fine Sunday morning) up to the church steps, and then everyone went home, safe in the knowledge that their respective pets were now well protected by the blessing of the church. It is days like this – sunny skies, warm weather, good friends – that I realise how lucky I am to live here. And I think I need a puppy.

It has been a relatively busy week for me. On Tuesday, I flew to Germany to meet with a client. Yes, I actually left my island. Miracle of miracles. I won't even get into the weather as I think all of you have a good understanding of my views on acceptable levels of temperature; but the trip itself was quite good after a tentative start. The flight itself was fine and because I only had a carry-on bag – I never check baggage when I travel as the delays at the baggage collection conveyors can be abysmal, and the risk of losing baggage it too great – I was able to scurry through the terminal to find my client-supplied driver. As I walked through the glass doors, I began to look around at the group of drivers that were holding up signs with the names of the people they were there to collect. No, not that driver. Not the next one either, nor the next one in the queue of drivers who didn't look that happy about being there either. Actually, I scanned the signs of the dozen or so drivers and couldn't see any signs that had "Rieley" printed on them. I have learnt that spelling doesn't count in these situations, so I also scanned for "Reilly," "Ryley", "Wyley," and any other aberration of my surname. Nothing. This was, to quote Stan Laurel, a fine mess.

Here I was in Frankfurt; it was past the time when I could ring my client to see if there was a car-glitch; and I was getting cranky. I began to walk around, trying to be obviously looking for someone, with the hope that the driver, who must have forgotten to bring a sign, would spot me. After about ten laps of the passenger area, I was still driverless. By now, the number of passengers from the Palma flight had been exhausted and a new group of passengers on an Istanbul to Frankfurt flight were coming out. I reasoned that if I didn't find the driver soon, I would have to simply find the taxi rank and manage my own way to the hotel that I had been booked into. Another ten minutes drifted away, and as my frustration level was reaching a new high, I saw a man with a very small company logo on his suit-coat…and the logo was of the company that had brought me to Germany. Apparently he thought it was my job to find him. An interesting customer service concept.

After reaching the hotel, I had a near-life-threatening shock. The Wi-Fi system that the hotel was using was not functioning. Now I don't know about you, but it is 2007, and my expectation is that any decent hotel that caters to business people has a functioning broadband system, and it is wireless. And whilst this hotel did have a system, the service provider was having a problem, so there I sat, in my hotel room, unable to connect my computer, and having CNN the only English-language station on telly. And if that wasn't enough turmoil, I realised that in my rush out of the house earlier in the day, I had forgotten the phone charger for my mobiles, and my Spanish phone was about dead.

So let's recap. I had left La Antigua; I was in Germany, where the temperature wasn't even near my low level of acceptability, I almost didn't get a ride to the hotel, I would be unable to recharge my phones, meaning in short order, they would sink into uselessness, and I couldn't connect my computer and check my messages. Hmmmm, it was a good thing I deal well with stress. Right.

Things did look up the next day. The extremely competent P.A. of the client I was in Germany to see went out and bought me a phone charger; the internet service provider managed to get things sorted out by the time I returned to the hotel at the end of the day; my meetings went very well; and I was booked on a flight home the next morning.

Okay, let me explain what "morning" means in this context. My ticketing was done through Air Berlin, which I have found to be a brilliant airline. But for some bizarre reason, the only flight that they had from Frankfurt to Palma the next morning was to depart at 0630h. With all the travel prob-

James B Rieley

lems that we all deal with in today's world, a 0630h departure means you need to be at the airport before 0500h; which means that I needed to leave the hotel at 0430h; which meant I needed to be awake well before 0400h. Ahhh, the joys of business travel. The good news was that Tabea (the one who saved my life with the phone charger) had made arrangements to have a driver at the hotel at 0430h. The bad news was that I would have to be ready to go by that time.

I reasoned that I would need a wake-up call from the hotel, so when I ordered my evening's room service, I placed a request for the 0400h wake-up call as well. I had them repeat my dinner order as well as confirm the wake-up call time, and then settled back into responding to emails. By 2000h, I figured that I had better think about going to sleep, so I turned everything off and closed my eyes, opening them only to see what time it was. 2100h. 2230h. 2315h. 2355h. 0030h. 0130h. 0215h. Scheisse…I was still awake and the amount of potential sleep I could get was slipping away faster than support for the Iraq war. I think that I must have fallen asleep at that point, as the next time I looked at the clock, the segmented green numbers said 0345h. Fair enough; 1-1/2 hours of sleep was better than no sleep at all, so I dragged myself out of bed and popped into the shower. At 0400h, my phone alarm went off. I was now getting dressed, trying to figure out how to get into the mini-bar to have some orange juice, and wondering why the wake-up call didn't come through. By 0425h, I was downstairs in the lobby waiting for the car to take me back to the airport, and asking the desk clerk about the wake-up call. "*You didn't receive the call?*" he said. "*Strange, it is written down I think.*" Dick.

I did arrive home safely and on my drive back to La Antigua, I realised that this trip provided me with several solid travel lessons, and I think they all begin with the tag line of the credit-card advert…"*Don't leave home without it.*"

1) Your phone charger, so you can be sure to have a wake-up alarm: don't leave home without it.

2) A good book, so when your computer can't connect you have something to do: don't leave home without it.

3) A language dictionary, so when the country you are in doesn't have television programming you can understand you can find out what is going on in the world (without having to sink to the level of watching the news of CNN which repeats itself every 15 minutes): don't leave home without it.

Then there always is the option of simply modifying the American Express advert to, "*Just don't leave home.*"

After several "interesting" things occurred, I was going to look up the word "bureaucracy" in my dictionary, but then I realised that the past several months have provided me with a good idea of what it can be. In late December, I decided to change one of my mobile telephone providers. I have, besides a proper home phone, a UK mobile and a Spanish mobile. I use the UK mobile for my trips to England and my Spanish mobile when in Mallorca. I know it is a bit complicated, but this keeps my roaming charges down to a minimum, and therefore, they seemed like a good idea to have. But shortly after moving to La Antigua, I noticed that my Spanish mobile, which is on a contract through Vodafone, didn't function well at home due to the immensely thick stone walls of the house. So realising that the easiest way out of a problem sometimes almost makes sense, I went out and picked up a "pay-as-you-go" card from Movistar to use with a spare mobile handset that I had. All I had to do was forward all the calls from my Vodafone handset to the Movistar handset, and all would work well, as for some unknown reason, the telephone signals from Movistar make it through all the walls of La Antigua. I really can't figure out why this is, as there is only one real mobile tower in the village and both Vodafone and Movistar have antennas on the same tower. Regardless, my plan worked, and I was able to receive calls made to my Vodafone mobile by forwarding them to my Movistar mobile. Confused yet? Don't be…this is the easy part of the story.

After almost two years of paying my monthly charge to Vodafone and buying the odd pay-as-you-go recharge for my Movistar phone, I decided that this was plain silly, so I decided to finally drop the Vodafone contract and convert the contract to Movistar so I could stop buying the recharges every so often. My biggest concern was that I would keep my same Spanish mobile number, but as phone service providers are under regulations in the European Union to do this, I figured that it would be a piece of cake. So…I went to the big Carrefour store in Palma (where all the mobile service providers have their own sales and service counters) and explained what I wanted to do to the man at the Movistar counter. To make sure that he understood my request, I actually practised what I was going to say whilst driving to the store, and his reaction showed me that my language skills have indeed improved. All I had to do was fill out a form and all would be set into motion I was told. Oh yes, one more thing…I needed to provide a copy of my residency number and my existing Vodafone contract information. Of course, I didn't have that stuff with me, so I went home. Two days later – I really try to only go into Palma if I have more than one thing to do…pollution, global warming, and I just don't like leaving the village unless I have to – I was back at Carrefour with all the information. Of course, the first man I spoke to wasn't there this day, so I explained my cunning plan to the current Movistar sales-type guy. He said something like, "*okay, I will take care of it. We will notify you by text message within a week when the contract and number have been changed to Movistar.*" I was impressed, not only by my ability to do the transaction in Spanish, but also by the apparent efficiency of the changeover service.

After a week, I still hadn't received a text message, and I assumed the reason was obvious. I realised that when I forwarded my phone calls from the Vodafone phone to the Movistar phone, the text message function doesn't forward as well. Buggers. I got into Amelia and drove to Carrefour, with the expectation that they were trying to contact me but were unable. Part of the excitement of having the number switched was that I would get a new phone as part of the deal. Not that I need another mobile – I have three or four old mobiles that I don't even use, but hell, I am a male, and new electronic kit is always fun to have, especially when it is free. I arrived at the store, when gleefully skipping through the doors to the Movistar counter in anticipation of having my phone problems sorted once and for all. Alas, another new person at the counter greeted me. Luckily, this person was aware of the situation and pulled out some papers and then began to explain to me that Vodafone couldn't find any record of the contract information I had supplied; and because of this, hadn't made the changeover to Movistar. I couldn't understand what the problem was until I remembered that when I first took out the Vodafone contract – when I had first arrived in Barcelona several years earlier – I didn't have a residency number and used my passport to validate the contract…my American passport. Okay, so now I understood the problem, but this understanding only surfaced another problem. The clerk (number three if you are keeping track) said that all I needed to do was produce my U.S. Passport and they could sort out the problem, but, as I am now a British citizen, I hold a British passport and had turned my US passport in at the Consular office as soon as I could. I explained all this to the clerk – yes, in Spanish – only to see him look mystified. He knew what I was saying but was at a loss as to what I should do next. I told him I would return home and see if I could locate my old passport number or a photocopy of the old passport.

The next day I returned again and Praise the Lord, it was the same clerk on duty as the previous day. I had my old passport number (but no photocopy). We exchanged information and he told me that I should have my new phone and changed contract within a week. He would let me know. Right. Another week passed and I hadn't heard a thing so I drove into the city. Yes, if you are now assuming my frustration level was hitting new highs, you are right; but I am living in a different culture that I was raised in and patience is a virtue, so I remained calm. Well, the JBR -living-in-the-culture-of-Mallorca-type-of-calm.

Another week passed and after still not hearing anything, Amelia whisked me back to Carrefour. It was clerk number two again, who, after checking the paperwork, told me that Vodafone was still struggling with the switchover process, still due to the complications of an old contract based on a passport I no longer held. I was told to wait a week and it would all be straightened out. Another week, another trip to see who was working the counter, and another trip home without my contract being changed over. In mid-week, I received a text message directly from Vodafone requesting me to ring Customer Service to explain what I was trying to do. By this point, I thought that what I was trying to do was clear to just about everyone in the solar system, but I rang the number and went through my request to switch my service and phone number to Movistar, and why. *"Ahh, entiendo"* the voice on the phone replied, and because she was saying that she understood, I assumed that the switchover was as good as done. Silly me.

Still another week, another drive in, followed by a drive home with nothing having changed. I was beginning to think that the free phone I would receive from Movistar as a bonus for switching to them would be out of date by the time they actually were able to activate the number in their system. But, as someone who does putter around in the world of business, I knew that this would eventually get sorted out. And besides, it wasn't as if I was phoneless; my forwarded calls were still coming through. I was just trying to make my life a tad simpler...and to save the cost of the pay-as-you-go phone cards.

So let's recap: this process began in late December, and I am writing this letter in early March, and tomorrow I plan on driving to Carrefour. No, I haven't been told that the contract has been switched. I just thought it might be nice to say hello to my new friends at the Movistar counter.

In between trips to Carrefour, I have been rather busy. Busy doing what you ask? Well, to begin with, I have had guests here at La Antigua and one of them did occupy a bit of my time. The good news is that Holly was a wonderful guest. She and I would go for long walks each day; we have great talks about just about everything; she didn't bother me when I was writing; and she would let me rub her back as much as I wanted to. Holly is, of course, a dog. When my friend Millie asked if I would take Holly for a bit whilst she (Mille) was away, I jumped at the chance. I have thought for quite a while about having a dog, and this seemed to be a good way to see if the idea really was a good one. Millie's instructions were quite clear: brush Holly everyday, take her for occasional walks, and talk to her a lot.

Everyday, we would venture out from La Antigua 3 or 4 times, with each walk being almost 2 kilometres long (which I think was more tiring for Holly than it was for me), and whilst walking, we would talk about what was going on in the village and make incredibly cheesy comments about the other dogs who would be yelping their heads off as we strolled past. When it was nearing dinner time, I made sure that I gave Holly options about what I could make her, usually explaining how I would prepare that evening's taste treat delight...which ended up being the same thing night after night, but hell, she is a dog and probably regardless of what I would say *("oooh, tonight I am going to prepare roast lamb with fresh rosemary from the garden, accompanied by fresh green beans and a side salad")* she only heard *"blah, blah, blah"*. Holly left last weekend and will sorely be missed. But my work schedule is pretty full for the foreseeable future, and it didn't seem fair to have Holly locked up in the house.

David Bowie said it years ago, "Ch-ch-ch-changes. Pretty soon you're gonna get a little older." He was right, and for a while, I have been thinking that I had better get cracking once again on making some changes in La Antigua. The house has two bathrooms, one upstairs as an en-suite to my bedroom, and one downstairs just off the kitchen. I had already made changes to the upstairs bath and now I wanted to do something with the one downstairs. Don't misunderstand me, it was a nice bathroom. It had a loo, a basin, and a tub-shower, but there were a couple of things that I thought I could do to make it better.

First, the bathtub. The bathtub was, well, small. It reminded me of the bathtub I had on Angelina, and a bathtub on a 17-metre sailboat is, almost by definition, quite small. I suppose I could have taken a bath in it, but it would have meant that my body would have to have gone into a near foetal position. Not a good thing. Friends who have stayed here had told me that stepping out of the tub was a seriously risky adventure, and as I had never suffered a slipping-moment myself, I just attributed the comments to some misplaced fear of ceramics. Regardless, what I wanted to do was replace the bathtub with a large shower. So the tub had to go.

My second issue with the downstairs bath were the tiles on the walls. The entire room was tiled when I bought the house – a good thing; but the tiles on the walls were all white – a semi-good thing; and decorated with cute little flowers in the corner of each tile – not a good thing. So I had decided that the cutesy-white-floral-cornered tiles had to go.

It didn't take me too long to come up with a plan. All I needed to do was remove the wall tiles and the tub and then re-tile the room. But when I began to really think about the part of the plan that would require removing existing tiles (now quoting from William Shakespeare) I realised that *"there's the rub."* Please notice all the literary references, and I am only on the fourth paragraph so far. Last year, when putting the shower into the bath upstairs, I had managed to tear a tendon (which in Spanish is "un tendon se rompe" for all you who might want to feel bad for me) in my shoulder and now months later, it was still plaguing me. My options were clear: A) ditch the plan and wait a few hundred years until my shoulder was completely healed; B) modify the plan by just changing the light bulbs to a depressingly low wattage so I wouldn't see the tiles; or C) hire someone to do the serious work. It didn't take me – the holder of an earned Ph.D. - long to realise that one option was the best, and I opted out for choice "C."

Yesterday afternoon (afternoon here seems to begin yesterday around 1900h apparently) Big Tony came over. You will remember Tony from the upstairs shower extravaganza of last year. I have added the "Big" to his name because, well, he is big. Tony's job was to disconnect the water supply to the existing tub/shower, as well as disconnect and remove the loo and the basin. I suppose I could have done these parts of the job, but it would have been my luck to not have the correct size plugs for the pipes and ended up with a flooded bathroom, so using Tony again made sense. Then this morning (morning began today just before 0800h), Salvador and Elio came over to start the wrecking process. I was ex-pat heaven, as neither of these workmen speaks a bit of English, so I knew I would be able to increase my Spanish skills. Okay, maybe I would be forced to increase my Spanish skills or else I might end up with God-knows-what for my new bathroom.

It only took a few minutes to see what the work plan was. Salvador, el jefe (the boss), told Elio, el trabajadore (the poor bugger who the boss tells to actually do the work) what I wanted to do and which walls to lop the tiles off of (all of them actually), and then he left. Elio and I chatted a bit about Uruguay (where he is from and where I know absolutely nothing other than the capital being Montevideo) and then he proceeded to take this rather heavy hammer and metal chisel and began to whack away on the walls. It didn't take long before there were shards of ceramic tiles flying around the room so I (again, using some of the knowledge I learnt in my doctoral programme) got the hell out of the way. After about 30 minutes, Elio came out of the room and asked me if I had a plaster (bandage) for his bloody finger. As I gave him one, I asked why he wasn't wearing leather gloves or safety glasses. His response was short and to the point; *"Why?"* Silly me. Apparently he has spare hands and eyes at home. I left the room again.

Shortly after noon, I decided to venture into the room of destruction. Elio seemed to be about 30% done with breaking the tiles off the walls and did stop long enough to tell me that most of the tiles are so firmly attached to the walls that the work is very difficult. Or maybe he was telling me about his sister...it is times like this when I wonder if my Spanish will ever be as good as I want it to be. Whilst I felt sorry for him, I realised that my choice of having someone else wield the hammer was one of my better decisions since moving to La Antigua. He then asked me if I had a something-or-other. I didn't have a clue what he was asking for so I decided to use the tried-and-true process of elimination response and started tossing out terms that I assumed to have something to do with wall-tile demolition. When I mentioned *"escalera,"* he smiled and said, *"Si, si. Una escalera pequeno."* I luckily was the proud owner of a small stepladder, so after getting it for him, he then began attacking the tiles that were above his reach. I did ask him why he wasn't using an electric-hammer-chisel thing to do all this, and he said that they had one and it was a good idea. And then kept beating the tiles into submission. I thought I would observe his hammering style for a bit, but after nearly being impaled by a tile piece as it flew off the wall, I retreated once again to the land of safety (which was just about anyplace outside the bathroom) and went back to working on a client project.

After lunch, Elio returned and again continued to make more noise than human ears were designed to absorb. Salvador stopped over to check on progress – as bosses tend to do when they aren't making those big decisions, like which wine to have with dinner later – and told me that this afternoon (meaning about 1800h or 1900h) another person would come over and help Elio clean up the pile of broken tiles that were now making it difficult to even open the door to the bathroom. Tomorrow, they (whomever "they" means) will most probably install the new tiles, and on Friday someone would come to make the walls that I want to paint smooth enough to achieve the semi Venetian-plaster look that I am after. I am not sure what is taking place on Thursday of this week, but if this week is like most others on the island, there will probably be a holiday of sorts. This week's holiday might be a celebration for St. Elio-the-Tile-Breaker for all I know. But hey, a holiday is a holiday.

It is now just after 1500 (still on the first day of fun-with-ceramic-tiles), and Elio has just returned after getting an electric jackhammer thing. Looking like something straight out of a Star Wars movie, the tool is big and powerful, and probably capable of putting out several hundred decibels whilst acting like a weapon of mass destruction. I decided to turn up the music in the sitting room.

Pepe just arrived. I have no idea who he is other than he seems to work for Salvador too. After the usual courtesies (I speak in Spanish and they wonder what Spanish I am speaking), he said that he was the man who would put the new baldosas (tiles) on the wall and floor of the shower. Apparently, Elio rang him to come over to figure out how to actually take the bathtub out. Tony had disconnected the water supply, but hadn't done anything with the drain, and even I was worried about how to disconnect it. Pepe looked at the tub for about four seconds, and then took a firm grip on the exposed end and…he just pulled it out. A demonstration of either years of experience in removing tubs, or he has children who get into things they shouldn't get into. Either way, the bathtub was out. Progress.

Elio arrived on day two and began breaking up the remaining wall tiles at 0730 today. How nice is that? There is just nothing like an electric jackhammer pounding away so early in the morning, especially inside the house where the sound reverberates as if there were a dentist standing over you with a loud-speaker connected to his drill. I was going to say something to him about the noise, but decided that progress was more important than saving headache pills.

Suddenly, I noticed that it had gone all quiet on the bathroom front (a cheesy reference to Mr. Hemingway, to keep up the literary quality of this story). Yes, Elio was done breaking up the wall tiles. Of course this meant that now the floor was covered with broken bits of ceramic and it was time once again to get out the escoba y pala (broom and shovel). This could have been a good opportunity to fill up the carretilla (wheel-barrow) several times and make a huge pile of rubble in the courtyard as was done yesterday, but today rain is bucketing-down outside, and it appears that the plan of attack will be to fill up as many bolsas (heavy-duty plastic grocery bags) as I can find for to use for disposal later. I decided that I would be a good little assistant and help Elio clean up the mess, but had forgotten that the air in the bathroom was so laden with pulvo (dust) that it was almost impossible to breathe...so I went back to the living room to have a cigarette - don't even think about asking for my logic in this.

The rest of the day went right on plan (or at least it seemed to). Just as Elio was picking up little bits of ceramic tiles that he had smashed off the walls, Tony stopped over to see what plumbing bits he would need to relocate the water supply lines and desagua (drain). I was on the phone at the time, but Elio told me that Tony said he would be back in about an hour to make all the connections. That was at 1100h, and it is now 1900h and he has yet to reappear. Luckily, Pepe came in the afternoon and did the preparation work for las baldosas nuevas (the new baldosas). Tomorrow should be an interesting day.

Day 3 began, once again, at 0730 with the arrival of Elio and Pepe. Tony, large as he is, was nowhere to be seen. Pepe set about to begin to install the baldosas that would not conflict with Tony's plumbing work, and Elio set about to carry cement back and forth for Pepe. Right about now, I am very thankful I hired Salvador's merry band of workers to do all this as my back has been aching just watching these guys. I retreated to the relative safe area of my computer to attempt to get some work done, but within minutes, the lads in the bathroom beckoned me. It was question time.

Pepe wanted to clarify how far up the wall he was supposed to install the baldosas, or at least that appeared to be his question. Then he asked about the size of the gap I wanted between the baldosas – this would be the gap for mortar – and I said that I thought that it should be the same as the existing floor tiles, or at least that it what I thought I said. Neither one of us appeared to know the exact questions and answers, but we were all more-or-less understanding each other, and after all, that is what communications are all about. I swallowed two more mega Ibuprofen pills to counteract the incessant pounding of Elio's hammer, I went back to typing, wondering what I had actually said to Pepe.

Day 3 had begun as the others had, with Elio and Pepe arriving at La Antigua well before the sun began to lighten and warm everything. By noon, the baldosas were all on the walls and the fun job of packing mortar between the tiles, and then the always horribly messy job of wiping off the excess began. And then Pepe was done.

Saturday, the fourth day of reconstruction of the downstairs bath, and all is well. Felix came this morning, but as he had never been here before, and to make sure that he knew exactly what his task was, Pepe brought him over. This was especially nice as it was clear when I saw Pepe that this was his day off. How did I know this? Well, I came to this conclusion because Pepe was dressed in his pyjamas, dressing robe, and slippers. It was beginning to look like the beginnings of the Mallorquin version of The Village People, but I knew that a cheeky comment at this point would be lost on them so I kept my observational wisdom to myself. After going over the work plan –

James B Rieley

Felix is the one who will make the non-baldosa-covered walls smooth as a baby's bottom so I can paint them – Pepe left to undoubtedly go back to bed, and Felix began to mix up a huge tub of what best could be called a Barrél of plaster slop. I resumed my role as peon apprentice and started bringing buckets of water to him and then went to clean up the water that I had so cleverly splashed on the kitchen floor. By the time the bathroom work is completed, having survived hourly episodes of feeling the need to clean up the broken ceramic tiles that keep appearing in the most obscure corners; having survived the veritable dust storm that has been floating around the entire house like the arrival of a cloud of locusts; and having survived the various leopard-like spots of new plaster all over the floors where workmen have tread; I will have the cleanest house on the island I think. Right…in my anal-retentive-home-cleanliness dreams.

Felix had told me that I would need to let the new gesso (HEY-SO, providing a dead-smooth plaster finish) walls dry before I painted them, which did make all the sense in the world to me. So I spent days five, six, seven, eight, and nine waiting for the stuff to be completely dry. Well, I didn't just wait…I put a small heater and fan in the bathroom and then checked on the drying process about fifteen times a day. I suppose I could have followed the tried-and-true message of *"a watched pot doesn't boil,"* but I usually only abide by sayings like this when I am not eager to get a project completed.

At last, my new plaster walls were smooth to the point of .0003 microns. Not really – I just made that up, and don't even know how smooth that would be - but they did feel really smooth, and finally dry. I actually was able to paint them and install some trendy profiled wood trim along the wall where it met the floor and then spent several days waiting. This "waiting" period has been a real test of my acclimation to the island culture. With Easter fast approaching, I knew that things would be closed, which meant that besides not being able to shop, Tony would not be working, and as the re-installation of the loo, sink and shower plumbing being the only things that were needed now, I was anxious to be able to complete this project. But we do like our holidays here, and getting things done around holidays can be a challenge. Thursday was when everything closed, apparently to get ready for Friday's holiday. Saturday is a day that Tony doesn't normally work, Sunday was Easter, and Monday was, well, the day after Easter. Nice. By Tuesday morning – yes, the Tuesday after the Monday after Easter - I was beginning to think that Emerson was right when he said, *"How much of human life is lost in waiting,"* but then Tony called.

He said that he was sorry he been unable to come to complete the reconnection work of the plumbing, but the holidays and blah, blah, blah. He did say that he would be at La Antigua at 1100h, more or less. And then at 1115h, he rang again to say that he would be a little late and would now arrive around 1530h. Well, at least he called. I ironed shirts to kill time. He did come and he complete the work. Job done. Fab.

So the downstairs bathroom reform project is now complete and I am proud to report that the waiting siege at La Antigua has ended. Unless of course you count the fact that Movistar and Vodafone still haven't managed to get my mobile phone issues sorted. Asi es la vida.

If there is one thing I have learnt since moving to the village, it is that sometimes the older ways are the best to get things done. Good learning opportunities for me, but frustrating as well.

Learning opportunity number 1: **How to deal with pest problems**. Last year, whilst sitting on the roof terrace of La Antigua, I noticed that they sky was getting dark. This did seem a bit odd, as it was mid-day. It seemed even odder that the approaching darkness was accompanied by the sound of what seemed to be a jumbo-jet that wanted to land in my courtyard. It wasn't until I opened my eyes that I realised what was occurring...it was a huge swarm of bees. For a moment, the movements of the swarm dazzled me and it weaved it way across the sky, rapidly changing direction causing the huge black cloud to make swirling patterns that were most impressive. This moment dissipated quite quickly when I realised that the swarm was only 5 or 6 metres away from me. I almost managed to set a world speed record for getting up from the lounger and getting inside.

After a few minutes, the swarm had gone and I ventured out to the terrace again, only to discover that the grupo de abejas (swarm of bees) had entered an attic air vent on the house across my street. I felt compelled to be a good neighbour and the next day told my neighbour. Job done. Good neighbour relations. Problem solved. Or so I thought.

This year, the bees were back and I decided to escalate my approach a bit. I went to the Ajuntament (town hall) and reported the bees, and after a few days of nothing happening, I tried again. This time I was told that I should call the Bomberos (fire department) and they would take care of the bee infestation. On my way home, I decided to primero habla con mi vecino otra vez (first talk to my neighbour, once again). I did stop in, finding the family sitting outside cleaning their pool. Well actually, the father was cleaning the pool and his wife and children were watching him. I explained that the bees were back, only this year, they were here with a vengeance. Okay, so as I don't know how to say they were back with a vengeance, I told him that the bees were back and they were pissed off. He told me that he would take care of it very soon. Wonderful. In the village, very soon could mean anything from the same day to sometime before he dies, but I was at pleased that we talked about it (actually I was pleased that he understood what I was saying...assuming he really did understand what I had said). That evening, whilst doing some typing, I heard this loud sound of whooshing air, sort of like the mother-of-all-aerosol cans was being emptied. I jumped up from my desk (okay, I don't jump up for anything anymore) and went outside to see what was happening. It was my neighbour, standing on the very edge of his roof tiles, with a compressor-driven spray doo-wah filled with I found out later to be bee poison, doing what appeared to be hand-to-hand combat with the nasty little guys.

I had mixed emotions about the ensuing battle. From one perspective, I was happy that he was doing something about the bees, but from another perspective, I was terrified that he would slip and do a reverse-double-flip as he careened down on to my street. My fears almost came true as suddenly he dropped the spray thingy and began to do what appeared to be the funky-chicken. A bit odd I thought, until I realised that he was being stung by the bees that apparently were not that keen on being gassed.

He danced to a flat part of his roof and ripped off his coat and scarf, muttering something about being stung in his oreja (ear). Ooops. Whilst waiting for the bees to regroup (a polite thing for him to do), he began talking to another of my neighbours who had also come out to watch the festivities. Sadly for me, they were speaking in Mallorquin, and I was only able to pick up some of the conversation. What I did find out later was that the neighbour with the little bee infestation had been aware that there was a problem when his son noticed honey was seeping down through the ceiling in his room into a wardrobe! Well, duh.

After about ten minutes, he scampered back onto the tiles and went at it again, this time with a large hammer to break the ceramic vent in his wall that the bees had been using as a doorway to their attic hive. Teetering on the edge of the roof, you would have thought that his favourite movie star was Charles Bronson in Death Wish. By now I was contemplating what I could do to help. My options seemed to be, 1) be ready to call the paramedics when and if he fell of the roof; 2) go up on his roof to help with the bee assault; or, 3) go back inside and hope I didn't hear any screaming. The DVD I watched was fabulous.

The next night, he was out there again, but this time he waited until it was dark out. His reasoning was that the bees would be asleep and therefore easier to kill. Right, as if the bees couldn't hear the footsteps on the roof tiles and the sound of the compressor. By this time – this is after two nights of mortal combat with the little Kamikaze-like honey-makers – there was a literal mound of dead bees in the street, and a lump of honeycomb that he had dislodged that was the size of two human lungs. I decided that again, discretion was the better part of valour and went in to watch telly.

I can't wait to see what his plan of attack is for tonight. I just know that my neighbour will be out in fighting kit again because no matter how many bees he has sent to pest Valhalla, the following day reinforcements appear on the scene. I found out from someone in the village that in Esporles (a nearby village), exterminators managed to annihilate a bee infestation that resulted in 50 kilos of dead bees and honeycombs. 50 kilos!!!! (For those readers who do not think in terms of kilos, 50 kilos is the same as one-hell-of-a-lot of weight) Nice. Now I don't think of myself as a total wimp, but if I was the one with the pest problem, I would have followed the tried-and-true remedy; which is, call and bee exterminator and then go to a hotel for a couple of days.

Learning opportunity number 2: **How to determine what the weather will be**. My friend John and I talk almost daily, and there are times when the bulk of the conversation revolves around our frustration of hearing conflicting weather forecasts. The most obvious way to find out the forecast would be to look in the newspaper, or watch the weather person on telly, or what we both tend to do, look online. Looking online has several options: There are a plethora of websites that have actual forecasts, there are some listings that have projections of what the weather in the rest of Europe will cause to appear here, and there are a small handful of visible and infrared satellite photos that can be viewed, giving an idea of impending cloud cover. I tend to like the satellite photos, as they show the actual cloud patterns. And whilst it is nice to see the massive swirls of storms as they cross the Atlantic, it would require an almost 24 hour per day viewing to stay on top of what the island weather will be.

For a while I decided that perhaps the best online forecasts are the ones that actually have temperature expectations, along with cutesy little graphics of either a smiley-face sun, the sun with a small cloud obscuring part of it, or a nasty-looking black cloud with a bolt of lightening creeping out of it. The problem is that there are quite a few sites like this, and they all seem to have conflicting information. One site will say that the next two days will be sunny and warm, and another site may forecast overcast days, and still another site may have sun one day and storms the next. If that isn't enough, it is not that unusual to have the various sites have temperature variances of up to 5 degrees. This all seems a bit odd, as this is not an island the size of Australia and, as we only have one serious airport on Mallorca, logic would dictate that we only have one weather reporting station. I was thinking of giving you the web-site address for these various sites, but suffice it to say that their forecasting reliability would leave one to believe that they address names are things like: *"completely-useless-information.com,"* or *"what-a-bunch-of-bollocks.com,"* or *"we-are-just-guessing.com."*

My frustration about weather forecasting information really only is an issue in winter and spring, as the rest of the year it is quite predictably sunny, but the past several weeks have brought a veritable potpourri of weather. As I am having houseguests next week, I thought I should get to the bottom of what the weather might be whilst they are here, so I went and talked to several village locals. After several conversations with neighbours and shop-owners, I discovered that there was consensus: it was going to rain this weekend. Okay, fair enough. Now I knew, but I was curious so I asked the next logical question; *"How do you know it will rain?"* The responses to this rather brilliant but inquisitive question all seemed to revolve around something like, "*Because it will.*" Right. On my way home from my weather lessons, I looked to see if there were any tell-tale signs that I could learn from… like sheep standing on one leg, all reciting phrases from Don Quixote, whilst carrying mini-umbrellas. Nothing. I guess that sometimes you just know.

This past week, two friends came to La Antigua for a visit. Becky and Jeff live in Michigan, U.S.A, and are about as close to professional birders as I have ever come across. Their visit was a real treat, not only because I was able to catch up with them on old times, but also because I learnt more than I thought I would about birding.

Jeff used to be a professional bird guide who would take cash-money paying bird fanatics on tours where the main objective was to see birds that they normally wouldn't be able to see whilst looking outside the windows of their houses. This all made sense to me until I found out that he used to conduct these tours in places like Venezuela, Madagascar, and Cuba, not to mention all over the United States. Okay, so it was beginning to be clear to me that birding is some serious stuff. This revelation was firmed up when they started to unpack and out came the binoculars, telescope, iPod with speakers, and camera. This unpacking demonstration was followed by ay a trip up to the roof terrace of La Antigua for a cursory glance around. Yes, when doing serious birding, you do need a telescope, as often it is possible to see the bird you are looking for through your binoculars, but a telescope brings them right into your eyes. And what you can see truly is impressive, even to me. I was intrigued.

I had known from previous conversations that the real birding effort on Mallorca would take place on the eastern side of the island near Alcudia and Pollensa where there are some apparently substantial bird breeding grounds, but whilst trying to help me understand what the attraction to all this birding thing was, Jeff spotted a Blue Rock Thrush flitting about on a neighbour's roof. In what seemed to take a tad less than a nano-second, we all had our binoculars focused on the little bugger. Two things to note here; 1) I said WE ALL had our binoculars focused on the bird because even I had been drawn in by the opportunity to see what this was all about, and being an ex-boater, I still had the binoculars I had whilst living on Angelina; and, 2) my reaction time to a sighting was miserably slow compared to Jeff and Becky. They would be all over the bird in question and I would still be trying to figure out where to look…clear evidence of a rank amateur at birding.

The Blue Rock Thrush was pretty flippin' spectacular, and my level of intrigue was escalating pretty quickly. Jeff, in about 2 more nano seconds, had the telescope focused on the BRT (this is not what true birders call a Blue Rock Thrush, but I am getting lazy in my typing). He had brilliant, almost iridescent, looking feathers that seemed to change hues in the sunlight. By now I was getting worried that I was having too much fun so I sat down and just marvelled at my houseguest's ability to notice what was surrounding La Antigua that I hadn't even paid attention to previously.

Just before dusk, we set out in Amelia so I could show them some of the scenery on the back roads near Puigpunyent, but it didn't take too long for a request from Jeff for me to stop the car. So here we were, three grown adults, standing outside with our brollies protecting us from the rain that had materialised, listening for bird songs in the forests. If you had asked me two weeks ago if I thought I would get into this, I would have replied that birding was right up there with getting meningitis probably, but here I was, gobsmacked that all the twitting and chirping that I previously considered background noise, was clear and distinctly different, and to make it even better, Jeff and Becky were telling me which songs were made by which birds. Bugger me. There we were, standing in the rain, listening to and watching birds in the trees. The worked like this: Jeff would say, "there is a (insert the name of some exotic bird here) in that tree; Becky would spot it in the tree; and I would, upon borrowing Becky's binoculars, say, "wow, it is a little porky-looking-black-and-white-striped-brown-bird-with-a-red-thingy-on-its-head." I don't think that they were too overly impressed by my knowledge level.

The next several days, Jeff and Becky spent over in swamp-land on the other side of the island doing their birding thing, returning on Friday evening with a list of over 110 species of birds that they had seen, including several "lifers" (LIFE-ERS) When I heard that their list included "lifers," I was very impressed. Of course, my glee was only surpassed by my ignorance about what "lifer" was. Quite logically, a "lifer" is a bird that you (as the birder) have never seen before, and with over 10,000 bird species out there, I suppose that seeing a new one is a big thing. But hell, I was still impressed that of the over 110 species they had seen whilst on the eastern side of the island, none of them included a Blue Rock Thrush. Specific evidence that Puigpunyent is special. And to solidify my village's position as a good place to bird-watch from, the day after they returned to La Antigua, the three of us (yes, I actually was out walking around looking for birds, but at least I was in the company of two people who knew what they were doing) saw another "lifer" for them.

We walked along a village path looking for a Wryneck that Jeff had heard from the terrace. It didn't take long before Jeff produced his iPod and played the bird's song, which, astonishingly to me, caused the little bugger to sing back. After a few duets, we were able to see it. A big "tick" in the "lifer" category for all of us. Of course, just about every bird I saw with Becky and Jeff were firsts for me, but it was fab that they were able to see quite a few birds that they came to see.

I thought it would be helpful to identify the classification system used to identify bird species, but I don't think I was listening that closely to what I had been told. Instead, I will share the Dr. JBR personal bird classification system: two wings, two legs, one head, and feathers all over the place means it is a bird. Now having said that, for those readers that are not as cheeky as I can be, and do have a sense of what this is all about (the birding thing), here are some names of birds that were seen by Jeff and Becky whilst in Mallorca. Leonora's Falcon; Booted Eagle; Audouin's Gull; Marmora's Warbler; Golden Oriole (this is interesting because I always thought they were chocolate wafers on top and bottom with a white cream centre...oh, that's right, I was thinking of Oreo's...never mind); Woodchat Shrike; Hoopoe; Linnet (the porky-looking-black-and-white-striped-brown-bird-with-a-red-thingy-on-its-head) and the fabled Blue Rock Thrush.

In all fairness, whilst I was extremely impressed with even my lame ability to spot birds after their visit here, I think I will still keep listening to Van Morrison, Linda Ronstadt, and the Commitments on my iPod.

The past couple of weeks have been interesting in the village. I have been going back-and-forth with a local architect/builder over some plans I put together several months after moving into La Antigua (which was, as I recall, a bit over two years ago now). Obtaining permission from the local authorities in the village to make a change to the house has been challenging to say the least. But it appears that progress has been made and hopefully (hopefully being the key word here), and I can make La Antigua more comfortable.

Then there was the birthday party. Whilst living in Barcelona on-board Angelina five years ago, I was extremely fortunate to have met several very special people. One of them was Addy. And whilst most of us (the marina group of friends that sort of came together into a life-long friendship) have left our nautical ways, Addy and his partner Gilly still do have a boat in the harbour there, but also have a home in Andorra (yes, this is the part of the letter where you stop reading and open Google to find out where Andorra is if you don't already know). It was a very special birthday for Addy last weekend and they decided to have a little party to celebrate. When I received my invitation, I thought instead of going out and buying a present or a nice card, I would make something for him. Well, my little project took on a life of its own and I ended up making quite a few birthday greetings. Not your usual "Happy Birthday Addy" cards; I decided to do something a bit more creative. With the magical assistance of my computer, I took magazine covers and movie posters (and even had to make some fictitious ones) and inserted Addis photo in them, and then, as you might have imagined, wrote new (and terribly cheesy) text to accompany them. My initial plan was to make one per week and send them to him via email, but, as the adverts on telly in America used to say, "*A Mind is a Terrible Thing to Waste*" – I ended up making 44 of these little buggers. The party itself was fab. I flew to Barcelona and then drove to Andorra with friends for a very relaxing weekend in the mountains.

When I returned, I thought I should take care of some soon-to-be-pressing business here on the island. Like most countries, Spain has a programme of inspecting automobiles every couple of years to ensure that they comply with all the safety and anti-pollution laws that seem to make life more complicated that it might need to be. When I purchased Amelia (two years ago this month), I had made sure that the inspection process had been updated so I wouldn't have to worry about it until June 2007...which it is now. Buggers, it was time to have Amelia re-inspected.

I asked my friend Barry (who has lived on the island since before recorded time) if he would go with me to the local ITV station (ITV is the equivalent of the UK"s MOT programme). Barry, being a good friend who apparently needed a break from his ongoing house saga, said he would; which was very good for me as I didn't even know where the ITV locations were, not to mention I had no clue how the re-inspection process went. Yesterday, we drove to an ITV location in Palma and after rotting in the queue for a while, found out that I didn't have the correct paperwork with me. Brilliant. It seems that the missing bit was the actual registration title that shows that I own the car. I professed that the paperwork I had with me was all that I was given when I bought Amelia, but the woman at the counter explained that what I had was a photocopy of the title. Right. Even I could see that it was a photocopy, but that is all that I had received I said to her. Unless I could produce the original, I would be stuffed; which, with the current inspection sticker expiring at the end of this month, could be problematic.

My options at this point seemed to be: 1) Go home and pout. Whilst this option was highly appealing to me, it really didn't seem to be too bright; 2) Go to a gestoria (HISS-TOR-EE-YA), noun, a type of solicitor who sorts out legal documentation for a fee) and have them get on the case for a duplicate. Another intriguing idea, but it seemed like it could be both costly and time consuming; and 3) Go back to the dealer who sold me the car and whinge a lot. I went for option 3, largely because when I bought Amelia, the owner of the dealership spoke a bit of English, and his daughter was highly fluent in my native tongue. I reasoned that they at very minimum would be able to steer me in a direction to get this whole looming mess resolved. I left Barry and drove to the car dealership only to find that the owner and his daughter were both not there, leaving only a salesman who spoke Mallorquin. Right. As I don't speak Mallorquin, I attempted to dazzle him with my Spanish, explaining what had occurred at the ITV office. He replied that, yes, the photocopy I had that stated that I actually did own Amelia was given to me when I bought the car and that the actual original document had been sent to me a couple weeks later. Fine. I replied that I never received it and asked what could be done (as well as asking when the owner or his daughter would return). He mumbled something and then opened a file cabinet drawer that contained a pile of car titles.

Just about the time he was flicking through them one at a time, a customer walked into his office (we really don't stand on too many formalities here, like waiting for you turn) and began to complain about the warranty he received when he bought his car. This caused my man to stop his exploration process and counter with what warranties came with a used car. This little

James B Rieley

"conversation" went on for quite a while, and whilst they were talking in Mallorquin, I realised that I was picking up quite a bit of the back-and-forth banter. It was pretty clear that the customer was not a happy camper, and the salesman was adamant – used cars do not come with ten-year warranties and if the guy had a problem with the car he bought years earlier, maybe he should have said something sooner. Really.

Whilst it was great fun to overhear all the arguments on both sides, all I wanted was for the owner or his daughter to get back from wherever they were so I could get my problem sorted. Just as the salesman was telling the customer to piss-off, or so it seemed, I noticed that on the top of the remaining pile of yet-to-be-checked auto titles was one that had my name on it. Now I interrupted and, with a sense of glee on my face, announced that there it was. I never did receive the original title to Amelia (which of course meant that for the past two years, I had been driving semi-illegally. Nice.

I was back in business, so-to-speak. I said thank you for finding my original title (I always do try to be polite, and besides, I wasn't sure how to call him a wanker for not sending it to me two years ago), and then asked him (kindly) if he would phone the ITV location to make an appointment for me to return. He asked me which one I had gone to previously and then told me that if I went to a different one, and arrived at no later than 0800h, I wouldn't even need an appointment. Fair enough. As by now it was almost 1100h, I decided to go home and do some proper client work.

The next morning, I was up before 0700h (dead knackered, but awake) and by 0800h was at the ITV location half-way to the other side of the island. There only were a few cars in the queue ahead of me, so I was feeling pretty good about the whole thing. But when it was my turn, I was told that I needed to go to the office first to "sign-in". Scheisse. I manoeuvred Amelia out of the now growing queue and walked into the office with all my paperwork, including the original title to the car. This only took a few minutes and I was back in the queue again (but at the end of it). I sat patiently, wondering if Amelia would pass the emissions part of the test. Last year I had the engine oil changed by a local mechanic and at the time, mentioned that there was a rattle coming from the exhaust system area, or so I thought. He told me at the time that my catalytic converter was buggered, but he couldn't find the right one to replace it with; and then I had forgotten all about it. I was beginning to whisk through all the potential scenarios that I might be facing if there was a problem. Would they tell me it had to be replaced? Would they confiscate my car? Would they force me to watch Fox News? I was beginning to become more than a bit concerned when the ITV mechanic/inspector person motioned me forward. Ten minutes later I was through the entire process, and was told to take my inspection report and go to the little booth to get my certificate. Right. I did exactly what I had been told, only to find that my certificate said that my car would not be approved for driving until I had something fixed on it. Catalytic converter? No, that must have been fine. I needed to have my head-lights adjusted. My flippin' headlights. Madre de Dios.

Am home again now, after going to the Seat garage in Palma and having them tweak the head-lamps, followed by a return to the ITV station to receive a sticker for the wind-screen that says I don't have to go through this again for another two years.

I could only assume that Tippi Hedren and Alfred Hitchcock were about to arrive at La Antigua. Some of the other cast of the movie had arrived earlier when two Blackbirds decided to build a nest in the courtyard of La Antigua shortly after my birding friends had visited. After learning what I had learnt from Jeff and Becky, I thought the idea of renting out some of the branches of one of my yellow Jasmine plants was a fab idea…you know, sort of a back to nature, ecologically sound commitment on my part. Of course I have been recycling religiously since moving to the village, so the move towards a sound ecological environment was already in place. And clearly, all the green lushness of the courtyard was, after all, pouring tons of oxygen back into the atmosphere. But now I would have house-guests (so to speak) that I wouldn't need to take for long walks multiple times per day. Yes, the birds were here and I was one happy Mallorquin camper.

Several times each day, I would see Mr or Mrs Blackbird zooming into the courtyard, diving head-long into the mass of leaves that almost completely hid the nest. I was under the impression that this was becoming a major building project and wondered how they managed to get a construction project permit when I have been struggling to get one for the roof terrace. I also wondered if what they were building was going to be a proper home, you know, with little children and everything (okay, little birds). Well yesterday I found out.

I had just returned from the market when I opened the courtyard door, and there, in amongst some of the plants was a small bird. It wasn't a sparrow or any other of the raucous chirpy birds that only seem to know one song. It appeared to be a little Blackbird. Whilst I was quite impressed that I could stand there and watch him hop along, I don't think he was too thrilled with the concept that el dueño (owner, pronounced, DWAYNE-YO) of La Antigua had returned home. I wondered why the little bugger didn't just fly away, but then I noticed that he didn't have any long tail feathers, which, not being an aeronautical engineer but also not being a total idiot, I realised would be needed to fly. Clearly, he (or she) was the son (or daughter) of the Blackbirds. How cool was that, I thought; it was like living with the family on Leave It to Beaver or Father Knows Best (with the minor exception that Mr. Blackbird was probably out at the pub all day whilst Mrs. Blackbird was taking care of the family). Then I realised that – think about this for a minute – junior Blackbird was in the garden hopping around because he can't fly yet, which meant that he must have been chucked out of the nest. (I was quite pleased that I wasn't there when he must have done a triple-lutz from the nest)

I went inside, thinking that at some point he (junior) would find his way up to the nest again, and didn't want to disrupt his (hopefully valiant) efforts. This morning I saw that he was standing on the back of one of the courtyard chairs. Cute. Suddenly I saw his mother (I was quite sure that his father was still at the pub with his buddies) land on the chair with breakfast for the tail-less one. Well I am assuming it was breakfast as mum was jamming some nasty looking shit into the little bird's mouth. I stood there for a few minutes, content in the fact that I was having my tea and toast, whilst this poor sod was getting grubs or whatever you get when you can't fly. After having a client conference call, I ventured outside, carefully trying to avoid disturbing the little bird that was probably trying to figure out how to digest the alleged food; but he wasn't there on the chair anymore. Well, I should clarify a bit. He wasn't physically there, but apparently his digestive system was working rather well as evidence that he was there was present on the back of the chair. Nice. I thought about going back inside to make a sign on my computer that said *"This is not a bathroom,"* but instead just cleaned off the chair. As I was doing the fifth rinse, I saw the little guy in the bushes, but at just about the same time, I heard a rustling sound near the cistern. Holy Ornithologist Batman!...today there were two little tail-less wonders hopping around the courtyard.

Immediately I began to think of the ramifications of the fact that my courtyard was fast becoming a bird hostel. I could, A) Apply for an EU funding grant to make La Antigua a Bird Sanctuary – the rule makers of the EU are pretty daft, but even I didn't think they were that daft; B) Corner the market on the island's guano production – at the rate the bird population of the courtyard was expanding, this could be an option, but a very messy one; C) Stay inside so as to not disturb the birds – sorry, until the birds begin to contribute to my mortgage payments, this option seemed out of the question; or D) Hope that the bird-children grow tail wings quickly so they can piss-off. This option did seem to make the most sense so I figured screw'em and went about my daily outside chores with the hope that the additions to La Antigua had not seen "The Birds." If anyone knows how long it will take for them to grow proper flying tails, please let me know. In the mean time, I think I will go buy some more cleaning supplies.

Things are just about back to normal at La Antigua...well, my version of normal at least. Upon my return from a business trip to Geneva, I was faced with one of those mixed emotions days. The birds that had been populating the courtyard were not present. This was both good news and bad news. It was really nice to have them around and watch the little chicks bopping around amongst the garden plants, but it was even nicer to know that once again I could leave my doors open and not have to worry that one or more of them would decide to hop in looking for a new place to defecate. Besides, if they were still here, by the morning, I am sure they would have become stone deaf.

The festival season is upon us once again. No, the other night didn't quite compete with the extremely well known and usually quite muddy Glastonbury Music festival, but from the usual quiet inside the non-permeable walls of La Antigua, I felt as if I was on centre stage. And because of the acoustics, I just about was.

I have learnt to read the handbills that are posted around the village, and it was there that I saw that the evening of 24 June was going to be a live music party of sorts...and it would be held in Placa Son Bru. As you probably remember, Placa Son Bru is virtually next to La Antigua. The good news is that I can see what is going on from the roof terrace; the less-than-good news is that because it is so close to my house, the sound comes streaming in. Windows open, windows closed; it really doesn't make much difference. Two hundred thousand decibels gets through anything. (Okay, perhaps 200,000 decibels might be an exaggeration, but it can get loud)

About 2200h, I was sitting in front of the telly, watching a DVD of the *"Best of Have I Got News for You,"* and the music kicked in. Don't get me wrong... the music was good, but I was trying to watch the DVD. Shortly after 2300h, I had put the next DVD of the box set into my player and turned the volume up. By midnight, I was on disc three and had adjusted the volume several more times. When I ran out of DVD"s in the set, I went up to the roof terrace and watched the entertainment for a bit. Well, I watched it until I noticed that I was dead tired, so I came back in and went to bed. I do remember looking at my watch at 0200h and the music was still floating around the neighbourhood. I went to sleep.

Then today, things really returned to my version of Mallorquin "normal." I had decided a while ago to declare my residency here on the island, well, technically, this means residency in Spain. The whole residency issue is quite interesting and does have some very specific implications. The law says that you can only spend 180 days per year in any country without declaring residency, and as I have in the past taken this number as sort of advisory, life has been okay. But as I had purchased a home here, and am very happy being here, (and want to avoid any legal problems); I decided that I might as well make the declaration. That is some of the good news. One element of the bad news is that, by declaring my residency, I will be liable for the collection of taxes in Spain. Okay, not a pleasant thought, but as I do live here, I am quite prepared to do this – besides, this will mean that my tax status will be more clear, which is always a good thing. This morning, I went into Palma to make the declaration.

I had spoken to my new abogado (solicitor) here last week. I was going to use the same abogado I had used last year to prepare an updated last will, but decided to switch my supplier of legal services when I discovered that my previous abogado was the subject of some very serious allegations of theft and corruption. Nice to see his name on the front pages of the newspapers, but not exactly thrilling to find out he would probably be relocating to the Spanish version of Devil's Island in the near future. My new person told me that the process was quite simple (I always shudder when I hear this here – my idea of quite simple has proven to be quite different apparently that life-long Mallorquins). All I had to do was go to one of the government buildings in Palma, making sure to bring with me my passport, two passport-type photos, and the original of my Empadramiento (EM-PA-DRA-MEE-EN-TOE, a legal document that shows I own a home here). So this morning, thinking that the earlier I was there, the faster the process would go, I left home at 0900h and drove into the city. After a bit, I found the building and walked in the door, only to find that I was standing at the back of a pretty long queue. Okay, I am used to queues and have developed a good sense of patience in waiting, so this wasn't a big deal; especially because the queue seemed to be moving along smartly. After about 30 minutes, I was in front of the line, and when the clerk motioned to me, I strolled up to the counter, quite pleased with myself for taking care of all this without experiencing much pain. My expectation was that the clerk would not speak English, and my expectation was met. I told him why I was there, and showed him all my papers, and then he said gave me a form to fill out and told me to go to the next office.

Okay, so the process wasn't over, but I moved outside to find the next office, which was only about 10 metres away. As I moved into the line (government offices are well-known for having massive queues), a guard asked me what I thought I was doing. I told him that I had been told to go to this line, apparently dazzling him with my command of the language. Right. He told me that I needed to take a number to get into the queue. I asked him where I would find the number dispenser. He said that he had them, showing me a huge roll of tear-off paper numbers. And then he asked me if I had paid the fee yet. The fee? *"What fee,"* I asked. He gave me (another) piece of paper that had to be filled out before I could dish out 6.70 euros. Not an outrageous fee, so as I reached into my pocket for the money, I asked him where to pay. He said at a bank. At a bank? I didn't see any bank on the premises and was wondering if I had misunderstood him (which is always a definite possibility). I could see his frustration increasing a bit as he told me that there were plenty of banks in the area and I needed to go find one. Geeez.

Okay. I went off to search out a bank. My first thought was to find a branch of the institution I use in Spain, but after walking several blocks, I decided that I would waltz into the first bank I saw. After standing in another queue at a bank, I paid the money and walked back to the government office to complete the process of declaring my residency in Spain.

The man with the tear-off numbers was quite pleased to see me again (and I thought I actually saw some pigs flying past) and he did give me a number and motioned for me to go into the door. Finally, I was on the veritable edge of the residency process. I walked through the door only to find myself at the back of yet another queue. As I stood there with the other 30 or 40 people, I looked at my number – it was B38. The time was just about 1000h. By 1030h, I was at the head of this queue and able to see inside the interior door, expecting to see another clerk, just waiting for me to hand over my paperwork. Well, surprise, surprise. Inside the door was a waiting room, chocker-block with another 50 or so people. On one wall of the less-than-comfortable-looking room, was one of those electronic number signs that banks and other businesses use to call people forward. The sign said A67. Hmmmm. Luckily, I overheard someone ask a security person the question that was in my mind; "*What is the significance of the letter "A?"* His response made all the sense in the world. The counter would tick off numbers from 0 – 100, and then reset to 0 again; with the current sequence being the first one (A). When the counter would reset, the letter would be changed to B. Of course, it didn't take me long to realise that, as the counter was currently on 67, but with the letter A, and I had number B38, I was 61 numbers away from being served. Madre de Dios!

I found an open chair and sat down, wishing I had brought a book with me, or maybe an entire set of encyclopaedias. I (foolishly) began to calculate how long it would take for my number to be called. For a while, it appeared that numbers were ticking over at the rate of about one per minute, but then there would be lulls of several minutes before it would change. So what would I do? I would re-calculate (yes, this was the point where I realised that had I brought my computer with me, I could have put together a floating algorithm that could have anticipated and predicted how much of my life would pass by me as I sat there). 1100h came and went. 1130h. 1200h. 1230h. And finally, just before 1300h, the number counter ticked over and little red lights showed 38. I stumbled through the archway and sat down at the desk of a clerk, who, in less than five minutes, printed out my certificate of residency. Done. Dusted. So let's do a little recap on my day: I went to a government office (always a mistake); stood in a queue (boring); was moved to another queue (additional boring); received a proper bollocking from a security person (bad JBR, bad JBR); walked to a bank and stood in another queue (growing older by the minute); stood and sat in the mother-of-all-queues (**B - O - R - I - N - G**). Residency paper firm in hand, I drove home, firm in the knowledge that "normalcy" on the island means a serious dose of patience will be required.

Someone once told me that if something is really important, it is worth waiting for...or something like that. Well, I have been waiting a long time to write this and finally it is time. As you probably have guessed by now as you have been reading, I really do like La Antigua. It has been a pretty great place for me to rest, to work, to be creative, and to explore new things in my life. But ever since I moved here, there was something that I wanted to do to make the house even a nicer environment. I was lucky in the fact

James B Rieley

that I didn't have to reform the entire house when I bought it – when I walked in the first time, I realised that this is where I wanted to live. Sure, I have done some re-modelling; I have designed and built some furniture bits, made some lights, made massive changes to the courtyard, but still I longed to make one more change. This week the construction began on a pool on my roof terrace.

Of all the bureaucracy and language challenges I have faced since moving to the village, this one has been the equivalent of climbing Mt. Everest. All I wanted to do was build a little pool on the terrace that I could use for exercise (Oh, sure. And if you believe that, I have this bridge for sale too). I researched buying a pre-fabricated fibreglass pool; researched the pros and cons of putting a traditional above-the-ground pool on the roof; but in the end, it was clear to me that the only sensible thing to do was just build a pool out of cement and block. I had even gone through the effort of making architectural plans of the construction of the pool, but then made a mistake. I decided to ask the village authorities for permission to build it. Now in all fairness, I really think that this was the right thing to do, but it has added almost two years to my timeline and the actual work has only begun this week.

Day one of the project: the whole concept of "day one" seems a bit odd to me, as I have been working on getting this bloody thing built for so long, it seems like this is actually day 500 or so, but none-the-less, the workmen actually arrived this morning. The plan was to reinforce one of the walls first. This really hadn't been an issue until visit number 5 or 6 by the architect. He was exhibiting a bit of panic about the weight of the finished pool after it was filled with water, and at that point, even I was thinking that a pool falling into my guest room or the kitchen was not the best of ideas, so the workers were first going to expose the top of one of the walls to install some reinforcing steel rods and hormigon (OR-MEE-GŌN, cement). They arrived just after 0730h, and after a bit of explanation from the architect of what they were supposed to do, out came the heavy tools and the fun began. I hadn't been too thrilled with the start time being so early, but because it does get very hot here very early each day, getting as much work done before the temperature crept into the 30"s did seem like a rational idea. So the workmen arrived, and as always I greeted them at the courtyard door to introduce myself and find out their names. I was a bit caught off guard when they introduced themselves as Andre and Valdic. Okay, so we are off to an interesting start – my workers are from Poland and they speak a little Spanish and tons of Polish. I, on the other hand, don't know a word of Polish and my Spanish is probably on a par with theirs...but probably not with the same vocabulary to work with. Well, life is a learning experience, so off to the roof terrace we went so they could get started.

After four hours they had managed to beat the crap out of the edges of the terrace where the pool would be going. As the technical architect had told me, the workmen would need to dig down inside the existing house walls to get rid of any rubble that had been hiding there for the past donkey's age and replace it with steel reinforced concrete. This was the excavation part of the project, and it made me nervous as hell. They started with a hammer and concrete chisel, the moved up to a small electric hammer; progressed quickly to a monster electric hammer; and by 1100h had brought in an electric hammer that looked as if one slip would take them all the way to the other side of the world. I thought it would be a smart move to let them whack away on the walls whilst I retreated to the relative safety of the living room. Sadly, I didn't have any earplugs so I turned on some music, but even that was drowned out by the pulsating hammer, sending vibrations throughout La Antigua. Clearly today was a two 1,000mg ibuprofen day.

Day Two: my new Polish friends didn't arrive at 0730 today - it was because they arrived even earlier. Luckily, I was up and ready for them (in my own way). Within a few minutes, the neighbourhood was filled with the sounds of their monster electric hammering tools, pounding the perimeter edge of the new pool locations into submission. I was becoming more and more impressed by the work ethic of these lads as they broke rocks straight through until they stopped for lunch at 1400h. Whilst I am always intrigued by how things are done – and this project is no exception – I did try to not appear to be standing over them, trying to avoid them feeling that I was just the Spanish island version of Simon Legree, overseeing my plantation workers. By the end of the day, the entire excavation project was complete and they were chest deep in the wall.

Day Three: Well this day was a bit of a problem as I was going to be away all day at a photo-shoot on the other side of the island so Heckle and Jeckle didn't show up. My problem, not theirs I guess.

Day Four: The plan for the day was to begin to fill up the now gaping trench with new hormigon and reinforcing steel rods. I really did understand the need to reinforce the walls as I didn't want to wake up some morning and find one of the spare bedrooms not having a ceiling anymore, but it also seemed a bit odd that only two days earlier, the lads from Warsaw (or wherever) dug all the rocks out. But by mid-morning, the trenches were filled with steel rods and the re-filling process began. Yes, this was a bit challenging for them as they had to mix the cement at the bottom road, then have it brought up "mi calle estrecho" (Spanish for "a street barely wide enough to get a scooter up") to the house, then hoist it all up to the roof terrace…in buckets. I was both amazed at their commitment to "alternate" building technology, and the speed with which they were able to complete this phase of the project. By the end of the day, the trenches were full and Valdic and Andrek were dead knackered.

Day Five: Shit…the steel reinforcing rod for the bottom of the pool was not delivered so nothing was accomplished on the project. That probably isn't a fair description of the day, as I was able to go into Palma and buy the skimmer-doo-wah thing and the pump assembly. Besides, I was thinking that the actual construction part of the project would take a week, so I set my mind on it taking two weeks...this is, after all, Mallorca and most projects seem to operate under a different time system than I was used to before moving here. So whilst it is day five of the project, the lads have only been on the job for three days – I think things are going well.

Day Six: Vaudic and Andrej (I really do need to find out how to spell their names I think) were here at 0730h again and within minutes were on the terrace talking through the next steps of the project in Polish. Well I am assuming that is what they were talking about; they could have been saying how much they hate the Brit who thinks having a pool on the roof terrace is a great idea. Today's project work turned out to be double-check all the reinforcing rod, followed by building a small retaining wall for the floor of the pool; all of which was completed by 1000h. By 1100h, they were mixing, carrying, slogging, lifting, and pouring the new cement. And then as a real treat, Vladik, after dumping ten or so buckets of hormigon onto the floor of the pool, used the mother-of-all-vibrators to get it to settle. By 1400h, they were done and buggered off to lunch, coming back to clean things up a bit and get organised for the next part of the project.

Day Seven: The project is quickly reaching completion. Well, the main phase is reaching completion at least. The way I have been viewing the project is that there are four main phases; the planning (which was painfully slow); actually constructing the pool (moving along smartly); the drying phase (which I am told could take two or three weeks); and the tiling. As I need to go to London and Frankfurt next week, my hope was to have the construction phase completed before I had to leave, enabling half of the drying phase to take place whilst I am away, and from the look of things, we are spot on with the timing. When the lads arrived, I asked them what their plan was for the day, and was told that they would be putting up the wood frames for the walls, inserting the reinforcing rods and then with some luck, pouring the hormigon. It turned out they were wrong.

Days Eight and Nine: V & A (I have given up trying to spell their names) have been assembling two large wooden boxes, one acting as the support for the inside walls and the other for the outside walls. I think their work was slowed a bit to install the piping for the skimmer assembly, the water jets, and the desagua (drain). My plumber (Big Tony) was supposed to do all this but as he is from the village and a Mallorquin from birth, he seems to operate on an entirely different time schedule. Twice he told me he would arrive at a specific time, with the second time being only three hours late. Actually, that wasn't too bad for Tony, but it was pissing me and the lads off a bit. Having said that, V & A operate on normal commitment work time (and with a work ethic I am more used to), so their framing work was delayed quite a bit. When Tony did actually arrive, we had another delay as he struggled to climb over the pool wall framework – Tony is a tad large – much to the amusement of the Polish lads. To catch up, the lads skipped lunch on day nine (now that is an exceptional work ethic I think) so they would be ready for the hormigon delivery. At 1500h, a dead-twin for Danny DeVito appeared with his magical mystery hormigon mixer and the fun began once again. A little mixing, a little driving the slop up the hill, a little hoisting it up in buckets, a little somewhat careful pouring the bucket-loads into the wall space, and a lot of words being spoken in Polish that I didn't understand (but I think I do know what they were saying, and, I will let you guess what it was).

Day Ten: This day began as other days the lads were here, with them strolling through the courtyard door at 0730h, rabbetting on in Polish. I was on the terrace, trying to help get things organised a bit. Yesterday had been a bit of a madhouse, with Valdic and Andrec tossing wood and metal bits around, desperately trying to get the wood framing up before the hormigon festival began once again. But they did manage to finish everything up, but only after a 12-hour plus day with no lunch break. The term "work-ethic" does spring to mind again. The plan today was to rip all the framing off (desencofrar), exposing the cement to the drying rays of the sun.

This project, whilst being a bit complicated with all the bureaucratic complications of getting permission to actually build the bloody pool on the roof terrace, then having to contend with the vacillating level of nervousness about the entire project on the part of the contractor, and then sort of being trapped at home whilst the work was being done. But as the lads were only here eight out of the ten days, and they still finished the work, I am nothing but pleased as punch. The next step will be to have them return in a week or so to do all the tiling of the pool and then turn my hose on and wait until it is full.

And in case you were wondering (as I have been for the past two weeks), I asked the lads how they spelt their names whilst they were on their lunch break – a cunning plan on my part to find out what they really were. They both smiled knowingly, and in Spanish, explained that their native tongue (Polish) was a real bugger, and then told me that they were Waldek and Andrzej. Right.

It is August, and in Puigpunyent, August means serious summer is here. We do tend to have pretty spectacular weather most of the year, but August is when summer really hits. A good time to be able to enjoy the new addition to La Antigua.

Last week, after all the tiling was completed, I received a phone call from Juan's office to tell me that I needed to go to the Ayuntamiento (city hall). I, being a good little villager, strolled on over one morning only to find that my project permit had finally been approved. "Approved," I said? "But the project is completed already." Yes, they knew that, but I needed to come in to sign the approval forms and pick up my construction permit. I did what I was told to do, and after signing several forms, was given a moderately large sign with a number on it to post on my house, so that any roving building inspectors would be able to see that the work being done was approved. Right. First of all, this is a little village and we don't have any roving building inspectors. Second, everyone in the village hall knows about my project. Third, my project was done already. I thought for a second, and then thanked them for the approval and the number (although I simply filed it away with all the paperwork on the project that I had been accumulating since I thought it up in 2005.

B.P. (before the pool), I had a group of Oleander in pots on the terrace. One reason was to make it a bit more liveable and Oleander plants are pretty low maintenance. The other reason was to help me keep my mental visual in place of where the pool would be. Once the work was done, I realised that I really didn't need them there anymore, and all the plants were a bit much. So, again, being a good little villager, I met with El Alcalde (mayor) of Puigpunyent and donated them to the village. No, I am not anticipating a "Dr. Rieley's Oleander Park" or anything; I just felt that the village might like it better to actually use them in their ongoing effort to make the village centre a nice place to visit. Besides, this was a better solution than hauling them to the recycling centre to be mulched away. The mayor sent someone over straight away to collect them and now they are waiting until the weather cools a bit so they can be planted.

August in the village also means the arrival of the summer festival. Last year I wrote about this and I think I emphasised the fact that some of the events – notably, the rather loud rock-and-roll band events – took place in the little plaza in my neighbourhood. This year, it was the same. Last evening it was the Gran Nit de Playback – sort of a combination of American Idol or the X-Factor, Puigpunyent style. I was torn between going to visit friends (last year it was pretty loud, with the sounds from the various bands wafting through my open windows at record-breaking decibel levels (or so it sounds like), or, just walking over to the plaza and enjoying the show. The event was to begin at 2200h (things do start late here), so at 2100h, I decided to just relax until the programme began...and I fell asleep, not waking until the programme was over. Either everyone forgot their amplifiers, or I was just dead knackered. I didn't hear a thing. According to the festival flyer, tonight it will be the CIRC MAGIC BLUES FESTIVAL, again located at my neighbourhood plaza. With luck, I will actually make it to this.

Today was something called "VI MERCAT DEL "TRASTO" in the village centre. I knew that this must be an open market, but I didn't know what would be there. A good reason to walk on over and take a look. This village is incredible; it seems that no matter where you go or what you do, almost everything turns into a social event. Go to the recycling centre, and there are several people who have brought their discardables in, talking away as if they hadn't seen each other in months. Go to the market, and it is the same thing. I reasoned that by going to the VI MERCAT DEL TRASTO, I would run into some of my neighbours and be able to chat away...and that is exactly what happened. The market? It was like a boot sale for children...and it was very special to see all the budding entrepreneurs selling their old stuffed dolls and old roller-blades and whatever else their parents probably told them to get rid of.

Three last minute post-scripts: 1) The Circ Magic Blues Festival (which turned out to be a musical jazz-based group) was simply fabulous. If they come to your city, and play in your neighbourhood, you really should go see and listen to them; 2) I have been thinking about the idea of a Dr. Rieley's Oleander Park, and whilst that does sound a bit over the top, I do think that a nice wooden park bench amongst the Oleander, inscribed with something like "una sonrisa le vuelve siempre" does sound nice; 3) After the clearly stated waiting period of twenty-one days to let the cement cure properly, I did begin to fill the pool, and yesterday after returning from the market, I was in it. It was, as my last letter said, well worth the wait.

I left Palma at just after 1400 today (Wednesday, 19 September) and flew to Lisbon where I took a taxi to the port. I had never been in Lisbon before, but I had known that it was claimed by the Portuguese to have been founded by Ulysses, and that during the Second World War, it had a reputation for being a hotbed of intrigue and espionage. My invitation to go to Lisbon had nothing to do with espionage, but it was intriguing.

A consortium of universities had contracted with Royal Caribbean Cruise Lines to charter one of their ships to use as a university, and I had been asked to come along to teach several courses in business leadership. The semester had begun earlier in September in Athens, and the ships course would take it to Lisbon, Panama, Ecuador, New Zealand, Australia, and then on to China. My contract was to teach on the voyage segment between Lisbon and Panama, and I was eagerly looking forward to the opportunity.

After the taxi dropped me off at the port – whilst Portuguese and Spanish are different languages, my Spanish did suffice to get me there – I stood in amazement at the walkway to the ship. The ScholarShip (really, this is the name of the ship) was built in 1966, had been christened the Kungsholm, but after being sold, became the Sea Princess, then its name was changed to the Victoria, then to the Mona Lisa, and finally to the Oceanic II, before it took on its current name. Clearly, this ship has been around a bit. I wasn't amazed so much at the ship; I was totally amazed that I had accepted the opportunity and was about to step on-board.

In the past several years since my GBS experience, I have only stepped on-board boats a few times, and until earlier this year, those experiences were not that great. One of the left-over side-effects of the GBS is a less-than good sense of balance whilst on a moving platform, such as a boat. But I had reasoned that the Scholarship (okay, this will take too much typing...from now on, the ship will be TSS), at a bit over 200 metres long would be about as stable as La Antigua. Well, that is my hope at least.

I walked up the gangplank with my briefcase and travel trolley and signed in. I was given a photo ID card and shown the way to what would be my home for the next fortnight. Years ago, I did quite a few cruises, and I have seen good and bad shipboard cabins. The one I have on TSS actually is rather nice. "Nice" in this instance means spacious but has no correlation to its decoration. Yes, it is an outside cabin, but the port is a tad small and I am sure that it will remind me of watching a programme on the Discovery Channel about whale hunting. I am not sure who actually did the cabin decorations, but I would assume that he is now down below pulling a large oar to the sound of a drumbeat. The cabin is decorated in what best could be described as a cross between the set of Father Knows Best and IKEA – lots of blond wood furniture, but in very 1960"s colours and patterns. I will undoubtedly keep the lights low whilst in the cabin. Before unpacking, I went off to meet the technology person to sort out how to be connected whilst onboard.

I have just finished my first meal on-board tonight. Dinner every evening I was told was sort of a buffet. It was...sort of. I am sure I will have more descriptive terms to use after a few more meals.

It is a bit after 2200h, and TSS is about to be underway. For my overly anal sailor readers who like to plot out waypoints (of which I am guilty myself), I will try to do daily updates on the ship's position, beginning as we depart Lisbon. According to the in-cabin display, TSS is at 38º43.02N, 009º07.01W, on a heading of 264º, doing 15.2 kts, and seawater salinity of 35.97 PSU (uncalibrated, of course). If you are not a sailor, this translates to "blah-blah-blah."

Day two.

Interesting…this is my first full day at sea in ages. When I went to bed last night, I could feel the movement of the ship as we ventured out into the Atlantic and it was a very soothing sensation. This morning, however, things were a tad different. We were plunging along still at over 15 kts on a course of 248º, and the seas were lumpy as roller coaster. There was a plenary session this morning for all the students to reflect on the experiences they had whilst TSS was in Lisbon. Even though this really didn't apply to me, I thought it would be a good opportunity to meet more of the students and faculty, so I went. If you guessed that it is cloudy and rather cool today, you are correct. The student presentations were pretty much what one would expect; sort of a mix between *"it was a great opportunity to meet local shopkeepers and learn from each other"* and *"I had a conversation with someone at a coffee shop who didn't speak any English, but we were able to communicate. It was incredible,"* and *"yeah, well like some damn taxi driver ripped us off."* Right. At the end of the session, one of the faculty in charge announced that the seas should calm down by late tonight and *"for those of you experiencing sea-*

sickness, there is medication available at reception." How nice to announce and then send everyone off to lunch.

I spent the afternoon with one of the academic organisers, trying to figure out what I could do to add a bit of value to the programme. It seems that this, the first semester for the TSS programme, is a tad disorganised and the administrators have been spending the first week putting out fires (that I think they have started). So, being pretty flexible, I said I would do whatever they thought might be helpful...and then I told them what I thought those "helpful" things would be, as you would expect me to do. I also met with one of the professors who asked me to come to his class tomorrow morning to introduce myself and talk to the class about "business stuff." Fair enough.

Tonight was fab. I had gone through the terribly long and confusing buffet line – by now I had figured out that if I use one plate for salad stuff, and one plate for pasta and other stuff, I don't have to make multiple trips through the line – and found a table to sit at when one of the students at the table next to me came over and introduced himself and asked if I would like to join them. I did, and within a few minutes, we were talking about the TSS programme, business, and how they could learn more that might actually be useful. And if you know me at all, you won't be too surprised to find out that by the time we had all finished our dinners, we had a handful of flip-chart paper and a marker sprawled out on the table, identifying the dynamics at play in the on-board programme. The small group and I will be meeting again.

Day three

My Friday began with sunny skies, and a bit of a smoother passage for TSS. The whole thing about the lumpiness of the departure from Lisbon had apparently been quite an issue, as last evening, as I was coming back to my cabin, I noticed paper bags that had been placed on the passageway handholds. Not just a few of them; they were all over the ship. Some students must be suffering more than others.

We went relatively close to Funchal this morning, but there was no reason to stop. TSS has a relatively tight schedule and during the first week of the semester, it already had to make two diversions from the plan, due to students who were extremely ill and had to be put off. But now, everything seems to be moving along rather well – with the minor exception that if there is an overall plan to help students learn, it hasn't been made very visible yet.

My on-board life is settling into a routine: Wake up, do some stretching, take a shower, get dressed, go have breakfast, listen to the teachers and staff complain about the disorganisation, listen to some students complain about the confusion due to the disorganisation, and then it is almost time for lunch. Actually, this morning, I was invited to a class on Sustainability and did sort of a question and answer thing with the students about business. I then listened to their presentations about the task they had to do: Develop

James B Rieley

a sustainable business that produced some type of product. The parameter was that the business that they had to develop had to follow the "model" in some textbook...a model that probably would be able to function about the same time as pigs are able to fly. Even the class professor was mystified as to why he had to follow the textbook model, but this was what he had been told to do, so this was what he was doing. One of the students, in the Q&A exercise, asked me if I was familiar with the model and what I thought of it. As I was not contracted to teach any specific courses but instead asked to bring the reality of business to the students, as well as bring a different perspective on this segment of the voyage, I replied, *"It looks pretty lame to me."* Ooops.

The afternoon brought a good dose of reading and lying on the fantail in the sun, with the solitude only disturbed by the group of students who spotted a group/flock/school/gang/bunch of dolphins swimming along side the ship. As I was on a relatively high deck, quite a bit above the water, it was hard to see if one of them was Flipper, so I went back to reading my book. Tonight's dinner was followed by a "students night" of sorts. Everyone (well all the students) have the ability to participate in one of many offerings put on by the students themselves, and I went to observe the "languages" one and the one titled "Model U.N." The students that were coordinating the offers are so full of passion around their hopes and dreams, and this almost makes the voyage worth it to me.

Tonight's voyage update – yes, the numbers bit – is as follows:

34º12.22N, 022º15.688W, 14.5 kts, heading - 247º (sort of toward Panama), sea temperature - 23.2c (important if you want to jump overboard I guess), sea depth - 5230m (really deep so not a very good place to jump overboard), salinity - 35.84 PSU (still an uncalibrated reading and I have no idea why it is important to know...and if it were so important, wouldn't you think they could at least calibrate their measuring instrument?), number of variations over the past three days they have prepared pasta – 5 (they are quite creative), the speed of the satellite internet connection – remember dial-up connections in 1995? More tomorrow.

Day Four: It is Saturday, or at least that is which day we all think it is. The students are living in a time "zone" that is divided into "Blue Days" and "Green Days," a way to help distinguish which classes occur on which days. I think the ship's crew keep track of days in terms of *"How many days until the ship stops someplace."* I am not sure how I am distinguishing the passage of days on-board, other than my somewhat important plan to write an update daily.

The weather has improved considerably, and by 1000h today, the clouds that had been covering the sky from horizon to horizon began to dissipate and by noon, TSS was chugging along under the warmth of the sun. I am becoming more and more impressed by some of the students I have met onboard. As their frustrations about the organisation, or lack there of by the school administration, increases, their motivation to do something about it themselves increases at the same rate. When I returned to my cabin from brekkie this morning, there was a card that had been placed under my cabin door inviting me to lunch. The card had been made by a group of students who were involved in an ad hoc interest group on the topic of marketing, and the invitation said they would like to meet me if it was okay. The prospects of doing more are very interesting, so I appeared at the designated place at the designated time, and was bowled over by the girls' motivation level.

After lunch, I met with several more students who are desperate to shift the direction and enthusiasm level in one of the courses they are taking. Hmmm, this sounded like a delicious opportunity, so I will go to that class tonight and show them how they can use system dynamics to help them sort out some of the challenges of globalisation. If all that wasn't enough, I spent several hours this afternoon on the fantail of TSS, doing serious research into the processes involved in the darkening of cutaneous surfaces when exposed to certain ultra-violet rays. And whilst doing this very serious research, I also met with several students and finished reading one of the books I brought along on the trip. If I were home, I think I would have been ready for a kip, but here, I came back to the cabin and changed so I could go off and do some mentoring before dinner.

Speaking of dinner, I am actually beginning to like the meals on-board. Don't mis-understand me...they aren't all that good, but there is a good selection of all the food groups, and I have noticed that I am eating rather well. This combined with the fact that I haven't been able to have any cigarettes (I didn't bring any with me), would cause me to gain weight, but I think I am actually losing a bit. Good enough. After dinner, I had been invited (by some students) to come and sit in on their class on "Communication & Social, Economic & Political Development." I went, the actual professor was late in getting there, and by the time he arrived, the class was already involved in creating a better understanding of the dynamics at play in the system they were learning about...yes, they were looping. Fab.

Number time:

Location: - 31º28.85N, 029º47.78W,

Speed - 15.0 kts,

Heading - 245º

All the rest is blah, blah, blah

Day Five:

It is Sunday, and that means we are on day five of my little sea-going adventure. I have been a bit frustrated today because the satellite that we use to upload and download email is acting a bit wonky, or so we have been told by the IT specialists on-board. Their information is a bit suspect, as they work for the TSS company, and there has been quite an undercurrent amongst the students and faculty about the company and their ability (or willingness) to resolve some fundamental problems that we are all dealing with. Tonight I was asked by several of the staff if I thought that there was anything I could to do calm things down a bit (I felt like screaming at the person asking to just fix the bloody satellite problem), so I had a problem-solving session tonight with some students to help shift them from problem-sufferers to problem-solvers. Tuesday and Thursday I will be holding plenary sessions with topics to be chosen by me. Right about now, it looks like the topics will focus on how we can all help ensure that the good idea that is TSS does survive. This is of special interest to me as I think they will be asking me to come back on future voyages..., which, assuming my GBS doesn't get silly, would do.

Day Six...

It is now Monday evening, well, almost Tuesday morning according to the clock. Keeping track of time has become a bit tricky on-board because the time zone we use is whatever time zone we are in. When we left Lisbon, the time was Mallorca minus one hour, so that was pretty easy to get your head around. But as the basic track of the voyage is West-South-West, and every 15 degrees of latitude equates to a time zone, where we are now is Mallorca time minus four hours...and we will be gaining another hour probably by tomorrow evening.

There was a faculty/staff/student advisors meeting tonight. It was meant to be a social event, but for quite a few of the attendees, the topic of conversation was the growing sense that there could be a mutiny afoot. This isn't too surprising as there is quite a bit of discontent going on due to the disconnect between students and staff, and teaching and learning. I have been working with the students to help them figure ways to avoid a serious conflict whilst at the same time, getting their concerns understood by management. This is becoming more and more fun for me as each day passes.

We are really ploughing through the water. According to the Executive Officer, we have another medical emergency on-board, and he had to make a decision to either head back toward the Azores or keep heading toward the Caribbean where closer to either location, there would be a way to airlift the ill person to a hospital. It looks as if the choice was made to race westward.

Whew, it is already Tuesday, which means the end of day seven. The reason for the race westward was confirmed to me today – we do have a potentially serious health problem on-board, and the plan by our Exec Officer is to reduce any risk by getting as close to a hospital as possible. We have been simply skating across the dead flat ocean all day today, and it has been fabulous.

Wednesday, or in ship's terminology, it is a Blue Day. The people who devised the on-board programme for TSS realised that with many students on-board, and only a set number of course and faculty options, it would make sense to divide instructional programmes into Blue Days and Green Days. Logically, something like this makes sense to keep things more functional, but one of the side effects has been that if you ask a student what day it is, the answer you get is either Blue or Green or Off. Being on-board with coursework and activities seven days per week has shifted the student's focus from measuring (or realising) time in calendar days to instructional days. Very interesting...except when I am asked if I can come teach a course and, upon my question of *"when,"* what I get is a *"the second Blue day from now"* and I am still in calendar day thinking mode. I suppose if I were to be on-board for much longer than I am now, I too would slip into this way of thinking.

When I was asked to participate in the TSS programme, I had said that I would try to respond to any requests on-board for me to help students learn (which is referred to here as "teaching"). The first few days were pretty lean in this regard, as the on-board managers didn't do a good job at letting people know I was here, and what I was here for. As this was pretty frustrating for me, I immediately began eating my meals with students and talking to anyone who had a question. This technique has worked rather well for me as I have been quite busy all this week with classes and workshops – tomorrow (a Blue Day by the way), I will be teaching three courses and doing a plenary session on the dynamics of building a sustainable floating university. With luck, I won't get too many people cranky, but it might happen. There are so many little undercurrents that are taking place here – just the kind of environment I love to deal with.

Tomorrow should be a rather interesting start to the day, as we are expecting a helicopter to arrive to evacuate two passengers who are ill.

Thursday, day nine. The rescue helicopter arrived shortly after noon today. We had been steaming at a pretty good clip for the past several days in order to get close enough to an island that had the hospital services that our on-board doctor thought were appropriate. Well, actually, we were just trying to get close to almost any island. By noon today, we were within about 150 miles from Puerto Rico and a U.S. Coast Guard helicopter appeared on the horizon racing toward us. The aft deck had been completely cleared of lounges and anything else that might get in the way and all the students were kept back a considerable distance to deal with the prop-wash. The ship slowly turned into the wind and the bright orange helicopter circled and then slowly manoeuvred into position over the aft deck, lowering a service person down to the ship. The student were duly impressed and provided a sound round of applause, but then was when the real rescue work began. A stretcher was lowered, followed by a basket. Each time, after depositing the item on deck, the helicopter would pull back and hover about 200 metres off the boat. Safety is a serious priority, and by hovering away from the ship, the helicopter crew was able to ensure that if anything would run amiss, it would not harm any of our passengers. After a few minutes, one of our ill passengers was hoisted up in the basket, and shortly afterward, the other ill passenger was hoisted up on the stretcher. The helicopter came back in one more time to pick up the serviceman and away they went, streaking back to Puerto Rico. We simply resumed our journey to Panama, in the knowledge that the two students would now be getting the health care attention that was required.

It has been a very eventful day for me as well as the entire boat population. I taught four classes today, every thing from Global Strategy to International Marketing Communications to Cross-Cultural Management. And if that wasn't enough, I did another plenary session that focused on the dynamics at play in the shipboard programme. Whilst my body has been telling me tonight that this all could have been a bit much, it was a fabulous day, and it was what I came here to do.

A final note for today. About the same time we were having dinner tonight, we passed Puerto Rico. It was the first time in quite a few days we had seen land, and because it was so close, a huge number of us gleefully turned on our mobiles phones to relish in the fact that we once again had a signal. How anal is that?

Day 10, a Friday, inside the Caribbean basin. We certainly did make good time during the medical situation earlier, and now we are well inside the Caribbean basin. After all those days screaming along the ocean – many of the days during windless, dead-flat sea conditions – we are now bobbing along at a somewhat comfortable speed through swells that are only a metre or two deep.

Tonight was a very special night on-board. One of the student groups that have self-organised put on a Hunger Banquet. I had heard about these previously, but had never been a part of one before. The entire complement of students was invited to participate, and over 80% did come to experience what so many people live with on a daily basis. When we arrived at the part of the ship where the banquet would be, everyone was given the opportunity to pick a small folded piece of paper out of a bowl, with each paper having either a pink, green, or yellow spot on it. After all the students (and faculty and staff who also had been invited) had their papers, Arturo (one of the students on this voyage that has impressed the shit out of me) announced that if you had a green spot on your paper, you should move to a stage area where tables had been set for the diners. If you had a yellow spot, you were asked to sit on the chairs that surrounded the dance floor area in front of the stage; and if your paper had a pink spot, you were told to sit on the dance floor – no chair, just sit on the floor. The people who had green spotted papers represented the 1% of the world's population who are not affected by food shortages and who have an income of at least 9,000 USD. These people would be served a full dinner meal, just as we had all been having for the entire voyage to date...they could eat as much as they wanted. Those people in the chairs (the yellow spotted paper holders) represented

Living on Rocks

the 30% of the world's population who are not faced with daily starvation and who have annual incomes from 900 USD to 9,000 USD. They would be able to walk up to a service counter and have rice and beans and water for dinner, with the ability to go back for more. The rest of us – I was in this group – represented the 60% of the world's population that barely subsist, and are faced with daily shortages of food. We were to have a small portion of rice and one cup of water for dinner.

Saturday, and I really can't believe that we are almost in Panama. Well, that isn't exactly correct…I can believe that we are almost here; I am just not sure I want us to be here already. It certainly looks like we will be at the beginning of the canal by this time tomorrow (evening), but as we are not scheduled to transit the canal until Monday, this might mean that we sit out and circle over night…which sounds pretty daft to me. I am sure that tomorrow, all will be revealed.

I had thought that today would be a semi-non-working day for me, but as things turned out, I was as busy as I have been lately. Meetings with students occupied most of my morning; a meeting with one of the faculty after lunch; a course in early afternoon; some coaching before dinner; solving world hunger during the time we were scheduled to have dinner; and a meeting with the student government people this evening. Okay, the "solve world hunger" item…I had been asked by one of the student advisors if they could use systemic thinking as a way to better understand how to leverage the efforts of people who are concerned about world hunger. I said it would be a good application, so then I had to show her how to do it.

Sunday evening, after 12 days at sea, covering 3968 nautical miles, we are only about 100 miles off the coast of Panama…and the end of my participation in the ScholarShip journey. It has been a very special time.

After a series of meetings with some students who had requested to talk, I had a class today that I had been asked to help out with, and a little tutoring example for the newly formed student government. Then tonight there was a "Latin Fiesta," which was pretty over the top. I was given a hand-painted card signed by many of the students whom I had worked with which was very special, and some of the lads on-board surprised me even further by buying me a series of The ScholarShip stuff that the on-board shop sells.

I have managed to accomplish several pretty important things on this trip. First, I was able to make it and survive it. I had some serious concerns about how my body would deal with the movement of the ship in light of the GBS leftovers that have plagued me for several years, but other than several times, I was able to deal with the leftover effects. I was able to, according to what so many of the students and faculty have told me, make a difference in both the educational programme and the lives of the students. And, most certainly not the least of things, I have established some very important relationships with both students and some faculty people. This trip has been more than I expected, and I am very happy to have accepted the offer to come.

P.S. There is a short epilogue to this story. Outside of the occasional person who suffered from mal-de-mer, all of us that were on-board TSS from Lisbon to Panama were suffering from the same malady; the ability to send emails was horrendously poor. For me, this was especially difficult as I was trying to stay in touch with clients as well as friends and family. So when we finally arrived in Panama, I thought that my ability to be in contact had returned to what my expectations for communications had been when I left on the voyage. After getting off the boat in Panama, I spent one night at the Marriott in Panama City before flying to Miami. That night in Panama City, I tried to deal with the most urgent messages, but finally gave up, realising that the following day I would be in Miami at some trendy South Beach hotel where broadband would function at lightning speed. When I checked into the hotel in Miami, I asked if there were any passwords I needed to connect to their network. The young lady at the reception desk said that there were no passwords, and that all I needed to do was make sure my wireless connection was turned on. And then she apologised, saying that for some reason the hotel's Internet was completely down. Nice. It took them over a day to get it running again. I will be home on Saturday…where I KNOW the broadband functions.

My life has been like the first line of "Learn to Be Still" by the Eagles: *"It's just another day in paradise."* There is no doubt that living in Mallorca is pretty special. But when I moved to La Antigua, I knew that I had found a very, very special home. I can remember saying to friends and family that I could see no possible reason to ever leave. But as I am sure we all know by now, the only phrase that makes sense in our lives is, *"never say never."* I am, with a sense of trepidation, moving from my village house.

I have some friends whom I have known since shortly after arriving in Mallorca that have a home overlooking the sea in Bendinat. From the first time I saw their property, I realised that if by some chance I could live there, it could cause me to re-think my choice of places to live. No, this doesn't mean I don't love La Antigua. Actually, I am so very fortunate to have lived there. I have been equally fortunate to have shared where I live with very special friends and family. But part of the property in Bendinat came on the market and I have decided to see if I could find as much happiness there as I have found in the village.

Most certainly, things will be vastly different living at Sol y Mar (the name of the new house). I am sure I will miss my almost daily encounters with the villagers whom I have come to know and talk with. I will also miss walking to Balthazar and Gilles's market and my "interesting" conversations with them. Whilst we always talk about the village, the weather, what is going on in the world, I have always been convinced that after I leave their market, they stand there and wonder about my Spanish grammar; even if whilst we are talking, they do understand me and I understand them.

But Sol y Mar is very special too. Quite a bit smaller than La Antigua, what Sol y Mar has that La Antigua will never have is the fact that it is on the sea. I think what sent me over the decision-making edge was my recent voyage from Lisbon to Panama. It has been several years since I have been able to be on a boat since my little GBS episode, and I agreed to the voyage with a real sense of trepidation. And whilst the trip was very special from the standpoint of being able to spend a couple of weeks with post-graduate students who were so eager to learn, what really made the voyage special was the fact that I was once again on the water. This may not make sense to those of you who have never lived on-board a boat, but there is an incredible feeling of looking out across the sea at the horizon, and for as far as you can see, all that is there is the horizon.

When I began writing, I spoke about the fact that I will never probably completely realise my vision, but being there isn't really that important. It is like the horizon – regardless of how much you try to reach the horizon, it is always out there, always out of reach, always a constant in one's life. My move to Sol y Mar won't get me any closer to the horizon…but I certainly will be able to see it more clearly. And that has to be a good thing.

2008

It is a new year already. It seems like the years are going whizzing past at breakneck speed lately, and I suppose that is okay. Since I wrote last, quite a bit has been happening here, and because I haven't written in a while, I thought I had better get my fingers clicking away.

I thought that whilst I was waiting to rent out La Antigua, I would spend a few days there, then a few days at Sol y Mar. It hasn't worked out that way. I have been out to La Antigua every couple of days, but usually only to check the post, sweep the courtyard, and make sure that the house is okay. Then it has been back to Sol y Mar.

Part of the gravitation to Sol y Mar has been the fact that it feels so good to be near the sea again, but part of it is also due to the fact that I do love projects, and getting Sol y Mar into shape has been just that – one massive project. In between my proper client work, the Sol y Mar project has occupied all the rest of my time.

I must admit, being next to the sea again has been very good for me. To wake up each morning and hear the sound of the water lapping (or pounding, as it does some days) on the rocks below Sol y Mar is perhaps the best sound in the world. Okay okay, so this is the perspective of someone who does love the sea and who lived on-board boats for quite a few years. It might be different for you, but it certainly has been working for me. Then there is the additional benefit of the weather itself. I had been told that Sol y Mar is located in its own little micro-climate, and often, when it is overcast at La Antigua (or even in Palma), it can be sunny and warm here. This bit of information has proven to be true. Each morning, I am able to sit out on the terrace and enjoy my tea, whilst being basked in the warmth of the sun. This does one of two things: it either gets me so energised to be highly productive, or it tends to make me so calm that I would be content to just sit and enjoy the view. I think I do a little of each actually.

Part of my big project of getting Sol y Mar put together in a way that is comfortable for me has involved putting something on the walls. I had thought that I would be able to take some of the paintings I had done at La Antigua and bring them here, but instead, I decided to just paint new pictures. Which I have done. With a passion.

I do find it interesting that my painting does seem to work in themes. When I came out of hospital four years ago, I did a series of big watercolours of plants. This probably had some subliminal connection to having another chance to be alive and well again. Then I dabbled with acrylics, doing some portraits and landscapes; and then I returned to watercolours and produced a series of paintings stimulated by the fact that La Antigua is near the foot of Galatxo (the tallest mountain on the island). But when I brought my watercolours to Sol y Mar, I found myself working with bright transparent colours and loopy-looking patterns. They seem to suit the environment of Sol y Mar, so most of them will stay on the walls here. I say most because I have made more paintings since moving here than I have wall space for. Oooops. The rest of my "getting the new house sorted" project has involved painting walls, building lamps and tables and other miscellany that would be pretty boring to list completely. The end result is that Sol y Mar is now home…and it feels so good. (Blimey, it is 2 January and I am writing this with my doors open and the sun pouring in)

Rafa and Kim (my friends who arranged for me to be able to rent Sol y Mar) had their woodsman friend Tomeo appear one day recently and Tomeo and Rafa climbed up several trees and whacked away at some branches that were obstructing my view of the sea a bit. Luckily, neither of them fell out of the trees, although at times, it did look a bit touch and go. Obviously, vertigo is not in their vocabulary.

My holiday was spent in America. I know, flying all the way to America is not exactly high on my list of fun things to do, but it was important for me to be there and to spend time with my family, some of which I haven't seen in too long a time.

So now things are back to (my version of) normal and routine. I have been able to avoid sweeping the courtyard daily, but have replaced that little task with cleaning the ashes out of the fireplace each morning and working on client projects. I would write more today, but I think I need to ring the estate agents that are supposed to be working on renting out La Antigua…I really don't think I need two homes on the same island.

Some of you may not realise it, but I really do "do that work thing." This week, I was doing just that. Yes, I actually left the calming warmth of Sol y Mar and travelled to Geneva Switzerland to meet with a client. This was followed by facilitating a two-day, highly intensive team meeting for one of the client's divisional heads. When I had been asked to do this, I said that I would be more than pleased to lead the meetings. It was then that I learnt that the two-day team meeting would not be in the extremely trendy glass office structure in Geneva, but instead would be near Megev, France. Which meant it would be in the mountains. Of France. In the winter. Where there is snow...because it is cold. Oh joy.

After flying to Geneva, my client and I left Geneva shortly after 1900 on Tuesday and after an hour's drive, were in Cordon, a very sleepy village-type place close to Megev. Megev (MEH-JEV) is a well-known winter and summer holiday location for the very fashionable people located near the foot of Mount Blanc. The hotel we all (there were eight managers from the client organisation and myself) stayed at was a wonderful example of a typical chalet-in-the-mountains, and you instantly had the impression that it was a very special place. Les Roches Fleuries has been in the same family for three generations, and they really do know how to take care of their guests.

The following morning, we all met in a meeting room in an adjacent building to the hotel for the beginning of the team meeting, and whilst I could go on and on about all the challenging things we talked about and did, to most of you it would sound like "blah-blah-loopy-blah-blah," so I will skip that and tell you what we did that night.

Francois, the head of the team, had arranged for some outdoor activities to stimulate the team. I always think that this is important, but rarely actually participate in them as I am brought in to do what I do and am not part of the team I am working with. The plan for that evening was to leave the hotel and drive ½ way up the next mountain for dinner. Okay, fair enough, that sounded harmless enough to me, even if it meant going outside in the middle of winter on some flippin' Swiss mountain. So we piled into two vehicles supplied by a hire company and drove down the extremely winding road from Cordon, past the town of Sallanches, and then up an even more winding road on the next mountain. Then we all got out of the vehicles (these were the type that have somewhat comfortable seats and heat flowing into the passenger compartment) and were met by three men in a somewhat deserted car park that had no illumination outside of the moonlight that was pretty much obscured by the clouds (that were dumping snow on everything). Luckily, the three young men each had a headband-equipped torch, so wherever they looked went quite bright...as long as they had their heads pointed in that direction. I was starting to think that this evening may not end up in the top 10 (or 20, or 2,000) of my favourite evenings, but I was there and I was going to have a good time.

The three lads packed us all into a retired army vehicle. I say retired, because it was clearly older than dirt, and army vehicle because it looked like the military lorries you see in the news used for hauling soldiers into some war-torn third-world trouble spot. This vehicle had multiple sets of massive tires, all wrapped in chains, to the point of looking like something from a mummy's tomb. We all tried to get comfortable on the extremely crowded bench seats that ran the length of the canvas covered (but open-backed) bed of the lorry. Regardless of the fact that the canvas top and the open back end didn't provide a massive amount of insulation form the cold, it wasn't that bad. Probably because of the fact that we were wedged into a space that was not that much bigger than a large (dark green) sardine can. (Hmmm, does this sound like it meets my criteria for a good time yet?)

We bounced further up the mountain via what felt like a show-covered cow path for about 15 minutes. When we finally ground to a halt, we were transferred to a two-compartment articulated vehicle with only tank-like tracks to move around on. Whilst it was pretty difficult to actually see – it was very dark and the snow was falling in what appeared to be a near blizzard manner – the vehicle did look like it had last been used in an Antarctic expedition. This part of the journey lasted another 15 or 20 minutes, and after grinding along, we crawled over a hill and came to a stop at a large snow-covered chalet. We all sort of fell out of the vehicle (and I am using that term very loosely here) and trudged along into the chalet for a traditional French-mountain-winter-chalet dinner…which was actually fab. It was after dinner that the team learnt about how they would return down the mountain. Francois had made arrangements for a group of "sledges" to be available, one per team member. Now in case you don't know what a sledge is, it is sort of like a mini tri-cycle on skis; and the plan was that the team would careen down the mountain on these tiny vehicles from hell. Nice.

Everyone in the team bundled up in their winter kit (they had been told earlier that they should be ready for an outdoor activity) and was given a headband torch and a sledge to try to figure out how to fit on. And then off they went. I had previous knowledge of the plan having been told by Francois when we were planning the meeting; and not part of the actual team, and being of sound mind (and a wimp) had declined to do the sledge part of the evening. Francois had told me that it wouldn't be a problem and someone would bring me back down the mountain in a vehicle.

One after one, the little sledges began flying down the "path" (and I use the term "path" euphemistically), with the occasional missed turn, many of them quickly ended up I a pile of snow most of them being upside down after their rather abrupt stop. I, the one who was still on the top of the mountain (1900 meters or so) and feeling quite confident that I would have a proper vehicle to take me down; then discovered that the vehicle that the guides had in mind was in reality, a snow-mobile. Oh good. As I knew I wasn't going to do the sledge thing, I was dressed in my warm and somewhat trendy topcoat, with only a scarf for additional warmth. Gloves? Don't own

Living on Rocks

any – remember, I live in Mallorca, and the only gloves I have are the ones I use to work in the gardens of La Antigua. Snow boots? Sorry, I only have Wellies, and I sure didn't bring them with me. Insulated underwear? HELLO? I live in Mallorca.

Okay, I got on the back of the snowmobile and the guide and I went racing down the hill, chasing the poor sledge-bound buggers in front of us. Being somewhat coordinated, I was able to use one hand to try to keep my coat tightly closed around my neck and the other hand being used to tightly grip a handhold to avoid being thrown off the thing as we ploughed along. Being an extremely courteous guide, we stopped whenever we encountered one of the team members that found themselves inverted in a snowdrift. Having said that, each time we did stop, all I could think of was how cold it was sitting on the back of the snow-mobile…in the cold, in the snow, at night, ½ way up the side of a mountain. (Yes, the term weather-pussy does come to mind)

Eventually we did all make it down to the embarkation point and transferred to the tank-like thing, which took us to the army vehicle thing, which took us to the cars, which took us to the hotel and warmth once again. Now, to be perfectly honest, whilst I will be so happy to be home again on Friday, I have been gobsmacked by the beauty of being so close to proper mountains covered with snow.

Yes, the return to what I consider "normal" has been pretty great. As I wrote, being in the French Alps was pretty spectacular, even if at times I felt as if I would run into George Michael and Andrew Ridgeley doing a remake of their "Last Christmas" video. Yes, it was a wonderful experience. But there is something about being at home.

I could be a bit jaded about this perspective. When I returned from the frozen tundra that is a skier's paradise, I found the weather on the island to be a bit more conducive to my idea of paradise. The sun was blanketing the island with 20c-plus degrees and after unpacking, I found myself just sitting outside, relishing in my choice of a place to live.

Last evening, just after midnight, I was back on the terrace, looking up at the millions of stars filling the evening sky. I couldn't help it…I went back inside and fired up my trusty camera. This sight was too good to keep to myself. There I was, trying to steady the camera on the terrace railing, making all sorts of adjustments to the normally automatic camera settings. After several painfully long-exposures, I knew I had captured the moment so I could share it. The moon was glowing, Orion was nestled amongst the other stars, all on a backdrop of pitch-black. And when I transferred the photos to my computer this morning, that was what I saw…pitch black with a speck of something that could have well as been a fleck of dust. So I cheated and went online and found a photo instead that looks just like what I saw.

I wasn't sure what I was going to do today. I had quite a bit of work to do after my client trip, but I decided that a break might in order so I went to lunch with two very close friends and then returned home to appreciate some of the miracles that surround us all. The Jefferson Starship had it right when they said, *"if only you believe..."*

I have started to feel like I am a coastal observer, sitting on a hillside, overlooking the sea-lanes as the boats of all sizes approach Palma, being on the lookout for those illusive submarines that might wreak havoc on the city and its inhabitants. Well, I could have been doing this during some war, but now I am just voyeuristically enjoying the view. On a good day (and I won't even get into what I consider a good day other than to say my bad days are something most of you might kill for after several months of winter), six or more boats are anchored out in the sheltered part of Palma Bay in front of Sol y Mar. By summer, I would imagine it would help if I had several more hands to count them all.

Things have been progressing rather well lately with the challenge of renting out La Antigua. My lovely and talented estate agent had brought over a couple who are currently living in the village, but don't like their current location and they will be renting out my home. With some luck, this week we will all be signing the rental contract and I will begin to empty the house. The word "begin" does seem a bit mis-used here, as for the past two months I have been bringing things to Sol y Mar to make my new home more comfortable and practical. But once the papers are signed (and the money is transferred...sort of an important part of the rental contract), I will put things into high gear. My plan (or is it "my dream") is to have La Antigua ready for them by the end of this month.

Between working on the rental situation and what has been a plethora of (proper) work lately, I have still managed to find some time to do a bit of creative work. Sol y Mar has quite a few windows, and from each of them, I have some pretty wonderful vistas. One of the vistas (that doesn't look directly at the sea) has been intriguing me ever since I arrived here. When I came out of hospital several years ago, my painting all seemed to focus on doing plants. It was almost as if whilst in hospital I took on the pseudo persona of John-James Audubon. I have no idea what stimulated this direction, but I suppose it had something to do with painting things that were alive, especially after having the less-than-good-fun GBS experience. So here I was, by all accounts quite healthy, back painting watercolours of plants again. Maybe it has some correlation to starting over again. Maybe it was due to some subliminal desire to put more structure to where I was. Maybe the plants just looked fab and I wanted to do a watercolour of them.

Not to change the subject or anything, but I just saw a bird land on one of the terraces and I didn't recognise it, so I quickly grabbed my camera...but he was gone in an instant. I did what any other person might do in this situation and I dashed off an email to my birding friends with a meagre description of the little guy, and within a few minutes received a reply that it was a Hoopoe. So, now I have two "lifers" for sure…the Blue Rock Thrush at La Antigua and now a Hoopoe at Sol y Mar. Just had to tell you.

I am all settled now. Everything has been moved from La Antigua to Sol y Mar. Almost all of the paintings that were hanging on the walls of La Antigua are safely locked in a secure storage facility. All the boxes here are unpacked. Now if I could only find my supply of Ibuprofen…..

It was Sunday, 2 March, and I was doing what any other self-respecting pseudo-Mallorquin would do who was living where I live. Yes, I was sitting on the terrace reading a wonderful book and once in a while looking up at the horizon under a blazing sun. The music was gently wafting out from the house, making me believe that I was as close to heaven as I could ever be whilst on this planet. My eyes began to drift down a bit, watching the various boats that were coming to anchor between Sol y Mar and the small island just off the coast.

As the anchorage began to fill up, I put my book down and started to pay more and more attention to the boats as they came in and dropped their hooks. It began to look more and more like so many fibreglass and wood animals that had come out of their burrows to bask in the sun. After a bit, I went inside to get my camera, as you do. It was then that I thought I noticed something on the shore of a small island across from Sol y Mar. I went back in to get my binoculars but by the time I had located them, I had lost track of where I had been focused on looking.

Feeling a bit like James Stewart in "Rear Window," I scanned the area, hoping to once again figure out what I had seen. I wish I had some type of turbo-zoom attachment for my camera, but then I realised that it is 2008 and I have extraordinary computing power on my side. My persona quickly shifted away from L.B. Jeffries (the character Stewart played in the movie) Besides, my leg was not in a plaster cast and Grace Kelly was nowhere to be found.

I downloaded (or is it uploaded?) the photos I had taken of the vista into my computer and began to do some electronic adjustments to the photos. My first step was to locate the photo that contained my area of interest of the dozen or so that I had taken. Step two was to crop the right photo so that what I was looking to find was central in the image. Step three was to continue to crop the right area, each time saving the resultant image. By now I had a series of progressively tighter and tighter photos, each of the same area, but with each one zooming in on the area. I had become the David Bailey-based character in Blow-Up, but without the nubile young things rolling around on a photo backdrop, and without the soft-top white Roller parked out front. I was like a man possessed; I had to see if what I thought I had seen I actually had seen. I cropped and looked. I cropped again.

By now, I was fighting the same thing that a traditional photographer would encounter; only my problem was the ever-increasing size of the pixels instead of the graininess that is inherent with film blow-ups. After an inordinate amount of iterations of the same scene, my computer screen was getting a bit blurry. Well actually it was my eyes that were struggling to stay focused and be able to interpret what I was seeing, so I went back to the terrace. By now, all the boats were lined up perfectly, with the gentle southwesterly breeze cueing all the bows to face the same way, almost as if they were all there worshipping the sun…which was what I was supposed to be doing. I took another look through my binoculars, hoping that somehow they had evolved from 7 x 35mm to something with the power of the Hubble telescope.

By now I was buggered for sure. I thought I had seen something, but couldn't locate it. I suppose I could have rushed down the hill to the shoreline below me and swum over to the spot on the shore, but I don't have a wet-suit and, regardless of what some might think, I do have a life. I went back to reading my book, but every once in a while, looking up, just on the oft chance that I would once again be able to see what was out there.

I just couldn't resist writing today. When I began describing the ongoing saga I was experiencing living in Mallorca, my intent was to only write when something interesting had occurred. No plan to write on a fixed time schedule, but instead when there was something that I thought you might be interested in "being here," even if vicariously. The past week seemed to meet my criteria.

A client group came to Mallorca and my charge was to help them assimilate into something that resembled a highly effective performance team. Okay, fair enough. That is part of what I do for work so I said yes. Clearly, the fact that they had decided to come to Mallorca instead of me having to fly off to northern Europe was especially tantalising for me. The week before they arrived, I had received several phone calls from the client leader, with part of each call focussing on the current weather. Each time, I marvelled him with the weather report – almost every time he rang me, it the sun was blazing down, elevating the temperatures into the low to mid-twenties. Shoot, it was so nice, I was wearing shorts and a light shirt and even then I was hot. It was almost hard to believe…here it was; the end of February, and it felt as if it was May. I was in heaven, and I faithfully (and teasingly) communicated this to the client. And then, the first week of March they arrived.

One of the planned parts of the several day meeting was a car rally. The client had made arrangements to hire seven upscale cabriolets for the event, and a route had been put together that went weaving around the northwest and central part of the island. When the time came for the rally to begin, the weather had turned exceedingly sour, with a strong wind pouring down on Mallorca from someplace north – which meant is was pretty cold. Up went all the soft-tops on the cars, and we set off to explore. One of the stops on the rally was in the town of Galilea, and if the wind pounding on the cars as we negotiated the incredibly high and winding roads on the way there.

Living on Rocks

When we arrived, there was something in the air. At first, it appeared to be almond blossoms that had been blown off the trees from the high winds, but then it became quite apparent that it was snowing. Yes, I will say this again, but with a bit more emphasis that might more clearly express my displeasure...it was flippin" SNOWING. I was gobsmacked, and whilst it wasn't exactly a blizzard, and nothing was sticking to the ground; but shit...snow... in Mallorca...in early March...damn.

Apparently, the whole climate change thing had run amuck. I think that all the ex-pats who have chosen to live in Mallorca (myself included of course) have become unbelievably spoilt with the weather we had been having most of the winter. And then to be brought back to reality was a cruel trick of the weather Gods. Hopefully, within a day or two, the weather we all have become used to will resume...or else I just may be forced to go out and order some more firewood.

Last week I was in Italy on a business trip, and whilst there, I stayed in a castle that dated from the 8th or 9th century. It was pretty spectacular, situated on a hilltop near Turin. On my way home, I began to ponder why some things last longer than others. Now clearly, the Castello de Pavona has had some work done on it in the past thousand years, but none-the-less, it is still there and will continue to outlast all the trendy and posh hotels that are constructed today.

I can remember when I lived in America, where, if you wanted to see old buildings, you would go to Williamsburg or Boston. Those buildings seemed so old compared to the ones in the city I was born in. But when you past the shores of America, it is quite evident that the entire country is filled with relatively new construction. I have lived in London (a city long before the pilgrims had a desire for clam chowder in Boston); stood in front of the Acropolis (a seriously old place) in Athens; marvelled at the remnants of mosaic floors in Crete; and climbed to the top of one of the pyramids in Oaxaca Mexico that date from 500 B.C. These places have lasted, probably far longer than anyone could have expected. And yet, whilst it can be quite inspiring to be at these past wonders, they are only places we have the chance to visit. For some, visit means to experience them vicariously through photos.

I think we all have important artefacts that are closer to home. They may not be some magnificent architectural remains that Tony Robinson has dug up on Time Team, but they are instead, artefacts of our lives. According to Wikipedia (don't you just love the fact that you can, through a couple of clicks, find out about anything?), *"an **artifact** or **artefact** is any object made or modified by a human culture, and often one later recovered by some archaeological endeavour."*

When I moved to La Antigua, one of the things I decided to do was change the garden areas of the courtyard, and in the process of digging up one area next to the house, I discovered several well-polished black stones. Then I found some more. And then still more. I was a bit perplexed how they all managed to find their way into the garden bed. I may not be the smartest person on this planet, but I have studied history and didn't remember reading anything about a glacier zooming through Mallorca, not to mention a glacier that deposited smoothly polished shiny black stones along the way. One of the workmen that were there with me saw what I was discovering and began to rabbit on that it was a sign of good luck. It seems that years ago, you would bury shiny black stones near your house to ensure good luck for the owner. Clearly this (in my mind) falls into the category of an artefact and I even brought them with me to Sol y Mar.

Whilst most of the traditional artefacts we have experienced are tangible, I tend to think that some of the best artefacts that we have ever experienced are those events in our lives that are indelibly etched into our minds. Discovering stuff from long-lost civilisations is pretty great, but remembering those things in our lives that have really made an impact on us is even better. These are the real artefacts of our lives.

Some wise man once said that the only thing that is constant in our lives is change. This wise man, probably some money-hungry consultant out hustling for work, interestingly was probably right. In our lives, or more appropriately, in my life, I have seen so many things change. And whilst I would like to think that most of the changes we have experienced are positive ones, the reality is that they are not better or worse, just different.

Take this for an example. I was just doing some research for an upcoming business piece I am writing. If I would have been writing this stuff years ago, I would have trudged off to the library to get the information I was after, but today I just Googled what I was after and 32-kazillion links flashed onto my computer screen (something else we didn't have all that many years ago. As I was gleaning the links, I saw a news-story about a new discovery by the Hubble Telescope. Shoot, I can remember when I had a telescope. With a massive 4" Barrél, my telescope was able to, on a clear night, see thousands of little white twinkling stars in the night sky. And now we have the Hubble doo-wah machine sitting God-knows how are up in space, seeing stuff that, according to the story, is 63 light-years away from Earth.

I was damn-near exhausted after reading how some scientists found methane and water in the atmosphere of some turbo-distant planet, especially when one of the scientists who had analysed the discovery was quoted as saying that the discovery was *"a crucial stepping stone to eventually characterising pre-biotic molecules on planets where life exists."* Right. The article continued by mentioning that one expert *"praised the work but said she would want more proof."* Really? Gee.

Even though I was a bit interested in the real message behind the article, I decided that if I kept reading about changes of that magnitude, I might hurt my slowly turning-to-mush brain, so I began to do something else. I was

Living on Rocks

going to go outside to enjoy the day, but I thought if I did this, then I would feel compelled to tell you all about it, and I have been told that my never-ending references to the weather here are not that exciting to read about so I won't. (about 21c, sunny, a few light clouds...no change there)

I suppose I could have embarked on some massive artistic project. I like art projects. They stimulate my thinking – what the scope of the project is; how best to accomplish it; what resources I need to apply to the project; and how all of humanity will be better off by my contribution to the world of art. But it didn't take long for me to realise that I didn't have any 15cm diameter white PVC tubing on hand, so I scrapped that idea.

Pondering my options, I thought; I reflected; I wondered how best to utilise a day off in Mallorca. The stores are all closed, so I had to come up with some project that I could do with stuff I had around the house. With Dusty Springfield wafting throughout Sol y Mar, I finally hit on what I should do. I would chuck the whole idea of doing something creative and go to lunch.

I would like to believe that in my life, I have learnt many things; some of them being very important. One of the most important things I have learnt is to always have a project to work on. My projects seem to run the gambit from proper client work to writing to doing creative things to keeping my life organised. Now what I find interesting is that I am able to move from project to project almost seamlessly. I have friends who are mystified as to why I am so project focussed; but my thought is that if I didn't have all these projects coming in and out of my life, I wouldn't know what to do with my time. I could probably spend a lot of time reading, but I would rather write. I could visit museums, but would rather paint. I could sit back and ponder the life I have chosen, but would rather work with clients. I could just do nothing, but I like to keep busy. Lately, my project chromosome has been in overdrive.

For some reason, before I actually begin to work on a project, I am able to have quite a clear picture of what the outcome will be. If I don't have the clear picture, I just don't begin. When I was contracted in 2006 to write three books for the Telegraph, I was able to "see" the completed book before I sat down and turned on my computer. Okay, so that isn't exactly accurate. My computer is ALWAYS turned on, but the part about seeing the finished books before I began was spot on.

For some time, I have had a very clear picture of something I wanted to make. This wasn't just another watercolour or acrylic painting, but instead it was a piece of sculpture. A big piece of sculpture. So after scouting around for the materials for the piece, I finally found them yesterday and today managed to finish the piece. Now the real trick will be to move the 2 x 2 x 2 metre piece a bit closer to where it will reside on the front terrace.

Then there was the relic I found when I moved into Sol y Mar. When I moved here, I found several spikey-things hanging from various points in and outside the house. I asked Kim what these were and she said they had been left by Naylene and Phil when they moved out a few years ago. Looking a bit like a shrunken head with electrodes all over it, they were, according to Kim, a natural way to keep flies away during summer. Okay, obviously this was something that was beyond my previous comprehension, but I am always open to learning new things. And this did seem like a good project, so as summer is fast approaching, I thought I would get with it. (Take notes; you could do this too). When I was doing my marketing today, I bought a spare bag of not-that-great-looking oranges and a bottle of clavos (cloves). After putting everything away, I opened the bottle and attacked one of the oranges, inserting the clavos through the skin all around the orange. I was going to put the clavos in the orange in some intricate pattern, but after the first 30-or-so, I decided to just stick them in wherever there was some space. Then tie the now firmly impaled orange to a string and hang it up. Easy-peasy.

I was about to begin a new project, but instead, thought that I deserved a vista-break and instead just admired the view from the sitting-room terrace just before a storm came racing through.

When I was young, I can remember my parents sending me off to have some aptitude tests. I think my father was thrilled when the results came back. I was told that I had good hand-eye coordination and a high aptitude for doing things with my hands. At the time I wasn't sure if that meant that I would be spending my life changing tires or digging ditches, but as things turned out, I think the tester-people were pretty much on target. I do like doing things that require good hand-eye coordination, and for me, that means spending some of my non-working time creating artsy stuff.

I (foolishly) thought when I moved to Sol y Mar that the new house would give me many opportunities to do so. Whilst being here has been highly motivating, it hasn't worked out as well as I thought. The motivation part is spot on – the weather at La Antigua was incredible, but at Sol y Mar it is incredible-er (is that even a word? Probably not, but you do get the point) due to it being smack in the middle of a micro-climate area. As for the actual doing new stuff, I seem to have produced more output than my walls can find space for. So, being of sound mind and body, I have adjusted my view of where to put things a bit.

I have previously mentioned some of the graphic art projects I have done, and I talked a bit about the rather large PVC tube sculpture that now resides on my front terrace. Well, making "Esteban Tenia Razon" was so much fun that this week I was at it again.

Back when I had the plastics company, my sons and I would scavenge through some of the scrap bins at the company during their summer vacation. We would look for cut-offs of fabricated and moulded parts, and then take them home and put them together and hang them on walls at home.

Interestingly enough, many friends just assumed I was spending serious money on these "artworks." Time has changed everything. I no longer have a plastics company where I can find cut-off pieces of stuff to re-create, so now I keep my eyes open for "stuff" that I can use to re-create into other "stuff." This week I was able to find something that was perfect.

A couple of years ago, I had make something I titled Gordian Beginnings, and the new piece was a logical complement...well I think it was logical. Besides, what I wanted to make was going to be way too big for the inside of the house but I did have a nice corner near the front door that was beckoning for something more creative than just another plant. After I finished it, I was pondering what to call it, and wanted to avoid just calling it "bendy-aluminium-tubing-doo-wah-thing," so after hearing from David about the new addition to his home, I sort of appropriated the same name they gave their daughter...oh, sorry...their cat. It is big, and it is shiny aluminium tubing, and it is now called Madeline-Sparkle-Pants. Well, it made sense to me at the time.

Then there was the other piece I made this week. This one is an inside piece, and whilst I did put it up so I could see it, it won't stay at Sol y Mar. A good friend had asked me if I would consider doing a picture of her son, and not wanting to do anything boring, I had asked her for several photos of him. "Rafael" was good for me to make as it involved many of the things I like. After applying some creativity, some geometry, some maths, and a lot of very smelly adhesive and it was done.

The other day I received an email from a good friend, and in it, he was telling me that he had overrun his hard drive capacity in his computer. Or maybe it was his digital camera. After reading this, I started thinking about what we all have taken for granted.

I can remember quite clearly (I think) when I had my first computer and it had a massive storage capacity for information...on an audio-cassette. And then it wasn't too long before some bright person came up with the idea of storing information on floppy-disks. Of course, in those days, a floppy disk was a bit over 5" in diameter, and as I recall, the amount of stuff you would be able to keep on one of these was 256,000 doo-wah bits or bytes or something. Then we went to smaller disks, then to CD-ROMs, to memory stick-things, to little chip-like things in digital cameras that can store shed-loads of photos on something that is only a couple of centimetres square. How times have changed. To me, what is even more amazing is that we just assume that the fact that one of those little postage-stamp sized storage chip thingy's have as much ability to store things as God-knows-how-many of those old floppy disks. And even though tomorrow will probably result in another massive jump in innovation for our computers, we just assume that this is the way things are. How soon we forget.

This thinking was probably stimulated by the fact that in the past several days, I have been re-reading some old family letters. By "old," I mean seriously old. In 2005, the best friend of an Aunt of mine sent me a serious treasure trove of family documents that my Aunt had before she passed away. Amongst the box were several sets of letters from family relatives that were their own version of my writings. Except in this case, they were letters written home whilst serving in the army during the American Civil War. Over the weekend I received another set, this time coming from a relative I didn't even know I had. Whilst I had read the letters when Sue first sent them to me, it was a good thing to re-read the set that Betsy had sent. It was whilst reading this treasure trove of information that I realised that we probably don't really appreciate all we have today.

The letters, written by both Frank and John Rieley who were both in the Union Army but serving in two different units, were written to their family to both keep them abreast with what was going on at the front and to let them know they were still alive. Whilst many of the letters relate just "stuff" about being where they were, some of them tell of serious exploits (Frank at one point had been captured and managed to escape from the enemy). It was also clear that there were two common themes in all the letters.

One theme was the almost desperate desire to hear from their family at home. The other theme was that they often didn't even have enough money to buy *paper, envelopes or stamps* to send the letters home. They couldn't call home because it was eleven years after the end of the Civil War that Mr. Bell finally figured out how to get his phone idea to work. They couldn't send an email home because it was almost another 100 years before someone sorted that out.

How times have changed. Today, we don't even think twice about whipping out a letter, although today we do it through the magic of email. We have the ability to send photos and videos back and forth electronically (from our mobile phones if we want) with no more effort than it takes to make a few clicks. 150 years ago, the best case scenario was to find someone who even had a camera and then wait until the image could be etched onto a thin steel plate and then have to post it…and then wait the several weeks it would take to arrive, assuming it actually did arrive. If you wanted to find out what was going on, now we just click on some news website. Then you had to find someone who actually had a newspaper or wait for a letter from home. When the Rieley boys went home after the war, it took them several weeks; the last time I flew back to America to spend time with my sons, it took nine hours. And yet, there I was, whinging about the time it took me. I think we often forget that whilst we have problems, we also forget what other people's problems were…and are.

I think we take so much for granted, and perhaps we shouldn't. Yes, it is 2008 and things are different than they were in 1863, and at the rate that technology is evolving, I cannot even imagine what things will be like for my grandchildren...and what their expectations will be because of it. At least they will be able to learn, through the letters and photos that my family has saved, that life has not always been as it is for them.

"The London Review of Books has been dedicated to carrying on the tradition of the English essay. In this respect, it is not very different from one of the great 19th-century periodicals. It gives its contributors the space and freedom to develop their ideas at length and in depth." This is the published description of a gift I received last autumn from my brother.

Whilst appreciating his thought of the subscription, I wondered at the time why he did this, but over the past 6 months, I have thoroughly enjoyed the myriad of book selections and essays that have been highlighted in the Review. A very good gift indeed. This morning I was trolling through the latest issue and came across a section at the back of it that had a series of adverts. I have no idea why I never noticed this section before, but there it was so I kept reading. As my "bucket-list" still has some things in it that relate to travel, I skipped past the "Specialist Booksellers," the "Out-of-Print Books," the "Readers Requests" and even the "Secretarial Services" and zeroed in on "Holidays." I thought it would be interesting to see what the holiday options were that might seem like interesting options for me.

"Pottery in Southern France. Short courses from May with Raku firing." Sorry, I have already done my pottery time, so that one didn't attract my attention too much.

"Sicily, Cefalu, delightful historic town. Two room flat, town centre, extraordinary view overlooking sea." Hey, I overlook the sea now, and according to my trendy map, it is the same sea. No thanks.

"Pollensa Mallorca, charming secluded spacious cottage to let." I live in Mallorca now so even the thought of going on holiday to the other side of the island did seem a bit ludicrous.

"Gozo, the hidden gem of the Mediterranean with cheap flights from the U.K. Luxury apartment with pool." Gozo must be hidden pretty well as I have never even heard of it. I will pass on that one too.

I did manage to go through the entire list, but all the adverts seem to have the same usage of pimply-hyperboles trying to let out their properties to somebody who wants to flee wherever they currently live for a while. I, on the other hand, am quite content to be where I live. I was about to fold up the Review and look at what else came in the post, but then my eyes drifted over to the next column of adverts. These were labelled, "Personals." I thought that I would share them some of them with you. I have, to avoid being yelled at (or worse) by the publisher of the Review, removed all the reply Box numbers.

"I've spent my adult life fabricating reciprocal feelings from others and I don't intend to stop now, nor at any other London Review Bookshop even I'm summarily ejected from. Yes, once the history section had emptied and we were left

alone his voice said, "I'm not interested," but his eyes very clearly stated "please follow me home and observe me from the shrubs in the park opposite until squirrels start to burrow into your legs, believing you to be a tree." Woman, 43. Reading between the lines even when the lines aren't actually there. Don't pretend you don't love me."

The next one was even more curious.

"As it happens, 11:34a.m two weeks next Friday is the first day of the rest of my life. Nuclear physicist (M, 40) on the brink of time-travel breakthrough. Write now to box no. XX but be aware that by the time I reply to you will be 98 whereas I will have aged just 12 hours. You may have a good-looking granddaughter by then though. Give her my number and tell her to look me up."

Some of the adverts did seem rather intense, but some were dead-straight to the point (whatever point the writer was attempting to make).

"This personal ad is the product of an entire evening spent eating acid. Man, 63."

Then there was this one. "The low resolution personal ad. When viewed from a distance it looks amazing, but up close its pretty poor. Man, 35, Gwent."

And then there was this man who didn't mess about. "Everyone in this column has an agenda. Not me. Man, 41."

This one must have been written by someone with very high expectations. "There aren't enough hours in the day for me to make love to all the women I want to make love to, so I'm going to start with you, nubile 21-years old choreographer and tantric masseuse, preferably French or able to adopt a French accent or not talk at all. Must know how to spoon-feed. Man, 78."

But this is the advert that should win the award…for something. "*The rumours are true! A scintillating love monkey does read the London Review of Books and currently has an opening in his life for a delicious lust vixen with whom to super-charge the static on his real nylon sheets. This advert is the recruitment process, and guess what, you just got the job (home-owning women only, 20 – 65, verifiable income, full credit history, no pets, no smokers, some knowledge of pulmonary medical procedures a distinct advantage). Man, 68. By reading this advert this far you agree to its terms and conditions and acknowledge it to be a legally binding contract. No loons.*" No loons?

For the past half-year, I have been reading the first thirty or forty pages of the London Review of Books, believing that it was a good way to increase my scope of learning. But now, after having finally taken a look at the last pages, I think that I have now found an entirely new form of entertainment…can't wait until the next issue arrives.

05

The Indefatigueable Mysteries of Being Here

I am sitting in my hotel room overlooking Lake Geneva in Switzerland right now. I was going to write whilst on the airplane, but as the seating was apparently arranged as an off-shoot of a Sardine can design contest, I thought the rather rotund gentleman sitting next to me might be offended by my fingers as they whizzed across the keyboard, clicking away madly.

What stimulated this writing – as you have discovered, I only seem to write when there is something stimulating going on in my life – was that I have been reading a marvellous little book that was given to me by a friend. The book is titled "Cuentos para Pensar," and it consists of a series of short stories that, as the title suggests, are stories to think about. The one that really caught my eye was called El Buscador (the explorer), but even before I got to that story, I was mesmerised by the introduction.

In the introduction, Jorge Bucay begins by saying that *"Todos los que hemos vivido buscando la verdad, nos hemos encontrado en el camino con muchas ideas que nos seduheron y habitaron en nosotros con la fuerza suficiente como para condicionar nuestro system de creencias."* This, more or less, means that we are all looking for the truth, and our mental models can cause us to create our own beliefs about what the truth is that we are looking for. I started thinking about this and realised that this little book is going to be chocker with wisdom.

We all are looking for the "truth." And we all have our own ideas of what that "truth" might be. Fair enough, but one of my mental models is that there are some "truths" that are applicable to everyone (Well almost everyone. I do know some people who believe that their version of the truth is the only one that is right). I kept reading.

The story of the explorer was enchanting. The explorer encountered a village where all the headstones in the cemeteries were noted by the number of years, months, weeks, and days that each person lived. I could go on and on about the story, but the underlying message was that many of us – regardless of how many years we have been on the planet – don't actually really "live." A very powerful message...for all of us.

I am now back home after spending several days in Switzerland. It was a business trip, and a good one at that. I was working with a group of managers of a client, and part of our time spent together took me into something I would have only imagined a few years ago. After a day of meetings, we went off in a motor coach on a journey of delicious discovery. And where did we go, you might be wondering? We went to Coulisses Gourmand. Yes, as they name implies, it was a cooking school.

James B Rieley

This part of my sessions with the group was planned as sort of a break from all the incessant story-telling that seems to flow from my upper orifice when I am working. The motor coach took us to Nyon, just north of Geneva, and after a short walk down some narrow streets, we were greeted by the proprietor – chef of the school Dominique Roué and his assistant Nathalie.

The plan was simple. The group was going to learn how to prepare a seriously complicated three-course dinner. Well that was the first part, and the only simple part of the plan. The dinner we would prepare was going to be OUR dinner, so if it was buggered up, we would go hungry. Clearly a good incentive to do well. The client team was divided into four groups, with each of us being responsible for one part of the meal.

So here is the menu we were given to prepare. The starter would be Noix de St. Jacques a la plancha, puree & chips de panais (Seared Scallops served with potatoes mashed and parsnip chips). The main was to be Agneu croustade with Provence vegetables and a ratatouille cake (Lamb, wrapped in a perilously thin pastry, stuffed with cooked vegetables, and served with a tower of cooked tomato, zucchini, eggplant, and peppers - all of which I pretty much will not normally eat).

After the chef had demonstrated how to do each part of the dinner, we were set free to become premier chefs for an evening. Now I do like to cook, but I have been accused more than once of eating to live (instead of living to eat), and because of this, my attempts at demonstrating culinary excellence usually falls into the category of "safe" things to prepare. I am pretty good at doing all sorts of things with chicken, but admittedly, I usually just make the same things over and over again. This was going to be a bit more adventurous, and even though I wasn't really part of the team, they had asked me to participate with them in the evening, and (luckily), I was put in the desert group.

The desert – Fondant au chocolat, Coeur de fraise – was probably designed by a cholesterol terrorist, as you will soon see. Ingredients for 5 people (there were 14 of us, but this is how the recipe was given to us) 200g of chocolate, 100g of butter, 3 eggs, 40g of sugar, 50g of flour, 50g of milk, 50g of cream, 500g of strawberries. For the English cream that was served with the treat, you will need 12 egg yolks, 220g of sugar, 1 litre of milk, and 2 sticks of vanilla. If you are not drooling by now, you must not be really reading this. I suppose I could go on about how to whip all this together into one of the best deserts that has ever crossed my lips, but the recipe is in French…but if you want it, let me know. Here is a hint; close your eyes and imagine taking a spoon and gently sliding it across a sliced strawberry so you can slowly cut into a small cake, only slowing down to watch the melted chocolate inside drip down the side of the cake onto the English cream that is surrounding it. Hmmm, I think I had better stop here, or I will need to take a cold shower pretty quickly now, but just know it was pretty damn good.

We sliced, we diced, we seared, we fried, we whipped, we whisked, we said *"Yes chef"* repeatedly, we baked…and then we feasted on what turned out to be a spectacular dinner.

I was at my doctor's office this week. Nothing overly dramatic, just one of my post GBS check-ups that I apparently will endure for the rest of time. I really like my doctor. He is pretty brilliant, after all, one of his specialities is GBS, and when I first went to see him several years ago as the evil-bastard virus was firmly entrenching itself in my muscles, nerves, and joints, he spotted what the problem was within minutes and his knowledge probably saved my life. But he has become a good friend, and I actually look forward to my office visits. We spend a few minutes going over the most recent test results, and then we sit around talking about just about everything. He practises his English, whilst I mutter away in Spanish.

This week's visit wasn't out of the norm of our usual agenda. One of his assistants did a DTC on me. A DTC for you non-medical types is a Doppler Transcranial test where they take a shiny stick-like-thingy and place it against the arteries going up my neck. The doo-wah instrument is connected to a high-tech bit of kit with huge speakers, so when it finds the arteries, I can hear the whoosh-whoosh-whoosh sound of blood pulsing its way up (or down I guess). They then make a colour print-out of what the blood flow looks like and the doctor looks at it and says, *"This is very good news James. You are doing very very good."* Nice.

He also told me that he thought I should go to a spa once in a while to alleviate my somewhat-off-and-on lower back pain. I thought it made more sense to not do anything stressful for my lumbar, like lifting anything that weighed more than a cup of tea, but when I mentioned that to my doctor, he smiled and said, *"British humour, si?"* Cute.

Today I decided to check out various spas near Sol y Mar, with the hopes that I could find one that was bugger-all cheap, and someplace that I would actually go to off and on. This was a very enlightening experience.

The spa is at a rather trendy and upscale hotel only about 5 kilometres from Sol y Mar (a real plus). I was ushered around as if I was some long-lost relative of King Juan Carlos, being shown every nook and cranny of the facility. I kept thinking all I wanted to know was what it would cost to go there once in a while, and after what was fast becoming an exhausting experience, I was given the very trendy "Treatment Menu."

This 15-page set of options read like a marketing whiz exercise in word games and was incredible. I thought it might be nice for me to share some of the options with you….ready?

"Cooling Ice Facial Therapy for Men – 50 mins – 120 euros. A contouring, tightening and firming facial achieved with our innovative Neurocosmetics Express Radiance Ice Cubes. Contour Serum tones the skin and our 100% Active Serum regains its youthful glow. This specialised cryo-therapy gives an instant tighten-

ing and lifting treatment boosting your visage." Okay, so let's just examine this one for a minute. "Neurocosmetics Express Radiance Ice Cubes?" What the hell are those? Ice cubes from the planet Xenon? And there is no doubt in my mind that if I plopped a bunch of normal ice cubes on my face, everything would tighten up too, but I think my "visage" would just turn bright red from the onset of frost bite.

Then there was this one.

"Deep Release Massage with Hot Stones – 75 mins – 140 euros. Heated black basalt stones are used to massage the whole body releasing deep-seated tension ideal for anyone suffering with muscular aches and pains. Working at relieving stress at the deepest level this treatment is designed to work on the body's energy channels." Right. I have no idea where my "energy channels" even are, but I think I would be a bit concerned if the spa person approached me with a light strapped to his or her head and was wearing long rubber gloves. I even Googled "black basalt stones" to see what they were, and came up with a link that said they are used for paving in China. I think if someone piled a bunch of these on my body it would increase my stress level, not release it.

And then the best of all (and I use the term "best" rather loosely).

"Firming Spirulina Booster Envelopment – 60 mins – 110 euros. An anti-ageing, firming and toning body envelopment idea for combating congestion, cellulite and maintain healthy skin tones after weight loss. Firming aromatic complexes treat the areas of the body that need skin conditioning combined with Spirulina seaweed to rebalance and remineralise the body, restoring a feeling of total well-being." Shoot, I can combat congestion in other ways that having someone cover my body with seaweed that they probably found washed up on some beach and put in a box marked "magical Spirulina beach crap." I also am not suffering from weight loss, but could I suppose if I would stop buying chocolate chip cookies, (which I only ingest for medicinal purposes, of course). And what is all that "aromatic complexes" about? Couldn't I accomplish the same thing by standing in a smoke-filled room that is littered with flowers and cow-manure? That would be complex-aromas, wouldn't it? And then there is that "rebalance and re-mineralise the body" part. Maybe that is done when you eat some of those black stones from the other option. And what is "Spirulina" you ask? According to an online dictionary, it is "the common name for human and animal food supplements produced primarily from two species of cyanobacteria (also known as blue-green algae)." Right, only 110 euros for something made from "cyanobacteria." Hmmm, sounds nummy.

What ever happened to swimming a few laps and then just having a rest in the sauna? I think I am going to pass on the spa options and instead just wander down to the sea (free) in front of Sol y Mar once in a while. I did go there today and did actually see some seaweed. I think I need to put a sign out on my front door stating, *"Dr. Rieley's Natural Spa and Trendy Health*

Centre." My doctor would be proud of me.

I have always been fascinated by geometry and maths. Note that I said "fascinated." This is, in my case, clearly different than "enthralled" or "enjoyed." I didn't like either of these subjects in school. But my father used to tell me *"There is mathematics in everything."* Okay, he was right, and this tidbit of fatherly wisdom has manifested itself in some of the art I have been producing. The interrelationship between geometric shapes and maths presents itself in many of the pieces I have done since moving to Sol y Mar. Such is the case with "Motown." But now you are probably wondering how I associate "Motown" with this latest piece. Well, this piece, along with "Madeline Sparkle Pants", are both related to "The Gordian Brothers," a two-piece sculpture I made whilst living in La Antigua. These were named because of their graphic connection to the fabled Gordian Knot, part of the legend of Alexander the Great. Okay, now follow this logic stream. The Gordian Knot was an endless piece of rope that was woven into an knot with no exposed end; Motown, was begun in the 1960"s in Detroit by Berry Gordy, Jr. Gordian Knot - Berry Gordy - Motown. Get it? Okay, now you are wondering how "Madeline Sparkle Pants" is connected to this stream of consciousness. Well it isn't. I stole the name from this adorable kitty that lives in Chicago because I just thought it was a great name.

Recently, I wrote about some of my ancestors, and I suppose you might have thought that I only had one set of family members. Well, that really isn't the case. My mother's side of the family had a tremendous influence on my life growing up, and whilst I don't have letters that they wrote more than 100 years ago, what I do have are very special memories.

My grandparents on my mother's side of the family had been best friends before they were married. Actually, the reason they were best friends was because they and their spouses were all good friends. But then my – pay attention now, this is a bit confusing – grandfather's wife passed away about the same time my mother's father died in an auto crash. My grandmother and grandfather ended up getting married to each other. My grandmother had two daughters, and my grandfather had a daughter and a son, so almost instantly, there was this family of four children. It never seemed to me that my mother and aunts and uncle were anything but naturally-born siblings.

When I was young, quite young actually, I can remember flying across Lake Michigan every summer to spend time at my grandparent's cottage. This was such a special time for me, and my memories of each summer are far clearer than just about anything else I can remember about growing up.

I think I learnt a lot about "doing stuff" with my grandfather. When I was about 11 or so, he and I planned a major travel adventure. No, he didn't take me to the Himalayas or anything, but at the time, it seemed equally daunting. One day, we got up and towed my grandfather's little aluminium rowboat to a spot on the Kalamazoo River, and motored all the way to Lake

Michigan. Okay, so you might be thinking, *"Wow, how many days did it take to do that?"* Well, the answer was one day. Hey, come on…I was young and this was a pretty big thing. And it got bigger. When we arrived in Saugatuck, on eastern shore of Lake Michigan, we tied up the boat at a quay and waited for my grandmother to arrive with the boat trailer so we could go back to their house. After a short wait, she arrived and I assumed that my grandfather would motor the boat around to the launching ramp so we could load it all up for the trip back. But my grandfather told me that I should bring the boat around. I think at the time my grandmother just about had a coronary, but my grandfather insisted that I was old enough to accept this responsibility. After some very polite excuses that gushed from my mouth, all the time my grandfather urging me on, I managed to head out into the lake (my grandfather did encourage me with all the confidence in the world to go pretty far out into the lake) and, all by myself, I motored out in a huge circle, and then motored back to the launch ramp. This was pretty high adventure for a young boy, and it left an indelible impression on me. Not just the fact that we went down the river. Not the fact that I was encouraged to bring the boat around all by myself. But the fact that my grandfather had immense confidence that I could do something that was pretty intimidating left a lasting impression on me.

Today, 20 May, is a pretty special day for me. Today would have been my father's 100th birthday. My father was, and still is, a huge force in my life. He was big on learning, and whilst he never received extensive formal education, he wanted both my brother and myself to learn as much as we could, and in anyway we could. In most cases, this meant by exploring what we didn't know, as opposed to just the formal educational system that we were raised in (he would be pretty mystified as to why I felt compelled to earn a Ph.D.)

He could be tough. I remember at one point whilst in high school, my grades for several classes were…well, the fact is that they were pretty abysmal. After an evening of being properly bollocked for my most recent grade reports, he told me that if my grades did not improve dramatically and immediately, I would be chucked off to a Military Academy to teach me some discipline. At the time, I was near panic-stricken. However, he could also be pretty sympathetic, as evidenced by the fact when my next grade reports arrived showing a less-than-energetic response to the threat on my part, I never did get sent away.

When I was younger than the Military Academy close-call, one day at dinner (this was in the days when families (mother, father, and children) actually sat and ate meals together) I announced that I was ready to learn how to ride my own two-wheel bicycle. I did have a small bicycle that had auxiliary wheels to keep it from falling over, but I was ready (I said) to ride a big bike. Without barely skipping a beat, my brother (two years older than I was) said that he would teach me after dinner. After finishing dinner, and my brother and I washing the dishes, he and I went outside and he told me to sit down on the stairs that went down from the front porch to the walk-path. He then took his bike and rode back and forth in front of me, repeating over and over again, "*See? See how easy it is?*" After a dozen or so rides back and forth, he stopped in front of me and told me to get on his bike and ride. I was primed and ready; after all, my older brother was pretty good at riding his bike, and he did show me. I got onto his bike and after almost going a whole two metres, I was laying on the ground with my brother's bike piled unceremoniously on top of me. "*No, no no. Do it like it did. Weren't you watching?*" he said as he helped me up. I ended up trying several times and thankfully, was able to stop when my father came outside and said to my brother, "*I will teach him. You can go inside.*"

My father told me to sit down on one of the steps and, as he sat down next to me, he reached in his shirt pocket and slid out his little spiral notebook and his mechanical pencil. He then began to make stick-figure drawings, one using the black lead of the pencil, and one using the red lead of the pencil. The drawings, he explained to me, identified the two central keys to bicycle riding; Balance and Momentum. As I recall, the drawings were pretty detailed and after listening to his explanations, he closed the notebook and told me to get on the bike and ride. I was feeling pretty good about his explanations, but at the same time, I wondered how his drawings would keep me from crashing out. Crashing out is exactly what I did after pedalling for almost ten seconds. My father walked over to where I was crawling out from under the bicycle and the first thing that came out of his mouth was something like, "*Weren't you paying attention? You weren't applying Balance and Momentum at the right levels.*" Oh for joy. By now, I was pretty convinced that I wasn't as smart or coordinated as my friends who could ride their own two-wheel bikes. Out came the notebook again, followed by more explanations of the two diagrams. But, luckily, before my father finished his second lecture on Balance and Momentum, I looked up when I heard my mother saying, "*I will help him. You can go in.*"

She initially asked me if I was okay and if I still wanted to learn how to ride my own bike. Well, yes, was the answer to both questions; and before I could profess ineptitude at bike riding, she stood the bike up and told me to get on. My mind raced….errr, I don't seem to be able to do this, why should I get on the bike, I wondered. This feeling was exacerbated by the reality that my brother had clearly demonstrated how he rode a bike and I wasn't able to. My father had shown me the two key elements of bicycle riding and I still wasn't able to. But my mother was standing there telling me to get on the bike, and I sure got the message. She put one of her hands on the bike seat and her other hand on the handlebars to keep it balanced and on I climbed. She said, "*Ready?*" I sort of nodded. She then said, in a no-nonsense voice, "*Pedal.*" And knowing my mother was using her serious voice, I did. Off we went, slowing wobbling down the street. When we approached the end of the block, she cautioned me to keep pedalling as we made a large, sweeping turn and headed back toward our house. I kept pedalling, and as we went past the house, I was almost feeling pretty good about all this. But at the same time, I was pretty nervous that one of my friends would see me and the image of my mother holding up the bike as I was pedalling was not anything I wanted anyone to see. At the other end of the block, we did another big sweeping turn, as my mother again instructed me to keep pedalling. We must have gone back and forth a handful of times when I noticed that the bike was really wobbly as I went around one of the turns at the end of the block.

I kept pedalling, even though I hadn't heard my mother's voice, and after heading back toward the house, I saw my mother standing on one of the front steps. It was then I realised I actually was riding my own two-wheel bicycle without auxiliary wheels or without any help. It took me years later to realise that whilst my brother and father had, in their own way, tried to "teach" me how to ride a bicycle, my mother had instead "created a safe environment in which I learnt how to ride. Big difference, and a difference that has stuck with me for the rest of my life.

I worked with my father for quite a few years, which was like the first lines of A Tale of Two Cities. These were the best of times and the worst of times, but never dull. He taught me about Leonardo de Pisa, a mathematician whom we know as Fibonacci. Fibonacci believed that there are sequences of numbers that are "natural." To drive the point home, he once sent me out to pick dandelions so we could count the number of petals on the flowers, proving out the Fibonacci theory. His sequence is, "*1, 1, 2, 3, 5, 8, 13, 21, 34, 55, ... defined by F(1) = 1, F(2) = 1, and*
F(n) = F(n-1) + F(n-2) for n = 3, 4, 5, ..." But you probably already knew that. Can you imagine me, counting petals on a dandelion to prove out the theory? Not exactly a pretty sight.

When I was faced with a problem or serious life challenge, he never provided me with a solution or gave me "the answer," but instead told me to go figure it out for myself. At times, this can be a pretty depressing response, but he taught me to be self-reliant and use my head to figure out how to avoid problems. By the time he passed away in 1974, I had realised that this was the best thing for a father to do for a son.

At times, he was pretty hard to live and work with, but he was, and always will be, my father, and he is missed.

The number 100 is significant in other ways as well.

- The number of subunits into which many of the world's currencies are divided; for example, one euro is one hundred cents and one Pound Sterling is one hundred pence
- The number of tiles in a standard Scrabble set
- Number 1 in the top 100 April's Fool's Day Hoaxes: The Swiss Spaghetti

Harvest
- In United Kingdom, 100 is the operator telephone number
- The first Chinese dictionary was written in 100 A.D.
- 100 is the HTTP status code indicating that the client should continue with its request
- The Huffington Post, head of the list of Top 100 blogs
- The 100-Series Highways are a series of arterial highways in the Canadian province of Nova Scotia
- The boiling point of water = **100°** Celsius (centigrade)
- In English slang, adding the number 100 to a particular skill or subject denotes introductory knowledge ("Physics 100", "Soccer 100"), akin to the name of a first year university subject.
- The Time 100 is a list of the 100 most influential people in the world, as assembled by Time. The list has developed into an annual event.
- Sum of the 1st nine prime numbers = 2 + 3 + 5 + 7 + 11 + 13 + 17 + 19 + 23 = **100**
- One Hundred Men and a Girl is a 1937 musical comedy film starring Deanna Durbin
- 100 Grand Bar (formerly known as $100,000 Bar) is a candy bar produced by Nestlé
- 100 is about the number of days since I rented out La Antigua and formally moved to Sol y Mar

It's almost summer and we all know what that means. Yes, reading a good book at the beach. Well, okay. Maybe that doesn't work for everyone, but it does for some I am told. For me, reading has always been important. No, reading is not everything to me...after all, I would rather write (and get paid to do it) than read, but sometimes, reading is a great way to expand one's views on just about everything.

I tend to order books from one of the Amazon sites – it is dead easy, and after a few days, the books appear magically at my front door. Yesterday, a new purchase arrived. Well, I should clarify that a bit. The book that I just ordered was first published in 1938, and I previously did have a copy of it. I first read the book, Richard Halliburton's Second Book of Marvels, when I was 11 or 12, and at the time, it filled my head with visions of a different world. Halliburton was an explorer-cum-journalist-cum-adventurer who wrote extensively about what he saw on his travels around the world. The Second Book of Marvels is not exactly classical travel literature. But it was at the time for me, a fabulous way to vicariously be part of Halliburton's journeys, and it (quite obviously) left an indelible mark on my brain...and probably was also the beginnings of my bucket.

This isn't the only book that had an impact on my life. In the late 1980"s, I read a book called Maiden Voyage, about a 18 year-old girl who sailed around the world single-handedly, in a 26ft sailboat. I can remember at the time that I was mesmerised by the photos and probably spent far more time looking at them than I did devouring the text. I never really had a desire to sail around the world, but the whole sailing thing resonated within me to the point that it wasn't more than two or three months after reading Maiden Voyage that I bought my first sailboat. I can remember years ago, after my second boat was a big enough stimulus for me to sell my house and become a liveaboard. We had gone to a boat show in Chicago, and there was Tania Aebi (the author of Maiden Voyage). After some prodding from my stepdaughter, I actually went up to Tania after her talk and rambled on for several minutes about how her book had changed my life. She listened intently to my story of how reading her book caused me to buy a boat and now live-aboard a boat and then said, "*Cool.*" And then she walked away. So much for meeting one's heroes.

I have other books that have influenced my life to be sure. They are pretty easy to spot amongst the random titles that litter my bookshelves. I seem to have quite a few books on the subject of far-eastern philosophy written by Thich Nhat Hahn and the Dalai Lama; and books in mid-eastern philosophy by J. Krishnamurti. These books are chocker with (what I believe to be) common sense ways to live one's life and I know they have been a strong influence on me.

Things have been pretty calm here lately (other than the excitement of receiving the Halliburton book). I would love to write about incredible experiences I have had, but the reality is that it has been as normal as one could yearn for. I did actually go out to La Antigua this morning. It has been several months since I have even been there and it did look a bit different than when I left it. My renters have…well, they have tried to make it "their home," which is a good thing I guess. Little do they know that no matter what they do, my La Antigua will always be firmly etched into my head. And then tonight, after dinner, I went for an evening walk and discovered what appeared to be the ruins of some terribly old fortress-type building near Sol y Mar. I thought it might be interesting to learn more about the construction; who made it, when it was built, and for what purpose. So I asked a neighbour, hoping to learn something incredible about the history of this part of the island. I was told that "*It is an old building.*" Right.

It has been a very busy week here, and like most weeks, it has been a real balance between good things and not-so-good things.

The good things: It has been culinary experimentation time again. I had been reading a Mallorquin publication – nothing overly challenging, just one of those free-distribution magazines that we find in our post-boxes and then either use for starting fires in the fireplace or send it off to be recycled (probably into more junk-post). After ploughing through the odd-articles about homeopathy and which celebrity is now on the island, I found a one-page story about food preparation. In the past, I perhaps would have only glanced at this page, using it as another way to learn more Spanish. But ever since my culinary experience in Geneva, I thought I would really see if I could prepare the recipe.

I have learnt there are two key elements to trying to replicate a recipe: the finished preparation has to be pleasing to the eye, and it has to be edible. The recipe in the magazine had a photo with it (always a good thing so you can figure out what your visual target it). After what seems to be another of my daily marketing expeditions (fresh is good), I had a go at the recipe.

Garbanzos a la Mostaza consists of a pile of garbanzo beans (chick-peas), an onion (I used one that was about the size of a cricket-ball), 2 fresh carrots, 4 small tomatoes, some extra-virgin olive oil, and a dollop of mustard. Now let me explain something…the term "dollop" may have different connotations to different people. To me (a lover of good mustard), a dollop is the amount you can pile into a spoon without much of it spilling over onto the floor. I have a big spoon. Chop up all the veggies, add them to the beans in a big bowl (I also chucked in some chicken), and then add the oil and the mustard. Here I would love to say that there is a real trick to blending all the components together but what I did was stir it all up until my arm was about to fall off, and then I ate it. It was fab.

Another "good" thing happened today. I have been walking a lot lately. I am not sure if I am doing the (allegedly) recommended 10,000 steps, but when I get home, my legs are almost in shock. Today I walked over to a beach where some good friends hang out almost daily, and we were talking, we looked up and saw something that I had never seen before. It was a perfectly circular rainbow around the sun. Actually, a rainbow may not be the right term (and I am sure some reader will tell me what it was), but it was pretty impressive to see. One of John's friends asked what it was (in Spanish). I quickly responded that it was "fin del mundo," (the end of the world). Obviously I was wrong, as this happened about five hours ago and I still have a broadband connection and am typing. I have decided to take this as a good omen. Not sure if I will go all the way and buy a lotto ticket or not, but thinking of it as good just has to be better than thinking of it as bad. I did take a photo of it with my phone, and whilst pointing a camera lens directly at the sun is not a smart thing to do, at least you can almost see what we saw.

I have, for a long time, thought that there are only two good reasons to leave home. One reason is when someone pays me to go, you know, like clients. The other reason is to see very special friends or family. Last weekend, I discovered another reason: When the reason to leave home is because the destination is Tuscany.

I have a very good friend whom, although we communicate several times each week, I haven't actually spent time with in several years. And although he and his family live in London, they now have a home in the hills of Tus-

James B Rieley

cany and this prompted the visit. One of the reasons that living in Mallorca is so good is that there is multiple airline options daily to most of the places I travel to on business. However, for some unknown reason (other than the old supply v. demand excuse that airlines use), it is pretty difficult to get to Italy from Mallorca. As a result, my flight plan first took me to Barcelona before flying to Pisa.

Pisa is just another town I think, except for the fact that near the centre of it lies a huge open area that is known as the Piazza del Duomo. The piazza contains a group of buildings that are recognised as masterpieces of architecture in medieval times; a cathedral, a baptistery, a cemetery, and oh yes, there is this tower that is a bit out of kilter.

Now I am usually not one to do "tourist" things, but when I read that Fibonacci was buried in the cemetery (and by now you should know about him and his numerical sequence), I was up for going there.

Outside of the fact that the piazza was chocker-block with tourists from all over the world, mostly there to see the Tower and have their pictures taken so it appears that they are holding it up (as if no one else had thought of doing it); and outside of the fact that the number of tourists was only equalled by the number of vendors selling almost anything that was supposed to be a memento of Pisa, or for that matter, anything that had some semblance to being Italian; seeing the Piazza and standing in front of where Fibonacci was buried was pretty special. My father would have been proud of me.

The next day it was up the motorway toward Comano. Zooming along the autostrade, it is amazing to see stone-works after stone-works...kilometres of them. I half expected I would be able to see the 2008 version of Michelangelo walking amongst the rows of cut blocks, looking for just that special piece to chip away at. But, seeing as how I was in a hire-car, going at about 30km over the speed limit – but being passed by just about every car on the road – I decided that it would be best to just assume that one day, one of the massive blocks would be fashioned into a very spectacular piece of sculpture. (Personally, I think working with PVC tubing is a bit easier, but that is just my opinion)

Comano is one of those sleepy little villages that so reminded me of Puigpunyent. Winding roads, houses that are so close to the streets that it seemed like a risky thing to step outside without looking carefully, and hills that were covered with green. Oh yes, on the weekend, the hills were also covered with rain clouds, but that wasn't important. Richard and I did what we do best, which is to say, plot out the future of the world, or as it must have sounded to anyone near us, babble on about business, life, autos, and anything else that seemed worthwhile.

On Sunday, it was off to San Terenzo at noon for a lunch by the sea. San Terenzo was one of those complete surprises for me. Nestled in a little cove on the Gulf of Poets (think Shelley), it is a sleepy version of Cannes or San Remo, or at least that is how it appeared to me. We had a wonderful lunch at a little café overlooking the beach – although Shelley was a strong advocate of vegetarianism, we all devoured seafood as if it were the nectar of the Gods with a brilliant sun pouring down upon us. And then the clouds found us, and after a downpour that looked like someone upstairs turned on a firehose, it was on to Lucca.

Not Luca, as in Luca Brazzi. Not even Luca, as in the young lad in Tea with Mussolini. Lucca is a walled city a few miles from Pisa that makes you feel that you in a time warp going back to the renaissance. The walls, which are still intact, provide the sensation that time has stood still. Narrow cobbled-streets, people pedalling around on bicycles, stunning architecture, all provided a wonderful feeling of warmth and solitude. And whilst I did really enjoy spending time in Lucca, by now I was longing to return home.

Spending time with Richard again was important to me. Seeing parts of Tuscany that I hadn't been to in the past was just icing on the cake…and I think it was icing that I would like to enjoy again someday. Of course, that would mean I would have to leave the island again, and right about now, nestled back in Sol y Mar with the sun reflecting off the sea in front of me as I type, this may not happen soon. It might be easier to "be there" if I would just go out and buy a Vespa, find some huge dark glasses, wear my blazer over my shoulders, and drive around saying "*Ciao.*"

Lately, the evenings here have been like living in the deep woods. Well, I suppose you are thinking that this couldn't possibly be true. *"Isn't Sol y Mar right on the water?"* Yes, of course it is, but when I say it has been like living in the deep woods, it is because there have been so many boats anchored out in front of the house that at night, it is beginning to look like a herd/flock/group/bevy/brood/litter/pack/skein (pick anyone that makes sense to you) of fire-flies hovering above the water. Truly a treat to see every evening.

A summer weekend, and things have only begun I am told. Today, by a little after noon, I counted 86 boats in front of Sol y Mar, and by the time I had finished, more were coming in to drop their anchors and bask in the summer sun. This vista, of course, for me is a mixed blessing. The views are spectacular, but sitting on the terrace and looking at all the boats does make me long to go sailing again. And whilst living on a boat was about the best way to grow old I always thought, being on land WITH THE VIEWS is pretty great too. I don't have to worry about big storms, although I have almost forgotten what rain even looks like. I don't have to worry about the never-ending saga of cleaning teak decks, varnishing bright work, or polishing stainless fittings to keep the salt air from doing nasty things to most things metallic. I don't even have to worry about an anchor-chain dragging, allowing a boat to go careening in to another one. Now, I just am able to sit in a comfortable chair, knowing that for quite a few years, I was able to do what many people only dream about.

James B Rieley

Having this house, like when I lived in La Antigua, can have its challenges. This is especially true in summer. Here at Sol y Mar, I have plants on three terraces that by the end of a summer day, are just about gasping for nourishment. So every night that I am here I do my watering regimen. For a while, I was doing this by filling up a 5 litre polyethylene watering-can, but due to some nasty lumbar things going on, I now simply haul out the hoses, set the nozzle pressure on turbo-blaster-fire-hose, and proceed to quench what seems to be the never-ending thirst of the plants.

Having this needed discipline is a good thing. It is sort of like the discipline that is required for me to put out my weekly business newsletter and other business-related things I do, as well as the artsy stuff I do when I am home. And speaking of the creative things, I recently became motivated to make some more ceramic plates. Regardless of how they may look, the whole ceramic project does require discipline. I have to make sure that the patterns are similar from plate to plate. I now have made almost enough plates with the grass pattern to cause Villeroy & Bosch to believe that they have a new competitor in the market place. And when I did the Galatxo pattern, I had to make sure that the contour-flow-lines were compatible from plate to plate.

I was thinking about writing more about the discipline required for all the ceramic things I have done, but just as I was about to keep typing, I realised that something that is that enjoyable and fun to do certainly can't be all about discipline…it is just a good way to spend my creative time whilst at home.

So here is the deal; I have this rooster painted on the wall above the terrace off my sitting room. It is big, and has a large piece of blue reinforcing rod stuck in it on an angle. I imagine that whomever painted it there had it in mind to make a sundial out of it, but I really don't know the story behind how it got there. I could let my mind race a bit and relate a story about the significance of the subject matter (a big orange rooster) or why the rod is painted blue and placed on the angle it is at. I could share with you the correlation between the rooster and the regime of Generalissimo Francisco Franco, who ruled Spain for so many years. I could alternatively explain how Mallorca, clearly part of Spain, has always thought of itself as a bit "different" that the Spanish mainland and how the rooster symbolises this independent feeling. But the reality is that long before I came to Sol y Mar, there was a German family living here and they thought that having a rooster sun-dial on the wall overlooking the sea was a cute thing to do. "*Oh*," was my reaction when I found out.

According to some online repository of (allegedly) information, a rooster symbolises pride, courage, vigilance, arrogance, strength, and flamboyance. I thought about these examples of symbolism and have "tested" them to see if they apply to my residency at Sol y Mar. Pride – well I do take pride in my house and both sweep the terraces and water the plants daily. Okay, almost daily. Courage – I do try to cook things that even a couple of years ago would have been quite intimidating to attempt. Notice I am not mentioning the quality level of what I have been making? Vigilance – I do have a turbo-powerful set of binoculars that I use to scan the horizon to see if there are any forces coming to invade the island. Strength – hmmm, I will have to think about this one a bit more. Flamboyance – well, the painted rooster is orange. Okay, so that bit of research didn't really yield anything I found to be illuminating, so I Googled *"Rooster meaning Spain."* Whilst this didn't yield too much that was enlightening, I did find a link that said that CID was a Spanish boys name that means God or rooster. All I could think of when I read this was the painting *"The Creation of Adam"* by Michelangelo. It was then that I appreciated the fact that Michelangelo did not have access to Google – can you imagine that painting on the ceiling of the Sistine Chapel with Adam touching a rooster? Neither could I.

One last bit of research did yield an important learning for me. Roosters in Spain say "kikiriki" instead of "cockle-doodle-doo." I am not sure why that is important, but it might prove to be a valuable learning for the next time I am in Puigpunyent and want to strike up a conversation with some farm animals.

The reality is that I have no idea on this earth why someone would paint a huge orange rooster on the wall overlooking my terrace. I just think some people do strange things.

We all do things that some others may interpret as a bit odd. I sure do; after all, I am the one who took some aluminium exhaust vent tubing and tied it into knots and put in on the front terrace…and then named it Madeline Sparkle-Pants. I really don't think that this is odd at all. In fact, I believe that we are all unique people who have likes and dis-likes that may be different than those of others.

Several years ago, I received a greeting card that said on its cover, *"Do what you can, where you are, with what you have."* I still have this card and look at it often, and lately, I think have looked at it more than ever before. I suppose it is because ever since I wrote about my "bucket list," I have really been thinking about what is in it and wondering if I will do anything about those things. The problem for me is that whilst some things seem to have been in my bucket for eons of time, other things pop-up once in a while and somehow, suddenly are added to my list. I think I am getting my head around this phenomenon (but am struggling to not get too analytical about it). This is what I have discovered.

We are humans. We have brains. Our brains, and their abilities are sort of one of those good-news, bad news things. The good news is that we have a pretty powerful tool for making decisions (the brain). The bad news is that most of us are pretty crap at using this tool (the brain). One day, everything seems to be quite normal and acceptable. Then one day, the same things that we thought were okay, we find to be completely unacceptable. I can remember years ago, when I used to spend time with my favourite family members (my Aunt Dorothy and my Uncle Ed) at their home on Paddock Lake in southeastern Wisconsin (yes, this was a very long time ago). In the morning, Ed would get up, walk across the road in front of their house, and go down to the lake for a swim. He would take soap and shampoo with him because after his swim, he would use the lake as a huge bathtub. At the time, it made all the sense in the world, but in today's world, this would be cause for the world's politically correct eco-police to lop off your head and put it on a stake.

Sorry to digress for a moment, but as I was writing this, I looked up and saw several identical power boats slowly motoring amongst some of the yachts moored out in front of Sol y Mar. It was if they were searching for someone or something. For a minute I almost felt as if I was transposed into a scene of From Russia With Love, with the Spectre boats searching for Mr. Bond and Tatiana Romanova near Trieste.

Not withstanding my little digression, I have learnt quite a bit in my time at Sol y Mar. My Spanish has improved dramatically (it is probably still total shite, but it is not as shite as it was). And having a greater capacity to converse in another language is a real treat. And now I know what to say the next time I come upon a rooster.

It happened again the other day. Well, it was sort of a variation of what I have been noticing off and on for the past several years. Suddenly, out of nowhere, something triggers a very special memory for me. The one that occurred the other day happened as I walked into the kitchen at Sol y Mar. As I walked past one of the counter-tops, suddenly my senses focussed on a bowl of cereal with sliced banana. It wasn't just the cereal and banana sensation; it was a flashback to being young and spending time at my grandparent's house in Michigan. I found this especially interesting, as I wasn't going to have any cereal, and didn't have any bananas in the house. But I can clearly remember my grandmother slicing up bananas and putting them on the cereal I would have for breakfast. And there it was again, albeit 50 years or so later…as clear as if she was in my kitchen that day.

I am not exactly sure what triggered that memory. It could be that Sol y Mar overlooks the sea, and the summers I used to spend as a young boy with my grandparents were mostly at a cottage they had on the shores of Pine Lake. It could have been that connection, but this isn't the first time something like this has happened.

Almost everyday, when I wake up and wobble through the sitting room with my morning cuppa, as soon as I open the doors that lead to the terrace, a gentle sea breeze wafts past me and I am instantly taken back to when I first was living on Peacemaker (which was the name of the boat that preceded

Angelina). And then there are the songs that I tend to play over and over and over again. Each song triggers a certain memory, and they all take me "someplace." When Pet Sounds comes up in my iTunes, I am instantly transported back to a different time and place. Listening to early electric Bob Dylan, Jimmy Buffet, and Dionne Warwick all gently float me back to a previous place in my life. And even when I hear a song that I probably knew about but never liked enough to buy (in the days when we purchased those round vinyl things), I suddenly find myself flashing back to a place and time that I remember very clearly. I think we all have these memory "triggers." Once in a while, the trigger takes you to a place you might not want to go to again, but more often than not, they are fab to have.

I need to clarify what I just wrote a bit. Most memories are great to have. Some, however, can give you nightmares. I received a call a couple of days ago from my friend John. He asked me to go up on my roof terrace and look down the coast. The reason was that there was a new yacht in the harbour near Portals Nous. I must admit, I do like to look at boats. I would also like to make it quite clear that I do not perceive myself as a bigot of any type. I am sort of a traditionalist in my boating views I suppose, and to me, some of the boats that are being cranked out now are nightmares in the making. The one that John called me about fell into that category. Later that day, I was talking to my neighbour Kim about what I had seen. She had heard about the boat and told me if I would use Google, I could probably find out more about it. Clearly, however, using Google is only good if you can figure out what to search under. Kim suggested I type in *"the ugliest yacht in the world,"* and it came up...for good reason. I guess the owner falls into the category of having more money than sense.

Things are getting quite interesting here lately. At the end of this month, King Juan Carlos will come to Mallorca, as he does every year for his holiday. His holiday home isn't all that far from Sol y Mar (okay, a couple of kilometres perhaps) and you can tell that his arrival time is approaching. Everyday prior to his arrival, some of the police services flies around in a helicopter looking for what I presume to be bad guys who may not especially like the king. I had been told by my neighbours that I might expect a visit from some men with suits and dark glasses sometime in July. When I asked why, I was told that from the air, the white tube sculpture (Esteban Tenia Razon) on my front terrace could be mistaken for a rocket-launcher. Oh my....

As you have gleaned, I am not keen on doing nothing. Some of the options for staying busy can include creative solutions to fundamentally long-term systemic problems, or simply applying some watercolour paints to a huge sheet of well-toothed rough stock. The creative streak, referred to as one of my demons by a friend in Australia, doesn't really require a specific challenge, just an outlet. Lately, the outlet has been ceramics.

I thought I was done with all the ceramic adventures I had whilst at La

James B Rieley

Antigua, but when some friends hinted that a ceramic house-sign for their property in Italy might be nice, the whole ceramic "urge" came back to me. After doing the house sign, I really lapsed back into ceramic mode and the past several weeks have resulted in the addition of 4 square bowls, 8 square plates, 4 ash-trays (I sent these to my brother), 6 large vases, 3 large round bowls, and 1 extremely large vase.

Now admittedly, I have been quite fortunate that these "creative demons" decided to rear their nasty tendencies at the same time that most of my client organisations decided to go on summer holiday. And whilst I still am connected to them and doing some behind-the-scenes planning work, summer has given me the chance to expand the scope of what I do like to do.

Just after the "James-does-pottery-festival" at Sol y Mar, I moved on to work on this year's holiday card. This has been a major challenge this year. Actually, truth-be-told, every year they are a challenge to design and produce, but this year it seems like an even greater challenge than before. I thought I had the design all sorted out last week, but then I could "see" a different design, so I began again. Now you are probably thinking, *"Hmmmm, isn't it a bit early to be thinking of holiday cards?"* Well, in my world, a world where you design and make your own cards, the answer is clearly no. And when the level of complexity of production of the cards increases, the time needed to produce them increases as well. With luck, I will have the final design sorted by the end of the month so I can begin making them sometime in September.

And then there was yesterday. I have no idea where this project idea came from, but suddenly it was staring me in the face. Now to clarify the physics of this, I am saying the project idea was staring me in the face, but as it was in my mind, that would be pretty difficult to do. How about this. I could "see" the finished project quite clearly in my mind. Yes, that is what I really meant (I guess). So mid-day, I went for a walk with my trusty turbo-digital-doo-wah camera and then staggered home in the mid-day heat (which yesterday was in the mid-30"s) to put the project together.

Yes, it is that time of year again…time for my annual talk about plants. Well, the reality is that there isn't an annual plant anything, but it does sound rather professional to have an annual anything I suppose. But seeing as how there isn't an annual entry for plants, the very least I could do is pass along some insights regarding my island that you could find beneficial for your own garden.

I discovered that I liked growing things when I moved into La Antigua. The courtyard gardens were abysmal when I arrived, and it did take some time to get them in the shape I wanted them. It became quite the challenge, as my plant background was mainly conducted with a weed-whacker whilst living in suburban America. But here I was, in the middle of the village, safely ensconced behind the courtyard walls, with my only fear being fear itself.

(Hey, that is a catchy phrase...I must remember that)

I did become rather adept at bringing some semblance of order to my gardens, and found special joy in growing my own cookery herbs. And after moving to Sol y Mar, I did work diligently to bring some green to the various terraces, even if all the plants are in macetas (pots). Again, I am growing some herbs, but here I am only growing albahaca (AL-BAA-CA), which you may know as Basil. I must admit it...I do love my albahaca, and put it on salads, chicken, and pasta. It is, after all, the big component of Pesto, and Pesto to me is right up there with puppies, Dusty Springfield, and chocolate-chip biscuits for good things in life.

My current albahaca crop is coming along quite nicely in three macetas. Growing it can be a tad tricky as the watering methodology is a combination of guess-work and pure luck (if you get it right). I have been quite lucky so far this summer with the herb, except that the other day, I noticed that some of the albahaca leaves in one of the machete's seemed to be getting smaller instead of larger. Upon some close observation, it was possible to see that someone or something was eating the leaves. This is not good, as I have a firm policy that states that only the gardener gets to eat the albahaca leaves, and I would be that gardener. In a near CSI-moment, I got out a magnifying glass and looked around the remainder of the leaves. Damn, they looked just like albahaca leaves look like when they are eaten by caracoles (CAR-A-CO-LACE), which are snails that have an albahaca-greed-complex. When they are in my gardens, they are also known as bastards. I hate those little guys, mainly because they not only eat my albahaca leaves, they do it at night when I can't see them.

I am not even sure what I would do if I could see the caracoles eating my plants. I don't think that they would be up for a lecture, even with flip-chart visuals that identified their errant ways. I can't imagine me presenting them with a petition (signed by me) urging them to stay away from my favourite herb. I suppose I could try to take them in front of the European Union court in Brussels, but they would probably win on humanitarian grounds or some other technicality. No, I think the only remedy is to annihilate the little buggers. When I lived in La Antigua, I found these cute little blue pellets that you sprinkle on the ground near plans that are under attack by caracoles, but I didn't have any of them here. I could have driven to the nearest garden centre, but I was afraid that I would come back with some giant palm trees or something else I really didn't need. Instead, I walked over to talk to Diego, a neighbour of mine.

Diego does speak English, sort of. He is quite fluent with phrases like, *"English, good;"* and *"Okay."* But I didn't" think that he would understand a lot of what I was describing, so I went with my Spanish. I explained what I was looking for (the little blue caracoles-killing pellets) and why I needed them (I hate those little bastards for eating my basil leaves). Diego said, *"Okay,"* and began to look around his little tool shed for the magical pellets. After a few minutes, a mate of Diego's walked into the shed and asked what he was looking for. I, being a good neighbour, offered my explanation…to which Diego's mate responded, in Spanish, with *"Use beer."* Okay, so he must not have understood what I had said. I reiterated my need to find some blue pellets to kill the caracoles, and then said, *"Entiendes?"* (do you understand?) He replied, again in Spanish, with, *"Yes I understand…use beer."* It was then that Diego got into the conversation, and after a few minutes, I learnt that if you sprinkle beer on the ground around your plants, it will get rid of any pesky snails that are raising havoc for you. Not having any beer in the house, I did do a bit of special shopping this afternoon and am ready for this evening. I hope those little albahaca-munchers don't like San Miguel.

Maybe I should have an annual plant issue. If the featured gardening tip this year is using beer to get rid of caracoles, perhaps next year the hot tip could be using red wine to forget where the garden is.

Some time ago, I wrote about my bucket list. I do enjoy sharing all these musings with you, which led to an unexpected phone call. It seemed that two friends of mine from Australia were planning a holiday and after reading about my bucket list, decided to invite me to come along with them. The reason was that they were going to Egypt. I hemmed and hawed, but after a bit, (and with some pretty powerful arguments from Lorraine and Kathy) decided I would indeed join them on the trip.

As it turns out, there will be nine of us going and the trip will include a couple of days in Cairo, a day in Luxor, seven days on a Nile cruise, and then a couple of days in Petra, Jordan. Sitting here in a hotel in Luxor, I was trying to figure out how to write about the trip. I have been sending my grand daughters post cards on the trip each day. Not real postcards – I figured that it could take ages for them to arrive, so instead, I have been making electronic post cards and then emailing them to the girls at least once a day. I suppose I could have sent these to everyone, but I didn't. So instead, here is sort of an abbreviated day-by-day diary of the trip.

Day One: I flew from Palma to Barcelona, and then on to Cairo. One of my struggles is the entire concept of travel. I don't think I mind actual flights, but "travel" is a real bugger for me. Here is what I mean. I left Sol y Mar at 0900h and with the help of a friend, went to the airport in Palma. My flight wasn't until almost 1100h, but with all the security checks, you never know how long the queues will be at an airport, so I knew I had to get there early. But as it turned out, the flight was delayed, so I didn't even arrive in Barcelona until well past noon. This was followed by an almost three hour wait for the Cairo flight. See what I mean? Travel = massive amounts of waiting time, and I really don't like that. Okay. So the flight to Cairo did take off more or less on time, and after another four hours, landed in Cairo Egypt. By now it was 2300h, and I was dead knackered. But was in Cairo. The hotel in Cairo (actually it is in the suburb of Giza) was the Mena House. If you ever want to go to see the pyramids, the Mena House is THE place to stay. Literally in the shadow of the pyramids, the Mena House is wonderful.

Day Two: This day was set-aside for two purposes. One was to just get some rest – the leftovers of the GBS do wreak havoc on me, so rest is always a good thing. Besides, this is supposed to be a holiday, so part of the day was dedicated to doing absolutely nothing. (In my lexicon, nothing is an all-comprehensive descriptor that includes doing writing work, of course). The first part of the day, however, was dedicated to visiting the Cairo Museum. When I lived in London, I had been to the British Museum several times and had been hypnotised by the antiquities taken from Egypt. But here I was in Egypt, and knew that the Cairo Museum had a huge collection of archaeological finds. I was quite eager to see them, so, with the tip to be at the museum for its opening smack at 0900h (not 0915h, not even 0905h we had been told...0900h), we arrived and began the process of paying for just about everything imaginable. After going through the metal detector, it became apparent that cameras were not permitted in the museum. I assume this was because of potential damage to some of the antiquities from flashes. So, cameras were turned over to the camera check-in desk just outside the building and then it was back in to see what could be seen.

The exhibition cases in the various rooms at the museum are filled with everything from small needles to chariots to amulets to jewellery to anything that a Pharaoh might need in the after-life. By the size and scope of the things that had been discovered in the various tombs that had been excavated in the past hundred years, a Pharaoh had pretty many needs. After wandering amongst the various artefacts – each one seemingly more marvellous than the previous one – we came upon an entire room dedicated to the Pharaoh Tutankhamen.

The room was an archaeologist's dream come true. Okay, I am not an archaeologist, but even I was gobsmacked by what was there. The two inner sarcoughogus' (sarcophagi?) that had housed the actual mummified remains of the Pharaoh were in separate display cases, as was the often photographically reproduced life mask. All of these relics were made of gold. Solid gold. To be in the same room as these relics was so special, but what made it even more special was the fact that there was no one else there. The throngs of tourist groups that were pouring into the museum hadn't yet made it this far yet, so being there, in the room, with all these relics was unbelievable. I quickly discarded the idea of nicking the gold death mask, as I figured it might set off the airport metal detector on my way back home. Instead, I just stood there in awe. And then the silence of the moment was broken. In a darkened corner of the room sat a guard, who said, in what sounded like a blend of Arabic and English, *"You have camera?"* As he said it, he looked around, probably making sure his supervisor (assuming he had a supervisor) wasn't nearby. They may have collected everyone's cameras at the front door to the museum, but they had not asked for mobile phones, so I whipped out my trendy iPhone and snapped away...and then filled the guard's out-

James B Rieley

stretched hand with currency, as you do for just about everything here. Within a couple of minutes, a throng of tourists entered the room and began their ooohs and ahhhs. We buggered off, the entire feeling of being there alone having changed.

I must tell you that whilst seeing all the archaeological finds is so very special, it does bother me that seeing all these things means that someone has dug up someone else's burial place. I do understand that this is the only way that we have learnt so much about the time of the Pharaohs, but I wouldn't be that thrilled with the thought of someone digging up my grandparent's graves, and consequently, I think it is pretty sacrilegious to know that it is through grave-robbing that we know all we know about early Egypt. Howard Carter, the archaeologist who discovered the tomb of the Pharaoh Tutankhamen, used to be one of my heroes. Used to be.

Day Three:

This was "visit the Pyramids day" according to the big travel plan. We thought that it might be nice to, instead of trudging around the pyramids on foot (it was hot and dusty and hot), to take a horse-drawn carriage ride, so the hotel manager arranged for one. At just before 0900h, this little man brought his carriage up to the front door of the Mena house – which, as it turns out, was the first time that this had happened. Apparently the "rule" was that carriages could only wait for passengers outside the secured gates of the hotel grounds, so it caused quite a stir amongst the locals that someone managed to be able to accomplish this.

Abdul (I have no idea what his name actually was, and calling him Abdul is no doubt a racist slur…my apologies) bundled us into the carriage and off we went. First it was around the Great Pyramid, then on to the second pyramid, and finally the third. There is no way to accurately describe what it is like to see the massively huge stone structures, so I will leave it to you to comprehend what it must have taken to build something with something like 3,100,000 stone blocks that weigh about 4 tons each, with each one being dragged to Giza by hand. The pyramids truly are one of the wonders of the world. As I was totally in awe of what was in front of me, I asked Abdul to stop the carriage so could get off and take more photos. It was then that Abdul 2 (again, apologies) approached. This man was on a camel, and in a flash, he dismounted and approached me, babbling on about me wanting to have my photo taken on his camel. I declined. He pursued the offer. I declined once again. And then in another flash, he put a keffiyeh on my head and a caftan-like robe over my shoulders as he thrust me onto his camel. Okay. So by now I was figuring *"What the hell. When in Egypt, and all that."* So there I was, sitting on the back of this camel, dressed as if I was about to enter the Lawrence of Arabia look-alike contest, and actually feeling like I would do rather well. We walked around for a bit – well Abdul 2 was walking; I was being thrown from side to side as the camel lurched along the sand dunes surrounding the pyramids. After determining that I would not be able to plant a flag and claim the land for the Queen, I managed to dismount and return the authentic garb to the man who probably last washed it in 1958.

The carriage driver (Abdul) then took us to see the Sphinx. This, once again, was a sight to be marvelled at. With the head being carved out of a single block of stone, and the body and legs being constructed of more massive stone blocks, the Sphinx lays in front of the pyramids, providing an image that is unforgettable. On the way back to the hotel, I managed to convince Abdul to return to the pyramids before letting us off. One of the images I had when I first saw photos of the pyramids when I was ten or eleven was being able to actually climb up the Great Pyramid. I didn't have a desire to actually go inside, but to be able to climb up loomed large in my to-do list. So he dropped us off as close as he could, and then it was on foot for a bit. Years ago – well actually not that many years ago – it was possible to do just about anything anyplace at the Giza site. But all the tourists have caused massive damage to the archaeologically important sites, so now access is restricted heavily. None-the-less, there is a way to climb up the massively huge stones a bit. And that is exactly what I was able to do. This was a day in which I was able to wonderfully tick off several items in my bucket-list. A day I will never forget.

Day Four:

This was to be the day to fly from Cairo to Luxor. And even though I hadn't written about this in my bucket list, something that was pretty important to me was to visit the El Zahraa stud of the Egyptian Agricultural Organisation. In the late 1970's and early 1980's, I had an Arabian horse farm in America. I was very proud of Pine River Farm and it provided many hours of enjoyment for me. The horses that I loved the most were all from Egyptian Arabian bloodstock, and to be in Cairo, the home of the El Zahraa stud and where most of the good Egyptian Arabian horses have come from, was too good to be believed. So before leaving, we took a taxi to stud at El Zahraa. With over 500 purebred Egyptian Arabians walking around in pastures was a sight to behold. (Now, if you are not a horse lover, you may just want to skip this paragraph.) What made it even more special was the fact that the stud, originally located on the outskirts of Cairo, is now surrounded by the city and it gives the feeling of being an oasis in the middle of an urban desert. Two staff members of the stud took us around, first to see some of the stallions, then the mares, and then the fillies and colts of this year. Whilst seeing the artefacts from the tomb of Tutankhamen was special, and climbing on the Great Pyramid was mind-boggling, being amongst all the straight-Egyptian horses was inspirational. I could have stayed there for hours…or days. But the Egypt Air flight to Luxor was not about to wait, so it was off to the airport for the next part of the holiday adventure.

Day Five:

Luxor is, well, Luxor. Located smack on the Nile river, Luxor is not exactly a pretty town, but then again, most places that survive solely on tourists coming from around the world to gawk at terribly old things wouldn't be. From a different perspective, Luxor was pretty spectacular. We stayed at the Winter Palace hotel, which is located on the Nile River. With an incredible history that dates back to, the Winter Palace is a classically designed Victorian structure that gives the impression that England still has a colonial empire. Whilst the building was pretty spectacular, the food was rather mediocre. On the other hand, breakfast was served on the terrace overlooking the Nile, so it wasn't exactly hard duty. Mid-day, a large black people carrier appeared and we were hustled off to the Oberoi Zahra to meet up with our friends from Australia that had arrived earlier.

The boat, one of 300 that we were told go back and forth between Luxor and Aswan, was wonderful. Whilst most of the river cruisers held 150 or more people, the Oberoi Zahra (the same basic size) has been kitted out to carry only 48 passengers, and yet the amount of staff was almost the same as on the typical boats. Needless to say, it was a tad posh. We all checked into our cabins and met for dinner and hours of conversation. (Some of our group had already been in Egypt for a week or so).

Day Six:

After breakfast, we met our group's tour guide. Rina Abou el Waffa was a lovely young woman whom we all fell in love with. On our first day we all piled into a large people carrier provided by the Oberoi people, and we went to see the Valley of the Kings. It was hot. No, seriously...it was flippin' hot. The daytime temperature on every day in Upper Egypt soared well into the 40"s centigrade, and there we were, walking around in the Valley of the Kings. No shade to speak of, just a lot of sun and rocks and tombs to explore. Each day after slogging around in seriously unbelievable heat at a tomb, we would be taken back to the Zahra to do whatever we wanted for a few hours. In my case, that meant plunging into the on-board pool to cool off a bit. Which I did. Every day. The swim that day was especially great for, as I was swimming in the boat's pool, the boat was sailing downstream to Quina. I suppose at this point, I need to provide a bit more clarification. We began the sailing part of the trip at Luxor and the overall voyage was going to be to Aswan. Aswan is south of Luxor, but upstream, as the Nile runs from south to north. Our voyage to Quina took us in the direction of Cairo, or in non-sailing terms, we went way out of our way and would have to come back toward Luxor. The purpose of this little diversion was to let us see another town, as well as see more of the river.

In the evening this day, we went to visit the Temple of Denderah, who as you may know, was dedicated to Hathour, the Goddess of music, love, and joy. Right. It was in fact, pretty spectacular, especially as we were there as the sun was going down and there were no other tourists around; something the

Oberoi people had arranged for us.

Day Seven:

(Just to keep track, this was the second full day on-board the Zahra...do try to keep up). We sailed back to Luxor and disembarked to visit Karnak Temple. This temple is far larger than the Denderah and covered an immense piece of land. Whilst most of the temples we saw did have what appeared to be a central building (the "temple" itself), the entire grounds around the structures were all part of what was known as the temple. This started out a bit confusing for first-time junior Egyptologists, but we did quickly understand the definitions of terms.

Later in the day, the Oberoi people arranged a quick tour of some of the back streets of Luxor. It is simply incredible to see the way that the locals who don't have direct contact with the tourist industry live. Actually, this was one of the real memorable parts of the trip (yes, one of quite a few). On the way back we stopped and did a bit more shopping and then sat for a bit in a very "local" café. Whilst sitting there amongst women walking around pretty much completely covered up, and men sitting smoking water-pipes, Russell and I decided that "when in Luxor, do as the Luxorian's do." Rina, who seemed to know everyone where we were, told a man who worked at the café that we wanted to try a water pipe, and within minutes, Russell and I were having some serious apple-tobacco through the interesting-to-operate water pipe.

Day Eight:

Another land trip, this one to the Valley of the Queens, which, as one might assume, is not that far from the Valley of the Kings. Incredibly hot, but even we were getting used to the mid-forty-degree temperatures as we would prowl around 4,000 year-old structures and tombs. Upon our return to the boat, we sailed to Edfu.

Day Nine:

At first light, we visited the Temple of Edfu. This had been billed as the "best preserved temple in the ancient world," and the hype was only surpassed by the reality of what we saw.

After returning to the Zahra, so overwhelmed by what we had seen, I barely could drag myself into the pool (yeah, right) as we sailed on to Kom Ombo. In the late afternoon, we visited the Temple of Kom Ombo. One side of the temple is dedicated to Sobek, the crocodile God, God of Fertility, and the Creator of the World. The other side of the temple is dedicated to the Falcon God Haroeris, who is (we were told) also known as Horus, the Elder. At each temple visit, Rina would whip out more facts than Wikipedia has online, and whilst we tried to listen intently to her stories, often some of our group would wander away to explore on their own and take as many photos as they could store on their memory sticks. I was usually one of those who would wander away, trying to simply get a grasp on all that was in front of me.

James B Rieley

About the time that Rina was notice that her group of nine was now a group of 4 or 5, she would, in a rather shrill voice, holler out, *"Hallo."* This was our call to re-group again, and being good little tourists, we always did. Well most of the time. Whilst we were having dinner back on-board the Zahra, we sailed to Aswan.

Day Ten:

This was going to be a bit of a touchy day for me, as we went via private coach to see the Philae Temple. I say we went by coach, but actually what we did was go by coach to a little harbour of sorts and boarded an old rickety wooden boat and putted our way to the island the temple is located on. This was the first time I had been on anything other than a seriously large boat since I had my GBS and found out that my equilibrium is pretty well shattered, so I was more than a tad nervous about this. But being on the little boat (about seven meters long) wasn't a problem. The problem arose when I went to step off the boat. Touring the temple was a bit wobbly for me, but it was worth the effort.

The temple was one that had been re-located during the construction of the low dam over the Nile. Quite a bit of land was flooded after the dam's completion and to avoid loosing the priceless Philae Temple, it was cut apart, block by block, and re-assembled on higher ground. The higher ground is now an island. (Just another side note here: When the high dam at Aswan was constructed from 1960 to 1971, it formed Nasser Lake, which is the world's largest man-made lake and doubled the countries power-supply because of its generators. The same thing happened to the four statues known as Abu Simbel, and they were cut, moved, and re-assembled on higher ground as well. I didn't get to see Abu Simbel on this trip…note the "this trip."

When we arrived back on the Zahra, I made an appointment for a serious leg massage, and feeling quite a bit better, joined some of our group as we did some serious shopping in the Soukh. The Soukh is, well, as with most things I experienced on this trip, pretty hard to describe. Close your eyes and imagine walking down very narrow streets, filled with traditionally dressed Egyptians, all rushing around getting ready for the arrival of Ramadan, with what appeared to be thousands of little shops selling just about everything you can imagine. Now imagine that every ten or twenty steps, a shop owner would step out in front of you and try to entice you in to buy something. It was straight out of a Casablanca-type movie. Some of the shop owners were a stitch. They would first accost you in German, English, Spanish, or sometimes French. Then after you responded with a courteous *"No thank you"* – the signal you spoke English, they would try just about everything in their limited English vocabulary to get you in their shops. That night, after thinking we had heard it all, one shop owner looked up from where he was sitting smoking his water-pipe and said, *"I don't know what you want English, but I have it inside."* Brilliant. As we walked along, simply cracking up at the rather clever approach, within 100 meters, his cunning approach was surpassed when a shop owner of a spice shop leapt out in front of us and said, *"Spices? Saffron? Viagra?"* Right. I don't think anyone bought anything that night, but we had a fab time in the Soukh, and when we were back on-board, all related our stories whilst on the top deck of the Zahra in the cool night air.

Day Eleven:

Whilst some from our group went off on an expedition of their own, most of us sat by the pool and simply did nothing. In this case, doing nothing included reliving some of the spectacular sights we had seen and comparing notes about this-or-that temple or tomb. Not a bad way to spend the day actually. That evening, it was "gala night" on-board the Zahra. Now this may seem like a rather naff way to spend an evening, but it was really quite special. The staff prepared a dinner that managed to out shine the previous evening's selections, which would have rated high marks in any posh restaurant on land...anywhere. And after dinner, we all gravitated to what had become our place on the boat at night, the top deck. We talked, we laughed, and we tried to digest all that we had seen on the Nile Cruise. And then it was over.

Day Twelve:

Our group of nine suddenly became a group of seven as we disembarked from the Zahra and flew from Aswan to Cairo. After some sad good-byes, four of us then flew to Amman Jordan and then took a car to Petra. It was a long, not-so-fun day, but Petra had been so high on my bucket list that even sitting in the car on the 2-1/2 drive south from Amman was filled with excitement.

On the way, I was talking to the driver, Mohamed, and couldn't resist asking him questions whilst his car hurtled along the King's Highway. One of the questions was something that I had asked Rina whilst we were sitting in the café learning how to smoke the water pipe. I had said to her, *"What do the people think of President Mubarek (of Egypt)?"* Her response was that the average Egyptian knew who he was, but didn't like him at all. They did like the previous president Anwar Sadat, and very much liked President Nasser. This made pretty much sense, as Nasser was the one who nationalised much of Egypt's economy following the devastation that King Farouk had bestowed on the country. I went on to ask if the average Egyptian knew who the Prime Minister of the United Kingdom was, and she said, *"Yes, it is Tony Blair."* Okay, so they missed that one a bit by a few years. Some people liked him, but some didn't she went on to say. And then she volunteered that no one likes the American president Bush. Interestingly enough, Mohamed volunteered the same answers, with the exception that in Jordan, the leader is King Abdullah II, the son of the late King Hussein, who the people also liked.

Day Thirteen:

Petra. I really have no idea what to write about Petra. When I was 10 or 11, I had read the book by Richard Haliburton that I talked about earlier. That is when I first learned about Petra, which occupied several pages in the book, and if there was ever anything in my bucket list worth wishing to see, it was Petra.

According to an information brochure, Petra was re-discovered in 1812 by a Swiss traveller named Johann Ludwig Burckhardt. I can only imagine what he felt as he walked along the deep, long, narrow gorge that leads to the site. After many twists and turns, (the gorge is 1200 meters long) all with the stone gorge walls looming overheard, you finally begin to get a glimpse of what the Nabataeans built thousands of years ago. Whilst I had thought that Petra was what is known as Al-Khazneh (the Treasury), it is really a very large site that is comprised of many buildings. Now here is the incredible part. All of the buildings were cut into solid sandstone canyon walls. No bricks, no mortar, just cut directly into the rock walls. Damn, it is simply incredible. We just sat there for a while, completely gobsmacked.

We had thought about walking in, but instead, we hired two horse-drawn carriages that had bounced along through the gorge. But once we were there, and after trying to catch our breath from the awe that we were seeing, we began to walk along through more gorges and down the road (and I use the term "road" rather euphemistically) through the rest of Petra. Some of the places we saw included the High Place of Sacrifice (always a treat if you are feeling rather frisky, as the term "high" does refer to the fact that you have to climb up quite high; the street of Facades and an amphitheatre that the Nabataeans built to hold 7,000 people. We also saw many Royal Tombs and the Palace Tomb, as well as a colonnaded street that was built with what appeared to be a heavy Roman influence.

We then plodded our way back to Al-Khazneh and just sat, speechless. We were quite lucky, as we had first gone through the gorge at 0730h, which was well before all the tourists (shed-loads of tourist flood there daily) had arrived, so we pretty much had the vistas to ourselves. But by the time we walked back, the area in front of the Treasury was filled with gawking tourists and after a while, we found our buggy drivers and went flying back up the gorge, feeling very much like Indiana Jones.

I have always liked writing mainly so others could vicariously experience what I have been experiencing since moving to Mallorca. And whilst I have never really struggled to share these experiences, this chapter has proved to be a real challenge. Not a challenge because I forgot how to type, but a challenge because my experiences on this trip have been so incredible, it is difficult to put them into words.

I have learnt so much on this trip. Many of these learning's have been about the cultures of ancient Egypt and the people who built Petra in Jordan. But perhaps my greatest learning has been that dreams are so very important, and so good to have as children. The only thing better than having those dreams is doing something about them whilst you still can. I will never forget this trip, and am incredibly thankful to my two friends who read the chapter on my bucket list, and then pressed me enough so I would be able to tick these two things off the list.

In the past several weeks, I have had two very interesting cultural experiences. The first one I wrote about; the trip to Egypt and Jordan is still on my mind, and it was truly an experience I will never forget. Just the fact that visiting some of the very special sites in Egypt and then being able to walk through the kilometre-long gorge to see the ancient glories carved directly into solid stone in Petra were both childhood dreams that have now become part of my realities. It was an incredible trip. And then there was the cultural experience I had the other evening.

I had gone to Munich to work with a client group, and after the very long day, we all went to visit one of the cultural centrepieces of Bavaria. Yes, we went to Oktoberfest. Oh my.

I was born in Milwaukee. When I was in my mid-teens, I can remember going to the first Summerfest event on Milwaukee's lakefront with my brother to see Freddie "Boom-boom" Cannon. Summerfest was an event that the city fathers developed as a way to both do something positive with the area, as well as stimulate tourism (which really means money) for the community. Summerfest was the brainchild of someone who had once visited Oktoberfest and had seen what a money-spinner it could be. I knew all this from growing up, but it wasn't until almost 50 years later that I actually experienced a bit of what Oktoberfest is all about.

My mental model was that it was all about thousands of people walking around consuming mass amounts of beer and having a good time. My mental model wasn't exactly right. There were tens-of-thousands of people, and they were consuming incredible amounts of beer. And whilst it did appear that they were having a good time, I think that many of them might not have a great morning the following day.

Oktoberfest is one huge party. Actually, a party on steroids. After making through a massive entrance area, we plunged through the crowds until we found the Hippodrom, a tent that we were scheduled to have dinner in. I am not even sure if the term "tent" is appropriate for what we walked into. The "tent" was the largest tent I had ever seen. It was filled with three-thousand people sitting at long tables. If they were not there, I am sure Airbus could use it to house one or two A380 planes in. *(Just a side note here. According to what I have found out, the Hippodrom wasn't the largest of the venues at Oktoberfest this year. There were eight tents, all sponsored by different breweries, that held about 6,000 people each, and one tent, sponsored by the Spaten-Franziskaner-Bräu brewery, that held a tad over 8,000 people. We didn't go to that tent, but I think it was the size of Lichtenstein.)*

As we made our way through the assembled throng, it was clear that these

James B Rieley

people were having a good time. It could have been stimulated by the obvious camaraderie of so many people coming together. It could have been stimulated by all the singing and loud conversations that were taking place (the level of noise in the tent was akin to sitting in a room filled with boomboxes set on turbo-high). It also could have been stimulated by the size and number of beer glasses that were being drained faster than the assets of a Wall Street bank. As I am not exactly a beer-fancier, I asked for something a bit less toxic, but I did actually try the beverage of the moment. I had been told that the best German brewers would put together special blends of their best products just for Oktoberfest, but to my less-than-finely-attuned-taste-receptors, it just tasted like beer to me.

On a riser on one side of the tent, a band was playing. Yes, this was a large group of men in lederhosen, serenading the throngs with their renditions of traditional Oktoberfest songs, such as, "Que Sera Sera," (I thought this was a French song?) "Achy-Breaky-Heart," (Oktoberfest meets Dallas Texas) and a true German version of "Roll Out the Barrél," or at least that it what is sounded like. At least this one was German. And then every few minutes, the band would crank up "Ein Prosit," which would cause everyone to stand up and clink their litre-sized beer mugs in a toast to something…probably the need to consume more beer. As our group got up to begin to walk around more of the grounds that had become Oktoberfest, a woman came up to us and asked if anyone in our group wanted to have their breath checked. For only 5.50 euros, you could "rent" a breath-a-lyzer so you could see if you were in any condition to drive home (assuming you actually did go home at some point). Whilst no one in our group felt the need to use this service, it did strike me as another clever money-spinning franchise, which Oktoberfest was full of. It also struck me that many of the people who probably did use the service would also need help standing whilst exhaling into the little machine.

After wandering around and stopping at another venue where I was told the beer was even more special than at the Hippodom (it still tasted like beer to me), the group headed off to discover what other fun things they could experience. I, on the other hand, being the party animal that I am, found a taxi and made it back to the hotel to do some follow-ups to today's meeting. On the way back in the taxi (whose driver appeared to be a graduate of the Henri Paul School of Driving), I began thinking…if I was not here on business, with a group of people who really wanted to experience Oktoberfest, would I have gone there? It didn't take me long to realise that the answer was no. But it also didn't take me long to realise that being a part of a real Oktoberfest was a cultural experience that I am glad I did. Ein Prosit!

I read someplace that *if you have enough desire, and put forth enough effort, you can succeed at just about anything.* For most of my life, I would have agreed with that statement. But for certain things, I would have said "bollocks" to that statement. I may have changed my mind.

Living on Rocks

When went to purchase Amelia a few years ago, I found out that you cannot purchase a car here in Spain unless you have a valid drivers permit. That made sense to me, but it was then I discovered that my driver's permit was not considered valid for this type of purchase. This seemed to be one of those diabolical governmental rules that plague mankind: I could drive with my existing permit; I could even rent a car with my permit, but I was unable to purchase a car.

The reasoning behind this regulation is that my permit – first obtained by myself when I was 16 years old – was issued in the United States. This means to those who are uninitiated in the intricacies of law, it was issued by a state government and not by the federal government. In most of the world, driver's permits are issued by federal governments, meaning that there is some standard of conformity between them, but permits issued by individual states potentially have variation in qualifications, and therefore, are not considered valid here. Bear in mind, the absurdity comes from the fact that it is okay to use a U.S. driver's permit to drive, just not okay to purchase a car. To me, at the time, this seemed like one of those daft regulations that only a bureaucrat could come up with. But it is Spain, and I am the one who chose to live here, so I did what any other self-respecting ex-businessman would do; I figured out a way to game the system.

After a bit of checking, I discovered that I could purchase a car with an international driver's permit. I made a few phone calls, and within days, received a FedEx packet with my international drivers permit in it and trotted off to buy Amelia. After about a year, I thought that, as I have chosen to live here in Spain, I should actually get a Spanish driver's permit. My first step was to simply exchange my existing permit for a Spanish one, but that wasn't to be. If it wasn't good enough to use to purchase a car, there was no way the government would accept it in exchange for a Spanish one. I tried to have it exchanged in the United Kingdom as well, but apparently they (and the French, Swiss, Germans, and just about every other European country) had the same view of the validity of a state-issued permit. Okay, not to worry, I would just take whatever test was required and would be on my way. Well, this brainstorm blew up in my face when I took the written test. Forty questions, of which you can only miss 4, and I mucked up 5 of them. As my existing (and apparently valueless) permit didn't expire until my birthday in 2009, I decided to just forget about it. After all, I was legal to drive my car with my permit – it was only a problem when I tried to buy it.

Let's fast-forward a bit. In mid-summer this year, and the whole driver's permit thing was on my mind again. So, with a massive sense of trepidation, I decided I had better resume my attempts to finally get a Spanish drivers permit. I registered at a driver's school. I bought the study books. I studied my little head off. And then I took the test. The test has changed, and is now only 30 questions, but the bad news is that you can only miss 3 or you fail. I missed 5. Buggers. I rescheduled for another test appointment, and proceeded to study harder.

I had never really learnt how to study whilst in school. I can remember doing exceedingly well on tests with innocuous questions abut current events but when it came to serious exams about things that a teacher thought were important (like the synopsis of Silas Marner, or doing partial differential equations), I usually only squeeked past, if that. I can remember one time being banished to my room by my parents to study for a big exam, only to promptly fall asleep at my desk. Several hours later, I awoke and crept into the sitting room expecting a proper bollocking, only to find out that my parents weren't aware that I had been sleeping and not studying. I think I barely managed to pass that exam. But now, far older and (hopefully) a tad wiser, I knew that I had to really buckle down and learn the rules for driving in Spain if I wanted the pass this test.

Part of the problem is that many of the questions on the tests (there are God-knows-how-many variation of the tests) just don't make any sense. Like the question about the sign that a vehicle must display when carrying a load that sticks out beyond the back of the vehicle. I knew the sign is diamond-shaped, with alternating red and white reflective stripes. I had seen this in the book and knew that it meant that something was sticking out at least 1 metre beyond the rear of the vehicle. But when I encountered a question about it on the test, I was flummoxed to find that the question asked how big the sign was. Who cares how big it is? Wouldn't you think the appropriate question would be something like, *"What does this bloody sign mean?"* I thought so. Another fun question was *"In a four-wheel drive car, which wheels do the driving?"* The answer choices were, A) the front wheels. B) the rear wheels. C) all four wheels. Well duh…it is a four-wheel drive car, so the answer would be C, all four wheels. Right? Wrong.

Okay, so I took the test again and again mucked it up. I began to try to figure out how difficult it would be to obtain a UK driver's permit. Of course, as they wouldn't exchange theirs for my existing one, I would have to travel to the UK. And then I would have to get a provisional license, so I could take a written test, so I could take a practical (behind the wheel) test. And of course, I couldn't do all this the same day, or even the same week; so that meant multiple trips to the motherland. This was getting rather depressing.

I have discovered that the whole driver's testing system here is a bit wonky. I recently heard that one ex-pat who was attempting to obtain his permit and after several attempts, was convinced that he had passed. This was even though each time he had been told that he had failed. Because he was so sure that he had done well enough, he actually found an abogado (solicitor) and marched in to see the Head of the Driver's Testing Bureau. After the abogado was finished explaining the law, el jefe (the chief) turned over the man's results and guess what? He had passed the tests…all of them. I was tempted to contact the abogado myself to do the same thing, but then realised that this might not be the smartest of moves as long as I want to live here – not a smart move to piss-off the authorities. Instead, I decided to resume studying the Spanish driver's code.

I think (I hoped) part of the problem was that initially, I was just studying the "Test Sample" book, but after two attempts, realised that there were so many potential variations of the actual test, that many of the real questions were not in the sample book. I began to read the "Learning to Drive Manual." Oh my....only 224 pages to memorise. Give me an interesting book on some random topic that interests me, and I will remember the contents forever. Force me to memorise something that I am only reading because I have to will usually result in a good demonstration of short-term memory loss.

This week, I had another go at the test. Feeling totally screwed by this system, I hadn't even opened the book in the past month. As a matter of fact, I was becoming so apathetic about the whole permit thing here I was ready to make plans to fly to the UK in the near future.

There I was, standing outside the Driver's Testing building along with the other 100 or so people who wanted to obtain their permits as well. As I was wondering how many of them had been here multiple times as well, the test proctor came out and began to call names. As I heard my name, and went up to collect the test form, I felt like saying hello again to this very familiar face, but I thought that was tasteless so I simply took the one page form and went into the queue at the door. Just before you step into the room and are told where to sit, a test administrator checks your identification – probably to make sure that someone who actually could pass the test wasn't taking it for you. Because I am a foreign national, I have to show my residency permit (original) and my passport (original). And because I wasn't really expecting anything other than another psychologically devastating result, I only had photocopies with me, but I think she was taking pity on me, so I was shown to a seat.

There they were...the evil thirty questions, some of which I had seen before. Some of them I would swear are not even in the bloody book. Screw it. I checked which boxes seemed to be rational, and drove home. This morning I went online to check my results and there it was, written in a little box that explains the test results, "Apto." Oh my...I passed the test. I had actually passed the flippin"-mentally-torturing-non-sensical test. At first, I was incredibly excited. And whilst I had actually gotten past this major stumbling block, I realised that now I get to experience the road test part of getting my driver's permit. Having driven for God-knows-how-many-years, this test will have to be easier than the theory test. Right.

It is almost winter here. Well, our version of winter that is. So I did what any logical thinking person would do who lives here (and who has a fireplace). I ordered leña. I used to do this several times a season when I lived at La Antigua. Actually, last year I ordered wood more than once as well, but last

James B Rieley

year I was just getting use to how much wood I needed to outlast the desperately cold months. Okay, again, our version of what desperately cold means. It wasn't that I was out of leña, I probably had enough to last several weeks, but I thought I would get ahead of the weather for sure. You just never know when the temperatures will begin to drop.

So last week, Tomeu, my friendly leña-supplier, pulled up at my front gate with his carry-van loaded down with a ton of wood. Please don't ask if it was a "ton" or a "metric-ton." All I know is that is was pretty flippin' heavy. After filling his little black rubber buckets with four or five logs for what seemed to be hundreds of times, the wood was all piled up on the front terrace. It was then that I asked Tomeu if he was the best one to talk to about getting someone to clean the chimney on my fireplace. It is great talking to Tomeu. Even though his English is limited to the occasional *"Okay,"* and my belief that my Spanish is pretty remedial, we seem to understand each other very well. After discussing the world's financial mess and local politics (another mess) we moved on to discuss how best to *"Limpear mi chiminea"* (clean my chimney).

When I was living in La Antigua, I had asked someone to come and clean out the chimneys above both fireplaces. When I had asked a village local, I was told that there were two basic ways to do it. One way was to hire someone who had all the appropriate chimney-cleaning kit. You can imagine what this is. A large brush that attaches to a flexible handle mechanism that can be extended. A variation of this method is to have the brush, but connect it on top and bottom to long cords. In this variation, you lower the bottom cord through the chimney and one person on the bottom tugs and releases his end of the cord, whilst on the top of the chimney, another person does the same thing. By doing this, the brush is worked up and down, knocking all the chimney crud off the chimney walls. Okay, I thought that this made sense and as I was about to call the chimney-cleaning-person, I was told about another method. This method involves the use of a long cord and a (get ready for this)…chicken. Yes, a chicken. I was flummoxed. I was told that the way chimneys had been cleaned for years was to go outside, select a chicken from your yard (preferably one that you would want to have for dinner that night) and ties its legs to a long cord and pull it up through the chimney. Okay, so I understood the physics of it all – the chicken would undoubtedly not be too happy about being tied up and dragged up through a dark stone-lined tube covered with soot stuff and would undoubtedly flap its wings like crazy, knocking all the built-up soot off the chimney walls. I even understand the logic that when the chicken is pulled out the top, it will be filthy and covered with creosote residue, but if you are going to cook it for dinner anyway…well, needless to say, I didn't go for that idea and instead elected to tell the chimney cleaner to use the brush and cords method.

So when I was talking to Tomeu, I very quickly mentioned that I didn't want to have anyone come to my house with a chicken. He laughed and

Living on Rocks

said something about small villages. He also said that there was another alternate method to clean a chimney. This method simply involved going to the local ferreteria (iron-mongerers for Brits, hardware store for Americans) and buying a container of chimney cleaner. I was intrigued so after finishing stacking up all the wood (neatness in woodpiles is an important human trait I seem to think) I walked over to my local ferreteria and bought a container of the magical mystery stuff. It came in a medium-sized blow-moulded polyethylene bottle (sorry, too many years in the plastics business I guess) emblazoned in big letters, "Producto Ecologico" next to a picture of a flower, so you know it is safe to use. Right.

Today I decided to give it a go, and after carefully (attempting to) read the directions, I began the process. After all, it was cloudy and misting rain today, so it seemed like a good day to do an inside chore. Paraphrasing the instructions, Step 1, build a roaring fire. Step 2, thrown on more wood to make the fire blaze like an arsonists wet-dream. Step 3, empty the contents of the container onto the fire.

Okay. I did build the fire; I did get it blazing so it was pumping out more flames and heat that I could imagine. I did empty the contents of the container. The flames did singe me. I did become almost blinded by the ensuring flares and sparks. It was as if I had poured a bottle of gunpowder onto the fire.

I was going to read the extremely fine Spanish print on the container that the mystical-Merlin-like-pellets came in to see what this mystical product contained, but I was afraid I would see the words NAPALM or WHITE PHOSPHORUS with a mild reference to Ministry of Defence surplus, so I decided against it. The good news is that I would like to believe that my chimney did become a bit cleaner. No inhumane treatment of chickens, no brushes to mess with, no mound of dislodged creosote on the floor to clean up afterwards. I was going to go up on the roof terrace with a tall ladder so I could peer down into the chimney to see how clean it actually was, but my "too-much-fun-in-one-day" quotient had been reached so I decided instead to do something more practical. I went back to the ferreteria and bought three more containers…Guy Fawkes night is just around the corner.

We all have an addiction of one form or another. Mine is to be connected whenever I need to be and wherever I am. Since living in Mallorca, I have worked through several ways to feed my addiction. Whilst living on Angelina, I had a Vodafone wireless PCMIA card-thingy that I would slot into my computer on the boat. It was bog slow, but it did work. When I bought La Antigua, I installed Telefonica's version of ADSL and then immediately adapted it so that my entire house would be wireless. Life was good. And then I moved to Sol y Mar and repeated the process – order ADSL from Telefonica and then install a wireless router so I could be connected without being bogged down by a cable. Again, life was good.

James B Rieley

But because I am a bit cautionary at times, this summer, I signed on to another broadband service. This one did not rely on a telephone line. It was a service that operated through a system that has a huge tower located on a nearby mountain. Because I can see the tower from my roof terrace at Sol y Mar (okay, I can see the top of the mountain and I know the tower is there), I was able to receive the wireless broadband signal. The signal then goes down a wire into my house where it is plugged into a wireless router. Voila! After going through all the installation issues, I now had two broadband sources, ensuring that I would always be able to be connected. And then last week happened.

We had this little storm go crunching across the island. I say little, but the winds were clocked at in excess of 120kph on parts of the island and the rain came down as if a huge fire-hose had been opened above Mallorca. The storm was great to see as it was occurring. The rain came down in various angles, mostly of the horizontal variety; the waves of the sea were 3 metres high and were pounding onto the shoreline below Sol y Mar at the speed of a locomotive gone mad; and the wind was sending branches and chairs flying about. And then two of the trees across the street fell down…and landed on the electrical lines feeding the neighbourhood…and on my telephone line. Interestingly, the phone line, although stretched so taut that it could have been part of a guitar and almost touching the ground, still was working. But that all ended when a work crew came out the next day to sort out the mess. They chopped the tree up, but in the process, cut through my phone line. Great. No phone, and consequently, no broadband. But, due to my cunning back up system, I was still able to stay connected. Life was still good.

I rang the phone company (Telefonica) and reported the "downed" line. They said they would send someone out as soon as possible…and you know what that can mean. I did realise that I was the only person in the neighbourhood whose phone service was interrupted, so my problem may not be a priority on an island where parts of it were seriously messed up from the storm. I phoned them again the next day. I had a neighbour phone them, reasoning that if a native Spanish-speaker rang, they might be better able to communicate my problem. All through this turmoil, things were still okay for my connectability because I had the back-up system functioning as if nothing had happened. And then yesterday my back-up system went down. I don't know if the mountain-top tower fell over or what. All I know is that suddenly, I was not connected. It was then I realised how addicted I was to being connected.

I phoned the mountain-top-back-up-broadband supplier, but they didn't even answer their phone. I called Telefonica again, thinking that at least I had my mobile working so I could talk to someone, but also realised that the broadband people I was talking to were still busy sorting out the other communications problems on the island. Buggers.

Yesterday afternoon, I managed to find a wireless signal floating around my house from a neighbour, or so I assumed. I really didn't care where the signal was coming from, all I knew that I was able to tap into it so my computer was once again humming along. Sadly, that signal disappeared rather quickly. By last night I had developed a metaphorical twitch, which by this morning had turned into a near case of "no broadband epilepsy." Not a pretty picture, and good no one was around. I wasn't in the best of moods. My need to be connected was becoming a bit obsessive so early this morning, I took my laptop and went to a local café that kindly has wireless broadband for their customers. I ordered some tea and toast and found the signal. By the time I had answered the most important email traffic that had been plugging up my machine, I had finished by breakfast and went home, only to find the Telefonica man on a ladder installing a new line. I still don't know what happened to my back-up system – those buggers still aren't answering their phone – but at least life here as resumed to my version of normal…so to speak.

I realised through this entire episodic comedy that perhaps I am a bit too addicted to being connected whenever and wherever I want. And for a second or two, I actually thought about beginning to turn my computer off for several hours each day. I think I will do that…as soon as I see pigs flying.

06
Amèlie

It is just about the end of the year, and I haven't written in quite a while. It isn't because I have been in a coma or anything, I just have been busy doing what I like to do here. Sadly, that hasn't included spending as much time outside as I would like.

This part of the Mediterranean has been caught in a rather nasty weather pattern of late. It could be some of the nastier side effects of global weather pattern changes, it could be just bad luck, or it could be that I was a bad child. All I know is that the weather has been less than nice. This morning, after once again trolling through the various weather forecasting websites (all of which must be staffed by coin-tossing guessers) I eventually came across a site that showed the current flow of the jet stream. Apparently this is the real problem that Mallorca has been dealing with. Instead of the jet stream screaming from west to east along the higher latitudes, it is pouring down from the frozen climes of northern Europe and keeping us trapped in a set of persistent low-pressure cycles, which has brought the island what seems to be about 40 days and nights of rain. Of course this really isn't the case, but it did rain pretty much of yesterday, and I awoke this morning to dead-grey skies and a constant drizzle. Thankfully, Tomeu was here last week and brought me another ton of leña for the fireplace.

Today was a very good day otherwise. I actually passed my driving road test. Yes, I actually passed it. This whole experience has been…well, an experience. I wouldn't say it has been anywhere near what I expected it to be, but at this point, I really don't care. But in case you ever find yourselves in this situation, you may want to ensure that you learn patience…I certainly have. When I first registered for the "practical's" part of earning a driver's permit here, I was told that, like the written theory tests, I would have to go through a driver's school. Okay, fair enough. This did seem like a good way to keep the driver's schools in business, but this is the way things are done here, so I signed up for behind-the-wheel lessons.

Whilst I have had a driver's permit since I was 16, and have never killed anyone with my driving, I was prepared to take a couple of lessons, if for no other reason than to find out what the test examiners would be watching for during the actual test. So after two lessons, what I learnt was that you can never cross a solid white line (*"James, think of the solid white line as a brick wall"*), and pedestrians always have the right of way. I took the test. I failed. Why? One of my wheels touched a solid white line whilst making a left hand turn. Okay, fair enough. I had been told, and still managed to touch one of the lines. A fail did seem a bit drastic for just touching a line, but rules are rules. My instructor asked me how many more lessons I wanted to take,

Living on Rocks

and I – reflecting on my many years of driving and frustration with the "system" here – responded that I didn't plan on taking any more before my next road-test. This proved to be a less-than-smart decision. My next attempt at the road-test was even more "interesting" than the first, and once again, I was told I did not pass, but this time for an even more innocuous reason. And if that wasn't enough, I was then told that by law, I would now need to pay an additional test fee, and take five lessons. Yes, this is the law. I was going to ask to see the actual statute on the books, but then figured that this would just alienate the driver's licensing authority (something you do not want to do), so instead I just pondered the dynamics of the licensing system in Spain. Let's see: The more times you fail either the written or behind-the-wheel test, the more money you have to pay to re-take the test, as well as pay for the "lessons" that are supposed to help you pass. Not too much of an incentive to help people learn too quickly I thought. The good news (I suppose) is that it keeps many many driver's schools open, which keeps many many instructors employed and keeps funnelling money into the coffers of the licensing authority. This view was confirmed when I met someone who was on her 80^{the} lesson. Oh my God...EIGHTY LESSONS!!!! And I was whinging about having to take seven. What a money spinning system.

So today I re-took the behind-the-wheel test and passed. Didn't run over anyone, didn't touch any white lines (I guess), and the best of all was that I didn't vocalise my observations about the "system." The end result of all this effort and expense of euros is that now I will have a drivers permit in the country I have chosen to live in. I am completely chuffed...now if I could only get the weather to improve.

I thought you might like to know what else I have been up to lately. Yes, it has been graphic-arts time at Sol y Mar. After doing my Christmas cards (an 8 colour-layer serigraph that attempts to replicate the feeling of walking through the long, narrow gorge into Petra), I decided that it might be nice to put together a series of limited edition prints. My inspiration for these editions was pretty easy – I simply decided to make prints based on some of the watercolours and pen & ink drawings I had made since moving to Sol y Mar. Whilst this became a larger, more intense project than I had anticipated, I was pretty happy with the outcomes. After several weeks, I had produced a folio that contained two prints based on the Compound series of watercolours, one print based on an extremely large watercolour of part of the gardens here, and several black and white prints that were originally pen & ink drawings I had done of some of the views of the Mediterranean shoreline at my house.

And now, as the Christmas holidays are face approaching, I thought the very least I could do is to wish you all a fab holiday this year, with massive wishes for an even better year in 2009.

Oh my...I am now firmly entrenched in writing triple digit chapters. Who would have guessed? I thought, because tomorrow is one of my favourite days, I would write about other favourite things as well.

Have I mentioned that tomorrow is one of my favourite days? I am writing this letter on 21 December, and that means tomorrow is the Winter Solstice at a few minutes after midnight here. As I am sure you know, the Winter Solstice is the shortest day of the year, and for here, that means only about 9 hours of potential sunlight. The shortest day means the least amount of sunlight of the year, and many of you might wonder how that could be something I would like. Well, it works like this…if this will be the day when we have the least amount of sunlight that means that the following day, daylight hours begin to get longer. Okay, so this could be viewed as a highly optimistic way to view the situation, but it works for me.

I like spring too. I think for me, spring is the best season because everything begins to grow. Summer is great, because I do love having the house open and the sea breezes wafting through the windows and doors. But fall is the time that things begin to die out, even on my little island paradise. And winter? Well I do like to be able to put on a nice jumper and sometimes it is even nice to wear long pants, but the very thought of winter sends both physical and psychological shivers down my spine.

There is the whole thing about living with views of the sea each day that really works for me. On a sunny day, the sea shimmers with an intensity that is unmatched, each little ripple being able to whisper a story of what it has seen. Even on those nasty storm-filled days, just watching the sea waves come pounding onto the shore with the waves pummelling all in their paths, is an incredible site. I could spend hours just looking out toward the horizon, watching the boats slowly sail past Sol y Mar, and remembering how great it was to be able to do that myself. I truly loved living in La Antigua. The village was a very special place, but after having spent the past year being right overlooking the water, I am not so sure I could go back too easily.

Clearly high on my list of favourite things is doing things that I classify as "creative." I simply love to write, and whilst much of my writing is focused on business, over the years, I have found great pleasure in writing about just about anything. I am not exactly sure when this started, but I do remember that whilst in school, I hated writing with a passion. But I think it was when I took an assignment in higher education and was told I didn't have access to any serious budget that writing suddenly became easy for me. I was trying to convince the college's unions that the initiatives I had proposed were valid and worthwhile. In my mind, the easiest way to do this was to bring in a nationally-recognised speaker that the unions would respect who would add credibility to what I thought was important. But without a budget, there was no way I could hire anyone powerful enough, so I wrote an article and managed to get it published in a higher education journal that I knew the union leadership read. That article led to another, and another, and another.

Not that long after publishing my first book, I decided to write a monthly

Living on Rocks

business newsletter. I chose the monthly timeframe, because I wasn't sure that I would be able to come up with enough content to do them more frequently. But after identifying some topics I thought might be interesting to potential recipients, I realised that I might be able to do the newsletter weekly. That was five years ago, and I am still finding a never-ending supply of things to write about. I won't even mention these epistolary process other than to say my intent when I started doing them, I had planned on doing about 12 per year. That was 4-1/2 years ago. Do the math.

When I am not writing, I am probably painting or making limited-edition prints of something. My Aunt Peg really drove me in this direction when I was 10 or so, and now, a few years later, I still get quite a rush by taking what I "see," and putting it on paper. I am not even sure why I enjoy this so much, but being told by others that they enjoy my efforts turns work into pleasure for me.

Oh yes, of course one of my favourite things is work. *"He likes work?"* you might be thinking. Well, for me, each day offers up a choice. When I wake up in the morning each day, I am presented with one of two options. I could think about all the things I have to do and the limited time I have to do them in. I could stress about external or self-imposed deadlines that may plague my plans for the day. I could worry about things that are well beyond my scope of ability to do something about. I could fall into the trap of being caught up in all these things, but instead I tend to focus on the fact that I am actually waking up to an opportunity to continue to do what I like best – which is learn and share and learn and share. By putting everything in a *"learn and share and learn and share"* mindset, time isn't important, nor are deadlines. Several years ago I received a card from a very special person that said, *"Do what you can, where you are, with what you have."* With that belief and a learn-and-share mindset, how could a day be anything other than fabulous?

We all deserve a treat once in a while. You do, I do, we all do. A few weeks ago, I was thinking what I wanted to do to treat myself. My mind raced with ideas, some of them a bit over the top, even I will admit. I have passed my driver's permit torture, and that was surely deserving of a treat, but all I could come up with was a newer car. You know, something a bit sportier, like a two-seater cabriolet something-or-other. But that did seem a bit impractical at times, especially when I make my somewhat frequent trips to my supplier of large artsy-stuff. Besides, Amelia has been a good car, and she is doing fine. So a newer car, for the sake of having a treat, seemed naff even to me.

I had just been to see an Aunt and Uncle in Florida, and on that trip, was able to spend time with one of my son's and his wife, so going travelling didn't seem to be special enough for a treat right now. Whilst on my trip to Florida, I did buy a new computer, and that was special because what I purchased was a Mac Air. If you don't know, this is the Macintosh laptop that weighs next to nothing and is thin enough to fit in an envelope…perfect for when I travel. But even that seemed like a functional business expense item and not a real treat. My house is already quite special. I could, I supposed, get a new desk, but that would be about as boring as watching paint dry. But then it hit me…one of the very special things about Sol y Mar is the views. The house has three terraces, all overlooking the sea, and the sitting room has large windows that let me see the Mediterranean from almost any perspective. The kitchen however, where I do spend some time, does not have a view of the sea. So after talking to a contractor, my plan was set…and today it kicked into high gear.

The plan was to knock a hole in the wall between the kitchen and the sitting room so that I would be able to see the Mediterranean whilst preparing my meals. And after receiving permission from the owners of the house, Juan and his two workers arrived the other day and began the project. I knew that this would be interesting, as it was going to be an all-Spanish adventure. I had piled up all the furniture in my sitting room, as I assumed that once the actual work commenced, the house would be filled with pulvo (dust), and had also applied masking tape to the sitting room side of the soon-to-be-porous wall where I wanted the new window would be. Juan studied the situation for about 3 seconds and then told one of his helpers to go out to his furgoneta (a furgoneta is a small van-type vehicle used to transport materials or equipment, FIR-GO-NET-A) and bring back a big sheet of plastic to cover the furniture. I was thinking of suggesting that instead of trying to cover everything, it might be easier to just build a tent-like thing around where the wall would be cut. But as I was trying to figure out how to say "tent-like-thing," Juan told his other helper to give him a drill. Oh my, this was like a scene from some medical programme on telly, with "the doctor" issuing instructions in an operating theatre. Before I could say anything, Juan had bored three holes in the wall – one in each of the two top corners of the masked off area, and one along the top edge. Okay, so I assumed he was testing the thickness of the wall, or even the composition of the wall itself so he could determine the best way to cut the new window. As I was pondering what was going on, Juan said something to one of this lads again and within a flash, there was a key-hole hand saw in his hand.

Just in case you are tool-knowledge-deprived, a key-hole saw is a hand saw in which the blade is very long and narrow, and is used to do intricate detail work. He jammed the pointy-end of the saw blade into one of the holes he had made and began moving it back and forth. In nothing flat, he had made it half-way down the masked-off line on one side. He then, as any good jefe (chief) would, told one of his lads to take over…and follow the line! The entire cutting process took less than 15 minutes. I was gobsmacked. After making the final few centimetres of the cuts, the two lads carefully lifted out the wall section, with Juan issuing instructions as they went. It was then that I began to realise why the project went so well.

Whilst the walls of La Antigua were made of stone and were a meter thick, the walls of Sol y Mar were made of a sandstone-like material, which submitted rather easily to the nasty little saw teeth. For the first time, I was able to actually see through the wall – something I had visualised for some time. It was everything I had hoped it would be. I would be able - whilst standing in the kitchen, attempting to make some incredible delicious version of proper food - to see not only into the sitting room, but I would now be able to see out through the windows of the sitting room that overlook the Mediterranean.

After a few hours of plastering the edges of the opening, Juan and his crew packed up and were on their way. I re-assembled my sitting room and kitchen and began to enjoy my Christmas treat, pondering what my next project would be.

2009

Dateline, Mallorca, 5 January, 2009. (this is where you should be making the sound of a teletype to reflect the immediacy of the news herein written... that is if you actually are old enough to know what a teletype used to sound like at the beginning of the big news programmes).

It may only be a bit past noon today, but the sun is out and I am completely chuffed. Yes, today was the day I have been waiting to arrive for the past six months or so. Whilst the process I have gone through has been a tad tiresome at times (like every day), in today's post, I actually received my Spanish driver's permit. This just has to be a great day.

I was thinking over the hols what I really would like to accomplish this year. I am not one who gets too wrapped up in making New Year's resolutions but it is still okay to reflect on what you want to do. I think that I don't make a huge written list of resolutions because in the past, I have rarely managed to realise them. This could be for a variety of reasons, with the number one reason being that in the past, many of the resolutions I have made have been pretty daft. There is the tried-and-true "get into better physical shape" resolution that many of us make each year. Several years ago, when I was still in resolution-making mode, I decided that this would be a good thing to focus on. I analysed what I ate and the amount of exercise I did. The food thing was pretty easy to sort out, but the whole exercise thing is pretty structured for someone like me. Whilst I am quite disciplined about some things, the very thought of following some exercise regime was a bit much for me to deal with. So I did what so many people do, and actually considered joining a health club.

Right. The health club thing. I did find one on a website that looked interesting. I was having some concerns when I found the website had a virtual tour of the facility, and the young incredibly fit woman doing the tour announced that her name was Seven. (Who names their child Seven?) It had a pretty well kitted-out weight room that was chocker with what appeared to be machines designed by Dr. Mengele and racks and racks of shiny weights. The club even had a pool, sauna, and running track. Hmmm. The cost wasn't that oppressive, but just as I was about to metaphorically put euros on the table, I realised that in order to use all this kit, I would have to actually go there several times a week. Each week. Every week. I re-thought what I was about to do and realised that this just wasn't for me. Instead, I decided to consider joining one of those yoga or Pilates groups that most cities have in about the same quantity as a Starbucks. Hmmm. After talking to several people who rambled on about how good bending and stretching my body in ways that God had never imagined, it became clear to me that this wasn't the answer either. So I did what any other self-respecting, quasi-clever person would do. I decided to open my own health club.

The "Dr. Riley's Health-Club-Fitness-Centre-Sunny-Terrace-Smoking-Lounge" is pretty great. No real equipment to get tangled up in. No outrageous monthly fee just in order to sweat. No paranoid litigiously-driven disclaimers to sign. And no other members. Just me, working once in a while on being more fit. The daily work plan (on the days when I actually do it) includes a bugger-long walk. I do have a car (and now an actual legal drivers permit) but there is the whole ecology-carbon-footprint thing, so I walk what feels like 32,000 kilometres each day. I used to have one of those step counters, but for some reason, after walking for an hour, it would never display how many steps it felt like I had taken, so I binned it. I also do some stretching exercises each morning when I wake up. I was thinking about ringing my solicitor to see if I could get a patent on them, but I was afraid he would say something less-than encouraging. Besides, my stretching exercises are more to ensure that my body will actually be able to get me out of bed in the morning than to tone up those abs and pects and whatever else I have lurking under my skin.

And by now, some of you are probably thinking, *"Why doesn't he quit smoking if he wants to become more fit?"* From a non-smoker's perspective, that could be a fair question. But I am not really too sussed about the smoking thing; largely because of my "be healthy" ace-in-the-hole. Years ago as part of my work research, I learnt how to do visioning. Yes, visioning. Each day, I see myself as healthy. (*If you are shaking your head wondering which planet I am writing this letter from, don't worry…I am still here in Mallorca on the planet Earth*). The whole visioning thing can be a bit tricky, but what I do is almost the same as seeing myself doing what I do each day, but I see myself as healthy whilst doing it. You could say it is like seeing yourself on telly. You have to adjust the focus to make sure that you can clearly see, but with some practise, anyone can do this. To do this well, it means that I look at myself from several perspectives but always focussing on my physical, emotional, and spiritual health. Now if you are a doubting Thomas (or someone with another name but who thinks I have eaten some bad paella), you have to realise that it really doesn't matter how scientifically promising this is…it works for me. I actually told my doctor about my visioning a couple of years ago, and his response was that if it works, keep doing it. This visioning does require some effort, but from where I am sitting, it is one hell of a lot less effort than getting up each day and being faced with the spectre of sweating along with a group of other people at some health club trying to avoid being eaten by a multi-tubed chrome pain machine.

I used my visioning process whilst I was going through the entire driver's examination process. Each time I had to put up with some completely ludicrous government-driven exercise in draining my checkbook, I kept focused on seeing myself buzzing around the island with a proper Spanish driving permit. And now I have it.

Life is full of good news and bad news, and often they are the same thing. My good news is that I now have my driving permit here; the bad news is that now that I have my permit, I will have to come up with something else to envision besides just being healthy. Hmmm.

Before I get into this, I must ask you if you have ever seen a movie with Arnold Schwarzenegger and Danny DeVito called "Twins?" It is a comedy in which Schwarzenegger seeks out his maternal twin he was separated from at birth, only to find that it is the character played by DeVito. Try to keep that visual in your mind as you read this letter.

Well, she is here. Yes, Miranda has arrived at Sol y Mar, and I am pretty happy. I had been thinking of Miranda for some time now, and even put quite a bit of effort into finding here. The effort was worth it. I found Miranda on a trip to Barcelona. I had flown over for the express purpose of meeting her and when I did, I was convinced she was the one for me. Oh...sorry, forgot to say this part...Miranda is a car.

As you have read previously, when I purchased Amelia, she wasn't my first choice. But as luck would have it, the car I had been looking at was sold by the time I managed to get my car-purchasing-act-together and sort out the legalities of owning a car in Spain. But Amelia did turn out to be a wonderful purchase, and has given me several years of safe, sound transportation. And in fact, Amelia is still doing well, but we are now slipping deeper into a serious financial crisis almost all over the world. The financial mess has landed solidly in Spain, and I began to ponder how the crisis would impact auto dealers. Well, it has impacted them pretty heavily...which has proved good for a potential buyer.

So I recently began trolling around looking for a fun little car and after locating several of them in on-line auto websites, began developing some mental criteria for a possible purchase. Lo-and-behold, my list of potentials was narrowed down to four and after eliminating one here on the island, I flew over to the mainland to look at the other three. Car 1 was pretty nice, but it looked too much like a posh, up-scale car. I was looking for something that had the appearance and feel of a proper British sports car; two seats, compact, convertible top, manual transmission...but I also wanted to have a car that would not bankrupt me on maintenance or purchase cost – which completely eliminated anything made in Great Britain sadly. Car 2 fit most of the criteria, except it was so old it could have been buried in the Valley of the Kings, and the colour was a bit too flashy for me (actually, the car doors, boot, and rear fenders were all different shades of the same colour which implied it had been shunted several times and re-painted). Not a good purchase for me. Then there was car 3, Miranda. Miranda fit all my criteria. Brilliant condition, low number of kilometres, dead comfortable, and the highlight was that the dealer that had her apparently was suffering from a dire cash flow situation, so they were pretty desperate to improve their cash flow by selling whatever they had in inventory.

It was pretty clear of how much they wanted to sell, because they actually brought Miranda to the hotel instead of me going to their facility. I sat in the car; I looked in the boot (terribly British as it was only big enough for a couple of servings of fish and chips; I looked under the bonnet (not exactly British as there weren't several side-draft carburettors leaking petrol all over the place); checked the paint (just the few and almost mandatory dings); and then began the time-tested bargaining process. I won.

Now your mind might be pondering two questions: 1) *If he bought the car on the mainland, how did he get it back to the island of Mallorca?* 2) *What is the deal with the name Miranda?* Okay, fair questions.

1) Miranda came home on an overnight ferry from Barcelona to Mallorca. The ferry ride is another whole story that I won't bother you with, other than to say that the Iscomar Barcelona-Palma ferry is not exactly the QE2. Out of 800 potential passengers, there were only 83, so there was tons of space, but most of the eighty were drivers of the many lorries that make the transit daily and the communal spaces did have this feel of a Teamsters union meeting. The way the loading process worked was "interesting" at best. Everyone drove their cars up this massive 45-degree ramp onto the top deck of the ship...and were told to park them there. On the deck, in the open, exposed to the elements. Bastards. So whilst Miranda was still there upon the ship's arrival in Mallorca, she (as well as all the other cars parked on the deck) had become covered in salt spray. Nice and sparkly in the sunlight when it dried, but as it is not a good thing to have a car covered in salt, I had to wash her when I was back home.

2) The name thing. Right. When asked why I have named my cars, my reply is usually something like, "*Why not?*" And when asked why the name Miranda, my response has been, "*Well, look at the car. See? She is sleek, with a dash of excitement about her, cloaked in a bit of exotic intrigue, and oozing a sense of fun...clearly, she is Miranda.*" Enough said.

So to recap, I managed to survive the rather convoluted (and disgustingly

Living on Rocks

bureaucratic) driver's permit process; I pay taxes here on the island; and now I have managed to find Amelia's twin, in a sort of Schwarzenegger and DeVito cinematic sort of way. Things are well in hand here on the island.

I hate wasting things, and because of this statement, you might be thinking that this is going to be about how I am re-using plastic bottles, or making old newspaper into paraffin-laden logs (not a bad idea actually), but that is not exactly what I am not wasting. As I was growing up, I was pummelled with parental messages. As I recall now, some of them included, *"a penny saved is a penny earned,"* *"eat everything on your plate, there are starving people in (fill in this space with which ever country you were told about),"* *"if you make that face anymore, your face will stay like that for the rest of your life,"* and one of my favourites, *"if you don't study more, you will never get a good job."*

I also learnt quite a bit from what I would see on our family's black & white Muntz telly. Some of this proved to be completely useless, but for some reason have stuck in my mind all these years. I can still remember watching the Spin and Marty episodes on the Disney programme (I learnt the benefits of wearing undershot cowboy boots); the terrible scenes from Dallas, and Memphis, and Los Angeles all are as clear today as they were when they were flashed into our sitting rooms (I learnt that there are some pretty sick people out there); the horrendous images that filled our television screens nightly from Viet Nam are still etched firmly in my psyche (I learnt that power can be used for good, but rarely is); and sitting outside at a friend's house, watching when Neil Armstrong first set foot on the moon will always be with me (I learnt that one can achieve anything if they really want to).

I can also remember seeing some pretty bizarre adverts on telly. Dancing tooth-paste tubes; effervescent tablets that would sing, extolling the benefits of taking them; famous people explaining how most doctor's really did think smoking was a good thing; and then the advert that probably make the biggest impact on me. In the late 1960"s there was an advert for the United Negro College Fund that talked about education. In the advert, the key message was that *"A mind is a terrible thing to waste."* I think of all the "messages" I heard growing up, this is the one that keeps coming back, sometimes to haunt me.

I am at my best (whatever that means) when I am busy. I do love my projects and keeping busy. I think I would just whither away without things to do, and instead of waiting for them to happen, I create them. Last year, just after moving to Sol y Mar, my mind cranked up into proactive mode and I came up with a little project to increase the benefits of my sitting-room fireplace. I am not sure if I was distracted by a few other projects or what, but the idea sat and festered inside my head until last month.

So here is the scenario. It is winter. Winter means cold weather and short days. I don't like cold weather and short days. And whilst I do believe that the mind is a very powerful thing, I haven't quite figured out how to keep the cold away and keep the days long (well, I did figure out how to completely cover Sol y Mar with a huge Plexiglas dome, but that is another story). But to counteract the temperature and lessening amount of light, every night I have a fire in my fireplace. This is good for me (a nice warm feeling), good for the economy (by now I must be one of Tomeans best customers for leña), and good for the carbon footprint of Mallorca (burning wood is just putting nature back into nature). But as I was sitting in front of the fire one night, the *"A mind is a terrible thing to waste"* message came back to be like a bout of bad chilli (okay, sorry about that, not the prettiest metaphor…the message came back strongly…yes, that is better). I needed to resurrect my idea from last year, but this time, actually do it.

This idea involved physics (yawn). My fireplace is old, and is typical for one that was built years ago. You put some wood into the brick cave-like opening in the wall, light it, and most of the heat goes up the chimney. The reason is that heat rises. Well duh. So whilst it always looks very pretty, more heat is going up the chimney than actually wafts out into the sitting room where I am. I can remember seeing something that was sold in the 1960"s, when ecology began to become more than just another "–ology" word. I decided to build one.

I bought some copper tubing. Okay, I normally would have done this out of PVC tubing, but plastic tubing and the heat from a fireplace don't co-exist well. So I bought the copper tubing and an assortment of copper elbows. With my trusty hack-saw, I cut the tubing into the lengths I needed and then joined them with the 45-degree and 90-degree elbows. And then I stuck the convoluted-looking tube contraption into the fireplace and built a fire. The side-view shape of this "thing" was sort of like a big "C." My plan was that the bottom of the "C" would be exposed to the cooler air on the floor, which would then travel up and around the "C" as the fire heated the tubing, and would exit from the top of the "C" into the sitting room. Well, it worked. But then, because I sure wouldn't want my mind to go to waste, I reasoned that if I forced air into the tubing from the floor, I would be able to realise even more heat out of the top of my new trendy and ecology neutral heating system. I also reasoned that if one tube was good at moving heat into the sitting room, two tubes would move even more.

So after buying more copper tubing and more elbows, and a very small computer muffin fan, I now am the proud possessor of the Dr. Rieley"s-carbon-neutral-turbo-somewhat-passive-but-incredibly-efficient-fireplace-heating-system. I was thinking of naming it something, but shoot, it isn't a car, is it?

And after all that, then I realised that during the day, when the sun is pouring in through the windows, the heat that is built up goes sneaking up through the chimney, so I decided to creatively stop that too. I cut a sheet of carton-pluma (foam-core) into an arch shape, and then painted it to match the rest of the brick fireplace structure. After a few minor adjustments, I was able to have it fit exactly into the fireplace opening, effectively sealing it off from airflow up or down. I keep it in the opening during the day and remove it when I build my daily fire each evening.

With some luck, my parents are proud of me for not wasting my mind, but probably still a bit flummoxed that I do have a good job and didn't study all that hard.

It never ceases to amaze me at the way we, as humans, can focus on so many things at one time. Being able to focus on more than one thing – the much maligned at times multi-tasking – is something that some can do better than others. At times, I am crap at it.

I do try to multi-task as much as possible. This probably has a connection to my belief that I have a lot to accomplish. If it isn't keeping Sol y Mar organised, it is trying to get my pseudo-garden flourish, or do something artistic, or something literary (in my business-sort-of-way), or working on a client project. There is so much to do, and whilst I am usually pretty good at keeping things sorted in my mind, once in a while, I do become completely distracted by...well, by stuff.

I was about to write a letter, but after a while sitting in front of my computer (which is on my desk in front of one of the windows overlooking the Mediterranean), I realised that I wasn't typing. I was just sitting looking out the window at the waves coming into shore.

Watching the sea can be very calming, almost hypnotic. Regardless of how big the waves are, I just love watching them. Some days, the gently ripple in almost mirroring a soft ballad, slowly coming to shore in a peaceful rhythm that could almost lull you to sleep. Some days they are more like a flotilla of steam engines, forever racing their high crests to shore, where they mimic massive hammers pounding the rocks on the shoreline into submission. And then there are the days like today...a light breeze out of the South-West, causing the surface of the water to look almost like Monet is flicking his brush back and forth making the waves appear to glisten like millions of little diamonds as they flutter toward the shore.

And if the visual isn't enough, the sounds are even more incredible. I could spend all day listening to the water as it meets the shoreline and watching the waves descend onto the rocks in a tactile greeting that only something greater than you or I could have ever devised. I cannot do anything other than believe that I actually must have been a good boy growing up to be so privileged to hear the sea sing its lullaby everyday. *(A cautionary note to readers: the soothing effect of the sea is magnified incredibly if your CD player is stuck on repeat during one of several songs by Dusty Springfield softly in the background.)*

I would have continued to sit here and watch, but I managed to come out of my near trance when I realised that I needed to light the evening's fire. Right. Fire. Another almost hypnotic-effect-generator. I love watching the fire in my fireplace at night. The flames dance around as if they were part of some delicate ballet, gently streaming upward into the darkness of the chimney. I could go on and on about this, but you might think I am acquiring pyromaniac tendencies – which I am not. I just am amazed of the calming effect a fire can have. Luckily, this effect wears off quickly in the morning when I have to shovel out all the ashes from the previous evening's flame-dancing-extravaganza.

Okay, the fire is going, and I am resisting sitting in front of it falling victim to its hypnotic qualities, and instead am trying to complete this piece… but I think I have lost my train of thought. Perhaps I should have left my computer on the desk instead of taking with me to the sofa in front of the fireplace, with the rhythmic sounds of the gentle waves coming to shore. Buggers….

It is so hard to believe, but it is already almost mid-March. I am not even sure where the time has gone, but it has been passing quite quickly lately. Having said that, today almost seemed like Christmas was here again as in the post, I received six holiday cards from friends. Okay, so you may be wondering how that is possible. A fair question. After I moved from La Antigua to Sol y Mar last year, I thought I had given everyone my new post address, but these cards were addressed to La Antigua. Last evening, I received a call from the family renting the house saying that I had some post. I assumed that it was something that had just arrived, so I met Melanie (my renter's wife) in the car park of Carrefour today. I was beginning to feel like Guy Burgess as she passed me a plastic market bag that was chocker with post that they had been saving for me. Well, at least I now have the cards, and actually, it was kind of fun opening Christmas cards in March.

I just came back from another business trip. I really don't mind the trips, after all, this is how I get to the client offices. But whilst I do like being there, if truth be told, I really do hate going there. High on my list of travel whinging is all the waiting at airports as some incredibly underpaid person tries to figure out what the geometric images are that come up on their scanner-doo-wah screens. I guess that I am not too keen on standing in the endless queues that fill the airports I seem to frequent either. And if those two things aren't enough, my last trip to Geneva was, well, interesting.

Whilst standing in the boarding queue, I could overhear a rather well-dressed businessman-type talking to an attractive young woman who he was obviously travelling with. No doubt it was his niece. I came to this conclusion because she was incredibly attractive but far younger than the man in the tailored glen plaid suit. As they were standing there, the young woman (whom I began to think had a tattoo that said, "1st-class slapper" hidden somewhere under the skirt that only covered about 6" of her kilometre-long legs) was pouting because the boarding process would require that we all would be packed into a motor coach for the trip to the plane. I would have been far happier to simply walk through the air-bridge that connects the terminal to the place as well, but this is the way it was that day. So the old guy was offering her reasons why we had to do this, all of which were about as realistic as my comment about her being his niece. After about ten minutes, we were on our way across the tarmac to the waiting Airbus turbo-blaster-take-off A320. How these planes manage to accelerate from zero to a kazillion miles per hour in a second or two is beyond me, but that is another whole story. I managed to get off the coach and board the plane, lofting my travel trolley in the overhead bin above seat 3C and sat down.

As the people shuffled past me toward the back of the plane, my right shoulder was only pummelled a dozen or so times, but I wasn't too concerned about that. An aisle seat is always prone to having that happen during boarding. Getting off the plane isn't a problem because I am in the front and only guess at all the chaotic pushing and shoving that is taking place behind me. As the last people from the coach boarded the plane, there was the fun couple. I could have figured out it was them even if my eyes were closed as soon as I heard her whinging about something and him putting forth another bollocks-filled explanation. And then they sat down in the row immediately in front of me. How nice. My expectation was that for the next two hours, I will hear explanations about everything from global warming to the financial crisis to how planes manage to stay in the air to God-knows-what. As we taxied toward the runway, I found I was right. Lucky, lucky me. I was almost tempted to ask if I could switch seats as the plane took off. The Lolita-look-a-like, who was in 2A, let out a sound that was reminiscent of Meg Ryan in the restaurant scene of "When Harry Met Sally" as the plane surged into the sky. I just prayed he wouldn't try to explain the dynamics of thrust to her.

Less than ten minutes into the flight, her uncle-father-boss-mentor-customer (you can pick which ever of these you think how this guy views his "relationship"), who was occupying the seat immediately in front of me, began seeing how far back his seat would go. It wasn't that he just reclined the seat. It seemed as if he thought that if you keep pressing the button and bouncing against it, eventually it will go dead flat. It was as if the seat in front of me was occupied by an ADD-laden hyper-active adolescent that was out of control.

I had planned on using my computer on the flight, but it didn't take too long to realise that the repeated back-and-forth of the seat back in front of me would smash the lap-top screen. I was filled with options as to what I could do. I could have; A) Asked to change my seat; B) Asked the bloke to stop the back and forth activity; C) Slapped him on the top of his head. I almost opted out for option C, but then I realised that my hand would need to be sterilised to get all the grease off of it from his rather dire comb-over. I instead decided to just close my eyes and think about something more important…like how good it would be to be home again in a couple of days.

First, my apologies. I began writing this in mid-March, and because of a few

JBR-projects (that you know I do love), I sort of became sidetracked a bit. But now, almost a month later, I decided I had better get my fingers clicking away on finishing this letter.

Yes, I flew to Geneva again. (This was in mid-March) This was going to be a relatively short trip, but an important one. And extremely importantly, I had very high expectations. The weather forecast for the two days I would be there was exceptionally good, and I was relishing the opportunity to once again see the city in a different light than the past several months of trips. Well, actually, I was relishing the opportunity to see the city in any light. Winter in Geneva are not all that fun for someone who lives in Mallorca. Granted, I am quite weather-spoilt, and equally granted, I don't really do winter outdoor sports. I suppose if I lived here, I would love the fact that in a one-hour drive, I could be well and truly on top of some snow covered mountain and in winter sports heaven. I have been told by some local friends that when the weather is at its gloomiest, all they do is go up to one of the mountains that encircle the city and you can actually be above the clouds and in brilliant sun. Okay, I am sure that is quite pretty, but it must be colder than a freezer. So I don't do it. In winter, I seem to shuttle back and forth between client offices and my hotel…, which has quite speedy broadband, interesting room service, and a good heating system.

On Thursday, it was so nice that I walked to the office from my hotel and back. It was wonderful. A bit chilly – all the locals were rabbiting on about how warm it was…10c – but the sun was out and whilst walking along the lake, it was very nice. As I was walking (3,850 paces return trip, and please don't even ask how I know that) I began noticing that the worldwide recession hasn't really impacted the city too much. I managed to see more Maseratis, Maybachs, Aston-Martins, Ferraris and Bentley Continentals buzzing along my route that I could count. It was if I was walking in the midst of the world's largest mobile used car dealership. I was beginning to think that this must be testosterone city, but then noticed that most of these cars were being driven by women. It is, I suppose, possible that there was a Barbi-lookalike convention in the city, but probably not. More likely, it is just Geneva.

Immediately after the Geneva trip, there was a short stop in Andorra to see some friends. I have been to Andorra before, and the first time I thought it was sort of a *"Wal-Mart-surrounded by mountains."* That was almost ten years ago, and if it weren't for my friends there, I am sure I wouldn't find any reason to go, because not much has changed. But when the sun is out and I am not in the midst of shoppers from France and/or Spain who zip across the frontier to buy alcohol or cigarettes, it is a pretty spectacular place. Having said that, it did snow one day for a bit and that did, for me, sort of deflate my view of it. But the little side trip to Andorra on my way home was very special and we all had some fab food and good conversations over the weekend.

After my return home, I became pretty focused on some Sol y Mar projects.

Living on Rocks

Now you may be thinking that it is almost mid-April, and that means that we are on the edge of summer weather. But none-the-less, I had ordered another ton of leña for my fireplace. It isn't that it is desperately cold or anything. I just do like to have a fire at night and I reasoned that if I bought the wood now, I could chop it all up with my trusty new axe and have it all stacked neatly (neatly being the key word here) so that by next winter, it would be dead dry and ready for when I crank up the fires again. When it arrived (the ton of leña), I wasn't home (cleverly), so Tomeu just chucked over the wall at the front of Sol y Mar. That was really okay with me as if he would have stacked it up, I would have had to unstack it during my orgy of chopping. I am not sure exactly how Tomeu calculates the weight of all this wood, because this "ton" sure seemed a lot heavier than previous deliveries. This may have something to do with all the carry-wood-from-the-pile-to-my-chopping-block-and-split-it-and-then-stack-it activity. Regardless, I now have five nicely organised rows of wood ready for this winter. I won't even get into the condition of my back if that is okay with you.

This morning I went on one of my semi-occasional visits to see my doctor. Toni has become more of a friend than a medical advisor for me. He is the one who saved my life when I contracted the GBS, and my frequent check-ups to make sure that the evil bastard virus doesn't somehow return to plague me have been not only good for my health, but have ended up in long conversations about just about anything good friends talk about. When I arrived at his office this morning, they had just opened the doors so I filtered into one of his salas (waiting rooms) with the other people who had also arrived a bit too early. After a few minutes, one of Toni's staff came into the sala with a clipboard and went to each person, asking them who they were, and what they were there for. After asking the other four people, she came up to me. I was already to dazzle everyone in the room with my Spanish – "*Me llamo James Rieley y estoy aqui para pruebas de sangre*," but before I could utter a word of my well practised statement, Antonia said, "*Hola señor James*" and walked away. Everyone else in the waiting room just looked over, probably wondering how many times you have to come to get recognised. The answer of course is, far too many.

After one of Toni's phlebotomist's sucked some blood from my arm, Toni and I went out for coffee, and in my case, tea. I was dead hungry as the blood test required that I didn't eat anything after midnight and I typically eat shortly after I wake up in the morning. We talked for a while about building alignment around initiatives in organisations – no, really, this is what he wanted to talk about – and then back to his offices for a "nerve conduction" test. I was ushered into an examination room that had more computer kit in it than I even own and after a few moments, had electrodes attached to my elbow and the fleshy bit at the bottom of my thumb. Then his nurse placed yet another electrode on my wrist and said I shouldn't worry. Then she pressed a button on one of the computers. I was going to ask the nurse if Toni had bought the machine at the (hopefully upcoming) Guantanamo electrical apparatus sale because the electric pulse wasn't all that fun. She then switched the electrodes to my other arm. I was ready this time for the blast of current and when it came, I was so tensed up that I barely noticed it. Then she hit the button again, and looked at me with a smile that roughly translated into "gotcha." Cute. I did find out that electrical current flows through nerve bundles at 45 meters a second. I also learnt that trusting attractive nurses is not always a good thing to do.

It is Sunday. Almost the end of April, and things are moving along quite well here. Having said that, last evening was one of those nights when nature plays her own game. Mallorca is an island located about 60 miles due east from Valencia on the mainland of Spain. Which also means that it is less than 300 miles from the coast of Africa. Enough geography. When the weather patterns drive winds from south to north, we sometimes get some bits of Sahara sand plopping on the island. This is rarely noticed unless the sand comes along with rain. This apparently happened last night. When I was having my breakfast this morning, I didn't have a clue of what had happened until I received a call from a friend who told me to go out and look at my cars. Both Amelia, my white car, and Miranda, my black car, were completely dirty-sand-brown, So, after doing a thorough washing of them, I thought it was time to move on to more of a planned project.

Between client work and visits, I have been working on a couple of projects that have been nothing but pure enjoyment for me. One of them has been another book. Most of my writing (other than these often cheeky stories) has been confined to business things. The six books I have done have all been about business, and whilst I do like sharing some of what I have learnt in my years in the business-world with readers of this genre, I also have dabbled off and on with fiction. In January, I had decided to focus on fiction for a bit. I toyed with the idea of writing a novel and after a few attempts at beginning it, finally settled on the project's direction.

The validity of my idea was reinforced on my birthday this year. My brother had written with an offer. For my present, he would publish a book of all my stories from Mallorca. A fab offer, but not what I was leaning toward. I was working on a novel. The novel centres on David Somerset who, interestingly enough, lives on Mallorca. (who would have guessed that?) I was thinking of telling you more about the book (which I finished writing several weeks ago), but I think you will have to wait until it is available on Amazon (which should be in several months – feel free to buy many and buy often).

Oh screw it...this is what will be on the back cover.

"Letters from the Village" is the story of David Somerset, a double ex-pat, relationship-challenged author, who was hired to write a screenplay based on a bestselling book he wrote of the same name.

The chapters are interspersed with some of the actual letters that he wrote to friends and family over a five-year period so that they could vicariously experience what it was like for someone who was raised in a fast-moving, high-tech, "go do it" environment, and then moves to an island in the Mediterranean where the term slow takes on a whole new meaning; weaving a story that tells how he copes with relationships, culture, and happiness on the island of Mallorca...and survives.

Okay, now you can get ready to contact Amazon in a few months.

I have also been catching up on another bit of creativity. If you remember last autumn, a rather testy storm blew through this part of the Mediterranean, and in its process, left a path of destruction. Destruction is a relative term, and whilst it did wreak havoc on other parts of the island, the bulk of the damage near Sol y Mar was a couple of downed trees and...one of my terrace sculptures was blown apart. Yes, one of the large sculptures I made for my terrace was pretty much obliterated by the winds and as luck would have it, it wasn't actually completely destroyed. But it did come apart, leaving a pile of big white PVC tubes laying about on the terrace. Last week after returning from a client visit, I set out to put it back together. So, once again, the front terrace is back to normal (if you consider normal being having a large white sculpture-thingy on it).

It is Spain, and things are a little different here. Not everything, but clearly some things are different in other parts of the world I have lived in. One difference manifests itself quite often...and that is public holidays.

In the UK, we have Bank Holidays. This terminology was developed long before British banks went on mental holidays where they decided to not do anything that was worthwhile apparently. In the 1870"s, someone thought that bankers should have a break once in a while from all that stress of counting money, and over time, these original four days became the current eight. Now of course, bankers use the time to celebrate the fact that when they are closed, they can't muck things up any more than they currently have been.

Spain took the concept of public holidays a bit further. Here we have sixteen public holidays. Quite a few of these are probably a result of the church, with the country basically shutting down to celebrate San Juan (St. John); San Pedro y San Pablo (St. Peter & St. Paul); Santiago (one of my favourites as it is the celebration of St. James, the patron saint of Spain); and the Immaculada Concepcion (Immaculate Conception).

When I first moved here, I thought this was pretty brilliant...more than one holiday each month. Not a bad thing. But then I moved to Mallorca, where we have not only these holidays, but a few that seem to be specific to the islands. In Mallorca, we also celebrate holidays for San Sebastian, (20 January), Dia de les Illes Balears (Balearics Day, 1 March); Lunes de Pascua (Easter Monday); and Segunda Fiesta de Navidad (St. Stephen's Day). This plethora of holidays escalates even further as some communities on the island have their own holidays as well.

Now I must admit that often, faced with the prospects of an island culture that has 20-plus days per year where everything shuts down, it can be a mix of good news and bad news. The good news is that no one is supposed to be working (but the entire concept of work here is often suspect anyway). The bad news is that on any of these days, it is a bugger to find any stores open. Of course, this isn't a serious problem unless you get caught out with an empty refrigerator on one of these days. When I first encountered this little problem (it does seem like a little problem if your refrigerator is not empty), I decided that I would always ensure that I have enough food in the house to last through any siege of holidays that the local government could devise. This clearly has led to the fact that my kitchen shelves do take on the appearance of a supermarket for the certain non-perishables that I tend to consume.

This morning, after relishing my tea and toast, I began to think about what to make for dinner. I usually don't think about this until my stomach is screaming out for sustenance in the evening, but it is overcast and drizzling today, and my mind began to ponder what I could do to occupy myself later in the day. I settled on which culinary delight I would whip up, but then realised that I was missing several component elements of the soon-to-be-feast. Bugger…today is the first of May, which means it is Labour Day here. Which means that everything is closed. Which means I wouldn't be able to whip up my dinner-delight. Which means I just wanted it more. So, being a man on a mission, Miranda and I set out to find a market that was open.

Luckily, there is a local market only a few kilometres from the house, and they were open. Actually, they always seem to be open. Quite obviously, the owners either A) Have no respect for the government's public holiday missives; B) Lost their calendars and had forgotten that it was a holiday; C) Are concerned about the people who may run out of some food-stuff and stay open to serve them; or D) Are blatantly greedy. I am not sure which is correct, but I tend to think that letter D could be spot on, and thankfully so.

Regardless of their motives, the market was chocker-block with people, all apparently planning parties to celebrate the holiday. I wound my way down the aisles, desperately trying to find what I was looking for before someone else scooped it up. Instantly gratified, I had found what I was looking for, and then whilst standing in the incredibly long check-out queue, I also plopped some impulse purchases into my basket…as you do.

So now I am home again and everything is put away…and have already changed my mind about what to make for dinner. So instead of making my previously planned food extravaganza for the evening, I have decided instead to help out my chosen government by coming up with some additional holidays to celebrate. High on my suggestion list would be to hold a celebration on any day that's name ends with a "Y." Good. Job done. I think I will have a kip.

Well, I did it...again. No, I didn't buy another car; Miranda and Amelia are quite enough, thank you. But I did fly to America last week. It had been several months since I had seen my grandchildren and thought it might be a nice idea to hop on a jet and buzz over to see them. Well, that was my thought at least. I had forgotten the minor part about travelling to middle-America requires two flights, and one of them lasting nine hours.

I left Mallorca very early one morning (sorry...it was VERY early) and flew to Madrid, where, after a hour or so, I boarded another jet for the seemingly never-ending flight to Chicago. After watching several movies (whose names I can't even remember now), and two meals, we touched down and after negotiating the maze that is O'Hare Airport, and deftly getting through customs and immigration, I went through the gates to find my son's wife standing there with a "Dr. JBR" sign. Adorable. We drove into downtown Chicago to meet David for dinner and as my body clock was going into shut-down mode, we made arrangements to have breakfast the following morning.

After devouring a plate of blue-berry pancakes for breakfast that probably was big enough to feed most of the people of Darfur, David went back to work and Nancy and I drove to Milwaukee so she could spend Mother's Day with her mum. I, on the other hand, had dinner with some old sailing buddies and then went back to my hotel to see if I could actually sleep through the night. Right. As if.

The following days were spent with some very special old friends whom I hadn't seen for too long, and because I was in America, I thought I would begin my own financial stimulus programme. I have read that Mr. Obama has chucked out ka-zillion upon ka-zillion, but I thought I should help out. I went shopping. I did manage to stay away from any and all computer stores and instead went for clothes. Well, whilst the selection there is unbelievable, and the prices are considerably less than they are here, I was about to give up until I noticed that my shoes were sort of dying. I plugged on and went to numerous shoe stores, but after realising that I really did like the shoes I was wearing and hadn't found anything I liked more, I went to a shoe repair shop and this little old man sat on a stool and hand-sewed them back together. Wednesday I drove to Sheboygan. My son Matthew, his wife Melanie, and their two daughters live there. Years and years ago, I kept a boat in the harbour of Sheboygan, and I have fond memories of being there. But last week, the weather in Sheboygan was not fit for man nor beast so we all went to dinner after stopping in at the Post Office. Yes, we went to the Post Office. For some time, I have been saying that it would be fab if my granddaughters would come to Mallorca to visit, and the first step was to apply for their passports. I am really looking forward to having them visit, although because they are two teenage girls, and I am neither, I think we will do this one at a time. Besides, Miranda only has two seats, and I can't imagine them being too keen on seeing the island in Amelia.

James B Rieley

Then the next day I drove back to Chicago's crazy airport and began my flights home, arriving in the early afternoon yesterday. By my calculations, my body will have shed all the jet lag about the same time I will lose all the weight I gained from the enormous servings of food that America seems to exist on. I am betting on Christmas.

Today I actually finished unpacking and resuming (my idea of) normal life again. This, as you may have imagined, involved getting back into my Sol y Mar routine and after washing the cars, I settled down on one of the terraces to sleep in the sun. A good day so far, and whilst it was great to visit with everyone, it sure is good to be home.

The beginning of this week was the culmination of several months of preparation, hours of logistical planning, and several cases of Coke-Light. Yes, it was running of the First Annual Non-Classic Car Rally of Mallorca. Okay, so maybe it wasn't as official as it sounds, but it was meant to be a fun get-together of friends who would spend two-days and one-night travelling around the island...and it was great fun.

The flyer that was sent out tried to make it clear that this was meant to be a fun couple of days

What you need to participate:

- A car
- A desire to do something different with friends (old and new)
- A driver and a navigator (who can read directions)
- Enough money to pay for your food and lodging for one night.
- A mobile phone (just in case you manage to get lost)

What you don't need to participate:

- A map - we will supply you with the maps and rally instructions that you will need
- Crash helmets - if you think you need a helmet, you are in the wrong rally
- A compass - this island isn't that big
- Any sophisticated auto GPS system – this rally is not all that complicated
- A calculator or Time-Speed-Distance wheel - sorry, this isn't that competitive

The rally began Monday morning, when all the participants gathered at Sol y Mar for some pre-rally snacks and a "participant meeting." Seeing as how none of the participants had been told where the rally would take them, or what it would entail, this meeting was pretty important. Truth-be-told, I think some of them were a tad concerned about what they had signed up for, but everyone seemed prepared (whatever "prepared" means).

Living on Rocks

There were seven teams of people who had agreed to participate, and each team was given a sealed envelope that contained the information for the first day of the rally, as well as a wax-sealed Panic envelope, in case they somehow managed to become totally and utterly lost. At 10:30h, with strict instructions from myself, the teams set off from Sol y Mar at three minute intervals, and the rally was underway.

Putting a rally like this together (I thought) was as much fun as participating in it. Part of that fun was constructing the "rally book." With 25 pages of instructions, the teams were led step-by-step from the front of my house to the planned evening stop in Pollença. Whilst some of the actual instructions were easy, *"when you see this, turn right,"* or, *"after about 5km, you should see this. If you do, you are on the correct road;"* whilst many of them were connected to questions the teams needed to answer. *"What number should you ring if you have electrical needs?"* was asked accompanying a photo of an electrical supplier, but with the phone number on the wall blocked out. *"What is the name of this tunnel just after kilometre marker 23?"* again, with the name in the photo being blocked out, was another typical example of some of the questions. All the teams had to do was see what were in the photos and write down the correct answer on their (very trendy looking) answer sheets. All in all, there were 34 questions to answer over the two-day event, and it was remarkable how many of the teams were able to get most of them.

By the end of day one, all the team's had assembled in front of a hotel that was nice enough to accommodate the entire group. Well, almost all of the teams. One team's car had developed an electrical fault, so they had to drive back home instead of risking leaving their car all night with open windows. The rest of us sat around and talked about what they had encountered during the day, being careful not to share the answers they had recorded. Then we all went to dinner, helping to financially stimulate the economy of Pollença.

After devouring the hotel's fab breakfast the next morning, Tuesday's rally instructions were distributed and the rally was on once again. By now, the teams had driven about 180km, with another 140km or so to go. Keeping track of the whole distance thing was important, so at the end of the rally, it would be easy to see which team had pretty-much stayed on course for the entire rally...and which team(s) managed to get lost.

The rally took everyone to Cala Figuera, where we all met for lunch, then on to the last leg before finishing the rally at one of the participant's home. And then, as one would imagine, prizes were given out. The winning team (most number of correct answers) were presented a bowl that had been acquired from the La Antigua Ceramica studio (yes, that is me), but the poor other participants all received prizes as well...although, the term "cheesy-prizes" doesn't even capture the silliness of them (a pair of fuzzy dice to hang from

James B Rieley

your rear-view mirror isn't exactly a high-value prize). All in all, everyone had a fab time, and after having a few glasses of cava, the conversation did evolve to who would put on the next event. Can't wait to see this one – making this rally was great fun, but I think it would have been even better to be a participant. I will keep you posted.

Today is pretty special here. Well, actually I think everyday is pretty special here, but today is even "special-er" if that is a word. Today is the summer solstice. Yes, the day that many of us long for…it is the longest day of the year. For people who tend to love sunlight, the longest day gives us just what we are after, and in the case of my island, this means that from 0625h to 2116h in the evening, we all will be basking in the warmth of the sun.

Now in all fairness, we don't quite celebrate the day like they do in some other places. The morning news channels all reported that the number of people who had flocked to Stonehenge had never been higher. Stonehenge, located in southern England, is a very special place to see. The rings of stones date back four or five-thousand years and for many, represent "the" place to be on the summer Solstice. Sort of a blending of an all-night party and a semi-religious ceremony, this year an estimated 35,000 pseudo-Druids, New Age aficionados and those who probably had nothing else to do at the break of dawn were there to watch the sun peek over the Salisbury Plain.

I can remember whilst living in London, driving out to see Stonehenge one summer's day and it was pretty spectacular. I have always enjoyed being in seriously old stone buildings (okay, so Stonehenge isn't actually a building, but stick with me for a few more sentences). What I have always tried to do is press my palm up against one of the stone walls. It is almost as if you can "feel" the history of the building and "hear" some of the stories that, if it could talk, have taken place within its walls. I really wanted to do this at Stonehenge, but when we were there, the entire site had barriers that had been constructed around it. There were signs that alluded to the fact that the site was being restored, but I think that there must be a lot of people who just wanted to touch it.

I didn't celebrate a Stonehenge-type Solstice – my wardrobe contains nothing that even looks like it has been made out of horse-hair, nor did I clink any little cymbals or do an serious chanting. Having said that, at one point during the day, I was considering humming along with Tina Turner's voice as she belted out *"boom-shuck-luck-lucka, boom-shucka-lucka-lucka, dah dah dah, dah dah day, dah dah day, hey-hey-hey"* on my iTunes. (Would that have counted as chanting? Not sure) What I did was do what I normally do on non-work days…I went outside and enjoyed the day.

The Solstice here was pretty great. Not too hot (about 30c) lots of sun, gentle sea breeze, and about 40 boats at anchor in front of Sol y Mar. I managed to sit out and relax a bit with a brilliant book (Jorge Bucay's "Cuentos para

Pensar") as well as reflect on the other night. I had just returned from a client visit and went to a little dinner party at a friend's house. Antonio, one of the participants in the recent car rally, had vowed at the end of the rally that he would put together a little dinner for all the rally teams that had survived the two-day event. Apparently, the term "little" didn't translate all that well, as he had made (all from scratch) Gazpacho, followed by two paellas that were each about the size of hula-hoop. It was brill to see everyone again, and the food was incredible – someday I really would like to get off my bum and do more proper "from scratch" cooking. I sort of have taken the first step.

One of the things I miss about not living at La Antigua is not having a proper garden. So a week ago, I went out and bought some more large macetas, a few bags of proper dirt, and a melange of seeds to plant. And because of my diligent efforts, I am now proud to report that I am eagerly awaiting the arrival of the two different types of tomato plants, lechuga (lettuce) and two different types of cebollas (onions). What I find is amazing is that the lechuga is already beginning to come up. "Coming up" is a relative term when talking about planting vegetables from seeds I suppose. In my definition, this means that there are some small green bits that have made it up through the soil. And to be perfectly honest, I am not even sure if what is coming up is the lechuga...I neglected to label with maceta has which seeds. But that is okay. Life is full of adventure and surprises...and I will certainly be surprised to find out what I will be able to harvest first.

Back to the party. The food was simply fabulous, but what I really enjoyed was talking with friends. Whilst everyone there did speak English, the vast majority of the guests were Spanish, and they courteously always drop into my native tongue when having a conversation with us ex-pats. This is nice, but it certainly doesn't help my Spanish. I have found that my Spanish is far better when I am speaking to someone who doesn't speak English. Because native Spaniards speak, in what sounds to us like rapid-fire, no-stopping-for-breathing, endless streams of words, I find that it doesn't even permit me time to think in English. Therefore, my Spanish is far better. So at the paella extravaganza, I tried to avoid English as much as possible. I am sure that they all thought that my Spanish is still crap (something I am quite convinced of), but the evening was far more rewarding when I would (you can pick one here...) A) attempt, B) mess-up, C) butcher a beautiful language with poorly conjugated verbs, or D) sound like I really am trying to learn the language of the country that has been nice enough to let me live here.

The "best-by-date" thing. Oh yes. We have all experienced shopping in a market (or in some cases, the supermarket) where almost all packaged food has a "best-by-date" stamped on it. I suppose this is a good thing, but it has also proved to be a real nuisance for me. I tend to read these dates very carefully when I buy something. And then to make things even worse, I read them even closer when I take something out of the refrigerator. I have been told that I am a bit over the top about this and have noticed that I had either stop buying too much so I don't discover things that have expired in my larder, or don't be that picky about something that has a date that is only one day past. For sure, I do need to be a little more thoughtful when purchasing some items. The other day I looked at the jar of ginger paste when I was making some salmon and saw that it was "overdue" by about 6 months. Oooops.

I think the "sell-by-date" thing applies to other things besides food. Last night, this thought came to me quite visibly. It is Glastonbury time in England. No, not the town in Somerset, that is always there. It is the Glastonbury music festival, and I couldn't help but let you all know. The reason is that for many of you, the performers are people we have known through their music…and for many of us, their music made a major impact on our lives.

Now to be fair, I am not there. I am watching some of the performances on television and tonight I have been watching Crosby, Stills & Nash. And then I was watching Neil Young. (It was almost like listening to CSN&Y of days gone by) And then I was watching Bruce Springsteen. Whilst many of the songs are so familiar and do "take me back" to a different time and place, it is pretty apparent that some performers have gone past their best-by-dates. Loved much of the music then, and in many cases, still do. But I am not so sure about the new images of the aging performers. Clearly, some performers need to check their own best-by-dates and when they are well past them, stay home.

The whole best-by-date thing extends to even more things I think. I have noticed that there are some things that I used to be brilliant at, that now I am not so good at. I used to be really good at remembering things. I was damn good at names, dates, phone numbers, and the like. But now I think I would be at a bit of a loss without some sort of back up system. I suppose I could use something like putting Post-Its around the house as little reminders, but that may not work because I am not sure where I have put my pad of Post-Its. I could tie a string around my finger, but I only have ten of them, and would probably run out of space too quickly. Instead, I have decided to exercise my brain. Yes, brain exercise. I tried getting deeply involved in doing Su-do-ku, but that drives me a bit bonkers. I was pretty involved in the world of crossword puzzles for a while, but when I kept encountering questions like who was the second son of some obscure person in English literature, or, what is the Latin name for a plant that went extinct in the 1500's, I gave up. Now my brain exercise seems to fall into two categories; writing (a very good brain exercise), and,…a…oh shit, I forgot the other one.

Earlier this week, I had to go to the mainland to attend a client meeting. Okay, that isn't exactly accurate. I chose to go to the mainland to attend a client meeting. I really didn't *have* to go…but I did because I was asked and it is what I do. Being a clever bugger, I went over the day before and we went to dinner with some friends in Sitges. Addy had suggested that we all go to dinner at a very nice restaurant near the waterfront, and in his words, the food was very good and the entertainment was better. The restaurant – Monroe's, named after the cinema icon – had a very typical English menu we were told, which would be fine. Sometimes a proper English meal is a good thing to have I have realised.

So we drove into town and after finding a parking spot, walked down the narrow but heaving streets until we found Monroe's and were greeted by the host…or was it the hostess? I can honestly say I haven't had such a good time in ages. I guess Cindy Lauper did have it right…girls just want to have fun.

I have managed to take some time off work to resume painting. My latest expedition into the world of acrylic on canvas was interesting. When we all got together in Sitges recently, I had taken some photos, and one of them intrigued me no end. I was so taken by it, I thought it might be a good opportunity to do an acrylic portrait. After spending several long nights playing with texture and colour, I thought I finally had it sorted. And whilst it does look like the photo of the subject, neither the photo or the painting look like her so I think I will keep this one for myself.

Second, I have written often about what I am lucky enough to see from my terrace. Well, today the vista in front of me was a bit over the top, even for me. Each day, I get to see boats of all shapes, sizes, and types anchor out in front of Sol y Mar. As an ex-sailor, some of them cause me to wish desperately to once again be able to have a boat, or at very minimum, be able to sail again. But equally, some of the boats I see are flat-out yachts that boggle the mind. Today I saw one of these. The boat's name is Iona, and she is 73 meters long (3/4"s the length of a football pitch) and as I was wondering how anyone can afford such as piece of kit, I heard a helicopter's whirly sound. This sound isn't all that unusual as police helicopters often go zipping past the house. But the sound I heard today was very close…because it landed on the stern of the boat. So sad that some people have to live like that….he says sarcastically.

Third, next week I may attend a reunion. No, not my high-school reunion, but a reunion for some of the graduate and post-graduate students I met when I sailed from Lisbon to Panama a couple of years ago. I have stayed in touch with quite a few of them and received a note recently about a planned reunion that will be held in Barcelona. As it is only a 30-minute flight, and it would be great to see some of them again, I just may hop on a jet.

Fourth, and most certainly not the least important. I like to read. I do tend to stay away from reading business books, and I wouldn't want their content to pollute my business-writing tendencies. I do, however, like to read the outputs of authors like David Baldacci and Nelson DeMille and tend to get my hands on their latest efforts as soon as they come on the market. But there are several other authors whose books I have in my collection, and there must be some deep-seated theme thing going on that drives me to

James B Rieley

have them. One is Beryl Markham; another is James Barrie. And right now, I am trying to get my hands on an early copy of Robert Louis Stevenson's *Treasure Island*.

Markham was a contemporary and friend of Karen Blixen, who wrote *Out of Africa*. Markham's books are marvellous stories about how one can overcome what are perceived to be insurmountable odds. Barrie, of course, is the author of *Little White Bird* and *Peter Pan in Kensington Gardens*, both wonderful books about hopes and dreams. And then there is Stevenson. His *Treasure Island* is a wonderful story of adventure and discovering the unknown. I suppose one of the reasons I really want to find a good copy of *Treasure Island* is because the 1911 edition was illustrated by N. C. Wyeth, and the illustrations alone are marvellous. So, every once in a while, I troll through Google searches trying to find a good copy of the 1911 edition at a reasonable price. I am not holding my breath.

I know I have written about my adventures with the mysteries of language. For me, it has been quite a journey so far. I was raised and educated in middle-America, chose to become British, and now live in Spain. Right. First, the whole thing about English. Upon my arrival in London years ago, it became painfully clear to me that what I thought was English, really isn't English at all. Not that either one is right – the real essence of language is that it is simply a way for people to communicate.

When I was growing up, I was able to communicate with family, friends, and teachers (well, not so sure about my communications ability with teachers, but that is an entirely different thing. When I moved to England, I was also able to communicate. But I did discover that there are little nuances that seemed to lurk around, waiting to catch me out. One of them surfaced the other day when I was talking to a friend. I had said that an Aunt was in hospital. I didn't say she was in *the* hospital, only that she was in hospital. (she is okay by the way, thank you very much). There are other little variances in how the English language is used between the USofA and the UK. One example is that we watch *"the rugby"* on telly. I know that if I said to a British mate *"Are you going to watch rugby on Saturday,"* he would understand. But because I have always tried to learn how to assimilate into a chosen culture, I try to use the local language of choice. Which brings me to the fact that whilst I chose to become British, I don't live in Britain, but in Spain.

As I have probably said before, I did learn some Spanish in school whilst growing up. But the Spanish I learnt was more Mexican that proper Spanish. So when we moved to Spain, I thought I would be completely buggered, but I wasn't, and it didn't take that long for me to pick up some of the nuances of the language as it was spoken. But there was a minor problem…I was living in Barcelona, which although is in Spain, it is actually in Cataluña. The Catalans are very proud of the fact that they are different and part of this pride manifests itself in their desire to hold on to their own language.

Catalan (or Catala) does have some commonalities with Spanish, but the key word here is "some." The same holds true here in Mallorca (where they speak Mallorquin, which is sort of like Catalan on steroids). The good news is that according to my experience and some data point that I heard, almost everyone understands Spanish (Castellano) and only 75% of them speak their local language.

So just to expand (or confuse) your understanding of the complexities of language here, I thought I would give you some examples of what I encounter when I leave the house (and then you may understand more why I am content to not go out). And so you know, I promise not to get into any of the specifics like when to apply unstressed vowels, the correct usage of post-consonantal "X"s, inchoative endings, or the use of medieval nasal plural in proparoxytone words. *(When I read this collection of confusing and barely understandable terms online, I realised that some academics must have way too much time on their hands, which is probably why I almost failed English in school).* On to the examples I have heard since coming to Mallorca...

When apologising, what is often heard includes:

Spanish (Castellano) – Lo siento

Catalan – Perdó

English (UK) – Sorry

English (America) – Yeah, right.

When asking where a bathroom is, you may hear:

Spanish (Castellano) – ¿Donde esta el aseo?

Catalan - ¿On és el bany?

English (UK) – The loo?

English (America) – Gotta pee.

Other language nuances apply to the actual level of speaking.

Spanish (Castellano) – quite animated, usually with some hand movement

Catalan – very animated, usually with hand gestures

English (UK) – soft spoken, not wanting to sound offensive

English (American) – very very loud

Don't get me wrong. I do love languages, and I do love to hear them spoken. But I have never been too big on going to classes to learn a language. Several years ago I attended a full-immersion French school for several weeks. No, full immersion does not mean I simply fell into a vat of a nice Bordeaux. The classes were brutal, but as no one was allowed to speak any native language at any point throughout the day, the full-immersion thing did wonders. My French soared and I was able to hold my own in just about any conversation. Of course when it was over, I flew back to Spain and my French knowledge drained away faster than a good Chardonnay on a hot day. I guess I am con-

James B Rieley

tent to just surround myself with a new language. Just hearing the sounds or seeing the words is wonderfully helpful, and I try to read as much as I can in the Spanish media. I don't know about everyone else, but this works for me. I may not understand all the words, but it doesn't take long to figure out what is being talked about.

So this morning, I was trying to adjust something on my desk telephone (in which all information in the little digital read-out is in Spanish). After trying just about every combination of button-pressing, I finally thought that perhaps the easiest way to make the adjustment was to first switch the read-out to English. I pressed the "menu" button and began to scroll through the various options at my disposal. After several clicks, there it was – idioma. Fab. I clicked on "ok," and as I began to look for "ingles" I saw "Euskara," "Gellego," Valenciá," "Catellano," and "Catalá." No choice for English. I was about to think that I was so screwed but then realised that part of being here is all about exploring and learning. So, as we say in northern Spain, Txin-txin!

Charles Dickens first line of A Tale of Two Cities has once again come zipping into my mind. The past week truly has been "the best of times and the worst of times."

On 30 June, a bomb was set off under a Guardia Civil (sort of like federal police) car, killing two officers. Several people in the vicinity were injured. I am quite aware of the location of the bombing, as it was in front of the Guardia Civil office next to the post office I use frequently. The government immediately clamped down the island, with the airport and ports closed. I have a good boating friend who phoned me to say that even the yacht harbours were not allowing any boats to come in or go out.

Even a week on, the police presence here has been substantial. The Spanish media is full of daily stories about who they believe are responsible for the bombing, and the other day, they published photos of the suspected terrorists.

Because Mallorca is a strong tourist destination for Brits and Germans, this bombing will undoubtedly play havoc with the island economy. Within two hours after the bombing, the story was receiving massive coverage on UK television stations. The immediate suspect organisation that the authorities believe was behind the bombing is ETA (Euskadi Ta Askatasuna, which roughly translates to "Basque Homeland and Freedom). This year is fiftieth anniversary of ETA"s founding, and for years, they have been terrorising the part of northern part of Spain, but lately, their reach has grown. Regardless of whom is responsible for the car bombing, it was not a good day on my island.

A few days later, the other aspect of Dickens intro line surfaced. Did you ever see the movie Amélie? I loved that movie. It is the story of a young French girl who tries to help others, but lives a very introspective life. I liked the story so much that I almost named my first car here after her, but

Living on Rocks

instead settled on Amelia (which actually does suit her more). And whilst Amélie the movie was very special and great entertainment, there is now a real Amélie in my life.

If you think back, you know that one of the lingering side-effects that I have had to deal with from my GBS experience was a little problem with balance. For the past four or five years, I have been able to do almost everything, with the only lingering issue being that my body didn't like it when I tried to be on a boat. Yes, I was able to do the Lisbon to Panama cruise of two years ago, but that was on a ship of 200 metres. I was even able to do well on the Nile cruise of last year but that was on a pretty stable riverboat. The thing that I missed was that I haven't been able to be on a "normal" sized boat. I have terribly missed not being able to be on boats, and have longed to have that balance problem go away. I think it may have.

A couple of weeks ago, I had dinner on a friend's power boat, and noticed that, whilst I still had some balance problems, things were better than they had been in the past. The next day, I found myself on another powerboat and it was miraculous…I didn't feel the need to hang on for dear life for fear of toppling over. A few days ago, I was back on the second boat and again found that I was able to stand without wobbling. And because of the fact that my newly found "health" had come at the same time the boat I was on was for sale, I decided to once again resume my boating life. I bought the boat…and am going to name her Amélie.

A good friend who saw a photo of the new boat said, *"But where are the sails?"* Well, there aren't any. I never was that keen on powerboats, largely because you didn't get to experience what sailing is all about (sails, winches, polishing stainless and varnishing teak). Amélie will not require these efforts at all, which at this point in my life, truth be told, is just fine with me. I will at least be back on the water, even if it is on a motor yacht.

My brother used to have a statue of an old smart guy in his garden. The massive bronze casting appeared to be of an old man, sitting, pondering something or other. But when you walked up to it, you could almost feel what was going through the man's mind as he was thinking. As for me, I would like to believe that the statue of Voltaire was whispering, *"Le paradis terretre est òu je suis."* I was reflecting on this today when I realised that paradise is where I am.

After several weeks playing with Amélie – actually getting to know her better and discovering what secrets she has hidden away in the many lockers on-board – I am pretty comfortable with the whole *"spending time in Andratx as well as Sol y Mar"* thing. And because of my escalating comfort level, I thought I would tell you a bit about where Amélie is on the island.

First, she obviously isn't *on* the island. Amélie is currently on a swinging mooring in the harbour of Port de Andratx. There is a town of Andratx, but that is a few kilometres inland, and I think I have only been there a couple of times. But the port is where I am currently spending about one-half my time lately.

According to a massively in-depth (five minute) Google search (does anyone actually look stuff up in books anymore?), I discovered that Andratx *"has been inhabited since pre-historic times. It was initially part of the Ahwaz Al-Madina district when the Muslims were in power. This district was then awarded to Berenguer de Palou, who was the Bishop of Barcelona after the Catalan reconquest."* (Okay, don't worry, I promise there will not be a test on all this) *"Andratx was at the centre of the "Barony of Andratx". This area also included; Calvià; Puigpunyent; Estellencs; Banyalbufar; Marratxí; some areas of Pla de Sant Jordi; and the parish of Santa Creu.*

For the most part the people on Andratx settled on the coast. During the fifteenth century continuous pirate raids pushed them inland in search of safer places. A defence system was built all along the coastline. Today the famous watchtowers are one of the areas main tourist attractions.

The Bishop of Barcelona controlled this area up until 1835. Then Mendizábal permitted the State to expropriate and sell Church lands off in public auction.

Tourism arrived in Andratx in the 1960"s (yadda, yadda, yadda). Okay, enough of what I found on Google. What I found on my own exploring is a bit more in line with what Voltaire said.

Andratx, or more appropriately, the port of Andratx would be a wonderful sleepy little fishing village, if it weren't for all the tourists. The port covers two sides of a natural harbour, with one side being almost completely occupied by the Club de Vela (where all the up-your-bum yachties seem to hang out) and the other side filled with shops, restaurants, and cafes. This side is also where all the non-gold-braid-adorned sailors and boats are. And amongst these boats is still a little fleet of fishing boats. They look so adorable as they all stream out each day at 0500h in a long line; repeating the same basic manoeuvre 12 hours later. When I say the part about them looking adorable, that means if you would be standing on shore. If you are on a swinging mooring, as Amélie is, you get to experience what is often a pretty wild ride, as the line of boats go plunging past twice a day. I am still not sure about the preciseness of the 0500h to 1700h thing. Apparently the fishermen here are members of a pretty powerful workers union and get to knock off work each day at the same time; or, the fish have a strong lobbyist in the EU Parliament in Brussels who says that fishing after a certain time would infringe on their rights. Right. It is probably an EU thing…everything is these days.

So, back to the reality of where Amélie is…I think I like the town better at night than during the day. This is not to say I actually go into the Port at night, but the lights of the little town do look fabulous each night as they shimmer across the water. Amélie is close enough to the centre of the Port to get a sense of all the activity, but far enough away to avoid actually getting stuck in it all. The vistas are pretty great.

And for those of you who are probably wondering how I am actually existing when I stay on-board, there are two clues. One is that Amélie not only has eight extremely large solar panels that make enough electricity to serve all the refrigeration needs of the boat, but she also has a water-maker.

I used to think that having a water-maker was some luxury that only ocean-crossing boats would need to have, but I am so chuffed that instead of having to come to shore every couple of weeks to refill the on-board water-tanks, now all I have to do is press a button and this machine begins to turn sea-water into clean potable water. And when I do want to go to shore (usually to have a fab pasta salad with Pesto at a restaurant on the sea-front), I just step into the tender and motor on in. There are other situations when I use the tender (other than the never-ending quest for pasta con pesto). Every morning I get into the tender and row. Yes, this is like having a rowing machine in your house, except this is a real rowing machine. If you know anything about hard-shell inflatable tenders, you already know that they were not mean to be propelled for any great distance with oars. But I figure that this is brilliant exercise, and each day I row between 1.5 and 2 kilometres. And if that isn't exercise enough, when I return to Amélie, I usually then fall into the sea and go for a swim.

Speaking of swimming, I thought I would leverage my swimming exercises and the other day bought a pair of swim-fins. I found one pair that looked okay, but as I was walking to the check-out, I saw another pair that looked even better. These puppies are long and I reasoned that the longer they were, the more exercise I would get from using them. Well, the first day I plopped them on and then slipped into the water (25 degrees centigrade, which is wonderful to swim in), I realised that with the fins, I feel like a rocket-man. Okay, a speedy-swimmer might be more appropriate. Zoom, zoom, zoom…just call me old-smart-turbo-swim-fin guy.

I have a good friend who, admittedly, has had some problems lately. The other day we were talking and I told him about a programme that used to be on telly in America. Each week, the returning cast and whomever the guests were would sing the same song. The lyrics would change based on either the guests or on current events, but the refrain was always the same. The refrain contained the lyrics, *"If it weren't for bad luck, I would have no luck at all."* As I have been told more than once, this line doesn't seem to apply to me. And whilst I don't feel that is completely true for some areas of my life, some areas have been doing brilliantly lately.

I have some very close friends in various parts of the world who are very special to me. I have a wonderful home, with spectacular vistas of the sea. I am once again able to be on the water, and Amélie has come into my life. I get to work with great clients; get to paint and do ceramics and write. Things are going pretty well.

James B Rieley

Speaking of work (and I do mean "proper work,") as I began to write this chapter, I was in Geneva again. Whilst I would rather be home (who wouldn't I suppose) than have to travel for work, Geneva is a very special place to spend time. Having said that, when my plane landed this morning, the skies were completely overcast and the temperature was only 14c – I can't even remember when it was that chilly in Mallorca this year. But shortly after getting settled in my hotel, I went for a walk along the lake. I am writing this on Sunday, and everyone was out enjoying the sun that had begun to peak out from behind the clouds, and it did feel great to be part of the wonderful Swiss culture again. I even managed to get something to eat from my favourite pannini shop in front of the omnipresent fountain. The fountain symbolises Geneva, well, along with chocolate, watches, secret bank accounts, and extremely expensive black cars with middle-eastern registration plates of course.

When I returned to Mallorca, I had a plan in mind. First, I needed to finalise plans of where to keep Amélie for the winter. The good news is that when I bought her, part of the deal was that I would own the swinging mooring in Port de Andratx. The bad news is that the gap in the harbour faces southwest, and in winter, that is the direction of all the nasty weather that hits the island normally. Last year, the harbour was not a good place to be, so I will be moving Amélie to a marina berth somewhere on the island. I wanted to get all that sorted the week I return. I also wanted to install something I just made for Amélie.

The aft cabin has a relatively large opening port on which the previous owner had put a rather tacky translucent photo of the Caribbean. As the term "tacky" is pretty appropriate, I had decided to replace the photo with some louvers. I suppose I could have sourced them from a marine supplier, but instead decided to build them myself. So after some clever geometric calculations and fine cutting with a small saw, I built the louvers just before flying to Geneva. Installing them is part of my plan for my return to Mallorca (let's hope the luck holds and I can actually figure out how to do it).

A few weeks and two flights later, I was just back from Germany. My trip there was good, but it is always good to return home. When I booked my flights, I found a flight that left Frankfurt at 0430h in the morning. A bit of a shock to the body, but it was worth it to be back at Sol y Mar. I had planned on heading out to Andratx right away to spend some time on Amélie, but I have been caught up in some work projects so I haven't made it yet, and don't plan on it until the end of the week.

In between work projects, I have spent some time cranking up the ceramica once again. I had previously made some ashtrays for my brother and after one of them broke, he had asked me to make more for him. Okay. Then I had been thinking about the plates and cups on-board Amélie and wasn't all that thrilled with what the previous owner had left – they are very nice,

Living on Rocks

but…. So I decided to make a new set of dishes and cups and serving platters for the boat as well.

The ceramica process is great fun. Actually I think doing anything creative is good fun, but this is special fun for me. I take stock, un-fired materials, design a pattern on them, paint the pattern on them, then put several coats of glazing on them. I used to use a pink glaze but apparently the government where the glazing liquid is made discovered that it contained lead, so now they have reformulated the liquid. Not too sure about the green colour, but it really doesn't make any difference – once they are fired in some turbo-hot oven for a couple of days, the glazing turns dead transparent…and if I put it on correctly, extremely glossy. So tomorrow (I need to put a couple more coats of the glazing on) I will haul this load to the oven facility and a few days later, should have more fun kitchen things to figure out how to store. Aha! Another project. How lucky am I?

En este capitulo, quise intentar escribir todos en español. Después de pensar en él, decidía que puede no ser el mejor de ideas. Cuando he traslado a Mallorca, pense sit u vives en un otra pais, es importante aprender la idioma del pais. He encontrado que mi español es mejor cuando estoy hablando alguien que no entiende inglés. Un dia, estaba hablar para 45 minutos con un amigo solamente en español y era muy feliz. Sin duda, yo sé mi español es malo, pero la única manera de mejorar es practicar. Es verdad, que algunas veces necesito utilizar un diccionario para encontrar la palabra correcta, o pregunta mis amigos españoles, pero estoy intentando apprender mas. Pero, porque muchos de los personas que leer mis cartas no hablan español, entonces pienso es mejor escribir en inglés. ¿Si? ¿Vale contigo? Bastante español….para ahora.

There are a couple of new things to write about. As you know, the ceramica has been busy once again. Yesterday the fruits of my labour came out of the oven and I was able to see the finished items at last. I had made a set of six dinner plates and four cups to keep on Amélie. When I bought the boat, it did come with a pretty full complement of dinnerware, but they weren't exactly what I thought would be nice to eat from, so I had decided to produce my own set. I also had made several other items as well. I had decided to make a couple of very formal-looking serving platters, one of which involved coming up with a new design. The design so intrigued me that I then produced four tazas (coffee or tea cups) with the same pattern.

Also worth telling you about is the move of Amélie from Puerto de Andratx to Palma. The journey wasn't all that big of a deal. After casting off the mooring lines in Andratx, we eased out of the harbour and began to motor toward the marina. I dearly would have like to say that I raised the sails, but Amélie has no sails to raise. But instead, she has these two monster diesel engines. I say monster, as each one of them is considerably larger than even my car has. But the good news is that they are quiet, and after turning the corner that attempts to shelter Andratx from strong winds from the east, Amélie was

James B Rieley

on a course to Palma.

The past weeks since Amélie came into my life has been different. Good different, but different none-the-less. I don't even think I can explain the feeling of once again being able to be on a boat. I do miss being on sailing boat, but the very fact that at least I can be on any boat is a good thing. And Amélie has turned out to be a wonderful improvement in the quality of my life.

The journey itself was not a big thing. I had checked the distance between Andratx and Palma several times, and depending on how far out to sea Amélie would go, the distance covered would be about 23 miles. At a speed of 10 knots, that would mean that the trip should take a couple of hours. I had also checked with some boat friends in Andratx and had been told to plan on a 3 – 4 hour trip. So, a couple of hours v. 3 – 4 hours. Hmmm. Obviously, there was a disparity in assumptions about how long it would take, but it didn't make any difference. I had decided to move Amélie into a marina in Palma for the winter, and move her I would do.

One of the things any (somewhat) smart boater does before any trip is to check the weather forecast. I did this, on just about every website weather projection I could find. The range of predictions spanned the entire gambit: clear skies, low winds, smooth seas were included in the best-case scenarios; all the way to overcast, light rain, and serious waves. But one of the things I have learnt since weather forecasts began to appear on line is that these forecasters must be using quija boards or coin-tosses when they make their predictions. The day before the move, the weather in Andratx was a mixed bag. Sunny skies quickly degenerated to strong winds and storm clouds. I even saw seven waterspouts that began to descend to the sea just outside the harbour, but after a couple of hours, the skies cleared and all looked good for the next day's voyage. But at some point overnight, the weather went completely downhill.

In the morning, the skies weren't all that bad, but the swell that was pouring into the harbour of Andratx made it brutally difficult to even get into Améliña (I had named the tender the equivalent of "little Amélie" – pathetic, isn't it?). But the word of the day was "persevere," and after an hour of waiting for things to settle down, off we went. Once outside of the harbour, the water began to settle a bit and after 80 minutes or so, we pulled into the little bay in front of Sol y Mar, and within another 40 minutes, we were in Palma.

I had been told that I would be able to tie up Amélie on the quay directly in front of the clubhouse of the Royal Club Nautico in Palma, but upon arrival was told that the regatta boats that had been occupying that quay during the previous week were still there. Buggers. So Amélie was relegated to a berth out on the end of one of the floating quays in the marina. Yesterday, when checking with the marina, I was told that most of the regatta boats had departed, so in the next day or two I will take Amélie over to where she will spend the winter. All in all, a good week so far.

Yes, it is almost here once again...the end of yet another year. I can remember when I was younger, I would always marvel at how "older" people would comment on how fast time flies as they aged a bit. Well, I am here to agree with them. The past couple of months (since I wrote last) have been "interesting." My client work has kept me far busier than I had planned on, but that is a good thing. Actually, work is a good thing. Even when it means that I haven't been able to spend as much time on the island as I would like to. Having said that, I do enjoy being in different cities occasionally. Luckily, it is almost winter and the airport in Palma isn't all that bad now that the throngs of holiday-makers that seem to pollute my island all summer aren't here. Certainly, the economy has contributed to this drop-off in tourists coming from northern Europe, but it doesn't make any difference to me...it is almost as easy to get through the airport here as it used to be years ago.

My work hasn't solely been focused on clients. I have been writing and doing artwork as well. I have wanted to have another party at Sol y Mar since the one I put on last year, and the idea that kept floating through my mind was to have a bowl party. Yes, a bowl party. The thought process I went through included my belief that it would be fun to have a party in which every food-type thing would be served and eaten in bowls. So after having my idea trashed by friends several times – *"You want to have a party where everyone must eat out of bowls?"* – I ventured ahead and made up some invitations and sent them out. My reasoning was that if I actually sent out the invitations, I would have to sort out the food and serving logistics. The food sorted itself out (with culinary expertise assistance, of course), and for the serving issue, I decided to make my own bowls. So a while ago I cranked out 26 new bowls, all with the same pattern on them. So with the new 26 bowls, and the ones I had made for Amélie and for Sol y Mar, I now had 42 bowls of the same size. My plan is to have my neighbour Pacha help by washing bowls as soon as they are used so the guests can always have a clean bowl for their next taste-treat-delight (none of which I am actually making).

I have also tried to get over to see Amélie as much as humanly possible. Having her moored in Palma for the winter has made things easier, but the other day I did run into a minor problem. (Note: I am using the term "minor" very sarcastically). It was basura day. For me, basura day is any day I have more than one bag of sorted garbage or recyclables. That day there were five I think. After loading everything into Miranda and dumping the appropriate bags into the colour-coded appropriate containers, we went to fill up the car with petrol, then to the alterations shop where I had some over-sized jeans being made to fit and then into Palma to see my printer. It was then I realized that I was missing my house keys.

Ever since moving to Sol y Mar, I have kept two sets of keys – keys to the house, and keys to the car. And I have always been pretty good about making sure that I put the key rings in my back pocket, but that day, I had apparently dropped my house keys into one of the designated basura bags. I went crazy. Not so much because the keys were now lost, but because I had managed to lose them. Buggers. I wasn't all that worried about the house keys as I knew that I could get another set from Rafa and Kim. But on my house key ring I also had my key to Amélie. Okay, I did have a spare key but…you will love this…I keep the spare key on the boat. So let's recap a little bit. I have lost my key to get into the boat, where I keep my spare key. How daft is that? Rafa did help me get into the boat eventually, and I now have revised my key handling procedures. On my car key rings (I do have one for Amelia and one for Miranda) I also have the house key and the boat key. So now, as long as I don't lose my car keys, I will be able to go home or to the boat. Fingers crossed on this new plan.

The holidays typically are times when we all rush about, trying to do all those last minute things that we have slagged off earlier; times when we get together with friends; and times when we manage to acquire those nasty holiday colds. For me, the past several weeks have managed to cover all these things.

I have been highly motivated, and with the end of the year meaning client issues have fallen off a bit, I have been focused on art projects. Just before the gran Fiesta del Cuenca (Festival of Bowls) at Sol y Mar, I managed to produce several pruebas (tests) of a new series of Cadres Doblados (folded pictures). I have done quite of few of these in the past, and have been quite happy with the results. After an excursion to one of the local markets in Palma where I took photos of various food groups, I decided that several of the photos would lend themselves quite well to the Cuadro Doblado concept. So with my trusty lata (can) of cola-lite in hand, busied myself on making them. My plan is to make an entire series of them in a larger size – the pruebas are only 20 x 30cm and I would like to make them about 70 x 100cm. Yes, a bit too big for Sol y Mar, but my vision is to have an entire series installed in a restaurant.

The Fiesta del Cuenco went along brilliantly. The menu consisted of shrimp-fried rice, Thai green chicken curry, beef terryaki, Basmati rice, chocolate brownies with pralines-and-cream ice-cream, and puff pasty with red-berries and vanilla mascarpone cream. All the bowls were set out in place before anyone arrived and because I had made so many bowls for the party, as guests finished with one bowlful of whatever they wanted, they could use a clean bowl for their next attack on the food extravaganza. (Yes, I did have Pacha here helping to wash bowls for the entire afternoon to keep a supply of clean ones ready). Lots of good conversation, great friends, fab food – it was a very special afternoon. And as each couple left, they were given two of the cuencos that I had made for the party.

About the only problem with the party was that the day before, I started to feel like I was getting a resfriado (head cold). By the time the party began, my head was about to explode. By the time the party was over, I felt like it actually had exploded. This wouldn't have been too much of a bother except for the fact that two days after the party, I flew to Paris with a friend

Going to Paris is always a special thing. Wait, I should re-phrase that....BEING in Paris is always special. Going there can be total shite. The flight from Palma to Madrid wasn't all that bad, but the connecting flight to Paris was delayed over two hours, and then the terminal (Madrid has two terminals, which feel like going between them is an excursion on its own) was changed. Even with the delays and the terminal changes wouldn't have been that bad, except my head was now so full of cold that I felt like the Centre for Disease Control would have identified it as a weapon of mass destruction. None-the-less, the plane did arrive in Paris safely (just a couple hours late).

Paris over the holidays was crazy, but in a good way. It was cold in Paris. Now in all fairness, even I didn't expect that the temperature in Paris would be anything close to the weather that I have in Mallorca in winter, but geeez....it was below zero when the plane landed. And for someone who is well-weather-spoilt, experiencing zero and below is not a good thing, especially when you are filled with cold. So I did what any good traveller would do and kept taking the potpourri of meds that I had taken along. The city, even with the dire cold weather, was humming like a well-honed instrument with throngs of people filling the Champs Elysees doing their last minute shopping. Well at least that is what one would think on Christmas eve. But it is Paris, and the Champs Elysees is usually chocker-block with people anyway.

2010

Okay, okay, okay...It has been several months since I have written anything... actually since the end of 2009. I could offer several rather brilliantly concocted excuses, but the reality is that I have just been plain focused on other things.

One of the projects that has been occupying time of late began in autumn. I had developed (an incredibly powerful client curriculum – but I would say that, wouldn't I?) and have been flitting between client sites delivering it. This project will come to an end in March, which should enable me to put more time into the other projects that I have had my head buried in lately.

The first project I focussed on was fixing the Sol y Mar web-cam. Late last year, we had one seriously windy storm, and apparently, there was so much salt spray from the sea in front of my house that some of it landed on the tiny web-cam lens. The picture was still there, but it was looking like an old movie that starred Doris Day...nice and soft, almost impressionistic, but pretty much devoid of any detail. I tried to clean the lens several times, but to no avail. Finally, I took the camera down and brought it inside so I could do a proper cleaning of the almost miniscule lens aperture. I used hot water, serious window cleaner, tiny scraps of soft cloths...everything I could think of. Sadly, this has resulted in an even worse picture. I could just get a new camera, but fixing this one does seem like a project worth pursuing. The vista is still incredibly beautiful, even in our crap winter weather. I will let you know when I get this bugger sorted out.

In the past, I have talked a little bit about one of my projects. I first made one of the Cuadros Doblados several years ago when I actually was living in the village of Puigpunyent. A "cuadro doblado" is a "folded picture," and the first one I did was a portrait of my brother. Then I progressed a bit and made a very large one that hung in my sitting room at La Antigua. This was done in water-colour and was part of the entire Galatxo series of water-colours I had done whilst living there. Every so often, I would crank out another one, but in January, I became mesmerised with how I could use the concept to make an entire series of them. Part of this was due to the fact that several friends here on the island had been pressing me to do an exhibition of some of my art outputs. They had found a location for the exhibition, but the wall space wasn't conducive to many of the pictures I had painted, so I didn't press forward too hard. But then the whole Cuadro Doblado idea came to life and my work began.

Whilst during a visit to one of the larger markets here, I had taken a series of photos of some of the various food-stuffs that were for sale in stalls. Whilst these pictures were taken with my phone, resulting in less-than-optimal quality, I could already see how I could use them as part of this new series of works. After uploading them into my computer (is it "uploading" or "downloading?" Who cares...) I started to make small *pruebas* (tests) of how the finished cuadros would look. After seeing these, I became even more committed to the project and after figuring out how to do them with a minimal hassle, I began to work on full-size Cuadros Doblados. After completing seventeen of them, I then realised that they would all need *marcos* (frames), so this became yet another project.

And if that little project wasn't enough, the Cuadros Doblados project led to yet another one. This one may be a little harder to explain. Many (many many) years ago, whilst living in America, I had toyed with the idea of making women's outerwear. Formal and "sporty" jackets to be specific. Even though I didn't own a sewing machine, I made the first three jackets myself – very long nights with a needle and thread. It was a great project, and I was convinced I could make them. After all, I was able to read a blue print, and a clothing pattern is just like a blue print, only full size. By the time I sorted out the design problems, I figured that I would need to hire a full-time seamstress (which I did) and set up a little jacket factory in some spare space at my company. At the time, every jacket that we made would sell within a day or two (good news and validation that I wasn't totally crazy), and because of it, I realised that there would be no way we could ever keep up with production needs (bad news for a start-up company idea). I subscribed to Women's Wear Daily to better understand the clothing business, and then began to investigate the options of producing these jackets off-shore. After a while, it became apparent that the whole thing about dealing off-shore seemed terribly complicated, so I chucked the whole jacket idea. But as I began to make sketches of the products for this new project, I also began to look for sources off-shore to produce them. After lots of research, I decided to scrub the entire idea as it was becoming way to complicated. That was then. Right about now, you might be thinking, *"Okay, so what is the flippin" project you are working on now, James?"*

It is scarves. Large (90cm square) women's silk scarves. I whipped out several designs, and then contacted a silk scarf producer in China and after trading messages, finally did authorise them to produce a sample. They did, and sent me a photo of the completed sample just before it was sent out. The photo blew me away, and I commissioned samples of five other designs, which I am waiting for as I type.

All but two of the designs for the scarves come from other pieces of art I have produced, which is fun because it is like having multiple outlets for previously produced designs. The big issue, which of course is a project in itself, is how to market the scarves. I do have options for this: market them myself through a web-site; market them through word of mouth (too slow); find distributors, and/or align myself and the designs with a recognised brand in the marketplace. I am working on this, and will let you know when I have it sorted (just in case you want to begin buying them soon).

It happens to everyone. Another year passes on the calendar, and we are another year older. It happened to me this week, and it was very nice. The whole birthday thing is something that we either enjoy or dread. I tend to think of them in terms of just the way things are. I suppose I could fall into the "dread" category, as the older you are, the more aches and pains we tend to discover. But the aches and pains are just something that happens, and we have little control over them. So it doesn't make much sense to get all frustrated about them. Shoot, this is why we have Ibuprofen, isn't it? I had planned to have a nice quiet day at home, but just after noon, I heard the doorbell ring. When I opened it, expecting a neighbour who was going to stop over, I found a dozen friends all standing outside with pressies and singing Happy Birthday in English and Spanish. Quite the wonderful surprise. After some bubbly and snacks, we all went out for a late lunch together at a local restaurant that I tend to frequent. All in all, a very special day for me.

Let's see...what else is new here? Right. Groundhogs. No, not the actual animals (I don't even know if we have groundhogs here on the island). I mean groundhogs as in Groundhog day. Like the movie, where you think that you keep re-living the same thing over and over again. Well, this seems to happen to me each year. Remember when I first moved to Sol y Mar? After a short period of time, I built this rather large sculpture for the front terrace. All in all, it was a very fun project to build. That winter, there were a few storms that blew across Mallorca, and one of them relegated the sculpture to a pile of PVC tubes. My magnificent Estephan Tenia Razon had been reduced to a pile of scrap plastic tubing.

Not one to let the weather beat me, I rebuilt it in Spring 2009. Of course, because of the type of sculpture it was, the second version did appear to look a bit different. That was okay with me; a little variation on a theme can be a good thing. But then this winter the same thing happened again – big winds led to a pile of tubing. So I, completely undaunted by those nasty bugger winds that don't seem to like PVC tubing sculptures, rebuilt it once again. And once again, it is the same basic sculpture, but it clearly does look different. I suppose I could have numbered the various pieces and recorded them all so it would make re-building easier, but I guess that is part of the whole project experience. This time, I did devise a new way to keep the tubes together, and with some luck...well, will let you know next winter.

And if all that isn't enough, I have also been getting ready to move Amélie back to Andratx. The term *"I have been getting ready"* means that Rafa has come over to the yacht club where Amélie has spent the winter and done all sorts of fun (for him) things that needed to be done. Amongst the list of "fun things" are changing all the engine filters, changing the oil, changing the fuel filters (not a good thing to have dirty diesel you know), and finally, installing new engine anodes. We will go back this weekend to finish some other routine maintenance tasks and then all I need to do is count the days until the middle of March so I can fire up the engines and go back to the harbour on the southwest side of the island.

Right...almost forgot to update you on the scarf project. I have received six samples of my designs from a supplier I have been talking to, and whilst they are nice, I have also been toying with making some other designs. The latest designs are more conducive to being screen-printed and form a grouping that would be comprised of the same patterns, but with multiple colour combinations. So with the new designs, I have been in contact with the previous sample supplier, as well as two more potential suppliers of high-quality silk scarves. All this has been going pretty much as I had assumed it would, with the minor exception that the delay between figuring out the design and the time it takes to have a sample of it in my hands is way too long for my liking. I was tempted to have the screens made here and then actually do the screen-printing myself, but I really don't have the space here to set up to do it. So for now, I think I will have to just rely on (or contend with) external sources for the samples.

There is something else. I recently saw something online the other day that stuck in my mind. You may now be reflecting on how our world has changed quite a bit and so much of what we see is from some online source. Crazy. What I saw was a quote from St. Augustine. *"A man may lose the good things of this life against his will; but if he loses the eternal blessings, he does so with his own consent."* This was especially personal, as the day after my "big day," my sons lost their mother to a long illness. We will all miss her.

Oh, how I wish I could write to tell you that summer is here again, but the past several weeks have been like a weather rollercoaster here on the island. I do understand the implications of the dynamics of Climate Change, and because of this, I am quite aware that as the ice cap surrounding the North Pole melts, it is sending fresh water into the Atlantic. And I am equally aware that all this fresh water is mucking up the normal flow of the Gulf Stream, which in turn, is playing havoc with the weather patterns that skip across the ocean to Europe. But geeeeez…the weather lately here has been pretty flippin" depressing. Overcast skies, excessive winds, nasty cold temperatures sinking down from northern Europe, and today a phone call from a friend alerted me to the fact that he could see snow falling in Palma. To borrow a line from the overly abbreviated spelling text messaging formats, WTF? Okay, so it is crap here, but the good news is that whilst it is crap here, in most of mainland Europe, it is serious CRAP. And as with most things, it will pass.

On a different subject, when I bought Amélie last year, I discovered that she had so many "extra" things, some of which I struggled to figure out what they were for. One of them turned out to be an old, hand-operated, manual washing machine. Here is how it works. You take a big bucket, and fill it with soapy water. You then put in whatever clothes you want to wash, and then take the magical-mystery-washing-machine-doo-wah-thingy and plunge it up and down for a while. It works just like a washing machine (I have been told) and does represent a massive technological advance over what was used in the 1800"s I suppose. As Amélie already has a washer-dryer onboard, I really don't see a need for this thing. So, if you have a boat and need a hand-held washing machine, or if you know someone who really needs this soon-to-be-classic-collectors-item, let me know.

My burgeoning hand-made silk scarf business is going very well. Well, the term "business" may just be a dream at this point, and may represent a sense of great optimism on my part. So far, I have received samples of various designs from a supplier in China, and have just authorized more samples from an Italian producer of high quality silk products. When I say, "more samples," this refers to the fact that this week the cute little concept became pretty serious. The Italian supplier really does have their act together, and a sample run for them is 120 scarves. Yikes! 120 scarves. I agree, it did seem like a lot, but they are a serious producer and only set up to run based on a minimum of 100 meters of silk. So, with the scarves being 90 x 90cm that means I had to agree to them making 120 of the little beauties. The good news is that the 120 scarves will really mean I will receive 40 of each of three colour combinations of the same design. Yes, this is a consolation for me, as now I will be able to see if the entire scarf project concept is viable. If it isn't, be prepared to receive scarves for birthdays and Christmas and whatever days you celebrate.

James B Rieley

Also of note, this was a very important week in other ways. A good friend, and fellow author, who lives in the UK asked me about some of the letters I have that were written by two of my relatives during the Civil War in America. I scanned several of them and sent them off. His reply was that we should consider putting them together in a book format to enable more people to understand what it was really like for soldiers during those turbulent times. I am thinking about it. An excerpt of one letter, from July 1863, is below.

You have probably heard of the movement in this Department long before this. Well we have had considerable skirmishing with the rebels since we left Murfreesboro. Our regiment had one man killed and eight men wounded. We are now stuck in the mud. It having rained every day since we started but one. We are camped about five miles from Winchester and forty miles from Huntsville, Ala., waiting for rations. We have had pretty hard times lately, having been seven days without rations. What little we had to eat we got from Secesh farmers. I expect that you can get much better accounts of the movements from the papers than I can give you. I will write again as soon as the mail route is open.

P.S. The sun is here again, so I just finished cleaning the roof terrace of Sol y Mar and now plan on heading over to Club Nautico to do the same on Amélie.

Have you ever wondered why some things happen the way they do? I used to ponder this all the time. I read voraciously to find the answer. I consumed books that some might consider to be a bit "out there;" I talked to people who I thought have a sound view on life; I spent time practising the Transcendental Meditation I learnt years ago. And then one day I thought I found the answer (no, it was not 42). The answer, or more appropriately, my answer, was that things are the way they are because of the choices we have made. And with that bit of wisdom firmly implanted into my head, I then got on with doing what I do. What I do is, as you may have surmised, is to enjoy my life and remain close to those people who are in it.

I also do projects, but you already know that. With summer approaching at the speed of light (a very dim light some days I fear), the sun's rays have stimulated my productive genes. So having said that, a few updates.

Whilst I think I have told you that I am all set for the exhibition this October of my Cuadros Doblados, the past week saw four more of them materialise. Okay, so "materialise" isn't exactly the right word. How about, *"I busted my butt to make four more?"* Yes, that is more like it. These were heavily stimulated by the fact that I have been spending more free time on Amélie, and being surrounded by boats is the best stimulator for anyone with the sailing gene firmly embedded in his or her DNA.

Next, I have spent quite a bit of free time working on the scarf project. This was a bit trickier, as I am still waiting the delivery of the 120 initial production run from Italy. So instead of just sitting waiting for the delivery agent to ring me, I began to put together some thoughts on how I would sort out the distribution model if this project takes off. The reason I said it was tricky is that this has always been quite easy for me to do when I am working with a client, but to figure it out for yourself whilst balancing your own mental models about what works can be challenging. After hours,…no, days…of consideration, I knew that the first step would be to raise visibility around what I was working on. Let's see (I undoubtedly said to myself), to raise visibility, one needs to let people know what you are doing. Right. I contacted several extremely bright friends who are in the fashion industry in Paris, London, and New York and told them what I was up to. They all expressed interest, but also wanted to see what I had been designing. Buggers. But, as a big believer in the far-eastern philosophical statement *"When the student is ready, the teacher appears;"* I was ready, and a solution was in front of me.

Earlier this week, I went on a couple of photo shoots. With the kind and gracious assistance of two pretty fabulous friends, we went off and took a couple of hundred photos of them wearing the sample scarves I have in my possession currently. With those in hand, I then slammed together a "test" website so other people could see the output of my scarf project. Whilst this site is only temporary, at least now there is a way to show the scope and direction of the project.

Last week also brought me a flashback of sorts. I had received a note from someone who, years ago, I knew very well. She had been reading these chapters and wrote to tell me that she still had in her possession, one of the Shar-Pei coats. Okay, so now you are probably thinking, *"What are the Shar-Pei coats?"* Years ago, and I do mean years ago, I had considered expanding my horse breeding business to include dogs. Not any dogs; Shar-Pei dogs. These are the adorable little dogs that have shed-loads of extra skin that hangs on them like an oversize coat. One of my sons and two of my friends had gone to a Shar-Pei breeder to learn more about the breed. That evening, after our visit, we went to dinner and whilst ravishing a pizza, I discounted the dog breeding idea, but then realised that someone (me, of course) should be able to design women's jackets that would have multiple folds and overlaps on them. Bingo. The next day I went to a fabric shop and bought a sewing pattern – the fact that I didn't sew didn't bother me. That evening I made my first Shar-Pei coat. It looked like…let's see, what is the right word here? Right. It looked like shit. The next night I made another one. The third night I made another one, and finally I knew I was on the right track. Not owning a sewing machine was making this difficult and I was getting frustrated by having to use a needle and thread to whip these out, but the third coat wasn't all that bad. The fourth day I hired a seamstress to do these properly, and I bought a sewing machine to make her life easier. After several weeks, my seamstress had finally developed a pattern that worked and began to produce these coats in two styles; one formal, and one that was done with fun in mind. So last week, "la femme blonde" wrote to tell me she still had one of them, and then sent me a photo of it. Quite the flashback from 25 years ago.

I would write more today, but it is time to go out and wash Miranda and Amelia, and then head over to Amélie to enjoy the day.

Oh my. No tengo palabras describir este (I don't have the words to describe this). In my barrio (neighbourhood, although where I live could hardly be called a "neighbourhood"), there are quite a few building restrictions. I can almost understand most of them, after all, Sol y Mar is a "front-line" sea home and gladly, the local authorities do put restrictions on what can be built in the area so the flavour of the coast is not destroyed by abysmal looking properties. Sol y Mar itself is quite an old house, built in a traditional Spanish style. I always thought that the building restrictions applied to the houses on the other side of the street as well, but for the past year or so, my beliefs have been put to the test.

Down the street, there was quite a large home that looked in disrepair. Last spring, it appeared that someone had decided to tear the house down, as crews of people appeared and began to dismantle it. I say "dismantle, as it wasn't as if a wrecking ball suddenly began to blast the house into piles of rock, but instead, the windows were removed, the walls disappeared, and we were all left with an empty shell to look at as we drove past. And without missing a beat, the house began to re-assemble itself. Sort of. What rose from the pile of rubble on the site looked as if it was the same house, but on steroids. As I didn't pay that much attention to the old house and what was coming together, I can't be sure but I would be willing to wager that the new house is a good 50% larger than the old one. Okay, fair enough. Quite obviously, the owners (new owners?) had some serious money and were spending it faster than a government could bail out a bank.

The completed construction is sort of a fusion of classical architecture and Le Corbusier on heroin. Extensive use of fenestration, combined with huge marble-y looking walls. And then the oddities began to appear. First, it won't be that difficult to find out who the owners are, as they have had their initials carved into a section of one front wall facing the street. Even that wouldn't be all that odd, except the initials are about 2 metres high. Then, as the workmen were installing the Spanish version of a cobblestone drive, it was evident that they were putting in water tubing…you know, the type you would use for under-floor heating. This is Mallorca, and unless the ongoing climate changes that we are all experiencing bode poorly for my part of the island; this seemed a bit ridiculous. And then it was done…or so we all thought. Next to the extremely large pool, a equally large rattan elephant appeared one day. And then, the ultimate in "What is Wrong with This Picture?" appeared. Workmen delivered a truckload of wood poles, like the kind that are used to support telephone lines. And the very next day, just between the dry-stone wall fence and the pool, there was a log cabin. Yes. This massive new and trendy property has a little log-cabin in the front yard. What is that all about?

Moving along, (other) things are pretty good here. This weekend was the annual Hublot Maxi-sailboat regatta and even though this really played havoc with my ability to park near Amélie at the yacht club, it has been wonderful to see. For hours today, sailboats were skipping past Sol y Mar desperately looking for favourable winds so they could whiz back to Palma and collect the big prize (which, because the race is the Hublot Regatta, is probably a big watch or something).

And then there is my little scarf project. I decided that if I was going to see if this project makes sense, I needed to really go for it, so I authorised the production of another of my designs by the Italian screenprinters. This week, I will probably authorise the production of two more designs. And then I began to look for packaging options. This was like searching for the Holy Grail, but not finding diddly-squat. What I wanted was something that would be elegant, smart, simple, and yet of a quality that would match the quality that I am putting into the scarves themselves. Finally, after what seemed to be looking at all 32-ka-zillion options that came up on Google, I decided to just get on with it and design the packaging myself. Which I did. And then, just to make sure that the design would work, I made up about 50 of them. So now it is just a matter of time to find out if all this has been a good investment of time and money, or just a fun project.

I do like my technology. And even though I say that, it often seems to run amuck in my life. This past week was a case in point. Shortly after moving to Sol y Mar, I installed a webcam at the house. As you probably already know, this was as much for my viewing whilst traveling, as it was for friends and family. Well, as I have already written, the picture had gone all wonky a while ago. I am pretty convinced that this was due to salt spray from the Mediterranean, and have tried to clean the lens repeatedly. The end result was that the picture looked as if I was directing a movie starring Doris Day... a hazy, out of focus picture is an understatement for what I could see. So, after contacting the lovely (sarcastic comment for sure) people at Panasonic, I broke down and bought a new camera.

With that solution in hand, I began thinking about doing the same thing for Amélie. Putting a webcam on-board a boat that is typically on a swinging mooring out in the middle of the harbour in Andratx was a bit more complicated. I did find a solution, and through a friend of mine, bought a webcam that functions with a mobile phone SIM card. I was in business, or so I thought. After taking delivery of the camera-thingy, and looking at the installation instructions, I wimped out and asked my friend Graham to set it up for me. He did so, and the other day I actually installed it on-board Amélie. This part wasn't all that difficult, except for the part about stringing 12VDC cables behind hidden panels and up to where the camera would be mounted. With everything set, I turned the camera on. My plan was to have it point toward the bow, so that if I was traveling, or even just at home, I would be able to view the weather environment the boat was in. The only minor glitch was that all the windows on Amélie have summer screens over them. These screens – made of substantial white woven plastic – allow you to see out, but keep the summer sun at bay. And as much as I had wanted the camera to "see" through the forward screens and focus on the sea, the screens are a bit distracting. So my revised plan is to simply remove one screen so the view is unobstructed. Excellent solution, and the picture was crystal clear. So after finishing all this installation work, I set the camera to "on" position, and came home. As you might imagine, the very first thing I did after returning to Sol y Mar was turn on my computer to play with my new technological tool. I remembered the website, and entered it into my home computer. I entered the "user name" and "password," and waited for the picture to pop up on my screen. What popped up was pitch black. Hmmmm, that didn't look right, so I refreshed the picture, but again it was black. And it was then I realised that I had put the camera lens cover on before leaving the boat. Daft idiot. Needless to say, the next day I was back on the boat and removed the lens cover.

Don't mis-understand me, I have been doing things that don't require massive technology. More scarves have arrived from Italy – a very good thing; and I have been cranking out new designs with a passion. I still haven't made the decision whether to make this project into a proper business, but that isn't all that important quite yet. Don't worry…I will let you know once I know.

This week I am planning on moving Amélie back to Andratx. Well, at least that is my plan. I am still waiting to hear from the man who will put the mooring back in place in the harbour. He was stranded in the UK due to the recent eruptions of the volcano near the Eyjafjallajoekull glacier (don't even think about expecting a pronunciation guide from me for that city in Iceland) Shortly after the volcano went off, air travel in most of Europe was cancelled due to the ash floating around in the skies. I can understand that nature is often chocker with surprises, but I do think it was rude for Mother Nature to kick that sucker off when I am waiting for Terry to fly back to Mallorca and re-set my mooring. Buggers. But with some luck, he should be back this week and Amélie will finally be back home.

Update: It is May Day. Yes, that's right, the first day of May, and this can conjure up all sorts of images in one's mind. My mind always seems to fall into one of two pictures: either an flower-filled alpine field, complete with a tall May pole that has ribbons wafting down from the top, and young children running about. The other picture is a bit different, as it is the annual May Day parades from Eastern-block countries during the Cold War. Rows upon rows of soldiers doing some precision goose-stepping along a wide boulevard followed by what appeared to be a never-ending stream of massive tanks and rockets showing the rest of the world how strong those countries were. But today's May Day images are different. This May Day was the day that Amélie finally went back to her swinging mooring in Andratx, and even though it was dead overcast most of the way over, the sun came out as soon as she was moored...and I was smiling.

There have been some other non-technology-related things occurring lately here. A good Welsh friend here on the island had asked me a couple of months ago if I was going to participate in this year's Europa Day event. I think I replied at the time that I would consider it, but didn't know what he was even talking about. Right...after a short verbal tutorial, I found out that Europa Day was a celebration of sorts on 9 May in Palmanova (a sea-side town not far from where I live). There would be artisans of all types displaying their wares I was told. So I contacted the event people and on Sunday did just that. As the past couple of years at Sol y Mar have been rather creative for me, I didn't have to worry if I would have enough things to bring. After the DrJBR sorting and culling process, I ended up taking along some of the new pañuelos, some of the Cuadros Doblados I have been making, as well as a few of the aquarellas and pen-and-ink drawings I have made since coming to Sol y Mar. My expectations weren't high, as I assumed that Europa Day's typical exhibit would be more like 3 candles for a euro instead of 200 euros for a scarf or 850 euros for a Cuadro Doblado; but I had thought that this would just be a fun day along the sea...which it was.

More importantly than the fun, of course, was that the day was wildly successful. The feedback that was received was extremely positive – "que chulo" was heard repeatedly (roughly, "how fab"). Some pretty great friends helped out, bringing all the Cuadros Doblados and pañuelos to the site, staffing the La Antigua Design exhibit, and bringing everything back to my house after it was over. Pacha, Cris, Richard, Kim, and Fernando's help was very much appreciated. (note to myself...having two cars is great, but having two small cars and making large pictures doesn't mix well.)

There was a dark side to the day, however. Well, not so much "dark," but "big and pink." Throughout the day, Pacha and I were gobsmacked at the number of overly obese (if that is even possible) and sun-burned tourists that were strolling along in various states of undress. Not a pretty sight. Big and pink are mild adjectives for the state of much of the humanity we saw. But we did desperately try to avoid making cheesy comments under our breath. No really, we did try (but often failed miserably). Overall a good end to a great week.

It is a bit past 2030 on a Wednesday evening, and I am on-board Amélie surrounded by an incredible stillness. The sea is as flat as I have seen it in a long time and my floating neighbours are all just bobbing about. The only sound is the odd ripple of water as it brushes against the hull of Amélie... things are pretty good. As the sun was beginning to drop behind the headland, I thought it was a good time to begin to write.

It is probably hard for anyone who does not have boating as a key chromosome to understand how nice this all is. Sitting on the aft deck, just watching the world revolve makes this whole thing about being alive pretty incredible. About the only discernable noise came from my CD player gently surrounding me with Carl Wilson's "Heaven."

Today was meant to be a busy day for me. I had been here at the beginning of the week, but then had to go home to deal with some client things (and clean the house, of course). But this morning I was all caught up, so I came back in Amelia. The drive here from Sol y Mar is pretty much all motorway, and it is an easy 25 minute drive. I would like to bring Miranda here, but when I stay on-board, it would mean that I would have to leave Miranda on one of the narrow town streets overnight (or for multiple overnights), and I am not too keen on that. It isn't that Amelia is an "expendable" car, only that I think that because she looks so normal, no one would do anything.

After arriving, I went to my meeting point and found Améliña waiting for me. I use her to get from boat to shore or the reverse. I have a good friend here to sort of watches over my boat when I am away, and when I do come back, he brings Améliña to shore for me and ties her up at the same place each time. So I plopped my satchel into Améliña and motored out to where Amélie is moored. (Sorry if all these names are confusing…you really do need to pay attention.) After doing my mandatory (self-imposed, but mandatory none-the-less) cleaning chores on-board, I decided that I was due a bit of fun, so I rowed Améliña from my mooring to the other end of the harbour. It isn't like crossing the Channel or anything, but it is over a mile each way, and rowing a hard-bottomed inflatable boat isn't exactly all that great. But for me, it is cheaper than having a land-based rowing machine, and the exercise is clearly good for me. The row there wasn't that bad, as there was a breeze behind me all the way. But the way back was a real bugger, but that is what exercise is supposed to be about. Isn't it? Anyway, I did make it back and had some lunch and then sat down to get some client work done. And then tonight, the stillness set in. I was thinking that this would be a good time to do some TM, but just being on-board is the best meditation there is, so the Maharishi will just have to wait.

So I was once again faced with a major conundrum: *Should I just relax a bit and enjoy the incredible stillness, or should I do something a bit more constructive.* Just to clarify, something "constructive" means using my brain for something other than a repository of too many creative ideas whilst sitting in the sun. I seem to run into this conundrum quite often, but in all fairness, I found quite a few years ago that being surrounded by sun and water are incredibly stimulating to me. So, like many humans who are faced with massive conundrums, I compromised. This doesn't mean I just defaulted to the sun-solution. I decided to use the sun and the gentle waves of the sea to help me get cracking again. And it didn't take long to get those brain cells to deliver a solution to me.

When I was researching for my Ph.D., I spent a considerable amount of time studying far eastern philosophy. One of the things I learnt has stuck with me as if it was super-glued to my psyche ever since. The phrase I had discovered was, "*When the student is ready, the teacher appears.*" After about 30 mins, I was apparently "ready" for what I needed to do, and off I went.

I had received the most wonderful little book from my son David. The book is titled "My Dad," and after opening it, I discovered that it was full of lined pages. Almost completely devoid of text, the only writing consisted of questions on every other page. At first, I thought, "*What cute questions.*" They were things like "*What was it like to grow up,*" and "*Which one of your parents are you most like,*" Cute. Some of the questions were a bit more inquisitive, but none-the-less, it looked like answering them might be a good thing to do.

The intent of the author (assuming there really was an author) was to have a "Dad" fill out the pages with answers to the questions. Very cute. But it didn't take me long to realise that my answers would require more space than the book allowed, so I fired up my computer and began typing. I do like to write, and after quite a few hours, I had managed to get a good start. I was now ready to finish my little question-driven essays. I went below and grabbed the computer I have on Amélie and went up to the aft deck to finish what I had started when I received the book. I did this with the best of intent, but here technology mucked up my plans. I do have a relatively good computer on-board, but whomever designed these laptops must have never considered that they could possibly be used outdoors. The brightness of the sun made trying to see what I was typing damn impossible, so I had to go below to do my writing. This "modification" to my conundrum wasn't anticipated, but I figured that I could finish up the questions in short-order. I was wrong. When I finally did finish, long after the sun had gone down, I had whipped out 18 pages and 12,000 plus words...and was exhausted.

Upon reflection, and the main reason to tell you about this, this "exercise" was brilliantly cathartic and I would encourage any father to do something similar for his children. I never realised until I had encountered each question how little our children really know about who we are, and how we managed to arrive at where we are in life. At the risk of promoting a book in this letter (especially a book that I did not publish), if you are a parent, go buy the book and get writing. It will be good for your children, and very good for you.

I do have an exercise programme; one that is boring, but a programme none-the-less. I know that some of you might now be thinking, "*Hey, exercise programmes are not boring.*" Okay, fair enough. Even I like to exercise. My own exercise programme is very structured. No, really. JBR and a structured life in the same sentence. Really. My exercise programme consists of massive amounts of stretching when I wake up, as well as sporadically throughout the day. (This would not be the time to knit-pick about the obvious conflict between the words "structured" and "sporadically," thank you very much).

The reason I have developed this exercise programme falls into two central categories. The first one is that my body does have a few miles on it, and if I don't stretch first thing each day, the creaking sound would be deafening.

This age thing, for me, is complicated by that little episode I with the evil Guillain-Barré Syndrome. Whilst my doctor continues to assure me that the chances of it coming back are about the same as achieving world peace in the next few minutes; it can be a worry. Especially because every once in a while, I wake up and my legs and back feel like they did as the GBS began to attack me before. The second reason for my exercise regime is that having Amélie requires that I am a bit more fit than I needed to be when I just sat in front of my computer writing books a few years ago.

This morning, I awoke to the usual alarm. My alarm system consists of a large extremely bright yellow light in the sky. I suppose I could close the persona's (large wooden louvered shutters, in Mallorca, usually green) each night on the windows in my bedroom, but that would block the view when I wake up – if this logic seems confusing and a bit contradictory…well, it is. Keep reading. First, after noticing the fact that I am still on the planet and breathing, I began the day's stretching. To make sure my stretching programme isn't counter-productive, I did do quite a bit of research about the correct way to stretch. I could have, I suppose, actually put more structure into my exercise regimen by enrolling in Yoga or Pilate's class, but I am saving those options for when I am seriously old (don't even think about saying anything right now). After zipping into about a dozen websites and then printing out what I perceived to be the pertinent tips about bending (without breaking) and stretching (without tearing), I thought I had it all sussed. Back to this morning.

So I began my usual routine. 60 of this, 60 of that, followed by another 60 and 60. This is usually followed by a Yoga position that I had discovered that I had been doing for years. This description of this position, the Savasana, probably would appear to be me lying on my back after being run over by a lorry…which is typically how one feels after all this other stretching. I don't do this *"Oh-my-God-he-looks-dead"* position too long. Actually, just long enough to remember what is next in my highly organised exercise system before I repeat the whole thing over again.

I have looked into several Yoga positions that, according to their online descriptions, and was pleased to find that I had already been doing several of them before I became so highly motivated. It seemed that I was already doing the Sukhasana and the Pavanamuktasana, and off and on, even the Salabhasana and the Ardha Matsyendrasana. I was going to try the Boogity-boogity-boogity-shu, but that one requires me to have Chubby Checker blaring on the radio, and that seems a bit inappropriate in the morning.

I used to have a DVD about Pilates. It was one of those DVD"s that celebrities who no longer have proper jobs seem to gravitate into making, and for a time, I would plug the DVD into the player and stretch out on the cabin sole (this was when I was still living on Angelina) and try to follow the moves. I am not even sure that it did anything for me, but that could have something to do with the lack of excitement when you watch the same movie

Living on Rocks

over and over again. Having said that, I was thinking about getting another Pilate's instruction DVD, as it has to be a good thing to do (and the names of the positions are in a language that I actually understand). So this morning, after feeling exceptionally well-stretched, I went into the Amazon.com site to look for one that seemed like a logical purchase. Okay, problem one: Amazon has 1,583 DVD"s listed under the search entry of "Pilates." Problem two: The first 52 offerings had pictures of women on them that either don't even have the term "flab" in their lexicons, or have been Photo-shopped to the *nth* degree. Offering number 53 was titled "Pilates for Men." I kept scrolling when I saw this one too, because the bloke on the cover of the video looked like a cross between Superman and Christiano Ronaldo. I am not looking for abs of steel; I am just looking for abs that allow me to see my feet on occasion after a big meal.

Number 72 was called "Real Pilates: System 27." Holy shit. The implications that the makers of this video either have 27 different Pilates systems to offer, or that they have just put out 27 versions of someone bending their body into strange positions in order to sell more DVD"s was impressive. But not enough to buy it. By the time I had scrolled through over 125 of these videos, I gave up.

I next went to an actual Pilates website, just to refresh my memory so I could see if I even needed to buy another DVD. I found one that listed quite a few Pilates moves, along with helpful hints about how to do them correctly. I especially liked the "Tips for Rolling Exercises" and "Swan Dive." Although neither of them mentioned what I believe to be a key tip (don't do this on the edge of a very tall building), they were helpful...in an Ilsa, She-Wolf-of-the-SS sort of way.

Being fit means more than just being physically fit of course. There is also the mentally fit component that needs some focus. Years ago (and I do mean many years ago...like in the early 1970"s) I learnt how to do Transcendental Meditation. And whilst the whole way that it was taught then was a bit over the top, the basic premise is pretty powerful. My expectations of the classes were pretty high. But when I saw my teacher, whose name was Steve and not Maharishi-something, write *"cosmic consciousness"* on the flip-chart, I began to wonder a bit.

There are two main key points to doing TM (I was told). One was to devote 20 minutes in the morning and 20 minutes in the evening to meditation. The other key point was remembering the mantra that I was given by my TM "teacher" (and I do use the term "teacher" pretty loosely here). Shortly after being given my instruction (the term "given" doesn't really apply here as I had to pay for the bloody class), I was pretty good about the whole 20 mins each morning and 20 mins each evening thing, but that degenerated after a month or two. And then there was the day that I forgot my mantra and went into near panic mode. I phoned Steve and was just about to admit my ineptitude, when it suddenly popped back into my head. Since then, I must admit, I don't do TM every day (much less twice a day), but I have found that it is very good at clearing out my head so I can be more effective at whatever I am doing. I would tell you more about the mantra aspects of TM, but as we were all told in the TM class I took that our mantras should never be shared, that would probably unleash the anger of some guru on a mountain-top in India, so I think I will pass on it.

Because I already do TM (once in a while), I thought I should either get seriously serious about all this healthy exercise stuff and join a class, or just follow the guide to life on a card I received years ago, and still have. The card said, *"Do what you can, where you are, with what you have."* I like that. I like it a lot. Good sound advice. So, a part of actually following this wisdom, I went out for lunch and had a fab ensalada pasta con pesto (pasta salad smothered in pesto). Hey, doing all this typing burns up a lot of carbohydrates. Doesn't it? *Jai guru dev.*

The past week has been filled with extremes for me. First, I have been experiencing quite a bit of pain. At times, the pain has been rather extreme. Having said that, it has been a wonderful week. *"Hmmm"* you are probably thinking. *"How can he have a week of pain that has been wonderful?"* A fair question, and the answer is inter-related.

For the past week, I have been on-board the Seabourn Legend cruising the Mediterranean (which was the wonderful part). The pain has been a result of the fact that whilst on-board, I partook in some Yoga and Pilates classes. Actually, the first day I signed up for an on-board Yoga class (the only Yoga virgin in the group); which was followed the second day by a Pilates class (again, being the only Pilates virgin in the room). By day three, I had signed up to have the Yoga/Pilates teacher give me one-on-one instruction for the rest of the trip. But enough of the painful part of the trip; you might be more interested in the "wonderful" aspects of the cruise.

Addy, Gilly, and my friend Gillian and I decided that a little holiday break might be a good thing, so we all met in Villefranche-sur-Mer (France) and after two days, took a car to Monte Carlo to begin the little holiday. For all of us, it was admittedly a "neighbourhood cruise," as the itinerary was Monte Carlo to St. Tropez to Antibes to St. Raphael to Mahon (Menorca) to Palma de Mallorca to Valencia to Barcelona.

Thursday-Saturday: Villefranche-sur-Mer is one of my favourite places, not only in France, but probably anywhere on this little planet we all inhabit. Having a hotel right on the harbour made the stay there even more enjoyable. The opening scenes of the movie "Jewel of the Nile" were filmed in Villefranche, and from our rooms, the views of the harbour were spectacular. After two days, it was time to get to Monte Carlo to begin the cruise so we all piled into a taxi and drove the 6 kilometres along the coast road to the principality. After checking in on the Legend, we all settled in and at about 1800h, we set sail.

Living on Rocks

Outside of the itinerary – neither Addy nor I were too keen on having to travel any great distance to have a holiday – the main reason that we had chosen the Legend was that it is a very small cruise ship. The typical cruise liners that are plying the seas these days have two to three thousand passengers, and the Legend only holds 220 guests (on this cruise, there were only 208 of us).

Sunday: The planned itinerary was for day one to sail to the Poquerolles (a small group of islands off the Cote-de-Azure) but due to some foul weather, the Captain announced that we would instead sail to St. Tropez. No, we didn't see Brigitte Bardot, but St. Tropez is a pretty buzzing place, and well worth the visit. Lots of trendy little shops, and a fab harbour.

Monday: We arrived at Antibes shortly before 0800h and we went to shore. One of the joys of the Legend is the fact that, due to its size, we were able to anchor quite close to shore.

Tuesday: If you look on a map, you will see that St. Raphael really isn't that far from Antibes, but the Captain managed to sail the 53 kilometres in only 9 hours (note the sarcasm here as if there was a walk-path, you could have arrived in the same time on foot).

Wednesday: Even though Menorca is a short hop from Mallorca (the largest of the Balearics), I had never been there before, so this was going to be a treat. After winding our way deep through the harbour (one of the most secluded natural harbours in the world) we tied up at one of the cruise-ship quays.

Thursday: This stop was pretty anti-climatic for me. Have no doubt, Palma de Mallorca is a very special place, but shoot, I live here. Clearly (at least in my mind), there was no reason to get off the ship and explore the city. I had, however, received a phone message from the Marina where I first kept Angelina when I moved to Mallorca. The message was a bit intriguing – *"James, we have received a letter in the post that was sent to you here."* As I haven't lived there in six or seven years, this was incredibly intriguing, so we walked to the Marina, only to find that the letter was in reality a Christmas card that had been postmarked 22 December 2008. So much for the postal service. So back to the Legend for another day in the sun sipping cranberry and orange juice (mixed together, of course).

Friday: Valencia is the home of the European Formula 1 Grand Prix, and the Legend tied up next to a section of the racetrack that winds through city streets along the harbour. When I say "next to," I mean...*next to*. As the actual race was this weekend, all the teams were there practising, and the howl of Formula 1 cars screaming past the ship was fabulous. After watching the cars go whizzing past for a couple of hours, we dis-embarked long enough to walk to turn 8 of the track and stood about six meters from the corner. (I am sure my hearing will return in several weeks) If you like Formula 1 racing, it was a pretty special thing to be a part of.

Saturday: The Legend slipped into Barcelona just before 0800 and after breakfast, it was time to pack up and leave the ship. Sailing into Barcelona was pretty special, as I had spent several years living there on-board Angelina. But I knew that in a few hours, I would once again be in Mallorca and on Amélie very soon, so for once, having this voyage finish wasn't a bad thing.

Overall, this little holiday was fabulous. Great weather (after we left France), an incredible environment on-board (the staff ratio to passengers was almost 1:1), good friends…a very good holiday. I would be remiss if I didn't mention the food on-board. I had cruised the Caribbean quite a bit in an earlier lifetime, but those cruises were all on monster-sized boats. Because of that, the food, whilst pretty great, was produced in such quantity that it rarely gave you the sense that it was prepared for you. The Legend was quite a bit different. With several dining areas (a large restaurant, a stern veranda restaurant, and even dinner on the main deck), the choices and menus were quite spectacular. The only disappointment was one night when we chose to eat in the main restaurant. This evening's menu was billed as the specialities of the Head Chef, but his "specialities" clearly missed the mark with everyone we spoke with afterwards. Having said that, the breakfasts and lunches were un-matched each day.

I think that one of the reasons I liked the Seabourn Legend, outside of the brilliant ambiance and service, was that there were so many comparisons to Amélie. My boat holds a little over 1,000 litres of diesel fuel; the Legend holds 1.34 million litres. A good thing when it is time to fill the fuel tanks I guess. Legend has a crew of 197 people; Amélie has…well, me. Not a good thing when it is time to scrub the decks I think. Legend, when full, generates about 400,000 USD per week of income. Amélie…well, let's just skip the comparisons, okay?

Perhaps it would be better to write a bit more about the pain part of the cruise. I have known for some time that I could probably be in better shape, and have been desperately working each day to stretch enough so my body doesn't creak too much. So when I found out about the Yoga and Pilates options on the ship, I thought I should give it a go. After the first two days of actual classes, I was becoming addicted to it all, so I signed up for the personal coaching offer. The on-board guru-ette was pretty incredible. It didn't take her long to put together a regime of Pilate's actions-moves-postures-stuff (pick anyone that you think is accurate) that she said would be very helpful for me. And even though Jacqui's talents were on a par with Dr. Mengele for inducing pain, every day I became more and more addicted to the programme. Of course, my challenge now will be to continue to practise what I was taught, which I plan on doing (as soon as I can get to the chemists to buy more Ibuprofen).

Stars. The sky was full of stars. Being on Amélie, especially sitting on her swinging mooring in the harbour in front of Andratx provides a perfect environment to sit and watch them all as they whisper gently as they twinkle. The night was clear, and the moon was yellow, oh, hang on…those are the opening lyrics to Stagger Lee. Sorry. Just sitting there the other night, my mind began to be filled with all sorts of questions.

"I wonder how many stars there are?" Counting stars, or more appropriately, trying to count stars can be a bit tricky. I was going to try to mentally segment the evening sky into sections to make my counting easier, but being on a swinging mooring did make that a tad difficult as Amelia's position kept shifting as the gentle breeze slowly moved her around. I then moved on to a different counting method that involved simply counting up one small area of the sky, and then extrapolating that amount by the size of the area in relationship to the entire sky. I counted as far as 32, and after my clever extrapolation process, came to the conclusion that there are multiple ka-zillions of those little buggers up there. I had even thought of using the Drake equation to calculate how many stars there are in the heavens. As I once saw online, the equation is $N = R^* \times f_p \times n_e \times f_1 \times f_1 \times f_c \times L$, with all those letters and symbols meaning something way beyond my capabilities that night. Whilst I am not sure, I believe that if you actually run the equation completely, you will see that the answer is indeed multiple ka-zillions of stars. I went on to the next question that popped into my head.

"How many constellations can I pick out?" Well, I was able to pick out Ursa Major, Ursa Minor, Orion, Leo, Dopey, Grumpy, Sleepy and Doc, but the other ones must have been hiding or something. The next question that surfaced in the maze of brain cells that were admittedly getting pretty worn out from the previous questions, was, *"What were the ancients smoking when they named the constellations?"* but before I could even contemplate that, I moved along to *"What is it all about?"* By *"it,"* I meant *"everything."* Right. This should have been an easy question to answer, but I hadn't been consuming mass amounts of vino tinto, which clearly would have enabled me to come up with something that made sense at the time. Instead, I went to bed.

The following morning, my ability to see the stars was obliterated by our own star, the Sun, which even early in the morning, was blazing down upon the harbour. After a suitable breakfast (tea, toast, a sliced orange, and a thin layer of number 2 sunscreen) I went on deck to get cracking.

The past week has been pure, unadulterated bliss. No sir, don't get me wrong. The past week hasn't been all fun and games. My days on-board haven't just been chocker with relaxation. As I have a computer on-board Amélie, I am able to keep up with my client and writing work. And on top of that, I have been semi-religiously practising all the Pilates positions/movements/pain-inducements that I learnt on the Seabourn Legacy. But I have also been able to do what any boat owner does the most of, which is, of course, cleaning. Luckily, the amount of teak on-board Amélie is about $1/10^{th}$ of my previous boats, but there is plenty of stainless to polish. And then there is all that deck space. This week I did manage to come up with a brilliant way to keep the foredeck clean. Note to all my boating friends, you may want to make note of this. What I discovered, through massive

James B Rieley

and intense research, was that if I would go for a swim in the crystal clear (and warm) water of the sea, and then immediately lay down in the sun on the deck, it prevents any dirt from accumulating on it. This process clearly needs to be repeated on all deck sections that are exposed to the sun, and in the case of Amélie, that meant quite a few dips in the water. The things I have to do to keep the boat clean can be exhausting, but I do try to keep a clean boat, so I would repeat the process multiple times each day.

Of course, this process has been made easier due to the fact that the weather has been brilliant here. The other day, I did look up from my deck protection duty and did see a cloud, but luckily, it wasn't coming my way.

I have also been reading. Reading voraciously I might add. As I have a selection of books on-board, whose numbers do seem to increase every time Amazon makes a delivery to Sol y Mar, I did take some time away from my on-deck duties to expand my knowledge of all things important. This depth of research expansion has included some of the works of Carlos Ruiz Zafon, David Baldacci, and Ian Fleming. Right about now, my sons are thinking to themselves, *"Oh my God, he is re-reading all the Fleming books for the n-th time. Oh my."* Why save them if you don't re-read them is my motto. You, however, might be thinking, *"Hey, those authors don't write about business stuff."* Clearly. But to quote someone, *"Man does not live by bread alone;"* or in my case, by business stuff alone. Besides, I write about business stuff, and to read about the beliefs and assumptions of others could cloud my brain. Can't have that happen, can I? Especially when there are all those stars out there that need counting.

A few years ago, there was a book that was made into a movie, and it had some crazy title. Okay, so a lot of movies have crazy titles. I believe the one I am thinking of was the *"Unbearable Lightness of Being."* I was thinking using this as a theme to write about. Maybe *"The Unbearable Heating of Summer;"* but that title would be a little silly because I like the heat of summer. How about *"The Unbelievable Process of Thinking?"* I actually liked that one for a few minutes, but then realised I would be getting a headache pondering the question too long, so I skipped it too. I could have used *"The Insatiable Desire to;"* but then realised I wasn't sure what I had an insatiable desire to do right then. Shoot. This theme-picking thing was becoming a bit of a problem. Then it struck me like an out-of-control-train-on-a-downward-sloping track (nice visual there)..."*The Ever-Increasing Word Count Conundrum."* Like it? I hope so because here is the deal.

Conundrum, according to an online dictionary, is defined as *"A paradoxical, insoluble, or difficult problem; a dilemma."* In my case, the problem is how to keep coming up with stuff to write about. The answer to this conundrum (which by the way, probably means that it isn't a conundrum anymore) is to just write about the stuff that is going on around me. So, for the 133rd time, here goes.

Living on Rocks

I discovered, or actually rediscovered, the best way to tell when summer officially arrives here. I say rediscovered, because this happens every year, and for some reason, I have managed to block it out of my memory every time it happens. One might think that to tell when summer officially arrives here, the best way is to check the calendar. But you see, according to the calendar, 21 June is the official beginning of summer, and this can be a bit misleading. For most of us in the northern hemisphere, summer is the beginning of good weather, and in most weather-context definitions, this means sunny and warm. One way to check this would be to make a simple graph. On the bottom line of the graph, you would write in the days of the month. On the vertical line of the graph, you would put down the percentage of cloud cover (or the amount of rain that has fallen) on any given day. Then by plotting the cloud cover (or rainfall) each day, it would be possible to get some idea of how sunny it has been lately. I will save you some time here....the graph for the past couple of months would have no line at all.

There is another way to tell if summer has actually arrived. For my island, the official start of summer is when you go to the airport, and the arrivals area is full of motor coaches that will take the holidaymakers to their respective corners of Mallorca. Seeing the airport arrivals area literally chocker-block with tour coach's surfaces two mental models for me. One is that, as this island really does rely on tourism to survive, all the arriving holidaymakers are a good thing. The other mental model is that I sure am glad that I don't live near where the tourists like to go.

The Sol y Mar webcam is finally up and running again. As I had written about a chapter or two ago, the new replacement camera did arrive after waiting a month (so much for good customer service from Panasonic), but then there were problems getting the signal to be able to be accessed by any web browser. I could see the camera image on my home computer, but that didn't seem to be worth the investment. Why? Well, when I am home, I don't need to go online to see the view; I just look out the window. The purpose of having the bloody webcam is to be able to see it from anywhere. So, this afternoon, a computer tech-y person came over and after gesturing hypnotically a few times, voila! The whole system is again working.

One of three things have seem to have happened lately here. The choices of what this is all about include; A) I am suffering from the onset of Alzheimer's; B) I am bored beyond possible belief; or C) I have slid into serious money saving mode. The reason that one of these must be going on is that I haven't been smoking lately. I actually ran out of cigarettes on the first of July, and for some reason, didn't rush out to get some. The next day I flew off to Geneva, and that meant I wasn't going to smoke for two days as I can't buy the brand I smoke there. When I returned home, I forgot to buy some on the way back from the airport. A few more days passed, and I still hadn't bought any, and every time I would think about it, I would be doing something, or it would be at a time that the tobacconists were closed. Then I went off to

Geneva for another two days and just returned home again. I actually did think about buying some fags on the way home from the airport today, but missed the exit from the roundabout. Now for those of you who believe that smoking is bad for you, or evil, or something not good; rest assured, I haven't quit smoking. I just am not smoking.

I think there is a clear distinction, at least for me. I once stopped smoking for nine years; and then a couple of years ago when I did the ocean crossing from Lisbon to Panama, I didn't smoke either. But in both cases, I never thought I was quitting. Actually, I am fine not quitting smoking. But apparently, I am also fine just not smoking sometimes. I must be in that mode right now. I will let you know if I return to smoking mode one day.

The other day Sunset Boulevard was on telly. You know, the black and white movie from 1950 starring William Holden and Gloria Swanson. Geeez... what a movie. If you haven't seen it in years, well, it is worth watching. Whilst in Geneva, I saw "The Family Stone," which was wonderful, but in a very sad depressing sort of way. And then I recently watched "Jewel of the Nile" for the umpteenth time. I always thought that one of the reasons I liked this movie and the one before it (Romancing the Stone) was due to the name of the sailboat at the end of the first one, and the beginning of "Jewel of the Nile." But it recently came to my attention that the first part of "Jewel" was filmed in Villefranche-sur-Mer, and having just been there, not to mention that it is one of my most favourite places, I just had to watch it again.

I should call this item, the "music" item, because that is what it is about. I have done it. I have gone over to the dark side. Yes, I have actually downloaded a couple of Lady Gaga songs into my iTunes. I have always considered myself to be more of a middle-of-the-road, easy listening, soft rock, Corrs kind of listener. My iTunes does represent an almost eclectic selection of music, however, with songs by Mana, Dionne Warwick, Alex Ubago, Frank Sinatra, and (of course) the Ronettes interspersed with Linda Ronstadt, Brooks & Dunn, Dusty Springfield, La Oreja de Van Gogh, and George Friderich Handel. And whilst I tend to vary my listening tastes, there are some artists whose music I could listen to for days on end.

A long time ago, and I do mean "long," I had purchased a record album by Carl Wilson. Yes, Carl Wilson, brother of Brian and the late Dennis Wilson. I can't even remember if it was on vinyl or cassette – it was a LONG time ago – but I can still hear some of the songs every so often. They just slip into my consciousness like a shell appearing on the shore. No big fanfare; no flashing lights; they just appear as if they had never been gone. Last month, my son David found a copy of the album and is sending it to me, and soon, it too will be in my iTunes (which means I won't have to worry about wearing it out).

In my work with clients, I have always said that questions are more powerful than answers, and this belief is largely based on my experiences in business.

Living on Rocks

But I have had personal experiences that have led me to the same conclusion. Years ago, one of my sons came to visit and after some time trying to be polite to each other with just "talk," he said, *"Dad, can I ask you a hard question?"* I replied, *"Is the question hard to ask, or hard for me to answer?"* His question was sort of a breakthrough and, respected him so much for being able to ask it. Enough about that; one of the questions that I have lived with for many years now is, *"What should I read?"*

I do like to read. And although my selection of recurring readings is pretty varied, much like my choices in music, there are a few authors and publications that I do seem to be attracted to. When I lived in the village, I subscribed to "Casa y Campo," which is sort of a variation of Country Homes or Architectural Digest for Mallorca. But when I moved to Sol y Mar, I stopped buying "Casa y Campo," and now, I tend to buy whatever magazine strikes my fancy at any given moment. Having said that, I do still receive one publication through the post each month. It is

"Vanity Fair."

I am not sure if you read "Vanity Fair" or not, but I do find it especially interesting. And there is one page of each issue that piques my interest every time the magazine appears in my buzon (post box). The page that I always go to first, often before I even see what is in the issue, is the Proust Questionnaire, located on the last page.

Marcel Proust (who lived from 1871 to 1922) is the person who is credited with putting together a series of questions that are designed to reveal quite a bit about the person responding to them. Although it wasn't Proust who began to do this, the questions are now known as the Proust Questionnaire. These questions, or more appropriately, and adaptation of them, have also been an important part of James Lipton's questioning on The Actor's Studio programme. I could just continue to rabbit on about that else uses these questions, but instead, I thought it might be nice for me to answer them myself. So, in the spirit of full-disclosure and all that rot, here are Proust's questions (and my answers).

What is your most marked characteristic? *Confidence and ability to focus I think*

What do you consider your greatest achievement? *Earning the respect of some pretty smart people*

When and where were you happiest? *When I found out I was to be a father*

What is your greatest regret? *Not having been able to see more of my boys as they were growing up*

What is your idea of perfect happiness? *Spending time with those I love*

What is your most treasured possession? *Something my father gave me; the ability to figure it all out*

Where would you like to live? *I live there now*

James B Rieley

What is your greatest fear? *Living too long and becoming well and truly ill*

What is the trait you most deplore in yourself? *I do struggle with the whole patience thing*

What is the trait you most deplore in others? *When someone says they will do something, and*

then they don't

What is your main fault? *That's kind of an accusatory question, isn't it?*

What is your favourite occupation? *Going there*

What is your favourite colour and flower? *Blue, unless it is a flower, then yellow*

Who is your favourite author? *Well, I am I guess*

Who are your favourite heroines in real life? *Beryl Markham, Dorothy Kosher, Margaret Ann Dennis, Tania Aebi*

Who are your favourite heroes in real life? *Thich Nhat Hahn, Nelson Mandela*

Who are your favourite painters and composers? *Anyone who has truly mastered water-colours; Burt Bacharach, George Gershwin, and of course, Brian Wilson*

What is the military event I admire the most? *The turning of swords into ploughshares*

What do you consider the most overrated virtue? *Sincerity*

What is your greatest extravagance? *I haven't found it yet*

What is your favourite journey? *Petra was pretty great, but I don't think I have experienced my favourite journey yet*

What is it that you most dislike? *People don't take responsibility for their own actions*

What is the quality you most like in a man? *Honesty and integrity*

What is the quality you most like in a woman? *Honesty and integrity*

What do you most value in your friends? *Just knowing they are there*

If you were to come back as a person or thing, what do you think it would be? *Not sure I would even want to come back*

If you could choose what to come back as, what would it be? *Someone who makes others happy*

How would you like to die? *Just going to sleep as my father did seems pretty great*

What is your present state of mind? *Floating*

And then from Lipton's variations of the questions:

What is your favourite word? *Yes*

What is your least favourite word? *No*

What turns you on? Quite a few things actually; how much time do you have?

What turns you off? Vegetables that are green, and begin with A

What sound or noise do you love? The sound of waves lapping against the hull

What sound or noise do you hate? I try not to hate anything, but gunshots are not nice to hear

What is your favourite curse word? I think you should ask my friends this one

What profession other than your own would you like to attempt? I have changed mine several

times already so I am not sure anymore

What profession would you not like to do? Anything where thinking was not a requirement

If Heaven exists, what would you like to hear God say when you arrive at the Pearly Gates? Welcome home

This week I found out that my very good friend Richard passed away. You are probably thinking, *"Oh, that is too bad, but why are you telling me?"* The reason is that you have missed out on meeting someone very special.

I first met Richard when I accepted a position with one of those big global consultancies. I was brought in to head their Leadership Development efforts, and Richard, I had been told, was one of the key internal people. Within a week or so, I had asked that everyone in my department be brought together so I could tell them who I was and what my plans were for our departmental future. After the day-long meeting was over, Richard sat with me in some little outdoor café and told me that he thought the meeting went well, but that he thought he would be leaving the company. I wasn't too happy at that news, and spent quite a bit of time trying to convince him to stay. He did, and the several years I spent at that company were pretty great, and this was largely to do with the fact that we held each other in rather high regard. Even after we had both left that company, we stayed in weekly contact. Richard was one of those special friends that, even though you may not see each other on a regular basis, when you are together or even when you are on the phone, it seemed like we just picked up the last conversation where we left it off.

Having said that, anyone who would have seen the email traffic that buzzed between our respective machines would have been confused beyond belief. An email might begin with "Dear Keith" and end with "Love, Mick;" or "Dear Julius" and end with "See you on the 15th, Hugs, Brutus." Of course, then there were those that really challenged me to greater response heights, as Richard was educated in proper English schools, and I was...well, certainly not educated in proper English schools. We would communicate about damn near everything, from the state of the government at home (in the UK), to which E-type Jaguar would be a safer investment, to the rather dire state of management in most companies, to how Christine Keeler was

James B Rieley

doing. Not much was beyond the realm of our conversations.

For the past year, I was very lucky to have been able to actually see Richard on a monthly basis. I have a client who had asked me to develop a curriculum for them, and then deliver it. My first thought was to ask Richard to do it with me. Working together again (after our common experience with that (allegedly proper) consultancy was a high priority for both of us, and when the opportunity came up, I rang Richard immediately. It was during one of these sessions that Richard explained to the assembled group, just before they were released for a coffee break, that for the two of us, *"coffee" is code for Come Outside For Fag Exhaling Exercise.* I had known for a long time that Richard's doctors were not all that keen on his smoking, and we used to talk about that too. But his response to my concerns was that, he was too old for many other vices, so what the hell.

Richard had four real loves. His wife Annette, and his two daughters made up three of them. Nothing else did, or could, come close to his love for them. Having said that, a while ago, he did buy a Royal Enfield motorcycle. His initial description of her to me verged on the edge of soft-core pornography, but in a loving way. When I heard the news that he had passed away, my first thought was that I hoped that he was on his motorcycle, raising all sorts of chaos on the winding Tuscan roads near their house in Italy. But even though that wasn't the case, when I was speaking to his daughter Rose, she said that that was probably what he was doing right now.

One last thing, just so you "can" know Richard a little bit. This is something he sent me once, describing what it was like for him in school.

As a youth, first day of autumn term at school and we had a new teacher filling in the register. This was a boy's grammar school and she was a female in her twenties (a great rarity in those days). She duly went round the room asking names and religion (as a C of E school everyone had to attend morning assembly with prayers so anyone not C of E was catered for separately). I think as she went round the room there may have been a couple of Catholics and a Jewish boy, the rest being solidly Anglican. When it was my turn I gave my name and said "The old religion". She looked up and smiled. "Catholic?" "No, Druid". First day of term, first detention.

God, how I miss my friend.

I saw it in the headline of La Vanguardia (a Spanish newspaper)....*La Aurora boreal podrá observarse esta noche, también en bajas latitudes. Los científicos sospechan que se apreciará desde bajas latitudes, ya que la onda de radiación y viento solar puede crear una tormenta geomagnética.* (the quick and dirty translation is that due to the crazy solar storms that are taking place right now, it might be possible to see the northern lights from right here in Spain). My first reaction was how fab it would be to actually see it. My second reaction was that I was quite lucky to already be on Amélie where there would be less light pollution, just in case the magical light show is on.

Most things astronomical have always fascinated me. When I was a young lad, I had a massive 5" reflecting telescope – which when I think about it now was pretty crap and certainly not massive, but when you are 10 years old, it was like having the Hubble telescope in your own yard. The fact that the tube was a bit out of straight, and my lens selection was meagre at best, didn't lessen the fact that I could actually see the stars. I can also remember when I first read about Halley's comet. With an orbit of 76 years or so, I quickly did the maths to figure out when it would return to be close to Earth so I could see it. (It did whiz past in 1986, but by then, much of my astronomical tendencies had dissipated apparently because I missed its visit). I had a 3" refracting telescope when we lived near Houston in Texas, and did manage to see the rings of Saturn several times. But now, the third of August, 2010, it was going to be possible to see the northern lights that have intrigued mankind for eons. This was going to be especially exciting, as normally, you can only see the lights from some place in the frozen tundra, but thanks to the craziness of the Sun, it might be possible to just sit on my aft deck and be mesmerised.

It was a very nice evening on the aft deck of Amélie watching the millions of stars, but the fabled northern lights didn't make an appearance this far south. Besides, if they had been visible here, I wouldn't have been able to document the event very well as the only camera I have on-board the boat, other than the trendy camera in my trendy iPhone, is the underwater camera I wrote about a while ago. This camera, whilst pretty great for capturing stuff going on below the surface of the sea, would be pretty crap for snapping photos of the astronomical light show of the year.

Having said that, I have found that Amélie magical underwater camera does take some pretty fair photos above the surface as well. In the past couple of days, I was playing around with it to see what it really could do when not submersed in the warm waters of the Mediterranean. Of note was yesterday afternoon when I welcomed a group of visitors to Amélie. I have always tried to have a *"Come when you want to come"* policy on the boat, eschewing the need to formally invite visitors at certain times. Although in fairness, as you can't exactly walk up to the boat at some marina, my policy does, by default, require some advance warning of a visit. But yesterday was different. As a matter of fact, I didn't even realise that they had come over until I looked up from the project I was working on. There they were...the Patos family. Well, I do suppose it is more appropriate to say a family of patos (ducks). They paddled around for a bit, and then buggered off to visit someone else I guess because by the time I decided that it might be polite to feed them, they were on their way.

Earlier in the day I had a little not-fun water encounter. I have, as I think I have written about, been doing quite a bit of swimming of late. This is all part of my two-fold programme of trying to beat my not-exactly-abs-of-steel into shape, and to just enjoy swimming in a pool with no sides to it. I used to just plop into the sea and paddle around a bit, but lately have been doing my version of power swims. With a chart programme on my computer, I have identified various distances from Amélie and then I can tell how far I have been swimming. All this seemed fine until the other day when I decided to swim over to a friend's boat. I had been doing about 200 metres out and back a couple of times each day, but that day, I found that my friend's boat was actually a little over 550 metres return. So later that day, instead of doing another big distance adventure, I decided to just scrape some of the feathery-looking week-like things off my propeller shafts. This did seem like an easy task, and after taking a wire brush with me, dove under the boat a few times. I was almost done when I noticed that I felt like I had been stung by a few hundred bees. I found out from a friend that some of the underwater weed-like-doo-wah-thingies do like the warm water of this time of the year, but do not like being attacked with a wire brush. Lesson learnt. Once the itching stopped a few hours later, I vowed stick to my swimming regimen, and will get rid of the little bastard underwater growth things by using the Donald Campbell method.

And if that weren't excitement enough, last evening I watched the most spectacular sunset. Sunset's here do sort of become a bit monotonous, with virtually every evening being so high on the Richter scale of sunset beauty that my expectations are exceedingly high. But last evening, the scale was shattered as the sun decided to slowly sink into the glass-like surface of the water, falling directly behind one of the lights of the harbour entrance.

This morning I decided that I needed to come home for a couple of days. Actually, the "come home" is correct, but the "couple of days" is sort of just an idea. I think the reality is that I came home to make sure the house is still there; sort through any post that had been delivered whilst I was away; do a bit of cleaning and watering; and meet some friends tomorrow. After that, who knows (but I would not wager against my immediate return to Amélie if I were you).

It has been an interesting time lately. I know, I know…the word "interesting" can carry a huge amount of implications. But in this case, I really do mean it has been interesting this week. And for me, that is a good thing.

I had flown to Geneva in July for some meetings, and because the weather was pretty brilliant there that day, immediately went for a long walk down to the Lake. Lake Geneva is one of those good news-bad news bodies of water for someone who would rather be on the water than doing just about anything else. The good news is that the lake is incredibly long and the scenery along its shore is pretty spectacular. The bad news is that the lake is rather narrow, so no matter where you are, you can always see some part of the shore. The only reason I call this bad news is that years ago, the first time I sailed out of sight of the shore on a boat, I realised that this is what sailing is all about. Well for me at least.

I think that the "sailing without seeing land" thing is so important to me because of its connection to something I learnt when I was younger. My father firmly embedded in my mind the belief that I could solve whatever problems were put in front of me. Well, he didn't really teach me like that... what he did was not solve my problems for me and instead, forced me to learn the point. And the connection to the "out of sight of land" thing is that when you are out there sailing, it is your responsibility to bring the boat (and yourself) back in one piece. If that isn't having to do problem solving sometimes on the spot, I don't know what is.

Then there is that advert that said, "*You can never discover new lands if you are afraid to lose sight of the shore.*" The first time I saw it years ago, I realised that it was one of those DNA-things going through my body. And whilst admittedly, I am not all that big on some types of variation in my life, I do like the concept of exploring. The difference is that for me, sometimes I am quite content to explore whilst never leaving my own comfort zone.

Part of my exploring has been the whole boating thing. I remember when I first began to delve into learning to sail, I devoured hard-core sailing magazines. These were the magazines that had articles by serious sailors about how they rigged their boats, and how they handled some of the challenges they encountered whilst cris-crossing the worlds oceans. One of these people was a man named Steve Dashew, who had made quite a reputation for building serious ocean-crossing sailboats. In mid-August, I looked up from the aft-deck of Amélie and saw one of his boats. Several days later, after returning to Sol y Mar for a few days, I noticed the boat was in front of my house, so I called him on my hand-held boat radio. Within a couple of hours, we were talking in the middle of a boat-yard in Palma, and I was again wishing that Amélie had two masts instead of two diesel engines.

Since I wrote last, I also "discovered" a singer that really impressed me. Okay, so I really didn't discover him, but I heard him for the first time. I had gone to a charity golf outing for Fundacion Handisport (no, not to play; just to support the charity) and a friend of the founder of the Foundation came and sang for the assembled people. Jaime Anglada is pretty special, and I was blown away by the reality that almost everyone at the charity event knew the words to his songs. After the event, I did, as you do, go online and bought everything he had on iTunes.

And then there is my art stuff. Lately I have been exploring how to get the upcoming art exhibition set up. I think I have written about this previously, but now it is almost here and I have been working my brain cells overtime figuring out what pieces to exhibit, and how to have the venue arranged to show the work. I have visited the venue a couple of times to get a feel for the salon, and actually made a $1/10^{th}$ scale drawing of the space in order to mentally position my work. But that seemed so flat, so I decided if I was going to do this, I should do it right (my father apparently was leaning over me that day), so I built a scale model of the actual space. I then printed scaled pictures of the pieces I plan on exhibiting and tried them out in different places on the model.

After multiple changes to the big layout plan, I thought I was ready, and was ready to move on to the other pressing issues. First, the end of September meant the turnover of La Antigua. The family that had been renting it for the past two-plus years were moving out and I needed to go out to the house to make sure that it was in the same condition as it was when they had moved in. The same weekend required Amélie to move from Andratx to her winter location. This is one of those mixed emotion things for me. I had spent over ½ of my time during August and September on the boat and had loved it. Not only was spending all this time good for me mentally, it was very good for my physical health. Every day, I would row around the Andratx harbour in Améliña Rowing the tender is a real pain as it is not designed to be propelled by two oars, but even that made the rowing exercise a good thing. One day I had taken my portable GPS doo-wah-thingy and plotted the distance to various points in the harbour, so I would be able to track how far I was rowing each day.

Due to the fact August and September were pretty warm here, after my morning rowing expedition, I would plop into the water and swim a bit. Initially, I began swimming from Amélie to shore and back. Then I found a different place on shore to swim to (a bit farther, of course); and it didn't take too long to start swimming a longer and longer path each day. Then one day some friends had brought their boat to Andratx and I swam over to see them. I knew that it was a bit of a long swim, so that afternoon, whilst on my third rowing penance of the day, my GPS told me that their boat was almost 500 metres away. And this was on top of the other two swims each day. Right. The next day I decided I had better have more of a structured exercise regime, so I managed to get it down to a kilometre of swimming and several kilometres of rowing each day. I could actually feel like I was getting fitter. I did find it strange that after one of my rowing or swimming episodes, I did think it would be nice to have a cigarette, but even as I write this after three plus months, still haven't bought any. So all this exercise was good, but then the weather began to degenerate a bit so I didn't spend as much time on the boat. Less time on-board resulted in less time rowing and swimming, so it was back to Pilates at home.

And then it was the end of September, and time to bring the boat to its winter mooring. The trip to Sta. Ponça was pretty easy, with the minor exception that one of Amelia's engines would not start, so the trip over was "interesting"…and, at least it used less fuel and did manage to get her into the slip without bashing into anyone else's boat.

That brings me to the recap of the art exhibition opening night. Several days before the actual opening night reception, we had dragged all the pictures over to the exhibition venue and set everything up. Two nights later, it was

Living on Rocks

the reception, which went very well. I didn't have high expectations for the evening, other than people coming and enjoying some of the pieces I had made over the past five years. But my expectations were met and exceeded as a friend from Puigpunyent who had come over purchased one of my cuadros doblados. All in all, a very good night. I guess it was a good idea that I started making them.

I was thinking about Ethel the other day. I could be cheeky and let you guess, but after exhausting all the typical Ethel's; (Mertz, of I Love Lucy fame; Rosenberg, of the electric chair fame; Merman, of unbelievably loud fame), you still may not have managed to think of Waters. Yes, Ethel Waters. And why, are you now thinking, did Ethel come into my mind? In the early 1930's Ethel Waters was the first person to have sung "Stormy Weather," and oh my, that is what it has been here for the past two days.

Stormy weather, in the form of wind and rain, isn't a bad thing. Actually, for an island that pretty much dries out all summer, the rains of autumn are a good thing. The problem is that those of us who have chosen to live here are pretty spoilt and even though we know intuitively that rain is good, it still does disrupt a nice daily routine.

I, being dead bored because it was overcast and wet, decided to listen to music this morning, and after looking outside at the same time the Ronettes were singing "Walking in the Rain," decided to put on my Wellies and grab my brolly and go for a walk myself. I wasn't even sure why I needed the umbrella as the rain had let up, but it seemed like a good idea just to have it with me. So there I was, walking along looking terribly like someone in Somerset (Wellies, Barbour jacket, James Smith and Sons brolly) when the skies re-opened and began to bucket down once again. Serves me right for venturing out I guess, but even though I still managed to get a soaking even with all my protective kit, it was great to be out. But enough talk about weather.

I know I have written several times about astronomical phenomenon, but this blurb, whilst about stars, is a little different. It all began with a flashback, and I am not sure exactly what caused it. It was probably the fact that "Grease" was broadcast the other night on telly. All I know is that I found myself flashing back to the late 1950"s and early 1960"s. My brother had, for as long as I can remember, been involved in the music business, and even growing up, he was somehow connected to the music scene where we grew up. He used to receive demo records in the post on an almost daily basis from record companies. And whilst he seemed to know everyone who was anyone in the music business that came to Milwaukee, I was relegated to just being one of the throngs who sat in the cheap seats of a venue. Of course in those days, a live performance was not what it is today.

I can remember going to see the Dick Clark's Caravan of Stars when they were on tour in the late 1950's (I think). The acts included, Frankie Avalon, Duane Eddy, Fabian, Connie Francis, and just about everyone else who had a hit record then. This was well before what we now know as "band tours." Way back then (and it does seem like a terribly long time ago), music promoters would put together these huge shows that had many artists playing their stuff. Each group would play a song or two from their pseudo-massive repertoire (usually a repertoire of two or three songs) and then the next singer/group would come on stage. This is the way it was until a certain English group came on the scene. And then it changed once again when there was this big music festival on a farm in the state of New York in America. But even with all those changes, and the current flood of incredibly expensive live performances of big-time artists, there is still nothing that can compare to the way things were.

And speaking of "those times," this morning, I decided that I needed to do more of looking up. I am not exactly sure of the connection between "those times" and my sudden need to look up, but it is my chapter, so you will have to just keep reading.

For all three years I was living in Puigpunyent, one of the constants was Galatxo. Galatxo is the highest point on the island, and soars almost 1,000 metres toward the stars. Compared to say, Everest or K2, 1,000 metres isn't all that high, but when it towers over a little island village, it is pretty impressive. I remember many times thinking that I should see what the village looked like from the top of Galatxo, but for some reason, I never did. Today, I decided it was time.

I have a friend who recently went to Galatxo so I sent him an email asking his advise about the easiest way to get on the right road that would take me to the mountain. He responded with what I thought were pretty concise directions, so this morning, I packed some fruit, a big bottle of water, and a jacket, and drove off on this adventure. I found the right road, and after driving for a bit, parked my car at the large stone gate. With my camera and rucksack, I went off to begin my big climb. I knew before getting there that it would be quite a hike, but I had no idea how long it would be. This was complicated by the minor fact that whilst the directions I had been given were good, they were not going to get me to where I wanted to go. My directions took me to a place called Finca Publica Galatxo, which is a unbelievably large finca that had been given to the government of Calvia, probably to avoid potential tax problems. After about 1.5 kilometres, I came upon the finca and after a quick view, continued to follow the path noted by the signs. The path I had chosen was to Pou de Ses Sinies (PO-DAY-SAYS-SEE-KNEE) and according to the distance noted on the wooden sign, I should be able to get there in about an hour. I had decided to head in that direction as it was the highest spot identified on the signs at the finca, and my reasoning was that the higher the better. After all, I was going to the highest point on the island, and I assumed after reaching Pou se Ses Sinies, there would be another sign pointing the way for the rest of the journey. I was wrong.

I did stumble along the rock-strewn path as it wound its way up through the scenery, and after a little more than an hour, I encountered some bloke running along the path coming toward me. Running. Shit, I was struggling walking on the rocks and this guy was running as if there was a lava flow chasing him. I knew that lava was not an option, so I just assumed that this guy was some psychopathic health freak and kept stumbling along. Within another 15 minutes, I came to a clearing where there was a couple that looked as knackered as I felt. They asked if I spoke English, and with a great look of relief on their faces, I said that I did. After a few minutes of chatting about how pretty it all was where we were, one of them produced a trail map (something I didn't have) and I discovered that whilst I was definitely climbing higher and higher (something my legs already knew), there was no way I was going to make it to the top of Galatxo today. Actually, I was on the wrong side of the topography completely. Apparently, when I had asked for directions to "Galatxo," my source gave me directions to the Finca Publica Galatxo, and not the mountaintop. Right. That was okay, as I had had a brilliant hike through some spectacular scenery, and had most probably worn off 32 kazillion calories.

As I hiked back down the hill, I began to think of what lessons I had learnt on this little expedition. This thinking process was only interrupted once, and that was when four men on mountain bikes went whizzing past. What was that all about? I must have been on the path for health freaks. Lesson 1: Know where you are really going. I had asked for directions, which were spot on. They just weren't going to get me where I wanted to go. Minor problem. Lesson 2: Carry a dictionary. This would have been quite helpful as all the hiking trail signs were printed in Catalan (Mallorquin) and not in Spanish. I do love the language, but the language I do love is the national language (Spanish) and at my age, learning one new language is hard enough. Lesson 3: When hiking up mountainous terrain, do not wear boating deck shoes. I didn't see a single piece of teak along the path, and my deck shoes and the rocks I was walking on did not seem to get along well. Lesson 4: Having an entire team of Sherpa guides to carry supplies is a good idea. This may be a bit overkill when out on an afternoon hike, but I would have liked to have them today.

Day Two. I awoke this morning and all I could think about was finishing what I started yesterday, so, lessons well learnt, I put on thick socks, put on better shoes for climbing, packed more pears and some chocolate bars (for energy) and headed back to Galatxo. It was 0930 and I was ready. This time I headed to the road from Puigpunyent to Galilea, where, I had been told by another friend, I would find a turn off that would take me up the mountain. My directions were clear (again). Take the turn off toward La Reserva and follow it for 3.4 kilometres, then take the turn when you see the sign marked Es Cucui. Okay. No one bothered to tell me that the road toward La Reserva hasn't been maintained since the Moors were here apparently, other than the odd patching job. Sadly, the patching of the tarmac must have been done with marshmallows. The road was just plain terrible and Amelia was none-too-chuffed about trying to survive the potholes, some of which appeared to be deep enough to swallow Ibiza. I have no idea what the grade was, but at times, it did feel as if I was driving up a 45-degree hill. Just after I had gone the 3.4 kilometres, there was a sign that said Es Cucui, and I obediently turned and found myself heading up an even steeper hill.

After another few kilometres, the road sort of ended in a huge pile of gravel that held a sign that said Puig de Galatxo, 1 hr. 15 min. Right. I could almost taste the looming excitement as I began to hike up the path that extended upward from behind the sign. At the time, I was thinking how treacherous this path was, but was soon to find out that this path was quite a luxury for what lay ahead. It was now shortly after 1015 and I found myself really struggling as the angle of the hill that I was climbing kept increasing at the same pace that the path became smaller. It wasn't too long before I realised that the real plus to my packing time this morning was including a very long wooden rod that I was using as a walking stick. As it was still early in the day, and the path was pretty slippery in spots, having this assistance was a real plus.

At first, there was the rather infrequent wood signpost with an arrow that I assumed pointed the direction to follow, but after a while, the arrow indicators became simple piles of stones that someone had made for the hikers who came up here. After finding yet another pile of stones, I saw something through a break in the trees. It was an observation tower, and I knew that all this effort had been worth it. I was almost there. Having said that, after another 10 minutes, I could see that the observation tower was not actually at the top of Galatxo. No doubt about it, it was pretty flippin' high however. Although the tower – a fire prevention vantage point – was locked, even from its base the views were pretty spectacular. To the south, I could see the sea near Sta. Ponca. To the east, I could see parts of Palma and Palma bay. To the north it was easy to see where Soller was behind the mountain range; and to the west, I could see Estellencs and the sea. I had to keep going…I was so close to the top…or so I thought.

I still hadn't seen anyone on the path this morning and was beginning to believe I was the only one out here as I kept dragging my excessively tired legs up the side of the mountain. When I looked around after another 30 minutes, I was astonished to see how much further up I had managed to get. And that was about the time I heard voices. The sounds were coming from a different path that was snaking along the western side of the mountain. Undoubtedly, this was the path up from Estellencs I had been told about. The voices belonged to four young men who I saw were on bicycles. BICYCLES. Shit. I was struggling to do this climb on foot, and here were four guys on mountain bikes. Incredible. Feeling a bit wimpy about the fact that I was knackered and they seemed to be feeling no pain at all, I started to go back down so I could get to a spot where I thought they would stop. It took

Living on Rocks

a few minutes to get there, but as I negotiated my way around this big rocky corner, there they were. Luckily for me, they spoke Spanish (as opposed to Catalan) and I asked them how long it had taken them to get this far. Well, one of them told me, they had ridden their bikes from Palma to Puigpunyent and then up the mountain earlier in the day. Shit shit shit shit. Okay, in all fairness, each of these guys was less than ½ my age, but geeez. I took a photo of them and they jumped onto their bikes and went bouncing down the path. I just sat there, totally flummoxed by how these guys could do this. Right…the age thing. I turned around and continued my journey up. After a while, encountered a couple that appeared to have done this type of exercise before. They were both kitted out with matching spandexy-looking hiking kit, seriously impressive climbing shoes, a portable GPS-looking thing, and a map. I couldn't resist, and asked them how high we were standing on the side of the mountain. The man checked his map, and then the electronic thingy and said that where we were standing was 748 metres high. Right.

The peak of Galatxo is 1026 metres high. I was then at 748 metres. I needed to climb another 278 metres to make it to the top. After looking at the helpful couple, then looking at the remaining 278 metres, I decided that this challenge was for another day. I was at the level where what remained looked to be serious mountain climbing, and I wasn't quite prepared for that. Not quite prepared means that I didn't have the right kit, nor did I think my legs would be able to make it all the way up AND THEN make it all the way down. So instead, I devoured a pear whilst sitting on some rock, pretty chuffed that I had made it as far as I had. Quite obviously, I did make it back down the mountain, just in time to write this letter before I fall asleep for the next few days.

Note to readers: Due to clearly slacker writing behaviours on my part, this was written over several weeks, so please excuse the following two part structure. Okay? Okay.

Part 1:

Do you believe it? It is November. Geeez. It seems like this year has gone faster than all the previous ones, but I think that has something to do with perceptions as it appears that 2010 has the same number of days as previous years, and the number of hours per day hasn't shifted either. I suppose the perception of a massive acceleration of time has some correlation to the number of years I have accumulated. Could be, but the way my mind works; that is just a good reason to get cracking and not sit idly by. And with that in mind, I have been working diligently on a new project.

When I say a "new" project, this one is actually an annual project that typically begins in late summer and takes until about now to finish. This year, I think I was so busy with other projects that I lost the plot for a bit, but the past couple of weeks I have been working on this year's holiday card. I

James B Rieley

would like to be able to say that I have the design all set, but I am still playing with several different looks for the card this year. Now some of you may be thinking, *"Oooh, not like James to still be working on designs when it is already November."* Well spotted, but I at least have narrowed down my choices for what I want to do. The good news is that by the end of this week, I should have it all sorted and have my little production line set up.

I have also been working on my own Christmas present. You know, this is when you buy yourself a present. The good part of doing this is that you don't need to worry about receiving a beige jumper from your children (in retribution for the ones I bought each of them years ago) or even worse, a book or CD that you just positively hate. So screw it…you get yourself what you want. My present for myself this year is going to be a little trip. Nothing too over the top, but just an escape from the winter weather of the island for a bit. Winter is, after all, cold and grey and wet, and at the risk of sounding like a real weather-wimp, when you live where I live, even 12 or 15c does feel too cold. So my plan is to go away for a little bit.

Picking a place to go became a bigger challenge that I had hoped. I had thought about doing what I always recommend that clients do when they are faced with big decisions: make a matrix and use it to determine which of the potential locations does the best job of meeting my holiday requirements. Of course, in my case, the principle requirement is that the location would have better weather than Mallorca will have in the middle of winter. That means going to a different hemisphere, and as there are only two, and Mallorca is in the northern hemisphere, I needed to go south. It didn't take too long to figure out that my best options would be Australia, South Africa, or the Caribbean. Yes, I know that the Caribbean is in the northern hemisphere, but work with me on this, okay? My other criteria fell into two main categories. Friends, Cost and Distance (with less being good for both criteria). South Africa and Australia both did well in the friend's criteria. The Caribbean and South Africa did about the same in the distance criteria. And Australia (and staying home) did the best on the cost criteria. I will let you know when I decide for sure, as right now, I seem to have it all sorted in my mind and then waffle on the decision within minutes. Maybe I need a bigger matrix.

Back to something I wrote about earlier. It is now three days later, and I have begun the production line of cards. This is another one of those "geeeeez….." moments. Every year, I discover something new about making cards, and this year, the big discovery (and not in a good way) has been that the very trendy paper I chose doesn't seem to like my printing ink. That may not be a fair statement, as a couple of hours from now, all might be well with the world again, but right now, I am not exactly chuffed with my choice. Yes, the paper is quite nice, with a mild linear texture. Yes, the colour (a variation of cream) is very nice. The problem surfaced when I screened on the first colour. Within seconds (literally about 15 seconds) the paper decided that

Living on Rocks

it should begin to roll itself up. This isn't supposed to be like this. In all the previous cards and even this year's test prints, I put the ink on and the paper stays dead flat. But this time, I put on the first colour and the paper begins to act like a roller coaster at Alton Towers. And if that didn't generate enough excitement here in serigraph-central, after about two minutes, the paper goes flat AND THEN BEGINS TO ROLL THE OTHER WAY. Buggers. But using my wealth of postgraduate education (and some weights), I seem to have that sorted out. I can't wait to see what happens when I begin to apply colour number two.

Part 2:

Okay, so I managed to survive through the peaks and valleys of the card extravaganza this year. Remind me to not trust paper selection to anyone else in the future. But after several frustrating days of holding curling paper down, I did move on to several limited edition prints (on some seriously good dead-flat 200g/m2 paper).

I do have a couple bits of exciting news. First, on a visit to my silk-screen supplier I stopped at a new garden centre and picked up several packages of bulbs from Holland. I used to bring bulbs back from business trips to Amsterdam whilst living on Angelina and after that, when living at La Antigua. So now I have high hopes that in several months I will see the results of my gardening exploits on the main terrace of Sol y Mar.

Another bit of very welcome news is that the big holiday plans are finally sorted, and the winning destination wasn't even one of the three places I had first thought of. I had toyed with the idea of sort of modifying the Caribbean option to include Cuba, especially after going to a concert in Palma with the Buena Vista Social Club, but instead have decided to go to another place that was featured in *The Second Book of Marvels* I wrote about when I wrote about my bucket list. I think I will wait to tell you more about this until the trip (mid-January), but I think I need to find a pith helmet and lots of khaki for the trip.

One last thing. It is early December, and that means that the holidays are fast approaching. When this happens each year, my iTunes selections seem to evolve a bit. Other than the completely understandable amount of time listening to music by Ibrahim Ferrer, Compay Segundo, and Omara Portuondo (present and past members of the Buena Vista Social Club), I also have been listening to Christmas music. The whole Christmas music thing is pretty eclectic in my iTunes, with songs by everyone from Darlene Love (Phil Spector's Christmas album) to Handel's Hallelujah Chorus.

More or less, there are two types of people; ones who love *going* someplace, and ones who love *being* someplace. I have known for some time that I am part of the former population. I dead chuffed to be contemplating, planning, dreaming, and whatever about an upcoming adventure or challenge. Being in the midst of it is okay, but for me, the real buzz is in the anticipation. That is one of the reasons that today is so important.

Now, today is a very special day for several reasons. One reason is that today a once-in-a-lifetime event took place. Today was a total eclipse of the moon. The astrological phenomenon occurred for about 3.5 hours, beginning at 0733 this morning. Sadly, Mallorca was pretty well covered by some nasty clouds so I didn't get to see the eclipse, but I did look online to see the photos of the eclipse that were from other parts of Europe. The reason that this was a once-in-a-lifetime event is another big thing for me. Today is the winter solstice.

I am also pretty excited about getting ready for my upcoming holiday trip. As I had written in my last chapter, my plan was to go to Australia or South Africa, or the Caribbean. But for quite a few reasons, the end destination has changed, and as the departure day comes closer, I am feeling better and better about it. The big challenge will be to survive the next several weeks before my trip begins. Luckily, the number of sunlight hours each day will be increasing, so I think I may just be able to do it. Besides, right now I have to be content with getting ready for Christmas.

I won't be having a tree this year in the house. As a matter of fact, I haven't had one for quite a few years. One year whilst living at La Antigua, I did make some decorations and drape them all over a palm plant, but this year I probably won't even do that. But rest assured, my Christmas here will be filled with the sound of love. Darlene Love, to be exact. And the Ronettes. And Wizzard. Bob Geldolf and his friends. Mariah Carey. And of course, Georg Friderich Handel.

2011

"The Godfather" was just on telly the other night and I loved Clemenza's line, "Leave the gun. Take the Cannoli." Having said that, "Another New Year" is more timely I suppose. Whew, how many times have we said that? Well, for some of us, clearly more than others. The Christmas holiday and New Year rolled through my part of the island like someone with narcoplexy. Okay, that may not be fair to use to characterise the entire island, but for the inhabitant of Sol y Mar (that would be me), it was pretty accurate. I did hear from quite a few friends and family members, but largely, the holidays just sort of slipped past. Which can be a good thing sometimes.

And whilst the term "quiet" did reign supreme here, this doesn't mean I wasn't busy. The focus of my efforts have once again been on my art. It has been like a giant serigraph festival here…with the minor exception that I really don't have the space to properly set up for screen-printing and at times my screen supplier doesn't seem to have the same sense of urgency I do. But, it is Mallorca, so until I decide to produce my own screens, I think I will have to suffer through with the occasional delay. To offset the space issue, I do seem to have several options. Option 1 is to use La Antigua – which is currently renter-less – as a studio. This option would require me hauling

Living on Rocks

all my art stuff out there and it would be just my luck to have someone rent the house again. Option 2 would be to rent some studio space someplace nearer to Sol y Mar. This would cut down on any travel time and it could be a good time financially to do that. The economy on the island still isn't all that great and the number of storefronts that are vacant is pretty high. Option 3 would be to just keep my sitting room divided into two spaces: one for sitting and enjoying the vistas and the other for screen printing and painting. I suppose there actually is another option, and that would be to stop doing art things and go back to more writing. I will really need to figure out which option makes the most sense, but am sure I won't do anything until after I return from the big holiday trip in a couple of weeks. This brings me to Richard Halliburton.

I first wrote about Richard Halliburton a while ago. To recap a bit, when I was about 11 years old, I first encountered a book Halliburton had written. He was sort of an adventurer/author, and his "Second Book of Marvels" filled my mind with images of far away places that were full of intrigue and mystery. I lost my book many years ago, but in the 1990's, I found a copy at a bookseller and bought it, and then several years ago, after losing the replacement, I bought another one. The book tells about what Halliburton considered some of the marvels of the world, and amongst them were, the Great Pyramid, Petra, the Taj Mahal, the Potala in Lhasa, the Great Wall of China and in chapter 28, he wrote about Angkor Wat. Largely because of this book, several years ago I went with friends and explored the wonders of Egypt and Petra, and next week I will go to Angkor Wat in Cambodia as part of the big holiday trip. Needless to say, I will write about it.

I do like the serigraph process. It combines a modicum of creativity and a dash of technicality; all blended together with several heaping amounts of patience, of course. In the past, I have focused more on doing "one-off" pictures, usually in either watercolour or acrylic. But doing the serigraphs enables me to produce multiples of the same picture – that does assume that all of the multiples are good.

Well, what can I say. It has taken me quite a bit of time to write again after the trip, but I will plead exhaustion from doing the almost daily post cards. If you don't choose to accept this rather lame excuse, how about my dog ate my computer? Okay. I don't even have a dog, so that excuse won't work either I guess. I think I have just been lazy about writing.

The trip was, as I think I mentioned in one of the post cards, the best of times and the worst of times. Yes, clearly Cambodia was well worth the trip itself. I am not even sure if it was either the people, the places, or the serenity that seemed to pervade the environment...or even a combination of all of them. All I know is that if Cambodia weren't so far away, I would consider spending more time there. This is far more than I can say for Thailand. Well, that isn't fair. I guess the mainland of Thailand was okay, but Koh Samui was extremely disappointing on many levels. I suppose it wouldn't have been all

282

James B Rieley

that bad if it weren't for the completely over-the-top tourists who apparently don't understand that they are tourists in someone else's country; or if I had been a trained lion-tamer, complete with chair and whip to fight off the never-ending onslaught of creepy crawlies. A lesson's learnt experience I guess.

But the point is that I am once again back in Sol y Mar and life has resumed to its normal pace and feel. Well, that is except for a present I received on Koh Samui. Ever since I returned to Mallorca, I have still be plagued with the leftovers of my little bout of acute gastroenteritis. So, after a trip to my doctor and a visit to a gastro specialist, I am now scheduled to have someone stick a television camera down into my stomach to see what is going on.

I have experienced several types of medical procedures, some of them at the time seemed to be high on the list of Dr. Maglevs-Favourite-Party-Games. But previously never having had a endoscopy, or in my case, to be medically correct, an esophogastroduodenoscopy; it opened my mind to a whole new level of things not to do. (BTW, I think if you are a Scrabble player, you should remember that word…it must be well worth about 3 million points). According to my doctor (who is not related at all to the previously mentioned Dr. M., the procedure is pretty cut-and-dried. He (they?) simply put a camera down my throat into my stomach to see what is going on. Right. I was good with this explanation until I clarified what he said (he is after all Spanish). You put a camera down my throat? I will report back after I have reached my fun quotient for this month.

Let's see, what else is new. Ahhh, the terrace off my sitting room is worth talking about. Through the magic of good planning and some wood glue, I now have a rather piece of large latticework on the east end of the terrace. I put this puppy up largely to block out the view of the property next door, and it seemed like an easy rationale for having some Jasmine plants on the terrace. So with Rafi's assistance, the latticework is now up and I am in the process of convincing the Jasmine plants that they had better get growing pretty quickly.

Well, last week I again violated one of my cardinal travel rules. Yes, this is the rule about travelling more than 2 hours…and I broke it by about 12 hours. I flew from here (Palma de Mallorca) to Madrid, and then to Miami, and then drove for four hours. Now, in all fairness, I didn't do this because I was told to – I did it to spend some time with a relative. My Aunt who lived in Melbourne Florida suddenly passed away last week, and my Uncle was understandably shattered by what had happened. I had been in pretty constant communications with them for quite a while and had been able to speak to my Aunt on the phone when she had arrived in hospital. But shortly after our last conversation, she was rushed into operating theatre and as a result of too many problems to go into here, was put into an induced coma. She passed away within two days, and the third day, I was on a plane on my way to support my Uncle.

Living on Rocks

It does seem that all of my trips to the USofA are driven by family emergencies. And whilst this could easily be remedied if the remaining members of my family would move to Europe, the reality is that they haven't, so when things go wrong, I go there. It isn't so much the length of time it takes to get there that drives me batty (although I really do not do well on flights of more than two hours unless I am able to lay down, which does require sitting in the pointy-end of the plane). What sends me over the edge is the difference in cultures between there and here (or there and just about any other place on this planet).

A good example of this was the smack-in-your-face display I saw at a supermarket that I had gone to whilst shopping for my Uncle. I was pushing my cart down the aisles that, without too much exaggeration, did seem wider than some streets in Puigpunyent, when I came upon the frozen food section. This section alone filled two aisles (both sides of the two aisles, of course) that must have been the length of a rugby pitch. And there, right in the middle, was the section that contained breakfast foodstuff. I couldn't resist and took out my camera-phone-thingy and managed to get a photo of about ½ of the breakfast delights, much to the concern of the other shoppers who seemed to be very used to the amount of types of food for sale. A few minutes later (no, I did not buy any of the waffles or pancakes, although the blueberry pancakes did look pretty tempting), I had yet another in-your-face example of culture. I had been looking for something that my Uncle had asked me to buy for him, and whilst I knew I was in the right department, I couldn't find the specific item he had requested. After looking up and down, side to side, and then in both diagonal directions, I thought I would seek assistance. Just then a young girl who was wearing what appeared to be the store uniform (name badge and all) walked past. I said, "*Excuse me Susie*" (which is what was written on her name badge so it seemed like a safe bet to give it a try), "*I am looking for a package of (whatever-the-thing-was-my-Uncle-wanted).*" She never even slowed down but did manage to turn her head toward me as she said, "*I'm on my break.*" Nice.

I really shouldn't be too critical about customer service there, as in most cases, it is far superior to what we see here in Spain. I have never had an experience like my recent one with Susie-who-is-on-a-break, but I have had multiple experiences where clerks must think I am wearing a cloak of invisibility, because they simply ignore you. Nice.

Today, however, I did have a good customer service experience here. The new iPad 2 finally reached Europe and today at 1700, the local Apple dealer put them on sale. We ventured out to the store, arriving smack at the appointed hour, only to find out that there were 50 people who had apparently stood in a queue for some time. I was given one of those paper-tear-off numbers that signified that I was number 51, and the clerk handing out the numbers was courteous to a fault. I wasn't even sure I wanted one of the latest technology doo-wahs, but did stand around for about 30 minutes, only to then discover that they were then on customer number 26. Right. Perhaps I will wait until some of the impulse urge wears off the throngs that are desperate to always have the latest piece of electronic kit. Don't get me wrong; the iPad2 is pretty slick. But I actually need one about as much as I need another head.

When I chose to be a citizen of the United Kingdom, I knew at the time that the country was a bit "eccentric" at best in certain areas. Perhaps "eccentric" isn't a fair term to use, but after this long as being British, I don't think I can think of another term.

I, as you know, actually live on the island of Mallorca, which, as you also know, is a Spanish island in the Mediterranean Sea. And although where I have chosen to live is over 1,000 miles from the country I chose to be my home, due to the proliferation of technology, I can receive English television at Sol y Mar. And herein is the first example of eccentricity.

If you read the first two paragraphs carefully, you will have noted that I British, but can watch English television programming. This is one of those cultural nuances that is often missed by those who are not immersed in them. The United Kingdom is a constitutional monarchy and although it is a country, the country is comprised of four separate countries; England, Scotland, Northern Ireland, and Wales. I am not English, although when I lived in the UK, I always lived in England. I am British. If you were born in Wales, you probably identify yourself as Welsh, and possibly would acknowledge that you are British. A similar thing would occur if you were born in Scotland. You would be a Scot, and might be willing to acknowledge your British-ness. But for some reason, people born in England tend to think of themselves as English. Period.

This whole "belief" thing sounds even more eccentric when you consider a speech I gave to a business group not long after I arrived in London. After an extremely complimentary introduction, I went on the stage and opened with, *"Thank you. I am very pleased to be here in Europe, and..."* Before I could even go on, a man in the audience raised his arm and said, *"Excuse me."* I was a bit caught off guard, never having had that happen to me in the past. I stopped and looked at the man with a confused look on my face. I said, *"Yes?"* desperately trying to figure out what was occurring. He said, *"You said you were happy to be here in Europe. Europe is over there* (pointing to what I assumed was sort of south-east). *This is England."* I couldn't believe it. Here I was, just trying to give a talk that would make the group who was paying me think they were getting value for their money, and this person who was obviously up-his-bum with his English-ness mucks it up before I have barely begun. What a tosser. I couldn't resist and replied, *"Sorry. My fault. I was raised in a school system where one of the required courses was geography. In that course, we had this very large map of the world, and the multi-coloured land mass just to the east of the Atlantic Ocean was noted as Europe."* No more comments from him that day.

English television programming can also fall into the category of "interesting." There are several programmes that I have told you about in a previous letter that are pretty special. One of them is "Coast;" another one is "New Tricks;" and of course, there is the BBC"s "Have I Got News for You." I do try to make it a point to see these. But then there are several programmes seem to be rather bizarre. In that category are programmes such as "Lambing Live" – a programme from a farm in Wales about sheep giving birth. Right. Not exactly something that I would find entertaining, but I can send you the satellite channel number if this is of interest to you.

I used to watch a programme titled "Master Chef" in which chefs – both amateur and working – are given cookery challenges over a series of weeks until the "Master Chef" is crowned. This programme used to be pretty good, but this year it has degenerated into just another reality-type programme, full of those pregnant pauses when someone is kicked off the programme each week. Too bad, as I really liked learning dishes that even I could prepare. About the only other programming offering that I consistently watch from the UK is the BBC news. Of course the stories seem to be slanted occasionally, but as least when they say "World News," they mean news from other parts of the world. This varies considerably from when I lived in the USofA, and he World News seemed to mean any story that took place between the Atlantic and the Pacific, and the Canadian and Mexican borders. Sort of like baseball's "World Series," which hasn't involved a team from any country other than the US since the Mayflower landed.

Other television programmes that might fall into the category of "car-crash-telly" include; "My Big Fat Gypsy Wedding" – a series about the over-the-top weddings of British travellers (gypsies) with the highlight (highlight?) being a 17-year old getting married in a 20 kilo (44 pound) wedding dress complete with built-in lights; "Pop Goes the Band" – an incredibly innocuous offering in which old pop groups will be transformed with the help of fashion stylists, trainers, and plastic surgeons. My all time least favourite British telly offering is "Deal or No Deal" in which a TV presenter tries to convince the game show participants that they really do have a chance at winning lots of money. I could probably go on and on about the lack of any sense of culture in some of these programmes, but I did spend countless years in a country that produced "Hee Haw" and "Jersey Shore," so best I end this ranting now.

There is, of course, Spanish television. I used to try to use Spanish television as a key-learning tool so I could increase my capacity to speak and be understood here in the country I have chosen to live in. But admittedly, I have decreased my time dedicated to watching local programming but – this is a good thing – have increased my time dedicated to listening to local radio programming. Not just music stations, as the ratio of English-language songs to Spanish-language songs is probably in the 4 to 1 range or more. I have instead been listening to local talk radio programming, and whilst I do not understand every word the announcer or programme host says, I do get the drift of what the conversation is all about. This is like reading Spanish newspapers. By getting an understanding of what is being talked about, it is very helpful in seeing how some words are used in context, and even what some words are.

There are big things afoot in the United Kingdom in the next month, and they centre around the upcoming wedding of HRH Prince William, and Catherine Middleton. William and Kate, as the whole of the British media call them, really do seem like a neat couple. Of course, the last time there was anything this big in the UK was the wedding of Prince William's mother, Diana to Charles, the heir to the British throne. Already you can purchase commemorative plates; cups; thimbles; swans (I have no idea how anyone would possible rationalise buying a commemorative plastic swan, but as Mr. Barnum said, *"There is one born every minute*); reproductions of the dress that Kate wore when their engagement was announced; T-shirts with a photo of the happy couple emblazoned on the front; serving platters; and my favourite (said extremely sarcastically)…a commemorative wedding mouse-pad for your computer. As one website said, *"We have never seen so much wedding crap for sale before."* Spot on observation.

Right. One more thing, the reference to Blighty. Blighty is the term used by British troops that served overseas that has been appropriated by ex-pats to refer to where they were born. In my case, this would be the country I chose to consider my home…except for the weather…and the politics…and the taxes…and mushy peas….and………….

I wanted to comment on the near saturation of news stories about the wedding between Prince William and Katherine Middleton. It was beginning to seem that nothing else was going on in the world. But today was the wedding, and I found myself feeling quite proud to be British. We do know how to do proper celebrations. I don't feel the need to write anymore about the ceremony because unless you have been living in a cave, on Neptune…you will have seen the wedding coverage yourself. Cheers.

One of Paul Young's songs has the line *"Always moving, but going nowhere."* This kind of sums up where I am now. The good news is that I don't feel I need to go anywhere now, and I do like to keep extremely busy. The bad news is that some of these same projects do tend to take on a life of their own at times. An example might be a current project that I am working on diligently, albeit a bit early. Yes, I am working on this year's holiday card already. I really don't think I can do much about it really…the "picture" of the card and what I would say on the inside just floated into my mind the other day, so I was half-way there already. I suppose I could have written myself a note, so that when November came around again, I would not need to come up with a card idea but that isn't the way my head functions. Have an idea… do something with it. Besides, this way I won't have to worry about the cards anymore this year.

I have been putting quite a bit of time in on (hopefully) getting rid of that stomach-bug thing I acquired in Thailand. Yes, it is almost the end of April, and I am still plagued by whatever it is. Part of this "challenge" has been to tick off possible options as fast as my doctors can think of them. This means I have had more ultrasounds of my insides, cameras stuck down my throat, and been poked and prodded more times that I want to remember. The big strategy – eliminating possible reasons – is working (I assume). I do feel better, but will be well pleased when I am back to the same condition I was before the big Thai adventure.

I was walking past the little calita near Sol y Mar on my way to lunch at Puerto Portals – all part of my self-imposed dedication to walking great distances - and suddenly I felt as if I was in Portmeirion watching the filming of The Prisoner. But as Patrick McGoohan wasn't in sight anywhere, I was forced to believe that someone just had the most fab water toy known to man. The "toy" was huge, almost like some floating castle with several ramps that people could slide on into the sea. I suppose it would look great in a huge pool in Las Vegas, but here, overlooking the little bay at Puerto Portals, it just looked out of place or part of a semi-science-fiction programme.

And finally, just a bit of wisdom...A teenager once asked an old man, *"In a relationship, which is more important, to love or to be loved?"* The old man replied, *"Which is more important to a bird, the left wing or the right?"*

For the past week, I have been toughing it out on Amélie, and my time on-board usually is pretty busy. Last summer, it became apparent that the bimini that covers the cockpit had taken on another function. You may know that a boat bimini provides shade and acts as a huge umbrella... but because we typically don't receive any rain here in summer, being the shade provider is its biggest function I suppose. The additional function last summer was to act as an aseo (bathroom) for pesky gulls that apparently thought that sitting on the black bimini and defecating all over it was great fun. When I bought Amélie, I saw that there was a blow-moulded owl on the radar arch, and having the boating chromosome firmly flowing through my veins, I knew that the purpose of the owl was to scare off gulls and other birds that like to leave white deposits on bimini. Apparently, the gulls of Mallorca either are super-smarter than gulls in other countries, or no one bothered to let them know they should be scared of the plastic owl-like thing (which really isn't all that intimidating anyway).

I spent much of last summer trying to figure out how to keep the gulls from landing on the bimini. Now to be fair, I don't want to give you the impression that I was having a Tippi Hedren moment or anything. The gulls didn't show up in large groups, but even one or two gulls with a loose bowel problem and a black bimini do not go well together. I needed to find a way to keep those flying defecators away. One rather festive solution (that I was dead convinced would work a treat) was to buy a water squirt gun. I found one at a children's novelty store and after filling it with water, proceeded to sit on the aft deck waiting for the first gull to make the mistake of messing with me. I am not sure if the gulls weren't not all that scared because the gun, in an almost day-glow green and red, looked more like something that Flash Gordon would have used on his exploits. It could have been that or the fact that the range of the water stream was about 2.5 meters and the gulls would sit on the water at a distance of 3 meters and then quickly zoom in to crap all over the bimini as soon as I had to go to the galley to refill the very low capacity squirt gun. Once in a while I would get lucky and actually hit one of the birds as they were in their final dive-bombing formation, but you could almost hear them saying *"Thanks for the drink James…all this flying and crapping was dehydrating us."* Bastards. One day, after the gun began to leak all over me, I realised I was looking at the problem incorrectly. The squirt gun wasn't the answer. Actually anything that I could do manually whilst I was on-board was a bad solution as I don't spend all my time on Amélie. What I needed was some passive gull intimidator…you know, like a plastic owl. Right. The owl was supposed to be the natural enemy of gulls, but my plastic owl was acting more like a gull magnet. What I needed was something *like* the owl, but far more intimidating.

After some thinking time, I decided to see where I could find a scaled-down replica of the robot on Lost in Space. I figured that with some minor modification, I would be able change the audible warning from *"Danger Will Robinson"* to something like *"All Gulls Who Think that this Boat is a Bathroom Should Bugger Off,"* but in a robot-like voice, of course. But when I went on-line to see what the robot actually looked like in case I had to make one, I realised it looked pretty much like home hoovers made by Dyson, so I abandoned that idea.

It was then I realised that the name of my boat was Amélie, and therefore, what I needed was a garden gnome. If you are one of the 18 people in the world that did not see the movie Amélie, this won't make any sense, so either Google it or just work with me a bit here. A garden gnome. That was it. All I had to do was find one.

I looked online for anything that looked like "Garden-Gnomes-R-Us" but kept striking out. I did find a supplier of cutesy garden gnomes, but being a sentimentalist, I wanted one like in the movie. When David and Nancy flew over and surprised me for my birthday, I told them about my garden gnome quest, and about a week after their return to America, I they told me on one of our calls that they had found one and were posting it to me. I couldn't wait. Those pesky gulls were in for it now, I kept thinking whilst waiting for the package to arrive. Then one day, I checked my buzon (post box) and found a notice from the post office that I had a package there that I needed to collect. I could understand the fact that I needed to go collect my new family addition, as there was no way that the box would have fit into the

Living on Rocks

little buzon, and because I was required to sign for it, the post-office-people couldn't just leave it in front of my door. The next morning I was standing in front of the post office door when the employees staggered in, each of them probably wondering what was in the post for me that would warrant such a demonstration of eagerness to get a package. After returning home, I gently opened the large package, and there it was; my own garden gnome. Those gulls were so screwed I thought…as I began to figure out how to mount it on the boat.

Okay, the mounting thing instantly proved to be a problem. The owl was blow-moulded out of an olefin compound (sorry…it was plastic) and my new garden gnome was moulded out of resin and almost completely solid… which meant I could not mount it where the owl had been. Buggers. I named my new family member Norm, and put him on the terrace where he could lurk amongst some of the plants and went to the boat to come up with another solution. My next solution was so simple, I was a bit mystified that I hadn't thought of it sooner.

What I did was take a blank CD and hung it from a string over the radar arch. I suppose I could have used a recorded CD, like something from the Bay City Rollers, but that would have resulted no doubt in a huge fine by some anti-cruelty-to-birds-political-lobby, so I went for the blank CD. Because there is almost always some form of breeze in the harbour of Andratx, the CD, all shiny and sparkly, spins around in the wind, causing sunlight to flash off it like a high-powered laser. I was dead chuffed at this solution at the time. I was a bit less chuffed several days later when I had returned to the boat only to find the CD was gone. No, I didn't think it was due to an assault by the gulls. More likely it was a wimpy string that broke, and because of this, I made a more impressively mounted version two. That one disappeared after another few days, so when I came out earlier this week, I was committed to making a version three that would be able to scare the shit out of gulls for the rest of the summer. When I connected it to the clever little hanging hook that I made out of a coat hanger, I just knew that the gulls were going to get the surprise of their lives. It was if the light reflecting off the CD tracks was functioning like a Laser-Based-Gull-Destroyer (LBGD) that would make the gulls constipated and impotent at the same time, or at least that I what I was hoping would happen to the birds. I might have been right, as the gulls do come sweeping in out of the suns rays, only to be near blinded by what must look like a LBGD. Now all I have to do is scrub off the remains of guano that appeared between CD attachments. I hope your summer has started well (for those readers in the northern hemisphere. For those south of the equator, well…bundle up).

In several past chapters of this *"Incredibly-fun-little-stay-connected-set-of-randomly-generated-chapters-of-my-life,"* I have written about the preponderance of holidays that we are forced to abide by in Spain. Okay, so the word "forced" isn't really appropriate, because we all love the number of them;

James B Rieley

but even I must admit that some weeks, we do seem to just about shut the country down due to our incredible love of not being able to go to work. The other week was a prime example.

In a one week period, we had the summer Solstice, dia de St Joan (St. John, for you non-Spanish-speaking readers), and some other holiday, whose namesake totally and completely escapes me (no doubt due to holiday overload). The first one to appear during the week was the solstice. Although there is no definitive way to know who celebrated the solstice first, scientists and conspiracy theorists believe that it was celebrated by the Druids. Those Druids really knew how to celebrate. Every year at this time, they would put on their very best animal skins and hunker on down to their local Stonehenge-y-like site and party on until the wee hours of the morning. Apparently, there is not archaeological evidence of the Druids doing much of anything, but seeing as how they were here during the Iron Age, it is pretty clear that their robes must have been well pressed. I was thinking about this when it was the longest day of the year again. For those of you who missed it, it was 21 June. Technically, today wasn't any longer than any other day, but the hours of sunlight extended the "day" for everyone in the northern hemisphere. It kind of makes you wonder how the Druids knew that today was a day worth celebrating. It isn't as if they had set their iPhone alarms to ping them on the longest day of the year. No iPhone alarm meant they weren't even able to be reminded of when Fiona Bruce did the evening news or when Have I Got News for You was about to begin. They just knew. It kind of makes me wonder how could these people – actually any people who were living on our planet hundreds or thousands of years ago – could figure out so much.

I know people who, even with the massive amount of available technology, can't keep their calendars sorted. But those Druids without iPhones or computers (no archaeology, so we can only assume but this would be a safe bet), managed to know when the longest day was every year. The Egyptians had this sorted well too. Ask any sane conspiracy theorist and they will tell you that aliens built the Pyramids, so perhaps they also told the Egyptians which was the longest day of the year. Not sure about that, but I don't know any sane conspiracy theorists to ask.

The longest day of the year was clearly a time to celebrate, and Robert Bell (you really didn't think that his parents baptised him "Kool" knowing he would one day head up Kool and the Gang?) had it right when he sang
"There's a party going on right here;
A celebration to last throughout the years;
So bring your good times, and your laughter too;
We gonna celebrate your party with you."

My celebration of the Solstice began by waking up on Amélie and following my daily regimen of all things healthy. Okay, some of you may be rolling on the floor in hysterical laughter, and I will excuse that, but I really have been working on my health (again). I am not sure if this year's health drive is a result of the fact that I seem to have quite a few friends who have been hammered with health problems, or maybe it is out of boredom. Regardless, this year's regimen whilst on-board Amélie includes multiple-times-each-day rows in the harbour and at least two major swims. The difference is that Améliña is meant to be driven by an outboard motor and rowing her is about as easy as pushing treacle through a strainer. But all the drag generates resistance, which generates real exercise. The swimming is brilliant and I now do at least two swims each day from Amélie to shore and back. My exercise programme when not on-board Amélie is a bit different, and consists of watering the plants on all three terraces and waiting for the current rerun episode of The Gilmores to be on telly. I think being on-board Amélie is good for me.

Another potentially "interesting" point of health information for you. Last week, it was exactly one year since I ran out of cigarettes, and then began to forget to buy more. Have no doubt, I have not quit smoking, but it is quite evident to me that I have made the conscious choice to just not smoke for a while. Well, as of last week, for the past year. I "stopped" for a long period of time once before, not smoking for nine years. Then I hadn't quit either, just wasn't smoking. Admittedly, I do think about getting some cigarettes off and on, but I never do. Choice...what a gift. I have no idea how long I will extend my smoking cessation this time, but as with many things in life; it is what it is.

And now, because I have been spending more time on Amélie that at home, one of the summer nautical thematic information bits. Bobbing around in the harbour with lots of privacy as Amélie is – she is on a swinging mooring as opposed to being tied up in some tacky marina where your nearest neighbour is inches away - one of the things that one does is watch other boats. If you are a non-boater, this may seem like an utter waste of time. But if you have the boating chromosome coursing through your veins, this can be high entertainment. Whilst this harbour has its share of the big, the small, the sleek, and the rubbish (that barely is floating); the other day a real treat appeared on the horizon and then anchored just outside the harbour entrance. It wasn't Capt. Jack Sparrow, but it sure looked like it could have been. There aren't too many sights as great as a tall ship, and it was quite a charm to have the Stad Amsterdam so close.

It was dark and the rain kept pouring down on the city. As he stood against the wall, desperately trying to stay as dry as possible, he had to place his hand over his ear in order to hear the voices from the hidden microphone that he had placed in the restaurant earlier that afternoon. Suddenly, a car came around the corner and its lights shown through the rain, lighting him up as if he was on stage. His cover was blown, and he knew it. There was little he could do other than to turn and walk down the alleyway. Within seconds, the car had begun following him, and with every step he took, the car closed in on him. Ooops, sorry, this isn't part of a chapter of the latest

Robert Ludlum book, although it would make a fab story line...some evil group of neo-whatever's plan to genetically modify the world's supply of gluten until an ex MI-6 operative finds out about the plan and...okay, sorry... am losing track. No, this chapter isn't a book title; it is the conundrum I have found myself facing. Here is how it all started.

Remember my intestinal horror story from Thailand? The one that no one can still seem to sort out? Well, I decided to take things into my own hands, and did a quick inventory of (alleged) food stuffs I consume, and, voila! I realised I consume mega amounts of Aspartame (as in cola-lite) and gluten (as in just about every food stuff I like). So, being in a seriously take-charge-of-my-own-health-situation, I decided to cut back on both the cola-lite and the amount of gluten I consume. Well, that lasted about a day when I realised that if I was serious about adjusting my diet, I would need to either do it or not do it. I chose to do it. This of course meant, to banish both cola-lite and gluten-laced foods from the list I products I consume.

Now on the surface, this decision wasn't all that difficult, until I discovered that gluten is in flippin' everything. Well, everything I like at least. So after stopping purchasing cola-lite, I began to look for gluten-free anything. Admittedly, I really didn't even know what gluten was, so being a tad anal-retentive about using my computer, I Googled it and came up with this: *Gluten (from Latin gluten "glue") is a protein composite that appears in foods processed from wheat and related species, including barley and rye. It gives elasticity to dough, helping it to rise and to keep its shape, and often giving the final product a chewy texture.* Right. Not exactly the most helpful thing for me, especially as this makes it sound like gluten is the food equivalent of Super-Glue. As I wasn't getting the answers I was after, I took a different tack and went to the market. Gluten-free bread is available, so I loaded up on a couple of loaves of it (one for Sol y Mar and one for Amélie). That was the good news. The bad news is that I like wheat bread and gluten-free bread only seems to come in white bread here, and if that wasn't enough, was the consistency of the bread is very similar to either indoor-outdoor carpeting or a slice of very old cake. But it is available, so I bought it. I did discover this morning that one of the best things about this gluten-free bread is that you cannot tell if it has gone stale. Fresh, stale...it all feels and tastes the same. This might be a bonus, but I am not quite sure how as yet.

Pasta, another food I quite like and again, it is available here in gluten-free, but to date, I have only found one type. The pasta I like the most is fresh tortellini (which I prepare with fresh pesto, also by Buitoni...they both are really good, you should try them) but here all I can find is spaghetti. Gluten-free spaghetti to be exact. Not bad actually, but it is like eating an entire game of limp pick-up sticks. Now to be fair, meats, fish, fruits, and vegetables are all gluten-free, but I am more of a toast-for-brekkie and pasta-for-dinner kind of guy. Having said that, in summer, I do eat my fair share of salad, and it is summer, so I might be okay for a while. I also do like to have fresh tuna, but admittedly I do shy away from preparing multiple things for one meal. Don't get me wrong. I do prepare (my version of) complex meals (chicken, with potatoes and peas is kind-a-sort-a complex, isn't it?) But those are meals I make as comfort food in autumn and winter. And with the spectre of autumn coming in some months and my food options slipping away, finding acceptable foods is a bit daunting. I suppose that this all would be so much easier if my new diet, plus all the swimming and rowing wasn't working. But I do feel quite a bit better. Good news? Normally this would be considered to be good news, even by me. But as any problem solver worth his salt (or salt substitute) knows, by changing multiple variables at the same time makes it pretty tricky to see which variable is the one that is really making the difference. But for now, whether it is the gluten-free diet, or the elimination of Aspartame, or all the swimming and rowing, I really don't care. Maybe soon I will find out.

Other non-gluten conundrums here include how to spend my time onboard Amélie. Therefore, my time-spending-options include: writing; painting; doing something else creative; reading; sleeping, etc. Because I already do the first two items, I decided to also do some of number 3 recently. Of course the next challenge is to think of something creative to do. In my case, I began to look at the pile of dock-lines that I had decided to throw out. It didn't take long to realise I could actually make something with them. (I know, I can appear to be a bit pathetic). After a while, I had made a rug. And then I made it bigger. And then I made another one.

I was thinking of doing something different for this chunk of the story, but after pondering the idea for either six consecutive 24-hour days, or about 3-1/2 seconds, I decided to just continue down the same random literary notes as in the past. After all, this all started as a way to let readers know what it was like for someone who was raised in an upbeat, fast-moving, technologically-laden, large city environment, and then moved to the little (but adorable) village of Puigpunyent where, as I had said long ago, "slow" takes on a whole new meaning. But then several years ago, I left La Antigua and moved to Sol y Mar but kept clicking away on these little computer keys. The (alleged) direction of these chapters did have to change a bit (as I no longer was in the village), but the basic concept of writing when I thought there was something worth writing about. Which brings me back to this entry.

I just found that writing about cool stuff is good and often is something worth remembering as well. This is the case of today, but almost one-hundred years ago. To be specific, as in what happened on 24 July, 1911. What happened was that Hiram Bingham "rediscovered" Machu Picchu in Peru. The story is that Bingham, a lecturer at Yale University, had been a delegate at some science conference in Chile and decided to wander home via Peru. His guide convinced him that a fun way back might include a stop off at Machu Picchu, which had been largely forgotten by the locals so the chances that there would be rooms available were pretty high one would imagine.

James B Rieley

Shortly after Bingham went public with what he had found, other "re-discoverers" came out of the proverbial woodwork (or in this case, Peruvian mountaintop stone work) all stating that they had "re-discovered" Machu Picchu first. Regardless of who was first in "rediscovering" Machu Picchu, Bingham was credited with being the one who publicized it around the world through his connections to the National Geographic magazine, and because of his work, had a windy road that leads to the site named after him. Well done, Hiram. I don't think we will get into the tasteless part about how many artefacts that Bingham managed to take out of the country or how even today, Peru is still waiting for many of them to be returned. Perhaps a slight change of topic might be in order. When I sailed to Mallorca many years ago, I recall that I stepped ashore and claimed the island for the Queen, as any good British subject would do. Did I get a road or harbour or tapas bar named after me? Shoot, I never stole any local artefacts nor even shop-lifted anything from the local IKEA or Carrefour stores. Have I been listed in any history books as a person who "re-discovered" Mallorca? No sir. Perhaps I should have had some P.R. spin-doctor with me who could have made me out to be the good-guy instead of just another Brit who wanted to live on this wonderful island.

The whole thing about "rediscovery" is important, as there is little in this world that was not discovered, or lived on, or seen, or known many many many years ago. But for some reason, the history books that we read (and our children still read) list those important "discovery" dates in history as if no one at all was aware that these places existed. The year 1492, when Columbus "discovered" the new world springs to mind. The fact that this and the many other claims to this "discovery" do seem to fall short of the mark when you consider that all these explorers encountered people who were already living in "the new world." Maybe it was assumed that those people didn't know they were there. Or maybe, those people didn't count because, as my brother wrote in one of his songs, *"They're not like me."* That is probably another topic not to get into too much now.

The past couple of weeks haven't been the best here. A couple of really good friends passed away. One of them was the mother of my neighbour Rafa. Merche (MER-CHE) was brilliant, and whilst she was older than I (which is an understatement), she was great fun. She and I used to sit in front of her house and talk. Okay, the word "talk" could be an oversimplification of what we were doing. Merche was from mainland Spain and would speak in some rapid-fire-anything-but-staccato-constant-stream of consciousness, usually telling me about the current corruption of government or the days when Franco was in power. I was mesmerized by her stories, and whilst I would ask questions about her opinion on this or that, I am sure that she was just being polite when she heard my meagre Spanish attempts. My Spanish competence at the time really didn't make any difference to Merche, and she would just go on and on about several topics at the same time. And if this wasn't enough, she would do this whilst keeping up a near flow of cigarette after cigarette. These were in the days when I was still smoking, but she could outdo me to the tune of 3 or 4 to one.

I have found that my Spanish actually improves when I am talking to someone who I know doesn't speak any of my native language. I am not sure exactly how this happens, but it consistently seems to. Perhaps it is because when I know the person I am talking with doesn't speak any English, my brain seems to kick into overdrive. Maybe overdrive isn't the right word for what happens, but I know that I stop trying to find the right word or trying to translate what they are saying. It just seems to all fall into place. This is how things would go when I was talking to Merche. Her English vocabulary consisted of *"Hello"* and *"James,"* and because of it, everything fell into place for me vocabulary-wise. Having said this, I am sure that after one of our talks, she would tell her family that her neighbour's Spanish was pure shit. Merche was great, and I will miss her quite a bit.

I lost Clive recently as well. Clive was about as Welsh as they come and had arrived in Mallorca many years ago. He and I would have these wonderful esoteric conversations about things that really didn't mean much at all to anyone else. Once Clive lent me copies of several of the books his brother wrote. The books (hang on, you may suddenly become very envious) "Wave Scattering by Time-Dependent Perturbations," "An Introduction to Echo Analysis: Scattering Theory and Wave Propagation," and, "Green's Functions: Introductory Theory with Applications" – were full of equations and I can remember Clive telling me that whilst he didn't understand the subject matter at all, it didn't make any difference; he had the film rights. And he said it with a perfectly straight face. Clive was another one of those people who we probably don't appreciate enough when they are here with us, but will miss terribly now that they are gone. All of us who knew Clive are richer from just having him as part of our lives.

This week it has also been the celebration of Verge del Carme. This celebration is so typically Mallorquin and if you ignore the number of motorized rides that appear out of nowhere on the back of a group of lorries, or the vendors selling God-knows-what, it is pretty great. Part of the celebration involves a sea-land procession in honour of the Patron Saint of seafarers and fisherman. The term "sea-land" means that a statue of the Virgin is carried out of the sea on the shoulders of some pretty hearty types who allegedly are fisherman. This is a pretty spectacular sight if you haven't seen it before. Not exactly the same sight as Ursula Andres walking out of the sea in Dr. No, but it is fab to see anyway. And if all that vista doesn't get you going (I am talking about the fisherman carrying the Virgin out of the sea...pay attention here), there are the semi-requisite fireworks that accompany just about any celebration on the island. As I was on-board Amélie at the time, and as the fireworks were set off just across the harbour, the sight was pretty spectacular.

James B Rieley

Yes, it once again is "un aglomeracion de cosas," or for the Spanish-challenged amongst you, a collection of miscellany from my life on the island. This time the collection seems to all be connected to maths. My father loved maths. Well, maybe that isn't exactly true. What is for sure is that he loved to try to get me to love maths. Or at very minimum, to understand that maths are everywhere, and either I had better get my head around them or I would be buggered. At the time (I first remember having to practise writing minor maths equations at the highly intimidated age of ten), I just hated all the structure my father wanted to expose me to. Fair enough; I did understand that I needed to understand maths when I went to the shops, or when I wanted to get paid for shovelling my neighbours snow-filled drive in winter, or later, when I would need to fill up my car with petrol. But that is about as far as I could see that I needed maths in my life. But, like any good son (who was trying to avoid family strife), I soldiered on and would look quite interested when he would expand my potential maths knowledge base. And then one day, he introduced me to Fibonacci.

I think I mentioned Fibonacci previously, but he is well worth writing about again. Born Leonardo Pisano Bigollo in 1170, he must have been a very bad boy because his name seems to have changed quite a bit over his lifetime. He was also known as Leonardo of Pisa (a nice touch…I wonder if I will one day be known as James of Bendinat?), Leonardo Pisano, Leonardo Bonacci, Leonardo Fibonacci, and most commonly as the way my father talked about him, Fibonacci. He was, according to Wikipedia, *"Considered by some "the most talented western mathematician of the Middle Ages."* He has two pretty serious claims to fame. One is that he wrote the Liber Abaci (a book about maths calculations). The other is the sequence of numbers that he figured out. My father was fascinated by Fibonacci's sequence and believed, as Fibonacci did, that the numbers in the sequence appear in nature repeatedly. For those of you who didn't have a father who was really into maths, the numbers in the sequence that Fibonacci identified are the sum of the previous two numbers; i.e. 0, 1, 1, 2, 3, 5, 8, 13, 21, 34, 55, 89, 144, 233, 377, 610, 987, etc.

As my father was never one to just "tell" me something, he would instead get me to do something so I could "discover" for myself what he wanted me to learn. This may have been a good way for him to get me to buy into his ideas, the fact is that this methodology of helping me learn was pretty annoying at the time. A good example was my father's belief that the numbers of Fibonacci's sequence appeared in nature. Instead of my father just telling me this, he told me I should head over to the park near our house and pick a pile of flowers and leaves from trees. I must have been pretty easy, or perhaps I just accepted my father's way of helping me learn, because I did as I had been instructed. After returning with my assortment of nature's produce, my father sat with me and we counted petals on flowers and "spikes" on tree leaves. My father was right…almost every example I had brought back with me did turn out to match with Fibonacci's sequence. There were a couple of examples that didn't match up and when I, as a young rebellious (in my own way) teen-ager, would say, *"Excuse me father, but this flower has six petals* (a non-Fibonacci number)," he would not even raise an eyebrow but just softly say *"an Aberration of nature...keep counting."* Nice.

Okay, so how does all this Fibonacci-maths-numerical sequence qualify to be typed out by yours truly? Easy-peasy. The other week, the weather in Andratx, where Amélie is moored, was...well, it was interesting. Not rainy or even cloudy. It was windy. And with sustained winds comes waves. And because Amélie is moored to a swinging mooring in the harbour, the wind and waves meant that it was a bit "bouncy" on-board. Now I use the term "bouncy" with a certain amount of cheek, as for a person who does not have the *"Being-on-a-boat-is-better-than-just-about-anything"* chromosome, the term would have been knock-down-hang-on rough. Whilst the weather norm is just the opposite and usually Amélie just sits there in the sun with its bow facing into the direction the breeze is coming from, gently turning as breeze shifts from one direction to another; that day it was different. The winds (some serious blowing shit of 30 kts) were from the south-east, but the waves were coming in from the west-north-west. This resulted in Amélie being hit broadside by the never-ending train of waves rushing to shore and beating the crap out of anything in their way. Amélie and I were in the way. When this happens (which is not often at all), I tend to go find a book to read or fall asleep. Which is what I was about to do, but then I remembered my father's not-so-subtle stories about the Fibonacci sequence. I started wondering if this sequence, because it appeared so often in nature, might also be the key to the wave patterns and they kept whacking into the side of Amélie. I sat on the aft deck and started to count the number of big waves and smaller waves, and then began to try to determine if there was any pattern between them. After about 15 minutes of this, I said screw it and took a kip.

Changing direction a bit (and this has nothing to do with anything); I just finished reading "1000 Years of Annoying the French," and now am immersed in "Talk to the Snail," another book by Stephen Clarke. Both of these books are quite good, and whilst they should be read with your tongue comfortably nestled in your cheek at times, they are quite revealing about life in my neighbouring country. An excerpt from "Talk to the Snail" explains it all.

"The differences between what you can expect from the British and French national-health services in the case of various common ailments:

"France: Call your doctor, get an appointment for the next day, or maybe even the same day. Go to a small private-looking apartment, and wait in what looks like a living room with an abnormally large number of magazines on the coffee table. Look at the fashion pages of a recent Elle or news magazine. Be welcomed personally by the doctor, who comes to fetch you, probably just a few minutes late if he or she is not an especially popular or inefficient practician. Explain

your problem, have your throat examined, your ganglions felt, your temperature taken with a thermometer pressed on the forehead or in the ear (the days of the rectal probe are gone, much to the chagrin of some). Listen while your doctor tells you the Greek names for sore throat and runny nose (which all the French know). Watch him or her write out a prescription for aspirin, throat pastilles, nasal spray, chest rub, tablets for a steam inhalant, antibiotics in case things get worse, and (probably only on request these days) suppositories. Ask for, and receive, a three-day sick note. Pay the doctor by cheque, and leave the surgery, shaking the doctor's hand, promising to return if the cold doesn't clear up in the next few days.

Go to a pharmacy, get a rucksack full of medicine, watch the pharmacist swipe your social-security card so that your refund is credited automatically. Go home, have an aspirin and a hot drink and wait for the cold virus to go away naturally. In the case of recurring snuffles, request a stay at Aix les Bains health spa.

Britain: Call the doctor's surgery, be told that there are no appointments free for the next week and to call back in forty-eight hours if you're not cured or dead. Go to the supermarket, but a medicated drink, go to work and sneeze all over workmates. In the case of recurring snuffles, try acupuncture. So true...

And lastly, from the *"How-good-can-one-man's-life-be"* department, I have made a discovery that has the potential to be more impactful than just about anything. Yes, this has to do with my self-imposed Gluten-free dietary exploration. One of the hardest parts of the whole Gluten-free diet thing is finding foods that I might like that are indeed not laced with Gluten. I don't mean things like meats – whilst not a vegetarian, I am able to exist rather well without eating meat. What I mean are things that I would "like" to eat; with the emphasis on the "like." The other day, whilst on one of my searches for acceptable food products, I found the Holy Grail of Gluten-free foods... Gluten-free Carrot Cake. I have no doubt that by day I type again, I will have gained 34 kilos. At least it will be a Fibonacci number weight gain.

Since the tenants that were renting La Antigua left, I have been going out to the village once a week to check on the house, collect any post that has been delivered for one reason or another, and...yes, sweeping the courtyard. I cannot even imagine how many times I have swept that courtyard since buying the house, and at least when I lived there, sweeping it seemed to be more appropriate than it is now. But sweep it I do. After all, *"Tengo agulloso con mi casa"* (I have pride in the house I own) and in case someone decides they want to rent it or buy it, the very least I can do is keep it looking nice (which might make it easier to rent or sell I suppose).

I had a real flashback the other day when driving through Puigpunyent on the way to the house. I was slowly negotiating my way through the construction work taking place on the high street (if you remember my previous stories about the village, I suppose I could have said *"The construction work on one of the two streets"* but that would be a bit cheeky so I will say *"the high street"* to make the village sound a bit classier) when I had to stop in the centre of town as a front-end loader was moving a pile of dirt just in front of the market.

In fairness, I must say that Puigpunyent must be becoming a metropolis of sorts as it now has two (counted...one, two) markets. The market I was stopped in front of was the one I used to shop at, the one owned by the brothers, Balthazar and Guillem. As the front-end-loader was doing what it does best (spilling half the dirt before it was dumped where it was supposed to apparently be dumped), Balthazar came out of the store carrying someone's groceries. When he recognised me sitting there watching the dirt-spilling contest, he came over to say hello. (I know...if you are reading this in London or some other real metropolis, the very chance of a store owner coming out to say hello to an ex-customer must be about as real as winning the lottery.) This is the second time that Balthazar has wandered out into the street to say hello, and it was, as it was the previous time, great to see him again.

Balthazar was one of the reasons that made living in the village so good for me. His little market didn't have too many options for food products, but when I couldn't find something I really wanted, I would tell Balthazar what I was after and the next day he would have it for me. One time, not that long after moving to Puigpunyent, I had asked him if there was any possible way he could make something similar to what I would buy in the Sta. Catalina market when I lived in Palma. That market had a stall that sold chicken breasts, stuffed with bacon and dates and they were sooooooo very good. Balthazar said that of course they could make these, but it did take several false starts. Finally I went into Palma and bought one to take back to Balthazar so he could see exactly what I was after. I am not sure if it was Balthazar or Guillem who made them, but they were brilliant. Of course, the new version was about twice as big as the ones I had previously been purchasing in Sta. Catalina which at first was a bit disconcerting, but the fact that they were bigger only meant that there was more of them to devour...the ones from my little village market were better than the ones from Sta. Catalina.

I can remember just before I moved away from La Antigua to live by the sea at Sol y Mar. I had gone to Balthazar's to pick up something and kibitz with the locals – shopping was more of a social thing in Puigpunyent than it was a replenishment-of-the-larder activity for most people. As I was perusing the massive selection of foodstuffs in the two-aisle store, I suddenly heard Balthazar talking to a customer in English. I was gobsmacked. Balthazar, a good local Puigpunyent native, speaking English. I couldn't believe it. I even looked over to the meat counter to make sure that what I heard was really happening. It wasn't even just rudimentary English. It may not have been the Queen's English, but it was clear that Balthazar did know English quite well. I was desperate to talk to him to ask about his new language skills, but being a good Brit, I waited for the other people in the meat queue to be served. When it was my turn, I sauntered up to the counter, only to hear Balthazar say, "*Hola James. Como va? Que tu quieres hoy?*" (Hi James. How are you? What do you want today?)

I was beginning to think I had suffered a momentary brain aneurism. I could have sworn I had hear Balthazar speaking English to the woman at the counter a few minutes earlier, and now my ears were filled with Spanish. "*Balthazar, hace cinco minutes, pienso he oido tu habla en ingles. Es verdad? Tu sabes ingles?*" (Balthazar, five minutes ago I think I heard you speak in English. Is this true? Do you know English?). Balthazar's mouth crept up into a little smile as he said, "*Claro James. Tengo otras clients Britanicos.*" (Of course James. I have other British clients too). "*But Balthazar*" – I had broken into English for some reason, probably because this was a real WTF moment – "*in the three years I have been coming here, you have never spoken English to me*" I blurted out. He responded, also in English, "*James, when you first came into our store years ago, you introduced yourself and said that although your Spanish wasn't good, you would try to improve your Spanish by living in our village. Your Spanish has improved very much and that is why we have always spoken Spanish to you. Isn't this what you wanted?*" Well of course it was, and had I known that Balthazar spoke English, I am sure I would have used that as a crutch to avoid learning more Spanish. Geez, I sure do miss that village sometimes.

Recently, I received a note from a friend in France who asked why, if I miss the village so much, am I not living there. The reason is a bit complex. I do miss the village and La Antigua. But at the same time, I am quite content living overlooking the Mediterranean Sea each day, whether the sun is out or not (it is usually blazing brilliantly in the sky, showering all of us that are lucky enough to live here, with the inspiration that only sunlight can give). When I bought La Antigua, it was the right thing to do, at the right time, for the right reasons. When I had the opportunity to move to Sol y Mar, that too was the right thing to do, at the right time, for the right reasons. I really don't have a clue what I will be doing in the future, or even where that will be. But I do know that if something changes in my life again, it will be the right thing, at the right time, for the right reasons.

Last evening, after watching just a few of the 32 ka-zillion stars that seem to hover above Amélie as they sent their Morse-code-like twinkle watching over me through the millions of miles of space, I watched "Under the Tuscan Sun" for the umpteenth time. In the movie, there is a line where Diane Lane is questioning why she bought her house when it hadn't brought her everything she wanted. Her estate agent friend said, "*Signora, between Austria and Italy, there is a section of the Alps called the Semmering. It is an impossibly steep, very high part of the mountains. They built a train track over these Alps to connect Vienna and Venice. They built these tracks even before there was a train in existence that could make the trip. They built it because they knew some day, the train would come."* Think about it...

I know in the past I have written about my quest to become a bit more healthy. I have told you about my *programma de ejercicio cuando con Amélie (my on-board exercise programme)*. Well, today my programme could have become a bit over-the-top, or, as my neighbour Sayana said, "crazy." She might be right.

I came back to Sol y Mar the other day. I have been doing this all summer. Several days on the boat, then a quick drive home to check the post, water the plants, and make sure that the house was still standing. Then I would often whip together a highly entertaining pasta dish and then rush back to Amélie. Yes, of course the pasta dish would have pesto. Is pasta ever served any other way than with pesto? Really? This visit to Sol y Mar is a bit different.

I came back with a plan to actually stay here for a few days. You know, sort of a *"List-of-stuff-to-do-that-was-easier-to-do-from-the-house-than-from-the-boat"* plan. And because I assumed that this list would take me far more than a few hours, I thought it would be smart to just enjoy being home again (for a while). Now, because my exercise programme has been running a bit out of control (in a good way) whilst on-board Amélie, and with the realisation that I would be at home for a few days, I thought it would be best to bring some elements of my programme home with me. Now in all fairness, as my exercise doo-wah-programme consists of swimming and rowing; and as the dinghy I row is as big as my car, it was clear that this wouldn't be the part coming home. Instead, I brought home my swim fins and turbo goggles. (Just a note here: there is nothing turbo about my goggles at all, but "turbo goggles" just sounded better than "goggles.)

Yesterday, when I awoke, I laid in bed listening carefully to see if I could hear the sea pounding against the rocks on shore. I heard nothing, so I sprinted out of bed and went to the terrace to check the sea conditions (Okay, another clarification: there is no way I could "sprint" out of bed, but I wanted to convey the image that I was eagerly moving from bed to terrace, as opposed to dragging my rather aged body around the house). Sadly, the wind was coming from the east, which meant pretty good-sized waves and rollers skipping across the bay in front of Sol y Mar. The good news was that now I had an excuse why not to go down to the sea and attempt to swim to the island. The whole "swim to the island" thing had become one of those personal-best-mission-things that we, as humans, often do to wreak havoc on our bodies in the name of health. In my case, for someone who never was a good swimmer, the past summer has increased my competence and confidence about swimming and I had calculated swimming about the same distance in the harbour of Andratx several times. If I could do it there, I could do it here. So yesterday was out. And today it didn't look all that much better.

But today I was convinced that I had to do something physically challenging, so after looking at the waves, I decided to do a long walk. When I am home, I do go on long walks, but today when I set out, I formulated a plan to walk from my house to Mood (a restaurant/night club/bar/God-knows-what). I have done this walk in the past and I knew that in August, which we have now found ourselves in, the only time that this walk is doable would be first thing in the morning. It was 0730h, so I set off. After making it to the car park of Mood, I turned around and headed back, barely breaking a sweat. (Right, still another clarification point: it is a long walk, and I was pretty knackered, but I knew if I slowed down, it wouldn't be good, so I just kept plugging on. The actual distance is only a few miles according to Google Earth, but using the "Dr.-Rieley"'s-ready-to-patent-distance-energy-consumption-calculator," it is considerably further. Here is how this works… you take the actual distance in kilometres (I do live in Spain you know), which was 5.9, multiply that by your postal code, which in my case is 07181. This gives you a number of over 42367.9. Seeing as how I think any number greater than 8 is too far to walk, this walk was WAY too far.)

After returning home and peeling off my now-ready-to-be-put-in-the-washer-or-the-trash-bin shirt, I just happened to look out the window and buggers…the sea had calmed a bit. I was full of endorphins (or some other chemically-laced-health-hallucinogen) so I thought, *"What the hell? I think I will go swimming now."* In hindsight, the term "daft-bugger" does spring to mind. I grabbed my flippers and my turbo-goggles (now it was the health-hallucinogens speaking) and went down to the beach below Sol y Mar. The first thing that came to mind upon arriving was that there was "evil deceptive waves" and they were certainly bigger standing there on the rocks than they looked from my terrace. But by this point, I was already there and those psycho-babble-health-endorphin-guys were still whispering, *"Come on James, you can do it. It is only to the island. Come on. It will be fun."* Right. I trudged out over the rocks and managed to put on the fins and goggles and plunged in.

As always, the fist two or three dozen strokes feel brilliant, and you can see the sea bottom whizzing past at a speed that Donald Campbell would have been proud to do. And then I looked up to see that the island was somehow further away from me than it had been when I started. Obviously, this was just an optical illusion because of the fact that instead of seeing the island from shore or from my terrace, I was now literally at sea level and through goggles that were already fogging up. Or it could have been due to the fact that those health-freak-endorphins had stayed on the beach and were splitting their sides with laughter as I slopped my way through the waves. I carried on, as you do.

I did make it to the island and back, even considering the fact I had to stop about eight times each way to de-fog my shit-goggles (Notice how the need to repeatedly defog the goggles may have changed my mental model about how great they are?). One more thing: I do think that it is only fair to let you know that when using the previously mentioned distance formula as it applies to swimming AFTER walking, you need to also multiply the result by your age, and then the national debt of Greece. Can I rest now?

So I am reading this book. I think I have told you about some of my reading choices in the past, and most of them shy away from anything to do with business - (don't want to pollute my mind with somebody-else's rubbish theory on why managers continue to make crap decisions, or relish in their own mega-mania. I do like a good mystery, but in this category, I do shy away from the Ann Rice or Stephen King genre – probably too much like being with some of those business people I mentioned before. I do like the odd historical novel – I still have the copies of the books about Beryl Markham that I bought quite a few years ago) and just about anything that has (or may have) links to my work. Just a reminder…my work is all about helping people and organisations realise their potential. There.

So, back to the beginning of this chapter. I am reading this book. This book is a bit challenging for me because it is in Spanish. The book, "Ingleses, Franceses, Españoles" (the English, the French, and the Spanish) was written in the late 1960"s, and explores why the three population groups, and the people of them, act, think, and behave in the way they do. Whilst I am not sure that some of the points made by the author in 1969 have been proven to be exactly accurate, many of them do ring true (at least from my experience).

Reading a book in a foreign language, especially one that you are not all that competent in, can be a slow process. I have done this in the past with the Da Vinci Code, but only because I had already read it in English, so I thought it might be easier to understand. That was sort of a "cheating" approach to learning by reading. This book was more of a full-frontal-assault-on-my-brain. I wanted to read this for a couple of reasons. First, the somewhat obvious one (to me) was that the subject matter sounded pretty intriguing to me, from both a work perspective, and a learning perspective. Second, I thought that seeing as how it had been a couple of years since I stumbled through Dan Brown's book, perhaps my Spanish knowledge had improved enough to make the reading time more pleasurable. Third, …. well, there is no third I guess. So I borrowed the book and began reading it a couple of days ago. (Just so you know, I am only about ¼ of the way through it as I begin to write today).

The author puts forth his belief that the English are closely aligned to demonstrating actions (although I tend to think that many Brits older than my generation do seem to enjoy talking about the way things used to be; the Empire, ruling the waves; etc.). The author also believes that that the French are all about being intellectual and thinking (although from my experience in the business world, I have no idea what they have been thinking about); and the Spanish are all about passion. This proposition could be rather accurate, or at least it might appear that way. Spanish people are very passionate

James B Rieley

about just about everything. They are passionate about their food, their sport, their families, politics (although this passion didn't do all that good for them in the 20th century). The book's author helps to make this point in one section where he makes a little comparison; *"Cromwell is England, Hernan Cortez is Hernan Cortez."* I love it.

So, the reading thing. I have found that it actually is easier for me to read this book than it was to read the Da Vinci Code, even if I already knew that story. Most certainly, there are words I don't understand (words? Sentences more like it), but for some reason, I do seem to "understand" what the author is talking about and I do get the major drift of the book, and am pleased I have been doing this. The book is pretty great, by the way, and perhaps I will report back later when I finish it.

The other day, I was coming back to the Port of Andratx after a quick water-the-gardens, check-the-post, and perhaps even cook something trip to Sol y Mar, and lo-and-behold, I was stopped by the police. Actually it wasn't just the local police or even the serious police. I was stopped by the Guardia Civil at one of their roadblocks. I don't remember seeing many of these until a couple years ago when four ETA people came to the island and set off a bomb that killed two Guardia men. (Note to anyone who does not want to really piss off the authorities; don't kill a couple of them. These guys do hold a grudge and I would venture that you would rather jump off the Eiffel Tower than be caught by them.) I had just come off the motorway and was about to enter the Port of Andratx (where I keep Amélie, and which is actually a separate town than Andratx) when I went around a round-about, only to find this Guardia guy standing in the middle of the road, waving to me to pull over.

I have seen the roadblocks in the past, but always from a passive observer perspective; as in driving past. But now I was one of the lucky ones that was pulled over. (Note that I use the term "lucky" with my tongue firmly planted in my cheek) I did what any other driver should do when this guy with a dark green uniform and huge gun motions to you to roll down your window…and rolled down my window. He very politely asked me for my permission to drive (license) and my automobile papers (certificates of car-worthiness, ownership documents, and insurance papers that show that the car actually is insured). I very politely hand them all over as I managed a near-impossible physical manoeuvre (of having a smile whilst watching the guy's hand on his gun). He started to look at the papers and then again asked for the auto papers. I, still with my almost genuine smile, replied that I had already given them to him. Of course at this point I was beginning to think that I misunderstood the man with the big gun and would in a flash be on a plane heading to the Guantanamo Bay Resort and Spa. But, not to worry, he looked again at the pile of paperwork that by law we must keep in our cars, and then said okay as he looked through everything.

All must have been in order because el Capitan Civil (not his real name obviously but it does very official, don't you think?) handed the pile of papers back to me with a very courteous *"muchas gracias caballero."* I smiled and said *"muchas gracias"* as well. Then, for some unknown reason, I added my apology for having crap language skills. His expression changed in an instant and then, after glancing back and forth a couple of times looking for something or someone, said, *"Caballero, su español es bueno. My eeenglish it ees sheet."* We both smiled, having bonded forever,...and I drove off before my new very best friend could try to introduce me to his sister.

And the last of the "C" guys...you would think it was time for a full moon here. I know that it is a weekend, and all the weekend-boaters seem to come out of the woodwork, but this Saturday has been flippin" incredible. I have no idea what kind of boating or mooring instruction some of these people have had, but it sure isn't that great. One guy, let's call him Dick (as I did under my breath) clearly must have not bothered at all to learn about mooring his boat. Apparently he is from the train-of-thought that says that "parking" a boat is like parking a car on a crowded street – just get as close as you can and everything will be okay. I was going to say something clever to him, but my French is pretty limited, so instead I just smiled and said *"See you next Thursday"* as he finally had decided to move on. He probably is still trying to figure out what next Thursday is.

Because so many things have been happening lately, but none of them have warranted a mega-amount of writing, I have been saving them and thought that today might be a good day to unleash them upon you. So....by the numbers...these are a few things that have been happening to my life on the island (in increasing numerical order)

0 – the number of usual parking spots available at Cris and Richard's house tonight. I had been invited over for dinner along with some other friends and after finding a place to put Amelia, had a wonderful evening, even with the festival music blaring from the calita near their house.

1 – the number of times I have driven Miranda to Andratx and left her parked there unattended. I usually drive Amelia there, but this is just based on some wimpy mental model that Miranda would somehow be vandalised if she were parked on the street for several days.

1.3 – the number of miles I swam the other day. Earlier this year, I had decided to go to battle with the lingering stomach effects of the Thailand trip. I have told you all about this. The three big things I decided to do were, cut way back on my intake of Coke-Lite (only 2 cans in the past three weeks), cut out as much gluten as I can from my diet (a bit challenging sometimes but it is turned out to be doable), and crank-up the level of exercise I do. This last part was pretty easy, as I was starting from a pretty low value. The two main exercise things I have been doing are rowing Améliña, and swimming. At first, I was over the moon with the fact that I was able to swim from where Amélie is moored to shore and back. For a non-swimmer, being able to do

200 metres was pretty great, even if it was pretty tiring. I have kept at it and, as I already wrote about, swam from Sol y Mar to the island in front of my house, and recently did 8/10th of a mile (about 1200 kilometres) in Andratx. This week, I did a wonderfully satisfying 1.3 miles of non-stop swimming (which felt like about 48 billion kilometres, more or less). And then I rowed the boat a bit over two miles. I think the endorphins have taken over my body.

1.5 – the number of days it took the whiz-kids at Apple to replace my iPhone. My phone had for some unknown-to-me reason, decided to go a tad wonky. I looked on-line for remedies to the problem, but after resetting the entire phone to no avail, I phoned the Apple service-centre for Spain. They said it wouldn't be a problem. They would send a UPS driver to my house with a empty package to put my phone in, and then it would be transported to their service-centre (someplace) where it would be checked. I was assured that either it would be repaired or replaced and I would have it back in 3 – 5 working days. (I assumed that would be if it were re-delivered to me by a flock of pigs flying overhead.) On a Tuesday at 1700h or so, a UPS driver appeared at my front door with an empty box (that was clearly labelled "iPhone"). He placed my phone in the box and gave me a receipt and was off. By Wednesday morning I had checked the online tracing link for UPS and found that the package (assuming with my phone) was in Holland. By shortly after 1400h, I received a note from Apple that my phone was being replaced and was going to be sent back to me that afternoon. Thursday morning, a different UPS driver came to my door with a replacement phone (which has worked brilliantly). Apple....pretty high on the list of companies who really understand customer service I think.

2 – the number of gouges that were left on the driver's side door and near wing from the %*&@$£ vandals who keyed Miranda on the one day she was parked in Andratx. Lesson learnt. Want to guess which car I will drive to Andratx next time I go to the boat?

230 – the amount in euros it cost me to fix the door locks on Amelia. For some time now, the clever little push-button-electronic-door-locker-ignition-key thing for Amelia hasn't been working. It first went to sleep last autumn, so I went to the local SEAT dealer who kindly sold me a new battery for it. And just to be a nice guy, he even put the new battery in the key. This was probably either due to the fact that he wanted to demonstrate that Spain does offer sterling customer service, or he just didn't want to answer the phone at his counter (that all the other technicians seemed to be avoiding as well). The new battery lasted a month or two, and I just resorted to locking and unlocking the car by putting the key into the door...the way we all used to lock and unlock cars. That was fine until one day when I almost couldn't remove the key from the driver's door, so, being cunning and resourceful, I simply started using the passenger door to lock or unlock the car. That clever system worked until last month when the passenger door de-

cided it wanted to go on strike as well. But using my superior brain power (superior to the door), I pumped a couple of litres of WD-40 into both doors and for the next couple of weeks, one of them would work. I really didn't get what was going on as one day the driver's door would work, and the next day it was the passenger door. I wasn't bothered and did carry on…until one day in Andratx. After coming to shore, I walked to the car with a load of things to take home. I tried to unlock the doors but neither of them seemed to want to cooperate. I looked through the driver's window and saw the little pin-like thing sticking up in the air. I figured that either the car was happy to see me, or that the door actually was unlocked. Apparently the second option was the one that was most appropriate, as the door did open rather smartly. But equally smartly, the car alarm began blasting, causing all the German tourists to look over at the person breaking into the nice white SEAT. I quickly started the car (the alarm kept wailing) and slammed the shift lever into first, as I wheeled my way down the coast street. By the time I had made it to the corner, the alarm must have become exhausted from all that noise-making, and stopped. By then I was well on my way home, all the way wondering just where is the actual horn located on the car, and what wires should I cut to stop it if it goes off again. Which it did as soon as I reached my local market, by which time I must have wiped the nasty incident out of my mind. As soon as I turned off the car and opened the door, the flippin" alarm went all postal again. I just walked away from the car with a look on my face like *"Whose car is that making all the noise?"* Of course, when I came back from the market with a bag full of gluten-free things, the alarm went off again. My local garage did manage to fix it (but it did take them longer than it took Apple to replace my phone).

250 – the number of people who came out to watch the races at the Fiesta de Portals. I am actually guessing at this number but it did look pretty close. Here is what this is all about. You may recall me writing about the crazy party every year in Puigpunyent. You may also recall me writing about how the sound from the live bands would permeate even my metre-thick walls of La Antigua at night. Well, every year about this time, each village/town/whatever has their own party, and this weekend, it is the party for the village of Portals Nous (which is more or less next to Bendinat). There is evening entertainment (item "O" above) and this afternoon, there was the village version of the Mille Miglia. Actually, this was more like a soap-box derby, with kind-of-sort-of motor-less vehicles that careened down the streets of the village that led to the seafront at the calita. I say it was like the Mille Miglia because people were lined up along the streets, and in some cases, barely avoiding being hit by the driver of one of the "cars" (and I use the term euphemistically) as they scorched their way to the sea. Judging by the way the vehicles went, I think there must have been three different classes of racers: Racers who, A) throw caution to the wind; B) have more guts than sense; and, C) have no sense at all.

408 – the number of days since I had my last cigarette. Don't worry, I still have not quit…I am still just not smoking.

625 – the number you get when you multiply 25 by itself. I have no idea why that has always stuck in my mind, but it is great to know when someone asks you what is the square root of 625.

Life is full of choices. Usually, at the time, we are convinced that what we have chosen is the right thing. The reality is that we rarely truly know if it was the right choice until much later. I chose to live in Mallorca six or seven years ago, and, as I have discovered, this was a good choice. Whilst living here was never part of a big plan; I do think it was the right choice, for the right reasons, at the right time.

The sunset. Again. What might seem like the endless spectacular sunsets. I was looking for a good omen that would ensure that today was a good one, and I found what I was looking for when I went out on deck last night. The whole "old sailor" thing about *"Red sky at night, sailor's delight"* is cute, but the reality does seem to be that we have had quite a few evenings where the sunsets are beyond fabulous. I read someplace that there are over 250 shades of red, and that night, they were all evident as the sun slowly slipped down to the horizon. The sailor thing does seem to hold true, and when the early evening sky does glisten with the warm glow of red, the next days do seem to bring good things. Well, good things within reason, of course. Today wasn't much different.

I struggled to get out of bed this morning – too many aches from probably too much swimming distances more than the length of a pool. Yesterday I had done my now-almost-standard-mile-long course in the morning before breakfast, and then again in the afternoon. Just so you know, I do not restrict my exercise routine to just the swimming and rowing routines I have establish; I also get exercise by popping open several of those blister-pack units that contain 600 mg tabs of *ibuprofena* multiple times each day. So after all my aches this morning, I staggered into the galley but on the way, did manage to look outside and saw that the sea was pretty much dead flat, so….into the water I went. After doing the mile thing, I did have breakfast and then set out for a pretty much chocker day.

First I drove back to Sol y Mar. Yes, it was one of my every-two-or-three days back to water the plants and check the post and do other miscellaneous house-stuff. Then after ticking all those boxes, I drove out to La Antigua to see if that house was still standing and if the courtyard was filled with leaves from the bougainvillea plants that have grown this summer even larger than they were before. Then it was back in the car to drive to the port again. But instead of heading back on the Puigpunyent-Palma road, I decided to take the more scenic route.

The term "more scenic" is pretty apt, but like many things seem appropriate at the time, there are some unintended consequences. Today was one of those times. The "scenic" route I took went from Puigpunyent, through Galilea, to Es Capdella, and then on to the other side of Andratx. The reason I call it the "scenic" route is that this little road (little meaning narrow-as-shit) should be in the Oxford Dictionary definition of serpentine. And if all the windy-bits are enough, the road takes you up and over one of the minor-mountains here on the island. When I first discovered this road just after moving to Puigpunyent, I quickly also discovered that about the only safe way to drive it was to hit your horn a couple of times as you approached a spot where the road twisted around some rock wall. For some reason, the brain-trusts that designed this road didn't think to make the road a tad wider on the corners, and because all the twisty-hairpin-like corners through the mountains do not allow for seeing who might be coming the other way, using your audio indicator is about the only way to let someone know that you too are trying to avoid either scraping your car along the rock-side of the road, or, if you are going the other way, trying to avoid having one or more of your wheels slip over the edge of the road (which would, of course, cause your car to slide down some massive hill to the valley below). I suppose that when the road was built, cars were quite a bit smaller than they are now (or maybe the road at the time was well-and-truly wide enough for two donkey-carts). All I know is that whilst I do love driving on that road, several times that day I found myself slowly going around a corner only to encounter someone in an over-sized car who must have had his or her iPod on turbo-decibels preventing him or her from hearing my little horn go beep-beep. And if those experiences weren't enough, I also encountered an amateur peloton of crazed, matching-spandex-wearing bicyclists who thought that riding 3 and 4 abreast was clear evidence of their manliness. Right. Whilst it was quite tempting, I did decide to not cause some of them to careen over the edge. But after another dozen or so twists-and-turns, I was over the top of the mountain and the road began to straighten out as I cruised along the valley. And that is where it all hit me.

The valley was…well, it looked like a Robert Altman painting or Diane Arbus photo. Stark. Lonely. Desolate. Almost alien looking. And whilst even the starkness and desolation of what I was looking at was majestically beautiful, I realized that it seemed so removed from what most people believe that Mallorca is like. If you believe all that you read about Mallorca, it might be understandable why you might think that this is an island chocker with incredible calas and beaches. Well, there is no doubt that we do have some spectacular calas and fabulous beaches, and they hopefully do entice tourists to come here on holiday (and leaving their euros or pounds or dollars for sure). But this is one of those "context" things. Our calas and beaches are fabulously beautiful, but they are just two parts of what Mallorca is all about. What it takes to discover the real Mallorca is the willingness to get out of the tourist areas and explore a bit. In other words, in order to really be here, you need to really "be" here. This was one of the big reasons of why

James B Rieley

I moved to Puigpunyent (no metropolis or touristy areas there); and it also is the reason I live where I do now.

And on a side note that is not entirely unrelated to my story…I recently was reading a book in which the author wrote about the fact that one grain of sand from any beach compared to all the sand in the entire world, is still bigger in proportion than the earth is in relationship to the universe. He went on to mention that dinosaurs had roamed our planet for over 600 times longer than we (man) have been on "our" planet. And we still call it "our" planet. The term "delusional" does come to mind. Perhaps it is time for all of us to adjust our mental models folks and put them all into some type of context. Personally, I think it is pretty great to know that we are just a tiny speck in a huge something. In all fairness, a bit of clarification here: Admittedly, when I first came to Mallorca in 1970 or 1971, I also thought that the island was all about the calas and the beaches. It took me pretty many years to return, and to finally "get it."

Years ago, I realised that as we achieve higher and higher birthday numbers (yes, this is just a nice way to say we get older), time seems to whiz past faster and faster. This summer reconfirmed this belief for me. It seems as if it was just yesterday when I (more or less) moved onto Amélie for the summer, and now it is already October. My summer was (again, more or less) the opening of *A Tale of Two Cities*. Being on the boat all summer was incredibly good for me. My exercise regime went into warp-drive and I found myself swimming and rowing daily, and to greater and greater distances. But as September arrived, I also found that I had somehow totally and completely buggered up my left arm. Common sense would dictate that I should be able to figure out how this occurred, but swimming is such a non-stressing exercise, at times, I have been mystified how paddling off to do a mile one or two times a day would cause so much grief for my left appendage. Having said that, rowing Améliña, my dinghy that admittedly wasn't designed as a rowing machine, could have been seriously counter-productive, especially at the distances I was rowing her. After having to stop these two methods of being healthier due to my fear of tearing something that shouldn't be torn, I finally decided to find out what was going on. And because I have a computer, I went first to Dr. Google.

According to a website (one of the potential 257,000 results that popped up) I found the following bit of information. *"Many tears are the result of a wearing down and fraying of the tendon that occurs slowly over time. This naturally occurs as we age. It can be worsened by overuse - repeating the same shoulder motions again and again."* Right. This explanation must have been clearly written by someone who is the Head of the Anti-Rowing-and-Swimming League; so with that less-than-good news, I then decided to throw away my computer (not really) and get someone to see if they could somehow magically reduce the pain I had been living with. Yesterday, the knock on my door signalled the arrival of Maria.

Living on Rocks

Maria is una masajista (trained massage therapist) who was recommended to me by a couple of friends. She arrived at Sol y Mar yesterday afternoon, complete with massive carry bag that contained her massage table/bed/thing and an assortment of tools of her trade. After explaining my problem to her – in itself an interesting thing as she began by telling me that her English was limited to a few words, and as we know, I am not exactly as fluent in Spanish as I would like – she set up the table and told me to climb on. She then began to (not sure if the appropriate adjective here is "gently" or "forcefully") massage my back and arm with a passion that almost sent me into dreamland. At times, her finger movement did result in a non-Dr. Mengele level of pain that did result in me staying awake. Other than that, the experience was better than good.

After what seemed to be either a minute, or an hour, I began to be aware that there was the incense wafting through the air. This awareness corresponded with the sensation of heat being applied to wherever her hands were working. Maria had begun to use two thin metal tubes with burning incense in them, which understandably felt as hot as molten silver being applied to my arm. And then, sadly, she was done and left Sol y Mar in the downpour that had erupted outside after she had arrived. I awoke this morning, wondering if my arm would be better. My first thought was that if it was better, I could roll out of bed and plunge into the sea and do sort of a "make-up" mile to compensate for my recent lack of swimming activity. But as I realised that, whilst my arm did feel better, moving it certain ways still showed that there was something amiss. This realisation hit me about the same time I remembered that I wasn't on-board Amélie and in fact, yesterday, my friend Rafa and I had moved Amélie from the wonderful swinging mooring she was on to the marina at Club de Vela in el Puerto de Andratx.

Sometimes things just don't go as one has planned, and even though Maria's magic fingers did make my arm feel a bit better, the pain was still there. So, feeling that enough was enough, I went to see a specialist to try to figure out what was going on. I have always had high regard for competent people, and the specialist I saw fell into that category. After my usual "my Spanish is crap, do you speak English" question, to which he said no, I soldiered on in Spanish, describing (or trying to describe) the pain in my arm. He had me stand up and asked me to put my left arm behind my back, which was pretty difficult. He then took his thumb and pressed a spot on my shoulder, only to hear me exclaim in the universally understood, "*Arrrrgh*." Right. Easy-peasy (he didn't say that, but that does rather describe how tricky his diagnosis was.) Torn tendon. Wonderful. He even made a drawing for me that explained what happened, and then told me I needed to have an MRI and then with some luck, an injection of cortisone. He alluded to the fact that the injection would only work out if the tendon was seriously ripped up. So, hopefully by the end of this week, the MRI will be completed and I will be all cortisoned up and back to normal (or at least my version of normal).

James B Rieley

Moving the boat to a marina is an acknowledgement that summer is indeed slipping away. Now for those of you that don't live in a climate as I do, the term "summer" carries different meanings. Here, warm weather and virtually constant sun continues almost to the end of the year, and for some of you, "summer" seems to last for a couple of hours on one day in August. When winter actually does arrive here, it sets up an almost contradiction in visual terms. Tourists from northern Europe arrive in the dead of winter and instantly throw on shorts and sandals and can be seen walking about in Palma thriving on how warm and wonderful it is. But for those of us who live here throughout the year, the weather is relatively depressingly vile and we are all bundled up with long pants and jumpers. Luckily, it isn't winter yet.

The actual reason that I move Amélie to a marina at this time of year is that, ever since I have had Amélie, I have seen that one or two fools have kept their boats at anchor in the harbour, only to discover that the winter winds and storms that blow in from the southwest have sort of "moved" their boats closer to shore. Actually, what I should say is that each winter at least one boat that was left on a mooring has ended up smashed on the rocks along the shoreline. Being in a marina is just a safer place to be, and does allow me to still go on-board and enjoy the gentle movement of Amélie. Besides, I can always take her out and putz about the island if I want to. The chances of this in reality are about as good as me winning the lotto, but I am sure I will pop over to Andratx once in a while to sit on the deck and read (well after I have made Amélie all sparkly clean. This is a far better solution than leaving Amélie on her swinging mooring and at some point having to ring my insurance people and tell them that my boat is now on the rocks in many pieces and then asking them if they would kindly send me a check.

Today is el día de la Fiesta Nacional de España, which means that because we haven't had enough holidays this summer, we are now able to celebrate National Spain Day. Which means that everything will be closed. Which means that hardly anyone will be working and making money today. Which means that the Spanish economy will continue to languish on the edge of something or another. I am not saying that holiday's are a bad thing…actually I like the idea of national holidays. Although in the case of today, there were some things I would have liked to accomplish, and now I will be forced (note the use of the word "forced") to just go to lunch and then sit outside and ponder what to do tomorrow. So…Viva España.

In order to ensure that I could be completely supportive of the National Spain Day, after all, this is the country in which I have chosen to live, I decided I should talk to a neighbour this morning, so I went down to see Rafa and Kim. When living in North America, on the national holiday everyone went on a picnic. In England, it seemed appropriate to go to a cricket pitch and be bored to tears. I am in Spain, and I wanted to get this right and appropriate. When I arrived at their piso, it was clear to me that this holiday must be very special. There was Rafa, sitting on their terrace with a pair of

Living on Rocks

panelled-racing goggles, looking quite a bit like T. E. Lawrence about to get on his motorbike after all those years in the desert. How this all connects to National Spain Day was beyond me so instead we talked about the weather (which by the way is pretty flippin" brilliant (but I would say that, wouldn't I?)

Corcovada. No, not the National Park in Costa Rica – haven't been there. Not even the mountain top overlooking Rio de Janiero with the huge Imagen del Cristo Redentor. The Corcovado I am referring to is a song written by Antonio Carlos Jobin in the 1960's and it has arisen to the "most played" number on my iTunes. Whether the original version by Jobim, Astrud Gilberto and Stan Getz, or the remake by Frank Sinatra and Jobim, the song is, in a word, wonderful. So wonderful in fact that you really need to Google it or find it on iTunes.

And now, a medical update. No silly, this is not an advert from telly, this is a Dr. JBR medical update on my wonky shoulder, which I touched on a bit ago. I did have the MRI, which is always a treat, and leaves one nearly deaf. After collecting the test results, I went off to see my doctor, who after reading the report, immediately had a smile on his face. He told me – or at least this is what it sounded like as he doesn't speak a stitch of English – that the good news was that the pesky offending tendon was not torn into pieces, but was in fact simply buggered a bit. He also explained that somehow (the term "rowing-a-boat-not-designed-to-be-rowed" does come to mind) my tendon had become dislodged from the neat little groove it should reside in and was now all tangled up where it shouldn't be. Right.

Whilst "knowing" is always important, what I really wanted to know was what we could do about it. I was thinking I could try to find someone like Mandrake the Magician to gesture hypnotically and force the tendon back into place, but I have no idea where to look in the Paginas Amarillas (Yellow Pages). So instead I asked the doctor what we could do. Another smile appeared on his face when he said, "*Cortisone infusion.*" Infusion? Well, I had seen the trial of the doctor who "infused" Michael Jackson a bit too much so I had a clue what the term meant.

I really don't like to get shots. Not sure why, but I just am not all that keen on having them. But, as someone who has had multiple spinal taps in my life, I figured that nothing could be worse than that, so I said okay. A few minutes later, we were sitting at his desk again and I asked how this shot would get the tendon back into its appropriate resting place. Again, the smile. This infusion wouldn't do that. The infusion was only to try to reduce the inflammation that might (and I should have put "**_might_**" in bold, underlined italic just to show that my mental model was pretty low of success) allow the tendon to slip back into place all by itself. This is where you can begin to watch for pigs flying overhead that will signal success. He also told me I should come back next week for another infusion of cortisone. When I asked what we would do if the tendon still was acting naughty, his smile became

James B Rieley

even bigger when he said, "Operacion," Which of course means Operation. Oh good. It would be my luck that the surgeon would be Hawkeye Pierce. Will keep you posted.

So at this point, I am still not swimming nor am I rowing, which has put a serious crimp in my self-imposed exercise programme. But because I know that all the exercise I have been doing has been good for me, I have reverted back to my typical winter exercise regime and have been walking again. A lot of walking. When I was living at La Antigua I bought a cheap-as-chips pedometer after reading that we all should walk 10,000 steps per day. Well, that is what I have been doing. At least 10,000 steps of walking each day, not counting all the walking I do around the house. My walking is more like a forced march and I have by now plotted out various distances from Sol y Mar so I don't have to attach the pedometer to my pocket when I go out. The little "click-click-click-click" as the ball-bearing bounces back and forth recording leg movement is really annoying. The big challenge of all this walking is to do it either first thing in the morning, or early evening. The rest of the day is still consumed by our idea of autumn, which for most of you, would be a bit warmer than mid-august during a drought year.

First, a medical update....Head nurse Gillian arrived Wednesday and Thursday we went to la clinica for the procedure on my shoulder. Relatively short waiting time, and then I was whisked (wearing a fab bluish-gown thingy, as you do) into theatre. After some doctor-wanna-be enquired as to which shoulder they were supposed to play with (which he duly marked with a big black "X," I was wheeled into the surgical suit where another doc-wanna-be lathered up my shoulder with an iodine-type solution. I an not sure if he was being cautious or just wanted to use up a 55 gallon drum of the stuff, but my body was then 1/2 orange and I am sure Paris Hilton would have been completely jealous of the festive pumpkin colour.

Next it was the administration on the anaesthesia. I had been told that I would be completely under for the procedure, as they would use Propofol (assuming that Michael Jackson's doctor hadn't used it all). But as I was lying there waiting to drift along to la-la land, I noticed that I could feel someone who was apparently sitting on my left-side holding the shoulder in place. Then I became aware of a sound of a disk grinder, which was chipping away at the bones that were aggravating the tendon problem assumedly. I luckily did not hear anyone mutter *"Oops"* in Spanish. This went on for almost an hour, and then I was taken to a recovery room for a while, and then to a hospital room where I spent the night. After the surgeon stopping in the following morning to ask how I was and give me several scripts for the pain, I was whisked away safely to the Sol y Mar Rehabilitation facility, which is my home, of course. On Wednesday it was back to see my doc to check out how things are healing, then hopefully a plan for some physio-therapy (this one handed typing lark is pure shit). His examination verified that all was healing well and (thankfully), he said I could stop using the rather pesky sling.

All in all, I think that the surgeon did a brilliant piece of work and the whole healing process does seem to be moving along.

Since that exam, I have stopped taking the pain meds – they just messed up my stomach as much as they took the edge off the hurt – and made the major accomplishments (for me at least) of being able to put on a jumper by myself, and on Saturday, driving a car for the first time. Needless to say, after my auto excursion, my shoulder was feeling pretty buggered. Oh well...all part of the healing I assume.

Yesterday I went to the doctor's office and he pulled out the stitches. I had told him that I drove there by myself, and he just rolled his eyes. I am looking in my Spanish-English dictionary to see what that means, but I assume he didn't think I could (or should) be doing that already. Ooops.

On day four after the op (it is now day 10), I decided to attempt something constructive. For those of you who know me, and I do mean really know me, you are probably aware that I do have a fair bit of computer technology at hand. One of my computers has, for the umpteenth time, gone to computer heaven and this time it appears to be for good. Sadly, I cannot even get it to fire up to clean off the hard-drive, so I thought I would simply remove it before binning the computer. Taking a laptop apart with two hands probably isn't all that easy (especially if you don't know what you are doing), but with one good hand, it was a bit of an adventure. I did manage to retrieve the hard-drive (and the disk-drive, but not sure why I saved that) and later that day, conducted a memorial service for the remains.

Well, almost another year has whizzed past and whilst this one has presented some challenges, overall, it has been pretty great here. The biggest challenge ("biggest" is admittedly a term grounded solidly in my mental models) has been my shoulder problem. I have been doing the physio-therapy every day, and all the effort has been paying off big-time. I must clarify a bit about this...I had been told my Joaquin, the guy who has been bending my left arm in ways that I am sure God never had in mind when she came up with the human body concept. Of course, if Joaquin were here right now, it wouldn't be too happy about my description of him "bending" my arm. Joaquin says we are "exercising" the shoulder area, but it sure feels like bending to me. The "every day" concept is also interesting. When he first told me that I should come everyday, I asked if "everyday" meant seven days per week. This would have been an attractive option for me as I had been told by my doctor I would probably need 15 days of therapy, so the "everyday" plan meant I would only have to drive to the rehabilitation place for a day more than two weeks. But when I queried Joaquin, he said, "*Yes, everyday except for weekends, when the centre would be closed.*" And then he informed me that the following week, the centre would also be closed on Tuesday and Thursday for holidays. Right. So last week it was only three days of contortionism. Never the less, I was given a set of "exercises" I could do myself at home and I do have considerably more mobility every day. All good there I think.

James B Rieley

I must admit that the whole rehabilitation thing has flashed me back to when I was recovering from the evil-bastard GBS that I had shortly after moving to Mallorca. Then the physio-therapy was pretty critical as I could barely walk upon my being released from hospital. What would normally take a minute or so to walk from point A to point B then meant it might take me ten minutes, and all the time I would be careening all over the walk path, looking incredibly pathetic and in need of assistance (which I did need to negotiate even a simple walk). When I began my physio this time, I was surprised to see what I thought was a familiar face. It was Andres, my therapist years ago and it was his work that helped me get better as quickly as I did. When I saw him, I walked over and said hello and he said, "*Hola James*." Not a bad memory on his part. Nice to be remembered, but my preference would be to not have to even go to the rehab facility, so as soon as I finish writing this chapter, I think I will do more exercises.

Shortly after getting rid of my sling, I was interviewed about a workshop I had agreed to do here on the island. Doing the workshop was a real treat for me, and as you might imagine, it was rather systemic in nature, with the delegates learning how to use some of the 7 M7P tools and loops...my kind of a fun day. The interview appeared in the paper here, and other than the fact that the editor had apparently miserably failed in punctuation class, and had been a bit too creative with my biography, the article covered two pages and even I was impressed. And on the subject of work, I have been writing quite a bit lately. Most of this writing has been in the form of articles (about business leadership, of course). I wrote one of them after watching parts of the Conrad Murray trial in Los Angeles on telly. During the testimony of one of the expert scientists who had been called to testify about the relative strength of the drugs that Murray had been using on Michael Jackson, the expert started talking about "bioavailability." It didn't take long to figure out that what he was talking about was the amount of actual drug that Jackson was getting – the bioavailabilty of a pill is low compared to that of an intravenous injection as the IV method gets the drug straight into the bloodstream. I kept hearing that term – bioavailability – used repeatedly during the experts testimony, and became so intrigued by it, I wrote an article titled "The Bioavailabilty of Leadership in Organisations." After I had finished writing it, I decided to send it to a friend who is an editor of a business journal that I used to write for quite a few years ago just to see what she thought about it. She apparently loved it and it will be published in February (even after I told her how I came about to use the term bioavailabilty). Business journal publishers around the world need not fear, I do not watch the X-Factor (although, come to think about it, that could be a nice "hook" for an article).

Today, for the first time since before my shoulder operation, I went to see Amélie. I hadn't been there because getting on-board would have been a bit too much of a challenge, but today I was feeling pretty chipper, and after

Living on Rocks

stopping at the local Correos (post office) to post some letters, I drove on to Andratx to make sure that all was well with Amélie. I did manage to lower the pasarella on the bow and get on-board, but after a quick look to make sure the bilge wasn't full of water (it wasn't) and that the solar panels were still pumping electricity into the battery banks (they were), I decided that overdoing it wasn't the best for my shoulder, so I closed up the boat and drove back home. On the way home, I thought, as it was almost Christmas, I should do something special for Sol y Mar. Yes, I replanted several albahaca (basil) plants. Nothing better than pesto for the holidays.

And speaking of the hols, when Matthew and David were young boys, Carol and I had hired some guy to play Santa on Christmas eve. The plan was to make some noise and then I would burst out of our front door to find Santa there bringing presents to the boys. A nice plan, but he sure didn't look as good as David did in his Santa suit helping out at a centre for developmentally challenged children this week. I mentioned that to David in an email, and he quickly responded with a one-line message – *"You HIRED somebody?!?!?!?!?"* Oooops. I best not say anything about the Easter bunny I guess.

Today is the last day of 2011, and it has been pretty clear to me that this year whizzed past pretty quickly. This year I have lost two good friends; have been lucky enough to see some special old friends who now live far away; seen some friends move away from Mallorca; and met some pretty neat new friends here on my island.

Admittedly, I have slagged off on my weekly regimen of weekly business writing, and perhaps even not been as disciplined on writing these notes. I would like to say that I have continued my artistic endeavours as much as I should, but probably haven't done that either. But I have done some things I never expected I would, or could. My summer on-board Amélie was wonderful and it did result in a serious amount of physical exercise of swimming and rowing. Having said that, all that swimming and rowing (probably rowing the tender to Amélie that was never designed to be rowed) was the cause for my shoulder woes. The good news is that after Joaquin, my physio-therapist, doing contortionist-type things on my injury, have improved things dramatically.

One more thing that was pretty wonderful this year was that a couple of weeks ago, I decided that I really should see my sons over the holidays. So, after some pretty brilliant planning, we began the big tour. After flights from here to Barcelona, then to London, and then to Chicago, followed by a three-hour drive north, we spent a few days with my son Matthew and his family. Sadly, Matthew was recovering from a hospital visit, so he and I didn't get as much time together as I would have liked, but it was good to see them all again. One highlight (although I am not sure that is the right adjective to describe what was seen upon awaking the morning after arriving) was the snow that had fallen overnight. Even I thought that freshly fallen snow is pretty great, but the fact that there was snow was a tip off that the temperature was now well less than freezing, and cold weather and James Rieley do not seem to get along well. Then it was a flight to Los Angeles where we spent several days with David and Nancy and enjoyed the wonderful weather and just hanging out in the city of Angels. Just a note about the time in Los Angeles…whilst there, David and Nancy took us to a restaurant where we had to arrive no later than 1900. When I asked why the urgency about arrival time, David said that at exactly 1900, and then again at 2000, there would be a snow-storm. Right. This was Los Angeles and the daytime temperature was 25 degrees plus, so a "snow-storm?" But sure enough, whilst sitting eating outside at the restaurant, at exactly 1900, a series of machines located on the roofs of the buildings surrounding the mall suddenly began to spew snow on the throngs of people that were enjoying Christmas outside. And if that wasn't enough, as the snow was falling, some speakers began to pump out Bing Crosby singing White Christmas. Only in Los Angeles in California. Then after a quick visit to finally meet a long-lost relative from my extended family after several years of trading emails, there were more flights – Los Angeles to London to Barcelona and on to Mallorca – and the trip was over.

It would have been great to spend more time in both cities and see some of the other friends that I haven't seen in a while, but that wasn't to be. So for those of you whom I didn't see, my apologies. Maybe next visit (although even I can't believe the number of times in the past I have said this is my last trip to the states. I guess that is why "never" isn't really part of my vocabulary).

So tomorrow it will be yet another new year. I would love to be highly eloquent and impart some tad of wisdom about all the good things a new year can bring, but I think I will just let it slide and wish everyone a year where all your dreams and wishes come true.

Besos y abrazos a todos, JBR

2012

It is 2012, in case somehow you have managed to avoid all the fireworks and news stories about the celebrations around the world. And with most new years, this one is chocker with opportunities. Stress for some, but opportunities none-the-less. I actually began with the opportunities a few weeks before Christmas by cranking up my computer – this assumes that you might actually believe that I turned my computer off for more than a few minutes over the past twenty years. What I did with my computer is write an article. Yes, it was a business article, but that is what I do. Then I wrote another one. And another one. And another one. And then yet another one. Five articles on substantial business issues in about five weeks. I sent one of them to an editor I used to work with at a business journal in New York, and they picked it up for publication. Then I sent another one to a friend who works for a UK-based publisher, and they picked that one up. And if all that wasn't enough,

Living on Rocks

last week I whipped out some loops that explain the dynamic complexity of the Global Financial Crisis and its impact on local businesses. Hmmmm, nice tasty loops, but an incredibly sad story. It has been a pretty nice start to the New Year.

And on a more cultural note, the other day I had been invited to go to Bunyola to a friend's house for a traditional Catalan dinner. It is the middle of January, and Bunyola is almost in the middle of the island, which means smack next to the mountains. Brrr. I was told that the meal was going to be a barbecue, so I knew I would need to bundle up a bit. But, being Dr. Adventurous (once every ten years or so), I accepted the invitation. After bundling up in enough layers to closely resemble the Michelin man, today I drove Miranda to Marta's house.

She had made Calçots (KAL-SHOTS is more or less the way to pronounce it), which are sort of like massively long sofritos (which look a bit like spring onions on steroids). As I had never had them before, I mustered all my adventuresome chromosomes and did as everyone else did. What you do is take one of the Calçots off the barbie, peel back the thin film-like skin layer that took the brunt of the heat from the coals, and then dip them into Salvitxada (SAL-VEE-SCHADA, a romesco sauce) before eating. Whilst eating calçots can be a tad messy (within seconds all my fingers were pitch-black from peeling off the outer-coating layers and totally slimed up by the Salvitxada), they were quite good. Yes, even I thought they were quite good, and I have been known to be a bit picky about foods (I have been known to have an aversion to vegetables that are green and whose name begins with an "A"). And if the Barbie wasn't producing enough, Marta had also made quite a few Butifara (BOO-TEE-FAR-AH, a spicy sausage) that were exceptional, especially after dipping in the salvitxada as well. After we had annihilated the local calçhot population, Marta announced that for our postre (PO-STRAY, dessert), we would walk across the road to an orange grove and continue our feasting on oranges straight from the tree (that we picked ourselves). A good afternoon, with good friends, and an increased cultural awakening. Loved it.

Monday it is back to the physio for more treatments to help get my shoulder to stop being a bit wonky. There is no doubt that the operation did wonders. There is equally no doubt that the physio-therapy I have been enduring has increased my mobility in that shoulder by a huge amount. But last week when I visited the doctor to get a review, she was astonished at the mobility I now have. As I moved my left arm into every possible position I could think of, she kept saying my progress to date was "phenomenal" and "incredible." Then she asked if I had pain when I was doing this, and I said, "*Of course.*" Right. Fifteen more sessions were put in the diary, so Monday it all begins again. Now to be fair, I really don't mind the fact that I have to go for the rehabilitation work. The reality is that I know it helps, so I am happy to do it. What irks me is that the first fifteen sessions began at 1400h each day, and this really would muck up my days. At least this second tranche will begin at

James B Rieley

1030h each day, which will leave me most of the day to do something else. Now all I have to do is figure out what to do with my afternoons.

I know that in the past, I have rabbited on about the weather in these musings on occasion. The reason that I have done this falls into one of several categories, including: A) I love the climate of the island, B) I love driving you into a state of high envy if you live where the weather is shite, C) The photos that accompany my weather-ramblings usually look pretty good. Well, as the saying says, what goes around comes around. The past two weeks have been more or less a comeuppance weather-wise. Now to be fair, the months of November, December, and even most of January, were pretty flippin' wonderful. But equally to be fair, the island has been dry and we have needed some precipitation in order to avoid a drought this coming summer. So you would think that a little winter precipitation would have been welcome. In most situations, I would agree with that statement, but...the weather patterns lately have been less than nice and the desperately cold weather that has pummelled northern Europe managed to sink south and cover Mallorca. The operational word here was "cold." Actually for me, two words..."fucking cold." And if you paid attention in your physics lessons in school, you will recognise that precipitation plus bugger cold means most likely snow.

I can remember five or six years ago it did snow in Palma, but I think I was in some client meeting in London and missed it. Besides, by noon that day, the snow had all melted away and island life returned to normal. But this year, the snow was a bit more aggressive and the cold air from northern Europe (who received it from Russia according to the weather-people) has blanketed the island for two weeks now. And to make things even worse, the forecasts all say that it will remain cold for yet another week. You might be thinking, *"He is such a weather wimp...and Mallorca still has better weather than just about any other place in Europe."* If you think that, you would be right. Fair enough. But part of being spoilt about the weather is that you want to continue to feel spoilt.

The weather has brought the classic good news-bad news tension. Good news...I have been using the chimenea (CHI-MEH-NAY-A, fireplace) nightly and the fires are both wonderfully warming and highly visual. Bad news... In the past two weeks I have gone through a half-tonne of wood whilst at the same time, running the heating system of Sol y Mar. More bad news...my firewood inventory needs to be chopped up into fireplace-sized logs, which I do. However, more good news...chopping all that firewood is better physiotherapy than going to hospital. So, other than I feel like the Michelin man with my jumpers, I am feeling pretty good (but would feel even better if the weather pattern would return to (my version of) normal.

And now, the real reason for this letter on this day. Today would have been my Aunt Peg's 95th birthday. Peg was my father's sister and a had a serious impact on my life...and impact that still can be seen when I do just about anything creative. Peg was an artist, and years ago, when I was 12 or 13 or some other rather young age, she had come with some of my family on a little holiday. My father had rented a cottage-like house in the woods in Gills Rock. Everyday, Peg would find some way to trick me into going off with her to paint or draw a picture of one of the commercial fishing shacks or boats that would be bringing in their catch of the day. After a couple of weeks, our holiday was over and it was time to pack up to go home again. At the time, I can remember my Aunt asking me if I would like to have her entire set of oil paints and brushes that she had been using.

Being a polite young man, I said thank you, but did turn down the offer of the supplies. Have no doubt, the offer was intriguing, especially because I think I was really getting into the whole art thing by then. Peg reiterated her offer, this time reassuring me that she really wanted me to have the supplies. My father was sitting near by and was subtly observing what was going on. When Peg made her second offer, I noticed that he was peering over his glasses to see what I would do. Right. This appeared to me to be some sort of parental test, and once again, I said thank you but I couldn't accept her kind offer. I knew I had done the right thing. Oh sure, I would have loved to have all her paints. After all, these weren't just a set of 6 or 8 colours in shiny tubes combined with three or four spiffy brushes of marginal quality. These were a proper set of twisted and bent over tubes with paint smeared along the sides and about a dozen of seriously used high quality oil painting brushes. Just the fact that I had spent my holiday time watching my Aunt use them meant that I knew that with this kit, my painting expertise (pretty crap at that point in time) would improve. My painting skills would never match hers but with all that kit, it would have a chance of getting closer I thought. But I also had it clear in my mind that one of the big lessons that my father had firmly implanted in my mind – you don't accept gifts from people who aren't in a position to give them...or something like that – was still in force. Whilst I was keen to have the paints and brushes, I actually did feel good that I had said thank you, but no. It was then that my father got out of his chair and came over and with a little smile on his face, told me it was okay to accept the most generous gift of my Aunt Peg.

Peg was pretty special and as I have said, a huge influence in my life. Even today, I make my own Christmas cards, something that Peg always did. There is no doubt in my mind what, whilst I do like the creative part of making the cards, I know that it is Peg's influence that is with me each year as I plot out the year's card. She had a fab sense of humour and in later life, was a devoted step-mother to her family. But most of all, Peg was my artistic mentor. One year I even drove for over eight hours to see Peg, just to talk about screen-printing and doing water-colours. What a joy she was, and even though she passed away in 2005, her best friend and I always toast her on this very special day.

The past week has been eventful here. Actually, you could say it has been a real eye-opener. First, the weather...back to normal for the first week of

James B Rieley

March, so that is okay. Next, the news…well, there isn't any big news from here other than I did decide to start up the engines on Amélie the other day. After sitting in the marina for the past several months, I thought it might be a good thing to do and after a few spins, they each kicked in and life was good on the boat. And now, the real subject of this entry.

Years ago, I wore glasses. It seems like I had worn them for most of my life. I can even remember when I was about 12 or 13, being told by an eye doctor that if I wore bi-focals for several years, my eyes would become all better. Well, that doctor was an idiot, as I wore both bi-focals with those nasty lines and the type where the two lenses sort of blended into one another for years. Then one day, whilst living on Angelina in Barcelona, I was leaning over the bow pulpit and my glasses slipped off my head and slowly danced their way to the bottom of the harbour. I actually had a diver come over and pointed to exactly where the glasses had disappeared, but after about 30 minutes of him sweeping the bottom, all I could assume was that when the glasses were on their way to the seabed, they landed on some poor unsuspecting fish and he (or she, to be politically correct) was now the only four-eyed atún (tuna) around.

After a few days, I decided to go get some replacement glasses and after an eye exam, did manage to buy another pair. But as I already had a pair of chemist glasses for reading, I only had the prescription set for distance. I thought that was a clever move, but as it turned out, the glasses were so bloody heavy, I decided to try wearing contact lenses. When I was in my teens, I had wanted to switch to contacts, but I never could quite get the hang of not flinching as my finger came closer and closer to my eye, so I gave up trying. But now, at a clearly more mature age, I decided to give it a go again. This time, I mastered the lens-insertion-technique and I was in well-sighted once again.

My ocular prescription was different for each eye and after talking to a friend in London who was in the midst of having that laser-surgery-thing, I decided to try wearing only one contact lens; the one in my right eye. My reasoning was based on what my friend had told me…the brain automatically distinguishes which eye is being used when only one is corrected for distance. So again, I was well-sighted, as well as not being as poor from the days of buying two different contact lens prescriptions all the time.

I was even more clever when I discovered that I could wear my contact lens (note, only one lens now) for days on end. The fact that the box my lenses came in was clearly marked "Daily" didn't bother me. I was just so chuffed that I didn't have to do the "hold-the-eye-open, drag-out-the-old-lens-and-stick-in-the-new-lens" routine every day. But one time, after not changing the lens for a bit more than a week (I know…bad James), I did decide to change it and I really struggled to get it out. So for a while, I wore no contact lenses. No glasses, no contacts…nothing. And miraculously, I could pretty much see. No, I didn't think that the first doctor's prediction was coming true, I just assumed that my eyes decided that it might be better to function properly than to risk having me stick things into them again.

So for the past seven or eight years, I haven't worn any corrective eyewear, and have managed rather well. When I went through the completely painful process of earning my Spanish driver's license, I had to take an eye test, but did squeak through, so there was no real reason to even contemplate glasses or contact lenses again. This was a real bonus as it enabled me to assemble a collection of trendy sunglasses. But (and this became a big "but") a few weeks ago, I went to an ophthalmologist for a check up and was told that I had a cataract in my right eye. I knew that this eye was playing up a bit, but attributed that to the possibility that the eye function of my brain was getting tired of figuring out which eye to use for focus as I tend to switch my focus from my computer screen to looking out at the Mediterranean multiple times each day. Sven (no, this is not a Spanish name...my eye doctor is from Sweden) gave me the options: I could, A) Do nothing until that eye was so buggered that I would probably need a pirate-looking-patch (which did, for a person with a set of nautical chromosomes almost seem an attractive option); B) Get some seriously corrective glasses (by this age I was pretty much over the Buddy Holly look); or C) Have cataract surgery. The last option seemed to make the most sense so yesterday, I went under the knife, so to speak.

The only real problem that occurred was that the equipment in the surgery theatre didn't seem to want to be calibrated correctly. Seeing as how his plan was to make a tiny incision with something smaller than a Swiss-Army knife (I hoped) and having all the magnification doo-wah stuff spot on was pretty important, all this meant was a 90 minute delay in Sven starting. The actual surgery went quickly and about the only discomfort was having a light that appeared to be brighter than the sun blaring into my eye whilst he was doing it. I had asked Sven to describe to me everything he was doing as he did it (I do like to learn about things) but have decided not to describe the entire procedure in this chapter, as you might be eating and it could spoil your dinner.

Ten or fifteen minutes later, I walked out like a new man. Okay, like an somewhat older man with two good eyes. Okay...like an somewhat older man with one good eye and one eye that was dilated to about the size of Barbados. This morning the dilation had reduced so that my right eye lens was only the size of St. Thomas, so by tomorrow I should completely be in focus.

Well, what can I say? Not much actually, other than I am very aware I have not done much writing in months. It wasn't that there was nothing going on. I just thought at the time, what was happening was just so normal for here that it might not be too interesting to read about...that and I had become a tad lazy about writing I guess. Mea culpa. Disculpame. My apologies.

It is now nearing the end of April, and it seemed like a good time to write again. Nothing massively going on here, but there are a few updates that I thought might be of interest…so….here goes.

After my little shoulder surgery, I still have been experiencing some mild discomfort when I work on increasing my mobility so I thought instead of going through more of the electric-impulse therapies, I would do something about it myself. You know…the "mind-over-matter" solution that I often employ, and in most cases, this works wonders. The key to doing this is a combination of some intense visualisation efforts, accompanied by increase mobility exercises. Whilst this has been more-or-less providing me with a bit more pain-free mobility, I recently decided to increase my efforts a bit but with some assistance.

Whilst on the cruise a couple of years ago, I had attended several on-board Pilate's sessions and found them quite beneficial. I was thinking about signing up here for a Pilates class, but that seemed like a bit too much structure and discipline for me. I looked around and did find about a kazillion Pilates videos, but I thought that would just be a waste of money. Instead, I began to look at Yoga as potentially good vehicle for me. Again, the spectre of trudging off several times a week to a yoga class wasn't that exciting so instead, I decided to find a yoga instructor who could put together a programme for me that I might actually follow. My reasoning for going in this direction all made sense: I would be able to do yoga when I wanted, and because I have these terraces here at Sol y Mar, I could almost picture myself being up on the roof terrace stretching and bending and whatever in the sun whenever I felt like it. Of course the challenge would be to find a yoga instructor who was up for this.

*And then in May or June….*Today was my first session with my yoga master. Swami Yubendalot Maharishi was brilliant. Okay, that isn't actually his name; his name is Kevin, but Swami Yubendalot sounds much more Indian. Kevin came over this morning and we went through a series of stretchy-type things I could do and after a couple of hours of him checking out my current bendable limits, gave me several exercises I could begin to do. My next session will be later this week, at which time he will give me an entire programme that I can follow (or at least attempt to follow). I am pretty chuffed about this and will keep you posted as things progress.

*And again in August….*This summer certainly hasn't been like last summer, or even the summer before. No, this has nothing to do with the weather, which has, as usual, been pretty brilliant. I am not sure I can even place my finger on it, but I know it has been different. I have been to Berlin a couple of times to see my brother and been busy working on a couple of projects and the combination of the two sort of has kept me from spending my summer months on the boat. Last month (this would have been in July), I did become highly motivated and began sorting out what I wanted to do for this year's Christmas/Holiday card. A bit premature you say? Perhaps, but when a project manifests itself in my head, it is time to get cracking on it. So, after

Living on Rocks

several trips to my screen-maker and the lads who do my foliolitos (colour separations that are used to produce the screens I make the cards with), I was making pruebas (tests) of the image on the card. Once I had those sorted, I put everything away in storage as even I think that actually making Christmas cards in July is a bit over the top. I must remember to pull everything out and actually produce them in a few months though.

And now today (which is late October)....Last month something did happen that is worth writing about. I have sold Amélie. Yes,...me....boatless again. This wasn't an all-that-difficult decision as I didn't spend that much time on her this summer (which you just found out about) and when you are offered a bit more than you paid for a boat, it is always time to sell. So I did. I think a lot of my friends were speculating how many days after the sale I would begin to twitch uncontrollably, but I was fine with the sale. She was a wonderful boat to have, but truth-be-told, I didn't actually take her anyplace. To me, Amélie was more like having a beach cottage...without all the sand. Each morning I would get up and dive into the sea and do a lap (hey, my laps this year were a bit more than 1/2 mile) and then have breakfast on deck in the sun. Okay, I am missing that, but it is now late October and I wouldn't have been swimming too much now anyway. I have received a couple of SMS"s from the new owners on their way to Gibraltar (*"James, I can't find the keys to the engines"*) (*"James, do you remember where the manual is for the air conditioning?"*) (*"James, can you tell me again how to switch from the main diesel tank to the reserve tanks?"*), as well as an invitation to visit *his* boat the next time I am in Gibraltar. I have been in Gibraltar, but once is enough so I don't think that will happen. Besides, he would probably want me to try to help him look for something he can't locate on-board.

This summer I also managed to see the iPad app I developed actually get completed and listed for sale on the iTunes store. I (cleverly) named the app the System Dynamics Loop Generator as it enables users to create bespoke causal loop diagrams, which as I am sure you all recognise as a principle way to help understand the dynamics at play in organisations. I was thinking of writing more about the app, but I think I can hear some of you dozing off about now so I will move on.

In the past week, I did drag out all the Christmas card paraphernalia and cranked up the Sol y Mar holiday-card-production-line. Whooo-weeee!!! The plan was to do a five-colour serigraph, but I eventually ended up by using six colours. They are all resting in the sitting room now so that they dry thoroughly. Probably tomorrow or the next day I will pick them all up and fold them...and then wait until it is closer to Christmas to send them out.

Keeping Current... Actually, the lead of this chunk of words is a tad misleading. It isn't about saving electricity, although I suppose if I would turn off some of the computer kit I have constantly running, I could do that. No, this chapter is about me desperately trying to avoid falling into the treacle-like minutia of daily life that caused me to delay getting cracking with the last chapter. So, even though I have often been accused of not keeping up, it has only been a week since my last writing and here I am writing to you again.

I think I recently said that I was working on a new project. (Perhaps I should go look myself to see what I said. Okay, I did check, and I did mention that I was working on another book). Well, I have just about completed it. Yes, speedy fingers-on-the-keyboard in action here. I do like my little projects, and I most certainly am enamoured with writing, but this project took on a special sense of doing something more important than just writing about business decision-making. This project was to write a book about what it was like for two distant relatives who lived in the United States during the Civil War. First, to clarify something that I wrote previously, the subjects were not my Great Great Grandfather and his brother. No, I clearly buggered that up. They were my Great Grandfather and his brother, John Rieley and Frank Rieley.

First a little background. My Aunt Peg, who sadly passed away in 2005, and as the apparently self-appointed family historian, had collected a group of letters that John and Frank wrote home to their Mother during the Civil War. I had seen some of these letters years ago, and actually had a couple copies of them in my possession, along with other Rieley family memorabilia. But when Peg died, her best friend Sue sent me this rather voluminous carton containing transcripts of all the letters, along with military documents and photos from that period of time. When I received them, I read them voraciously (finally, after all this writing, I found a good place to use the word "voraciously" – well done me) and stared at the photos…and then I put them all back into the carton and taped it securely so that one day my sons would be able to have them. Shortly after this, I sort of electronically met Betsy, who is the Grand-daughter of another line in our family, and she started sending me more family information from the Civil War times. Then, not long ago, I was talking to a friend who lives near London who had written a book about aerial photography during the First World War. I mentioned to Nicholas that I had this veritable treasure trove of letters from the American Civil War and he suggested that I do something with them. I pondered his comments, but probably was distracted at the time by some other project that I was focused on. And then a few weeks ago, stimulated by something, I re-opened the carton and decided that this was the time to compile them into a book.

When I become involved in a project, I do really get into it. "Getting really into it" means that I can be like a dog with a bone and short of a tsunami rushing madly toward Sol y Mar, not much will cause me to lose focus. Well this project was like that, but on steroids. This was more than just an exercise in writing…this was real stuff about real people in a pretty depressingly desperate situation; and the real people were relatives of mine. So after sorting through the contents of the carton, one night I cranked up one of the computers and started typing. I just finished writing the book yesterday and thought that this was indeed something worth sharing.

Doing this book was far more challenging for me than writing the other books I have done. This is probably due to several things. First, when I have written my previous books, the process sort of looked like this. Step 1. Think about what to write. Step 2. Visualise what it would look like. Step 3. Type. But this book required very little thinking about what to write – John and Frank had written the letters already. Okay, so I did have to "see" what the finished book would look like, but that was pretty much driven by the letters, so all I really had to do was input into my computer what the brothers said in their letters…and this is why it was so challenging. The letters were written long-hand in the late 1860's when literacy probably wasn't the most important thing; especially if you were slogging up some mud-filled hill with your sabre drawn, dodging musket fire from the enemy. So even though my computer's spell-check programme kept vomiting error messages at me faster than that guy fell from the balloon on the edge of space the other day, I kept at it…and now I am done.

So right now you may be thinking, *"I wonder what he will do with the book now that he is done?"* A good question. There is no doubt I will publish it, but am not too concerned about that right now. For now I am a bit to occupied writing to you and pondering what I will do next.

And just because you are nice enough to read all these ramblings, I thought I would share one of the letters with you. This letter was written by my Great Grandfather's brother Frank to his Mother. P.S. Don't take out your red pencil…all I did was write up the letters as they were written.

Pittsburg Landing, Tenn.

Camp Shiloh

May 7, 1862

Dear Mother:

Received your letter of the 8th a week after date and was very glad to hear from home and also to hear you were all well. The reason I did not answer it then was that I expected we would cross the Tennessee River and I did not want to write until after we crossed it. We are on the other side of the river for about three weeks, scouting and guarding a telegraph line. We crossed to this side on the 25th to Pittsburg Landing. It is composed of two log houses one of which is the postoffice.

We camped on the battle field of Shiloh the first night. The next day we moved about three miles and rejoined our division. We could not see much signs of the battle except on the trees which were full of bullet holes, and some of them cut in two by cannon balls. The graves were very thick. I saw one hole where there were twenty of our boys buried. The men who were in the battle told me some holes had fifty buried in them. Our men did not half bury the Secesh soldiers. I saw where one was buried whose hands stuck out. I went over to the 41st Ohio last week and saw Dick Neville. He was in the fight but was not hurt. He feels first rate and is ready for the next fight. Michael Miller was wounded in the arm. He started for home soon after the fight, so I suppose you have seen him before this. We moved to our camp here on the 29th. We camped about six miles from Pittsburg Landing and about twelve from Corinth, and two miles from the Mississippi line. I was on the picket line night before last and was in Mississippi.

There is a report in camp today that Corinth is being evacuated, but we do not know for sure. If it is, we will have to follow them three or four hundred miles further I suppose. I should a good deal rather fight them here than follow them three hundred miles further, and then have to fight them. I think that the next time they are whipped, it will finish them.

I am well and in good spirits. We were paid off today for two months and I will send twenty five dollars home with this letter. Our Chaplain is going home on furlough and I will send it with him to Monroeville and he will send it by express to the same directions as before. If you get this and the money, write and let me know.

Give my love to all.

Frank Rieley

In the past couple of days have been adding foot-notes (more about that in a minute) and an overview of the Civil War action that their two respective units saw during the conflict. And then today, whilst going through my treasure-trove of information about them, I came across a photocopy of a three-page letter than Frank's mother had written to a Mr. Graham, who apparently was the person who convinced Frank that enlisting was a good thing to do.

The good news about this find was that it was a copy of the actual handwritten letter, as opposed to the previously typed transcriptions I had been working with for the letters themselves. The bad news was that it was bloody hard to read. But, a project is a project, and I have always believed that once a project is begun, it must be driven to its completion. So after several hours, and the assistance of a huge magnifying glass (and then the application of common sense to the word choices), I managed to sort it all about; and then put it into the book as yet another appendix item. Am feeling pretty well chuffed about it.

Now, the reason that I earlier said "more about that in a minute." After completing the transcription of the letters themselves, I was in a pretty good mood and told a few people about what I had been up to. One of these people is a good friend who lives in the UK. Nicholas is the author of a fabulous book about aerial photography during the First World War (The Western Front from the Air, in case you are interested), and quite a while ago, we had been talking about historical records and I had mentioned that I had all these letters, but really wasn't sure what to do with them. He had encouraged me to put them into a book. So, when Nicholas phoned me to say hi at about the same time I had more-or-less finished the book, I told him that I had indeed written a book about the letters. He then mentioned that in a few days he was going to see his publisher to talk about his book and wanted to know if was okay with me if he mentioned my project. I said *"Sure, why not"* but expected that his publisher would just chuckle or at least avoid using language like *"Oh, cute,"* or *"So?"* But later rang me to tell me that the publisher did want to talk with me about "Letters Home," and the next day in a phone call, I was told that they did indeed want to publish it. Nice...and perhaps one of the easiest publishing arrangements I have ever made. Now, the foot-note thing. The publisher did say to me that he would like me to foot-note selected words in some of the letters, and add the "action" record of the brothers units, and this is why the book is now a tad fatter than it was before. Overall however, I think the publisher was right and I do feel even better now about the project than I did before...which was pretty flippin" good then so I am feeling extremely chuffed now.

By the way, Frank's mother was none to happy about him enlisting, as can be seen in her letter...which I thought I, as a parent, would share with you.

Wednesday evening, Sept. 4th, 1861

Mr. Graham,

Sir

Having heard that you and Mr. Clark advised Frank to go and enlist I should like to have you let us know if you can where he is. No doubt if you were interested in his going away you were also enough interested where he went and in what regiment and company he has enlisted. After having advised him to go it is quite likely he would confide in you that much that he would tell you of his whereabouts. Of course I would not wish to concern you in the least if you are not to blame but if Frank was controlled by what you said to him in regard to his being so suitable a young man you ought to have consulted whether his mother was willing first and not begin to praise him and advise him to go.

I supposed he was taught at Sabbath school to obey God's laws in preference to any others and had he learned them he would know that one was to obey his parents and I think you as <u>professing Christian men</u> ought not to persuade him to break these. I have reared Frank with as much care for him as Mrs. Clark has her son and it is just as hard for me to part with him as for her to part with George or as it should be for your mother to see you or your brother go off to be engaged in this act of taking other men's lives and sending poor souls into eternity perhaps unprepared to meet the living God. If that is what your Sabbath school teaches I think it high time to with draw my other boys from it that they may not in <u>Sabbath school</u> at least be taught such principles.

Frank has for so far been our obedient and good boy and had he obeyed his own impulses he would I think never have left home in the manner in which he did. He had not told us he was going or enlisted or anything of this kind and we have been to every camp and place around town where he would be likely to stay but could find nothing of him and if you know where he is you will confer a favour by letting us know.

Mrs. M. Rieley

The joys of parenthood. I assume that Mr. Graham's reaction when he read the letter was something like "*Ouch*" and apparently, deservedly so.

I previously wrote about how I had decided to move from La Antigua to Sol y Mar. Well, after almost four years, I am moving back to the village where this all started. This hasn't been the easiest of decisions, mainly because I simply adore living on the sea. But as I have often said, the key to making sound decisions is to make them at the right time, for the right reasons. Every time in the past few years when I have driven out to Puigpunyent to make sure my house is okay, I have stood overlooking the courtyard and felt how much I missed being there, and clearly, owning a home and renting another one is a bit daft…so…time to go back. And once I know I am doing the right thing, for the right reasons, at the right time, I don't see any reason to doddle around. I started packing a couple of days ago and the movers are coming on the 12th. I am, as if you couldn't tell, pretty chuffed about the prospects of being "home" again.

07

La Clinica, Otra Vez

2013

It is only hours away from yet another New Year. About nine or ten hours, but that isn't important. What is important is that tomorrow will be the start of something special for many of us, or at least we would like to think it will be. For me, 2012 was a year of many changes, some of them okay, some pretty great, and some just...well, different. I sold the lovely and comfortable Amélie; moved back to the incredibly special La Antigua; and met some pretty special people. Like most of us, 2012 was a year of loss as well, but dwelling on loss isn't a good thing, and seeing as how we only seem to get one chance at this life thing, I am going to get my creative juices flowing and make tomorrow the start of something pretty flippin' great. Now just to clarify a bit, this does not mean I am already working on next year's Christmas card (but I am thinking about what it might look like in all fairness).

Coming back to La Antigua was all part of the creative process for me. When David was here, and I had more-or-less indentured him into the "getting the house organised" effort, at one point, he asked me what this big tube was for. He was holding a rather long square tube that I had made several years go out of carton-pluma (foam core). I looked at what he was talking about and then flashed back to when I was considering the potential of the pañuela project (the scarf project). I had been thinking about a potential design and decided that the best way to communicate it the Italian company I was having make the prototype scarves was to make a full size water-colour of the design. So I found this massively large piece of watercolour paper and made the design. Shipping was going to be a problem as I couldn't find a commercially available shipping tube of the right dimensions, so I made one myself (as you do). I think David asked where the painting was, but I wasn't sure...until we looked in the tube. After scanning the design, the Italians had returned it to me and I simply put it away.

The next day, whilst in Palma, David and I took the painting to a framing shop. My vision was to have a frame made that was more-or-less compatible with the other frames I have littering the walls of La Antigua, but David (who apparently has inherited the "influencing gene," convinced me that something "different" was in order. So here it is hours before the New Year, and the framing company rang to tell me that the painting is all mounted in the frame, and due to the fact it is far too big for either Amelia or Miranda, they are bringing it out to the village in a couple of hours. (It is now several hours later, and the painting is here and hanging on the wall...and whilst the picture looks great (I think), the frame is just perfect for it.)

And because I am writing about artwork, I had mentioned another picture in the last chapter a cuadro doblado that I made. Well, truth-be-told, I wasn't the photographer of the two photos, but when I first saw them, I knew that they should be "together" in a cuadro doblado, so after getting permission from Samantha, who had taken the original photos I was using, I had them printed quite large and then proceeded to (carefully) make the folds. Of course, because the finished piece is very large, I then had to commission a local village carpenter to make the frame for it. (mono-colour, 115cm x 131cm). Perhaps the size and complexity of these two most recent additions to La Antigua will result in me producing things a bit smaller again...or drive me on to even bigger pieces.

So here we are, a new year and all the rest of our lives are just waiting in front of us. Will we (as in the Royal we), A) Continue to plod along, figuring that the life we have is what was dealt to us and we are stuck with it; B) Try to get better at whatever we have chosen to do with our lives, but often just giving up; or, C) Take advantage of the opportunity with the skills, brains, and hearts that we have and make a difference in both our lives and in those of our friends and family? It is amazing what we can accomplish in our lives...and with our lives if we only make the choice to do so. And on that almost lecture-like note, I wish you all a wonderful New Year, filled with joy and love and whatever you really want.

Normality is a term we all long for, well sometimes. Today, normality returned to La Antigua, or perhaps more appropriately, to me living in La Antigua again. Now to be fair, I must begin with a bit of context. It is winter here in Mallorca. Okay, let's begin...

Having said that, today did begin with a bit of a shock. I awoke to find....rain. Yes, even though it is early January, which by any account in this side of the equator is the middle of winter, the fact that when I looked out one of my bedroom windows I saw lluvia (YOO-VEE-A, rain) bucketing down as if I were at the bottom of Victoria Falls. Okay, so perhaps that is somewhat of an exaggeration, but it was raining and because I had three different groups of workers coming today, I wasn't too chuffed about it.

My "plan," and I do say my "plan" as if this was the way I actually expected the day to go; was to have my clever satellite internet guys show up at between 0900h and 0930h. Then around 1100h, I was expecting my fontanero (FON-TAN-ERO, plumber) to arrive to do something magical with a drain from the clothes washer that was acting as if there were a couple of meters of sludge in the drain line. And then around 1300h, the blokes delivering my first tonne of leña (LANE-YAH, firewood) at the house were scheduled to show up. But as we all know, the best laid plans of blah, blah, blah....

Just before 0900h, I received a phone call from the firewood guys. They were out in the street trying to figure out which house was mine. Buggers. I told them to wait a minute and I would be right out. Grabbing a jacket and umbrella, I scooted across the courtyard only to realise that I didn't have my key to unlock the courtyard entrance door. Back into the house for the key and then out the door in a flash that Superman would have marvelled at and there they were, parked at the bottom of my street trying to figure out how they could squeeze their camion (truck) up the narrow street to my door. I took a quick look and told them that it wouldn't fit. They said "good," and proceeded to attempt to back up the street.

I can remember years ago when I lived here, trying to back Amelia up the sloping narrow street, and all I did was bang off the walls on either side whilst at the same time, inhaling the rather pervasive odour of clutch that was about to burn up. So I just stood there in the rain, complete with my Barbour jacket, umbrella, and Wellies, looking very proper watching the two guys repeatedly jam their truck between the walls. After several attempts, they gave up and one of them walked over to me with a less-than-happy look on his face, muttering something about the street being too narrow for them. Well no shit.

So instead of parking in front of the Puerta Principal (main door) to the house, they left the truck on the street and proceeded to fill up large black rubber buckets with my firewood supply (that will probably only last me a month anyway as I do love having a fire going. And with a fireplace in both the sitting room and kitchen, I do tend to go through quite a bit of wood). There were only able to put three buckets in the wheelbarrow they had with them, and then trudge up Es Forn and into the courtyard, where they then proceeded to unceremoniously empty the buckets with the tried-and-true dumping method. So whilst they were making repeated trips back and forth, I was, as any well-intentioned homeowner would do, trying to stack the wood neatly. Of course the on-going rain meant that all my stacking efforts would mean I would have this nice set of rows of wet wood that I could then cover. Aaaaargh.

A tonne of leña takes about ten trips via the wheelbarrow and just about at trip three, the satellite guys showed up. They have been here before, so I just pointed to the kitchen doors and sent them up to the roof to do whatever they were going to do. (Note, still raining) As the last set up rubber buckets cleverly deposited their fill of wood onto my courtyard (my stacking was about 50% behind the unloading and dumping process), the plumber and his helper arrived. I did take a quick look up at the roof terrace to see if the satellite twins were having fun as they were adjusting the signal receiving disk (the rain was falling a bit harder now) and then paid the wood guys and rushed to the corner of the courtyard where the plumber was standing, trying to avoid becoming thoroughly drenched.

I had communicated with the plumber via email (and in Spanish, thank you very much) about the problem, but there, standing in the rain, he again asked me what the problem was, and yes, because he is Spanish, he asked me in Spanish. He said, *"¿Donde es tu problema?"* (Where is your problem?) and I think I said something like *"La desagua de mi lavadora no funciona."* (The drain on my clothes washer doesn't work.) He responded by giving me a look like *"No kidding, you brought me out in the rain to tell me what you already told me in your email? Where is the flippin" drain?"* Right...my mind suddenly was filled with the picture on the cover of the book *How to Make Friends and Influence People*. Well done James. I showed him where the washer was, and where the spin cycle water was supposed to exit the through the drain pipe, which was clearly plugged up. After 45 minutes, he somehow magically managed to remove two years of sludge that had packed in solid from lack of use and at the same time, the rain let up and the sun began to come out.

I was suddenly feeling pretty good about the morning. Yes, it had been a bit chaotic with everyone coming at the same time, but the firewood was more or less stacked up, the satellite internet doo-wah was more aligned, and my washer would be working better again. And the sun was starting to peak through the clouds a bit more. Of course, to accompany the feeling good thing was a feeling-a-bit-poorer feeling, but I would now be able to tick three things off my list of things that needed to be done at La Antigua. I was feeling so good, I decided this would be a good time to go to the village market, and because the sun looked like it might totally and completely displace the evil rain clouds, I decided to walk to the market...which I did. The rain didn't resume until I was about half-way home...just another winter day in the village. The return of normality.

2014

I can remember about four weeks ago pretty clearly. I was in a pretty good mood, standing in the courtyard in the sun, realising how terribly lucky I was. I can even remember at one point, listening to Van Morrison doing "There're Be Days Like This" and thinking to myself that Van was right, and thankfully so. Of course, that was before I contemplated the minor reality that whilst there are "days like this" in a good context, as well as "days like this" that are totally and completely un-adulterated pure shite. Within twenty-four hours, I would find out.

(Now just as an editorial sort of note...from this point on in this story, there are quite a few days I don't remember so I have reconstructed this rather depressing diary from conversations with the few people who were there at the time. This would also be a good time for you to go download "Day's Like This" by Van Morrison....Good survival music)

The next morning, I had a series of med-appointments. Nothing serious at all actually, but my right shoulder was getting all wonky so I had made an appointment for an MRI to see if the shoulder was just acting up or would require something more in line with surgery. My lumbar was also acting pretty sassy, and even though I put this down to its age (note I said "It's age",

Living on Rocks

and not "my age") I thought it best to have checked out to see if I should buy shares in some ibuprofena manufacturer or get it fixed. Then there was this pesky sore throat that I had been plagued by for a few days. The day after the dolor de garantha (sore throat) appeared, I began taking Amoxicilina, but the soreness didn't want to go away, and it made sense to have this checked out as well.

So, on this very sunny and warm Friday, we had driven into the city, making the rounds of medical facilities. By 1700, MLR and I were back at La Antigua and I was trying to figure out what I could actually eat that wouldn't feel like it was ripping up my sore throat and decided on eggs scrambled. Mary, who had been visiting, offered to whip up the eggs for me, and I settled down in front of my computer. Literally, within a minute or so of her bringing the plate of eggs to me and then disappearing back into to the kitchen to make something for herself, the room began to spin. Spin may not even be the right word, unless you think of "spin" in terms of a centrifuge running amuck. I learnt along time ago, when one feels that they are becoming dizzy, one of the best things to do is drop down to the floor enabling more blood to get to the brain, and probably avoiding falling down onto the floor. I had no time to do anything, and the next thing I realised was that some of the filing cabinets I have behind my desk were laying on their side. I couldn't figure out how they managed to get on their side, but sure enough, there they were. It was then I realised that the filing cabinets were just fine – I was lying in a heap on the unbelievably substantial baldosa floor. Oh right, I also realised at the same time that I was throwing up whilst laying on the floor. I did manage to call out and in a bit, Mary came rushing in to find me in not my best form I think. She told me later that at first she thought I had been throwing-up blood, but I moved my head a bit to find out that when I unceremoniously hit the baldosas, four places on my head and nose had nicely acted as shock-absorbers, and because head wounds bleed quite a bit, were making quite a mess on the floor.

We had the common sense to ring my doctor, who after hearing a short summary of what had occurred, immediately said "*Ir a la clinica*" (go to hospital). It wasn't "*If you have some time…*" or "*After you do the dishes and clean up his head, you may want to consider…*" No, Toni's message was pretty clear and within a minute or so, we were on the way to the Urgencies (A &E) of the hospital I had been at when I had GBS years ago.

Other than sitting in Urgencies waiting to be called on and watching little children stare at me (no doubt due to the fact that I must have looked a crash-test dummy with dried blood all over my face) the next couple of days were pretty unremarkable, as I look back at them now. Not unremarkable because I had listened to Eric Clapton in the 1960"s, but more unremarkable because nothing really happened. I felt during those days that I was in some hospital programme and telly. A doctor would come in the room (nice rooms, b-t-w), take my pulse, scribble something down on a scrap of paper,

James B Rieley

and walk out. Then an enfermera (nurse) would appear, take my temperature, check my pulse, connect me up to a new IV, and occasionally, wipe off some of the blood-mess that had really made a mess of my head. And then they released me. Mary kept asking me why I don't ask them to take a throat culture, as I reflect on it now, a logical thing to request but at the time, I just assumed that they knew what they were doing and whilst I still did have a sore throat, it was either lessening or I was just thinking it was lessening. Regardless, I was just happy to be going back home so didn't say anything. Mary flew back to the EEUU that morning, and after being released, I drove home shortly after mid-day, thrilled beyond belief that I was once again safe within the walls of La Antigua. That evening, I wasn't all that hungry, and actually don't remember eating anything, but I do remember feeling pretty knackered and going to bed around 2000h.

I slept pretty soundly, all the way until about 2100h (yes, here is where the sarcasm begins to seep into the story). I did manage to fall back to sleep and added another 30 mins or so to my sleeping total for the night. This pattern went on all night with this near constant cramping-like abdominal thing going on precluding any chance of getting some real rest. At some point, I do seem to recall thinking *"Errrr, I think I may have been released from la clinical a bit to early,"* but that thought quickly disappeared with the next wave of unbelievable pain that ripped through me. The good news (note: more sarcasm approaching) was that this only lasted until 0700h in the morning when I finally figured out that something was not right and decided to do something about it (other than hoping for a 747 to be dropped on my body from 42,000 metres).

By 0800h, I was in Amelia and slowly and cautiously, making my way back to the clinica. I say slowly and cautiously largely to placate the friends who have since bollocked me for driving in by myself. The reason I did not (pick any one you like) A) Call a friend to come and collect me and take me into the clinica; B) Ring an ambulance to come and take me in to Urgencies; C) Ring the local Policia to come and take me in to the clinica; or D) Hope that in the next few minutes, all the pain would disappear and my life would be okay again. Right. I might have actually opted out for option (D), but it would have been to complicated to both drive into Palma whilst at the same time watch overhead for pigs flying, which as we all know, would be demonstrated when highly ludicrous desires are thought of as potential realities at the same time. So I drove, slowly and cautiously *because I just needed to get to the clinica and that was all I could think of.*

I did make it to the clinica and unceremoniously staggered out of Amelia, leaving her smack in front of the door in a no parking zone. I do assume I turned her engine off, but am at the time wasn't really sure. This little chronicle gets very hazy here as I barely remember going into the building, much les what happened next. What I do remember is finding myself in a small UCI room (Intensive Care Unit) surrounded by a team of people in UCI uniforms, and my upper body pretty well covered with wires and connectors. I found out many days later that I also had restraints connected to my arms and legs as I was desperately trying to rip all the wires off of me and get out of the room. Could be safe to say I wasn't doing all that well.

Day-Two in the UCI. Okay, to be fair, this could have been day three, or even day six I guess....I really don't know. What I do know is that on this day, I began to realise what was going on and truth-be-told, I wasn't too overly happy. I do remember that I was in a lot of pain and no matter what position I tried to be in, it didn't provide any relief. I can also remember that just about the time I would be drifting off for a few minutes of desperately desired for sleep, someone from the UCI team taking care of me would come in, take some reading on my body, ask me a shedload of questions, and then proceed to tell me how good I was going. I can quite clearly remember one man from the team who said multiple times something to the effect of *"You must be so happy that you are doing so well."* I am still expecting to hear from his solicitor regarding the content of my tasteless replies. I can also remember seeing my friend Cris about this time. I couldn't at the time figure out how she was in the UCI care room, but there she was, and she told me that everything was going along well and that my Son David was there. This was even more confusing to me than everything else.

Quite a few years ago, I had made an arrangement with David that in case anything happened to me, I wanted him to jump on the first jet available and get his bum over to Mallorca. The key words to this semi-explicit agreement were *"anything happened to me."* I had always interpreted this to mean I had either just passed away or was about to. And now I am in a hospital that seems like it must have been designed and built by Lewis Carroll and my friend Cris (I was still trying to make sense why she was there) was telling me that David was there. My reaction wasn't all that good, and I think I told her that I was not happy he was there or something to that effect. I didn't find out for many days later that when it became apparent that I had gone ill (clearly I was ill), she had gotten in touch with David after being told by the head doc on my case, that if she had the contact information for my relatives, she had better get them over here as my prognosis was pretty grim and it was marginal that I would make it to the next day. Oh....okay, so when I heard this I realised that perhaps I was a bit more ill than I had previously assumed. None-the-less, I was pretty pissed off. I was ready to go laying in the sun on the roof terrace; ready to go driving Miranda on some winding but exceptionally fun mountain road; I was even ready to go standing in front of a flip-chart doing loops; but to let go in some environment which made no sense to me didn't seem right. Besides, at this point in time (I think), I still didn't even have a good grasp on what was going on with my body.

I do remember hearing the med team talking about a Liver infection, but when I first heard that (or think I heard that), I think I think I chimed in with *"Guess again lads, I don't even drink."* Then I heard the term "meningitis" and I think another couple of less-than-exciting medical terms, and whilst I would love to have this record spot-on accurate regarding my comments and reactions, as I think back about those days, it really is just a blur.

By Day Four (or Five?) I recall one of the med team dropping hints that they might be chucking me out of the UCI and send me to a "normal" room. This was the first point in this flippin' nightmare that I actually thought that things might be getting better. Please note that I said *"thought things might be getting better"* is the operative sentence and at this point, it was as if they were continually teasing me by increasing my hopes, only to have them be dashed within hours for some reasoning that was only clear to the people with UCI uniforms.

To quote Mr. Dylan; *"You don't need a Weatherman to know which way the wind's blowing."* My days and nights were the same. The level of pain barely seemed to change, regardless of the amount of pain meds that were flowing through one of the IV lines. The bed was abysmal and had a sagging trench that probably rivalled the Marianas Trench for depth and scope. The food choices (okay, the food was what they chose for me and I had no input, which at that point even I recognise made sense) were like the Oxford Dictionary's definition of "bland." Things were not good and, truth-be-told; they were beginning to look like they wouldn't be getting better. I wanted out of this place and was desperately trying to show that I was ready to be moved to a "normal" hospital room.

It was Day Six (Seven?) when I was finally chucked onto a gurney and sent upstairs (literally upstairs to a normal room as opposed to some metaphor for a pain free place, thank you very much). By now, I did have a pretty good grip on what had happened to me. Apparently I had some form of Liver infection (that they have no idea how I could have managed to contract). My body had been staving this off pretty well until I then got a sore throat. Then all hell fell in, and much like a house of cards, my defences began to fall faster than....well, pretty quickly.

I have been in this "normal" room now for just under four weeks and it appears I will be released completely next week sometime. My arms look pretty much like I could use them to strain pasta after all the IV lines and blood-test entry (exit) points. My body is about as pale as someone without a stitch of melanin standing in a snow-storm. But I am better. Not only, just to be clear, am I better, but I actually feel better and am so very keen on getting out of here and getting on with my life (which apparently isn't over quite yet).

And just in case you are wondering, yes, I did learn several really important lessons whist getting through this nightmare of a month. The most important lesson that we all need to remember is that, when it concerns your own health, you had better get your bum as active as possible and take charge or it will not end well. In my case, this meant that as soon as I was able to get a grasp on what was going on, I had to start asking questions. Admittedly, some of the questions were not well received by the docs but it is my life and I should be able to know what is going on with it. Every I was told they wanted to do a test or procedure, I would ask "*Why?*" and "*What will this tell you?*" I also tried to better understand how all the tests I was undergoing worked and what they were supposed to identify. Part of this little process of "*Ask a question, then ask a better question, and then still a better question*" proved to be especially beneficial after one of the enfermeras had come into my room to check my temperature last week.

Years ago, if you wanted to take someone's temperature, you would take this very narrow glass tube and put it under the tongue and wait for a minute or so. Extremely accurate, but not especially quick. Now, with the marvels of technology (and the rather obvious pressure to get more done in less time, hospitals use something a bit trendier to measure temperature. The glass tube has evolved into a phone-like handle with a digital readout and a conical tube that sticks in your ear. The staff person presses a button and after a couple of seconds, the unit sends out three adorable little beeps signalling that it has calculated your body temperature. Easy peasy. Well, sort of, I discovered. That night, the nurse was in my room and whipped out her temp-taker-doo-wah-thing. After a couple of seconds, it beeped, and she said, "*Oh James, tu tempuratura es muy alta.*" (*James, your temperature is quite high*). I asked her what was indicated and she said that the machine said it was 38.3. With 37c being the acceptable norm, this did seem high, so I told her I thought the machine was broken and could she please redo the test. She did and this time it indicated 36.7. Now I was really puzzled so asked for a third go and this time, the machine indicated 37.4. I said thank you and immediately wrote down the three very disparate readings. Now to some, this may not seem like a big deal, but when docs are making treatment decisions that are partially based on daily temperature variations, knowing that the machine that is recording the temps is accurate is pretty important. Now, every time a nurse comes in to take my temperature, they dutifully take it tree times and record them all. Quite obviously, I have explained all this to my docs and key nurses (and can't wait to get out of here and write a tasteful letter to the manufacturer of the temperature reader.

A couple other lessons learnt seem to be that (something we all know already) everything is connected to everything. My lumbar pain was most probably connected to the Liver thing and the sore throat. When one of them went totally wonky, the others fell like they were being sucked into a Black Hole.

When I look at the actual chronology of events with help as I don't remember so much of this, it is pretty clear that whilst I instinctively knew something wasn't exactly right, just popping Ibuprofena like they were M&M Peanuts isn't as smart as seeing someone who just may more about the whole health thing.

James B Rieley

Could life be better right now? Of course it could. I have just lost about a month of time for no apparent reason and my body will need a bit of care and exercise to recover from it. But more importantly, could things be worse right now? Of course they could. Life is full of choices and these are our choices to make...and if we choose not to make them, then we will just get what we get. Sorry, but I am just not up for that. Mr. Morrison had it so right....."*When all the parts of the puzzle start to look like they fit, then I must remember, there'll be days like this.*"

After three weeks back in the village – which once again does feel very much like "my" village – I thought it might be good to reacquaint you with Puigpunyent. After all, it has been about four years (most of them living in Bendinat at Sol y Mar) since I really wrote about what it is like to live here.

I was thinking about how to do this and for some rather bizarre reason, Clint Eastwood came to mind. Not really Clint Eastwood the actor, but to use a format that sort of follows one of his early movies. The movie was, "The Good, The Bad, and the Ugly." But due to the fact that even when I lived here previously, I don't think I ever saw anything ugly here, I think I will just settle on the first two categories of Eastwood's movie.

The Good

We have our own post office (Correos) here in the village. This means I no longer have to hop into Miranda or Amelia and drive half way to Andratx to post a letter. A very good thing.

The Bad

My village isn't exactly a metropolis (which in itself is a damn good thing) and it would be unreasonable to think that the local Correos would be open all day. Having said that, it is only open from 0800 – 1030 Monday through Friday, except of course when there is a holiday; and even after living in Spain for a decade, it does still seem like we have a holiday just about every week.

The Good

Puigpunyent has one of the most impressive recycling efforts in all of Europe. Within walking distance from La Antigua (shoot, everything in the village is within walking distance from my house), the recycling centre enables villages to actually feel as if they are making a positive contribution to saving the environment. Definitely a good thing.

The Bad

When I first lived here, you could just walk in (or drive in if you have too much to carry...which often happens, especially if you have just moved back to your house after being away for several years and had to do a lot of cleaning) and plop your recyclables into one of the many big containers that were plainly marked with what goes in it. But during my absence, the village fathers (or as we say here, the old boys) must have decided that too many non-villagers were using our centre so electric gates were constructed and now you need a pass-key to get in. Now the reality is that this isn't all that bad, but it does mean that if you walk all the way down there without your little plastic magnetic card doo-wah, you must then walk home and get it so you return and throw stuff away. Okay, fair enough. But for some reason the old boys also decided that the electric gates should not work between 1400h and 1600h. Not sure why that decision was made as the centre is largely unattended anyway...perhaps the random cats that prowl around it need a siesta.

The Good

As you may remember if you have been following me since the beginning, one of my prime movers for moving to the village was to ratchet up my Spanish. When I was living in Bendinat at Sol y Mar, the need to speak Spanish wasn't all that important. This was largely due to the fact that I rarely saw people on the street when I would go for my walks, and if I did, they were usually tourists who were lost, or some staff member of my excessively rich neighbours. But here in Puigpunyent, when I go for walks into the village centre (a term I use with my tongue firmly in my cheek as this village doesn't really have a "centre") to go shopping, I typically see a dozen people and everyone says hello. This is a wonderful thing and it always does make me feel as if I am part of the community I have chosen to live in.

The Bad

Puigpunyent is a village on the island of Mallorca, which is part of the Balearic Islands, which are part of Spain. So wouldn't you think that the language of choice would be Spanish? Think again. The native tongue of Mallorca is Mallorquin, which is just about the same as Catalan. So whilst everyone here does understand Spanish (even my version of Spanish which everyone says is very good but I still think it is rubbish), the locals all seem to speak Mallorquin to each other, and this language is about the most difficult thing on the planet to understand. Not exactly in the category of a "romance" language, Mallorquin is...well...not really pretty, but as they say, "when in Rome..." so I suppose I will have to start paying more attention to learning and speaking what the locals have had since birth. This should be about as much fun as getting polio.

The Good

The village has its own sports centre, complete with a seriously large pool, several tennis courts, and a full-sized football pitch.

The Bad

It is (our version of) winter...and the pitch is dirt, not grass...but I only walk past it so it really isn't my problem.

The Good

I just found out that some clever entrepreneur has made an arrangement with the Ajuntament (town hall, so to speak) to cover the village with Wi-Fi. This is a brilliant move and should be a successful venture (and be a good back-up system if the satellite internet signal I now use ever goes all wonky).

The Bad

I can't seem to find out whom to talk to in order to test out the village Wi-Fi system.

The Good

I get to live here.

The Bad

Can't think of a single thing....well, perhaps living on a smaller rock?

2015

Traditions are good things I guess. They seem to be solid and add a bit of comfort to our lives. We all seem to have them, and that alone could cause one to think that they must be relatively nice to have. We have traditions relating to holidays – we may go to Grants house for special holiday dinners, or we may open presents a bit earlier than our friends. We may always wear the same thing on the first day of class, or after we survive the first day of class, we may go to the same pub with the same friends each term. These repetitive patterns of behaviour, over time, represent traditions. Quite often, the reason that something is a tradition is that we have planned and planned and planned to make whatever it is very special; something that will become a special memory that we will want to relive; and when we do, it becomes the start of a new tradition.

Sometimes however, traditions just sort of evolve over time without any pre-planned idea. You know what I mean: "X" occurs, and because of it, we react to it and do "Y" for some reason. If and when "X" happens a second time, and we do "Y" again as a result, it can be the start of a tradition. Every time "X" happens in the future, we sort of do "Y," *or a variation of "Y"* for some reason. Often the rationale for why we do "Y" when "X" happens is lost, which simply leaves the rationale as, *"We do "Y" when "X" happens because it is a tradition."*

Personally, I would like to think that I don't have all that many traditions. Having said that, I am aware that there are several things that I do that are directly interconnected with events, which because I have done them more than once or twice, do seem to be traditions. One of them has been writing an essay during or after some form of less-than-usual medical experience.

I started doing this about eight or nine years ago after spending several weeks in Clinica Palma Planes here in Mallorca. The reason behind doing this the first time was, I suppose, my desire to keep friends and family who, in some cases, lived thousands of miles away, more or less informed with what was going on. I was very aware that if I didn't explain all that was happening, my friends and family that were not with me could come to some conclusions based on bits and pieces of information; conclusions that were "very wide of the mark." This could cause them undo worry, so I, at the time, decided to write a little essay about my experience. That essay – "Patients and Patience" – was not only great fun to write, but it also was a good way to make sense of the not-so-great experience for me.

Then last year, I wrote "Days Like This" after another less-than-fun medical experience. This essay was a bit shorter than the first one, which I do find strange as the time spent in hospital was more than twice as long. I think I had actually hoped that, even though I do love to write, that my second hospital-based-surprise-event would be the last. But here I am, lying in a bed in Palma Planes again, so in the best desire to not want to slag off what appears to be a tradition, I am writing again.

Ever since my little hospital experience of 2013, I really have put effort (effort, as in serious effort) into living healthier. I made the conscious effort to exercise more, to eat better, and to just take care of myself. Even now, I find it interesting that years ago, whilst facilitating a conference on making choices, I was standing in front of a group of people telling them that everything we do in our lives, and everything we experience, is a result of choices we make. One of the things I had said to them was that *"Everyday we make choices about our physical, emotional, and spiritual health."* I also said something like *"The only way to have any sense of physical, emotional, and spiritual health is to make the conscious choice that you want to have it."* I had the participants at the conference move into groups of three, and then tell each other their own story, and then, if they wanted to, verbally make the conscious choice to be physically, emotionally, and spiritually healthy. I was feeling pretty good about this little exercise, but as I walked around the room, I noticed that in one of the groups of three, there was a woman who wasn't doing well. Being a good little facilitator, I stopped to ask if everything was okay.

At that point, the woman who I thought wasn't doing well began to cry quite openly and another member of her group told me what had happened. They were taking turns telling their individual stories and when it became time for the woman, she blurted out that a couple of weeks before the conference, she had been told by her doctors that she had terminal cancer. At this point, the woman sobs that whilst she would love to be able to make the conscious choice to be healthy, that wasn't really an option anymore for her. As a facilitator, these are the times when you wish you had become a librarian, but as I think being a librarian could be pretty boring these days, I decided to crank up my best facilitator skills and opened my mouth. *"So, just to make sure I understand, you would like to make the conscious choice to be healthy, physically, emotionally, and spiritually, but your doctors have said you have terminal cancer. Is that more-or-less right?"* The woman was pretty deeply in sobbing mode again, and the two others in the group were looking at me as if I was up for the Most-Insensitive-Person-On-the-Planet award. The woman did bob her head a few times, which I took to mean that I did have the situation right. Then I went for it.

"Again, I apologise, but I want to make sure I understand. Did your doctors say that you would die this afternoon?" Now the looks of the other two people in the group shifted to a look that normally would accompany a mental model of "you daft insensitive prick." The woman was startled apparently and her sobbing stopped long enough for her to say that her doctors had told her that she had perhaps 6 months to a year before she would pass away. *"Ahhh, thank you for sharing that"* I chimed in with. *"So let me ask you a question. Whilst I am really sorry that you have been given this news, I don't understand why, if you want to, you cannot make the conscious choice to be healthy for the time you have remaining. If you want to live as healthy as possible, physically, emotionally, and spiritually, you can still choose to do so for that time, can't you?"*

I just hate it when what I tell others they can or should do comes back to me as something I can or should do, but after being released from hospital last summer, this is what happened to me. Those words about making health choices words sort of flashed in front of my eyes, and I did make the conscious choice that I wanted to be healthier. This is where the whole daily-semi-marathon-ish forced walking thing came from. This is where the swimming-as-often-as-I-could thing came from. And this is where I discovered that you can actually cook green vegetables and eat them...who would have guessed that? After a year of this, I admittedly, was pretty chuffed. I had made the right choices and felt healthier. And then I started getting tired.

I began to notice that whilst doing my almost-as-fast-as-a-speeding-bullet walks around the village, I would become a bit tired and feel pressure on my upper chest at times. My assumption at these times was that I was, after all, getting older and as my goal was to get the exercise and not to necessarily break any village walking speed records, doing the walk faster and faster wasn't as important as just doing the walk. So I would slow down a bit and then wouldn't feel the tired or pressure feeling. Life was good.

When MLR arrived in September, I noticed that I was staying at home whilst she was doing her walking/running tours of the village, but wasn't overly concerned as much as a tad frustrated that I didn't feel up to doing all the hills around the village. Things sort of changed when I contacted one of my doctors to make an appointment for my semi-frequent blood tests.

I have known Toni since my little GBS experience years ago. I knew something was amiss but had no idea what it was and by chance, had picked his name out of the Paginas Amarillas at random. After struggling into his office for the first time, he asked me some questions, told me to try to do some stretches and squats, and then announced that the thought he knew what I had. As it turns out, Toni has two medical specialities: Parkinson's Disease

Living on Rocks

and the evil Guillain-Barré Syndrome…which was what I had. Toni literally saved my life and our relationship shifted over the years from just doctor-patient to good-friends-who-happen-to-be-doctor-and-patient. So, I made the appointment and on Wednesday of last week, MLR and I went into the city, she to do a spot of shopping and me to have a bit of blood sucked out of my body.

I have had so many blood tests since my GBS experience that I swear my veins sort of yield themselves up whenever I enter a medical facility, and last week was no different. Then, as part of ensuring that the non-returning GBS is truly non-returning, Antonia connected me to a machine that was shocking. No, literally. She had put straps on my left wrist and just below my elbow and then after smiling at me, quickly turned a dial on the machine and some serious amperage when whizzing down my arm. We played that game a few times, then she moved the wrist-located strap down to my individual finger tips and did it for a few more times. I was then given the ultimate pleasure of having the game played on my right arm. I was about to tell her where all the WMD"s were hidden in Puigpunyent, just to avoid the possibility of water-boarding being the next fun thing, when Antonia said, "*Es todo*." (That's all.) Nice. I was about to leave when I asked if I could talk to Toni for a minute. She explained he had to go out (hard to believe that there are people who are actually sick on the island) and asked if she could relay a message for me. I said sure, and mentioned that when I do my walking, I seem to somehow acquire this pressing feeling on my upper chest that goes from shoulder to shoulder. She gave me sort of a quizzical-are-you-out-of-your-mind look and told me to go to Urgenicias…and tell them…and do it that day.

I rang Mary Lee, who was at the Mercado Oliver, and then walked down to meet her there. She asked how much fun I had at the doctors and being a good partner, told her what Antonia had said. MLR said that we should just treat the day as a doctor-day, and after walking back to where Amelia was parked, we drove to Clinica Palma Planas.

Upon entering the Urgencias area (the equivalent of an A & E department only without desperately ill people laying about in beds because the department is understaffed), I went up to the desk and told them what I had told Antonia, and within a dozen minutes or so, was ushered into a consultation room, where I repeated my story. Nice looks of concern, followed by instructions to go to another (a different) consultation room. In this room, my blood pressure was taken along with a serious of pretty comprehensive medical questions. Just about the time boredom is setting in for me, I am hustled off to a room where they take a few dozen litres of blood (yes, this could be a mild exaggeration) and then plopped into a silla con ruedas (SEE-YA CONE ROO-EH-DAS, wheel chair) and whizzed down to x-ray. There they took a couple of chest x-rays and then wheeled me back to a waiting room in the Urgencias department so I could play Solitaire on my phone whilst waiting.

Three games later, I was ushered into another consultation room where the doc on duty said that they blood test and x-ray both looked good, but he thought I should do a stress test. I did my best to put forth a nice and solid "for joy for joy" outward appearance, but may have failed a bit. This could be due to the fact that in the past, I have taken stress tests and have found that they tend to induce stress, so this doesn't seem logical to me. The doc that was telling me that he thought I should have a stress test didn't have any urgency in his voice, so I said that yes, of course I would have one, but not that afternoon, thank you very much. I signed eighty-seven disclaimers of liability (a possible exaggeration I suppose) because I wasn't going to have the test the same day. On the way out of hospital, we did stop in at Patient Services and told my friend Santiago what was going on and he said he would make the stress test appointment for me. Good man, thank you very much. We then went home and talked about what all this medical stuff was about. This conversation didn't take all that long as we still didn't know what was going on, but figured out that we would know the next day.

The following day, we went back to hospital arriving about 15 minutes early for the stress test. After sitting in a waiting room for about 30 minutes (bastards, they probably make you sit and wait just to build up the level of stress), I was ushered into a room where a doctor took an ECG, followed by being taken into the evil treadmill room. I twisted my mouth into the complimentary "*Ahhh, the treadmill*" expression, but it may have looked suspiciously like "*Ahhh, the fucking treadmill*." We (the doc there, the staff person there, and myself) went over the procedure, which, if you have never had the opportunity to take one of these, kind of goes like this.

1. You stand on the treadmill rubber track.
2. They wire you so they can monitor your vital signs.
3. They turn the treadmill on and you begin to walk.
4. Every couple of minutes, the speed increases, as does the elevation angle of the walking surface.
5. You desperately try to not be thrown off the machine as the treadmill path goes up to about 150 kph (yes, this could possibly be a slight exaggeration).
6. They turn off the machine and you gasp for air and softly curse the doc and the technician for being cruel to you.

I have had treadmill stress tests previously and as they were wiring me up, I was trying to remember how long I lasted before running out of breath, but before I could remember, the machine started and the fun began. A few minutes later, the machine thankfully slowed down and I was put on a chair to catch my breath. This was followed by the technician spraying something under my tongue (which turned out to be nitro glycerine), which was the clue to me that something wasn't especially good about the test results.

Living on Rocks

Later, once I could again breath, the doc said that he wanted me to have an angiogram.

Whilst I had never had one of these, I knew what it was all about. For the uninitiated, an angiogram is where they slide a catheter in through a large vein, in my case, near my wrist. The catheter sneaks its way up to your heart and then through the magic of technology and chemicals, the person administering the test can visibly see if there are any arterial blockages. I didn't have to ask why the doc wanted me to do this test, as I knew that an arterial blockage would explain the pain I had been feeling in my upper chest, and usually was an indicator that a stroke or heart attack were looming.

The attending doctor made it perfectly clear, first in Spanish, and then in a smattering of English, that the plan was to look for and possible blockages in arteries near the heart, and if any were found, he would then push a stent up the catheter to the blockage spot and then inflate it. This, just as a side note, changes the procedure from an angiogram to an angioplasty. The inflated stent (sort of a wire mesh tube) would hold the artery open, allowing a proper blood flow, which would be a good thing. He asked me if I had any questions; I said no; and he got on with it.

I, someone who loves machines and technology and how they work, thought that this would be kind of a fun test to take because I knew that the patient gets to see the monitor showing the catheter winding its way through the body. Well, I did get to see the catheter and I was able to see the contrast liquid as it was dispersed through the catheter, but I struggled to understand how to spot some of the blockages.

When it was over, the doctor gave me a less-than-smiling-expression and proceeded to tell me that he didn't install any stents because the test showed that I would need between 9 of them, and at that point, using stents seemed highly inappropriate. I was sort of mystified as he was saying this as I had assumed that if there were more than a blockage or two, there would be a greater reason to install the stents. He explained that because I had so many blockages/arterial restrictions, it would make more sense to have heart bypass surgery. Fucking hell.....

Things suddenly began to happen in quick succession, but as this is Spain, this would not continue for long. I was checked into the hospital as a patient. Boom. I was taken to a hospital room. Boom. I was given a hospital gown. Boom. I was given dinner. This warranted a "pfft" rather than "boom" I found after taking the lid off the food tray that was brought to my room.

Saturday was spent in the very-nice-but-horrendously-hospital-feeling hospital room doing absolutely positively nothing. We had been told that the cardiologist and the surgeon (who I will undoubtedly refer to as "the cutter" later in this story, even though I am sure he will not look like either Eliot Gould or Donald Sutherland) would come to talk to us at some point during the day, but only the cardio showed up. Sitting there waiting is pretty boring but the good news is that I was the only one that had to actually be there. Mary Lee had the common sense to drive home to have a bit of a break, although "a bit of a break" included, she told me later, watering everything in the gardens, doing some wash, packing some clothes and driving back. Not exactly a "break."

Sunday was almost as boring as Saturday was, with the minor exception that it was Formula 1 day and the telly in my hospital room did have the F1 race in my choice of English or Spanish. MLR had walked over to a local workout gym for a few hours of spinning and whatever else those healthy people do. Then some friends stopped in and chatted for a while, and whilst it is great to do something, at this point, what I really wanted was to just get on with it all. If the heart bypass operation was what was required, then let's just go do it.

I really shouldn't complain, and I certainly don't want to make it seem that lying about in hospital was terrible. It isn't terrible at all, just boring. The days waiting for the cutter to decide when we do the operation are filled with "preparation for the surgery." Right. Preparation seems to mean an inordinate number of blood pressure tests; an injection into my belly before each meal that I believe I was told was an anti-coagulant; a hand-full of pills, and a low-salt diet. Sounds like all sorts of fun, doesn't it? In between this regime of pills and shots and shit food, I spend time reading, watching the news on telly, and talking to friends who try to assure me that heart bypass operations are so commonplace now there really isn't much to worry about. Actually, I am not worried. Have no doubt, I would rather have the stent option but I suppose that there is a limit as to how many stents make sense, so the operation it is.

Monday, and things should begin to happen. Well, at least this would be the day in which we had more answers to the ever-increasing number of questions that keep popping up. Shortly after my breakfast (and I do use the term quite loosely here) was delivered, a cardiologist came in and introduced himself. A very informative visit and he said that the cutter would be here later in the day to discuss the details of the operation. Fair enough. So now I am sitting in my room, not doing much of anything other than writing this part of my little health essay for 2014 (and thanking Steve Jobs for incorporating iTunes into his computers and phones).

The cutter was just here (and no, he did not look like either Gould or Sutherland). He actually looks like a good Uncle that we would all like to have. Everyone we had spoken to during the day who asked who my surgeon was rabbited on about the fact that this guy was the best, so meeting him was almost pre-destined to be a good experience and other than the fact that he didn't show up until well past 2100h, his visit was welcomed. If you know me, you probably realise that I am the kind of person who would rather "know" than be in the dark about something. (This is where some of you

Living on Rocks

might be guffawing hysterically) I don't have a big need to be in control, but I don't like to "not know" what is going on and the past several days of wondering what the surgery would actually entail and when it would be had been a real pisser. So when the doc (he may be a cutter, but after meeting him, he is far more than that in our estimation) walked into the room and introduced himself and asked if we had any questions, we pummelled him with them (but in a courteous way, of course).

We went through the basics of the operation:

- I lie on the table and someone puts me to sleep.
- I lie there and the doc cuts through the chest wall a bit.
- I continue to lie there and he separates my rib cage.
- As I am by now becoming expert at laying there doing nothing, I will carry on whilst the doctor will reach into the small circular opening with his little metal tweezers, being careful not to touch the sides, which would ring the buzzer and make the red light on my nose flash...no....wait...that is the game Operation. Skip this bullet-point completely.
- I, who will have become quite proficient in demonstrating my lying-there-skills, will continue to do so, and the doc will take a vein or two from one of my legs and put them (the veins, not the legs) in my chest, bypassing the wonky veins/arteries that have caused all this.
- I, in my final operating theatre contribution to the procedure, will remain lying there whilst the doctor sews everything up and then has a cervesa (beer) or two. (He didn't actually say that is what he would do, but if I was doing all the work and the other person was just lying there, I would sure as shit consider going out for a drink or two afterward).

We then asked a few non-process questions about the operation:

- When the operation will take place: Thursday afternoon or evening. It is now only Monday so waiting until Thursday seems like pretty grim prospects, but at least we now know. By Thursday I should be pressing the limits on the Bored-O-Meter.
- Number of bypasses: most probably three, but could be four. At least three is a Fibonacci number, so that is a good thing.
- Length of surgery: four hours probably, but you never know. Seeing as how I will be totally under, I guess I won't care.
- Length of time in UCI (intensive care): about two fun-filled days. Note the sarcasm in the words "fun-filled".
- Length of time before I can get the f**k out of the hospital and go home: maybe a week, maybe a little longer, all depending on whether or not I am a good little patient. Don't even think it.

So, more or less, all good news. Well, okay, maybe I should say, So, all good news because now we have a clue as to what is going to happen and when it will take place…which is damn good news.

You will love this little footnote: Remember earlier when I wrote that after having the blood test and electrical shock nerve test in my doctor's office, I had said that he wasn't able to see me because he had to go out? Well, as I was typing some of this yesterday (of course I have my computer in hospital), I received a text message from Toni. My first reaction was that he was concerned about me and was going to come and visit, but as it turned out, he sent the text message from a hospital room just down the hall from my room. The reason that he wasn't in his office on the day that I was there was that he had suffered a mild heart attack and he was going to have the same surgery I will be having. Unflipinbelievable….

08
A New Rock

2016

Leaving Mallorca has not been easy, but as I said when I told friends, *"You cannot discover new lands if you are afraid to lose sight of the shore."* As a sailor, I love sailing the most when I so far off shore that I cannot see it anymore, so this move has made all the sense in the world to me. Moving almost 7000 km to a country where I only know a few people is clearly "losing sight of the shore" I have come to know and love. But after taking a couple of flights after weeks of getting ready, I am finally home. Of course, the key word here is "home."

When I moved to Puigpunyent in Mallorca, I really did feel at home. And in my dozen or so years there, it was a wonderful home. But at one point, it became clear to me that it was time to move along and after a pretty nice year living overlooking the sea in Illetes, I am now "home" again. After successfully applying for legal residency in the British Virgin Islands last autumn, my application was approved and MLR and I flew down in February to see if this would feel like home for me. After visiting several islands, it became clear that "home" would be Virgin Gorda.

Whilst Virgin Gorda is the second largest of the BVI, this ranking needs to be put into context. The British Virgin Islands consists of about 60 islands, 16 of which are inhabited. The BVI has a combined area of about 153 square kilometres, and for a frame of reference, Ibiza itself is more than three times as large as all of the BVI combined. With a population of a bit over 32,000, the BVI has been a British territory since 1672. Our capital is Road Town, on the island of Tortola.

When I said that my new home is in Virgin Gorda, that was a tad misleading. My new home is a sailboat and she is moored about 150 meters off the coast of Virgin Gorda. The entire concept of actually living on-board a boat may seen foreign to many, but for me, it is more of a déjà vu experience. In this case however, there is a pretty big difference. When I have lived aboard previously, I usually had a land house or flat that I could retreat to if the need arose. But now Saphir will be my only accommodation, my only protector, and my only retreat. Saphir will be home. Having said that, living on-board Saphir is not exactly tough duty.

Saphir does have all the comforts of home, and over time, I will try to share with you how this home is different than where you live. For now, however, and for non-sailor friends, Saphir is like a three bedroom, two bath home. Big sitting room, great office, pretty fabulous kitchen, and an outside terrace that overlooks…well, it overlooks the entire flippin' world. Living on Saphir will be the latest in a pretty great line of floating homes. First there was Peacemaker (summers, on the very long Lake Michigan), then Angelina (Barcelona and Mallorca), then Amélie (Puerto de Andratx), then another Angelina (last summer in Puerto de Andratx) and now Saphir, in the North Sound of the British Virgin Islands.

I had thought about writing quite a bit more today, but the sea beckons and I think it is time for a swim.

According to the online Merriam-Webster dictionary, paradise is defined as *"a place of great beauty and perfection"* or *"any place or condition of great satisfaction, happiness, or delight."* In Dr. Rieley's EUDSIS (Exhaustive and Unexpurgated Dictionary of Seriously Important Shit,) the definition is, "being on Saphir in the BVI." But enough about that….here are some musings from the North Sound.

On day two of being here, I needed to go into Spanish Town (on the other side of Virgin Gorda), so I took the water taxi to Gun Creek (really loving all these names left over from pirate days), then was met by Nigel. Nigel is a young lad who drives a taxi here on the island. MLR and I met him when we were here earlier in the year, and I had made arrangements with him to be my driver when I needed to get some place on land. After getting off the water taxi and walking through the terminal (Gun Creek is one of the Customs Offices in the BVI), I saw Nigel and walked over and sat in his car. Wanting to make a good impression, I went full on courteous.

Me: *"Good morning Nigel, how is your morning?"* whilst extending my hand to shake his hand.

Nigel: *"Good, James"* whilst extending a fist to me.

Me: *"Really? Nigel, really?"* said with a look of scepticism on my face.

Nigel: *"Hey man, you are now one of us,"* and with a big smile, kept his fist clenched until I reciprocated. I trust he won't be too terribly disappointed when dreadlocks do not appear on my head.

The British Virgin Islands include a shedload of little, uninhabited islands. This results in a myriad of bays (calas), harbours, and coves. There is no doubt why the likes of pirates Calico Jack Ratham, Edward Teach, Ann Bonny, Israel Hands, and Benjamin Hornigold loved this part of the world.

This first week on-board again has been pretty much dedicated to settling into a routine. The biggest challenge of settling into a routine is figuring out what that routine should be. After the initial few days of discovering what wasn't working after non-use for the past several months since last here, and whilst the list was not all that long, it was polluted with nuisance tasks. The gas line for the hob and oven didn't want to flow, outboard motor on the tender decided to go on strike, and there were quite a few things that I couldn't find. But by the weekend, things were ticking along pretty well and the new routine began to take shape. Wake up, shower (well that is

Living on Rocks

actually go for a morning swim), have some tea and toast, ponder the state of the world (that usually takes place whilst on another swim), make sure things are put away in their proper places, check over the outside of the boat (which, because the boat is in the water, does involve yet another swim), lunch, relax (from the stress of all the morning's activities, of course), do some other boat stuff. Then it is just about dinnertime and time to sit in the cockpit and read. It might also include going for a swim.

Time seems to be different here than it was in Mallorca. Oh, have no fear, it still does have twenty-four hours and everything, but where Virgin Gorda is longitudinally as compared to artificial time zones means that the sun sinks pretty quickly after 2130h, but comes back about 0500h. With the sun going down so apparently early, even as the longest day of the year is quickly approaching, the early evening is a perfect opportunity for a sailor who happens to be on land at the time. That perfect opportunity does involve rum. One of the reasons this is a good thing is that the staff of the BEYC will take you back to your boat in one of their launches if your rum consumption becomes a bit blurred. Nice customer service to go with their nice rum drinks.

Several days before MLR left for her home in the states and I began my "flights" here, we did ship a collection/pile/group of boxes to each respective destination. Most probably because I studied geography in school, the routing that the boxes followed amazes me. I do understand the hub distribution of shipments concept, but geeez...Palma to Barcelona, to de Llobreg (Spain), to Koeln (Germany....clearly the wrong direction), to Newark (EEUU), to Louisville (a bit far off track I would have thought), to Carolina (Puerto Rico), to St. Thomas (US Virgin Islands...which is almost walking distance from the BVI if it weren't for all the water). So it does appear that the boxes are at least close. Having said that, am a bit terrified about placing a wager when they actually will arrive.

Random information, number 144; today, whilst sitting in the cockpit reading (more about that in a sec), the usual peace that envelopes the mooring basin was disturbed by one of the delivery vessels bringing some serious heavy equipment to this part of Virgin Gorda. As I am pretty confident of telling you previously, we have roads in parts of Virgin Gorda, but there is this very narrow strip of land just to the south of where Saphir is, and the rest of the island. The very narrow strip of land is also very low; as in, there is no road connecting the two parts of the island. So whenever something needs to be delivered here, it must come by boat. My shipping boxes from Mallorca all arrived on one of the BEYC"s motor launches, as does quite a bit of food and drink supplies for the resort/yacht club. When it comes to needing bigger things, it requires a bigger boat. I swear that these delivery barge-boat-things are left over from the invasion of France during the war, but even if they are, they sure do the job. This one seems to be delivering a tanker full of diesel (for boats) and a cement mixer (not for boats), and what appears to be a pretty large lorry of some type. Probably getting ready for when the BEYC closes and the annual fix-it-all-up-for-next-season begins in August.

When I heard the landing craft/delivery boat, I was in the midst of finishing a pretty good book…a book that I was happy to have bought/down loaded. *Eleanor Oliphant Is Completely Fine*. You will smile if you read it.

Being on-board Saphir all the time does cause one to think about some things that one would normally never even give a half-second to. For the past couple of days, I have been thinking about wind. This may seem logical, as I am on a sailboat, and if I don't have the engine on, the wind is the way the boat moves. Makes sense I would think about that, doesn't it? Okay, but the dynamics of wind on sails is not what I have been pondering. I have been thinking about how you (You? Me? Anyone?) would describe wind to someone who has never experienced it. You can't see wind, but you can see what it can do. You can't taste it, but it can bring flavours to you in the air. You can't smell wind, but you can smell stuff in the wind. You can't touch the wind, but you can feel air rushing past your skin. So the question is (in a Buddha-like way), how would you describe wind to someone?

I did my swimming lap today. Yes, one complete lap of the pool. Okay, to be fair, my "pool" is the sea, and one "lap" is from Saphir to the landing at the BEYC pool…about ¼ mile each way. So one lap is enough I thought. When I returned to Saphir (a bit knackered), I did have a healthy brekkie (tea, toast, nice marmalade, and ½ melon. Then it was time to get busy…. "Busy" here today meant go over to Gun Creek (must have my greens I have been told) and then back to the BEYC to try to get this website-scrolling-mess all sorted. Hopefully, the solution that you are looking at will suffice.

On the way to Gun Creek to find my greens, I was totally and completely amazed at the blues and greens that were in front of my eyes. Actually, I am not sure why I am amazed as this is what I see every day. Eighty-six hues of blue and almost the same number of greens; every flippin" day. I swear the people at Pantone must love this place.

It rained today. No, not the silly-sun-rain that comes and buckets down for five minutes and then buggers off – just about the time you get the hatches all closed, it is time to open them again. No, today's rain was, well it was proper rain. It started off with the sky to the south turning a very non-festive blue-grey. This caused me to tap into the Rain-Alarm app on my phone, only to see s multi-coloured blob of bright green and yellow, with blotches of blue and red, sort of like a disfigured artist's colour wheel. I zoomed out in the app and saw that this was clearly not going to be another five minute wonder, so decided it might be smart to close down the hatches…just in case the rain, that according to the app was heading here, actually did inundate the North Sound. About ten minutes later, Saphir suddenly emulated the part of the Exorcist, and spun around on her mooring as the wind when from a nice breeze of 8 knots up to 25 knots in a few seconds. Then the rain came. Then more wind. Then more rain. It was apparent to me that this was going to be a repetitive theme today, so I went below and opened up my Kindle.

And now, something from the "more-money-than-sense" department. Sadly, I don't have a photo of this, but I wish I did. A big chartered catamaran just came in just behind Saphir with eight people on board. Four men, and four women. When they tried to tie their catamaran to the mooring, all fun ensued, but as anyone who has sailed here has no doubt had their own trying-to-tie-up-to-a-mooring-in-a wind horror story, I won't even try to relate all of the conversation between the four men who apparently had not won a Merit Badge for knot tying, and the four women, who apparently had won a Certificate in making cheesy comments to their boy friends/partners/husbands/whomever. I decided to write about them because not fifteen minutes after they finally did get their catamaran secured, I heard a buzzing noise. It was pretty loud and did sound a bit familiar, so I sprinted up the companionway steps just in time to see one of the lads trying to control a drone-thing that was being tossed about in the wind. And then he tried to control it back to the catamaran. And then he tried to keep it away from the mast. And then he tried to keep it out of the shrouds. And then they all watched it crash to the deck. I was half expecting (read "expecting" as "hoping") it to crash into the sea. Never a dull moment here. Can't wait to see what they all do tonight. Idiots.

This afternoon (it is a Friday here, but that really doesn't make any difference I guess) I was sitting in the cockpit after doing a series of "boat stuff" chores. I wasn't just sitting there doing nothing, I was reading *The Constant Gardner*, which did require a modicum of concentration. But then for some reason, I stopped reading and just focused all my faculties on what was going on around me. On the surface, an observer might have said that not a lot was going on, but the reality was that it was pretty clear, pretty quickly, that there was far more going on than I had recognised at first. There was a nice breeze that sent gentle ripples across the surface of the sea, making a soft rhythm-like sound on the hull of Saphir. And as the ripples went past the boat, the sun reflected off the little wavelets, making the surface of North Sound appear to be a vast fractal-like surface of diamonds, sparkling in the light. The silence was only broken occasionally when the little bell that was a gift from Karl & Vikki from when they were in Thailand would move enough to result into a soothing, almost serene "ping." It was as if my mantra had somehow changed, and it was now everything that was surrounding me instead of the one I had been given in the 1970"s. Not a bad way to spend an afternoon. The Maharishi would have been happy.

Side note: the peace that had filled my afternoon did slip away as the rather testosterone-filled Cigarette-type-racer blubbed and gurgled into the mooring field with its four four-hundred-horsepower-each motors hanging on the back....geeez.

James B Rieley

Well, the day I have been anticipating/hating/waiting for is here. Today we left BEYC and sailed over to Nanny Cay. The trip was especially nice as MLR decided to fly in and spend a few days with me and her trip overlapped with my moving Saphir, so I didn't have to make the trip single-handedly. I have, since my first sailboat, tried to ensure that the boat (whichever boat it was) could be single-handed. This means sometimes changing some of the winch locations and routing of lines; but in the case of Saphir, it meant I didn't have to do anything, as the previous owner had the same thoughts I did about sailing. Having said that, it is always nicer to be sailing with someone. The preparation for the sail was pretty easy. The previous day we had gone over to the fuel cay and topped up and then checked everything over when back on the boya. Then it was pretty simple...tote that barge, lift that bale...in nothing flat, we were ready.

The sail over was pretty non-eventful. Nice breeze, moderately nice seas, several relatives of Flipper who appeared along side to say hello. Pretty nice. And after a few hours, we were in Nanny Cay for the duration of the (potentially) nasty hurricane season. The forecasts for this year's bit of wind and rain (excessive wind and rain actually) still are not all that evil. Having said that, the other day, Phil, one of the managers of yacht management here, did stop over to ask if we had been paying attention to the latest weather reports. It seems that some forecasts are (were?) projecting some semi-serious weather this weekend. The real concern, he said, would be obvious when other sailors began to strip all the cloth and cloth-like things off of their boats. It is now Friday afternoon, and about the only excitement here so far has been a family from Puerto Rico on a powerboat, yelling at each other (but not about the weather). So, life goes on, day after day in the sun.

Right. The "sun" thing. Yes, it sun seems to be out a lot here, but to be fair, it has rained each day since arriving here in Tortola. The thing is that the rain starts out as a couple of London-like spits of rain, then in moments, evolves into a serious downpour. That lasts for about five whole minutes, and then the clouds bugger off and the sun comes out and dries everything off again. And the temperature here? An interesting question as the weather in Mallorca has turned seriously, as our favourite weather reporter Poula used to say, "scorchio." It isn't scorchio here. We are considerably closer to the equator here, but the weather has been quite normal, with the summer mid-day heat offset by the breeze. More than tolerable. Having said that, when MLR was here, the air conditioning on Saphir was on quite a bit.

Enough weather talk. Today was one of those days where it seemed to be good to go for a long walk....long, as in the evil 10,000 steps walk that is (supposedly) a good thing. So it was down the quay where Saphir is, along the main quay to the hotel, then through the boat yard where all the boats that are on the hard are stored, then over to Captain Mulligan's (an outdoor pub that is pretty great), then along the main quay again, but with detours along all the perpendicular quays. When I finally made it back to the start-

Living on Rocks

ing point, I saw that I still hadn't done enough steps, so I carried on and followed the same basic route, but with some minor side visits to other quays and parts of the boat yard. Back to Captain Mulligan's (which was not open yet as it wasn't even 0800h), and then back to Saphir. My plan was to change into swimmers and then walk down past Peg Leg's (a restaurant and outdoor pub on the grounds of the pool and the beach) and go for a swim in the sea. The pool is nice, but it is a pool…and I am in the Caribbean where the water is wonderful and its little wavelets consistently beckon. Did the swim, back to the boat, and bingo, had done the 10,000 steps and time for some brekkie.

Something else that does fit in with the entire concept behind these chapters about what it is like to be here. My friend Kay Newton runs an online programme called "The Midlife Retreat" in which she talks to people who have "interesting stories," and for some reason, she said the whole "living on a boat in the BVI" would be interesting. As Kay lives in Zanzibar, which I find seriously interesting, I thought I would do this. Kay sent me an advert with all the pertinent information about the programme. I found the photo of me that Kay used to promote the programme interesting as I don't even own a suit, much less a tuxedo anymore…(but do have some pretty wicked red sailing shorts which I probably will wear as this isn't video anyway).

Last night was pretty special. Well, to be fair, not really any more special than the other evenings I have seen since arriving in this part of the world. But special none-the-less. It had rained about 2000h, for the becoming-regular-timing-of-five-minutes, and then cleared up again. But sitting below, doing some loops and watching a movie, I could sense something was up so I went up to the deck and saw that another group of storm clouds were about to encapsulate Nanny Cay and its environs. I quickly clicked on the Rain-Alarm app, only to see that it was just another storm cell moving rather quickly from east to west (as most of them do here at this time of year). It rained for (interestingly enough) about five minutes and then the skies cleared showing an elegant moon keeping all that could see it safe and content.

Yesterday was an exercise day. Is it not that I haven't been exercising, it is just that yesterday afternoon I felt like I had spent an excessive amount of time doing inside stuff, so that meant I should got out. As I don't have a bicycle, roller-blades, or a track-suit, the logical thing to do was to walk. Well, that seemed to be the logical thing whilst I was still down below in the air-con environment of Saphir. When I went up the companionway and felt the blast of warm, I almost began to rethink my logic, but then that silly *"You can never discover new lands if you are afraid to lose sight of the shore"* statement flashed into my brain. So, grabbing a hat and a bottle of water, I stepped off Saphir into a world to explore.

I have been on the road that goes from Nanny Cay (this, by the way, is pronounced NANNY-KEY) toward Road Town, but in the past, it has always been in a taxi, so walking down the road on foot seemed like good proper exploring. Out of the marina and down the road. That's the plan. Hot spit. Off I went.

Here, as this is one of the British Virgin Islands, we drive on the left side, which means I would walk on the right side toward the incoming traffic. This did seem like an appropriate application of logic, good Boy Scout training, and the reality that there was a walk path on the right side of the road anyway. I walked along, smiling away, looking at all there was to see. It didn't take to long to realise that either these intermittent rain showers during this time of the year cause plants to grow at a fearsome speed, or some people simply park their vehicles and must forget where they are.

When walking, I also paid more attention to all the sleeping-policemen that seem to populate many of the roads here on Tortola. They are in other lexicons, speed bumps, but here they seem to be a bit taller and broader. It also seems like many drivers must have memory lapses about them because it seemed like every third car/pickup/lorry that approached one waited until the very last minute to slow down, and then felt compelled to resume their normal, quite excessive speed within four milli-seconds after going over one. Of course this driving style does result in lots of screeches, which are always fun to hear when you are new on the island and have no clue what is happening.

Whilst walking, I would check my handy-dandy-trendy-iPhone-pedometer, hoping against hope that it would magically announce I had done ten thousand steps. Well, I did say hoping against hope, didn't I? I did manage to go past several interesting businesses, many of them almost completely hidden by the undergrowth, with one sign announcing a business that offered "FOOD, DRINKS, INTERIOR DESIGN." Really? Went past several "restaurants" (note the inverted commas, as I am not sure if even the locals would eat in them), with a couple of them having tables under a tree with men playing dominoes. At the taxi rank here at Nanny Cay, there is a shaded area under a huge tree where drivers play dominoes whilst waiting for someone to take into town. What is fascinating, especially whilst walking down the road, was that when a player would put a tile down, it went down with the sound of an AK47. Slap! Crack! Bam! Some serious domino players here. I kept on walking, knowing that my water bottle, which was by now almost half empty, was not going to last the distance unless I wimped out and turned around. I checked the pedometer thingy and it said 3800. Oh shit.

I bit further down the road, I did stop for a minute to ponder a project. Yes, it was a house, and it did involve some fix-up work, but it certainly did have potential. All it would need would be flippin' everything to make it habitable, like…well, like everything. Not a good idea worth pursuing, especially with the law here that states that every property for sale must be made available to a "local," which means that it is pretty difficult to acquire a home when even after you make an offer to purchase that could be for the asking price, you can't get it until all the locals have had time to make their own offer. It

Living on Rocks

is not about price, it is all about ensuring that tourists don't end up owning everything...which reflecting on what happened in Mallorca with tourists buying everything, probably isn't a bad thing to have a law like that.

Categories. You know, things like meats, fruits, dairy, or, animal, vegetable, and mineral. Categories. For no particular reason other than this popped into my mind one morning, I thought it might be interesting to share some different categories that are impacting a new-kid's life in the BVI.

Getting Stuff Done....When I moved from Barcelona to Mallorca years ago, it became quite clear quite quickly that things would be different. I don't mean to imply that things would be bad (whatever "things" actually encompasses), just that they would not be the same as they had for me for years. Some of the "things" do include how you get stuff done. For years, I had lived in pretty good-sized cities, cities that had appropriate infrastructures and people who had sets of policies and procedures to follow. Okay, so that doesn't always hold true, but in most cases, "things" seemed to have some semblance of order and "getting those things done" also seemed to follow a semblance of order. Then I arrived in Mallorca.

Living on the first Angelina was pretty easy, but when I left the boat and bought La Antigua, was when everything changed. Coping mechanisms are wonderful things, and perhaps the most powerful one was patience. We can hope and wish and dream all we want; if the system (whatever that might entail) doesn't match up with one's expectations, kicking, screaming, and pouting do little other than increase ones stress level. By putting everything into the context of, "it is different here" and "patience" is worth exhibiting, doesn't necessarily fix things, but these two contextual tools do make everything tolerable. And in some cases, quite interesting. After fifteen years in Mallorca, I had pretty much learned to cope rather well with the quirky way some things are done there. Some challenges did take longer than I would have liked, but what-the-hell, it was just a bit of extra time that really, in the big scheme of things, didn't result in anything serious. After than length of time on Mallorca, and those experiences I ran into, I also became quite adept at gaming the systems that would have driven me crazy years earlier. When I began to plan on moving to the BVI, I did reflect on the "Oh-my-God,-some-challenges-might-need-patience-here-as-well." Having survived Mallorca I was pretty confident that being in the BVI would be a piece of cake. And then today came.

The day began like most of them do...the sun illuminating the view from the forward cabin hatches at a bit after 0500h. Lay in bed for a while, ponder what I would need to do during the day; and then get up and have my tea and toast/bagel/whatever. On today's agenda, I was planning on staying near to Saphir as there was a Customs bloke coming over to check the boat. Nothing overly dramatic; just government bureaucracy in action. About 0900h, I receive an email from the agent who did all the documentation that was required when I bought Saphir. Transfer of title, change of registered flag from Canada to the BVI, and some other miscellaneous stuff. I had been told that the way this all works here is that a Customs official would come over, look at the boat, check the paperwork, and then sign off on everything. Easy-peasy. The email asked if I had all my paperwork in hand, and because the guy was coming at 1000h (I had been told) and it was now a tad past 0900h. Instead of replying via email, I rang the company. The conversation went pretty well:

- Me) Yes, of course I have all the paperwork.
- Her) if you have all the paperwork, you can send it to us and the Customs guy won't have to come over.
- Me) That makes no sense to me. If that were the case, why was the appointment set?
- Her) sorry, this is the way things are done here.
- Me) seeing as how this all should have been done when you did the initial paperwork, you don't plan on sending me an invoice as I won't pay it.
- Her) if we do the paperwork for this, we have to send you an invoice.
- Me) well, sorry about that, but if you would have done all this when it should have been done, this wouldn't be an issue.
- Her) why don't you take all the paperwork and go to the Customs office in Road Town and you can do it all yourself.
- Me) Thanks, I think I will.

And after gathering up all the bits of paper that possibly could be needed, I called a friend and we went into Road Town. Phil dropped me off and I walked into the Customs office with a huge smile on my face, full in the knowledge that things were actually getting done. Well done me...or so I thought.

I explained why I was there, and was promptly told that I needed to call the phone number of one of the Customs officers to make an appointment. She gives me a phone number and I ring this person. He answers, but it is virtually impossible to hear him because he is on holiday and is taking care of his children. He tells me to call a different Customs officer. This one doesn't answer his phone. Next I am told I really should be talking to a Customs agent. I say *"Okay,"* followed immediately by *"Is there one here in the office right now?"* Silly me. A Customs agent is really a company and the nearest one is on the other side of the harbour in Road Town...which means a taxi ride. Okay, I can do this. Into the street to find a taxi, and then a relatively short ride through town to the Port. I walk into this office only to be asked if I have already met with a Customs officer. To cut this story short, this went on for a couple of hours, with one person telling me something different from another person. At one point, the clerk in the Customs agent's office said, *"You have remarkable patience."* Nice. Not sure if that is true, but I did have good training over fifteen years on that nice island in the Mediterranean...and by the time I returned to Saphir, it was Happy Hour.

Staying Healthy...Today at Yoga class, it was pretty brutal. The instructor could have been having a not-so-great day, or it could just be that some of the positions were a bit different. I wasn't sure, but I could almost feel that everyone in the class was struggling. Well, at least it seemed like that to me, reading on one of the loungers at the pool. I suppose I could have joined the class, but I could have sworn I heard the lounger whispering in the morning Sun, *"James, James, come over here, it will be wonderful."* So I did. And it was. Now just to be clear, it isn't like I just laid there and did nothing. Every few minutes, I did tap my Kindle to turn the page on the book I was reading. I suppose I could have at least been reading a book about yoga or Pilates, but the mystery had hooked me just after I hit page 10, so I wasn't going to change. Later, after the yoga class was over, and everyone rolled up their mats and staggered away from the beach past me, I realised that perhaps I should be doing something more physical than just laying here reading. So I walked over to the beach bar for a cool drink. Thank you.

I am still doing the walking lark. Having said that, sometimes the 10,000 per day number of steps does slip away from me. But today, I thought I would go for the fabled "extra credit" count, so about 0720h, I headed out to crank up the step count. My plan was to take the direction toward Road Town, largely because of the sea breeze and I thought it would be nice to do this direction early in the morning. Because I have been doing quite a bit of walking, I didn't even feel the slightest bit tired until I made it to the end of the dock and stepped on land. But as the poster from the War said, my plan was to Keep Calm and Carry On. And that I did. After strolling well past the furthest point I had walked previously, I kept going until I realised that I was almost half-way to Road Town, and as I would need to come back by foot because I didn't bring any money for a taxi, I turned around and began the walk home. Doing all this pays benefits that make it more than just a health thing. I get to see things whilst walking that I wouldn't normally pay attention to if I were in a car. For example, today I found what looks like a great place for a catered dinner; several wrecked cabin cruisers that I think I could buy pretty cheaply; and even several families of chickens out for their morning walk as well.

Meeting New Friends...When I first moved to Mallorca after living in Barcelona for several years on-board Angelina, I knew no one. Not a soul. For someone who is pretty far over on the "I" scale of an INTJ, this could have been daunting, but the key to just about anything in this life is to just soldier on. It did take a while, but two friends from Barcelona also moved here shortly after I arrived, and they introduced me to a couple of old friends of theirs. Then I ventured out to a business lunch and met some more people. Then I met Vicki, who introduced me to Kay, who put on some workshops with me as the speaker/facilitator, which were attended by....and suddenly, I knew people. Some semi-crazy people, some very special people. I assumed that if I could survive the Mallorca experience, I could do the same in the BVI. So far, it is working a charm. Have no doubt, there are parts of the Mallorca experience that I don't see how could ever be replicated. Living in Puigpunyent was one of the best decisions I have ever made and I do miss it terribly. Having said that, living on the water again is right up there with life's best things. Here is how my process of assimilation has gone so far here.

When we flew into Tortola after I received notification that my application for residency had been accepted, I met the senior immigration officer at the airport...who confiscated my passport. The next day she gave it back to me and we have been friends ever since. My solicitor in Road Town is pretty connected and has been more than helpful. And then there is the boating community. Being part of a boating community is something very special. Everyone has a common bond; they either are on boats, or work with boats, or buy and sell boats. It is kind of like living in Puigpunyent, with the main difference being that everyone here speaks (some form of) English, and in the village, everyone spoke Mallorquin. But the point is, when walking down a street in the village or walking along a path in Virgin Gorda or walking along a quay in Tortola, everyone says something. They don't bury their heads into the ground (or in their iPhones). They actually look at you and say something. In Puigpunyent, it was often a variation of *"Holabondia"* (said at incredibly high speed, hence the run-on spelling of it here). In the BVI, it is usually a variation of either *"Morning mon"* or *"Howyoudoin?"* The point is that people here, as in Puigpunyent, want you to feel comfortable. It is working pretty well.

The grail. The subject of a book I just finished. It is hard to believe that anyone would not know about the Holy Grail. According to Wikipedia, *"The Holy Grail is a vessel that serves as an important motif in Arthurian literature. Different traditions describe it as a cup, dish or stone with miraculous powers that provide happiness, eternal youth or sustenance in infinite abundance."* Whilst all of us may not believe in the concept of the grail being real, I tend to think we all have our own version of a Holy Grail and it is something we strive for in our lives...which is good, because if we are not striving for something, well...you know.

If you are concerned and kind enough to ask, my answer to your questions is a quote from Haruki Murakami. I first heard quote this in some movie quite a few years ago, and realised it did fit me sometimes. Sadly, I cannot for the life of me, can't remember the name of the movie. The actual quote, without the movie reference, will have to suffice. The quote, my answer, is, *"I'm all alone, but I'm not lonely."* Perhaps the reason is that I know you are all where you are, and whilst it may be far away, it is only so in some man-made measurement. Perhaps the reason is that I am pretty adaptable (well we know that is rubbish). Perhaps I know that some day, to quote the Supremes, I know *"We'll be together."* And, seeing as how we are peeling back the multi-

Living on Rocks

layered onion of "why?", here is another bit of wisdom from Murakami..." Dreams are the kinds of things you can – when you need to – borrow and lend out." Sharing some of my dreams with you in this multiple-chaptered-artefact, does keep us as connected as if we were all on the same island.

I can remember being in London giving a speech on organisational effectiveness to a large company group and when I was being introduced, the CEO mentioned that I had all these years of experience, was an expert in systems thinking, and other blah blah blah stuff. And then he said that whilst I do sound American, I am actually British and live on a yacht in the Mediterranean. I just hated introductions like that. Not only the business bull-shit hype, but the personal stuff as well. It sets up all sorts of mental models in the brains of those people who I would have rather had paid attention to my talk than drift off to being on a boat in the Med. When the speech was over and I had managed to survive the Q&A stuff, I was ready to get out of there back to my hotel but first had to deal with the group of people who had questions that they didn't feel comfortable asking in front of the assembled group. Okay, I could deal with that, so I went through them one after another. The last one was a man who came up to me and said that he just wanted to say how envious he was that my life had turned out the way it did. Well, for starters, I said that I didn't think that my life was even over yet. I then asked him why, if he thought that "this life" was so great, he was in London working his life away and not living on his own boat someplace. *"Oh, I would love that, but I have a job."* I replied, *"Okay, so you have a job. If you would rather live on a boat someplace, quit the job and buy a boat." "I wish I could, but I am married and we have children who are in school." "Okay, I know quite a few people who live on boats with partners or spouses, and have children that are home schooled on their boats."* This went on and on until I blurted out something about how we as humans, are in love with our dreams but are pretty shite about making them become reality. We all have the ability to have a vision of what we would like our lives to be like. We also have the ability to make choices. It does stand to reason therefore that we have the ability to make the choices that will enable us to live our vision. Just saying....

Today (a Friday) was another day at the pool. The pool here at Nanny Cay has proven to be a wonderful place to read and relax and I seem to be showing up there almost every day of late. The pluses of the pool are that it is about 20 meters from the sea; there is the Beach Bar about 4 meters away; and there are some big brollies for when the skies open up for those five-minute showers.

There are a couple of downsides to the pool I have discovered and I thought it only fair to share them with you so you have a balanced view of what this is like here.

1) The water temperature of the pool feels like it is a tad warmer than your bath water might be. Having said that, it is still pretty nice.

2) There is a young-persons sailing school around the bend of the inlet, and each day, the school takes a break mid-day and the kids come running and diving into the pool. This is actually kind of fun to watch as these kids are totally and completely fearless. I was speaking to one of the instructors of the school and he said that the kids are anywhere from six to 10 years old. SIX YEARS OLD....geez. I wish my parents had brought me here. (or that I even knew about sailboats)

3) The Sun is so bright here, and with the reflection off the water, even I often consider buying some sun-screen with a higher SPF number than 6... like 8 or maybe even 9.

Next week on Monday (just a couple of days away) should be interesting. I am going into Road Town with one of my stops being the Post Office. Living on a boat means that you don't have a proper address to receive post. That isn't always a bad thing, as the vast majority of the time I was living in Mallorca, I never received post. Just the odd advertising piece, or during the holiday season, Christmas cards. The reality is that most things that we tend to think of as important come electronically now, so the need to have a proper address is about as important as having a land phone number. Having said that, since being here, I have experienced several times when I am asked when filling out a form for something what my address is. When I knew I was moving here, I did a couple of things. First, I asked if I could receive post at the BEYC, and was told yes and was provided with a P.O. Box number I could use. Next, as soon as we were back in Mallorca, I sent myself a letter as sort of a test to see how long it would take to get from an island in the Mediterranean to an island in the Caribbean. That was in March. As of a few days ago when I rang the BEYC, that letter still had not arrived. Upon arriving here again after disposing of everything in Mallorca, I rented a P.O. Box in Spanish Town on Virgin Gorda. As soon as I had that box number, I passed it along to some people and one of them immediately sent off a test letter to that address. I rang them and they said that yes, I did have something in my box. Well hallelujah. Of course, I am on Tortola now until October and my P.O. Box is on Virgin Gorda, so that isn't helping. The lady at the post office in Spanish Town said she would be happy to simply forward the post there to me here by sending it to the Road Town post office with my name on it. Hence my trip Monday to see if this works. Fingers crossed. Will let you know how it goes. If you are in Europe and want to send me a letter, the best method might be to find an empty wine bottle with a usable cork, and after checking the circulatory flow of the Atlantic for the best dates of currents, put the letter in the bottle and chuck it into the sea. Or, if you forget all that after drinking the wine, use DHL or FedEx.

The other day I was talking to friends about the weather, both in Mallorca and here. After hearing about the heat that was blanketing his island, and sharing the rather glorious weather on my island, Karl said, "*So, this is the fabled hurricane season?*" or something like that. I could tell by his voice

Living on Rocks

that there could be a smattering of sarcasm coming through my phone, but truth-be-told, even I had been wondering where all the bad weather was. Don't misunderstand me...I am not exactly wishing to be pummelled by massive winds and rain of Biblical proportions, and to be fair, I do understand the whole percentage-risk thing, but if this was the midst (or almost the midst) of hurricane season, I am all for it.

Later that day, I started reflecting on what he said and realised that I have been pretty reliant on the weather information that I pick up online or from other boaters here. That caused me to think back to when I lived in Puigpunyent and a local farmer and I were talking about the weather. When I asked him if he thought it was going to rain, he looked over at his chickens and said, *"Not until tomorrow morning."* I think I made some cheeky comment about the chickens telling him what the weather was going to bring, and he replied with something *"Look at them."* He was predicting (and planning on) the weather based on signs. Signs that I admit, I really didn't understand. I think I need to do a bit more research so I understand the weather a bit more, especially because I am in a place where for several months each year, the weather can be seriously testy.

It is Monday now, and I did go to Road Town as I mentioned I would. I had hoped to sneak a ride with someone who was going into town, and whilst I did manage to do that, it was a taxi driver. That's okay, must keep contributing to the economy you know. Ten minutes later, I was being dropped off at the Post Office and I was prepared for a moderate to substantial time in a queue. Surprise surprise, there was no queue. As a matter of fact, I almost thought that the Post Office workers had gone on strike. After several "Hello's?" emanating from my mouth, a clerk did come to the counter. I explained my situation – I had rented a P.O. Box in Spanish Town but had been told that it could take a while for the paperwork to come through. By the time it did come through, I was here on Tortola. Miss Waters of the Spanish Town Post Office said I could sign all the papers (and pay for my box, of course) here in Road Town. She had even told me that there was something in my box that she would have forwarded to the Road Town Post Office for me. When I finished my explanation of why I was there, the clerk explained that I would need to talk to her supervisor. Right. As I was waiting, I looked around at the interior of the Post Office. Not very big, it looked from the floor tiles to be about 12 x 30 feet; it had your bog-standard Post Office sales stuff (packing tape, envelopes, ribbons and bows), and seven surveillance cameras. Seven cameras? What is that all about? For the amount of action that was taking place, they could have had a courtroom artist capturing what was going on. Luckily, I was in no hurry, and as I was about to begin to count the number of envelopes in the gift-wrapping display, another woman came out and asked me what she could do for me. Very courteous customer service, but now I had to repeat the entire bloody story. Eventually, all became well, as I was able to sign the box rental agreement and pay for the key (which of course is at the Post Office in Spanish Town so I won't even get that until I return to Virgin Gorda), and, the highlight of the Post Office adventure…I was given a small package that had been in my P.O. Box and that Miss Waters had sent here. Nice. Now, thoroughly pumped by my early morning success at working the system, I headed over to Bobby's to do some food shopping, then a taxi back to Nanny Cay.

Apparently, tonight is a big night in Road Town. From 28 July through to 9 August is the annual BVI Emancipation Festival. According to what I have found out from talking to several people, this is to celebrate when colonialism ended in the British Virgin Islands. So from what I have been told, instead of having locals being owned as slaves, now it is locals who are slaves to "extravaganzas of local and international music, pageants, Food Fairs, j'ouvert (street jamming), parades, gospel celebrations and folklore presentations." Seeing as how I am here and you aren't, I am not sure how you will experience this fully, as even though tonight is the Torch Light Procession and opening of the Road Town Festival Village, I am sure I will not venture back into town again today.

I did wimp out about the opening of the big Festival….well, actually, that isn't completely true. I made dinner (salmon fillet with a bowl of creatively cut melon), and then became thoroughly engrossed in a movie, followed by several episodes of Modern Family before I realised that I had missed the celebrations.

Today (a Wednesday) is the first morning that I have woken up to an almost completely overcast sky. Pretty good wind, lots of clouds scooting along…an interesting morning for sure. After having some toast and tea, it was time for a walk after the 8-minute long rain stopped and hopefully before the Sun blasted its way through the clouds as if someone had set the overhead controls to bake. I was side-tracked a bit when I received a message that said my phone would not work as I had not paid the bill. The phone provider here is even less competent than most, so I had to race into Road Town to show them that the billing is an automatic account withdrawal. Sadly, the people who do that apparently do not talk to the people who do the billing. Idiots. All sorted and then it was back to Saphir to work on the current project. Okay, I should say one of the current projects. This project is pretty timely as it is August already, and that means it is Christmas card time. Yup. You read that right…Christmas card time. I don't send them now, but I do like to have my plan and design all sorted by now so I am ahead of the curve. I am struggling with how to pull this off this year as the post is pretty shite here and even more costly than the postal service in Mallorca. I have this year's card design pretty well sorted, and now am just trying to determine if it is worth trying to do them by hand or do them electronically (which means no mess, no need for massive space to let the cards dry between colour layers, and no need to wonder if the cards would even arrive. I was going to do some loops to look at the unintended consequences of each option, but instead I think I

Living on Rocks

will just wait for a sign.

I was just listening to the radio and heard a weather alert bulletin. It wasn't a warning that the weather was going tits-up, but instead it was an alert of what would happen and what we all would need to do in case of a warning. It began with something like, *"You may have only 36 hours to get ready for a hurricane from the time we issue the warning until the time it strikes. If you aren't ready now, you will not be able to be ready."* Nice subtle approach, but it did get me thinking. I looked at my check list, and think I am okay. Strip off the headsail; remove the bimini, spray hood, and connecting insert; lash down the wind generator; take down all burgees and the BVI ensign; throw on additional mooring lines; make sure all the ports are closed; fill completely the water tanks and the fuel tank; ensure battery banks are all at maximum; and get over to happy hour before prices change back. So my checklist is pretty complete. And not to appear to be an over-achiever, I actually did unfurl and strip the headsail off, fold it nicely (not really) and stuff it into the sail locker. Big tick there.

I wrote the previous paragraph yesterday, and today I find that the reason for all this activity could be approaching. I was talking to a neighbour (a guy whose boat in pretty near Saphir) and the conversation evolved to what weather sites are the best. He said that he likes the NOAA site, so after returning to Saphir, I did a few clicks on the computer, and after reading the text information and looking at the map, I thought it was worth thinking about. There was a picture on the site of a large vibrator shaped blob (a tropical storm) along with the potential path of said tropical storm that was coming our way. Hmmmm. I suppose I could be more concerned than I actually am. But the reality is that after all, it is all just percentages of risk management and the storm centre is at least five days away and its trajectory could change or it could just dissipate completely. Well, that and the fact that I will be in Mallorca for a few days during the time that this storm could materialise into something nasty. As the poster during the war said, Keep Calm and Carry On.

Now some of you might be thinking that I am not all that thrilled being here in Nanny Cay, as opposed to being on a boya in front of the BEYC on Virgin Gorda. Well, have no doubt, being effectively at anchor is far more desirable to me than being in a marina where it is boat boat boat boat boat, almost looking like sardines in a tin. Having said that, I have been pretty lucky here in Nanny Cay. The boats on both sides of Saphir (and behind Saphir) do not have liveaboards, so there is a moderate amount of privacy. The sense of being out there on your own certainly is not here, but the trade-off is that here in the Marina, I can get "stuff" done. It is the classic "everything is good news and bad news at the same time" dynamic. The good news of Virgin Gorda is that it is pretty remote. The bad news is that it is pretty remote, which in this context means, anytime I come up with some brainstorm project, the chances of getting it done at all, or at least at a moderate price, disappear faster than chocolate-chip cookies on-board Saphir. (Shit, typing that sentence made me hungry). Last week I was pretty irritated by the companionway tinted polycarbonate panel that you have to lift out to get out of the boat. Then once you are out, you need to re-install the panel to lock up the boat. Before I left Virgin Gorda, I had drawn up plans to have doors built to replace the panel, but that required someone coming out from Spanish Town (on the other end of Virgin Gorda) and then he wanted what I thought was a King's ransom to do the job. Last week I had decided I would look around here for a carpenter or Boatwright who could make the doors. I did, and a week later, I now have two very spiffy teak doors (each with a tinted polycarbonate window) that allow me to sail through the companionway like a real person. Very high quality workmanship by Miles and Lawrence (and at about ½ the other price. Then today, as I was working on some loop structures whilst sitting at the navigation station, I realised that the cushion on the seat was about dead and needed to be replaced. I rang my friend Miles and asked him if he knew of a foam cushion place here in Nanny Cay. He told me about one just on the big quay, and I hustled over there. Fifteen minutes later, I was headed back to Saphir with a brand new seat cushion. The ability to actually get stuff done here at Nanny Cay on Tortola is pretty nice I guess.

There are times that I feel that I am still in (or on) Mallorca. Like the next few days for sure. When I was getting the cushion replaced, I was chatting with the cushion-replacement-person (what do you call a cushion replacement person...a cushionista? No clue). I said that I felt lucky to have arrived at their workshop just before they closed. He said to me that I was luckier than I thought, as not only would they be closed on the weekend, they would be closed Monday, Tuesday, and Wednesday. The reason I was told was the Emancipation festival that I mentioned previously. In Mallorca, it seemed that there was a holiday just about every month and many of these did seem a bit of a stretch to me. Closing for three workdays here is right up there with "a bit of a stretch." The good news I suppose is that I really can't conceive of needing anything from contractors for a while now. The bad news is that, as someone who does not have a proper job, I don't get to take three days off of work. I think I will be able to deal with the bad news pretty well.

My average day's routine has expanded a bit. Maybe evolved a bit is more appropriate. Now, each day I do look forward to evening. Dinner, a movie, then a bit of reading before I put the book I am engrossed in away and drift into dreamland. I think the movie part has been the most interesting of late. Whilst many of the movies I am watching are so unmemorable that I can't even remember what they were about in the subsequent mornings. But some of them burn an image into my head that often causes me to rewind it a bit and then ponder what I heard. Last night was one of those. Whilst watching The Imitation Game, one of the characters said, *"Sometimes it's the very people who no one imagines anything of, who do the things no one can im-*

Living on Rocks

agine." It can be interesting to think about what others may think of you and your capabilities. More importantly is pondering what you want to do, and actually could do, if you really applied yourself.

Yesterday, whilst at the pool in the morning, I was talking to some friends here and heard about a big parade that would be taking place mid-day in Road Town. I was invited to join them, and admittedly, I was intrigued to find out what a "big parade" would be like here. When we were in St Martin, MLR and I saw a pretty impressive parade one evening and I suppose I was thinking about using that experience as a baseline for island parades. I said I would go along with them, and just as we arrived in Road Town, it started to rain a bit. I actually did look at my watch to see what time it was…and what time the typical five-minute rain would end. That was at 1300h. Yesterday. Monday. It is now 0730h on Tuesday and it is still raining. There were times yesterday, last evening, and even this morning when I realised that all the cute five minute tropical storms that we have been experiencing here are nothing compared to the m-f-serious rain that has been falling. I keep checking the Rain-Alarm app to see how fast this thing is moving, but the picture that comes up just looks like Nagasaki afterwards. But this dispatch entry is supposed to be about the parade in Road Town, so….the rain did let up more or less after about an hour and everyone (there was a pretty big crowd where we were) started to look down the street, half expecting for the parade to come whizzing past before the rain commenced again. After about thirty minutes, it did return, and with a passion. What felt like walls of water kept coming down with everyone huddled under whatever cover they could find. After hearing that the parade was called off due to the weather (completely understandable to me), I decide that this is going to not happen, so I elect to find a taxi to bring me back to Nanny Cay. By the time I get to the taxi rank, it is bucketing again but I do find a driver who is willing to venture out. Then we have to sit for a while because for some reason unknown to modern man, even though it is raining like I have never seen, the parade begins to float its way down the high street of Road Town. Unbelievable.

The taxi ride coming back was slow, mainly due to the massive river-like flows of water coming down the hills and rushing across the road, which in spots was littered with rocks that had been brought down the hills with the torrent. I did get an earful from the taxi driver about some of the other drives on the road…opinions that I did agree with…but we did get here in one piece. I sloshed my way to Gennaker's (an outdoor but under cover restaurant at the marina) and managed to talk my way into borrowing a huge black bin bag, and then made it out to Saphir. Around 2000h, the rain did let up enough for me grab a torch and go on deck to check everything nautical, only to find that Seraphina (my tender) was more than half-full of water, which did make sense. I grabbed a bucket and began to bail her out, and by 2030h, there was only a small bit of water left. I stopped at that point as the rain was resuming and came back inside to have some tea and watch a movie…as you do.

And seeing as how the topic of weather does seem to be pervasive this "chapter," I thought I would check that NOAA hurricane projection website to get the latest view on whether or not that big storm was still coming my way. Good news I think.

To begin with, and in an effort to ensure full disclosure, these paragraphs have almost nothing to do with the North Sound, or to be even clearer, nothing to do with the Caribbean. Having said that, the following text does reflect your diarist's experiences upon leaving (temporarily) the BVI, so that is why it is here. But to shed more clarity on what this "chapter" is all about, it could have been titled, *"James, who-you-may-think-is-always-on-holiday, takes a holiday."*

Well, so far, things are going well. I arrived at the Tortola airport (which is really located on Beef Island, which is connected to Tortola by a relatively new bridge) a bit early, but growing up, I was taught "better early than late." I arrived at the airport at 1530h (or so) and after going through the check-in process, said to the clerk, *"I know I am ticketed on the 1745h flight to San Juan, but is it possible that there is an earlier one?"* As I said this, I casually looked at my watch, making it clear that I recognised I was almost two hours early – not her fault. I also tried to have a semi-pathetic sad look on my face, in the hope that the clerk would take pity on me and let me fly earlier. Of course all these actions on my part (pathetic as they were) were based on a wild assumption that there even was an earlier flight. The clerk gave me a sly smile and said, *"Oh, I am sorry. You just missed our flight at 1530h."* Well shit. I guess I should have been even earlier. But before I could even give her an even more pathetic look, she said *"I can put you on our 1608h flight. Would you like that?"* Damn right I would flashed through my mind but *"That would be wonderful, cheers"* came out of my mouth. She stamped my boarding pass and sent me through to the gate. After barely making it through the security check point (six attendants and I was the only person in the queue did seem a bit overkill), I went and sat down at gate number 3. Just as I was pulling my phone out of my pocket to see if I had received an email or call, the gate person came over to me and said I should go with him. As he wasn't walking toward security, I thought that this might be okay, but as I was pondering his request, he semi-blurted out, *"Now, come quickly mon."* Right. I grabbed my carry on bag and went with him out the door toward the Cessna 402 that had just landed. Just a note here…I was flying on Cape Air and the nine-passenger Cessna 402 is a fixture in their Caribbean fleet. So Mr. Gate-Clerk and I are walking out toward the plane just as it was disgorging the nine people who had just arrived in it from Puerto Rico. Must be hearty souls to come here on holiday or just plain daft, after all, this is hurricane season. When the last person was off the plane, the Pilot stuck his head out the window and motioning to the north, said, *"Come on, let's go…that is a storm and*

Living on Rocks

if we go now we can avoid it." As it turned out, I was the only passenger and leaving immediately was fine with me, so after sitting in several seats to find something soothingly comfortable, we went screaming down the runway and into the sky.

Years ago (and I do mean serious years ago), I had taken flying lessons, and have always liked the whole cockpit thing so after settling on a seat in row 1, the Pilot and I chatted all the way to San Juan. He wanted to know what I was doing in Tortola. *"I live in the BVI and am actually flying to Mallorca to see some friends."* As I was answering his question, I could see Nanny Cay and mentioned that Saphir was there...so we sort of went off conversational course a bit. Had I ever flown on a small plane like the Cessna? *"Yes, and actually, this is pretty posh compared to some planes I have been on."* (I once flew in a two-seater where I was behind the pilot in a plane with a joy-stick sticking up out of the floor and cloth wings and only a compass for navigational instruments) What is the most special plane you have ever flown on? *"Oh, that is easy to answer...I flew on the Concorde from London to New York a long time ago.* That sort of stopped his line of questions, which I thought was fine, after all he was supposed to be flying not being a talk-show host. The rest of the flight was nicely quiet and, all in all, it was a pretty nice way to spend a bit less than forty-five minutes. That was all okay news....but the reality was that now, of course, the fact that I was flying earlier meant that I would have had to spend four fun-filled hours in some lounge waiting for my flight to Madrid. Feel free to note the sarcasm of "fun-filled." This could have been worse, but because of my tickets, at least I was able to sit in a lounge. But as fate would have it, as I signed in I found out that the Business lounge at the San Juan airport closed at 2000h, so I would be able to spend the last 90 minutes in some uncomfortable and decrepit row chair at the gate. So there.

The flight from San Juan to Madrid was pretty uneventful. Seriously uneventful. I boarded and was greeted by a member of the tripulación who said upon seeing my boarding pass, *"It is to the left and you can sit anywhere."* I knew it was to the left when you board, but I didn't quite understand the "you can sit anywhere" comment. Upon finding my assigned seat (the seat I had requested when I bought the tickets actually), the CSD person came an explained that of the twenty-four seats in Business on this flight, only three would be occupied. Damn...my first flight had nine seats, and I was the only passenger. Now I am in a huge plane (A330) that has 24 seats in the pointy end, and there are only three passengers. I was going to draw some loops to see if it had anything to do with my excessively grey hair or new spiffy jumper, but instead I figured that this was a Godsend to not be in a crowded airplane, so I just sat down and waited for some cava. After the rest of the passengers on the plane were finally boarded (and the other two passengers who were going to be near me on the flight boarded), the Airbus lumbered down the runway and in a flash (a long, lumpy flash perhaps), we were off.

A bit of irony here. The pointy end's configuration was 2-2-2, and I was in row 3. Twenty four seats, remember? Guess where the other two passengers were sitting? Really? Damn right…in row 2, smack in front of me. The entire flippin" section and we are lumped together as it we were a family. Unbelievable. I moved.

The inflight entertainment was only available on iPads (which were distributed to anyone who wanted one, and whilst I did accept the offer, the movie options were pretty grim so I opted out for the Pesto Ravioli and a nice Rioja before closing my eyes. What seemed to be minutes later (but was actually hours later), I awoke and was able to see the sun beginning to peek over the horizon. A pretty great sight early in the morning. I had zumo de naranja and tea and after a short time, we landed in Madrid.

Madrid's airport is, well,…never mind. For me, what was important was that I was in the middle of a story familiar to all multi-leg travellers; another city, another airport, another flight. After sitting in yet another lounge but by now, feeling the need to eat healthy food, I did have some proper breakfast before I boarded my last flight and after another hour, landed in Palma.

As the plane was coming into PMI on the usual north-to-south approach, I looked out the window at the vistas that I had seen on virtually every flight I had taken over the past fourteen years when returning to Mallorca. On every previous flight, the feeling I would get as the plane would swoop in over the fincas was one of warmth, knowing that I was home again. This time it was different. Even the ride into Palma past very familiar places felt different. I can't even explain what the feeling was, but it made me realise that I have indeed moved and Mallorca is now where I used to live. Having said that, the most wonderful thing was to now be with friends that I have known for what seems to be a lifetime. The whole sensation of time does seem to be relative to how one feels about a place or special friends. As I was planning this trip a few days before I left, it felt as if I had left Mallorca several years ago, and the reality is that I had left Mallorca 2.5 months ago. The friend thing can be summed up best by two expressions, "Friends are the family you choose," and, *"To know them is to love them."*

The flights back to the BVI (home) again were pretty much as expected, with the minor exception that going this direction does seem to be more attractive to others and on each flight, there were passengers travelling with me. Actually, I was getting quite used to the feeling of having my own Cessna 402 or Airbus 330 on the way to Spain that I think I was hoping it would be the same on the way home. Having said that, here is the flight summary. PMI to MAD was pretty much chocker and only a few screaming children. Had I been actually going to Madrid, I wouldn't have been that happy either. Luckily, all I was going to do was walk the 428,769 kilometres through the airport to get from my arrival gate to my departure gate. Reminiscent of Karl & Vikki's photos of queues at PMI recently, when I made it to Passport Control, it looked like Ellis Island in the early 1900"s probably did. I did enquire as to where the Fast Track line was, but only received dirty looks from those standing next to me...and a curt "No hay" (there isn't one) from a security person. With a common reason to whinge, I made a few friends in the very slow moving queue and eventually did get through in time to continue humping my way to the gate.

The MAD to SJU flight was an hour late in taking off, but it was pretty nice. Fab service, better-than-okay food, comfortable seats that go flat, but I thought the in-flight entertainment was not all that great. Now to be fair, the entertainment is presented on an iPad which the Purser gave me, but the number and selection of options weren't that great. Well, that is what I thought until I clicked on the movie "Table 19." If you haven't seen this, and do enjoy smiling during a movie, you really do need to download / go see / whatever this pretty great story. And because the selection other options wasn't that great, I ended up watching a second time after waking up after a kip. (I liked it even more the second time)

I suppose there were two highlights of my return to the Caribbean. Highlight number 1 was after deplaning in San Juan. As I had been in the pointy end of the plane on the flight, I was one of the first off and the people who did make it off before I did stopped to do something with their carry-bags, so I found myself to be the first from the flight to get to the immigration area of the airport. There were no queues at all...actually, there were no other passengers there, and for a minute, I was wondering if I was in the right place, but then several of the immigration officers motioned me to come to their windows. Of all the flights I have made in my life, in all the years I have been travelling, I have never experienced that before. Almost makes you want to travel more (okay, I am sure it is a once-in-a-lifetime thing so I won't hold it as a travel incentive).

So my return travel was pretty good up to arriving in San Juan. I checked into the airport hotel as there was no available connection to take me on the last 45-minute leg of the trip. It was there when I first heard the horrendous news from Barcelona about a terrorist attack. Having lived in Barcelona for several years, and having walked down the Ramblas many times, and, having friends who do live there now, I felt completely gutted by what happened, as I think it has done for us all.

Highlight number 2 was Friday morning, which admittedly, did come pretty early for me as jet lag pummelled my body by waking me at 0400h. But a few hours later, and after a tasty breakfast, I was off to the Cape Air gate of the airport. As fate would have it, my return flight on Cape Air to Beef Island was the same as my outbound flight. You guessed it....once again I was the only passenger. A very serious highlight for me, and I am trying to figure out how to make this the norm here. I suppose the only way is, according to Scotty the pilot, to fly only in the off-season. Not sure how that will work long term, but it is worth a shot. I had a great chat with Scotty and because of that, the time flew past faster than the plane was going. We landed, I went through Immigration, and jumped into a taxi for the ride back to Nanny Cay.

Now for those of you who have been looking to hear what I did whilst in Mallorca, I did what I came to do and was fortunate enough to see quite a few very good friends. And for those of you who now are wondering if all this was sort of a precursor to moving back….no. I have missed my friends terribly, but even though it often feels like I have been away for several years, being there with them wound back time and it felt like we were just continuing on with previous conversations without skipping a beat. After all, as I said a few paragraphs ago, friends are the family that we get to choose. For those friends I didn't get to see, I wish I could have but just ran out of time.

Mallorca, even as nice as it is, is just another island now and the one I have chosen to live on here is pretty special and it is quickly becoming "home."

One last thing….When, sitting on Saphir in front of BEYC before the storm season arrived, we were talking about what I would do to avoid being trashed in a hurricane. I do like having options, as you should know by now, and one of the options that I found especially attractive was to simply sail south toward the top of South America, out of the hurricane zone. I, instead, took the option of staying in the BVI and being in Nanny Cay, which is a recognised hurricane hole. To date, this choice has been pretty good as once again, I have dodged a bullet as all the tropical storms that have begun to come this way have dissipated or turned away.

Normal. I have no idea w-t-f that actually means for me other than I am back on Saphir again after my (mind-boggling-wonderful) trip to Mallorca. And now that I am home again, I am doing boat stuff, more or less. And for me, living on Saphir means doing boat stuff, hence, normalcy. Today's "boat stuff" included doing some maintenance on Sapphires batteries. Batteries on a boat (well, on a sailboat especially) are pretty important as no-battery-power-means-no-electricity. And in the case of Saphir, that would mean no freezer, no refrigerator, no lights, and perhaps most importantly, no watching episodes of Modern Family. Therefore, (and clearly logically as I am only on season 5 of MF) maintaining the batteries is something that needs to be done. The main battery bank on Saphir consists of eight monster batteries and is located under the aft-port berth, and because no one is visiting, I have been using that cabin as sort of a catch-all space. This should not be confused with the aft-starboard cabin, which is sort of like a storeroom, or the forward cabin, which is where I sleep. At about 0900h this morning, I started dragging stuff out of the cabin and piling it all in the salon. Then I dragged out the mattress cushions and piled them on top of the other pile of "stuff." It was then that I could finally uncover the battery boxes and check the levels of battery juice. A tad low, so, leaving the pile of "stuff" on the cabin sole, I went to the local Nanny Cay market to buy some distilled water. Yes, there was a tag on the appropriate shelf that said "128 oz. Distilled Water" but the shelf contained mineral water. After asking the clerk if there was any distilled water in the back, I was told most probably not, so I went to the Nanny Cay chandlery, which is almost next-door. No, they didn't have any either, but a clerk said that he thought I could get some at a different market that was *"Just down the road mon."* Well, great. When I (apparently foolishly) asked which way and which road, he said, "Come on mon, I show you" and outside we went. Barely making it through the door of the chandlery, he sees a friend of his slowly driving through the car park. I have been here long enough to know what happens next. The bloke in the car stops and the two of them chat about something that I could not understand. After a few minutes, the clerk says, *"RayJay"* (or something like that), *"my man here needs some distilled water."* Can you take him to the VI Auto shop?" RayJay (maybe it was RegGuy?) says *"Yeah mon, come on"* and leans over and opens the passenger side door of his car. I get in and, because I have learnt the drill, stick my fist out. He taps me back and off we go. Oh yeah, I'm back in the BVI. We end up going down the road toward West End and make two stops, neither of which have any distilled water, but the conversation along the way was pretty good. I felt like I was the host of a dating programme: RayNay (?) is from Dominica, has a girlfriend, an 8-year old son, works in construction but loves to sail, does deliveries in his non-construction work time for the Moorings and Sunsail, and was out last night until 0400h.

By about this time, we had turned around and we were now headed toward Road Town. Two more stops, neither of which had any distilled water, and by now, even though RayKay was talking about his recent trip to Dominica, I was beginning to think about buying a huge boiler and distilling water for the masses. We then stopped at another auto store and as we went inside (I think he wanted to make sure I knew how to say *"Do you have distilled water?"* correctly) I asked him why everyone in every place we stopped leaves their cars running when they go into a store. Because then you don't have to start it again was the response. I would have thought it had something to do with the air conditioning in the cars, but RayMay's car didn't seem to have air con so maybe it was just easier to leave the car running. Clearly it would be easier for a car thief as well, but on an island, if you steal a car, where are you going to go with it? This last stop didn't have any distilled water but it did have bottles of "Battery Water," which was probably coloured distilled water with a heftier price on it. I bargained (as you do) and managed to get the price down from 2.50 USD per bottle to 1.50 USD, which did impress RayTay quite a bit. We chucked the case of bottles into his car and then he drove me back to Nanny Cay. Not only was I chuffed that I now would be able to tick the "maintain-the-batteries" box, but it was just one more sign to me that the locals here are pretty great people. I can't imagine a local whom I have never met before in many other places I have lived drive me around for 45 minutes without asking first for a credit card and several letters of reference. As RayBay started to drive off, I was going to shout out

"*Thanks,*" followed by his name and "*I really appreciate all the help,*" but as I never really did figure out his name and didn't want to piss off my new best friend, I just waved and smiled.

Today, a Tuesday, is one of those doing-stuff-in-Nanny-Cay-days. A bit of shopping at the market, taking the laundry in (and collecting it later), the daily walking thing, and for a bit of relaxation, just sitting at the pool/beach reading. Okay, so maybe I do the sitting reading thing often. Truth-be-told, I do seem to be ripping through the books on my Kindle at a pretty good clip. This isn't because I have the time; this is because the books I am almost inhaling are written so well, they are difficult to put down. I read a couple of chapters, and then are so caught up in the story, I feel compelled to read the following chapter...and then often, another one. You might be thinking that this addiction to some books would keep me from other semi-necessary tasks here, but I think it simply causes me to do more stuff better than before. I have learnt, however, that there are some things that are well beyond my ability to control.

Years ago, a very good friend said to me, "*James, you shouldn't worry about things you can't control.*" That is very good wisdom, and I have passed that along to many people since hearing it myself. Sometimes that wisdom is pretty lame. Like this afternoon. (just a note here, it is Wednesday, the day after I wrote all that good stuff about doing stuff better here). I had Adrian over to the boat. Adrian is pretty switched on about all things technological...well, at least about internet stuff. Saphir has a system on-board that can capture boost existing WIFI signals, as well as a router so those signals can then me floated all over Saphir. A brilliant system, but for some reason, it hasn't been working all that well. Truth-be-told, it wasn't working all that well when I was at the BEYC on Virgin Gorda, but I didn't feel compelled (or rich enough) to warrant some repair guy coming out to look at it. I haven't worried about it since we arrived at Nanny Cay either as there is a repeater WIFI tower about 20 metres from Saphir and I do have a pretty strong signal. But because I am in "get-Saphir-all-spiffed-up-for-my-return-to-living-on-a-boya-again" I thought it would be a good time to have Adrian take a look at the system. Now the good news, other than he is in charge of all the WIFI at Nanny Cay, so he does know what he is going; is that I wasn't going to be hammered with travel time from one island to another, as Adrian's office is about 150 metres away from Saphir. So he came over with his computer and some electrical testing stuff, and after about 20 minutes, pronounced the system to be all good. Excellent news, and reinforced my belief that I had made the right decision about dealing with this here instead of over on Virgin Gorda. I opened my MacBook, and sure enough, the Saphir router signal was big and bold. Then I did the same with my phone, but the signal was pretty much non-existent. Then the computer dropped the signal. Then Adrian's computer couldn't find the signal either. He was non-too chuffed about what was going on, and before I could say anything, was running his computer

Living on Rocks

through a series of system checks of the entire Nanny Cay WIFI stuff. After a few minutes, he announced that the electricity was down. Down, as in "the power station on this end of Tortola had ceased to be working. I asked if it was simply overloaded but he said something like, *"it is summer and it can happen."* I then asked what we should do, using the word "we" meaning anyone here who was planning on using electricity. *"My suggestion would be to wait until it comes back on. We have a generator, which either has kicked in or will kick in within a few minutes, but that won't power up all these boats running air con. Waiting is good."* So waiting is what I did. After about an hour, I did phone the marina office just to see if their power was back up. To be extra courteous, I said, *"I believe there is an electrical service fault here on F-dock."* The receptionist who was on phone duty said she would immediately transfer me to someone responsible. Within seconds, a very solid-sounding male voice came on to ask what I wanted. I again said the thing about an electrical fault. He said that they knew about it and it was not just here at the marina. I asked if they had any idea when power would be restored, and he said, *"No, why don't you ask the government?"* I was going to say something appreciative like, *"Thank you, you dick,"* but didn't. I was going to send him one of my newsletters on the subject of building good customer relations, but instead just turned on the generator.

A couple of days later, two to be exact....the electrical fault thing is all sorted. I have my internet connection; I have my air conditioning, and I have my ability to watch a movie in the evening. As it turned out, the problem wasn't the Dalek-looking tower that my cables for shore power connect to; it was one of the cables itself. Apparently, or so I would like to believe, when the power dropped, everything shut off until the power was restored. That makes sense, doesn't it? Well when was restored, it must have surged a tad and where the cable that was the supply for the air con on Saphir connects to the boat basically blew out. Well, not basically; one of the three contacts within the connectors went to melted-connector-heaven. An hour after discovering the problem, all was well again on-board Saphir and life resumed as we (Saphir and I) were used to.

If you read up a few lines, I said that the connector *basically* blew out. I did try to correct it, in the next sentence, but as I was typing it, I realised that the way we use the word "basically" really drives me mad. "We" seem to use it a lot, even though how we use it is where I struggle. *"We basically went to the store and bought blah blah blah."* How can you "basically" do something? Either you did it, or you didn't, yes? "I basically decided to fly back to Mallorca for a week." No, I didn't "basically" decide, I did decide. "The connector basically blew out." No, it either blew our or it didn't. In this case, it fucking blew out. There. I feel better, as I hope that Mrs. What's-Her-Face, my English teacher from school should feel that I actually did learn something in that class.

And on a Saturday, I was talking to good friend about a photo I took of

378

their home. Admittedly, when I took the photo, I was pretty far away from the casita I had been staying in, but the detail just wasn't there for me to see well enough to do a proper watercolour of it. This inspired me to do two things; rummage through my hard drive to find any other photos of the property and keep enlarging them to see the detail I was missing, and, watch the movie "Blow Up" again. If you haven't ever seen "Blow Up," it is probably due to one of the following reasons. 1) You weren't old enough to remember when it came out in the late 1960"s; 2) You never had a real camera that used proper film; 3) You never had a dark room in your home where you wound your own film canisters and did your own developing and enlarging. I was there, and I did, and I did, so "Blow Up" is one of those pseudo-religious experiences of those times.

"Blow Up," in case you don't know, is a Michelangelo Antonioni movie from 1966 about a photographer (allegedly David Bailey) who…oh never mind. It is a fab movie…and better than fab if you were there.

Now, with so many column inches about a time long ago, one of you might be wondering if I would go back in time if I could. The answer is pretty simple…no. The 1960"s and 1970"s certainly were interesting times, but here is the problem with trying to go back and relive something you did once before. People often say that it would be great to go back in time knowing what we know now. Maybe, but if you would go back in time, the chances are 99.999% that you will do something that will send you on a different course than the one you took then. And if that happens, you will not end up where you are now. For me, this would mean that I wouldn't know any of my friends, and that is a risk I would never want to take for anything.

Time is one of those largely mis-understood things. To some, time whizzes past at near jet airplane speed, and to others, it drags on like a sleepy slug trying to go up a greased tree. For me, time and the way it feels, is pretty situational. There are days when it does seem to fly past faster than I would like, and yet there are other days where it doesn't seem to move forward at all. Today (a Wednesday) is one of those very special days where both of these sensations seem to be present. The morning, I could have sworn my watch had been infected by some steroid-like accelerator. I looked at my watch early this morning and it was a few minutes after 0700h. The next time I looked at my watch its little luminescent hands showed it was coming on 1130h. This could have been fine, but when I looked at it the second time, I thought it was going to show it was about 0900h. I have no idea where the time went. And now it is afternoon and I am reading in Saphir, whilst waiting for a friend who is driving into Road Town this afternoon to ring me to say he is ready to go. The waiting is what is making the time to almost stop. Of course the good news of that is that I am devouring a new book.

If you have been following my little weather updates, you know that we have been luckier that a lotto-winner (well, maybe not that lucky) as almost all of the Caribbean storms have skirted the BVI in fine fashion. Never-the-

Living on Rocks

less, I do keep checking on a daily basis what is going on near the Cape Verde islands, where all the nasty stuff begins. Most of the storms that appear on the NOAA website are just that; storms with rain and wind. Today, however, one of those pesky storms was upgraded to a hurricane already; Irma by name. The next few days will determine how close Irma comes.

It is a Thursday, and I went to Road Town today to get a few things done. Well, that was the plan at least. I really only had two stops planned, but as with many things in life, only two planned stops, even with the best planning, can sometimes become a bit more complex. The "plan" went off the rails before I even left Nanny Cay as yesterday a friend here told me that he would be driving in and I could ride with him. Always a nice thought, and a good way to avoid a one-way taxi fee. Of course I wasn't aware that his ability to remember some things was fleeting, so after not getting a phone call, I rang his number, only to find out that he was already in Road Town. I went over to the taxi rank and found a driver who would take me in. Sort of back on plan, I thought. My driver going into Road Town today turned out to be a belonger who was 76 years old. He told me about all the changes he had seen here in his life, which is a conversation I love to be engaged in. Just about the time we were entering the town, I brought up the hurricane forecasts and he said that the storm would bypass the BVI. I apparently looked at him incredulously, but he just tilted his head a bit and, pursing his lips, slowly shook it back and forth. Okay, here we go…scientific information in the form of computer weather projects v. an old boy who has seen it all. No judgement from me, but I sure hope he is right. One of the two big reasons to go to Road Town was to go to the Fed Ex office to send off two more watercolours of homes to good friends in Mallorca. I had looked on Google maps to find out where the FedEx office was and from what appeared on my computer screen, their office was just about a block away from the Digicel offices on the high street in the centre of town. I tend to compartmentalise things like this into location-proximity-to-places-I-know, and God knows, I had been to the Digicel offices multiple times to sort out their charges for my mobile service. So, as the taxi approaches the Digicel office, I tell my taxi driver (and meteorologist) that anywhere here will be fine. He stops his taxi as I am disconnecting my seat-belt, and I leap out. BAM!!!! It is only about 0930h and it feels as if I have leapt into the boiling cauldron of an active volcano. Cleverly (not really), I had not brought a hat or umbrella with me, so instead my body decided to begin to shed water weight in the form of perspiration. It couldn't have really been that hot, but it certainly did seem warmer than the 30c it turned out to be. That's okay, as I do like it warm, but some reason, this blast of "warm" felt more like the town had been set to "broil." I looked around for Station Avenue, where the FedEx offices were, but after not seeing it, realised I probably needed to go another block to find it. After finding myself on a different street (a street that the city fathers conveniently forgot to put an identifying sign on), I decided to walk a bit further. The term "a bit further" was a cute way to say that after walking for about 30 minutes up and down streets, I still hadn't found what I was looking for.

Now for those of you (probably women) who are now thinking, "what a daft piece of work for not stopping and asking for directions," the reality is that I did ask two different pedestrians I encountered and stop in at three stores asking them all if they knew where the FedEx offices were. The consensus was to keep walking in the basic direction I was going, with one person telling me I was going the exact opposite of where I should be, and the other person thinking it was a restaurant that sold really good jerk chicken. I kept walking. Now, with the realisation that I am doing all this without a hat or an umbrella to provide shade, I did try to think positive and assumed that after another block or two, I would have no water left in my body to perspire at all. I did finally go around a corner and find a big building (by BVI standards) with a massive FedEx sign on it. I staggered in with my A4 sized white envelope containing the two watercolours and was greeted by a very nice clerk whose first words were, *"Welcome to FedEx. You must be walking. Did you find us okay?"* How nice was that? I do have legal residency here but do recognise I am a guest in this country, so I figured that replying with sarcasm would be tacky at best, so I just smiled as I dragged myself to the service counter and enquired what it would cost to send this meagre envelope (that had almost no weight at all) to Mallorca. She smiled, did some calculations, and then told me it would be 97.50 USD. I immediately wanted to turn on my phone to Google if there is a direction connection between heatstroke and hearing loss but instead said, *"I am sorry. Did you say it would cost 100 USD to send this envelope to Spain?"* She looked at her computer screen and replied, "No, it is only 97.50 USD." So on my walk back to the centre of town with the envelope still in my hand and being used as a sun shield, I thought I would see what it would cost if I shipped it via standard (but express) post. It didn't seem to take that long to get to the Post Office, but I assume that was because I had lost so much water weight on the Sahara-like march that walking was easier. Or maybe I was seeing a mirage of a line of Piña Coladas with waiting for me on the counter of the Post Office. The clerk at the Post Office said it would cost a bit over 10.00 USD. Ahhh, that was more like it. Having not had the best of experiences with the post in the BVI so far, I felt compelled to ask about how long it would take for the envelope to arrive in Mallorca. She wasn't sure, but did say she thought it could be less than two months. Maybe. But she wasn't sure. Then she asked me where Mallorca was. My next stop with my envelope still in my hand was a company that does postal-like services and luckily, they were pretty switched on. A bit over 10.00 USD like the Post Office, but it would only take a couple of weeks to arrive in Mallorca (and this clerk actually knew where Mallorca was, so that was a plus for sure). Another real plus of using the postal-like services company was that they were smack in the centre of Road Town...actually, about 75 metres from where the taxi dropped me off when I started today's sweating festival.

My next stop was Bobby's Market, which is a pretty good-sized operation that usually has everything I could ever want. I was feeling pretty good as I walked into their heavily air-conditioned store (envelope-less for the first time today). My shopping list wasn't all that huge...some milk (which I could have purchased in Nanny Cay, but as long as I am here at Bobby's, I might as well buy some); some pasta and some pesto and salad dressing. So, to carry on from my already totally buggered morning, all they had that I was looking for was the pasta and salad dressing, so I went back out into the heat. I was going to think of what else I could do now that I was in Road Town, but instead, with sincere apologies to Mr Dylan, I got a coin to flip. *"It came up tails, which rhymed with sails, so I made it back to the ship."*

Today's scores. Exercise quotient: Super-duper-high. Satisfaction for task accomplishment: Yeah, well, not all that great.

One of the challenges that I face here is trying to think about what you might be interesting in knowing about. Every day here is new and pretty great, but I do recognise that what I think is pretty interesting (and therefore worth writing about) may not be interesting to you. And then there is the topic of weather. One of the reasons I have written about the weather is that it is pretty flippin' great here. Perhaps I write about it so you have context, or perhaps I write about it so that those of you who live in shite weather locations grumble. Or maybe I write about it because I simply love being here. However, as much as I would like to say all is totally and completely under control here, we are talking about Mother Nature...and she can be a bit unpredictable at times. So...here is what is going on here as of Saturday morning and what I am going to do about it.

As Bob Dylan said, *"You don't need a weatherman to know which way the wind blows;"* but when it comes to hurricanes that might be approaching, it certainly can help.

As MLR has said more than once to me, *"James, what is your plan if Irma comes exceptionally close?"* First, "exceptionally close" is one of those descriptors that has piles of baggage with it. To me, "exceptionally close" means that I would have to get off Saphir and find some place to spend a few days. In real terms, that, according to locals that have lived through seriously nasty tropical storms, is when the winds are in excess of 75 mph. It seems when the wind is that strong, it means that you can barely stand up, so the spectre of being blown over and chucked into the bay here is not really that attractive, so if the forecasts show that Irma is coming overhead with monster winds, I would leave. Clearly, this means you do need to stay on top of the forecasts, as by the time the wind would be that testy would be too late to leave. Second, based on where Irma is right now, and the speed and direction she is headed, we have been told we won't even know until Sunday or Monday how close "close" will be. So that means keep refining the plan and waiting. It is Saturday.

As of now, the big plan includes the following.
- I have already stripped off the headsail and would either strip off the main or simply lock it firmly into the mast where it resides.
- Take off the Spray Hood, the Bimini, and the Perspex insert that joins the two, and stow them.
- Empty the refrigerator and freezer.
- Lock and seal all opening hatches.
- Strip off any loose or non-essential lines, sheets, and halyards (including burgees)
- Strip off the davit hoist lines
- Fill water tank and diesel tanks (to increase stability of the boat just in case)
- Put about six old tires in large garbage bags and use them as additional fenders around Saphir. (the yacht management company will supply them to me and my neighbours)
- Make arrangements to find a place to stay for a couple of days, as I have been told that I would not want to stay on-board during a hurricane.
- Put on additional lines connecting Saphir to the marina docks. The word "additional" means every extra line I have on-board.
- Disconnect the two mains power lines from Saphir to the marina.
- Open the sea-cock on Seraphina (the tender) and let her fill with water. She is a Zodiac-type tender and will not sink when the interior is filled with water. This will give her more stability and reduce the chance that Irma could pick her up and send her flying through the air.
- Put together a small bag containing identification documents; important papers; books to read; and the usual stuff you would take if you were going on a little holiday.

Actually, there is a prequel to the big plan, and that is to talk to locals to find out what they think is going to happen, or could happen. I spoke to two more locals this morning, as well as several ex-pats who have been in the BVI for donkey's-years. The consensus is that there is no consensus. Part of this reason does seem to be divided into two groups....the people who rely on science and technology, and those who think science and technology is good, but not quite as reliable as nature. About the only thing that everyone does agree with is that it will take a few more days before it makes sense to do just about anything. I am good with that. Having said that, I am watching the NOAA site multiple times daily now, and am working on cooking up damn near everything in the fridge. Might also walk over to the hotel and see if I can get a room for the end of next week.

If this projected hurricane path does occur, the centre of Irma should (hopefully will) pass about 200 miles northeast of Tortola. After doing a quick walk-around survey of long-time residents, this would mean it would be "nicely messy" here. "Nicely messy" seems to mean windy and wet according to those in the know. That would be far better than having Irma roll smack over Tortola, but because it is Mother Nature we are talking about, I will continue to get ready in case she decides to be a real bitch and come closer.

Having said all that, when I checked the NOAA site this morning, I saw that Irma may not be the only visitor. So nice to be popular.....

09

Irma Comes to Visit

A visit from Irma.

Just a preliminary note about this part of the story. I haven't been giving titles to my chapters previously, but I thought that this one did deserve one. To me, it seems perfectly appropriate (and incredibly cheeky) to call it ***"Another Day in Paradise."*** If you don't live in a cave in the Himalayas, you probably know that a hurricane came through the Caribbean last week. This chapter is a bit longer than previous ones and it tries to tell the story of what it was like to be here during the hurricane. Spoiler alert: It wasn't fun.

So…I was enrolled in Hurricane 101, and not by choice. Well, that isn't exactly true….I could have left Saphir to fend for herself, or not even have come to the British Virgin Islands, so I guess enrolling in this "course" was sort of a choice. Best I start this over again… I have made it through intro to Hurricane 101, and it has been "interesting."

04 Sept, 1132h What I find so amazing is that all the weather reports are slowly but surely categorising the Irma situation as becoming Category 4 and having it pass about only 30 miles from Tortola. Everyday a new projection comes out and the situation is shifting from grim to grimmer. I would assume that by later today, the situation will be grimmest, but that would be kind of silly as we all know that Wednesday will be the real grimmest day. Not even sure if these are real words. Grim, grimmey, grimmest, grimmeyerest? As I look down the docks at the boats that are here in the marina, I am pretty tripped out that not many of them seem to be getting ready for the hurricane. Having said that, I give my neighbour John seriously big points for his efforts to get ready. He has experienced hurricanes previously and he has his boat lashed eighty-five different ways and has even chucked an anchor in to help keep his bow away from anything. And if his prep-work isn't enough, he is doing it all on his own, whilst being a Dad to a 3 year old daughter and a 5 year old son. Pretty impressive. So he is one extreme. The other end of the "getting ready for Irma" continuum is the seriously lackadaisical stance of so many others. If you didn't have a computer or smartphone (which means no news or storm projections) you would swear that today was just another day in paradise. Incredible. Maybe tomorrow (Tuesday), everyone will snap to and get cracking. Maybe.

I just went for a walk to the store and I did see that almost all the second story windows in the Nanny Cay complex have their storm shutters closed and more and more boats do seem to be adding lines and are being held

Living on Rocks

off their respective docks. Still, when I was in the store, I was talking to one of my buddies who works there and he said that they would be open from 0700h to 1900h every day, regardless of a hurricane or not. I assume that means as long as the employees can actually get to the store. Time will tell on that one.

I was struggling to get a good connection most of the day and finally around 1600h, I rang the office and was told that they are taking down the access points to avoid having them fly away in a day or two. The Internet is still working in the office, the plaza, and in the hotel, so I might need to take a walk later.

04 Sept, 1800h Not much to do now other than watch telly for a bit and get some sleep. This afternoon had been pretty productive, with doing last minute checks, removing things like the stainless Dorade vents, helping Travis (a man who works for the yacht management company here) set lines, and potentially one of the most important things: taking lots of photos of the preparations I have made in case. Always a good thing to have in case I need to (heaven forbid) contact my insurance company.

05 Sept, 0700h I woke up this morning to the sound of rain, but after a few minutes, it was clear that this was not really Irma rain, but just tropical storm rain; i.e. another one of those 5-10 minute rain deluges that we get here at this time of the year. After that cloud continued past, the sun was there, signalling another very special day. Of course in this case, the descriptor "very special" does mean something other than sunny-and-warm-with-nice-breezes. Irma is coming later today. Last evening, after watching a movie, I was able to get online using Sapphires network repeater to the system on shore, and was looking at information regarding hurricane rotation. Hurricanes north of the equator all spin anti-clockwise, and typically, this means that the winds to the north of a hurricane centre are worse than they are in the south. And because Irma is going to pass so close to Tortola, that could be to our advantage. "Could" being the operative word here.

It is now 1400h, and I have left Saphir and am in the hotel here at Nanny Cay. Actually, I have made three trips here, bringing over things I might need during the storm. The reason for three trips is that some of these bags were heavy and I am doing this alone, which meant two trips. The third trip was because I felt the need to go back and check Saphir one more time. But now I am in the hotel and am reflecting on what today has been like. It was pretty amazing to see that everyone suddenly showed-up and went to work on shuttering buildings, and lashing boats together and to the various docks here. Right now, the main centre of the marina (where Saphir is) looks like this huge spider-web, with lines going every which way securing everything before the storm hits. MLR sent me several messages during the morning, each one painting a darker and darker picture of Irma. So now she is a Category 5, which means seriously fucking big winds, and its path has again shifted a bit so now we are smack in the path of Irma. Am not overly thrilled but that is the way things have turned out. Never having been in a huge hurricane (never having been in any hurricane to be really explicit), I have no idea what to expect. Having said that, I have, since settling into the hotel, seen all sorts of doom and gloom hurricane stories, so I guess my expectation is that it will be shit. My plan is to be here for Tuesday, Wednesday, and Thursday, and then go back to Saphir (assuming Saphir is still here and not winging her way to Miami Beach. To paraphrase an old movie, I feel like I should be standing outside, clicking my Crocs together, saying, *"I sure am not in Andratx anymore."*

Still 5 September, but now it is 1800h. I went back to check on Saphir and the wind is picking up. Nothing overly dramatic yet, but you can hear the whistling sound as the wind weaves its way around all the standing masts and shrouds. And so it begins.

6 September, 0800h. So, this is the day Irma is supposed to hit. I have been up since 0400h. Unbelievable howling wind, on-and-off buckets of rain. All the electricity failed about 0540h, and as of now the generators have still not started up. The wind is from the north, so that means that we are still on the leading edges of the rotation. Some trees have blown down already and Irma is still 8-10 hours away.

6 September, 1000h (more or less). My friends Karl and Vikki (who live in Mallorca) called, and the conversation was one of those good-news-bad-news things. The good news was that they rang and were very concerned. Very good friends. The bad news was that they had been following any information on Irma and updated me on her path and what devastation she had wrought on St Martin on her way across the Caribbean. As we were on Facetime, I showed them live pictures from the marina, and updated them on what was going on here. They said they would put an update online as I had been receiving quite a few messages from other friends, and then they said they would ring back in a couple of hours. Not long after that, I rang MLR, and gave her the same update that I had shared with Karl and Vikki. I told her not to be scared as I had done everything possible to prepare Saphir and was now in the relative safety of the hotel at Nanny Cay. She said she would ring back in a few hours as well.

6 September, 1130h Things here are going downhill at an alarming rate. Not only is there no electricity, the phone service has now stopped, so this means no communications with friends and family. No electricity also meant no water, as water-pumping systems would be out. No water meant, amongst other obvious things, no functioning loos. No broadband, no way to get in touch with emergency services, no just about everything. I had, when speaking to everyone earlier and the previous day, said that if I am not in communications, the only thing to consider is that communications are all down from Irma's intrusion on the peace and tranquillity of the BVI. No one should think, assume, or wonder if, I was unable to communicate for some other reason.

6 September, 1200h I guess because I have never experienced a hurricane before, much less a Category 5 hurricane, I really had no expectations of what it would be like. For the first few hours after daylight began to lighten up everything, it was possible to open a window and its persianas (shutters) and see what was occurring. By noon, this option was clearing not on the table anymore. I did have my hand-held VHF radio (it is a boat thing and operates on battery) and was monitoring some of the traffic around the marina. What I was hearing was not good, with reports of boats sustaining some damage. That wasn't too big of a surprise, as the wind was howling louder than I had ever experienced in my entire life. Think of what it would be like standing next to one of the Rolls-Royce jet engines on a Boeing 787...and then double it or treble it. The descriptor "fierce" does not adequately describe what the sound was like. It was unbelievably loud, which made it doubly ominous because I knew what the wind could be doing. The last time I had been able to look out the window, I had seen good-sized waves screaming through the marina, accompanied by dead-flat-horizontal rain. Even though I did not feel that it was wise to try to open a window again, I was able to see a nice, constant flow of water coming in from under the balcony doors of my hotel room. And by the time I was placing every towel I had in front of the door, the doors blew open, ripping the locks off the doorframes. Right. Time to rearrange the room a bit. I dragged the sofa, table, two loungers, and anything else that was substantial into a nice pile with the meagre hope of keeping the doors shut. I probably am mis-using the words "meagre hope" here...I should have said "absolute and depressing hopeless effort" and the wind-speed was a function of Mother Nature, and all I had on my side was some semi-tacky rattan furniture. Not exactly the best odds to wager on. As I scurried around looking to see what else I could use to stop the now river-like flow, I heard the roof tearing itself off. The roof of the hotel looked to be semi-corrugated sheet metal, and it was a pretty safe bet that it was only screwed or nailed to a solid wooden support system. Inside my room (I was on the second floor, the top floor of the two-story hotel), the ceiling was a very nicely dark stained vaulted ceiling with big beams. But as soon as the sheet metal was viciously ripped from its mounting, it was clear that the gaps between the wood boards that made up the vaulted ceiling were big enough to let water through...and let water through they did. It was pretty obvious that being in the room was not a sustainable option anymore, and I retreated to the bathroom (that had a false ceiling) and tried to get cosy reclined in the bathtub. At the time, this made lots of sense, as it was undoubtedly the strongest space in the hotel room. So there I was, semi-reclined in the bath, in damp clothes due to the now incessant waterfall in the main hotel room, reading my Kindle, and monitoring what was going on with my hand-held VHF.

I started to hear conversations between someone named Althea (but right now am not sure that was her name), and various other people. Althea was in the shower block with several other people and was saying that they felt very safe and there was room there if anyone wanted to try to get there. Sitting in the tub, listening to the roar and knowing that the ceiling structure itself may not last too much longer, I radioed her back to say who I was, where I was, and that I was going to attempt to get to them. I packed up what I could in one briefcase; leaving the other two bags I had with me in the bathtub and went to open the door. It would not open. The amount of air pressure doing strange things due to the circulation of Irma was incredible, and after many tugs on the handle, I managed to get the door open. That was when I first saw some of the destruction that had been going on around me. More trees down, with branches and large segments of the sheet metal roof swirling around in some post-modern dance of death. I started to rethink my plan of getting to the shower block, but as I looked back into the rest of the room, I knew it was time to go; staying in the hotel room was clearly not a sustainable option. Down along the outside hallway to the stairwell; down the stairs, which were littered with pieces of the hotel building; and around the corner. The entrance to the shower block was about 40 metres away, but it was along another exposed hallway that appeared to be an airflow chamber for horizontally beating rain, and assorted pieces of railings, sheet metal, and three branches. This was one of those terrible life decision times; you know you can't go back (probably because it might be impossible to make it back to the room) and you know that continuing on to the shower block door is going to be the most difficult thing I had done so far. The decision sorted itself out when it became apparent that I could not stay standing there any more as too many things were flying my way. I radioed again to say I was almost there, but all I heard in response was that the wind was too strong and they couldn't understand what I said, but would be ready at the door in case I said I was coming. A big breath of air (hoping the breath would contain energy or adrenalin or something) and I plunged out…just as a large branch fell and blocked my path forward and backward. I turned a bit and went out from under the hallway and worked my way to the door. Three people were there and pushed the door open as I staggered in, completely soaked, quite exhausted, but alive. They immediate lashed the door closed again and I and the other seven or eight people tried to smile as we greeted each other. Lots of questions about what it was like outside and where I came from. My answers were *"Room 212, up there,"* and, *"It is pretty much like hell outside."* The main topic of conversation in the shower block hallway revolved around when the hurricane eye would arrive. We all knew by then that Irma had shifted her path so much that we would experience some lull of the eye, but no one knew if the eye would come in right over Tortola. With reports that the eye was more than ten miles in diameter, it was possible that we would be able to tell when it was here. That happened within an hour or so.

6 September, a bit after 1300h It seemed to take place rather quickly, but

Living on Rocks

upon reflection, it happened over a ten-minute period. The rain stopped going horizontally, and then the wind seemed to lessen considerably...and it became lighter. This all meant that we were either on the edge of the eye or damn near in the middle of it. Everyone in the shower block fled the dark, extremely humid environment where we had been huddled, and stepped outside. I decided I would go back up to my room on the second floor, but after turning the corner from the shower block doors, I could see that there was no way I would be able to climb over the massive piles of debris that had jammed themselves in a small walk path. I tried to see if there was another way to reach the second floor, but I knew that the clock was ticking away, and if the eye was 10 or 12 miles in diameter, and the storm was moving at about 16 mph (which is what we had heard), then there was damn little time to faff about outside. I returned to the shower block door and tracked down Althea. As she seemed to be the one that was de-facto in charge, I told her she needed to tell everyone what "the plan" was for when the eye moved on and we were in the shit again. She agreed and did have a plan. But now there was a new problem. When the eye came over, not only did all of us that had been in the shower block go outside, everyone else that was staying in the hotel materialised at the doors to talk, share, and ask questions. Now we had a group in excess of 30 people, and when Althea made her announcement, everyone started to pile back into the shower block to wait for instructions for when we should leave.

Standing in the eye of Irma was pretty incredible. It only took a few minutes to go from roaring, fucking hell, to a very surreal calm. The sun was out, there was only the gentlest of breezes, sensationally warm, and surrounded by downed trees, huge pieces of metal roofs, and people who were clearly shell-shocked. It was almost like Salvador Dali painting that had come to life. And in an almost good way. But we all knew that this surreal environment would not last for more than a short time. We also knew that when all hell broke loose again, it would be worse.

Althea's plan was to head over to one of the condominiums and hunker down there. Her rationale was that when the eye would pass over, the storm surge would come flooding across the car park and it most certainly would reach the shower block. No one was keen on being stuck in a dark space with water rising incredibly quickly; especially when there was talk that the storm surge could reach over 5 or 6 feet. It was at about this point in time that I saw that people were putting on life-jackets that some had brought with them, and it was possible to hear murmuring from some that they were in fear of drowning if the surge could come pouring in. Things were going downhill. This was complicated even further when I realised that the door opened outward, and if there was a wall of water coming, it might be near impossible to even open the door to leave. I mentioned this to Althea, along with the reality that it might be better to leave before the eye was completely past. She agreed and screamed out, *"That's it, we're going now,"* and proceeded to go racing outside. I was pretty close to her as she went out, and all I was carrying was my briefcase, but it was chocker with heavy stuff, and I realised quite quickly that I would not be able to keep up with most of the people, who by now were sprinting through the puddles, desperately trying to keep up with Althea, as she was apparently the only one who knew where the condo was. Around a corner we all went, with me the only one who wasn't running. Believe me, if I could have run, I would have. Across a small bridge and then around another corner, and suddenly I realised that I could not see anyone in front of me from the group of pretty panic-stricken people, who were, at this point, running for their lives. I kept going, with the assumption that I would see a condo door open with someone I recognised standing there. But as I was sloshing through what was now knee-deep water rushing at me pretty quickly, and rain pelting down again, even I was slowing down for fear of slipping and falling down, which would have not have been good. I came upon a group of condo gates and began to pound on each of them, yelling for Althea. I did realise that this could be a futile effort, as the roar of Irma was so strong that even I could not hear my fist smashing against the solid wooden gate door. At one of them, number 23 to be exact, a young man came to the gate and tore it open and hustled me into the unit. Quick introductions, *"Hi, I am James, and am sorry to barge in unannounced,"* followed by *"Hi, Dylan, and this is Cami…come in. Are you okay?"* Well no, but I said was something like *"I am fine to be out of that shit."* Dylan explained that they had seen me pounding just by chance because they had been on the second floor of the condo in case the flood surge came in too quickly. He had gone outside for a smoke when the eye came overhead and everything went all peaceful, but then had rushed back in when the eye wall appeared. It was just luck that instead of going back upstairs, he had stayed in the kitchen to see if he could see anything out the kitchen window of the condo. We actually kept talking in their kitchen for about 15 minutes and were about to go upstairs when someone else began to pound on their garden gate. Dylan rushed out in the now raging torrent and two men and two women staggered in, with one of the women almost collapsing on the floor once in the condo. She had fallen down into now more than knee-deep water and was clearly stressed. After a few minutes, we had all retreated to the second floor and waited, but didn't know what we were waiting for. After about 30 minutes of continual pummelling of the condo by the storm, the wind and the surge actually smashed through Dylan's front door, making the first floor a large swimming pool in seconds. Dylan and I ventured down the stairs a bit to see if there was anything that could be done but it was clear that there was no way we would be able to keep the door closed now that the door jam looked like a pile of floating toothpicks. We went back up and re-joined the group. We all just sat there, appreciative of the fact that we had made it through the first part of the storm, but the part after the eye went over was seeming much stronger and there was little we could do about it. By this time, I had heard on my VHF of the on-going destruction at the marina, but had no reports of where Saphir was (or used to be). Dylan went down to his kitchen-in-a-swimming-pool and about ten minutes later came up with cups of soup. Now just to clarify a bit here. Picture this: The front door of the condo has blown in from the wind and storm surge; there is over a foot of water covering the entire ground floor of the condo; Dylan is standing in the kitchen, in the foot of water, making soup on the gas hob. Damn. Back to the story...If you know me, you know I don't do soup. Well, I never used to do soup. I ended up having two cups of soup and it was the most welcomed food I could have ever hoped for. Good man Dylan.

6 September, 1800h (more or less) the entire hurricane time here could have been divided into three time chunks. The first was when the centre of Irma was a bit to the east of Tortola. Chunk 2 was when the eye was more or less transiting the island; and then there was the last chunk, which was the worst. The eye was moving past, which meant the rotation of Irma would now be pummelling us with winds from the West-South-West, and after a couple of hours, from the South. This is when the storm surge was at its zenith, and when the winds seemed to have so much more power than the first chunk of Irma. By 1800h, it sounded like things were beginning to calm a bit, but to be fair, "calm a bit" means that now it felt like the worst hurricane ever experienced by humans. Clearly, this is what the term "relative" is all about. What we were experiencing then, "relative" to what we had already experienced, didn't seem all that bad. The reason "relative" was so impactful was that by now it was pretty clear to everyone on the planet that Irma was the biggest, strongest, nastiest hurricane to have ever transited the Atlantic in recorded history. So in layman's terms, Irma was a real big bitch. And she sure was.

6 September, 1900h I went and laid down in one of the bedrooms that Dylan and Cami said were free to use and for some time, couldn't get this experience out of my head. Fair enough. It was beyond brutal. It wasn't until Thursday morning that it was possible to see what Irma left in her wake.

7 September, 0600h I was the first one up and whilst Dylan had told me the night before I should feel free to make something (toast, tea, whatever... they had a gas hob so it would still work), I decided I would take a little walk. Have you ever seen photos of the damage from the two atomic bombs that were dropped on Hiroshima and Nagasaki? This is what Nanny Cay looked like. Utter devastation. I walked past the hotel where I had been staying but was more focused on the marina side of the walk path. Boats under water, boats smashed into other boats, boats upended onto the walk path. I had seen photos of things like this, but actually being here seeing them in real life was a pretty powerful experience...and not in a good way. I kept walking...well, "walking" included feeling completely in a daze. This feeling was even more surreal as to get around, I was climbing up over boat parts and trees that had gone down...and finally, I saw Saphir. Interestingly enough, she was still connected to the boats that were on either side of her just be-

fore the storm hit. All three of them were there...but jammed in between another twenty or thirty boats that were in various states of disrepair. The good news was that Saphir was still floating. The bad news was that the entire super-structure of her was gone, and at this point in time, there was no way to know if she was floating on her own, or floating because she was still connected to other boats. I could not help but believe that Saphir will be rated as a total loss.

7 September, 0900h After trying to help out by carrying a six-gallon floor scrubbing bucket to the part of the Nanny Cay marina that was just constructed in the past year to fill it with water (as there is still no electricity, there is no water and in order to flush the loos, you need to fill the tanks repeatedly), I thought I would take a walk over to see if I could get into my hotel room. I had food and clothes still there. The food was something that Dylan, Cami, and I could use to stay going, and the clothes would be good to have because I was still wearing the same damp/wet/soaked (at various times during the previous day, each one of those descriptors was appropriate). So, climbing over ripped-off tin roof sheeting, downed branches and tress, and the odd nautical bits that had made it up on the grass lawn in front of the hotel buildings, as well as the odd-chunk of miscellaneous debris, I found myself at the stairwell that would take me up to the second floor. This stairwell contained less debris that I expected, and after making it to my room door, I tried my key card, but to no avail. There could be a bazillion reasons why it wasn't working, and it wasn't worth even trying to figure out what they were, so I went back downstairs. I saw a group of youngsters (okay, probably hotel guests who were in the mid-twenties, but to me, those are youngsters) and went to see how they were doing. Two of them had just married and were on their honeymoon. The new wife made some comment about *"Some honeymoon to remember,"* and I jumped in with *"This is a good thing to remember. No matter how much you get pissed off at each other in the future, you both need to take a breath and remember that you survived Irma together, and if that can't keep a couple together, nothing will."* Good deed done for the day. We chatted for a bit and then one of them asked which room I was in (or had been in). I said it was 212 and I was here to try to get things out of the room, but the door lock wasn't being overly accommodating to my plans. Brian, the newly minted husband said that he knew where there was a ladder I could use to climb up to my balcony. That seemed like a good idea, but I said I didn't think I wanted to be the one to climb up, so would he do it. Brian said sure, and a few minutes later, he and a friend materialised with this huge aluminium ladder, so I led them around to the side of the hotel that my balcony was on.

This was one of those seminal, *"Holy shit, this storm was more powerful than anyone could have imagined"* moments. Brian scrambled up the ladder whilst I went back up through the stairwell to wait for him at my door. When it opened, Brian had a strange look on his face, sort of a cross between pure fear and total amazement. It was because not only was the railing around the balcony missing, the entire wall and roof were missing. All that was left of my room – the room I had been trying to ride out the storm in – were two side walls, and a wall where my front door wouldn't even open.

We both stood there for a moment, looking around what all the fluffs of pink insulation that were embedded in the remaining walls and furniture that was piled up as if it had fallen from the sky...which I guess it sort of did. I asked Brian if he was okay, because it was clear he had never seen anything like this (nor had I) and he replied with a hesitant, "*Ah, yeah, yeah I'm okay.*" I told him he could go back down to be with his wife, but he said he would wait for me, so I began to look for the bathroom. I had spent the last 30 minutes in the room sort of lying down in the bathtub, as it seemed that it would be the safest place in the entire room. Well it was, because when I managed to bust open the bathroom door, the little space was intact and dry. After a few choice expletives, I grabbed my rucksack and cooler bag that I had brought with me to the hotel when I checked in, and then began to empty the refrigerator, which was still closed, into the two bags. Next it was dig through the pile and move furniture around to access the dresser where my clothes were and after grabbing my trendy straw sun hat and umbrella, we took one last look and left what remained as room 212 and both walked down the stairwell. I thanked Brian more times than I can remember and as I was walking away, I could hear him telling some of the others that had gathered around what he had seen in my room. I came back to the condo, probably a bit more shaken than I had been an hour earlier, and gave all the food to Dylan and Cami and then set out to find Saphir again.

It only took 30 minutes to find her and she was still floating, albeit totally jammed between numerous other boats, with all of them showing various levels of damage. Actually, there was nothing I could do but just look at her, and that didn't seem like it was a healthy thing to do, so I came back to the condo.

7 September, 1100h We (Dylan, Cami, and I) spent most of the rest of the day trying to sort out the condo that they are living in. It did take quite a hit from the hurricane, but all of the condos did surprisingly well compared to so many other properties here in Nanny Cay. The Condos and the new marina are only a couple of years old, and the construction methods used on them undoubtedly were different than the older units in Nanny Cay; which could have contributed to why they survived better. We can only imagine what the rest of the island looks like.

7 September, 2000h Chris and Marli, two of the (now) friends that were welcomed into the condo during the hurricane shortly after I made it in, stopped over with six bottles of Proseco. Not wanting to alienate new friends, we went through several of them as we "relived" the previous day.

8 September, 0700h I seem to consistently be the first one up in the morn-

James B Rieley

ing, and as I am a guest, I feel compelled to do something. Today, I wandered off to fill up our water supply. It did take three trips of hauling a very heavy water bucket, but by the time I was done, we were set for the day. And just as I was pouring the last bucket load into our hand-dandy water reservoir, there was a knock on the external gate. It was Dylan's neighbour who, because of our bout without electricity for a couple of days, had seen quite a few packages of frozen fruit defrost. And what do would you do if that happened to you? He made several pitchers of fruit smoothies and brought one over for us. A pretty great neighbour for sure. I had one glass, and kept the rest for D and C.

8 September, 0830h I decided that I wanted to go check out Saphir again, so walked around the complex until I found a squirrely path without huge piles of debris that I could negotiate down to the water. When I arrived, the first person I saw was my friend John, who with his two children, had been living on his boat in the marina as well. His boat did not survive well either and he was making multiple trips from shore to his boat to empty what he could. He said that he had seen Saphir – actually he said that he had crawled over Saphir and about six other boats several times on the way to his boat. Things on Saphir were not good, and John said he would take some photos of her if I wanted. I gave him my iPhone. About ten minutes later, he reappeared and gave me the phone and a fuller description of the hits that Saphir had taken. The description was not good and I asked him if he thought I could crawl over the other boats so I could take some things off my boat. John agreed and would help me get there.

Later, after John's help getting over the nautical mess, I was standing on the now completely stripped deck of my boat. No mast. No superstructure for the wind generator, solar panels, and all the antennas. A missing port. The toe-rails on both port and starboard destroyed. A longitudinal crack that ran the length of the top deck. The bow pulpit smashed into an almost Gordian knot looking mess. Water inside the cabin. I suppose the only good news was that she wasn't in immediate danger of sinking. After inspecting the external parts of my seriously damaged boat, I went below. Everything obviously tossed around. Water on the cabin sole. Water in the bilge. Water all over the navigation station. I found the missing smashed port laying on the cabin sole, along with just about everything else that had been below. I didn't attempt to turn anything on, as I agreed with John that Saphir was most likely a total write off. I did dig out of the mess several computers (right now my sons are wondering why I had more than one computer on Saphir.... well I have multiple computers and use them some times and it is always great to have a spare). I took a pillow out of a pillow case from the settee and chucked the computers in it and left Saphir, managing to get back to land without sliding into the (seriously polluted) harbour.

8 September, 1400h The three of us were feeling pretty rank after several days without showers, so we went over to the other side of the harbour

where Chris' (remember Chris and Marli?) boats were tied up. Chris manages a charter company and was fortunate as four out of his eight boats in Nanny Cay, only three had sunk. When Chris and Marli had been over for the Proseco-fest, he had told us that if we wanted to shower, we could do so on one of his remaining boats. Showering was like a gift from above, and to be clear, a gift from above was far better than an apocalyptic experience named Irma from above. Each one of us did try to be respectful and not totally drain their water system, and when we were all done and dressed again, standing on the deck of the catamaran, we all felt pretty good. We jumped into Dylan's car and headed into Road Town. We had heard that there were functioning mobile phone towers in Road Town, and each one of us needed to talk to family and friends to let them know we did make it through the storm, which by now had been recognised by whomever measures this stuff as the biggest, nastiest, and most powerful hurricane ever to come to the Caribbean.

The ride into Road Town was an eye opener. I had seen pictures of this kind of destruction, but had never really seen it before in person. It was, in a word, horrific. Best not to even try to describe it, and truth-be-told, it is very difficult to look back at the photos I took at the time.

After returning to the condo, and having...ready?...more soup. Damn, I am almost beginning to like soup. Damn. We walked over to the Beach Bar, which of course didn't even exist anymore, for a meeting called by the Manager of Nanny Cay. The turnout was pretty impressive in itself, with so many now familiar and friendly faces saying hello as we walked in and sat down. Not only were people polite and friendly, everyone has evolved a bit and asks how you are doing. We were doing the same to them. The sense of bonding after going through this kind of experience is pretty powerful, and I would think it is safe to say that I now have even more very special friends who I will be connected to for the rest of my life. The meeting itself dealt with weather updates – tropical storm Jose was supposed to arrive here on Saturday....tomorrow. Isn't that special? The good news is that the latest projections show it only brushing past Tortola with Category 3 winds. Two weeks ago, we would have all been rushing around preparing for this huge storm, but now, after the evil rage of Irma, if the projections are right, this will seem like a light breeze for us. We heard about all the security efforts being undertaken at Nanny Cay, which were pretty impressive. After the storm, there has been a moderate level of looting in Road Town, and the management team does not want that to happen here. We also heard that the water is supposed to be functioning tomorrow, which received a substantial amount of applause. Several other updates, then time for questions, and then we all walked back to wherever we were staying. For the three of us, it was a fabulous dinner prepared by Cami, and then just sitting around and talking about the day.

9 September, 0700h I awoke this morning the sound of an electrical fan

in the room I was using, and by this time, light was flooding through the windows. Two pretty nice signs to wake up to. One of the messages last evening at the Nanny Cay meeting was that the electricity generator for the complex would shut down at 2200h and return into service when Steve (the man responsible for infrastructure issues at Nanny Cay) would wake up. This made perfect sense. As we are getting our power from a monster generator on the Nanny Cay grounds, it made no sense to have it running all night when we are, or should be, sleeping. Refrigerators and freezers would be fine until the system would start up again the following morning. The part of waking to sunlight that was so good also related to something that had been talked about last evening. This was the news about tropical storm Jose. Even though the projections are for it to pass us with a pretty wide berth, as we all learnt a few days ago, projections are not necessarily the same as reality, so a sunny morning is a good thing. We shall see later in the day where Jose really is, as we were told that we could first feel him around 1400h, with his eye swinging past around midnight. Whilst 90% of the people at the meeting were pretty relieved at this news, you never know. There are a lot of fingers crossed here at Nanny Cay.

I thought it best to chip in and do something to help out my more than generous housemates, so I went out for more loo-flushing water after having a toasted bagel and some tea. The whole thing about the reality that we need to get our own water to fill the water tanks on a loo is really pretty sad. We are sitting here in Nanny Cay, a privately owned business, and we have electricity, will soon have water, and the rest of the island has neither, and probably will not have either for weeks or more, and we think it is a hardship. Pretty shite attitude. I tend to think that going to collect water from the new marina is really just part of a nice exercise programme. End of.

9 September, 1300h The three of us headed into Road Town again today. Dylan had a meeting that he had to attend, and Cami and I just were keen on checking in with family and friends. I did managed to connect with both of my sons, Matthew and David, as well as with MLR and several special friends before we then headed back to Nanny Cay. The kids dropped me off as they were going out to West End to check on their friends, and I wanted to check on Saphir again. After walking in past security (we now do have a security checkpoint to ensure that looters or potential looters cannot get into Nanny Cay), I found the spot in the marina where there is a monster-sized catamaran that is half on land and half in the water. When I was here yesterday, with John's help, I was able to negotiate my way to Saphir. So today, I found the catamaran, and after climbing on-board the boat that was literally sitting on a 45-degree angle, I carefully walked across the deck until I could get to the next boat in the multiple-boat-path-to-Saphir. Sadly, several boats had been towed away, and now it was impossible to even reach Saphir, so I had to walk back to the condo without being able to salvage anything else from my very sad boat. Being that close to Saphir but unable to board her left me

gutted.

9 September, 1700h There was another meeting tonight for all the residents of Nanny Cay. Most of the topics were security, fuel, and the water situation. These people are really doing a good job of passing along communication. Too often, organisations or groups of people don't pass along enough information about what is going on, and because we are humans, we tend to fill in the gaps in communication – the *"we don't know what is going on"* gaps – with our own hopes/assumptions/ beliefs, usually that are well off reality. By holding these nightly meetings, it enables us to not feel the need to fall into the rumour trap and consequently, feel that the people making decisions know what they are doing. One of the bits of information tonight was about tropical storm Jose, and I don't think there are any of us that are overly worried now.

9 September, 1900h Several other friends of Dylan and Cami came over to stay at the condo tonight. Two friends, Chris and Amanda, live on the island, with Chris working with Dylan. Their home was pretty much buggered in the Irma nightmare, so Dylan had said they could spend a few nights there at the condo to recharge their electronic kit and themselves. Then, just about the time that Cami had prepared another fabulous dinner, another friend stopped in and ate with us.

10 September, 0645h The electricity came on again this morning…always a blessing…but still no water. Perhaps soon. The big tizzy about hurricane Jose, which was really Tropical Storm Jose, evaporated faster than food on store shelves during a looting. I slept right through the night, and this morning, the only remnant of Jose (if any at all) was a nice breeze. This is very good for if we had tried to go through another hurricane, I am not sure that people here could have handled it. For sure, the people of the island have had more than they can deal with already and another one would have probably resulted in a total and complete breakdown of society.

I went over to try to see if there was another way to get on-board Saphir, but it is too risky now. Boats that are still floating are shifting a bit and now Saphir is well out of reach. My plan is to try to find someone who has a functioning tender and see if I can get a ride out to her.

10 September, 1230h. I rang up Chris, the friend whom I met during the nightmare of Irma, and asked if he could take me in one of his tenders out to Saphir. This seems like the logical way to solve the problem of not being able to board her. Chris, one of those over-the-top-generous-souls, said, *"Not a problem James. I will meet you at the bridge in 10 minutes."* Dylan and I walked over to the bridge and sure enough, Chris was coming toward us quite quickly. We jumped into his tender and we proceeded to track down where Saphir was. Just about halfway there, I looked up and here was Saphir coming toward us. The local salvage people were able to cut her loose from the Medusa-like tangle of shrouds, broken and downed masts, and dock lines

that were still attached to the numerous boats all jammed together. I had asked them to try to move her as every day that Saphir was in the mess, the risk of her sinking increased because boats she was connected to were slipping lower and lower in the water. If Saphir is a total write off, (which it does look like), I didn't want it to happen because I didn't try everything to save her. I leapt out of Chris" tender and onto the salvage boat and we slowly plodded our way to the new marina on the other side of Nanny Cay. About 30 minutes later, Saphir was firmly tied to a new pontoon and I set out to do a more thorough inspection of how she did in the hurricane. The reality is that she did pretty damn good. The evidence of that is that she was still floating. It was also clear however, that she had more damage that I first thought, with everything topsides shredded, crushed, or gone. Her hull is excessively beaten and abraded, and even worse, there was quite a bit of water in the bilges that won't come out from the pumps. I think that her hull could have been holed by something, and although it might be a small hole, it must be a hole none-the-less…and holes in the hulls of sailboats are not a good thing.

I emptied Saphir of all the bottles of water, soda, and beer so I could bring them to the condo for additional provisions for Dylan, Cami, and myself. Just after unloading them all at the condo, a neighbour asked me if I could help him move a boat. I, of course, said I would help. It was a big boat and there were only the two of us doing it, but we did get if to a new location as was needed. With some luck, my back will be pain-free again in a coupe of months.

By the time I made it back to the condo a few hours later, I was hotter and sweatier than I had been in my entire time in the BVI. Still no water in Nanny Cay, so I put on my swimmers (freshly liberated from Saphir) and went to the beach for a swim and cool down.

10 September, 1700h We went to the day's update meeting and were pretty chuffed about the news. The water system is almost ready to be turned on, and we might be full service again by tomorrow. We were also told that 150 Royal Marines were now on the island, and tonight, we would have 17 of them here at Nanny Cay. The management team really appreciates all the volunteering and helping that we residents have done, and we certainly have appreciate all their efforts to help get Nanny Cay running again.

11 September, 0630h It was very surreal this morning. There was a tension between knowing that I really need to leave Tortola, and wanting to stay and continue to help out. The first part of the tension is pretty tangible: my home is Saphir and, whilst she is still afloat, she is not liveable now, so staying on her is not an option. Whilst Dylan and Cami have repeatedly said I can stay with them as long as I want to or need to, that really isn't a sustainable option either. With no home/apartment/residence of any place, continuing to be here is in reality draining resources that could be applied better someplace else. There is the entire lodging issue, but there is also the

PTSD that is and will impact each of us that were here when Irma beat the crap out of the island. Living through something like this is pretty indescribable, but it will be difficult to expect that if you haven't been through a hurricane, much less the biggest and worst Atlantic/Caribbean hurricane of all time, that simply talking about it will make it okay. Then there is the self-imposed guilt that often strikes people who have lived through a major disaster. The guilt can strike because you don't understand why you made it through it in more-or-less one piece when so many others were devastated, and in many cases, lost their lives. I think the whole guilt thing contributes to people who leave when deep down inside, they want to continue to help.

On a less deep-thinking-psychological theme, I did go over to Saphir shortly after waking this morning. I rummaged around, trying for find more things to take off and keep, and whilst I did come back to the condo with a pillow case full of electronic things and some clothes, it really is a pretty crap feeling to know that you have to leave so much of what was important to you behind. Especially with the knowledge that if you leave it, you will never get it back again. A surveyor has not yet come to examine Saphir, but everyone who has seen here says she is toast. I have no idea what happens to boats that have been so beaten up that they are total losses. Perhaps insurance companies sell them for parts. Perhaps they are just towed out to sea and scuttled. I really have no idea. I might try to find out once I am out of here.

11 September, 1700. Not a lot happened today. Helped out some people with tier boats; talked to quite a few new friends about the experience that we all went through; and spent some time packing…and then repacking for my departure. Supposedly there is a boat coming for me tomorrow, but I did hear that the boat has been delayed again. Just before we went over to the nightly update meeting, Dylan, who had been in Road Town talking with Virgin people (and just to clarify, these are people he works with at Richard Branson's company). When he came home, he said that he could arrange for me to be evacuated tomorrow on a helicopter to San Juan. Clearly, I instantly had some real mixed emotions about his offer, but I did said okay…and thank you. Feeling pretty good about this, we walked over to the Beach Bar area where the nightly meetings are held. Usual announcement topics, good updates, and then the news that Adrian (our IT guy at Nanny Cay) had been working with Digicel (one of the mobile providers here on the island) and had set up WIFI coverage for about half of Nanny Cay. The coverage doesn't make it to the condo, but having to walk for a few minutes is a pretty small price to pay for communications. Especially when so many on the island still have no electricity, which of course means no communications. And whilst this news made everyone happy, what really brought a smile to our faces was the name that the WIFI coverage service has. Now what you do is turn on your phone, go to settings, go to WIFI, and look for F U IMRA. We all loved that.

Two other things happened at the meeting that made it different than the previous ones. First, a dozen Royal Marines were there. Seeing them there with us in person made us all very happy, as security on Tortola has become a serious issue. Restoring order on the island is a crucial step in starting the rebuilding process. And having a military presence here at Nanny Cay makes us all feel more secure. The other thing that stood out was that there were not as many people at the meeting. Quite a few people have been evacuated, which is a good thing, but also a hard thing when some of them have become friends. Apparently I am not the only one who noticed this, and there were quite a few of us who made it a point to talk to as many friends as possible, knowing that we might not see each other again for a long time.

12 September, 0600h I had been told that today was going to be the day I would be evacuated, and truth-be-told, I wasn't feeling too good about it. Have no doubt, I knew it made all the sense in the world for me to leave, but there was that little voice inside whispering, *"James, do you want to leave? Isn't there something you can do to help fix Nanny Cay and Tortola?"* Of course the answer is yes, but with the caveat that what I can bring to help fix it all can be done remotely. Staying meant that I would just be using resources that could be used elsewhere. Today would be my last day on Tortola for a long time. Or so I thought when I awoke. I hustled over to Saphir, took some more photos, looked for a couple of things that MLR had reminded me about in a message and as I was walking down the dock where Saphir is now, I could hear running water. Running water as if a 10cm diameter hosepipe was on. We had been told last night about the team's struggles to get our water system running, and that one of the last stumbling blocks was that there were leaks everywhere and they could not hold any level of adequate pressure. You know, like a couple of 10cm hosepipes that were broken. I looked around and sure enough, there were two pipes underneath the dock that would provide water to the various tie-up points for boats that were moored there…and both of them had been broken off during Irma's bitchy little visit. I immediately radioed the information in and very soon afterwards, a couple of lads came down and after looking, shut down the feed line and sealed off the pipes. By the time I made it back to the condo finally it was about 0900h and Cami had just gotten up. As I told her what I had found, she instinctively went to the kitchen tap and found that the water was now flowing and she went racing up the stairs to take a shower. When she came back down, I went to my shower and just stood there for an extraordinarily long time. Little pleasures people, little pleasures.

12 September, 1300h My evacuation process had been arranged by Dylan. Just a note here…first he literally saves my life because he saw me pounding on his gate during the hurricane, and then through his network, he manages to arrange to get me off the island. Dylan will always be held in high regard for what he did for me. Early on, a helicopter landing area had been cleared in Nanny Cay and it was immediately across the street from the condo that Dylan and Cami were cat-sitting in. He had told me that a helicopter would

Living on Rocks

land at 1330h and off I would go to San Juan. He also had said that I needed to be really sensitive about how much stuff I wanted to take with me, and I had packed accordingly. Then I repacked better. And then repacked again, each time, taking less and less stuff. By the time it was 1300h, I was down to one small suitcase, one rucksack, and one (bulging) briefcase. Dylan had buggered off around noon to continue his quest to save the world, so at just before 1330h, Cami and I carried all the bags out across the road to the landing zone. At 1400h, we carried it all back to the condo as no helicopter had appeared. Dylan returned and tried to ring someone to find out what was occurring, but we could not find out what was going on. We assumed that the helicopter had to be refuelled or something. By 1430h, one of us would go outside every five minutes and scan the skies, which in hindsight seems pretty stupid as a helicopter landing across the road is pretty flippin" noisy. Finally, just before 1500h, Maria (the pilot for Caribbean-Buzz, came swooping in out of the sky and after helping her strap in the other two passengers, we headed for San Juan. I knew that what I would see as we headed over West End and Sopers Hole would not be pretty...and it wasn't. It was one more unbelievably sad vista of what was paradise just a week earlier. Forty-five minutes later, Maria landed in Puerto Rico at SJU and I was on my way to a hotel room for the night with a long, desperately needed shower.

A closing note. A seriously massive thank you to all my friends and family who were so concerned and have worked tirelessly to keep in contact, provided invaluable assistance when communications were total shite, and sent me so many good thoughts and wishes. You are all appreciated. Thank you.

Now, sort of an epilogue to this chapter. Hurricane Irma has proven to be one nasty record-setting storm and its impact.

- Barometric pressure of only 914 millibars. Wind that hit Tortola was in excess of 180 miles per hour. Diameter of Irma was larger than 300 miles. Untold amount of financial damage
- When I decided to move to the BVI, I sold (or gave away) everything I had in Mallorca, car, furniture, paintings...everything. My entire life and everything I owned was on Saphir and is now gone. When I left the island, everything I had left, which was in reality, everything I own, fit into one small suitcase, one rucksack, and one briefcase. Fuck.
- I showed this chapter to MLR after writing it and she said that she found it so very sad. She asked me why I don't get into the sadness of the whole episode in the story...and I guess it is because it would be too difficult to write.

10

Wretched Excess of Waffles

Here I am, sitting in the relative comfort and safety (and luxury) of the Lake Home of MLR (from now and forever to be known as TLH), and I am unwinding, more or less, from the previous week's excitement. It was a week I will never forget for sure. This morning (a Thursday) was one of those "well this is different" moments. I opened my computer, went to my browser, and instinctively went to open both stormcarib.com and the NOAA hurricane projection websites. After those being about the only sites I had been looking at for some time, and then most recently checking them multiple times each day, not having to click on them seems so strange...but in a good way. And then as we were eating breakfast here in the land-of-plenty, the weather came on MLR"s telly. The pseudo-meteorologist (in reality just some hot babe who can read a teleprompter and stand in front of a green screen) was talking about this massive storm moving across the state. Yeah, right. Massive storm. What puppies.

Now, my reference to "the land-of-plenty." Yesterday, MLR took me to a department store so I could do some shopping. Not sure why; but could be because I came here with not exactly a full complement of clothes and stuff. So we walk into this store and find some shoes – yes, of course Crocs. Blue this time. The store doesn't have them in stock, but they will ship them to TLH (remember, The Lake House) within a week. We pay, but because MLR puts this on her store credit card, we get 30% off. Damn. Cheapest Crocs I have ever seen now. We then carry on and buy a jumper, a jacket, and a shirt. The shirt is 45.00 USD, but it is on sale for 4.50 USD. Yes, I will say that again....normally the shirt is 45.00 USD but now it is four dollars fifty. I couldn't resist. We take the lot to the check out counter and as the clerk is ringing it all up, MLR says that she has a advert-flyer coupon. The clerk mentions that there is another coupon, and then a discount for something, and then another discount because we were buying a punch of things from one department (the men's department). The overall total is 206.00 USD, but with the discounts and coupons, I only pay 40.00 USD. Do the maths friends...this is like a 75% discount. All I could think about was that it was a real shame that the store didn't have a satellite phone department or a new boat department. What is amazing (well, even more amazing) is that I would wager that the store still was making money on this stuff. Land-of-Plenty. I rest my case.

This morning, a Saturday, MLR and I are in Sheboygan WI where my son Matthew and his family live. We came up here to see everyone. I had mentioned

Living on Rocks

to MLR that this blistering thing going on with my lower lip was driving me crazy. She asked if it was sunburn, but seeing as how I had been in the BVI for months and the blistering didn't start to appear until a day or two after Irma went whirling through, that was unlikely. We decided it was best to go to a walk-in clinic, so we did. Nice people, fab facility (and free WIFI). We were barely in when my name was called and I went into the exam room and described to the nurse what was my concern, as well as the fact that I live where I live and hadn't suffered any sunburn from the entire summer to date. The nurse, and then the doctor who came in later, said that they thought that the blistering was some type of stress-related effect. I have no idea what might have caused me any stress lately. Any ideas?

After the walk-in experience, we decided we were hungry – yes, this will continue the land-of-plenty theme. We went to a cute little Chinese restaurant and ordered a cute little lunch. Orange chicken for MLR and orange beef for me, both with brown rice. After a short time, the waitress brings over two plates, each piled about as high as Mt. Everest with our respective lunch choices. Well obviously we weren't going to be able to eat all of these mountains of food, so we shovelled the excess of each of ours into take-away boxes and staggered out of the restaurant. We then drove over to a local cinema to kill some time by watching a movie and…get ready…yes, we went into watch the movie with a take-away box of orange chicken and brown rice. Yup, in the theatre. Only in America.

I spoke to the insurance company yesterday and the claims person provided some answers to questions I had about my claim on Saphir. I also said, *"As I have never filed a claim like this previously, could you tell me an approximate time frame for a claim that looks like it will be for a total write off on a boat?"* She replies that she has looked at the photos I had sent to her and that Saphir didn't look all that bad. I am thinking that there could be a real shit-fight looming here, but I will wait to see what the surveyor says when he arrives…which should be next week. Our current thinking is that depending on what the surveyor says, we both might head back down to one of the islands close to the BVI in case I need to get over to Saphir to deal with things quickly. Not sure yet when or where exactly.

Just about the time I was finishing up writing this, it became apparent that the weather news from the BVI is not good, and it may seriously impact our previously mentioned plans to return to the islands in the near future. After being brutally pummelled by Irma, now Maria is heading toward the islands. Currently, the forecast says that Maria will come through underneath the BVI and then swing up across Puerto Rico, and that it is currently not as strong and not as big as Irma. Whilst a weaker and smaller hurricane would normally be considered to be good news, when it follows Irma, it is more than the island may be able to handle. And Saphir is still there, now apparently against a wall with no protection at all.

Timing, as the saying goes, is everything. I think this saying might be correct.

I was pretty torn making up my mind whether to leave Tortola after Irma did her thing. There was (still is actually) so much to do to help sort out the mess that Irma left and knowing that I could help. During my decision-making process, I realised that where I can add the most value doesn't require that I stay on the island, and staying actually would sap resources. So I said I would go. And now, two weeks after Irma rolled over the island, Maria (the hurricane, not the helicopter pilot who evacuated me) is about to rip into the BVI. I don't think that the island and the people who are still there by choice, and the people who have no choice, can stand much more punishment from Mother Nature. Right about now, I am really glad to be not there (even though I still feel bad for leaving). Timing is indeed everything.

MLR and I have been listening and watching the weather forecasts for the BVI, and after the latest update (and upgrading) of Maria, we are both pretty saddened. To have suffered through a category 5 hurricane and then only a couple of weeks later, to find that Maria is now a category 5 and headed toward Tortola can only seem like a bit too much. Clearly, this isn't about what is fair, or what is tolerable…this is about nature, and as I have written previously, Mother Nature always wins, and there is nothing we can do about it.

Have no doubt, it is impossible to not think back to the Wednesday when Irma savaged the island. And often, it is the littlest of things that trigger some of the memories to appear front-and-centre in the mind. They aren't all bad memories, as there are so many parts of the story that are wonderfully positive news. Having said that, the positive news is typically about what went on within the Nanny Cay compound. What happened to the rest of Tortola would be hard to classify as anything other than "devastation." And yet, the people of the island are bound-and-determined to rebuild and once again have Tortola be the paradise it was before Irma came.

I heard from my friend Carli Muñoz who lives in Puerto Rico. He said that whilst he and his family did survive the wrath of Maria, things are pretty grim on that island with no electricity, no water, and only sporadic phone service. Even worse, he reiterated the stories on the news that it could take months to restore electricity to the island. It seems so odd that in 2017, it will take that long to bring electricity back. Yes, there is no doubt that Maria caused serious damage, but come on…perhaps all the available resources are busy on mainland east coast USA and not available for Puerto Rico… which is a US territory.

Today (a Tuesday), MLR and I drove to Sheboygan and spent the better part of the afternoon sitting in a waiting room at the local hospital. No, it was not for MLR nor was it for me. One of my two granddaughters gave birth to a 9 pound, 21" long baby boy. Cheyanne and Devin have named him Jasper and he is, I must admit, pretty cute.

MLR and I went into town to visit with some old friends, and to get back on the water. A friend has a large motor-yacht and he was getting it ready to be taken out of the water for the winter. His boat is on Lake Michigan, which as been known to freeze in winter, so sadly, people who have boats here need to put them on the hard for the coldest of the winter months. For Bill, getting it ready to be taken out meant that he took us for a nice ride around the harbour and the several marinas that are here. After all the recent traumas, being on the water again was very special, even if it was on someone else"s boat. And then, what do you suppose MLR and I did? If your guess had something to do with food, especially restaurant food in the USofA, then you are spot on.

And now, something observational about the US that is not food related (although I could write about this for the next year or two). A few days ago, MLR said that her left eye was bothering her, so after a couple of non-improvement days, we went to a local eye centre to have it checked. After about ten minutes, the doc said that she should put some eye drops in it several times a day and it should get better. The doc then wrote a prescription / receta / script (pick the term that fits your locale the best) and we went over to the local Wal-Mart to collect the eye drops. Note that we went to a local Wal-Mart, as they are the place of choice where MLR lives for anything inexpensive. The eye-drop bottle has a 5 ml capacity, which in layman's terms, is tiny tiny tiny. It cost MLR 110.00 USD. Yes boys and girls, the country that has everything apparently does not have health care for anyone unless you are seriously rich. One hundred ten dollars for a itsy-bitsy bottle of flippin' eye drops. Unreal. I sure wish the insurance surveyor would get to Tortola and figure out my claim so I can get back to the land where people really are appreciated. Besides, when I became a resident of the BVI, I was granted membership in the National Health Insurance programme…which means free health care. Damn right I am looking forward to being back in the islands.

MLR just read on Facebook that my insurance company does have surveyors on the ground in Nanny Cay, so perhaps I will have some answers soon. Fingers crossed.

As I finish writing today, it has been eighteen days since Irma spun across Tortola, leaving a path of destruction that will never be forgotten. In that time, some of the images that were burnt into my mind during and after the hurricane don't seem to go away. And it is some of those images that have raised questions in those eighteen days. Do you think that there will be lessons learnt by those who are working, or will be working, to rebuild this island and the other islands devastated by Irma? How long will it take to restore Tortola (and the other islands) back to the near-paradises they were? Why is it that there appears to be so much concern for the parts of the islands where a few live, but so little visible concern for the lives of those who had so little to begin with, and now have absolutely zero? And then a very personal question for you; seeing as how the issue of dealing with devastation is far bigger than solely those who inhabit the islands in a hurricane zone, what have YOU done to prepare in case a disaster of some form strikes

James B Rieley

where YOU live?

P.S. I promise to get back to writing about what life is like in the North Sound as soon as I can get back to the North Sound. Really.

Well, here I am, sitting in the middle of the USofA, still waiting for the insurance surveyor to make a determination about Saphir. As frustrating as this is, admittedly I am not exactly suffering here. Life here with MLR isn't exactly too terribly tough. Having said that, every time we go to one of the mega-supermarkets near her Lake Home (TLH), my head almost explodes. The variety of options for the same basic product is mind-boggling. I made a video on my iPhone of one aisle in the food section of a Wal-Mart that was about 20-25 metres long, but a bit more than two meters high. All that was in the aisle were crisps. Different texture crisps. Different shape crisps. Spicey crisps. Taco crisps. Bar-b-que crisps. Plain crisps. Textured crisps. Smooth crisps. Little packages of crisps. Monster bags of crisps. Crisps. An entire aisle of just crisps. O-M-G CRISPS!!!!! A few aisles over, it was like deja-vu, but this time it was candy-type treats. Then an aisle of frozen pizzas. Now to be fair, there was an incredible selection of fruits and veg, but no where near the variety or selection. I have no idea why there are so many "large" people here (he says as he types whilst eating the better portion of a raspberry Kringle that came from a three-meter long display near the door of the store).

Enough about all things edible, and back to the island situation. As MLR and I try to figure out the best options for moving forward, we have come up with a couple scenarios that do seem attractive. There is no doubt that, after going through all the residency process, I would like to live in the BVI. It is an exceptional place to live. The people are wonderful. The vistas are spectacular. The weather is exceptional. Okay, so it is in a hurricane zone but the fact that the BVI was seriously trashed in early September does not mean it will happen again...ever. We have not had anything like hurricane Irma for the past thirty-some years and it is possible that we won't have it happen again for the next thirty years. Or, because it is weather, it could happen tomorrow. There is no way to tell what will happen tomorrow to any of us anyway, so the weather thing is a risk that can be mitigated. The scenario we are looking at as mitigation would be for when MLR goes back to Wisconsin for the summer, I would head over to spend the time with my friends in Mallorca. This, by the way, does coincide with the highest risk times for hurricanes...which as we know, do not come to Mallorca. And because one of the worst things about being in a hurricane (or in that part of the world after a hurricane) is the total and complete lack of communications, I have already taken a step to fix that. Whilst living in Dylan's condo after Irma, his sat phone was the only way I could be in touch with the rest of the world, and because of it, I became a believer. This week I bought a satellite phone so even when there is no electricity and no mobile (cellular) phone service, I will be able to check in and be in communication. Feeling pretty good about that.

I still do a daily check of the 5-Day Hurricane forecast put out by NOAA, because, well…just because. Never having had experienced a hurricane previously, I admittedly had no context for what was about to happen in early September. When Irma was five days away, we did know that she was coming. What we (all sailors and NOAA forecasters) didn't know was exactly where she would hit. But we did know about where she would hit, and if I had it to do over again, I think five days out, I would have sailed south as fast as I could have. This time, however, as a hurricane-virgin, so to speak, I listened and watched the weather closely. The forecasts said that Irma could pass the BVI within 200 miles to the north. The next day the forecasts said she might pass 100 miles to the north. The following day it was possibly within less than 50 miles. Then less than 20 miles…and by then it was too late to leave. As it turned out, Irma went directly over Tortola, with the eye of the hurricane going smack over Nanny Cay. I should have taken a photo of what it was like when the eye went over, but I think everyone was too busy just being amazed that we all were alive. Little did we know that in less than twenty minutes, the eye would pass and Irma's real power would be evident. So (he types, trying to stay on track), watching the 5-Day Hurricane forecast is something that I just do. Today. Every day. And probably always will for the rest of my life. And if things on Saphir can be sorted out, the next time I see a forecast five days early, and the forecast says that some evil weather might be coming my way, I will raise my sails get the hell out of the way.

Things in general are pretty good. The weather here at TLH in the land-of-plenty has been pretty wonderful by my standards. All of last week it was in the high twenties (in Centigrade terms) and for me, that is about as good as it gets. But then yesterday the temperature plummeted and this morning when I awoke, my watch (more about that in a minute) said it was five degrees. 5 degrees C. O M G…it is like winter (well, I think it is like winter… everybody who lives here keeps rabbiting on about how nice it is after being so hot…pussies). The watch thing…Last week, MLR and I stopped in at the local (local here is a whole different thing as MLR"s TLH is about 45 mins from just about anywhere) Apple store. Every time I have travelled to the EEUU for business or to see family and friends, I do try to stop in at an Apple store to see what I need. I, like most humans, confuse what I "need" with what I "want," and the people at Apple are wizards at helping us stay confused. So there we were at the Apple store and MLR was thinking about getting a new iPhone. I was looking at a new computer, but seeing as how I have three of them with me right now, I wasn't looking all that hard. But then we both gravitated over to the iWatch department. Bingo. Do I need to say much more about this? (Mine is pretty nice and the best part for me is that is will be pretty water-proof for when I am back in the Caribbean… which will be soon).

Another observation from the land of plenty. MLR has this rather large telly, and in the morning and the evening, we have typically had it on to find out what is going on in the rest of the world. One of the things that I have seen in previous trips to the EEUU, but largely had forgotten about, are adverts for medicines. There are a LOT of medicine adverts on telly here. A serious LOT. Now, just to be clear, this is a pretty litigious country, so whilst the pictures that flash on the screen of the telly are wonderful pictures of happy, beautiful people doing things like walking through fields and riding horses along a beach, the sound is usually that of an announcer identifying some of the potential risks of taking the medicine. This is the list of one medicine that is advertised to help people cope with rheumatoid arthritis. As the list provided on the advert went so fast, I couldn't write all the risks down, I Googled the name of the medicine and found this.

"Along with its needed effects, (the active ingredient contained in the medicine) may cause some unwanted effects. Although not all of these side effects may occur, if they do occur they may need medical attention.

Check with your doctor immediately if any of the following side effects occur while taking (the medicine):

• Abdominal or stomach fullness • body aches or pain • cough or hoarseness • ear congestion • gas with abdominal or stomach pain • lightheadedness • blindness • bloating or swelling of the face, arms, hands, lower legs, or feet • blood in the stool or change in bowel habits • bloody or cloudy urine • blurred vision • broken bones • change in size, shape, or colour of an existing mole • change in skin colour • chest pain • chest tightness or heaviness • chills	• Abdominal or stomach pain • abnormal vaginal bleeding or discharge • agitation • arm, back, or jaw pain • black, tarry stools • bleeding from the gums or nose • mole that leaks fluid or bleeds • muscle cramps or spasms • nausea • new mole • night sweats • no blood pressure or pulse • noisy breathing • numbness or tingling in your arms, legs, or face • pain, redness, or swelling in the arms or legs without any injury present • pale skin • persistent non-healing sore on your skin • pink growth • puffiness or swelling of the eyelids or around the eyes, face, lips, or tongue

- clear or bloody discharge from the nipple
- cold hands and feet
- confusion
- constipation
- cough
- coughing or spitting up blood
- decreased urination
- decreased vision
- depression
- difficult or frequent urination
- difficulty with breathing
- difficulty, burning, or painful urination
- dimpling of the breast skin
- dizziness
- drowsiness
- eye pain
- fainting
- fast, slow, or irregular heartbeat
- fever
- forgetfulness
- frequent urge to urinate
- general feeling of illness
- hair loss
- hallucinations
- headache
- increased thirst
- inverted nipple
- irregular breathing
- irregular pulse
- irritability
- itching or rash
- light collared stools
- loss of appetite
- lump in the breast or under your arm
- raised, firm, or bright red patch
- redness or swelling of the breast
- seizures
- sharp back pain just below your ribs
- shiny bump on your skin
- slurred speech or problems with swallowing
- sneezing
- sore on the skin of the breast that does not heal
- sore throat
- sores, ulcers, or white spots on the lips or mouth
- spitting up blood
- stiff neck
- stopping of the heart
- sudden high fever or low grade fever for months
- sweating
- swelling of the face, fingers, feet, or lower legs
- swollen glands
- swollen neck veins
- tightness in the chest
- tiredness
- trouble breathing with activity
- trouble thinking
- unconsciousness
- unexplained bruising or bleeding
- unpleasant breath odour
- unusual tiredness or weakness
- unusual weight gain or loss
- visual disturbances
- vomiting
- vomiting of blood or material that looks like coffee grounds
- yellow skin or eyes

| • lump or swelling in the abdomen or stomach | |

I just love the "fast, slow, or irregular heartbeat." I am surprised they didn't list "no heartbeat;" and the "unconscious," and am wondering how, if you are unconscious, you are supposed to contact your doctor.

Lastly today, I found out that the entire story of Irma that I wrote has been reprinted in the magazine "The Islander." This publication is edited by a friend of mine and after I wrote about the less-than-fun hurricane experience, Simon asked if he could publish it all as a First-Hand Account of Irma. I said sure.

It is now a Wednesday; in a week, MLR and I will be heading south. First a stop in Nashville for a few days, then along on the way to the BVI. No real solid plans yet, other than I really need to get back to Tortola to see what the status of Saphir is, and figure out what to do next. Most likely, we will go to an island close to Tortola, and then I will fly over to see what is going on and hopefully meet with the insurance people.

It is the third or fourth Monday since I was evacuated from Tortola. The days do seemed to have gone into some time warp since I left my home and whilst living here at TLH isn't exactly hard duty; everything, including time itself, does seem to have gone into some new dimension. Today, as MLR needed to take a friend of hers to her doctor, I was left to my own devices here at TLH, and not wanting to just sit around and watch her internet continue to be slower than a handi-capped slug trying to work his way up a greased mountain, I decided to do some house-chores. Washing windows, raking up leaves, sweeping walks, taking one of MLR"s kayaks out for a spin (I know, this doesn't sound like a house-chore, but the waves on the lake were almost 1.5cm high, so it was pretty treacherous. Lots of fun things to do, but when I was done, it felt like I hadn't accomplished much at all. (Well, I could see out the sparkly-clean windows).

In today's inbox, there was a message about Saphir. It seems that the insurance surveyor (finally) arrived on the island and was shown over to my boat. After poking around for a while, he told the yacht management friend of mine that my wonderful Saphir is indeed, a write off. Of course, this isn't any thing more than my friend hearing the surveyor grumbling, so I won't know for sure for some time. Sort of yet another example of good-news-bad-news. But for sure, one element of the things in the "good news" category is that if Saphir is toast, I finally do have some closure on my current status of wondering what to do next. It isn't that I now know what to do next. Not at all. But I do have some closure in the sense that I know I won't be living on-board Saphir anymore. Time to get on with things and find the next adventure.

The past several weeks at MLR"s TLH have been pretty nice, and they have enabled me to really think about spending time here. Now to be totally and completely clear, when I say "here," I mean in this country. After being here for the past several weeks, it has been an amazing experience to be here for me. It has been one of those OMG times; mainly because I am gobsmacked at how much there is here. You name it, and you can find it here. And not just one of whatever you might be looking for; I swear that there are so many types of whatever you are looking for you would think you are in shopper's heaven. So I guess that is a good thing, if you are a consumer. But it is also pretty much consumers overload. I was talking to MLR as we were driving from an Apple store to TLH the other day and I said to her that I think after being here a while, it has made it pretty clear to me that I am more comfortable in less opulent settings. Have no doubt, I do like to have electricity, running water, and access to broadband, but all the rest is just a bit too much for me.

Tomorrow morning, MLR and I are leaving TLH and heading out on the road. The plan is to spend a day with her daughter Melissa and her family in the Chicago area, then continue south and spend several days with my son David and Erin. Logistically, this is a bit trickier than it might seem. The travel "plan" includes catching a ride with one of MLR's friends from TLH to a motor-coach terminal, then the coach into the city to a train depot. Then by train to Chicago, then the following day, by car to the airport, then a flight to David and Erin's. After our days there, we will...well, actually we still don't know what is next, we will make it happen. All we have to do is figure out what it is we need to make happen.

So, after lots of planning, changing, adapting, revising, and other mental pain inducing stuff, our plan has come together. As of today (the Tuesday known as the 17th), our plan is to leave here (Nashville) and fly to Naples Florida. We will be there (more or less) until 10 December, when MLR will return to TLH for Christmas, and I will go to Tortola for the month.

After sharing "the plan" (as it stands today), it made sense to get cracking, so yesterday (a Friday), we flew from Nashville to Ft. Meyers in Florida and then took an Uber-taxi-guy-thing to Naples and checked into our very spiffy condo. This condo is pretty far removed from life on Saphir in the BVI, but it is on a very large canal and only a five minute walk from the sea, so this is the closest we have been able to be to boat living again since I was evacuated from Tortola. The time since I left the island seems to vacillate between *"It seems like only yesterday"* to *"It seems like it has been years since I was there."* The first one is probably because the images of living on Saphir at Virgin Gorda and Nanny Cay are so crystal clear in my mind. The second one is probably because of being homeless and living out of a briefcase, rucksack, and small carry-on suitcase, and the fact that I long to go home again....boat or no boat. And speaking of the boat subject, I did hear finally from the insurance company and as it appeared to me, Saphir is being deemed a total write-off. This, as you might imagine, brings forth the old "good-news-bad-news" dilemma. The bad news should be obvious, at least to me. The good news is that I will not have to argue with some insurance adjustor about what it will cost to try to restore Saphir to her previously pretty-great condition. Even more good news is that it is once again boat-shopping time. Still not sure that buying another boat will be the best solution right now, but boat shopping is always a good idea.

And on other non-boat-related good news, our flight from Nashville in Tennessee to Florida went fine. After a short ride to the Nashville Airport (which for some reason has the airport code of MNA) via "Erin-Uber," the 90-minute flight landed in Ft Meyers, where another Uber person collected us and drove us to Naples. MLR had found this pretty spiffy apartment overlooking a huge body of water that has boats coming and going. Sadly none of them have masts, but my boat doesn't either, so I guess it is okay. The flat is pretty great and the broadband is ripping quick. It is only a less-than-five-minute-walk to the beach and each day since arriving, we have shucked off shoes and walked along the beach for a greater-and-greater distance each time. This is a pretty great way to try to figure out what to do next.

Yesterday, some friends we both used to know from previous work, and who now have a retirement home here in Naples, came to collect us and give us a ride to a large market, as well as a bit of a tour to see how the seriously rich live. They do appear to live pretty well, although their budgets for staff must be enormous judging by the sizes of some of the homes overlooking the sea. We saw one that looked to be about the size of Puigpunyent. And then last evening, we waltzed over to a restaurant overlooking the water and after a pretty fabulous meal, began the short walk back to the rental flat. In the car park, we saw a string of white cars, and I commented that it felt like I was back in Mallorca, and as MLR was talking a photo of them, I noticed that one of them had a matriculation plate that said "GOBVI." O M G ! I was gobsmacked and said I was going back into the restaurant to see if I could find out who had this on his car. Just then, a couple came out of the restaurant, and miracle-of-miracles, it was their car. I immediately asked if they were from the BVI or had a home there and was pretty gutted to find out that they weren't even conscious that the plate was referencing the British Virgin Islands. They just thought it was a plate with all letters on it. Damn. None-the-less, it was great to see and made me want to return even more.

At the risk of talking more about Irma, being here in Naples (Florida) keeps throwing the whole Irma experience in front of me. First, one of my friends on Tortola – the man whose leadership drove much of the immediate recovery process at Nanny Cay – send out a note and it in, he told about the real extent of Irma as she passed over the island. Miles wrote *"Irma was a monster - with 220 mph gusts, and 185 mph sustained winds recorded at Peter Island, we didn't have a chance. I read recently that a category 5 hurricane is 500 times stronger than a category 1 hurricane and causes 144 times more damage!"* And that brings me to Naples. Irma, after trashing Tortola and other islands, went on to cruise across the length of Florida. According to the Naples

Living on Rocks

Daily News, Irma hit land in Cudjoe Key (near Key West), then again when it reached Naples. At this point, Irma was a category 2 hurricane. Yes, there are multiple trees that went down, and we have seen some houses that lost roof tiles, but to talk to the locals (or read the papers), one would assume that Irma was horrible…which it was. But whilst many of the locals are convinced that they barely survived, the reality is that if a category 5 ever came through here, there would be a serious awakening. Pussies.

We have been doing a lot of walking. When I write "a lot," I men a serious lot of walking. Each morning, before brekkie, we head over to the beach and walk a couple of miles south along the sad and sea, then the same couple of miles back. One might think that, if we do this everyday, wouldn't it become a bit boring? The same two miles each way every day? The answer is not at all. The sea is always new and different and interacts with the sand, which exposes new and surprising mysteries each morning. The chances of me getting tired of walking along the sea are about the same as me getting tired of being on a boat….which are exactly zero. MLR, who really enjoys all this exercise lark, presses along each morning looking step-after-step for that one very special shell that the tide has brought in overnight. So far, she has found about 100 of them. After finishing up our daily morning roundtrip, we go back to the condo for some food and after a bit, we are re-charged to head out again. Then it was a bit of relaxing in the pool and hot-tub and a late lunch. Today was exceptional as just before dinner, we cranked up another 6,000 steps, so it was a 20,000-step day for each of us. I am, admittedly, pretty shattered as I write this entry, but I know in the morning I will be standing at the door waiting so we can hit the beach again.

It is a day that ends in "Y," so that meant another walk along the endless beach in Naples. The sand is so soft and warming, even early in the morning, it is the best advertisement to throw away all your foot attire. Today, we walked, and walked, and walked. And whilst watch the sun peak over some of the not-so-attractively-tall condominiums that line most of the east side of the beach, I did discover what could be the idea retirement job for someone who loves the sand and sea. It would be like making a Zen-sand garden with a rake, but here, the rake is a huge f**k-all tractor pulling a massive rack-like thing. I was thinking that the guy driving it was too focused on something other than peace and meditation because at no point did he make a nice design in the sand. Slacker…

On one of our "shell-hunting-beach-walks," MLR explained that when her parents would come south, they would walk along some beach and collect shells, and she was just doing her part to keep up a family tradition. I, in my never-ending-quest to learn, looked up what a shell collector is called. Google said it was a "*conchologist*" but I think it is "*A retired person with too much time on her hands.*"

It is (another) Sunday, and after an evening of rain (which didn't stop us from venturing out for dinner with friends), we decided that walking would be a good thing. We had shopping to do, so it wasn't going to be just another "fun" walk of a kazillion kilometres up and back on the beach. Besides, the wind was pretty strong (serious waves on the canal the flat overlooks). Instead, we decided to walk east toward where there are lots of shops. Because we are in the EEUU (USofA for some of you), everything would be open even though it is a Sunday. MLR had her shopping list and I elected to take my rucksack so there wouldn't be any need to carry a bag back with us on our return. As I have tried to make pretty clear previously, since being evacuated from the BVI, shopping here is quite the experience; mainly because they have everything here (as in EVERYTHING) for sale. After making it to a shopping area, MLR suggested we take a quick whip through a Whole Foods Store. My observations follow:

First, the Whole Foods Store is located in a shopping mall. Not like any shopping mall I can remember seeing. Ever. This looked more like a community of shops and flats, which of course was the intent of the designers. Lots of trendy, upscale shops on the ground level and flats to rent above them. Of course in this cute little ("cute" and "little" - two examples of sarcasm, just to be clear) shopping mall, the flats were for sale beginning at 1.4 MILLION USD. That is the price of the small ones. Go figure. The Whole Foods Store was mind-boggling. First, the foods were displayed in a way that you knew you wanted them. Fresh, bright, all looking exceptionally tasty. And then, about every 20 meters, there were people give out free samples of one food or another. The number of possible selections was crazy out of control. They even had a section where you could order food and have it prepared there for you to take away. I was surprised that they didn't have a loan officer there to give you the money to buy everything. It wasn't more expensive than other stores at all; but it all looked so good you just wanted to buy everything. With all this focus on health and organic food (their mission statement says they will *"Sell highest quality natural and organic products available"*), I did find it a bit off the mark that the shopping carts there are all plastic, so not exactly good for the environment. We did walk all the way to the end of the shopping mall and back to get the entire shopping experience and all I could think about *was "Why don't they have a sailboat store here?"*

Next week it is MLR"s birthday and I asked her what she wanted to do, and she said….get ready for it….no, seriously, get ready….she said she wanted to go across the state to Ft. Lauderdale to the Boat Show. Seriously. Well, if I have to. Will report back.

Well, you might have thought that I lost my computer or become so enamoured with living in Naples that I have given up writing this on-going story. Neither is the case, I assure you. It is just that my original intent was to write when I thought there was something interesting to write about. Being here in Naples does make one feel like they are in some "bubble-of-nice" or an "envelope-of-calm" because each day is pretty much like the previous ones.

Living on Rocks

Not that I don't like this...I am pretty good when the weather is constant. I have been known for claiming that I do love seasonal weather change. Of course, when a statement like that comes out of my mouth, what I mean is that in summer the temperature is about 30c and in winter it is about 27c or 28c. This isn't exactly what it is like here, but it is pretty close. Our days do drone on...we walk here to there, and then there to here. I sit by the pool or on the beach. MLR continually demonstrates an effort to become the Queen of Shells, although I have no idea how she will get them back to TLH. So our days are very much routine oriented, which is one reason that I haven't found a lot of "interesting" things to write about. There is that, but there also is the whole thing that this on-going story was meant to be about what it is like to be living on a boat in the Caribbean. Then Irma came along and there is no boat, and from the middle of September until early in December, I am not in the Caribbean. Soon that will change and I am keen beyond belief to get back there.

This whole exercise lark here is almost getting to be enjoyable. Well, parts of it. The parts where we are walking along a sun-drenched beach, listening to the waves from the Gulf of Mexico lap up onto the sand, where some pretty adorable little birds go scampering along the shoreline at about 200 kph, and where the sand nestles between your toes with each step. All that is great, and I actually do look forward to it. The not so enjoyable part yet has something to do with aches from doing all the walking. Having said that, aches or no aches, this is all pretty good. In yesterday's walk, MLR did go a bit overboard with her shell-collecting-endeavours and now the cute grouping of shells is now more than double in size. Can't wait to find out what her excess-baggage charges are when she flies back to Wisconsin.

On today's walk, we went all the way south that we could before encountering an inlet, which did block our path. And along the way, we came across a wooden elevated walk path that went across a pretty wide stretch of mangroves. Neither of us knew that there were multiple types of mangroves, but we were well educated after reading all the signage along the walk path. White mangroves, black mangroves, red mangroves...interesting as the all looked pretty much the same to the uneducated eye of a visitor.

We went over to Ft. Lauderdale on a Thursday as planned. This was what MLR wanted to do for her birthday, and who am I to deny a wish like that? Driving from Naples to Ft. Lauderdale is boring, as in B-O-R-I-N-G. The road, whilst multiple lanes, is dead straight for the vast majority of it, and slices through the everglades and seems to go on forever. Actually, it only took a couple of hours.

The boat show – after all, this whole thing is supposed to be about being on boats – was pretty crazy. First, it is purported to be the biggest boat show in the world. It covers six massively large marina areas in Ft. Lauderdale and had water taxis to take you from one area to another. We arrived pretty early but due to the size and scope of it all, we were only able to see part of one of the six areas before we felt like we were in the Exorcist, with our heads spinning at high speed. The good news was that just about everything nautical (or purported to be nautical) was available. The bad news was that this was not a show for sailors. We found only five sailboats and they were all monster-big catamarans.

About the only boat that even looked remotely interesting (that didn't cost massive amounts of money) was a go-faster boat that we looked at that wasn't even at the show. It was quite tasty, but am still looking.

It is a holiday here and MLR made reservations to go out to eat. In previous years, when we have been together during this holiday, we have joined with friends in Mallorca to have a "traditional" American Thanksgiving dinner. This year we are together and in the land of opulence, so I think that she thought it would be perfect to have a "real" thanksgiving dinner and it didn't take her long to find a restaurant within walking distance from the condo. Off we went and after settling in at the restaurant, ordered but neither of us requested anything to do with turkey, stuffing, cranberries, and the rest of the usual holiday treats. MLR had baked Brussels sprouts as well as roasted yellow beets. I ordered a Caesar salad. We did see other patrons at the restaurant being served these near monster platters of the turkey, etc. dinner, but we were quite content to have what we did. And then, as we were about to leave, MLR spotted a sign near the registration counter than offered cutesy hat-like things so you could have your photo taken as you were celebrating whilst gorging yourself on the pile of food. We couldn't resist.

It's now been two months since hurricane Irma savaged the British Virgin Islands, as well as many other islands in the Caribbean. After sixty days since I was struggling to get to safety, I have been amazed at how much progress has been made at Nanny Cay to not only clean up the mess, but to also restore the marina/resort to its previous condition. Even today, more photos are put online of the progress that the marina has made to untangle the mess of boats that were on-the-hard, that after Irma, were piled up in some sort of three dimensional jigsaw puzzle. We now have new docks in Nanny Cay, which in itself is a huge accomplishment. Having said all this, the rest of Tortola does not have much electricity and/or running potable water. Even so, I am very much looking forward to getting back there and am flying to Tortola on 10 December. I will be staying at the hotel in Nanny Cay (yes, the same hotel that I was in when Irma came through), but most likely, not in the same room.

I have very mild expectations for the weather when I return. It has been raining off and on in and around the North Sound of the BVI, but it is the ending phase of tropical storm season, so that is to be expected. Rain, but not rain in a hurricane. In fact, the hurricane projection maps that I was using daily during the height of the season, have been, for the past month, more or less the same. Which is pretty nice to see. The BVI was thoroughly trashed by Irma, and then blown to bits again when Maria went through a bit more than a week later. Enough is enough is what I think at least.

Living here for the past almost three months in the EEUU, for me, has been a real eye opener. Some of the things that stand out in my mind include;

- **the whole shopping thing.** As I have said previously, my head almost explodes when I am in a store that sells just about everything your mind can imagine. The term "huge selection" applies to just about every store we have been in.

- **the level of customer service.** This is so different than what I have experienced living in Spain and even in the BVI. In the BVI, people are very courteous, but they don't "get" the whole customer service thing. In Spain, I am not sure that the term is even in their lexicon. Here, in every town we have been in, shop employees bend over backwards to help you. Very impressive and it will be sad to not experience this more when we leave.

- **the weather.** Well, it has been pretty flippin' exceptional. As a matter of fact, the weather that we have had for the past seven weeks we have been in Naples is my kind of weather. Sunny skies, a very narrow band of temperature variation.

- **television adverts.** W T F ?!?!?! First, the number of adverts on telly are mind-boggling. Regardless of the programme content, there are what feels like a never-ending-slew of adverts. And if the number of adverts isn't enough, the content is even crazier. So many adverts for medical remedies; and, because this is a very litigious society, each advert features more disclaimers and warnings that you can imagine. With nice video of attractive people in the background, the audio rambles on about how this "pill" (most of them are pills) could cause…" followed by damn near every medical condition known to man. I keep thinking that it would be easier for the advert to say *"This pill may cause anything that begins with a vowel or consonant."* Crazy.

- **transportation.** This is sort of tricky as we haven't had a car here, so we walk to almost every place. Most of these walks do cover 3-5 miles, so this is good for the health thing. But whilst walking, something else has burned itself into my mind. Most of the roads are pretty packed with vehicles. The term "packed" is especially important, as crossing a road that has 4, 5, or 6 lanes each way can be daunting. Having said that, whilst you are dodging the cars racing along, you do get to see more posh cars than you see in London.

- **friend's visits.** Several sets of friends that we both have known who were in this part of the world stopped over and we were able to get together to catch up. Very nice.

In just a couple of days, I will return to where I decided to live a year ago. Very excited about that, and equally very much looking forward to getting this writing thing back on track about living in the Caribbean. Stay tuned.

11
Getting on With It

I am on my way home…to the place that I have chosen to be my home.
Day One.

God, this was feeling good. Okay, so it did mean getting up at 0200h, which seemed like going to bed at all just wasn't worth it. But a driver was coming to take me across the state of Florida, from Naples to Ft. Lauderdale where I would catch a flight to San Juan. The drive over was pretty uneventful and smooth beyond belief, making me realise why these monster black SUV"s were so popular in Florida. After having been properly bollocked by security at the FLL airport for having a small scissors and large knife in my carry-on trolley, I found myself in high defensive mode, explaining that I was going to have this trolley inside of a large suitcase and have them both checked. But yesterday, I came to the realisation that this bag-in-a-bag concept was seriously overweight so I repacked…. for the umpteenth time. And in the repacking exercise, I neglected to check what stuff was in which bag – the bag to be checked and the bag to carry on. The security man appeared to be listening intently but I think he was focused on something else as when I was done he said, *"Yeah, but you can't carry this stuff on the plane,"* and then he chucked them into a box with other contraband. The first flight was fine. Ft. Lauderdale to San Juan in an A320 only took 2-1/2 hours, and flying into the SJU airport gave me a good…no, make that a VERY good feeling. I wasn't home yet, but I was damn closer than I had been in three months.

After checking in to my next flight on a different airline, I wandered down to the airport hotel. I wasn't staying here overnight, but I had in the past and thought, as I had a couple of hours to kill before my next flight, it would be nice to say hi to Beatrice, the desk manager at the SJU Airport Hotel. (And now for an unsolicited advert…if you ever are flying in or out of San Juan, the SJU Airport Hotel is great. In all the times that MLR and/or I have stayed there, we have been treated really well, and Beatrice is very customer focused and does her best to make it a good experience. Okay, enough of that) After saying Hola, I began to walk back to the appropriate gate. The San Juan airport is like most large airports…lots of walking, but with food options about every twenty meters. Truth-be-told, I did stop in at the Starbucks food counter. I was hungry and thirsty and the thoughts of a hot chocolate and chocolate-chip cookie were most definitely messing with my head. As I stood in the queue (damn, there is always a queue at these trendy-coffee cafes), I began to rethink my potential order. The good news of Starbucks is that they list the calorie content for all their products on the big menu on the wall behind the scurrying employees. The bad news is that their products are not exactly "light" in caloric content. When it was my turn to order,

I had a bottle of juice and kept going to the gate, feeling a bit like a food wimp, but at least one that will not have gained a few kilos from the snack.

My last flight of the day was on Seaborne airlines, one of the niche commuter airlines that are laced around in the Caribbean. The plane, a Saab 340B, had 11 rows with 3 seats in each row. Luckily, the plane was less than ½ full. Of course for me, that was a real revelation, and most of the flights I have had to or from Tortola and San Juan have been in planes where I have been the only passenger. So 15 passengers seemed like a crowded telephone booth. The flight, all 27 minutes of it, was deliciously uneventful. After landing, I made it to the immigration queue and as I was only one of three people who were residents here in the BVI, I rather quickly was called forward. The officer at the immigration desk was none other than my old friend Ms. Richards. If you have been keeping up, you might remember that when we first arrived in the BVI in January, she was the one who confiscated my passport because one of the residency forms looked like a photocopy to her. We resolved that problem the following day, and since then, she and I have been friends. After about ten minutes of chatting (and consequently, probably pissing off the other people in the queue behind me), I went through and found my driver for the ride from the airport to Nanny Cay where I would be staying.

Admittedly, I had pretty low expectations of what I would see, especially on the East End of Tortola. Many of the homes along the road through the East End looked like a disaster zone before the hurricane came through in September and I didn't expect that they would look much different now. I was right. But not only were some of the ramshackle homes looking seriously "rough," there were quite a few commercial buildings that showed massive damage from the hurricane. And truth-be-told, I would not be surprised to see that they are not repaired a year or two from now…if at all. Even in the middle of Road Town, there were very evident signs that hurricane Irma had run smack over the island, smashing buildings as if they were made of plastic blocks. Having said all this – and my intention is not to paint an overly gloomy picture of what is going on here – there has been so much progress to fix up the island. Part of the problem (a very large part of the problem) is that Tortola, like the entire BVI, survives pretty much on tourism. The island-born citizens (belongers) don't have a lot of money to begin with, and when a natural disaster like a hurricane comes along, their standard of living takes a serious hit. The reality is that about ½ of the island still does not have electricity three months after Irma. The chances of belongers having enough money stashed away to be able to instantly rebuild to a standard that would withstand a hurricane, are about the same as the chances that you can win the lotto without having bought a ticket. The ex-pats who have chosen to live here, or have holiday homes here, typically do have enough resources to be able to rebuild quickly (or at all). And that brings me to where I am now.

Living on Rocks

I am staying in Nanny Cay, where I was when that bitch hurricane Irma came through and savaged the island. Investors who clearly understand the risk-and-reward equation own Nanny Cay, and since the day after Irma came through, they have been working to restore Nanny Cay to its former glory as THE nautical destination on Tortola. Actually, that isn't exactly right. They have been working to make Nanny Cay bigger and better than before. And they are succeeding. We have electricity. We have running water. We have broadband. This is pretty much of a different world than most of the rest of the island. And now I am here once again.

After completing the taxi ride, I checked into the hotel here and promptly unpacked my bags and then headed out to see what I could see. I saw a lot. Yes, there still are signs of the power of Irma (that bitch), but there are massive changes since I left the week after Irma did her thing here. After walking around quite a bit, feeling very voyeuristic mentally recording all that I could see, I went to the Beach Bar (as you do). It did feel like I had only been away for the week or two I had planned when I was evacuated. Lots of friends that I haven't seen since I left provided me with wonderful hugs and we all shared stories.

Later that night, after returning to the bungalow (my hotel room is, as I said, not in one of the big buildings but is one of a group of side-by-side bungalows) I decided this was enough for one day. I went to bed to read, and as I was opening my Kindle, I glanced up at the ceiling. The ceilings of the bungalows are identical to the ceiling of the hotel room I was in when Irma struck. I think I stared at it for some time, listening carefully to hear if the tin roof or the wood panels were being ripped off. I have no idea how long I just watched and listened, but it was one of those flashback times that are not great.

Day Two.

This morning, after waking and looking up (creature of new habit apparently) followed immediately by a somewhat soft *"Fuck you ceiling,"* I went over and had breakfast, followed by seeing more friends who were here. I also ran into the man who had coordinated the removal of our personal things from Saphir after the insurance company paid me for the loss. I had sent Travis instructions (with photos of locations) of the things that I wanted to have removed from Saphir. I had no idea how many of these things he would be able to get off, or even how many of them were not damaged in some way. He did good. I had to make three trips from the storeroom to the bungalow, dragging a very large wagon on wheels filled with boxes, plastic tubs, and bags. Lastly, I dragged a huge suitcase that MLR had brought to the boat when we moved it from Virgin Gorda. I am sure that if you look in the Oxford Dictionary under the word "heavy" you would see a photo of this suitcase. By the time I had finished my last trip, I was pretty shattered, but then the work was only beginning as I needed to find out exactly what Travis had saved. By the time I was finished going through everything and sorting out the things into categories (a pile of "save" things; a pile of things that are stinky and need a good washing; things to air out; things I have no idea what they are; and stuff that was ruined from water damage. All this work meant it was time once again to head over to the Beach Bar to have a well deserved bottle of something cool. Which I did.

A friend of mine who is the publisher of "The Islander" (a sailing magazine produced in Mallorca that is one of the best anywhere) read about my experience during hurricane Irma and asked if he could reprint it in the magazine. I said sure. Several weeks before coming back, he asked me if I would send him sort of a status report on the islands three months after Irma. This is what I sent him....

Hi Simon, I am back at Nanny Cay again, and quite happy to be here. I had been thinking about my return ever since I was evacuated. How would the island look? How much clean up has been accomplished? How would the locals be doing after not being able to even get away for a short time? I began to get an idea as my flight from San Juan descended toward the airport on Beef Island (Tortola). The hills of all the islands in the BVI and USVI are lush and green again, although you can see that there isn't quite the depth of green that there was before Irma came and savaged everything. This is a direct impact of the reality that nature is nature. The islands experience sun almost every day, all day. It is the end of the tropical storm season, and we have had quite a bit of rain. And it is warm. Every day. All day. Three things that virtually guarantee that plants will grow and do so with a passion.

But as the plane flew lower and lower, first passing over West End, then Nanny Cay, then Road Town, Paraquita Bay, and finally Trellis Bay, before touching down at Beef Island, it was clear that something very bad had happened here. In each of these harbour areas, it was possible to see boats that were still submerged or upside down , or partially on land. For a boater, these are not good visuals. The amount of boats in each area was pretty mixed. West End, largely due to the condition of the road (horrendous) that extends from Road Town and past Nanny Cay, is still pretty much deserted. Nanny Cay is doing the best of all these locations, most logically because the owners of Nanny Cay are very switched on and recognise the correlation between reinvesting in fixing the infrastructure and seeing a return on the investment. Nanny Cay also has a new marina area that was little used before Irma and now is the area with the best and most functional docks. The old marina at Nanny Cay is what took the beating during the hurricane and the new docks there will not be in until May. But Nanny Cay is full of life, which makes any inconvenience tolerable. Road Town is rebuilding, but the town itself still has very visible evidence of the hurricane, and could be many months to see everything cleaned up. Having said that, restaurants and pubs are reopening just about everyday, so for those who remember sitting at Pussers and consuming a nice cool libation, you can still do that.

Paraquita Bay was the tiny pond that had a very narrow entrance. This is where most of the charter companies would historically take their fleets and raft them all off in tidy rows. Very sheltered, Paraquita Bay had the reputation for being probably the safest place to be during a big tropical storm. Of course, that was before a category 5 hurricane ran smack over the island. It didn't help to then have another category 5 hurricane run right past the island a couple of weeks later. Paraquita Bay still looks, from the air, much like a disaster zone, with submerged boats, boats on land, and boats piled up on top of each other. Trellis Bay looked very quiet and far emptier than I had ever seen it before.

On land, the picture was far worse. From east end, where Beef Island is, to Nanny Cay (almost at west end), the road options are meagre, and many of the roads are in very rough shape. (the term "very" here means potholes that look like you and a car could easily be swallowed up). In some areas along the road, the buildings look exactly as they did the day after the hurricane, but to be fair, some of those buildings looked that way well before the hurricane. The "flukiness" of the hurricane damage is incredible. A house seriously damaged next to a house that looked fine, then two more that looked uninhabitable. It is the visual definition of devastation. The actual road through Road Town is brand new, and whilst it can lull you into a false sense that things really are looking up, many of the building along the nice, tidy, shiny new tarmac road are broken wrecks that look like they will need to be knocked down instead of repaired. From Road Town to Nanny Cay, the road is as it always has been, which is pretty much rubbish; massive potholes, with areas where big pieces of the tarmac are laying on the side of a hill. And then you get to Nanny Cay, and life is different. In Nanny Cay, there is electricity all the time, whereas much of the island still does not have it full time. We have running water, whereas parts of the island are existing on bottled water. And we do have broadband. The WIFI signal isn't saturating the entire Nanny Cay compound but it is in enough places so those who wish to be "connected," can be. By early summer, Nanny Cay will most probably be fully operational and 90% of the visible evidence of Irma's presence will be gone. But as with the rest of the island, the visible evidence of Irma may be swept away in some areas, the memories will be in your head forever.

Virgin Gorda is a good example of the dichotomy of trying to erase evidence of the two hurricanes. The island itself has been cleaned up quite a bit. Clearly there are still buildings that are obviously victims of the hurricanes, but largely the island has been made to look quite good. Having said that, it is a smaller island and because of that, there were less building, roads, and infrastructure systems to be damaged. But in the North Sound, sailors favourite destinations such as Bitter End show no signs of work being done to restore it to an operational level. Leverick Bay is sort of running, and there are boats that are coming in, but nowhere near like the number that you used to see in the North Sound.

Fogy's is open on Jost Van Dyke, as are many other well-known pubs on some of the smaller islands. One of them posted a picture only several weeks after Irma that showed a semi-broken table, in the sand, with a bottle of rum on it, and the caption, "Open for business." Nice.

Overall, if there were a Report Card for how things are after Irma, It might look something like this:

> *Amount of damage - monumental*
>
> *Amount of effort being expended to fix everything - monumental*
>
> *Chances of everything being "normal" again very soon - not so great*
>
> *Is it safe there - yes*
>
> *Is it worth coming back for a sailing holiday - for sure*

What the BVI needs more than capital investments and repair teams are customers. The reason that many of us have sailed in the British Virgin Islands was that it is simply one of the best places to sail. We all didn't come here because they had the best road system, or the best WIFI systems...we all came here because we wanted to sail. That hasn't changed...the BVI is still one of the best places to sail, and if we want to help the islands be restored to how we remember, the best thing we can do is come down and sail.

Have no doubt, it is so very good to be home again. You know, surroundings that feel right, weather that is mind-boggling great, and in a routine that does seem to work for you (well in this case, for me). Being in the hotel again (albeit in a bungalow with walls and a roof this time) may not be the geographic centre of Nanny Cay, but it certainly seems to be the centre of activity here. Every morning I can look out from my patio and see people scurrying about, fixing roofs, cleaning boats, in some cases, standing them up again, and getting ready as more and more owners and charterers come down for the season.

Four days after arriving in Tortola I have been out and about looking for places to live, and so far, things are looking up. Now to be fair, I am not sure exactly what "looking up" means but yesterday I saw three homes and all of them had potential. Now for even more clarity, when you are looking for a place to live on an island that had the shit beaten out of it by a Category Five hurricane, "potential" in this context means that it has a roof, walls, and electricity. Each of the three did have all three items, even if the electricity at one of them was provided by a generator. Each had pretty great views of the sea, with my reactions as an observer ranging from "Oh that vista is special" to "Oh that vista is so special" to "Fucking-hell, that vista is over-the-moon special." I am off again this morning to look at more options, but I fear I might be running out of descriptions of the vistas from today's selection. I will let you know.

Whilst driving around the island, my estate agent and I went past a place that is being used as the graveyard for all things destroyed when the hurricane(s) came through in September. The site is, sadly, pretty impressive. The pile of rubble (which is about the only way to describe it accurately), extends almost one half kilometre through some non-used piece of land west of Road Town and is huge beyond belief. Yes, this is clearly an O M G moment.

It is hard to see what "the plan" is to do with it all, as most of it will surely not breakdown over time, leaving this massive blot on the landscape in what was a beautiful piece of land on the seacoast.

I went out with a different estate agent in the morning, and then the original estate agent in the afternoon. By the end of the day, I knew that I was experiencing one of those "good news bad news" days. The good news was that I had been successful in finding places that could be suitable to live in. The bad news was that, of the six places (two flats, two condos, and two detached homes), all six of them would suffice. Actually they all would suffice very well. Damn. I love it when I have multiple options, but it can be a real bugger when there are too many good options to choose from. I did what any other person of sound mind and a systems thinking ability would do…I went to the Beach Bar and hung out with friends and a Coors Light or two.

Before I go on about my home hunt, this could be a good time for a short Primer on Home-Hunting-on-an-Island-that-Suffered-Through-a-Category-Five-hurricane-followed-by-Another-Category-Five-hurricane-all-within-One-Month. I suppose that a shorter title might be, "You-Must-Be-Kidding." The criteria for home hunting here falls into several key "this-or-that" categories. These categories include: home on a hill or home on a beach (there aren't any of the later anymore); homes with a view of the sea or a view of the hills (Hills? Thank you, but no); homes with some damage or homes with lots of damage (The term "lots" is pretty relative after the hurricanes); homes you can afford or homes that make you all wet inside but are still damaged; and the all time favourite category; homes that have electricity or homes that have generators. There is a third option for this last category, but I decided that "homes without electricity" just aren't my cup of tea. My choices in this "this or that" fiesta were homes on a hill, with a view of the sea, with some damage probably, something that was mildly affordable, with electricity (or a monster generator). The good news is that every day, more electric poles are going into the ground to replace the ones that broke, fell over, or just plain disappeared, and even if a generator might be needed now, it won't be for long.

Even with all these relatively obvious criteria to use to filter down the choices available, (or that might be acceptable), after looking for two days, I was thinking that this was a selection process of Gordian-knot proportions. But then, without a single matrix or set of loops, Saturday morning came and my mind was clear. I contacted the estate agent and made an offer on two of the properties. I needed to make two offers as timing played into the decision-making process. Instead of staying in the hotel until 10 January, which was the plan; I would now leave the hotel as soon as possible and move into a flat (it is really an up-and-down duplex, overlooking Long Bay, and stay there until the house I really want to rent is put back together, so-to-speak.

Whilst looking for places to live, it did land in my mind that having a spectacular view on Tortola most probably would require a way to get to it. So whilst I have been in between looking at homes to rent, I have also been looking for four-wheeled transportation. This has been a challenge. A challenge not because there are no cars for sale here; it has been a challenge because so many of the cars for sale have broken windows, smashed bonnets or hoods, or look like they are props for a remake of the Mad Max movie franchise. As I began to see some slippage in my perspective of what the term "acceptable damage" would mean, I received a call from a friend here who wanted to know if I could help him move one of his cars. I said of course, and then during the conversation, he said that he was moving it to Nanny Cay so it might be easier to sell. Sell? Well that word resonated in my head, and about an hour later, I bought it. Tania (Hey, I have always named my cars, and some day will explain why the name "Tania") only had one broken window and less dents than Amelia had in Mallorca. Four-wheel drive, estate-car configuration, right-hand drive, and all shiny silver…nice. Of course, having a car, living in the British Virgin Islands, and at the same time, having a carnet (drivers permit) from Spain, does raise the spectre of another nightmare as I had written about previously. Fingers crossed that the level of licensing complexity here is not as out of control as it was in Mallorca.

So, things are looking up a bit. The island still looks very sad and all messed up, but the people are up and working so hard to restore it to the way it was (or better) before Irma came. It is hard to characterise exactly what the collective mental model is here in the BVI, but what comes to mind (well, to my mind) is something that first produced during the war for printing on a poster in case of an invasion. Luckily Britain never experienced the land invasion and the poster never made it into print then. The message on the poster is still applicable to many situations that we has humans find ourselves in….it is worth remembering….Keep Calm and Carry On.

These words are very special and have no doubt been very helpful since 6 September changed so many lives. This story isn't over yet, but it is moving in a positive direction. And whilst it might appear that I will not be writing for a while from a sailboat, sitting at anchor in the North Sound, being here itself is not the worst thing in the world.

What can I say? I am, admittedly, feeling all Druid-like, and whilst there is no Stonehenge here to prance around, and I don't even own any sackcloth robes, the day I had been looking forward to for quite a while was finally here. The Solstice – this one being the shortest day of the year – brings life and new beginnings. Whilst I hate this day because it is the shortest day, I equally love it because every day from now on the days grow longer. More sunlight. More life. More smiles. *And for the purposes of this chapter, I will pretend to ignore that in six months, the days will begin to go the other way again.*

The move went okay today (the last Thursday before Christmas). When I say "it went okay," part of that is because I had put all the boxes, bags, and carryall containers into Tania early this morning and then actually found

Living on Rocks

the holiday condo that I had rented. This could have been a non-so-okay day if I had not found it but after driving along the coast road, then over the top of the mountain to the north side of the island, and then further along a different coast road, I was bobbing along the Long Bay road and shortly after, the condo. After unloading everything, I then headed back into Road Town. This was a shopping trip, and could have been avoided if I would have stopped on the way out, but I knew that doing the trip again would ensure that I would be able to get home on future days. So I went into Road Town and stopped at Bobby's Market, only to walk into a store that had for some reason, lost its power and was as dark as the middle of the night. Full of a new sense of adventure, I simply clicked on the torch feature of my iPhone and walked up and down the aisles, filling a basket with what seemed to be enough choices of proper food to get me by until Monday when I cook my 8-kilo Christmas ham. Oh, that's not exactly right. I did buy some wonderful fresh pasta and will undoubtedly have tortellini and pesto as my holiday meal.

After managing to pay the check-out person (as there was no power, she was adding up everything with a calculator, and as luck would have it, the total came to just ten cents less than an even dollar amount, so paying was not a problem. Then the drive back to Long Bay and the condo. Already, the road home feels like a road home, and that is a nice feeling.

After completing the task of unpacking and stowing clothes in logical places in the condo, I looked outside and low-and-behold, the other side of the bay was obscured by what looked like a mysterious cloud formation… which after a few minutes, became an adorable five-minute rain storm, with, I might add, a rainbow. And after the five minutes, the sun returned to bless my new home and life begins anew (again).

After a first night at the new home location, I awoke to see the sun starting to peek over one of the hills protecting Long Bay. It was going to be a good day, and that meant that music was required. And because today is only three days from Christmas, this meant that I clicked on the compilation of holiday music on my iTunes. So with the Darlene Love and the Ronettes wafting through the condo and out onto the porch, a good cuppa, and the sun beginning to stream across the water, I am ready to go.

I took a quick trip into Nanny Cay (I had forgotten to buy a couple of things when in Road Town yesterday, and there is a proper market in Nanny Cay… and it is closer) When I say "a quick trip," I do mean it. Driving Tania each day is helping me get used to some of the roads here post-Irma. Either that or Tania now knows where the larger potholes are and takes control of her own steering to avoid them. After my mini shopping excursion, I came home and realised that what was needed now was a walk along my new beach. There is something special, almost soothing, walking on the sand as the small waves scurry up to surround your feet. I was feeling that this certainly was what was called for today, so after putting things away and found a bottle of HT 0

(Hawaiian Tropic, sunscreen zero), and within minutes was strolling down the (rather long and steep) driveway to the condo. The adjective "steep" is pretty applicable on this island. There are some islands in the Caribbean that are almost dead flat (Aruba as an example is only about two meters high), whereas almost all of the BVI (and USVI) are like the tips of mountains that stick out of the sea. So when you want to build a home here, you more than likely will be doing it on a hill. Sometimes, a very steep hill. This was a prime reason for buying a car with all-wheel drive. Back to the story...

So here I am, slowly walking down the drive. After a few hundred meters, there is a hairpin turn to the right. Then another few hundred meters going down still at about 30-degrees, a hairpin turn to the left. After doing all this a third time, I felt like I was living the rakes progress, but not for the Hogarth reason. I did reach the road and as I crossed it to get to the beach, I did admittedly speculate about how much fun I would have climbing back up this Everest-looking driveway.

The beach itself was everything every beach aspires to (big assumptions that beaches actually do aspire to anything other than leaving sand in many places that you may not want it). The north side of Tortola (Long Bay is on the west-end of the island, but on the north side) does have the best beaches. Soft sand, no rocks, some shells (oh boy...MLR will be in heaven), and a semi-pounding surf. I am not exactly sure how to describe the sand here. When we walked the beach at Naples in Florida, the part that the surf had washed over was more-or-less, hard packed. But here, the sand where the surf has washed over it is deliciously soft and almost gushy, letting your feet sink in eight or ten centimetres, engulfing your feet in a warm, sensuous blanket with each step. I walked all the way to one end of the beach, then back past my starting point to the other end, and then back to where I crossed the road. Along this sojourn, several important learning's came to me...learning's that I felt I needed to pass along to you all.

Learning 1: I was surprised to see some new construction beach huts. I had been under the impression that there was no land available to build on, but apparently I was mistaken. I have no idea if these beauties are for sale, but I might check it out.

Learning 2: This learning could be extremely important for those of you that dream to one day have your own place on a Caribbean beach. Building in a tropical storm zone, and as we all know, the Caribbean IS in a tropical storm zone, requires making lots of choices. Which island to build on? What kind of vistas do you want to wake up to each day? What kind of construction materials to you think would be the best?

Learning 3: If you do want to build your own little romantic beach shack in a hurricane zone, the two words to remember are "reinforced concrete."

Christmas is only two days away now, and I was thinking I should have sent Santa a letter asking him to plead with Juracán, (the deity of chaos and disorder believed to control the weather) who was responsible most likely for Irma and her friends, to stay away from here next year. But it is probably good I didn't send the letter as that would be greedy of me. Having said that, a nice 20-meter Hinckley would be nice (but equally greedy I suppose).

Another day, another adventure. Today is a Saturday, and at the time, it seemed to be a perfect opportunity for some exploration of Tortola. I wasn't about to go all namby-pamby driving around...I wanted to drive over to Brewers Bay to see if I could find a house that the estate agent had showed me last week. For the purposes of full-disclosure, I hadn't been paying a lot of attention when we saw the house eight days earlier, but not being completely daft, I reasoned I could find it none-the-less. When I was there, I had taken a few photos of it and I first turned on my trusty repository of all things important (my computer, of course) and brought up all the photos on the screen. The house overlooked Brewers Bay and the vista in the photos gave me an approximate area that the house was in. I then opened Google Earth and began searching in the same approximate area until I found a home that looked like it could be the one. Same colour roof, same basic shape, a pool in the same area as the one I saw when I was there, and even more importantly was the assumption that if I was standing on the wrap-around porch, I would be looking down on the same part of the Bay I could see from the image on my screen. I "pinned" that spot on my computer, and then did the same thing, finding the same house on my phone. Then it was just a matter of firing up Tania and whizzing over to see the house again. And yes, this is where the "fun" began.

Instead of taking the road over the mountain to the Sir Francis Drake Hwy that follows the southern coast of the island from West End all the way to East End and then on to Beef Island (where the airport is), I decided to take the route that went along the northern coast of Tortola that, according to Google Maps, would take me all the way to Brewers Bay. And just a note of clarification; the abbreviation for "highway" in Sir Francis Drake Hwy means a moderately narrow two lane road. Cute adaptation of a descriptive word, isn't it?

Now, before I carry on, a bit of reminder of how hurricanes work. In the northern Hemisphere, all hurricanes rotate anti-clockwise. This means that as a hurricane marches past Tortola, the winds will initially appear to come roaring in from the north. This is what went on when (that bitch) Irma (notice the lasting resentment of her visit?) approached Tortola. The weather; i.e. massively powerful winds in excess of 180 mph smashing into the island from the north, and with them, huge waves unmercifully pounding the beaches.

The coastal road on the north side of Tortola is, in many places, only a few metres from the water. When the wind and waves came ashore back on 6 September, there are many stretches where the road was pretty much obliterated. Massive chunks of tarmac that had before made a nice smooth, seamless road, were ripped up by the combination of wind and waves, leaving gaping depressions that spanned both lanes and were in some cases, multiple car-lengths long. It is not as if they are deep enough to swallow a car or lorry, but one must slow down to a snails pace to avoid having the underside of your car being seemingly disembowelled. The seriously deep potholes require good hand-eye coordination; i.e. if you don't see one of these pits to the centre of the earth soon enough, you won't be able to evasively steer your vehicle out of the way. And if the potholes weren't enough fun, there are sleeping policemen scattered randomly around on many of the roads. Some of them have bright yellow paint on either side of the respective road, but the "bright" part was only valid the day that they were painted, and have no doubt, that was well before this year's onset of totally shite weather. If you fail to see one of these speed-bumps-from-hell, you have the sensation upon hitting it at speed that your car is being chucked into the air as if it were heading off into space. That can't be good for the car either. So the concept of caution-whilst-driving does apply here, especially if you are venturing out on roads you don't know. Lesson learnt.

So here I am, after only about five minutes of driving on the north coast road, wondering why I am going this direction. At one point I thought it wise to turn around and go back to my starting point and cross over the mountain/hill/whatever, but the road was so narrow there was no way I could accomplish this manoeuver. I soldiered on, but very slowly. Then a section of the road that looks like it did a bit more than three months ago. This false sense of security would be snapped away from me as soon as Tania would find a pothole that I never even saw.

When I had come out with the estate agent last week, we didn't come this way, and it was becoming quite clear to me that the other way (or *any* other way) would have been better. But by the time I am (or should be) quite near, it is a bit too late to start again, even if I could find a place where I could turn around. So, in the vein of a previous chapter's message, I simply decided to continue keeping calm and carrying on.

I did have my phone set to Google Maps and was hoping that the young lady who apparently is very small and lives inside my phone would talk to me, telling me where to turn. She, sadly, was on a work slowdown and wasn't talking to me, so now I was trying to avoid cavern-like potholes, sleeping policemen from hell, trying to avoid careening over some cliff, AND figure out where to turn. Yes, I do know how to have fun. I would have taken more photos of the vistas along these roads because they were (are) unflippinbelievably spectacular. But to do that, I would have had to either find a layby to park Tania (there aren't any on a road that is barely wide enough for one car) or simply stop, roll down the window, and click away. I almost did that several times, but each time, I noticed that someone was behind me and clearly in a bigger hurry than I was. I would attempt to pull over to one side as much as possible, but before I could even be partially off the road into some bushes, the respective people behind me would slosh around me and proceed on at a speed that I wasn't prepared to attempt. Clearly locals who have been driving these roads since the time they were built.

After what seemed to be ages, I thought I was about there. I found a driveway to pull into so I could check my phone's map programme, only to discover that somehow I had missed the turnoff from X to Y. (*You can insert your own names of choice for these roads as they do not have signs and even the map programme lists them as "unknown road."*) Not only had I missed the appropriate turn off, I was now quite close to the real road that I probably should have taken when I decided to drive out here today. I sat there for a few minutes, looking back up the narrow path-like road toward where the turn-off should have been, and then looking along the road the other way that would lead me toward Nanny Cay again. A real road. Wide enough for more than one car. Made from real tarmac. I wimped out and headed toward (relative) civilisation. After some nice new scenery, I did begin to recognise the road from when the estate agent brought me here. This road would take me down to Sir Francis Drake Hwy, which was the road home. But just before it gets there, you find yourself on a piece of road that is lovingly known by the locals as "the elevator." Let your mind wander on why it has that name.

The elevator is what might be called a "steep" road. I went back days later and tried to get a grasp on how steep was steep. I have an app on my iPhone that was designed to be a level, and there is one tab you can click on it that shows how much out of level something is. The elevator climbs up this hill at more than a 45-degree angle. Steep.

Just a few words of context about driving in the BVI. Are these roads totally and completely treacherous? Of course not. Actually, I find them far less intimidating than the first time I attempted to negotiate my way around the Arc de Triomphe in Paris, or the crazed multi-lane motorways in Los Angeles, or the roads to Galilea or Deia. Like so many things in this life, a little patience and everything is fine. At least Tania is right-hand drive, which does make it far easier.

It is the day before Christmas today. Long beach walk, continuing on to the Salt Pond at Belmont. As I walked along the beach, my feet were enveloped by the sea as its waves came rushing up every five or ten seconds, ensuring that I was not just someone strolling along but someone who was fast becoming one with the sea and sand. The sensation is wonderfully special. And then, as I continued on a small road (or large path) that went past the salt pond, it became clear to me that at no additional cost, I had joined one of those trendy health club places, with the minor exception that the one I was a member of is Mother-Nature's-Mind-and-Body-Rejuvenation-Spa.

And as amazing as it seems to be, Christmas sort of flew past. I had been invited over to my estate agent's home for Christmas dinner, but as she lives in East End, and I am pretty much on the West End of Tortola, the spectre of the drive at night was a bit much, so my dinner consisted of tortellini with pesto. Actually, I think it was the same last year, but then it was in the cockpit of Saphir, instead of on the terrace in Long Bay. Potato, potato. Tomato, tomato. Boxing Day followed and there wasn't much to report. I did a spot of food shopping, and then worked on finishing pictures, as you do. Back to doing what I like to do with combinations of colour, light and shadow, and shapes.

There are only a few more days this year, and then it will be 2018. Pretty amazing that we are all still here. Not necessarily, "here" in terms of being in the BVI, but "here" in terms of still above ground at all. And whilst it is pretty great that we are all here, this could be a good time to think about those friends and family who left us in 2017.

2018

Today began with great hopes for a good start to the year. The first thing was that I received an email from an organisation that tracks published papers, and as you may know, I have been rather prolific in this area over the past twenty years. The email said that some of my articles and papers have been cited in 56 academic papers that my work has touched on. I knew that some people had actually read some of my work, but to find out that now it had been cited that many times felt pretty great.

Then my local estate agent – the one who had been driving me around previously looking for places to live – arrived and off we went again. Today's circuitous routing took us to two places I had seen before with her, and two new options. All this looking is both tiring and extremely beneficial to keep narrowing down what our priorities are for a place to rent. One today was especially nice, but it would have been a nightmare for Tania to negotiate, with narrow marginally paved "roads" (and I use this term with tongue firmly in cheek). I could not even fathom how you would make it home in the dark. Incredibly spectacular and fabulous vistas, but thanks, no thanks. I did make a video of the one I liked pretty much and sent it off to MLR to peruse. Glad I did not video the "road." She would have slashed her wrists… or mine.

As my estate agent was driving me back to my temporary condo, she cut a corner a bit to close and by the time she was in my drive, her car had a flat tyre. An interesting finish to an interesting day. She did have a spare, and luckily a workman came past and helped in the changing process. I tend to not cut corners very close here whilst driving, but will probably give them an even wider berth now.

Whilst we were out looking for homes to rent, we stopped to get something to eat, and whilst it wasn't on the menu where we were, I did see a catamaran sandwich that looked interesting. How one catamaran can land almost perfectly on top of another one is one of Mother Nature's hurricane mysteries. I am quite confident that if a crew was tasked to do this with all the best equipment, they couldn't have managed an outcome as good as the one provided by Irma.

Yesterday, the year 2017 passed away and became just a memory. For some of us, the memory was a mixture of some real highs and some real lows. I had a blending of both, and whilst the lows were pretty flippin' low with the whole Irma experience, I have chosen to just get on with it…whatever "it" is for this year. So 2018 began with exactly what I was hoping for…sunny and warm days and more hopes and dreams for the future.

This whole thing about finding a place to live could be getting tiring, but it is all about making choices. Choices about how to live; choices about where to live; and choices about damn near everything in life. For me, the choices all relate to, and complement, the vision of living I have had for years. As someone who facilitates others making better choices, I do recognise that often, I feel like the shoemaker. The challenge is always to put my choices into a larger context to make sure the choices are the right ones, for the right reasons. Sometimes doing this can make you feel wonderful, and sometimes, it can come back and slap you back to reality.

Now to be fair, choosing where to live doesn't exactly fit in the same category as choosing to live with news of a terminal illness diagnosis, but the reality is – my reality, your reality – is that we may not be able to have a lot of control over getting old, _how_ we live is a choice we can all make.

And speaking of choices, this morning I decided to do laundry, wash Tania, and do other seemingly endless condo chores. Normally, I would do my beach walk early, but today it wasn't until past noon that I was ready to head on down to the beach. Now, just a bit of beach context for you. The beach at Long Bay is over a kilometre long, and at most points it is 25 – 30 metres wide, with about another 3 or 4 meters being where the surf washes up. So today, as I was walking down thinking about which way to start my walk – head West toward the Salt Pond at Belmont point, or head east toward the big posh homes – I was in my own little world. Incredibly sunny and warm does tend to act as a mantra and sends me to some very peaceful place where my mind can really function. And then I hit the beach and headed west. As soon as I made it past the big rock headland, I was gobsmacked. I had never seen the beach here that crowded. I didn't have any paper or pencil, but luckily my mental maths skills are pretty good and I was able to get an idea of how many people there were enjoying the beach. Seven. Well, six plus myself. Crazy crowded day.

I went into town with my estate agent for a last ditch attempt to find other living options. It isn't as if I haven't found a place. I did find a condo just down the driveway from where I am now, but I would be crazy as a loon if I did not continue to look. The looking is always fun (if it is for boats, but still okay if it is for land-based places), but all today's search did was eliminate everything we saw. That in itself is good, so I told the estate agent that the condo will do, and asked her to please get the paperwork in play. Today is the 4th of January and I do need to move in three or four days, so the timing is pretty perfect. And the reality that I don't have to worry about going to someplace completely new is simply brill. I know this barrio and feel very comfortable here. Actually, I had told MLR the other day that Tania pretty much knows the way to the condo all by herself, so that is a very very good thing. Moving day in three days…don't forget to bring some beer.

The first Sunday of the New Year, I went for my daily beach walk early enough to beat the sun coming up over the horizon. Of course, being on an island that is laced with mountain-like hills, in many places, the horizon is "over some hill." That is what it is here, so by the time the sun begins to stream across the sand, it is already quite bright out. And today, because I was the first person on the beach, the sand was still in near virgin condition, with the only disturbances in its soft, gently flowing surface were the small holes dug by little crabs. I am making an assumption here as I have yet to see any of the hole-livers…perhaps they have a different life cycle than I do. So there I was, walking along the pristine-feeling beach, feeling like I was part of a Daniel Defoe novel, of course with the minor exception that today was a Sunday, not a Friday. The peace that envelops you when you are the only person on the beach is amazing. All you hear are the waves breaking on the shore, making incredible patterns in the sand. I have been lucky enough to have had visited some pretty special places in my life, but being able to *live* in one is special beyond belief.

I moved today. Well, I suppose I should clarify that a bit. I moved from one condo to another in the same Long Bay area, and because of some booking complications (these condos typically are short-term holiday lets), this move might only be for a month. Time will tell, and I certainly am not going to get all wonky about it. Besides, the "move" didn't take too many minutes as it was only three hundred some steps from one to the other. But, as I packed up everything in Tania and drove over, it seems like it was more complicated than it really was.

I wasn't sure that this move was going to actually be required, as last week I received a lead on a pretty nice sailboat. About the same size as Saphir, with most of the same kit on her, the boat was located in Florida but the current owners said that they would consider sailing her to the BVI as part of a deal. That all sounded pretty nice…until I heard the price they wanted for her. Apparently they were living in some dream world of how boats are valued. I did try to explain to them that the only way to really know the value of anything is to find out what someone would pay for it. In this case, I did like the boat, but would have only offered them about 60% of what they wanted for it, and they were almost insulted. *"We love our boat and this is how much we think it is worth,"* came out of the man's mouth. I replied with a kind-sounding, *"Well good luck to you. I hope you find someone that will pay that much."* I wouldn't be surprised to hear from him again when reality sets in.

But for now, the new condo will suffice quite nicely, thank you very much.

I heard from MLR this morning. Her message did not bode well. She is on her way here and was told at the flight check-in counter that her baggage was overweight. No surprise there, as we have been talking quite a bit about what she wanted to bring and what it might be nice to have that is hard to find here. Her move is admittedly more complicated than mine was from condo 1 to condo 2. Mary Lee is flying from MKE to MIA, then an overnight stay before flying from MIA to the Cyril King airport (STT), and then the fast-ferry ride to Road Town where I will collect her from the ferry dock in the centre of town. So today I am sticking around the condo, getting things ready for her arrival. As I have been trying to clean and organise since I arrived, I support "getting things ready" could also mean working on one project or another. Hours of fun.

After MLR arrived, we started to settle in at the new condo. The new condo, only a hundred-or-so metres from the first one, is virtually identical, so for me, the change wasn't all that difficult. But for MLR, it was all a new experience. I had been living here in Long Bay for some time, and whilst I wasn't on a boat, nor was I on the North Sound, life here was pretty good. MLR and I would try to do daily beach walks, and that was pretty great as well. The beach at Long Bay is about a kilometre long, so a walk from one end to the other and then back again was a couple klics, and that was perfect. We also made quite a few trips into Road Town to go shopping for groceries or other things that we needed. Our first trip in was the day after she arrived, and it was quite an eye-opener for her.

When she arrived, the fast ferry (or perhaps I should say, the "alleged fast ferry") had been 30 minutes late coming in from St Thomas in the USVI, and by the time she had cleared customs here and collected her baggage, the sun was quickly settling behind the mountain-like hills that surround Road Town, and because of it, by the time we made it back to Long Bay, it was dark. So the next day, as we were driving into Road Town in Tania, MLR was getting her first looks at what used to be one of the most beautiful islands in the Caribbean. Have no doubt, things now are so much better than they were back in September, but just about everyplace you go, things are a mess. The term "mess" is about the only way to describe what MLR saw that morning.

Days slid on by, and MLR has done quite a bit of exploring the Long Bay area and has climbed up the crazy uphill roads that wind up the mountain whilst I, sensing that all that up and down hiking could be too much fun to handle, would stay home and absorb the vistas that were pretty incredible and reading some of the multitude of books I was enticed to buy for my Kindle in the past months. These first several weeks were not just all lazy days, and I began to do some "art-related" pieces. Pen and ink, coloured pens, and a limited edition set of prints were all outcomes of my need to do something creative.

The prints were the most challenging, largely because I have been unable to find a supplier of serigraph kit here on the islands. With no suppliers available, it was pretty impossible to come up with colour separations, much less the screens that I would use to print. When I was confronted with this dilemma, I flashed back to when I first was making multiple-run Christmas cards. When I started this annual project, I was living on-board Angelina in Barcelona and had no serigraph equipment either, so I made stencils out of flexible transparencies, and then applied the acrylic ink with a fine, closed cell sponge. Granted, the first couple designs I did look pretty rudimentary now, but that was what it was in those days. Whilst this did seem like a viable option here in the BVI, it also made me realise how spoilt I had become by having a set of screens and good suppliers in Mallorca. Replicating, or attempting to replicate, the serigraph process with stencils is very different. Making serigraphs gives you the ability to work with half-tones, and blending colour gradients by manipulating the density of the screens themselves. The stencil process, whilst great fun and satisfying the creative urge, is pretty much of a binary exercise in comparison.. Colours that go on the paper are pretty much limited by the colours that come out of the ink tube, and the reality that the only ink I could find here was opaque. If I had been able to purchase transparent colours, some blending of tones can be achieved on paper, but here, what comes out of the tube is what ends up as the finished product. Often, these are not the colour intensities I am after.

Having done all this whinging, I guess I am sort of pleased with the new pieces. But, as most artsy stuff is "graded" in the eyes of the beholders and not the eyes of the one that makes them, it really isn't up to me. Regardless, they have been, and will continue to be, good exercises in creative stimulation.

When I was in my young teenage years, one of the things my father taught me was the Elliott Wave Principle. This theory, not exactly as exciting as hanging out with my friends, has its basis on the belief (by Mr. Elliott) that "collective investor psychology, or crowd psychology, moves between optimism and pessimism in natural sequences." (You must be dripping with excitement by now). Elliott's belief was that these shifts happen in "waves," of either five or three. As we all know (or should by now), the five and three numbers are significant as they are part of the Fibonacci series of numbers that appear in nature. All that was to lead up to today's beach walk. MLR and I were about to head out from the condo when I suggested that we combined our beach walk for the day with a picnic, and she agreed that this would be a fun thing to do. She liked it so much that she said I could prepare my own picnic treat. (Some of the excitement began to slip away, but I did whip up a pretty fab sandwich) After walking along for a way, we found a place to sit down and, as we devoured our culinary delights (My sandwich and MLR's salad), she began to comment about today's wave patterns. I couldn't resist and brought up the Elliott Wave Principle, and after

Living on Rocks

a few minutes of observing, it was pretty amazing to realise that the Wave Principle not only is applicable in investor or crowd psychology, it appears that (at least for today), it was pretty much applicable for waves crashing into the beach from Long Bay. After our lunch, and its parallel very deep conversation about theories and natural sequences, we moved along to the end of the beach on the Belmont side and decided to contribute to the artistic endeavours of one or more other beach walkers by balancing rocks upon rocks, turning them into nicely balanced towers. For sure, this beach many need to be renamed the Zen Beach at Long Bay.

Living here is, as I have said repeatedly, it pretty nice. But to be perfectly fair and honest, living here in Long Bay is incredibly luxurious compared to the lives of many of the belongers whose lives were deviated by the three big events of last year. Three devastating weather events in one year, on an island that has been lucky for the previous 30+ years. So here we are, living in Long Bay, with electricity, hot and cold running water, enough money to live in a pretty special condo, and equally enough money so we never are hungry. Because we know how fortunate we are, it is sometimes pretty difficult to find something that we can do to help the locals get back on their feet. We do frequent shops and stores as much as possible, but since I bought Tania, I have also been picking up hitch-hikers who don't have transportation options. It is not unusual, whilst driving from the condo across the mountain to Sir Francis Drake Highway (the alleged highway) so see people standing on the side of the road, needing a ride, but not wanting to seem needy by putting their thumb out. So just before MLR arrived, I started pulling over and picking one or two of them up on my way into Road Town. Sometimes it is a chatty person, sometimes it is a very quiet person. Sometimes it is someone who appears to be older than I am, and sometimes (like today), it is school children with a parent. One day, whilst whizzing along the SFDH, I pulled over because there was this man who clearly needed a ride. He climbed into the seat behind me in Tania, and whilst driving in, I tried to engage him in conversation. It was a challenge, however, as within seconds after he stepped out when we reached Road Town, MLR and I were speculating if he had cholera, Ebola, or some form of any other contagion, as he wheezed and coughed the entire way in. Perhaps I am wise to screen people a bit more when seeing someone who needs a ride.

Today, the first Monday of February, we drove into Road Town because my residency permission certification needed to be renewed. When I was granted the residency, we went to the Immigration offices and had to wait in a queue for some time. Today, when we arrived, it was about 0945h, and there were people queued up outside the offices, as well as having the waiting room chocker. I sort of pressed my way to one of the three service windows. The verbal interchange went more or less like this:

ME: *Good morning. I am here to renew my residency certification.*
CLERK: *Did we call your number?*

ME: *No, I just arrived here.*

CLERK: *You need to take a number and wait until we call your number.*

ME: (as I looked over to where the number dispenser machine is) *I am sorry, but it appears there are no numbers in the machine.*

CLERK: *Really? The machine must be empty.*

ME: *If there are no more numbers what should I do?*

CLERK: *We must have already gone through all the numbers.*

ME: *Right. So what would you like me to do?*

CLERK: *You could come back at noon…*

We did walk out and went to a chemist to get some things, then to a café that had broadband and waited. Soon, it was nearing noon so we went back. The queue outside was about the same and after managing to find a place to sit inside, I sat and waited. And waited. And waited. And finally a security man came out and said that if anyone was in the room who did not have a number, that person should come back in the morning. Our new plan for tomorrow is for us to get there an hour before they open to get a low number (assuming they have numbers tomorrow).

We did arrive an hour before opening time, and the queue was more than 150 people. That was a tad depressing, but as luck would have it, by noon we were out of there with my passport stamped with my renewal, and MLR being told she can stay until she heads back to her Lake Home in May. All good news.

To close out this writing session, I thought it might be nice to tell you a little story about the beach. As the waves come crashing to the shore, they can make quite the impressive sound. And if you are standing in an area where there are rocks, the sounds are even more impressive when the water then rushes back out to sea. The sound as the waves retreat is hard to explain in words and about all I can describe it as is sort of a "ricky-ticky" sound of stones clicking as they bounce across other stones. One day, as we were standing there, marvelling at the sounds, I thought it might be best to make an audio recording of the sound, and because of the totally crazy technology we all have in our pockets, it made sense to do a video at the same time. So picture this….in order to get the video and audio to really represent what we were seeing and hearing, I took my phone out of my pocket and held it high in the air as I edged out into an area where the waves were crashing on the beach. I lined up what I thought would make a good video with audio track, and hit the little red button. The sun was pouring down on the phone's screen, making it impossible to see how many seconds were being recorded, so I sort of counted up to twenty, then hit the red button again and walked out of the surf. When I was back on the beach, I shielded the back of my phone from the sun, only to find that when I first hit the red button, I must not have pressed it exactly right, as the recording didn't begin

Living on Rocks

until I thought I was stopping it. Buggers. The following day, I was bound and determined to get this recording so I first plopped around until I found what I thought would be the best spot for both video and audio. Then I made sure I engaged the magically tricky red button and made the recording. The recording was okay, but I wanted it better than okay, so I did another one. And then I decided to do a third one. The third one was going to be a bit more adventuresome, so I went further out into the surf, ensuring that the sound of the stones as they clicked along making their ricky-ticky sound as the wave retreated into the sea. As I was getting my footing all set – when the waves would crash in, there was quite a bit of splashing and I didn't want to have a wave knock me know and kill my iPhone – I felt quite a few small pebbles bouncing past my foot. I was all set, but before I could engage the red button, the next wave came in and with it, brought several seriously nasty rocks. My left foot took several hits and I immediately hobbled out of the surf, not even thinking of the video idea. MLR asked me if something was wrong, but instead of describing what had just occurred, I showed her my foot, which was starting to bleed in several places. By the time we had returned home, the bleeding had stopped but the outside of my ankle now had a hematoma the size of Menorca on it.

Well, we are moving again. This move, as I had alluded to previously, won't be all that stressful as we will only have to go from the middle condo to the one at the top of the property...the one they (laughingly) call the Penthouse. Okay, so by definition, I suppose it is the Penthouse, but ...well...never mind. So MLR and I will carry up our boxes, suitcases, clothing, food, and miscellaneous containers of stuff from Saphir and within a couple of hours, and we will be all settled in again. Being upstairs will have its advantages, with the main one being the vista is even better than the ones from the previous two condos. The space is smaller, the kitchen is pretty much rubbish, but the vista is pretty remarkable...and this statement comes from someone who has pretty great vistas no matter which way I look. So we will be here in the "Penthouse" for the next three weeks, then back down to the middle condo again for the rest of this spring. Don't jump to some bizarre conclusion; we didn't move upstairs because we are charter members of "We-Like-to-Relocate." We moved because the condo that we were in had a previous rental commitment for these three weeks, so I had accepted it as one of the parameters of living there for the rest of the time.

Our routine has settled in pretty well now that MLR has been here for a month. We do the beach walk pretty much daily, except on days when my foot is trying to recover from being smashed to shit by some less-than-polite rocks in the surf, which of course was due to me being in the surf amongst the nasty rocks. MLR, who is a serious health-focused person, does daily walks all over the Long Bay area. I did a few of these with her, but no matter which way you go from the condo, a walk will encounter some pretty steep hills and I am quite content to just enjoy being here. Just enjoying being here does include doing artsy shit and talking to locals about business things, of course.

Part of our routine involves shopping, as one might imagine. When I was living on Saphir, or even after I returned to Tortola after Irma, shopping wasn't quite as complicated. I suppose part of this was due to my less-than-complicated dietary requirements. Juice, yoghurt, salmon or chicken, pasta (with pesto of course), salad, cereal…just the basics were fine. And admittedly, these basics were immersed in a routine of their own with me often having the same thing several days in a row. When MLR arrived, the food-shopping thing became a bit more complex, with new words entering my culinary syllabus. Words like, "variety" and "spices" and "healthier" again floating into my ears, as we would walk down the aisles of one of the local markets. Have no doubt, I do like the variety, and the healthier options, and of course, the addition of some spice into meals. Cooking for oneself is certainly different than cooking for two, and having someone preparing meals that does enjoy doing something different each day is quite the treat.

We do have to do other-than-food shopping on occasion. One day, we were in Bolo's, which is a semi-department store located next to Bobby's grocery. I say that Bolo's is a "semi-department" store only because its building was seriously trashed during Irma and I don't think they had insurance to cover the losses as now some of the walls (exterior and interior) are made of tacked on sheets of polyethylene.

Many of the aisles are a mess and in some areas of Bolo's, it appears that there are random things on shelves for sale. We had gone into Bolo's because I was looking for some acrylic ink to use on the prints I have been making. Amazingly, they did have some, and whilst not the same amount of options that I used to find during my years in Mallorca, I was pretty chuffed to find anything. Of course, the prices were a tad more than in Mallorca, but it is hard to tell if that was a result of Irma, or just the reality that the BVI is a bit pricey for a lot of things. So I picked out the colours that I wanted and then when I was about to check out, I remembered that I would need more transparencies if I were to continue making these prints. I had asked MLR to bring some with her, which she did, but when you are making multiple-colour prints, you need one transparency for each colour and the first two prints I had designed were going to almost completely exhaust the supply MLR had brought. When I asked the woman at the checkout counter if they had transparencies, she quickly developed a glazed look on her face, so I said I would go back upstairs to where the office-type stuff was and ask someone else. I did just that, and was pleased to find someone who knew what a transparency was. She said she thought there were some, but that was before Irma, so the two of us prowled around for a few minutes when she announced she found some. Her voice was all apologetic when she said that she was sorry but they only had one packet. My internal voice was mumbling "oh bugger" but that instantly changed when I saw that the pack she had in her hand contained 100-transparency sheets. Damn, that was great news. I did ask the price of the packet (You learn to ask the price of just about everything here) and she showed me the tag in the corner of the packet...$49.99. Shit. I was happy as Larry that they had the package of 100 transparencies, but I wasn't keen on spending a penny short of 50 USD for them. I am not sure what I said, or even what my expression was, but after a moment, the clerk said to me that I could just take them. *"Thank you,"* I said, *"but I really don't want to pay that much for transparencies."* She smiled (as everyone does here) and replied, *"No, you can just take them. Tell the girl downstairs I said you could take them without paying. We probably won't sell them otherwise. It is okay, just tell her."* I found MLR and we went downstairs and approached the checkout woman again, saying exactly what I had been told upstairs. She smiled and said okay, and out the door we went. God, I love this country.

The other day, on a Monday I think, we were in Road Town and sitting in the café in front of the Village Cay marina. I took two photos, which I tried to splice together. The reason I did this is to give yet another perspective on the situation here, which is in reality, the conundrum of Tortola. The photo (the photo combination) looks pretty nice, but if you look really closely, it is possible to still see boats that are partially underwater, boats without masts, and piles of empty moorings at the marina. This is where the paradox lies. Whilst things look from a distance like everything is fine again (like looking at the combined photos), when you really look closely, the devastation is so very visible. But for me, having been here during Irma's rampage and the week afterwards, I am so very impressed by what has taken place to help restore Tortola to what it was before September of last year. Yes, when you really look at it all, it is still pretty grim, but compared to what I saw days after it all happened, it is pretty remarkable. Sort of the ultimate in good-news-bad-news paradoxes.

Saturday, and that that means walking day. Okay, everyday is a good day to walk here, but today turned out to be very special. When I first moved to Long Bay, I spent the first few days exploring a bit. One of the walks I did was west, toward Smugglers Cove. The walk then was pretty special, and today, when MLR said *"Want to go for a walk?"* it seemed like a great opportunity to retrace the walk I had done to the Cove before she arrived. Sort of a blending between walking through the jungle down some muddy path and exploring uncharted lands, the walk was wonderful. It is wonderful because of the dynamics of Mother Nature. It is winter, so we get rain almost every day and night, even if for only five or ten minutes; and the rain and the sun's warmth make this an incredibly lush landscape. And since it is has been five months since Irma's wrath stripped all the trees of leaves, the combination of rain and sun have made much of the island green beyond belief. After going up and down some pretty muddy hills, we went around a corner and there was the beach at Smugglers Cove. This beach, not as long as Long Bay, is none-the-less, pretty spectacular. And because Smugglers Cove is in the wind and wave shadow of Belmont point, the surf is not as rough, making it a perfect place to swim. We weren't wearing our suits, but I did feel compelled to empty my pockets (no sense in risking losing a phone or important papers) and decided to walk into the sea for a few meters. Perhaps a few meters too far as one wave that was a bit larger than others, I was pretty wet, but it did feel wonderful. When I stepped out of the sea, MLR felt compelled to go in as well. Two pretty happy people. Walking back to the condo, we met up with quite a few neighbours. Three of them were a young couple and their daughter who are living near the Cove; one was a crab living in a fab-looking shell; and about fifty of them were little white butterflies.

I had to smile today on our beach walk. Today's walk felt like we were walking on what was to become a beach about a kazillion years ago. The surf was up substantially – full moon plays havoc with the tides – and because of that, the entire beachscape was different today than every other day. Now to be fair, every day, the beach changes a bit. A little more sand there, and little less sand here. A couple of new rocks over there. Some very special new driftwood in front of us. Nothing major, but it does change everyday, and it is these changes that make the daily beach walk so special. Today's walk was mind-blowing different. On the end of the beach where we have been building rock-Zen towers, there was a strip of rocks about 30 meters long. Today that strip of rocks is now about 80 meters long. Where the beach used to be (on average) about 20 meters wide, it is now about half of that. We found a Hamilton-Beach commercial mixer sticking out of the sand. We found an engine block from a boat (or a car I suppose) that had been washed up on shore. Some of the rock sculptures have totally disappeared. It was like the end of the movie Planet of the Apes.

This morning, before we did the beach walk, I had a follow-up visit appointment in Road Town, so we jumped into Tania and merrily drove along the (laughingly called) highway into town. The drive gets better and better each day with crews appearing out of nowhere to fill in potholes and areas of the roads that were washed away during Irma. We noticed that not only were the roads better again today, but there wasn't all that traffic today. When we arrived in Road Town, we discovered that it was a National Holiday to honour the first Premier of the British Virgin Islands and nothing would be open. Almost nothing, as the major groceries do have seem to learnt from the Americans and are open almost every day, so we filled up on a few necessities and whizzed home again.

Walking along the beach does stimulate one's mind, or I guess more appropriately, it can. This happens in multiple ways. One way is that the stimulation is calming beyond belief. It is the whole "grounding" thing: walking barefoot, along the beach, with the sand nestling between your toes, with the sound of the surf coming ashore, it like the most powerful mantra I have ever known. This is coming from someone (me) who did learn how to do Transcendental Meditation in the 1970"s. Another type of stimulation

Living on Rocks

comes from seeing "stuff" that is lying on the beach as we are walking. Sticks, driftwood, stones, shells, miscellaneous jetsam, berms of sand that were not there the day before...all these things can be highly stimulating. For me, it is all about making things from other things.

A bit of news now...in the middle of May, MLR and I will be leaving the BVI. MLR spends each summer at her pretty fabulous Lake Home in Wisconsin. She will be flying there to enjoy her home and spend more time with her family. I, on the other hand, will be flying to Mallorca so spend time with the friends that I left when I moved to the BVI. To be fair, by leaving the BVI at this time will mean I will miss the bulk of the 2018 hurricane season in the Caribbean. The reality is that the chances of an Irma-like catastrophe again are pretty slim, but having barely survived Irma, I am not all that thrilled with taking that chance right now. So, I will be Mallorca bound.

I had sent notes to several friends in Mallorca telling them of my plan and asking them to keep their eyes open for a home or flat I could rent whilst there. One of them did send me photos of an option...a sailboat that was for sale. This was a very intriguing option, and because of the six boats I have owned previously, I have live on board on five of them, and if that is not proof that I do love living on boats, not much else is. I did make an offer on the boat, and for a time it did look like I would be on-board for my time this summer in Mallorca, but at the last minute, the current owner changed some of the elements of the purchase contract, so I took back my offer to purchase.

Today's beach walk was...well...in reality, about the same. The sands had shifted as they do every day. Today, many of the rocks we saw yesterday were obliterated by tonnes of sand that have washed onto shore. And whilst we do love watching nature in action, today is was pretty special because we could walk out in the surf without the risk of getting our feet smashed by rocks being pulled back and forth by the surf's flow. The good news was that we were able to walk out pretty far. The fun news was when about every eighth wave was seriously high and made both of us pretty wet. Nice. The only bad news was that we didn't think we could just stay there forever. So we walked back and desperately tried not to pick up some brilliantly bent pieces of driftwood for yet another Medusa of the Beach piece.

This whole Medusa thing happened because we found some pretty special driftwood one day, and I could "see" that I could do something special with it. Then we found a few more pieces and in my mind, I could see the finished piece. The name for the project (everything is a project to me) was based on what I saw: crazy wild bent sticks of driftwood that, when assembled in some seemingly random (but carefully calculated) order, resembled the snake-head of the woman of Greek mythology, Medusa. Where the Medusa project (in my mind) was a "one-off" project, after making the first one, I then made a second. Then I made the third, which was almost double the size. The fourth was quite small, and nice for a desk or shelf. By then I was really getting into this as a project and very quickly I found myself making numbers 5, 6, 7, 8, 9, and 10. Ten was really a bit different and ended up being a gift to friends here. Numbers 11, 12, 13, and 14 all were pretty good sized like the first two.

I had put some of these on Facebook (as you do), and have received some (clever) comments about them. One comment suggested I make them in IKEA form, which I assume would be put some pieces of driftwood in a box with a tube of silastic cement. Several other people wrote to wonder how they could have one. Several others suggested I sell them here. We did talk to one gallery owner about having them sell them, and took several pieces over to them to put for sale. For me it is all about doing that "creative thing" and goes along with the limited edition prints I have made here.

In mid-May, MLR and I left the condo I rented in December and that we have been living in since then. MLR flew to Wisconsin to spend the summer at her Lake Home, and I flew to Mallorca to spend time with special friends. I am not exactly sure when I will go back to the Caribbean, but I will go back. The islands are very special to me, and I did become a legal resident there, so it is just a matter of time before I return. It could be two months, or four months or whatever, but I am going back.

The saga/adventure/exploration/whatever does continue. I did fly to Mallorca and it was pretty wonderful. One of my sons had asked back in April if I was excited about returning to the island I had lived on for more than 15 years. I replied that whilst I did love living there, going back was more about seeing so many old friends again. And that is what I did. I found an adorable flat in Sta. Catalina (ironically, a flat that I had lived in for a few months shortly after selling my boat so many years ago) and settled back into Mallorca-island life again rather well. And then one day, I received an email from an estate agent in the Caribbean that began to chart the next chapter in my life.

The weekend before MLR and I left Tortola, we had flown to Antigua to look at a boat that was for sale that I had read about. The boat, one that I would have considered a good liveaboard boat, was very special and I did make an offer on her. The offer was acceptable but then some of the other issues relating to keeping her in Antigua whilst I was going to be in Mallorca started to raise flags, and I cancelled my offer. But whilst we were there, we also looked at a couple of condominiums that were long-term rental options. One of them was very special, and after returning to Tortola (and then after arriving in Mallorca), I had kept talking to the estate agent. And one day, she wrote back with some pretty brilliant news. The condo/villa that we had liked wasn't available, but she did have one that was even nicer. Still in Jolly Harbour, it has two bedrooms, two-and-one/half baths, fab kitchen and sitting room, exceptionally large terrace, and a private boat dock. This was too good to pass up. I signed the rental agreement and will (finally) fly back at the end of August. I am very much looking forward to returning to the Caribbean, and now, my return will even be more special as I will be living on

Living on Rocks

a new rock.

I do want to return at some point to the British Virgin Islands, and I am sure at some point I will. But for now, just being able to continue living on rocks is pretty special, and the most recent addition to the list of rocks has not dampened the feeling.

Jolly Harbour, at times, feels like living in Nanny Cay in Tortola. A relatively self-sufficient community on the leeward side of Antigua, Jolly Harbour does have just about everything we need. Several weeks after arriving, MLR flew in and we immediately focused on settling in. Prior to her arrival, I walked everywhere here. "Everywhere here" sort of means that I walked from the condo/villa to the market and restaurants. I walked because I hadn't bought a car when I arrived, and after a couple of weeks, was pretty convinced there was no real reason to buy one. The roads outside of Jolly Harbour are not exactly two-lanes and are somewhat littered with potholes. Having lived on Tortola with a car after Irma wreaked her destruction, narrow roads with potholes aren't all that shocking, but I really didn't see the need to go through all that again. The fact that one doesn't need to leave Jolly Harbour for much made the decision not to buy a car pretty easy. For the times that we would need to head into St. John's or someplace else on the island, it is possible to take a taxi. Doing a cost comparison between occasional taxi usage v. cost of a car and insurance and petrol and matenance and God-knows-what-else, makes it pretty clear that taxi's are good. Having said that, when MLR did arrive, we went (via taxi) to a bicycle shop in St. John's and now are the proud owners of two bikes. The bikes are both old-school, and have one speed and coaster brakes, but Jolly Harbour is dead flat so the choices were fine.

Being here in the British West Indies is nice, but the past several weeks have reminded me of when I first moved to Mallorca. It was nice, but being "there" wasn't the same as "really being there." Let me explain. When I first came to Mallorca, I was in Palma, living on-board Angelina. That was the good news. The not-as-great news was that Angelina was in a marina smack in the middle of Palma, and because I was part of a sailing community, and because of that, everyone was speaking English. Get it? Living in Mallorca, which is in Spain, but being surrounded by the language of my birth. I didn't feel I was really "there" until I had bought my home in Puigpunyent where I was surrounded by locals. So here we are in Jolly Harbour in Antigua. Very nice and all that. The language of Antigua is English, so that isn't an issue. But there was something missing, so today, MLR and I rode our trendy bicycles to the commercial district of Jolly Harbour and then walked across the main road…and took a bus to St. Johns.

We had been to St. John's to buy our bicycles, but that was in a large taxi (we did need the space to bring the bicycles home again). This time we wanted to explore more of the concept of settling in, so we decided to take the bus into town. The term, "bus" is sort of a new experience here, as the "bus" wasn't exactly the same type of bus either one of us had experienced previously. Not a double-decker red bus from London; not a Greyhound bus that used to traverse the United States; this bus was in reality a 14 passenger people carrier. This was, as with many things we have experienced over the years in places we have lived either together or individually, not good or bad; it was just different. After parking our bikes, we started to walk to the bus stop, only to see it pull up before we were there. MLR went running ahead and jumped on, holding it for me. We then went bouncing along the road with the other passengers all the way to St. John's. We had been told that the ride could take 20 minutes, but after half of that, we pulled into the bus depot and set out to do some serious shopping.

St. John's isn't really a metropolis. Lots of people walking around; lots of shops with some "interesting" offerings in windows; quite a few open markets; and lots of new things to experience. After buying everything on our lists, we popped in for lunch at a harbour-side restaurant, and then made our way back to the bus depot. It only took a minute or so and MLR spotted a number 20 bus, so we boarded it and then waited. We new ahead of time that the bus "schedule" is more-or-less, "flexible." We found out what that meant when we sat in the back of another 14-passenger people carrier, waiting for the extra few seats to be filled. As soon as the last seat became occupied, the driver went ripping out of the depot just as the door was being closed. After multiple stops, we were the only remaining passengers by the time the bus pulled up at Jolly Harbour. We took our bags and made our way to our bicycles and rode home, making it just before it began to rain. All in all, a pretty great day of learning more about Antigua.

A couple of days ago, it was the equinox. The **September** equinox, which happens around the third week of the month, is the moment when the Sun appears to cross the celestial equator, heading southward. In most places north of the equator, the equinox foretells the onset of cooler weather. Here, in the British West Indies, it is the same. So far, the average day-time temperature has plummeted from about 28 or 29c all the way down to 27 or 28c. So not exactly jumper or long-pants weather I guess.

It is now early October, and we have been settling in quite well. The term "settling in" not only includes becoming more familiar with where we are, but also convincing the leasing agents to get their bums into gear to make the condo/villa more comfortable for us. They are doing what needs to be done, but it does at time feel like we are pulling a massive load up a mountain of treacle. But the important point is that the condo/villa is becoming nicer and nicer.

I have been spending quite a bit of free time editing this book, which, if you are reading this, you know about. And then last week, to break up the creative efforts a bit more, I pulled out my watercolours and went to work on some of the paper that we bought whilst in St. John's.

Living on Rocks

It has now been a month since I began to write these entries, and one way to look at this delay is that I have been bad. The other way to look at it is that there hasn't been all that much exciting stuff going on. I would like to say that the reason is the latter, but "exciting stuff" is a relative term for sure. What we have been doing has quickly become routine. Now to be fair in a recent phone call from some friends it was clear that what is routine here for us, isn't routine for others. Not too much we can do about this other than enjoy the environment we are in. And because of our routine, it is time to hop on our trendy bikes and pedal our bums over to the South beach for a swim and walk the length of the beach and back. Then, another swim. And yes, walking along the beach does include stopping in at one of the beach bar's to do some research on the quality and consistencies of Piña Colada's or Pain-Killers.

About the Author

James B Rieley is an advisor to CEO's and senior leadership teams both in Europe and the Americas. He holds an earned Ph.D. in Organisational Effectiveness, and was the President of a successful manufacturing company for over 20 years. After selling his company in 1987, his life changed dramatically. He purchased his first sailboat and learnt to sail.

He has lived in both big, fast-moving, technologically-driven cities, and towns and villages where the term "slow" takes on a meaning that few would understand unless they lived in them. He has written multiple books on the subjects of leadership and business decision-making effectiveness.

In 2003, he began to write a blog-like stream of experiences to friends and family so they could vicariously be with him during his life on an island in the Mediterranean. His writing output could best be known as "prolific," and he has continued this for the past 15 years. Rieley was living on Saphir, his sixth boat, when hurricane Irma came along. He currently lives on a rock in the British West Indies.

Printed in Great
Britain
by Amazon